SECOND EDITION

A HISTORY OF THE HUMAN COMMUNITY

Prehistory to the Present

William H. McNeill

The University of Chicago

Prentice-Hall, Inc., Englewood Cliffs, New Jersey 07632

Library of Congress Cataloging-in-Publication Data

McNeill, William Hardy, [date]
  A history, of the human community.

  Rev. ed. of: The ecumene. c1973.
  Includes bibliographies and index.
  Contents: Prehistory to 1500—1500 to the
present.
    1. World history. I. McNeill, William Hardy,
[date]. Ecumene. II. Title.
D20.M485   1987b   909   86–30230
ISBN 0–13–390287–0

Editorial/production supervision: Edith Riker
Interior and cover design: Suzanne Behnke
Manufacturing buyer: Raymond Keating
Photo editor: Lorinda Morris-Nantz
Photo research: Barbara Schultz
Cover photo: Art Resource, NY

Previously published as *The Ecumene: Story of Humanity*

Printed in the United States of America

10 9 8 7 6 5 4 3 2 1

ISBN   0-13-390287-0   01

Prentice-Hall International (UK) Limited, *London*
Prentice-Hall of Australia Pty. Limited, *Sydney*
Prentice-Hall Canada Inc., *Toronto*
Prentice-Hall Hispanoamericana, S.A., *Mexico*
Prentice-Hall of India Private Limited, *New Delhi*
Prentice-Hall of Japan, Inc., *Tokyo*
Prentice-Hall of Southeast Asia Pte. Ltd., *Singapore*
Editora Prentice-Hall do Brasil, Ltda., *Rio de Janeiro*

6-12-87 — MW-40672

Contents

Volume I: Prehistory to 1500

PART ONE
BEGINNINGS

1 Primitive Times   1

Emergence of Humans Upon the Changing Face of the Earth 1   *The Olduvai Gorge in Africa* 6   The Age of the Hunters—Old Stone Age 8   The Age of the Food Producers—New Stone Age 13   The Spread of Farming Techniques 22   The Beginnings of History 23   Conclusion 24

2 River Valley Civilizations: 3500 to 1500 B.C.   27

Sumerian Civilization 29   Egyptian Civilization 45   *The Decipherment of Hieroglyphic and Cuneiform Writing* 48   The Indus Civilization 53   Conclusion 55

3 The Rise of Civilizations on Rain-Watered Land: 2000 to 1200 B.C.   57

Civilization, Barbarism, and Cultural Diffusion 58   The Chariot Revolution 71   *Heinrich Schliemann's Success Story* 76   Religion, Writing, and Art in the Chariot Age 77   Conclusion 83

THE USE OF PLANTS AND ANIMALS IN AGRICULTURE   85

4 Empire and Religion in the Middle East: 1200 to 500 B.C.   93

The Iron Age—Importance of Iron 94   The New Relation of Village and Country Communities 98   Restoration of Bureaucratic Government—The

PART TWO
EURASIAN CULTURAL BALANCE:
500 B.C. to A.POBD. 1500

8 The Classical World and Its Expansion:
500 B.C. to A.D. 200   **211**

Volume II: 1500 to the Present

PART ONE
THE FAR WEST CHALLENGES
THE WORLD: 1500 to 1850

PART TWO
BEGINNINGS OF WORLD
COSMOPOLITANISM: FROM 1850

---

9 World Reactions to Europe's Achievements: 1850 to 1914   284

TRANSPORTATION AND COMMUNICATION   315

10 World Wars of the Twentieth Century: 1914 to 1945   321

11 The World Since 1945   357

12 Thought and Culture Since 1914   385

BREAKTHROUGHS IN THE USE OF ENERGY AND FUEL   407

Epilogue: Part Two The State of the World Today   411

Map List, Volume I

Map List, Volume II

Preface

This book is built around a simple idea: People change their ways mainly because some kind of stranger has brought a new thing to their attention. The new thing may be frightening, it may be delightful; but whatever it is, it has the power to convince key persons in the community of the need to do things differently.

If this is true, then contacts between different cultures become the main drive wheel of history, because such contacts start or keep important changes going. The central theme of human history, after all, is change—how people did new things in new ways, meeting new situations as best they could.

It follows that world history can and should be written to show how in succeeding ages different human groups achieved unusual creativity, and then impelled or compelled those around them (and, in time, across long distances) to alter their accustomed style of life to take account of the new things that had come to their attention by what anthropologists call "cultural diffusion" from the center of creativity. There remains a central mystery: How does important creativity occur? Accident, genius, and breakdown of old habit patterns all play a part in provoking inventions. Even more important (because commoner) is the need to readjust other elements in daily life after a major new borrowing resulting from some foreign contact has occurred. So here, too, I am inclined to emphasize the importance of contacts between strangers as a basic force in increasing the variety and multiplying the openings for all kinds of creative inventions.

This angle of vision upon human affairs came to me from anthropology. Thirty-five years ago, anthropologists studied simple, isolated societies; only a few of them tried to think about relations between such "primitive" peoples and the more complicated civilized societies that occupied so much more of the face of the earth. One of the people who did wonder about the relationships between simple and complex societies was Robert Redfield; my most fundamental ideas took form while sitting in his classroom at the University of Chicago in the summer of 1936.

But even very simple general ideas have to be applied to the data of history with some care before one can really be sure whether they are much use. This took me about twenty-five years: not till I had written *The Rise of the West: A History of the Human Community* (published in 1963) could I know how the history of humankind, insofar as modern scholars have been able to find out about it, would fit into this sort of anthropological framework.

The task was a large one. I had to acquaint myself with recent, more or less standard scholarly writing in all the different fields of historical study, and then look for relationships in time and space. This often meant going beyond the bounds of existing scholarly knowledge. Experts have to learn difficult languages and usually do not know very much about what happened outside the time and place where their own special skills allow them to make new contributions to knowledge. And different fields of learning developed different outlooks. Ancient India, for example, has been studied mainly by scholars interested in comparative religion and linguistics; they did not ask political, economic, or technological questions of the Sanskrit texts they used; and until quite lately, they did little archaeological digging. Chinese studies, on the contrary, were directed very much at political institutions and patterns of rule.

An outsider, like myself, asking similar questions of each time and place therefore had to be careful. Guessing too much would be a mistake; not to guess at all, even when available evidence and the state of scholarly knowledge left gaps, would prevent recognition of how the history of one part of the world fitted into the pattern of the whole. Yet in spite of such problems, in the end I felt that my effort had been worthwhile. The vision of human history that emerged from my work seemed simple in conception, yet complex in application. The simple pattern of interaction among peoples of different cultures could make room for all the multiplicity and surprisingness of human historical experience.

A lot of other people, ordinary citizens and even professional historians, agreed that my book was good, useful, persuasive. Thinking that such a vision might make the study of history in schools easier and more satisfying to the mind, I then set out to write *The Ecumene: Story of Humanity,* using simple language for the most part, and pruning out details, thinning proper names, defining special terms so that students could understand the ideas of the text more easily.

It is for you, students and readers, to judge how successful this effort has been.

WILLIAM H. MCNEILL
Chicago, Illinois

Note to the Second Edition

The importance of knowing about other peoples with whom we share the surface of the globe is self evident in an age when Americans interact with others everywhere more and more intimately and incessantly. Communications and transport make isolation impossible. Ignorance of others becomes more and more costly. Teachers and academic administrators therefore have begun to support efforts at more systematic study of world history, for only by knowing something about the past is the present intelligible. This book is intended to help such efforts.

Nevertheless, the task of learning about the whole human world is enormous. Students and teachers are likely to feel disheartened when they see how much there is to know. But if readers focus attention on the big picture—patterns of relationship across the whole of the intercommunicating human world, and take note of the big changes in those patterns that occurred only a few times in all recorded history—the task will become much easier. Details will fit into place without burdening the memory so heavily.

This book has been designed to make the big picture accessible. If you keep thinking about it as you study each chapter and read each page, history will keep its shape and proportion and remain intelligible; even interesting—perhaps fascinating. But it is up to you to keep the big picture in mind as you read each part: without that, confusion and boredom are sure to overtake you.

In revising this book for its second edition, many small changes were made to improve readability; and the two final chapters were completely rewritten to bring things up to date and keep proportions more or less in line for recent decades.

William H. McNeill

Volume I

A HISTORY OF THE HUMAN COMMUNITY

Prehistory to 1500

CHAPTER 1

Primitive Times

From the careful study of rocks, geologists know that the face of the earth has changed repeatedly. The earth itself may be about 4.5 billion years old—an unimaginably long time when measured against a human lifetime. During long ages of that past, changes in the earth's surface went very, very slowly. Yet across hundreds of millions of years, mountain ranges rose and then were cut down again by the slow action of wind and water on rock; seas spread their waters where dry land had been, and then withdrew as the land emerged once more into the atmosphere. Ice ages have come and gone; climates have altered. New forms of life evolved and old ones disappeared; even the chemical composition of sea and air changed.

EMERGENCE OF HUMANS UPON THE CHANGING FACE OF THE EARTH

Deep in the geologic past, conditions on earth appear to have remained stable for quite long periods—50 to 100 millions of years. But such periods of stability were separated from one another by other times of compara-

1

tively rapid and dramatic change. The most recent million years, which constitute the Pleistocene epoch (Ice Age) of geologic time, was a period of relatively sharp and sudden change—though by our human standards of time even these changes went so slowly that we may be living amidst them still without really being much aware of the fact.

Four times during the Pleistocene epoch great ice sheets, thousands of feet thick, formed in Europe and North America and advanced southward. Four times these glaciers melted back. The most recent melting time began about 25,000 years ago and is probably still going on in places like Greenland and Antarctica, where thick ice caps continue to cover the land.

The coming and going of the ice meant sharp and serious changes in the conditions of life for all kinds of plants and animals. Only those able to adapt themselves to such changes could survive, and, in fact, many creatures disappeared. Saber-toothed tigers and mastodons, for example, no longer exist. Other animals such as horses once galloped across the grasslands of both Europe and North America, but they disappeared in America a few thousand years before the Spaniards again introduced them from the Old World, where they had never died out.

Changes such as these were dramatic in themselves. But the rise of human kind, which took place during the same million-odd years when the ice advanced and retreated, also changed conditions of life in remarkable and far-reaching ways. For human beings learned how to alter the biological balance of the earth by making specially selected and domesticated plants and animals flourish in the fields and pastures of the world, thereby displacing wild species.

Such achievements often have unexpected and undesired results. Diseases and pests, for example, infested barns and fields; and erosion sometimes stripped the topsoil from whole regions where farmers had destroyed the natural vegetation in order to plant grain or other crops. In recent times we have even begun to alter the earth's physical geography, not only by building cities, highways, dams, pipelines, and canals, but also by polluting the air and water with all kinds of wastes.

In other words, human activity began to change the face of the earth far more rapidly than ever before. The slow-acting forces of unconscious nature were no match for conscious and cooperative human efforts to make the environment over.

Charles Darwin in 1859, after studying geological fossils as well as the differences among forms of life that existed in his own day in different parts of the world, proposed the theory of organic evolution in his book *On the Origin of Species*. He later wrote *The Descent of Man* (1871), in which he suggested that human beings, too, had evolved from other forms of life. Such an idea was shocking to most of Darwin's contemporaries. But more and more evidence has been found since then to support

Paleolithic tools and weapons. (*Courtesy of American Museum of National History*)

his theory, even though some of Darwin's ideas about how one species turned into another were later disproved.

Scientific thought is always subject to correction when new evidence turns up. Current ideas about human origins are especially uncertain, for the gaps in the evidence are still great. Nevertheless most experts on human evolution now agree that creatures enough like ourselves to count as prehumans began to walk the earth more than a million years ago.

Little is yet known about these prehumans or how they came into existence. Skeletons and bits of skeletons have been found in many parts of the world, from England to China and from Java to Africa. By far the largest number of such prehuman remains come from east Africa, but the distribution of the sites of these discoveries may be accidental. There are many parts of the world where caves and other likely spots for the discovery of prehuman remains have not yet been carefully searched. Still, the bones that have been discovered tell us something. For instance, skeletons indicate that a half-million years ago the various kinds of humanoid creatures differed from one another much more than human races differ today. There were both giants and pygmies, with teeth and skulls combining characteristics of modern apes and humans in different ways.

From Prehuman to Human

Prehuman communities presumably evolved biologically: that is to say, changes in genes were more important than changes in learned behavior. No one can say when evolution by learning to do things in a new way became more important than genetic changes. We can be fairly certain that prehumans had to be able to talk before learning could attain decisive importance. Our prehuman ancestors also had to be able to handle sticks and stones as weapons and tools.

But definite biological changes had to come before the legs and feet of our prehuman ancestors became strong enough to walk on, leaving their hands and arms free to explore the world, with the help of eyes and tongue. Other changes were needed to give the tongue free play for articulate (distinctly spoken) speech. Connected with these biological changes was an increase in the size of the brain. These changes did not come all at once. Nor can we tell whether humanoid creatures finally became fully human at a single place and time, or whether genetic strands combined and recombined to bring different groups, in different parts of the world, across the threshold of humanity at different times.

Tool-using is not exclusively human. Traces of fire and stones that had been chipped to make crude tools have been found in association with skeletons that are very different from those of modern humans; in fact, chimpanzees and other animals have been known to use simple tools.

The critical difference, perhaps, was speech. Language allowed relatively large numbers of individuals to cooperate more effectively by reacting to voice signals. Simple animal cries in the hunt helped to locate the quarry; but with language a plan could be worked out ahead of time, assigning one person here and another there to take the victim by surprise or to drive the game into a prearranged trap. Enormous improvement in the food supply must have resulted from the use of language for hunting. In particular, language allowed our earliest ancestors to hunt larger and larger animals, instead of having to depend only on small game.

As this change occurred, prehuman hunters could become fully human, because, for the first time, they could afford to support and train children for months and even years after birth. Thus the period in which children learned the arts of life and how to behave could be prolonged. And it was by learning more and inheriting less that prehumans became humans.

In the second place, language allowed people to refine and improve their reactions to the world around them. Different kinds of animals and plants, stones, and even actions were given names, and, having names, could then be recognized more easily; and their possibilities for good or evil could be learned ahead of time. Such words allowed our distant ancestors to organize their world according to general categories or classifications into which particular things could be made to fit. Knowing what to expect from each category, they could then act more efficiently in a particular case.

There is yet a third sense in which words and language made prehumans into human beings. Words can be combined and recombined in much the same way that people can use their hands to play with small objects and combine them or recombine them into new devices, patterns, and forms. As playing with things may permit someone to invent new weapons, tools, and works of art, so playing with words can provoke new ideas and feelings. Thus reason and invention, the bases for the extraordinary success that humans have had in dominating the earth, were let loose by the power of speech to classify things and by the capacity of hands to handle them. From the interplay between these two distinctive abilities, the human species finally and fully emerged, probably sometime between 500,000 and 50,000 years ago.

The Origins of Race

Modern races presumably descend from various mixtures of ancestral types. Some of the most obvious differences, such as skin color, which divide us today, are a result of adaptation to different climates. For example, Mongolian features and skin color are well adapted for survival in cold climates; African and Indian populations have dark skins that protect them from tropical ultraviolet rays; and the pale skins of Europeans are adapted to the scarcity of sunlight in a cloudy climate.

Race has recently become more of an issue in politics and social life, not only in the United States but in many other parts of the world. Skin color is obvious; hence our sensitivity to the shade of a person's complexion. But classification by skin color distorts and confuses the genetic facts of human variation, which are much more complicated than any difference indicated by skin color alone. Human beings cannot be divided into clearly separate races, for they show many kinds of intermedi-

THE OLDUVAI GORGE
IN AFRICA

The Olduvai Gorge in Tanzania, located a little southeast of Lake Victoria, has recently become the most important site in the world for finding out about human origins. The gorge itself is a narrow slash cut some 300 feet deep into the African landscape by the Olduvai River that runs through its bottom in the rainy season and then almost dries up for most of the year. The walls of the gorge expose layers of soft sediments that fell to the bottom of an old lake during the past million years or so.

Geologically, the gorge is remarkable because its walls are so soft. The change in earth levels that drained the former lake and allowed the Olduvai River to begin cutting through its bottom is very recent, as geological time goes, being measured in thousands rather than in millions of years. And because the change is so recent, the steep, soft sides of the gorge now stand almost bare under the African sun; they can easily be examined by human eyes and can be scratched with picks or dug with spades.

When Dr. Louis Leakey and his wife, Mary, began to examine the gorge in the early 1950s, they quickly found vast numbers of chipped stones that had presumably been shaped by men, or by manlike animals. Such a complete and lengthy series of tools was unmatched elsewhere in the world. The most dramatic find, however, fell to Mary Leakey in

ate types, involving every sort of variable characteristic. Moreover, variations in one physical characteristic, such as skin color, do not necessarily match variations in other characteristics, such as hair texture or head shape.

No satisfactory classification of humanity according to physical type has ever been devised. A common system recognizes white, yellow, and black races; but it is not really helpful, because each of these races includes many subtypes and local populations that differ from one another in important ways. The hairy Ainu peoples of Japan, for example, have white skins, but in other respects do not physically resemble European populations; and the Australian aborigines, called "black-fellows," are certainly black, but still are very different in their bodily form from black-skinned peoples elsewhere.

Small isolated communities may at times have been able to establish a nearly uniform genetic pattern among a few hundred or a few thousand human beings. But such communities never kept themselves apart from

1959, when, at the very lowest level of the Olduvai deposits, she discovered the shattered fragments of a skull that had once belonged to a humanoid creature. She named her find *Zinjanthropus*, though some experts denied that the skull really belonged to a creature enough like humans to deserve the name *anthropos* (Greek for "man"). From the position where she found the skull fragments, Mary Leakey argued that they must be about a million years old. Here, it seemed clear, was what remained of one of the makers of the earliest, crudest type of stone tools found in the lowest layers of the Olduvai Gorge.

At other levels in the Olduvai Gorge, other similar bones have been found. They differ from one another in important details. In addition, the types of stone tools changed with the levels from which they came. With so many finds in hand, the Leakeys were able to prove that with the passage of time the design and workmanship of the chipped stones consistently improved; but relationships between the different kinds of skeletal remains are not yet clear.

These discoveries in the Olduvai Gorge may show that humans first came into existence on the high plateau region of Africa in the neighborhood of Lake Victoria. This is what the Leakeys themselves believe, and many others are inclined to agree with them. On the other hand, the finds at Olduvai, dramatic and important as they are, also prove how very little we yet know about human origins. The discovery of a single new skeleton in some other part of the world can still change the whole picture, just as the Leakeys' discoveries in the Olduvai Gorge have done.

the rest of mankind long enough to become a different biological species; or rather, if any communities did so, they were later destroyed when they came into contact with a human population more open to the outside world.

When two or more different races live side by side for a few generations, biological boundaries blur. As time passes, more and more people of mixed blood combine features from the different races. This is as true in the United States, where whites and blacks have lived together for about 300 years, as it is in India, where light-skinned and darker-skinned populations have lived side by side for about 4500 years.

Wherever people mingle and move about, as has been happening more and more frequently in recent centuries, all sorts of intermediate mixed racial types come into existence. Until a few hundred years ago, most human beings were grouped in small village or tribal communities whose relations with the outside world were quite limited. As a result, ten or fifteen generations back our ancestors seldom saw anyone who did not fall within a well-defined local range of physical variation. This ceased to be true as ships and trains and airplanes made it easier to move about, so that all the different types of human beings began to mix more rapidly than before.

Racial purity among large and flourishing human communities is, therefore, a myth. Variations in physical appearance of course occur, and people react to such variations, thinking some persons beautiful or desirable and others ugly. But these opinions vary from time to time and from place to place.

The breakdown of age-old isolation is what created the conditions for modern race feeling. In more and more parts of the world, people of different appearance find themselves living side by side. However unreasonable, it is sometimes hard not to fear and distrust people who seem strange, or whose forebears have run afoul of yours—even (or especially) when they live next door or just a few blocks away. But the fact that differing human types are now living side by side more often than ever before means that the age-old process of biological and social mixture is going ahead more rapidly than in times past. If new barriers to movement do not arise, the physical differences among people will eventually become less than they are today, just as the differences today are less than they were when widely different prehuman types walked the earth.

THE AGE OF THE HUNTERS —OLD STONE AGE

The first humans were big game hunters. They lived in small groups, probably averaging no more than twenty to sixty people most of the time. Leadership rested with bold and experienced men who knew the habits of game and how to kill. Each group hunted within a fairly well-defined territory and rarely encountered strangers. Such communities probably had more or less settled campsites to which everyone came back at night; but from time to time, if game became scarce, the whole group might move to another hunting ground.

In such a life, hunger and fear were never far away. A wound or a broken leg was likely to be fatal, and those who fell ill had to recover quickly without help, or else die. At almost any moment, a sudden encounter with some fierce animal might end even the bravest hunter's life. Or strangers might suddenly try to take hunting grounds away, forcing the group to make a choice between fighting back, withdrawing, or trying to make peace.

Community Activity

Women's life consisted of fairly steady work. Searching for food—seeds, berries, roots, grubs, insects, and other edibles—was a main part of their task. In addition women made baskets out of twigs and grass, guarded the campsite, cared for infants, taught small children how to behave, and all the while kept a sharp eye out for any danger that might threaten.

Men undertook tasks that required muscular strength and endurance. Preparation for the hunt involved making or repairing spears, knives, and similar tools by joining sharpened rocks to wooden handles. Stalking animals that could run much faster than their pursuers—and that sometimes were far stronger and better equipped for combat than human beings—took much patience and prolonged cooperation. To strike an animal in an exposed vital part with sudden, sharp exertion required courage as well as precise muscular coordination.

After the kill came joy and a time for boasting, living over again the stages of the expedition, praising or blaming each hunter's actions, and reasserting the group's solidarity by dividing the flesh of the victim among the hunters and their families. After the meal, the men, and sometimes the women, danced around the fire. Their rhythmic voices expressed and reinforced the solidarity of the group, healed any individual frictions or frustrations the day might have brought, and prepared everyone for a sound sleep. Within a day or two the cycle began over again, when nothing but well-gnawed bones remained from the last kill.

PREHISTORIC BELIEFS   Ancient hunters probably believed the world was full of spirits that had to be dealt with carefully if everyday dangers were to be avoided, or at least kept to a minimum. How people first got the idea that spirits existed we do not know; and how they tried to deal with them we can only guess by studying how contemporary hunting peoples behave, and by taking note of the bits of evidence ancient hunters left behind them.

By far the most important prehistoric evidence can be seen in the famous cave paintings located in south-central France and in northern Spain. Here, about 20,000 years ago, artists painted beautiful and amazingly lifelike portraits of the animals they hunted and killed. These paintings are located deep in the earth, as much as a half mile from daylight. They may have been intended to appease the spirits of the animals portrayed. Or perhaps the paintings were meant to persuade the "Earth Mother" to give birth to deer, bison, woolly mammoth, and other beasts for men to kill and eat.

Everywhere, we may guess, humans felt a sense of mystery as they

Paleolithic art: A deer hunt from Castellon, Spain.
(*Courtesy of American Museum of National History*)

watched the change of seasons, the migration of game, the waxing and waning of the moon, and the growth and decay of their own bodily strength and skill with the passage of years.

TOOLS OF THE OLD STONE AGE   The cave paintings of France and Spain are, so far as we know, unique. Elsewhere, ancient hunters left no such record of their skills. From most of the world all we have is enormous numbers of stone blades and points dropped around old campsites or in caves. Some of these ancient stone tools look beautiful to our eyes, and the men who made them may have meant them to be lovely as well as useful.

Experts have classified these tools into sequences by determining that certain kinds of harpoon heads or fishhooks, found near the surface of a cave floor, were made by people who came after others who had used spearheads and knives of a different design, found further down in the earth. By digging still deeper, cruder tools made by still earlier humans sometimes turn up.

Precise sequences of this kind were first worked out by archaeologists comparing the remains from caves of the Dordogne Valley of south-central France, near the site where the cave paintings were found. Elsewhere not nearly so much is known, and we should not assume that the succession of tool types discovered in France corresponds to what happened in other parts of the world.

Still, scholars now know enough to say that in general, and all over the world, hunting bands developed more and better kinds of tools as time passed. This was particularly true when new materials like bone, antler, and rawhide came into use. But throughout the age of the hunters the fundamental tool remained a cutting edge, which was made by chipping bits away from a piece of brittle stone until the right shape and size had been achieved. In Europe and western Asia such tools were made by knocking a large flake from a larger block of stone, and then improving its shape by taking a lot of smaller chips from the large flake. In eastern Asia people preferred to keep on knocking chips from a core, and shape the core into the final form. This difference of technique lasted for hundreds of thousands of years and is almost all that can be said for sure about the earliest differences in human ways of doing things.

But whether the ancient hunters worked from a flake or from a core, the end product was much the same. Sharp and serviceable spearheads, arrow points, and knife blades could be made quite easily—as is shown by the incredible numbers of such remains that still can be picked up. With the right kind of stone to work with, it took a skillful hunter only a few minutes to make a new blade when an old one had been lost or damaged.

People later learned to grind stones into smooth shapes. This very obvious difference led the scholars who first studied early tools to divide them into Old Stone, or Paleolithic, and New Stone, or Neolithic, types. The difference was important, for, as we shall see, people began to polish stone tools only when they needed them for new purposes. But the rough, quickly made chipped blades of the Old Stone Age were, in fact, very well suited to the ancient hunters' needs, so changes in design came very slowly indeed.

If we assume that human communities developed as much as a half-million years ago, then human beings lived more or less according to the patterns we have just described for approximately 98 percent of their time on earth. Even if we make a much more recent estimate of the date at which human beings emerged, we still must assign at least four-fifths of humanity's earthly career to this primitive life. During most of that long time there is no trace of any alteration in the way people did things. Indeed, insofar as we have instincts and inborn traits of behavior, it is likely that they are attuned to the needs of life in a hunting band. One of the problems civilized populations have always had to face is how to reconcile the aptitude for violence so necessary for the ancient hunter with the requirements of peace and order within large, complicated communities.

The Appearance
of Modern Human Types

By the fourth period of glaciation of the Pleistocene epoch, humans had already come a long way. As climates changed and became cooler, some bands of hunters responded by learning how to sew animal skins together, thus making clothes to keep themselves warm. With clothing, almost hairless humans could live in climates where temperatures went below freezing for part of the year. The cold also required more elaborate shelters, either caves, tents made of animal skins, or houses built of mud and wood.

Tool types began to change, too, as stones of different sizes and shapes were used for new purposes—to drill holes in bone or skin, to whittle wood, to scrape animal skins. People developed great skill in splitting flint and other kinds of brittle stone into the right shape for a particular tool. Open-air workshops have been found where thousands upon thousands of "rejects" lie scattered about, just where they fell from the stoneworkers' hands.

The climatic change may also have stimulated considerable human migration. With better tools and the skills and knowledge needed to build warm houses and to make warm clothes, people were able to spread into new regions of the earth. In particular the part of Eurasia that lies north of the great mountain backbone of that continent opened for human settlement, up to the limit set by the glaciers. The Americas also appear to have been populated for the first time by people who walked across the ice that covered Bering Strait. Less is known about changes in human distribution in the Southern Hemisphere. Australia and Tasmania were reached at an early date, perhaps at a time when so much sea water was locked up in the glaciers that the gap between Australia and southeast Asia was narrower than it is today.

New physical types appeared during this period in Europe and other parts of the Old World. The most famous of these were Neanderthalers, named for a valley in Germany where this kind of skeleton was first discovered. Neanderthalers were short and stocky, stoop-shouldered and low-browed, and may have been very hairy. They lived in caves, which helped them to endure the glacial cold.

As the glaciers began to melt, "modern" kinds of humans moved into Europe and Neanderthalers disappeared. We do not know how this happened. The newcomers may have hunted the older type to death. Or they may have carried some disease into Europe that killed off the Neanderthal population. Or the two kinds of humans may have intermingled, but if so their descendants showed practically no trace of Neanderthal bodily traits.

Thus some 300 generations ago, hunting bands had learned to live in many different climates and to hunt many different kinds of animals. Yet they remained relatively rare in the balance of nature. Human populations were thinly spread and groups remained small, because the food they needed was hard to come by in any great quantity. Too many hunters soon meant too little game. Then the hunters had to starve until their numbers became smaller and the game could again increase. Human beings, in other words, were still at the mercy of the natural balances that defined the kind and numbers of plants and animals that could grow in a given region.

For many thousands of years this natural balance set limits that seemed to be fixed and absolute. Yet the next great stage in human development allowed people to escape from this limitation. They learned how to change the balance of nature deliberately by planting crops and domesticating animals. By doing so, they once more vastly increased the food supply at their disposal and created the basis upon which all later civilizations depended.

THE AGE OF THE FOOD PRODUCERS —NEW STONE AGE

No one knows for certain when and where human communities first learned to cultivate the ground and plant crops. Women probably took the important first steps. They were the ones who picked seeds and berries while the men hunted. And women may have known for a very long time how to pull out useless plants to make more room for those that produced good seeds or fruits. But as long as bands of humans moved to and fro across miles of country, always looking for the best hunting grounds, the women could do only a little to encourage the growth of edible berries, seed grasses, or roots.

Grain Farming and Herding

Not long before 7000 B.C., however, a basic change began to affect the part of the world now called the Middle East. We can tell well enough what came out of the change: small, simple villages of farmers. But no one knows just how or exactly where the change occurred.

The most favorable ground for the invention of agriculture lay on the western side of the numerous hills and mountains that lie east of the Mediterranean Sea, but to the west of what is now the central desert region of Iran. In this region, hillsides facing westerly winds caught enough rain to support a fairly heavy growth of trees. The plains were usually too dry for trees and could only support grasses, with occasional clumps of trees along watercourses or where underground water came near the surface. Toward the south, the land became drier and shaded off into harsh desert in southern Iraq and northern Arabia.

As to how farming was invented, we have to guess. The real breakthrough was the discovery of how to make seed-bearing grasses—ancestors of our wheat and barley—grow in places where they did not grow naturally. By preparing fields in forested land, where grasses did not ordinarily grow at all, people could plant suitable kinds of seeds and be sure that only food crops would grow. In such locations natural competitors (weeds) could not mix with and partly crowd out the seed-bearing wheats and barley. Such natural competitors could not easily pass through the forest barrier and establish themselves on the artificially cleared land.

The trick, then, was to be able to create at will special environments where useful plants could thrive. Men did this by cutting a ring of bark around trees of the forest. Slashing the bark killed the trees and opened the forest floor to sunlight. In such a place, wheat and barley could grow very well indeed.

But before agriculture could flourish, still another change had to take place. When shaken by the wind or by some passing animal, wild wheats and barley scattered their ripe seeds on the ground. This made harvesting difficult. But human action soon selected strains with tougher husks, so that seed no longer shook out of the ripened ears, even when the stalks were grasped by human hands and cut with a sickle. After all, only those seeds that stayed in the ear could be carried home by the farmers, and only seeds that had been safely harvested could be planted the next year. Rapid selection therefore took place in favor of varieties that suited human needs.

After forest clearings had been cultivated for two or three years, the cultivators found it helpful to burn the dead tree trunks and scatter the ashes over the soil. This fertilized the ground for one or two more crops. But after five or six years such fields usually became choked with weeds (whose seeds had come in on the wind) so that the soil was no longer worth cultivating. Instead, the early farmers killed the trees somewhere else in the forest and started the cycle of slash-and-burn cultivation all over again. Their old fields, abandoned, soon filled with trees again.

TOOLS OF THE NEW STONE AGE   The soft soil of the forest floor scarcely needed to be dug. A pointed stick to stir up the leaf mold and make sure the seeds were in contact with moist ground beneath was all that was necessary to make the seeds grow. Special sickles for cutting grain stalks had already been invented to aid in harvesting wild-growing grain. None of these implements required any fundamental change in tool types.

But cutting the bark around tree trunks was a different matter. An ax sharp enough to bite through into the wood, and tough enough not to shatter on impact against the tree trunk, demanded a different kind of stone from that used in making hunting tools. Arrowheads, knives, and spears could be made of brittle stone, for they were designed to cut soft animal tissues. They needed to be sharp, and even prehumans had discovered how to shatter a stone in such a way as to produce suitable cutting edges. But the techniques for shaping brittle stone would not do for an ax. Tough unchippable kinds of stones were needed to withstand the impact against a tree trunk. The problem was solved by grinding and polishing basalt and similar varieties of hard, dense stone.

Tools produced by this method look very different from those made by chipping brittle pieces of flint. Slow, patient work of grinding and polishing the natural surfaces of the stone produced smooth, keen, cutting edges. Obviously this took much longer than chipping tools into shape, but a well-made stone ax might last a lifetime and could be resharpened over and over again in exactly the same way that it had been made in the first place. Such axes were quite efficient. Modern experiments have shown that, when put onto a proper handle, ancient stone axes can cut down a tree almost as fast as a modern steel-bladed ax.

Needless to say, people did not cease to be hunters when they discovered how to make little fields in the forests and plant grain in them. Moreover, in places far away from the forest slopes of the Middle East, life went on quite unchanged by the fact that a few human communities had made this discovery. All the same, the balance of nature was seriously upset, for as food from the forest grainfields became more and more abundant, larger numbers of human beings could survive. Soon there were far too many hunters, fed partly by grain from the new fields. Wild game animals within range of the farming communities were nearly exterminated.

THE DOMESTICATION OF ANIMALS   This imbalance presented hunters with a great crisis. Some of them met it by domesticating a few of the kinds of animals they had been accustomed to chase and kill. Tame animals, protected by their human masters, led to the best pastures by day and herded together at night in some sort of enclosure, could be used in several new ways. In addition to providing meat they could be milked, and their hair could be plucked and used to make thread and cloth. Before long, people also began to use the muscular strength of the larger animals for carrying and pulling loads.

Only some animals could be domesticated; those that were too wild were killed and eaten. As a result, the physical type of domesticated flocks and herds changed rapidly from wild forms. The bones left by tamed sheep, goats, donkeys, and cattle became noticeably different from those of their wild ancestors. Consequently, experts usually can tell whether a particular pile of bones left around some ancient campsite came from wild or domesticated stock.

The fact is that as humans became dependent on food coming from domesticated plants and animals, domesticated plants and animals also became dependent on human beings. Wheat and barley that did not scatter the seeds naturally on the ground could not grow unless planted by hand. Domesticated animals, lacking the fierceness of their wild relatives, could not survive without human protection.

But when the new kinds of plants and animals had come into existence and when men and women had learned how to manage them successfully, the scene was set for comparatively rapid expansion of a radically new style of human living. Wherever suitable broad-leaved forests could be found, it was easy to carve out the fields upon which these little farming communities depended. Wherever grasses or leafy plants grew wild, people could drive their flocks and herds to pasture. Northern cold and desert dryness set limits to this kind of life, but within the wide zone that lay between these extremes, the whole world lay open to the first Neolithic farmers and herders.

As grainfields became more and more important, bands of people settled down to live in one spot for several years at a time. A prolonged stay made it worthwhile to build solid houses, often of mud or mud-brick, perhaps with some kind of thatched roof. It was also possible to furnish the house with breakables, such as pottery, and since grain had to be stored in a dry place to prevent premature sprouting, large storage pots became important. Domesticated animals also meant a greatly enlarged supply of hair and wool. Sheep with especially abundant soft undercoats could be bred for their wool, and soon were. A supply of wool allowed women to spin and weave cloth, providing a new artificial skin, softer and more flexible than the animal skins people had previously used to keep themselves warm.

Three Major Problems of the Early Farmers

The earliest farmers probably led peaceful lives, but not for long. While some human communities learned how to farm, others lived in drier, grassy areas where slash-and-burn cultivation would not work. But such communities could domesticate animals and pasture them on the wide grasslands that lay both north and south of the forested zones of the Middle East. Communities that specialized as shepherds and herders remained footloose, moving from place to place in search of pasture. The men in such communities kept much of the spirit and organization of the early hunting bands, for their daily task was to defend their animals against wild beasts and against other men. Warlike habits and the discipline of cooperation in combat naturally arose from such daily experience.

RELATIONS WITH HERDERS   Farmers' daily experience, on the contrary, required each family to scatter for work in the fields. Warlike habits did not find much scope when the daily tasks were to chop the trees, dig the ground, cut the grain. As a result, herders soon discovered that they could attack and defeat farmers, and then force them to part with their precious grain or other useful goods.

The balance between farmers and herders was by no means simple. Usually farmers were more numerous, but not so well organized for fighting. Walls could be built, as in China, and guards assigned to protect farming villages from surprise, but it was hard to combine constant readiness for attack with the tasks of cultivation.

Contact between herders and farmers was not always hostile, however. Instead of seizing grain and other goods by force, the herders might come as bargainers, offering cheese or wool or animals in exchange for cereal food or some other product of the farmers' skills. Herders were sometimes able to offer the farmers special stones or shells, or some other rare commodity, that they had found in the course of their wanderings. In this way rarities that were particularly valued, such as jade, often traveled long distances, passing from hand to hand several times en route.

ACCURATE MEASUREMENT OF TIME   Another critical problem for early farmers was deciding when to plant. In the Middle East, rains fall only in the winter months; grain must be planted in the fall; it ripens in early summer after the drought sets in. If, however, the seed grain is planted too soon, a chance shower might cause the seed to sprout, only to wither in the sun's pitiless rays. If, on the other hand, the seed grain is planted too late, the plants might not ripen fully before summer drought sets in again.

Such errors were disastrous; how could they be avoided? The answer was to watch the moon and count the months marked out by the moon's phases. But, of course, the waxing and waning of the moon does not exactly fit into the solar year, which determines the seasons. Every so often, communities that counted by the moon had to put an extra month in their calendar to adjust to the track of the sun.

Exactly how to do this in order to keep an accurate calendar was never solved satisfactorily by the early farmers. But, compared to what hunters had to know about time, the first farmers had far greater need for accurate timekeeping and they made great advances. In the hunter's life one day was much like the other. Whether it was sunny or rainy, hot or cold, made small difference in what had to be done. The farmer, on the other hand, had to look forward and learn to count and calculate. How much grain could a family afford to eat; how much should be set aside for planting? Farmers had to ration consumption so as to make the grain last until the new harvest. The year, instead of the day, became the fundamental unit of human time, and the annual measurement of time became vital.

Very likely certain individuals in the early farming communities became ritual experts—the earliest priests—and decided under which moon to plant the grain. But we have no certain information about this. We do know that the farmers' concern about planting and harvesting crops found expression in religion. Sun and moon, particularly the latter, were worshiped as gods or spirits with power over fertility. The earth, too, was thought of as a great mother, giving birth to the food people needed.

The parallel between the patterns of human life and plant life impressed itself on early farmers' minds. If seed, when planted, sprang again to life, only to die and then be planted once again, what of humans? If buried in a grave, would a person not rise again? Since dead relatives and friends often appeared in dreams, it seemed logical to answer Yes. After death a person's lot must be a shadowy life, perhaps in a dark underworld. Old Stone Age hunters, too, probably believed in life after death and may have conceived of the earth as a mother. Differences, therefore, were more of emphasis than of kind.

SHORTAGE OF SUITABLE LAND   The third great practical problem the early farmers confronted was a growing shortage of suitable forest land. As the population grew, virgin timber became scarcer and scarcer. It became necessary after a while to use abandoned fields over again, and at shorter and shorter intervals. This meant less abundant crops, since the soil was less fertile. It also became increasingly difficult to keep weeds under control: the closer together fields got to be, the more easily could weed seeds pass from one open sun-soaked patch of ground to another. Less fertile soils and weed-choked fields meant less food for the same effort. Each family therefore had to cultivate more land, but this only made the problem worse.

Not very long before 3000 B.C. a brilliant solution to the problem of land shortage was discovered—the invention of the plow. Probably it was not in the forested regions but in more open land along riverbanks that plows were invented. After all, the first fields were full of stumps. How could a plow do much good in such a place? But when men began to use animal strength to drag a spade or hoe through the ground, new possibilities opened up. Plowing could keep down the weeds. This, indeed, was its most important function. Plowing could also allow a single family to cultivate a far greater area than was possible with digging sticks. Finally, plowing allowed farmers to keep the same fields under cultivation indefinitely, for they soon discovered that a field left fallow (that is, unseeded) and plowed once or twice during the growing season, to kill the weeds before they could go to seed, would yield a satisfactory harvest next year. A simple rotation between fallowing one year and planting the next thus developed. And a single family, with a suitable plow and team of oxen or donkeys, could keep enough land in tillage to feed themselves and have something left over—on most soils and in most seasons.

The invention of the plow was fundamental to all subsequent Middle Eastern, Indian, and European civilizations. The plow was unknown in the Americas and never became as important in China as in western Eurasia. It brought animal husbandry (care and breeding) and grain farming together in a new way. It made men instead of women the main cultivators, for men followed their beasts into the fields and drove the plow, whereas before the invention of the plow women had probably done most of the work in the fields.

The plow also created the sort of field we know today. When the same ground was kept in cultivation, after a few years stumps rotted away, and the plow soon evened off the small hummocks that nature creates in any forest floor. Such fields could then become the smooth, open-land surfaces, one adjacent to the next, often laid out in a more or less regular geometric pattern that we think of when we use the word "field."

Finally, the plow enabled grain farmers to settle down permanently. Once plowed fields had been laid out and brought into cultivation, there was no reason to move on. Permanent village sites, fixed patterns of ownership of particular fields, and a structure of village life that has lasted to the present day in Europe and western Asia thus came into existence. At the same time, the possibility of empire dawned. Farmers who could not afford to move away could be taxed; and taxes could support courts, rulers, armies, cities. Civilization, in short, became a possibility.

The Root Farmers

Before the Middle Eastern style of grain farming and herding had spread very far, people in other parts of the world began a different kind of cultivation. In fact, cultivation of roots for food in the tropical regions of southeast Asia may be older than the grain farming of the Middle East. No one can be sure.

We know far less about how root farming began than about the beginnings of grain farming. It is a good guess—but only a guess—that this kind of farming started among fishermen who lived along the river edges and seacoasts of southeast Asia. The reason for thinking this may have been the case is that fishermen who use boats must come back to the land frequently, and they must come back to sheltered places where their boats are not likely to be damaged by a storm. Hunters were always moving on, but fishing communities tended to settle permanently around suitable harbors. When this happened the women could concentrate on finding good food crops and planting them near the boat landings.

The addition of root crops—manioc, taro, cassava, yams, and many more—to the food supply of fishing communities presumably increased the numbers of fishermen. If they became so numerous that there were fewer fish per fisherman to catch, then they had to eat more of the starchy roots, but they could not domesticate fish in the way hunters in the Middle East domesticated animals.

CONTRAST WITH GRAIN FARMING   The differences between grain farming and root growing are simple but important. Grain farmers harvested seed and planted some of their last year's harvest to get the next crop. Root farmers planted a live shoot from the parent plant in a new place and waited for the shoot to grow new roots. When the roots were big enough they were dug up and eaten. In the same patch of cultivated ground, therefore, plants at all stages of growth could usually be found— some freshly transplanted, some almost ready to be used, and others at various stages in between.

This kind of farming can flourish only where the difference between summer and winter is slight and plants grow all through the year. Grain farming, on the other hand, assumes a time in the year when plants do not grow, for only in such a climate will plants develop food-rich seeds to carry on the germ of life from one season to the next. Hence root cultivation fitted the tropics and must have started there, whereas seed farming started in the temperate zones.

Because the beginnings of root cultivation probably did not make very much difference in the way people lived, there is little indication of when it happened. There is no sign that population started to grow massively, as happened in the Middle East when grain cultivation got established. The east Asian root crops never supplied the basic foods for civilized societies in Eurasia. The development of root cultivation, therefore, was not nearly so world-shaking as the changes brought by the first farmers of the Middle East.

Rice Paddy Farming

At a later stage, however, the farming of the monsoon region of Asia achieved a much greater life-transforming power. This happened when Asian root growers discovered that rice, a kind of water-loving plant which invaded their fields when river floods put them temporarily under water, had a seed that was good to eat and worth raising for its own sake. They used the methods of planting they already knew; that is, they transplanted a growing rice seedling into the fields or paddies, instead of sowing the grain by throwing it broadcast on the ground.

To this day, the rice of Asia is first set out to sprout in special seed beds, and then each plant is separately put into the ground to grow to maturity in fields that are flooded by water brought from some nearby stream. Rice paddy farming feeds a third or more of the people who are alive today. It provided the agricultural basis of the Chinese and Japanese civilizations.

Its success rested on two technical facts. First, by creating artificially flooded fields in places where such flooding did not normally occur, the rice paddy farmers made an environment in which the rice plants, that naturally grow in shallow, fresh water, had no competition. Most weeds were eliminated by drowning. This method is comparable to the way that slash-and-burn farmers of the Middle East eliminated competing grasses by creating an artificial environment for their wheat and barley in isolated forest clearings. Second, the steady flow of fresh water into the paddies and out again brought dissolved minerals to the fields. The slow flow of water also provided an environment in which complicated interactions of light, water and innumerable microorganisms kept up the fertility of the paddies year after year. Once the fields had been laid out, farmers could expect a good crop each year. Unlike slash-and-burn grain cultivators who had to move on from time to time, rice cultivators had absolutely no incentive to move away and leave their carefully leveled fields behind.

People thus discovered how to change the natural balance of plants and animals in thoroughgoing and drastic ways. In the Middle East human communities invented grain cultivation and the domestication of animals between about 8000 and 6000 B.C. In southeast Asia root cultivation developed, beginning no one knows when. But rice paddy farming was probably perfected not long before 2400 B.C., when the earliest definite evidence of rice cultivation comes from China.

THE SPREAD OF FARMING TECHNIQUES

In other parts of the world, farming became important still later—often, and perhaps always, after people had heard from strangers how it was possible to plant and harvest seeds or roots. Rice paddy agriculture spread more slowly than slash-and-burn grain farming. It also spread less far, but where it established itself it took over the landscape in a much more thoroughgoing way than the early grain farming did.

By the standards of our day, life in tiny farming settlements of 200 or 300 people changed very slowly. When experts compare the bits and pieces left from Neolithic villages, they do find small differences from one layer to the next, or from one site to another, but the general impression is of a great sameness. This presumably reflects the fact that once the skills and tools needed for a farmer's life had been invented, nothing much more was needed. Year after year the same tasks had to be done: grain planted and harvested, new fields broken in, houses repaired or rebuilt; from time to time the whole community might have to move a few miles to some place where fresh forest land lay at hand.

But however unchanging Neolithic village routines may have been, the rise and spread of this new way of life worked great changes in the landscape. Slash-and-burn methods of cultivation required frequent relocation. A single community might move several times in a person's lifetime, perhaps twenty or more miles at a time. By comparison with any changes that we know of earlier, this meant a tremendously rapid transformation of the natural environment. Moreover, the new techniques could easily be imitated by neighboring bands of hunters. Grain farming therefore spread in every direction from its Middle Eastern place of origin. Farmers arrived in south Russia and the Balkans soon after 4500 B.C., and slash-and-burn cultivation reached the Atlantic coast of Europe about a thousand years later. A similar movement carried farmers across north Africa and into western Europe, where they met and mingled with those who came by the more northerly route.

We know less about migrations eastward and southward. Communities of Neolithic farmers drifted into northwestern India at an early date, but the record is still spotty and no exact time can yet be assigned to the earliest village sites in that part of the world. Traces of Neolithic farming, similar to that long established in the Middle East, have also been found in China. But the earliest Chinese farmers cultivated millet, a crop unknown in the ancient Near East, so agriculture may have been invented independently there. By about 2400 B.C. wheat and barley also appear in China; these crops came, presumably, from western Asia. But the few scattered discoveries in central Asia do not yet allow us to put the whole story together.

In the Americas and Africa people probably invented agriculture independently. When Columbus discovered America, the Indians in Mexico, and in part of what is now the United States and Canada, planted corn (maize), squash, and beans. This was a seed agriculture, rather like that of the Middle East. But the plants were completely different. In the Caribbean Islands and South America, root cultivation also existed. Sweet potatoes were the most important crop; but in the high uplands of Peru, the plant we call "potato" also flourished.

Most of the scholars who have studied the question think that American Indians invented agriculture for themselves, without any stimulus from Eurasia. Some, however, disagree. They argue that boats from southeast Asia (perhaps also from Africa) reached American shores before 500 B.C. Storm-tossed castaways who knew how to raise root crops would have found it perfectly natural to try out local plants until they discovered new and valuable foods.

The domestication of corn, however, was complicated and took a long time, since the wild plant had to be profoundly transformed before it could support large human populations. Yet the *idea* of seed farming, too, may have been carried from Asia to America, either by land or across the ocean by some boat's crew, driven before the winds to an unknown land. In the nature of the case we can never expect to know, for such an event would leave no evidence behind.

In other places, too, scholars have thought that farming may have started independently. In west Africa, for example, there are several crops, both roots and seed-bearing plants, not found extensively elsewhere. Does this indicate another center of agricultural invention? Or was it a matter of applying the idea of farming in a new environment, where new kinds of plants offered themselves, and the staple grains of the Middle East did not grow well? Scholarly opinion is divided, and the only way to settle the question would be to learn much more than is yet known about what happened in Africa before and after west African agriculture began.

THE BEGINNINGS
OF HISTORY

With the development of communities whose ways of life differed as radically as the lives of farmers differed from the lives of herders, and both differed from the lives of hunters, human society became much more varied. Interaction between different human groups could and did become a powerful stimulus to further invention and borrowing.

Usually strangers' ways seemed silly or useless; but every so often some new tool or idea, new style of art or new sound of music, new food or new game caught on. Anything borrowed had to fit in with all the things already known and done in the community. This frequently required numerous readjustments before whatever had been borrowed could work smoothly in its new setting. Sometimes the setting itself had to change; and all such changes provoked the possibility of brand-new inventions, because each new situation made people more conscious of what they were doing and forced them to make deliberate choices.

Earlier, when one band of hunters lived in almost the same way as every other band, contacts and collisions between such groups could do little to cause either party to change its ways. But when important differences began to appear, then contacts and collisions between different human groups assumed a new importance. People could and did begin to take advantage of what others knew; they were forced to invent new ways to protect themselves, or to seek more effective modes of attack. A self-sustaining process of action and reaction thus set in, keeping human societies from settling back to an unchanging routine. Historical change, in other words, assumed a new velocity; history, in the narrow sense of written records left by civilized communities, lay just around the corner.

People did not wait long before realizing the possibility and creating the first civilizations. How they did so will be the theme of the next chapter.

CONCLUSION

Prehumans became human when they learned to speak and then to hunt together successfully enough to feed children during their years of growth to maturity. This gave children a prolonged time to learn the arts of life with a minimum of reliance on sheer inherited instincts. Learning, in turn, allowed for flexibility and change, but at first changes came very slowly indeed. Hunters learned how to stalk their prey, how to ward off danger, how to make sharp-edged tools. They knew all they needed to know and could teach their children exactly what they had themselves been taught.

The first great change in this pattern came when people in the forested hill country of the Middle East discovered how they could make grain grow luxuriantly in the heart of the forest. More food meant more hunters; more hunters soon destroyed most of the game. Then people discovered how to domesticate some of the animals they had formerly hunted. This allowed certain communities to specialize as herders. They followed flocks and herds onto the grasslands that lay north and south of the hill regions of the Middle East.

Farmers soon had to deal with herders, either peaceably through trade or by taking defensive measures to guard against sudden raids. They faced other problems: how to know when to plant, and as population continued to grow, how to find enough good land for next year's harvest. Accurate time reckoning was not achieved until the first civilized societies emerged; but the problem of land shortage was met before that time by the invention of the plow. Plowing kept back weeds and greatly extended the amount of land a single family could cultivate. By planting only half of what they plowed, farmers could raise a crop every second year on the same land. Regular fields, settled village life, and the patterns of rural life that have lasted to the present in most of Europe and western Asia thus emerged before 3000 B.C.

In eastern Asia a different kind of agriculture arose, based on root crops. Later, these Asian farmers discovered rice and developed the style of paddy cultivation that supports the dense populations of that region today.

In other parts of the earth agriculture also developed, perhaps by independent invention, or perhaps by borrowing from either the Middle Eastern or the east Asian style of cultivation, with suitable adjustments to local climates and the array of food plants available in the region.

The net effect of the development of agriculture was an enormous increase in human numbers. Our ancestors first became the best hunters, lords of beasts; then people began to transform the natural balance by planting crops and domesticating animals, increasing their own numbers, power, and strength in the process many times over.

From this time onward, relations between different human communities became more important than interaction with the natural environment which, in the first stages of humanity's rise to dominion over the earth, had been the primary stimulus to improvements in ways of doing things. Human history, as opposed to the natural history of *homo sapiens*, thus commenced.

CHAPTER 2

River Valley Civilizations

3500 to 1500 B.C.

The earliest farmers were not civilized, and could not be. To build a civilization required far larger communities than could be sustained on the basis of slash-and-burn cultivation. Thousands of persons had to work together to build the monumental temples, tombs, and palaces that dominated the earliest centers of civilization. Only in large communities could specialists arise and develop the skills and knowledge that distinguished civilized from uncivilized peoples.

At first such sizable communities could arise only in geographical environments of unusual fertility. In the Middle East, where grain farming had first become important, the floodplains of large rivers provided such environments. Near the rivers, irrigation was easy and assured large and abundant crops. In addition, fresh silt renewed the fertility of the soil year after year, making it unnecessary for irrigation farmers to seek new land, as slash-and-burn cultivators in woodland regions had to do.

Consequently, it was not by accident that the earliest societies we recognize as civilized arose in three large river floodplains within the general region of the Middle East: beside the Tigris and Euphrates rivers in present-day Iraq; beside the Nile River in what is now the Arab Republic of Egypt; and beside the Indus River in present-day Pakistan.

Each of the ancient river valley civilizations had its own way of doing things, its own ideas, its own art. Yet ships carried people and goods back and forth, apparently from the earliest times, so that key

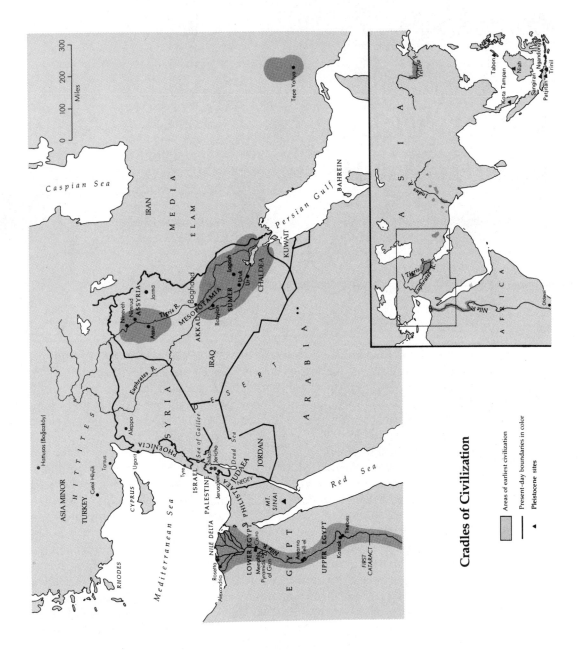

Cradles of Civilization

▨ Areas of earliest civilization

— Present-day boundaries in color

▲ Pleistocene sites

ideas and skills were able to pass from one civilized society to another, even across the long distances that separated them. This kind of contact explains, in part, why the rise of these three civilizations took place at nearly the same time: about 3500 to 3000 B.C. in the Tigris-Euphrates Valley and between 3000 and 2500 B.C. in the Nile and Indus valleys.

SUMERIAN CIVILIZATION

The first-known civilization arose in the lower Tigris and Euphrates valleys, in the land of Sumer which lies a few miles inland from the present coastline of Iraq on the Persian Gulf. This whole region is often called Mesopotamia, the name given to it by the ancient Greeks. (*Mesopotamia* in Greek means "the country between the rivers," and the term refers not only to Sumer in the south but also to Akkad, Babylonia, and Assyria strung out to the north. All these lands were bounded by the Tigris River on the east and the Euphrates River on the west.)

Before people began to change the natural landscape, the Tigris and Euphrates flowed to the sea through swamps, separated from one another by stretches of desert. Plant life was confined to the swamps and the regions near their edges where there was enough groundwater to make up for the almost complete absence of rain. The swamps were made by river floods, which came each spring when the snows in the mountains melted. Later when the summer drought set in up north, the rivers dwindled away until the rains of autumn and winter began to swell them once again.

When the rivers were in flood, the waters spread out from the usual channels. As the water left the main stream its flow became much slower, so that silt and sand sank quickly to the bottom. The effect was to build up a natural levee (or embankment) of higher ground close beside the main river stream. The levees in turn created natural basins on either side of the riverbed where swamp waters got trapped after each flood.

This was not the only peculiarity of the floodplain, for since the rivers flowed more slowly across the flat landscape than they did in the mountains, the heavier bits of sand and gravel carried down from the mountains by the waters came to rest along the bottom of the main stream itself. The Euphrates in particular tended to build up its bed in this way until the river might actually flow, between its natural levees, slightly above the level of the surrounding plain. Then every so often, when a particularly powerful flood occurred, the river would break through the levee on one side or the other and make a new bed for itself, leaving only a few stagnant pools to show where living water formerly had flowed to the sea.

Such an environment presented human beings with some useful resources. Fish were abundant and so were waterfowl. Date palms grew naturally along the levees and offered a richly nutritious fruit. Reeds abounded in the swamps and provided materials for constructing simple huts. Floods were a serious problem, but families with a boat had little to fear because no matter how high the waters rolled in a particular year, they would soon subside again, and in most years a few bits of higher ground remained above flood level all the time. The first thing needed therefore was a boat; hence, we can guess that the Tigris-Euphrates floodplain was occupied for the first time by human communities that knew how to make boats.

Unfortunately reed huts leave practically no traces for modern archaeologists to detect. The boats and nets upon which fishers and bird snarers depended were perishable too. The first settlers needed little in the way of stone tools, and any that may have survived are scattered far and wide underneath many feet of silt. Hence it is only by interpreting religious symbolism from later ages that modern scholars can find evidence for the existence of such communities in the very beginning of the floodplain's history.

Beginnings of the Sumerian Civilization

About 4000 B.C. the scene began to change. Large villages of mud-brick houses arose. Within a thousand years communities large enough to be called cities, and guarded by massive walls and gates, had come into existence in the land of Sumer. By that time, too, there had evolved a system of writing that modern scholars can read, thus opening up another path for the understanding of that ancient way of life which we can begin to call a civilization.

BREAKTHROUGH TO IRRIGATION FARMING   Irrigation was the key to this entire development. Crop raising was impossible without irrigation. Fresh-sprouted grain would wither and die under the fierce sun unless lifesaving water could be brought to the fields often enough to allow the crop to ripen. But as soon as men learned to water their fields at will, they could count on a regular and abundant harvest, for with enough moisture the soil of Sumer, which had been built up from river silt, was extremely fertile.

In the beginning, we may imagine, irrigation was practiced on a very small scale. The peculiar landscape of the lower Tigris-Euphrates

Valley made this easy. By digging a ditch through the levee, farmers could allow water from the river to flow onto the lower levels of the adjacent plain. When enough water had reached the fields, the ditch in the levee could be filled in, to be dug out again when more water was needed.

When, however, farmers became more numerous, they needed to irrigate land lying farther from the river. This called for more elaborate methods. By tapping the river a few miles upstream and constructing an artificial channel for the water, it was possible to irrigate land lying farther and farther from the river. The higher upstream the canals began, the wider the area of land that could be irrigated. But with the lengthening of every new canal and dike the task of maintaining the irrigation system became more burdensome. Soon it required the cooperation of thousands upon thousands of people to clean the irrigation channels each year and to inspect and repair the dikes.

The harder communities worked to extend the irrigation system, the greater the risks. Every spring flood threatened sudden destruction. The river might wash out vital dikes or obstruct a canal with fresh deposits of sand. Or if perchance the river changed course somewhere upstream, then every available man and woman had to be mobilized to repair the breach in the river walls in order to turn the stream back into its old channel; otherwise, the entire irrigation system would have to be redesigned—old canals abandoned and new ones dug—a task that might take years.

When everything went right the practical rewards were spectacular. Enough water, supplied at the right time, assured better yields than could be obtained from ordinary rain-watered fields. Irrigation agriculture, therefore, could support comparatively large and dense populations in the same place, year after year. Not only this: river silt was perfectly suited to the plow, so that a single family with a team of oxen could easily produce more grain than was needed for its own consumption. Farmers had to be able to produce a food surplus for civilization to get started. Only then could a substantial number of persons free themselves from the task of finding food and begin to spend their time doing other things. This, in turn, allowed specialized skills and new ideas to multiply until society as a whole became sufficiently complex, wealthy, and powerful to be called "civilized."

Sumerian Achievements of the Bronze Age

These factors all came together for the first time in Sumer between 3500 and 3000 B.C. During that 500-year period, the ancient Sumerians rapidly developed new skills and knowledge. Individuals who specialized in serving the gods, in laying out canal systems, or simply in making clay pots, had time to invent better ways of doing the job when they no longer had to work in the fields, but became full-time specialists instead. New crafts soon emerged: wheelwrights to make round, strong wooden wheels, boatbuilders and sailmakers, jewel engravers, scribes who kept written records, gold and silver smiths, and bronze founders who poured hot liquid metal into clay molds to make a great variety of tools and weapons.

Like the stone tools and weapons that had been used in earlier ages, bronze does not easily decay. Hence the first modern scholars who studied human beginnings invented the term "Bronze Age" to describe the period when people made their most important tools and weapons out of bronze instead of stone, or, as in still later times, iron. Recently, however, experts have played down the contrast between the Bronze Age and the Stone Age. Stone tools continued to be used in the fields long after warriors and kings began to use bronze swords and axes. Moreover, the use of metals did not begin with the birth of civilization, as scholars once thought.

Long before the first Sumerian cities took shape, various small communities of Neolithic villagers in the Middle East had learned that when some kinds of rocks were put into a hot fire, shiny metal would ooze out. In this way, copper, tin, lead, and silver could be produced from the right kinds of ore. Nuggets of pure gold could also be picked up in stream beds. The shiny stuff was good for jewelry, but it was too soft to cut or pierce hard substances and so had no use in the making of tools or weapons.

Not long before 3000 B.C., however, Middle Eastern smiths found out that a much harder material, bronze, could be made by combining copper and tin in a proportion of about 9 to 1. By pouring the hot, liquid bronze into molds, it could be made to harden into almost any shape. And such objects were so tough that even strong blows would not damage them.

Here was a material ideally suited for weapons. Soon, the Sumerians began to make bronze axes, spearheads, and swords for offense, and helmets, shields, and body armor for defense. As war became more important, a never-ending quest for tin and copper ores began. This quest drove civilized and semicivilized merchants far afield into the mountains north, west, and east of Mesopotamia, and, before long, to even more distant places, such as Cyprus, Sardinia, and up the Danube River to the Carpathian Mountains in modern Romania.

With these and similar improvements in technique went an accumulation of new kinds of knowledge, organized more systematically than ever before. The key breakthrough was the development of a body of full-time priests, who passed on their wisdom to their successors by formal patterns of teaching and apprenticeship. The priests' main concern was how to deal with the gods.

In addition to this, however, the priests accumulated many other kinds of knowledge. They employed the first scribes, keeping records of temple income and expenses. They learned how to measure space and time far more accurately than before. Without precise measurement of space it was impossible to build the great temple structures that came to dominate each Sumerian city; it was also impossible to construct really elaborate canal systems without being able to measure ground levels and slopes too gradual to be sensed accurately by the eye. As for the measurement of time, it was tied in with the calculation of the seasons and with the art of interpreting what the movements of the heavenly bodies signified for the future.

By acquiring and preserving such skills and knowledge, the ancient Sumerians achieved the essentials of civilization by 3000 B.C. Instead of small, isolated villages, in which everyone did almost the same things and had about the same abilities as everyone else in the community, Sumerian cities had become far more complicated. Experts and professionals knew how to do things that others did not. Most people continued to farm and dig and perform other kinds of heavy labor, and needed to know nothing their Neolithic ancestors had not already known. But a minority of experts and specialists had added a whole new dimension to human capability. Their skills and knowledge opened the door upon a new epoch of human history: the era of civilization.

Problems of Civilization

The success with which the Sumerians solved the problems of irrigation farming in the Tigris-Euphrates floodplain between 3500 and 3000 B.C. quickly created a whole new set of problems that had to be faced. Relationships between people doing different things and living in different environments became critical. The emergence of different social classes within the cities presented an obvious challenge: how could their different interests and outlooks be made to harmonize so that cooperation instead of quarreling would prevail? No less difficult was the relation between civilized society and the barbarians round about. How, for example, could the Sumerians acquire such necessary things as timber, building stone, and metal ores that could not be found in the floodplain? Simple seizure was one solution; trade with local inhabitants of the hill zones to the north and west, where trees and rock abounded, was another. Nor did initiative always rest with the city folk. Barbarian tribes could raid the floodplains, or might prefer to trade peaceably if the cities seemed too strong.

But no matter how important these problems became, and no matter how significant the new specialized products of city skills were for human history as a whole, it is worth remembering that nearly all of the inhabitants of the floodplain remained farmers. Basic to everything else was the fact that with irrigation farming, as long as the rivers were normal and enemies did not strike, more people got more food from a smaller area of ground than ever before.

Sumerian Social Structure and Technical Advance

By themselves the techniques of irrigation would not have made much difference if the Sumerians had not been willing to remodel the social structure to take full advantage of the new possibilities. Among slash-and-burn farmers, scattered plots of cultivated land, each cleared and tended by the members of a single family, worked very well. Each family controlled the grain harvested from the plots that its own members cultivated and saved the necessary seed for next year, or else faced the consequences. But when the same irrigation channel had to supply many families, irrigation farmers had to invent new patterns of planning and control. When everyone needed water, how much each could take had to be settled somehow. Means also had to be found to make each family do its share to maintain and repair the canals and dikes upon which all the fields depended. And the new skills and specialized occupations that made Sumer civilized could never have come into existence if ways had not been found to transfer grain and other food from those who raised it to those who no longer spent their time working in the fields.

Exactly how the Sumerians achieved the new patterns of living is not known. During the thousand years from 4000 to 3000 B.C., when the new type of society slowly took shape, no one had yet learned to write. Without texts that can tell us what people thought and did, we cannot know anything definite about Sumerian customs, and the ideas of property, duty, law, or prudence that defined their social relationships. Religious myths, which were recorded many centuries later, provide some hints as to how Sumerians may have looked upon the world in the formative centuries when they were learning how to construct bigger and bigger canals and how to construct a complex, civilized society that would both hold together and be able to defend itself from outside attack. But the myths are not very clear, and modern scholars do not agree on how to interpret them.

ORIGINS OF THE SUMERIANS   One theory holds that perhaps the Sumerians were invaders who came by sea from somewhere along the shores of the Persian Gulf or even farther away. Having better and more seaworthy boats than the older inhabitants, they may have been able to control movement by water. This would allow an easy concentration of force against the older inhabitants—whoever they were—who then were compelled to work for the Sumerian newcomers as farmers and servants. A few references in myths to arrival by sea from the south support such an idea, as well as the fact that mountains and domesticated animals play a much larger part in Sumerian religious symbolism than one would expect from a people who had always lived in the flat flood-plains.

Other scholars think that the Sumerians lived amid the swamps for a long time before they became irrigation farmers. After they learned to irrigate, according to this view, they developed their civilization under the leadership of priests who persuaded the people that unless they brought part or all of the harvest to the temple and gave it as a gift to the god, some sort of divine punishment would surely follow.

The question, then, is whether the farmers of ancient Sumer transferred part of the grain they raised to others because some conquering strangers forced them to do so, or whether they acted mainly from fear of the gods' displeasure.

There is simply not enough evidence to prove which of these theories is right. The important fact is that somehow the Sumerian farmers became accustomed to seeing a large part of their crop taken away to be used by others. And instead of reacting to this experience by planting and harvesting less grain than before, these ancient peasants kept on working hard, year after year. Only with such an arrangement could enough grain be raised so that the society could sustain the specialized skills and distinct occupations—that is, different social classes—that are a hallmark of civilization.

THE STATUS OF THE PEASANTS   The Sumerian peasants received little in return for their work. They may have been able to watch magnificent temple ceremonies from a distance, but the precious goods produced in temple workshops were for the gods (and their chief servants, the priests)—not for ordinary mortals. Peasants usually made their own tools and household articles, just as the earliest farmers of Neolithic villages had done. Wood for plows and sharp flints to put teeth in sickles had to come from afar, and farmers may have traded extra grain for such necessary supplies. They may sometimes have had enough grain to barter some of it for trinkets from town; but such exchanges were unimportant. In general, what the peasants received in return for the grain they handed over to their superiors was protection from the wrath of both gods and men.

THE ROLE OF THE PRIESTS   Sumerian religious ideas go far to explain how the system worked. According to myths, mentioned earlier, the world was ruled by a handful of gods. These gods behaved very much like human beings, but were more powerful and lived forever. Individual gods personified the great natural forces that mattered: earth, sky, sun, moon, thunder, air, and fresh and salt water. Each had his or her own temple. Here the god lived, inhabiting the statue that resided there, in the same way that human souls inhabited human bodies. Like ordinary mortals, the god had to be fed, clothed, and amused. Indeed, the gods had created humans precisely to perform these services. If, therefore, they did the job well, the god might be pleased and do his best to protect his faithful servants from danger. If for any reason a god was not pleased, then woe betide! Flood or famine or enemy attack—any or all such disasters— would surely come, unless extraordinary prayer and supplication could persuade the god to withhold punishment.

A god's house or temple stood near the center of each Sumerian city. Sometimes more than one divine household grew up within a single city. The Sumerians believed that these gods were very powerful and were liable to take sudden likes and dislikes, just as powerful persons might do. It was therefore important to keep track from day to day of just how the local god or gods felt. Special servants—the god's household staff—not only looked after each god's daily wants, but made it their business to watch carefully for any and all signs of their god's intentions. Only in this way could communities hope to head off possible disasters. These "special servants" were, of course, the priests.

They used several methods to discover the god's will. A priest might sleep in the god's house—the temple—and wait for the god to come in a dream and instruct him directly. Another method was to study the shape of the livers of sheep that had been sacrificed to the god. Still a third method was to watch the way the planets moved in the sky. Careful records of what these different signs had foretold on previous occasions allowed the priests to predict what the god intended by sending the same sign again. And they could also take preventive measures to ward off danger.

Granted the basic assumption that the Sumerians made about the world, the system was foolproof. If what had been predicted actually happened, this proved that the sign had been interpreted correctly. In such instances, any human efforts to change the god's plans had obviously been inadequate—too late or too weak to affect the divine will. If, on the other hand, what had been predicted failed to take place, the priests could claim credit for having warded off danger by acting wisely and quickly in the light of their special knowledge. Such doctrines obviously magnified the power and importance of priests.

Archaeological discovery shows that, under the stimulus of their religious ideas, Sumerians built and rebuilt the temples ever more elaborately. From rather simple beginnings—a mud-brick house set on a low platform—the temples grew higher and higher, until they became the fabled seven-storied *ziggurats*, temples reaching hundreds of feet into the sky. Around the temple clustered the god's storehouses. Here the priests gathered everything needed for running the temple household. Skilled artisans manufactured precious and semiprecious articles for the god's own use. They might also produce goods that could be bartered with distant peoples for the gems, metals, incense, lapis lazuli, mother-of-pearl, dyestuffs, and other luxuries that were needed to humor the god.

THE EMERGENCE OF NEW ARTISAN SKILLS Temple storehouses played a central role, therefore, in fostering new skills. Artisans who did nothing but carve gems, for example, quickly learned how to do so very skillfully. As a matter of fact, the Sumerians soon found a use for this skill that made the jeweler's trade an important one in all later Mesopotamian history. By cutting patterns into the sides of a cylinder, attached to a handle that allowed it to rotate freely, a pattern could be reproduced on soft wet clay by simply running the "seal" across it. When the clay dried, it formed a nearly indestructible record of ownership. Since no two cylinder seals were exactly alike, an owner could always prove his rights by running off a matching set of prints from the seal he carried with him. Everyone who had any property obviously needed such a proof of ownership. Hence it is not surprising that thousands upon thousands of these carved cylinders have been discovered. Some of them, their designs skillfully cut in reverse into the hard stone, produce an amazingly beautiful imprint even today.

We have far less information about other artisan skills developed in the ancient temple households. Weaving and dyeing were important; cloth seems to have been a major Sumerian export. A few examples of goldsmiths' art as well as some statues carved of stone have survived. But to our eyes, these two products of Sumerian skill are not particularly pleasing. Cult statues (statues inhabited by the gods) in the temples were probably made of precious materials, and none of them has survived. Hence, the masterpieces of Sumerian art have been irreparably destroyed. This makes it unfair to compare Sumerian art with that of Egypt, where stone played a much larger role and nearly undamaged masterworks still exist.

THE DEVELOPMENT OF WRITING As the size and wealth of the Sumerian temples increased, the priests had to keep track of what was delivered to and taken from the storehouses. To do this systematically they invented the world's earliest writing. It was not too difficult to prepare a tablet of moist clay and then make marks in it with a chopped-off reed stem, whenever a basket of barley came in or out. Nor was it difficult to develop a set of signs to stand for barley, basket, and for all the other things that came in and went out. But how could marks on the clay tablet identify the person who was making a payment or being paid? He had a name of course, but how could his name be written down? How could the chief priest know who had and who had not paid his dues?

But unless this sort of record could be accurately kept, as soon as the number of taxpayers got too large for a single person to remember who owed what and who had paid what, the whole system threatened to break down. If a farmer could get away without paying, others would surely try to do the same. Temple income would shrink; the god would get angry; disaster would ensue.

The problem was solved by drawing pictures of signs to represent sounds. A person's name could be broken down into separate sounds, and each sound (or sound cluster) indicated by a symbol. To illustrate this in English, take the name "Mitchell." This might be portrayed as a baseball mitt followed by a sea shell. Using this method (along with some bad puns), ancient Sumerian scribes were able to write down the names of individual persons and to draw pictures of concrete objects.

The next step was to find ways to express ideas and whole sentences. This they achieved by generalizing some of the picture signs as syllables— the pronounced sound—in any kind of word. To go back to our example, the picture sign for baseball mitt could be used for a lot of different words in English, wherever the sounds we symbolize as "mit" are spoken. Thus: ad-*mit*, per-*mit*, inter-*mitt*-ent, and so forth. And if such a sign were used often enough it might lose its original meaning entirely. This happened when the scribes simplified the original picture by leaving out some of the strokes, or changed them to make them easier to write, until the sign no longer looked like a picture of anything other than itself.

When a few hundred signs achieved this kind of flexibility, scribes could begin to write ordinary sentences, combining the syllable-signs with one another and with an indefinite number of picture signs that stood for particular, concrete objects.

This kind of writing was well worked out by about 3000 B.C. Since the total number of signs that could be used was very large, it took special effort to learn how to write and how to read. Scribal schools were established where young boys learned the art of writing by copying old clay tablets. As writing became an everyday skill, recognizable pictures disappeared. Written symbols were reduced to a few standard, simple strokes and imprints left by the reed stems that the Sumerians used to mark up the moist clay. Because the reed end made a triangular or wedge-shaped imprint, this kind of writing is called *cuneiform* (from Latin *cuneus* meaning "wedge").

The cuneiform script could be used to write any language, but unless the readers were well acquainted with the proper pronunciation and names to give to the picture-elements in the script, it was difficult to read. For this reason, at a later period, when Akkadian had replaced Sumerian as the standard literary language of Mesopotamia, the priests needed help in reciting sacred songs in the original tongue. Akkadian-speaking priests had to learn Sumerian with the help of dictionaries and bilingual texts, in which the words of their own language paralleled the Sumerian words. Recovery of such tablets enabled modern scholars to figure out how to read Sumerian. Of course, they first had to learn to read Akkadian. This was done partly by comparing it with Hebrew and Arabic—for Akkadian, like these modern languages, is a Semitic speech—and partly with the help of a few inscriptions that contained parallel texts in Persian and Akkadian.

The invention of writing marks the boundary between prehistory and history. Being able to read the ancient tablets enables modern scholars to know a good deal about the thoughts, customs, and actions of the Sumerians. However, we should keep in mind that written records developed initially in the temples. It is therefore possible that surviving texts overemphasize the role of temples in that ancient society. Temples and the service of the gods were important; we can be sure of that. But we cannot be sure that other groups and social classes did not also play an important role in even the earliest Sumerian society.

Despite this sort of uncertainty, it is clear that between 3500 and 3000 B.C. the ancient Sumerian cities established a social system that allowed for specialization. With specialization came a rapid improvement in skills and some basic new inventions. Wheeled wagons, for example, allowed people to carry heavy loads overland as never before and to get the grain harvest into the temple storehouses. Sails allowed boats to travel with unexcelled ease downwind, while the addition of a keel and steering oar allowed sailing ships to travel across the wind and make port more or less at will. Improved ships and wagons made it easier to assemble timber and metal from distant parts. This in turn meant larger buildings and better tools and weapons.

The Problem of Peace and Order
—The Rise of Kingship

In early times, so myths and stories tell us, each year, on New Year's Day, the gods met in council to "decide fate" for the year ahead. Perhaps such stories go back to a time when the priests of each temple gathered together annually at Nippur—seat of the important storm-god Enlil—to talk things over, exchange ideas, and make necessary decisions. As long as each of the cities was separated from its neighbors by stretches of swamp and open desert country, this sort of informal association probably worked well. But what happened when most of the land near the river came under cultivation so that the irrigation works of one city interfered with the water supply needed by another? Bitter quarrels broke out. Such disputes were matched by mounting foreign dangers, for the larger and richer the cities got to be, the more tempting they became to barbarian raiders.

THE RISE OF MILITARY CHIEFS   Tensions such as these opened the way for complicated diplomatic intrigue. A city at feud with its neighbor naturally looked for allies, and might find them among barbarians as well as within the circle of Sumerian cities. Old-fashioned priestly consultation at Nippur could not cope with such situations. Strong, violent men, able to lead the citizens in battle, were needed to seize and hold access to the life-giving water. Such leaders may at first have been appointed only for a particular campaign or for a limited period of emergency. But soon they were needed all the time. Indeed a successful captain might build up a personal household like the temple household itself. And when plunder from defeated enemies fell short, the great man might use his slaves, servants, and armed retainers to compel the citizens he was supposed to protect to supply his household from their own resources.

It was easy enough for a war leader or king to fasten his power on a single city. The revenue required to keep his personal household well supplied could come by diverting grain and other forms of income from the temple. This risked the anger of the priests and, no doubt, of the god; but it saved the war leaders from having to invent a tax collecting system of their own. Moreover, priests were not always against the kings. Sometimes they interpreted the signs from the gods as requiring the people to follow their king into battle against some threatening foe. In other words, among the ancient Sumerians, warlike and priestly forms of leadership often worked together. Only sometimes did priests and kings quarrel over how to use the resources of the city—whether for war or for the temple services.

But the rise of kingship within each city did nothing to solve the larger problem of establishing harmonious relationships among the separate cities of Sumer. Early kings sometimes overran a rival city and compelled its citizens to pay tribute, that is, grain or other valuable things. But after a few weeks a king had either to return home or else set up his headquarters permanently in the conquered city. In either case the king's household could control only the community immediately at hand.

To divide forces was to invite defeat. Furthermore, if an army stayed in a conquered city for very long food supplies were likely to run short. No less important, the god of the defeated city might not like to see a stranger encamped among his people. And the conqueror's god, who lived in another city, was, after all, far away.

Time and again, therefore, victory was undone. Conquerors went home, and the defeated city resumed its separate political existence, until some fresh quarrel provoked new wars and fresh conquests. For hundreds of years, nothing resembling a stable, central administration for the whole land of Sumer could be invented.

The Beginnings of Empire

KING SARGON I OF AKKAD   About 2350 B.C. the first imperial conqueror appeared. His name was Sargon and he came from Akkad, the region immediately upriver from Sumer. At one time or another he subdued all the cities of the floodplain and penetrated deep into barbarian lands. His soldiers may have reached the seacoast of the Mediterranean and the coast of the Black Sea. In Mesopotamia proper, they met no equal.

The secret of Sargon's success was partly the size of his army. He had more soldiers than any opponent could gather against him. Since they campaigned every year, Sargon's soldiers soon became veterans, more resolute, disciplined, and experienced than any enemy they had to face. In other words, Sargon's household became a standing professional army. Yet there was a serious flaw in Sargon's power. He could not feed his household for long in any one place, and he could not bring enough supplies to an imperial capital to sustain his army year in and year out. As a result, the great conqueror had always to be on the move, taking his troops to where plunder and food could be found.

As long as he lived, however, Sargon's power over the lands of Sumer and Akkad was never successfully challenged. But after he died his successors found it impossible to maintain supremacy. Mesopotamia soon broke up again into smaller political-military units. Some of these were tribal; some centered upon a city-state (which is composed of an independent city and the land around it); about others we cannot tell. The secret of enduring empire had yet to be discovered.

By Sargon's time, however, important changes in the structure of civilized society in Mesopotamia had begun—changes that were to pave the way for more firmly established empires. What happened was that when the formerly barbarian Akkadians began to share, more or less as equals, in the Sumerian style of civilized life, they brought new principles of social order with them. The Akkadians spoke a Semitic tongue and had been herders before they settled in the river valleys. Probably they were organized into tribal groups, led by chiefs.

Irrigation agriculture penetrated Akkad before and during Sargon's time. In Akkad, the peasants who did the work usually did not deliver their harvest to a temple. Instead, local warring chiefs put slaves and their other human servants to work in the fields and took a share of what they produced as rent or tribute. For the families that sweated in the fields, it made little difference whether their surplus grain went into a temple storehouse or into the hands of some strong-armed master.

For society at large, however, the Akkadian pattern meant that more resources were earmarked for military endeavors and less for religious uses. Warriors needed craft specialists too: metal-workers, especially, to produce weapons and armor on an ever-expanding scale. They also enjoyed luxuries of the sort the priests had once reserved for the gods. Hence the rise of a secular, military class of landlords and agricultural rent takers did not make much difference to the artisans either.

For a would-be ruler of all the land, however, the development of a more or less professional military class made the task of unifying the irrigated land a little easier. Individual landlords were not strong enough to resist the king's demands for military service and tax payments. They had no strong and deeply rooted local loyalty that made them resist such demands in the way temple communities, dedicated to serving a local god, usually did. And if perchance a landowner refused to obey he could easily be replaced, for many men were ready and eager to receive rent in return for serving the king as a soldier. But how could a king make sure of the obedience of landlords and cities scattered far away from the royal person?

THE UR III DYNASTY   The first systematic steps toward solving the problem of ruling distant subjects seem to have been taken under a line of rulers who governed from the ancient Sumerian city of Ur.* This dynasty, usually referred to as Ur III, ruled from about 2050 to 1950 B.C. The Ur III kings claimed rule over all of Sumer and Akkad. They made their power effective by appointing officials to represent them in all important cities. Such appointees held office at the king's pleasure. They had standing orders and instructions, that is, a set of rules to enforce. In addition, letters passed regularly between the monarch and his officials. This allowed the king to make his will known in particular cases of unusual importance, even at a distance, and applying, perhaps, to persons he had never actually seen.

The kings of Ur III, in other words, ruled by means of an elementary

---

* A government that rules over a number of different lands and peoples is referred to as an "empire," and a line of rulers who belong to the same family is known as a "dynasty."

bureaucracy. The bureaucratic principle is fundamental to all modern government. According to this idea, an official acquires certain powers by virtue of appointment to an office, and can command others to obey simply because of holding the office. Who the individual may be apart from the office is irrelevant. In other words, the official plays a role and ordinary people respond appropriately to that role. In this way the complicated relations of a vast and impersonal society may be regularized, peace can be maintained, and a degree of predictability can be achieved even among strangers who may never have seen one another before and may never meet again.

The delegation of authority from some central authority to officials stationed far from the capital may seem obvious today. It was far from obvious when rulers fumblingly first began to try to use the principle. It was not easy to convince strangers that some unknown individual could and should be allowed to exercise the king's delegated powers. Revolt, of course, was always a possibility. Officials might be disloyal or incompetent. Even at best, effective central control over distant cities was hard to maintain when communications depended on messengers who might be intercepted or delayed by rebellious subjects or by some other unusual occurrence. Nevertheless, the system worked.

HAMMURABI, KING OF BABYLONIA   Several centuries later another famous ruler, Hammurabi of Babylon (ruled *c*. 1700 B.C.), found it possible to disperse his soldiers over the Mesopotamian countryside without losing track of where each captain was and how many fighting men he had with him. Hammurabi did this by keeping records. Each captain was granted the right to collect what he could from the inhabitants of a particular district; in return he promised to supply a certain number of fighting men, equipped for war, when called upon to do so by the king or by the king's local official representative. On the basis of such records, the king could then summon part or all of his army whenever a campaign seemed necessary.

In this way Hammurabi overcame a problem that had been beyond the ability of Sargon of Akkad to solve. Instead of holding a large force around his own person and then having to keep forever on the move to find enough supplies to maintain such a horde, Hammurabi sent his soldiers to the places where food was available to support them. He kept control by keeping records. If one of his captains failed to come when called, his absence from the army could be detected at once. Drastic punishment would follow. Knowing this, everyone—at least in principle—obeyed the king's summons when it came.

From the point of view of the peasants and townsmen who had to support the king's soldiers, Hammurabi's system was preferable to Sargon's. The arrival of Sargon's army was like a plague of locusts—unpredictable and all but ruinous. Under Hammurabi's system the soldiers were on the spot most of the time. Soon people got used to supporting them, and the burden became more or less predictable. Even if over a period of years the demands for goods and services made by Hammurabi's troops exceeded the ravages made by Sargon's occasional visits, regular burdens were easier to bear and did less damage to ordinary civilian life and property.

Law, codified or systematized by Hammurabi and other monarchs, provided another important means of making human relations, even among strangers, more predictable. A rudimentary market whereby merchants organized interregional exchange of goods also emerged by Hammurabi's time. This was another way to coordinate human effort across long distances, often to mutual advantage. It is, however, difficult to tell just how effective these two devices really were. Recorded lawsuits, for example, do not seem to have been decided according to the provisions of Hammurabi's famous code; and anything like free-market exchanges may have been rare.

Despite these advances in administration, military organization, and trade, the balance of strength between inhabitants of the floodplains and the neighboring barbarians was very unstable. Barbarians learned much from living within range of Mesopotamian civilization. Many of them were especially interested in getting hold of better arms and armor and using their increased military strength to raid still deeper into civilized country.

Other factors also changed the balance of strength between the people of the irrigated floodplain and the inhabitants of surrounding rain-watered land. Sumerian methods of irrigation allowed the river water to evaporate from the cultivated fields. As a result, each year the water left small quantities of salt behind. Salt is present in most soils and is very easily dissolved in water. Hence rain picks salt up from the earth and carries it, in weak solution, via streams and rivers to the sea. But when the water evaporates into the air, salt remains behind. In the ocean, the result is that the seas are slowly becoming saltier. On the irrigated land of Sumer, too, salt slowly accumulated. Century after century these deposits increased until the soil, once so fertile, became too salty to grow anything. In this way the cradleland of civilization slowly became desolate. Wealth and power moved steadily north: first to Akkad; then, by Hammurabi's time, to Babylonia.

But as the center of civilization moved north, it approached a region where rains fall often enough to allow cultivation without benefit of irrigation. In such country the boundaries between irrigated and nonirrigated land became less sharp: the gap between what could be done with irrigation and what could be done without it narrowed. Little by little civilized social structures that had at first been possible only on irrigated land developed also on rain-watered land. The transition was gradual and extended from about 2500 to 1500 B.C. Its nature and consequence we shall consider in the next chapter. Before examining that breakthrough, however, we shall first look at two other river valley civilizations based, like the civilization of Sumer and Akkad, on irrigation, and like it, very old.

EGYPTIAN CIVILIZATION

In the area around Mesopotamia there were several small rivers with floodplains that could be irrigated. But these were not big enough to become the seats of independent new civilizations. Instead, settled life in the Jordan Valley, for example, although very old, was strongly influenced by the Mesopotamian style of civilization when the farmers of the Jordan became acquainted with Sumerian achievements and ideas.

The Nile and Indus rivers, however, were farther away from the Sumerian center of civilization. Their valleys were spacious and their waters abundant. Here, to the southeast and southwest of Mesopotamia, two other ancient river valley civilizations arose not long after the Sumerians pioneered the way. Contact by sea with Sumer helped. In Egypt, for example, the idea of how to make large buildings clearly came from the Sumerians, because Egypt's earliest monumental structures imitated the mud-brick buildings of Mesopotamia. But whatever Egyptians may have borrowed, they soon developed a civilization specifically and uniquely their own. So far as we know, the same was true of the Indus peoples and civilization.

Valley of the Nile

The lower Nile Valley differed significantly from the Tigris-Euphrates floodplain. The river flowed more gently; its floods were regular and slow. The Nile's narrow floodplain lay between high rock walls. Beyond the cliffs lay desert, even more barren than the deserts of southern Mesopotamia. Thus the lower Nile Valley was enclosed and protected, so that barbarian raids of the sort that constantly troubled Mesopotamia were no threat to the early farmers of the Nile Valley.

Another peculiarity of the Nile made political unification remarkably easy. The Nile flows north and, unlike the Tigris and Euphrates, was

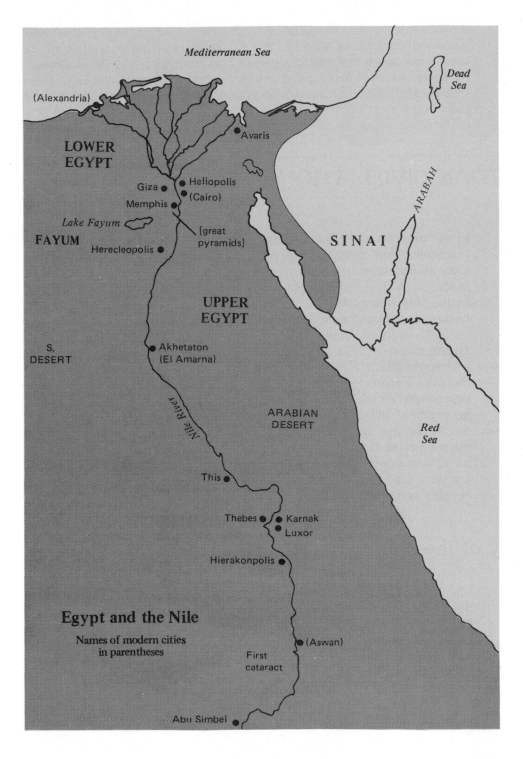

Egypt and the Nile

Names of modern cities
in parentheses

navigable to the First Cataract—which marked the traditional boundary of ancient Egypt. The country lies in the trade-wind zone, which means that a gentle, even breeze blows almost constantly from the northeast. By hoisting a sail, therefore, a boat may easily quarter across the wind and go upstream; by lowering the sail and allowing the vessel to drift it can go downstream with equal ease. Since the valley is only a few miles wide, anyone who controls shipping on the Nile controls the land of Egypt. Gathering the fruits of the soil into a single storehouse presented no difficulties for ancient Egyptians. Boats could easily move vast quantities of barley and other commodities up and down the Nile.

Even in flood, the Nile waters moved too slowly to damage dikes and canals. In fact, the ancient Egyptians never had to develop elaborate canal systems like those of the Mesopotamians. Instead, they relied on basin irrigation. This meant that they built low dikes all around a field and opened the dikes to let the Nile River flow into the field at flood time. When enough water had soaked into the earth, gaps were opened in the dikes to let the extra water run off onto a neighboring field that lay slightly lower because it was further down the valley slope. This method of irrigation prevented the accumulation of salt by evaporation— a fatal flaw in the Sumerian technique of irrigation, as we saw. Thus Egypt remains fertile today, whereas the land of Sumer has become a howling wilderness of sun-baked mud and sand.

The Egyptian cultivator seeded his fields before the flood. Later in the season, when the seed had sprouted and the level of the river had gone down, additional water had to be lifted onto the fields by hand. This water evaporated, but the floodwaters of the following year flushed away whatever salt was left behind by the comparatively small amounts of water that even the hardest-working farmer could lift onto his fields.

The Old Kingdom

Largely because of these environmental differences, early Egyptian history differed sharply from that of Sumer and Akkad. First of all, the land of Egypt was united by conquest before it became civilized. The name of the conqueror was Menes. His victory established what is called the Old Kingdom, lasting from about 3100 to 2200 B.C. During all that time Egypt remained politically united, with only trifling periods of upheaval as power passed from one dynasty to another. The capital was at Memphis, near modern Cairo.

Egypt's civilized styles of life and art developed far more quickly than had been the case in Sumer. About 2650 B.C. the kings of the Fourth Dynasty began to build the great pyramids, which ever since have symbol-

THE DECIPHERMENT
OF HIEROGLYPHIC
AND CUNEIFORM WRITING

Jean François Champollion (1790–1832) was an infant prodigy. At the age of sixteen he read a paper to a learned society in Grenoble, France, in which he argued that the ancient Egyptians had spoken a tongue ancestral to the Coptic language used by Egyptian Christians in their church services. Fifteen years later he proved that this theory was correct by deciphering hieroglyphic writing, after nearly 2000 years when no one had been able to read that ancient script.

Champollion performed this feat by studying the Rosetta Stone, found in 1799 near the Rosetta mouth of the Nile River. It carried inscriptions in three languages: Greek (which scholars had no trouble reading), demotic (that is, common) Egyptian, and hieroglyphic. Champollion assumed, first, that the two Egyptian texts were translations from the Greek. He then guessed that in hieroglyphic the names of rulers were enclosed within cartouches (that is, oval figures such as shown in the photograph of the cartouche from the Rosetta Stone). Then he simply assigned sound values to each hieroglyph inside the cartouches by comparing its position in the royal name with the corresponding Greek letters. The next step was to test the result on the rest of the inscription to see whether anything like a pronounceable text came out. It did, and sure enough the language of the hieroglyphs was enough like Coptic to prove Champollion's theory.

The meaning of the Rosetta Stone's hieroglyphic words could, of course, be established by comparing them with the words of the Greek text. But this did not solve all problems. Further difficulty arose from the fact that hieroglyphs sometimes used a single symbol to stand for a whole word or idea—like our use of "5" for *five* or "&" for *and*. But Champollion's key to the sound value of some of the hieroglyphs allowed him and other scholars to make guesses about the meanings of additional characters. Then what had to be done was to check the context in which the ideograph occurred elsewhere, to make sure that everything fitted and made sense. Within about fifty years, therefore, European scholars learned to read the ancient Egyptian writing very accurately, and sometimes could even correct the grammar or point out a spelling error the ancient stonecutters had made.

Roughly a generation later, other European scholars cracked the coded meanings of Mesopotamian cuneiform. They did so fundamentally in the same way. The key breakthrough began in 1835, when Henry Creswicke Rawlinson, a young English army officer, got interested in ancient writings. He had been sent to Persia to help modernize the Shah's army. His army rank allowed him to arrange an expedition to copy a long inscription cut into a cliff at Behistun, Persia, beside the ancient road that ran between Babylon and Ecbatana, one of the three ancient capitals of the Persian Empire. At Behistun there were three kinds of writing: ancient Persian, ancient Elamitic (used at Susa, another of the Persian capitals), and ancient Babylonian. The carvings loomed some 300 feet over the heads of passers-by, and the texts were rather well preserved because they were very hard to reach. Part of the time Rawlinson had to dangle from ropes let down from the top of the cliff, about 1200 feet above, in order to be able to copy everything carefully.

It took him eleven years to figure out how to read the Persian part of the Behistun inscription. He worked by comparing the words and spellings of the inscription with modern and medieval Persian words, and then guessing at the forms and meanings the same words might have had in earlier times. The method was perfectly OK, but not enough texts written in Old Persian survive to permit scholars to compare contexts. As a result, large uncertainties still exist as to how to read Old Persian. All the same, Rawlinson proved that the inscription had been made by King Darius (reigned 521–486 B.C.) and was a justification for his usurpation of the throne.

On the assumption that the Behistun inscription repeated the king's apology in the Elamitic and Babylonian languages, Rawlinson and others set to work to decipher these languages too. Elamitic raised the same problem as Old Persian: there are not enough texts to compare usages, so that its decipherment remains imperfect. Not so with Babylonian cuneiform, however. Vast numbers of baked clay tablets with cuneiform writing on them have survived; and with the key to cuneiform meanings that the Behistun inscription provided, it became possible to refine and correct first guesses by comparison with other texts, just as the Egyptologists had done with hieroglyphic. As a result, by about 1900 experts could read cuneiform almost as well as other experts could read Egyptian hieroglyphics.

Scholarly exchanges through learned journals allowed hundreds of men from many different countries to work together on each of these discoveries. Brilliant pioneering by Champollion and Rawlinson showed the way, but deciphering details took decades and systematic mutual checking among the entire company of scholars who engaged in the task. This kind of international collaboration, more than the genius of any individual, was what made the dramatic recovery of knowledge about the world's early civilizations possible.

ized ancient Egypt. By that time Egyptian civilization had achieved a perfection that later generations always took as a model.

THE ROLE OF THE PHARAOH   In Egypt the king, or Pharaoh, played the role reserved for the gods in Sumer. Indeed, the Egyptians believed he *was* a god—owner and ruler of all the land. As such he was immortal, and when he died his soul went to inhabit a blissful afterworld. The mighty pyramids were intended to preserve the Pharaoh's body, on the theory that his soul would wish to return from time to time to pay a visit to its former earthly frame. The Egyptians also believed that the departed Pharaoh would continue to need servants just as he did on the earth. Persons who had served him well were therefore allowed to build their own tombs nearby so that they might join the Pharaoh in the afterworld and enjoy eternal life in his service. This obviously encouraged strict obedience to the Pharaoh's commands and helped strengthen the political unification of Egypt.

The Pharaoh's court was like one of the Sumerian temple households. As irrigated agriculture spread, Egyptian peasants delivered vast quantities of grain to the Pharaoh's storehouses. Part of the grain was used to support skilled artisans and courtiers of every sort who ministered to the Pharaoh's wants and ran the country, much as the priests and temple servitors of Sumer ministered to their gods' wants and managed the local temple community.

In Egypt work on dikes and canals did not take nearly as much time as in Sumer. Hence the labor power of the entire country could be mobilized to work on pyramids during the seasons of the year when the Nile was low and there was nothing to do in the fields. Barley sent to the Pharaoh's storehouses was paid back to the peasants who labored to cut and transport the great stones to make the pyramids. Then, when it was time to begin plowing and planting again, work on the pyramids stopped (or at least slacked off) until the next harvest was in, after which the laborers reassembled to carry on their enormous task.

By concentrating wealth and skill so completely in the Pharaoh's household, the Old Kingdom was able to achieve amazing artistic perfection. From sculpture and wall painting, of which many examples survive, we can appreciate the extraordinary skill attained by Egyptian artists.

HIEROGLYPHIC WRITING   The so-called hieroglyphic style writing has the same high artistic quality as Egyptian art. Although hieroglyphic symbols were completely different from those used in Mesopotamia, the principles were the same. Signs for syllables and signs for whole words were confusingly mingled. Yet modern scholars can read hieroglyphic inscrip-

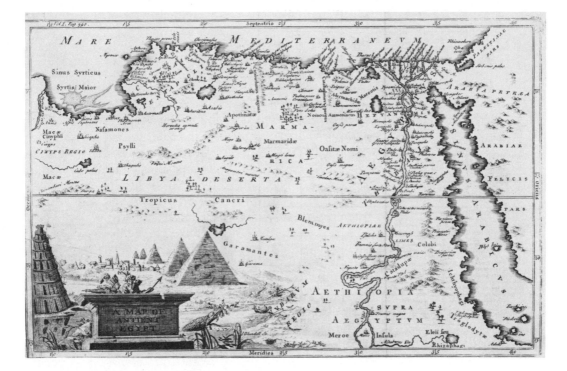

(*The New York Public Library*)

tions quite accurately thanks to the famous Rosetta Stone, discovered by the French when they invaded Egypt in A.D. 1799. (See pp. 48–49.)

Ancient inscriptions therefore tell modern scholars a good deal about Egyptian religion. Besides the Pharaoh, many gods were honored. Some of them had animal shapes; others were conceived in human form. Only a few gods had great temples like those of Sumer. As long as the Pharaoh, god and king, ruled the land of Egypt, the priests who served local gods could not obtain a large enough income to support elaborate temples. But after the Old Kingdom came to an end, local temples and priests sought more power and income—and got them.

The Middle Kingdom

The increase of local and priestly power brought many troubles to Egypt. Priests and nobles began violent struggles among themselves. Egypt became a divided country, and art and artisan skills suffered a severe decline. The struggle for power lasted from about 2200 to 2050 B.C. Then

Original pictograph	Pictograph in position of later cuneiform	Early Babylonian	Assyrian	Original or derived meaning
				bird
				fish
				donkey
				ox
				sun day
				grain
				orchard
				to plow to till
				boomerang to throw to throw down
				to stand to go

Some cuneiform characters: Origin and development. (Courtesy of New York Public Library)

Egypt was again united under a new Pharaoh, who founded what is called the Middle Kingdom. The new capital was at Thebes, in Upper Egypt, instead of at Memphis.

Pharaohs of the Middle Kingdom tried to imitate their predecessors of the Old Kingdom and claimed to be gods just as before. But in spite of the outward show, the Pharaohs of the Middle Kingdom were no longer absolute monarchs—owners and rulers of all the land. They had to share revenue and power with the priests and with new-sprung local lords of the Egyptian countryside. As a result, absolute control of Egypt under a single central authority was never restored. No new pyramids were constructed. The Pharaoh could no longer command the entire labor force of Egypt. Peasants had to stay home and work for their local lords and masters, each of whom, as best he could, tried to keep up some part of the artistic and other cultural traditions that had been established by the Pharaoh's household in the time of the Old Kingdom.

This compromise political order lasted for about 250 years (2050–1800 B.C.). Then, for a second time, local upstarts refused to submit to the Pharaoh's authority, and Egypt divided again into rival principalities. Something new to Egyptian experience then happened: about 1730 B.C. foreigners, called Hyksos, invaded and conquered the land. They brought unfamiliar ways and ideas with them—influenced, perhaps, by Mesopotamian civilization. The Egyptians hated their conquerors' foreign ways and, about 1570 B.C., were able to drive them back into Asia. Egypt was thus again united under the so-called New Kingdom.

THE INDUS CIVILIZATION

We know far less about what happened in the Indus River valley. The Indus River, like the Tigris and Euphrates rivers, flows from high mountains through desert to the sea. In its lower reaches, it behaves like the two rivers that cradled Sumerian civilization. The spring flood on the Indus was strong but irregular, and from time to time the main stream changed course by breaking through natural levees, created in the same way as those along the lower Euphrates River. As a result, the remains of the ancient city of Mohenjo-Daro, discovered in the 1920s, are located in a barren desert, several miles from where the Indus River now flows. A twin city, Harappa, lay some 600 miles upstream, near the bank of one of the main tributaries of the Indus.

Two obstacles prevent modern scholars from learning very much about the civilization that must have once flourished in these cities. First, groundwater has made it impossible for archaeologists to dig to the bottom at either Mohenjo-Daro or Harappa. Expensive engineering work would be required to drain the water off and permit further digging. Thus physical remains dating from the beginnings of the Indus civilization are still undiscovered.

The second obstacle to learning about the Indus civilization is that no one can read the ancient writing that was used at Harappa and Mohenjo-Daro. No bilingual inscriptions, like those that enabled scholars to decipher Sumerian and Egyptian ways of writing, have been found. Indeed, very little Indus writing has survived, for the ancient scribes probably wrote on palm leaves or some other perishable material. Only a handful of inscriptions, cut into cylinder seals like those the Sumerians used, prove that the Indus people did have their own kind of writing. Without more material to work with, even the most skillful cryptographic (deciphering) methods are unlikely to unlock the secret of how to read the ancient Indus script.

Several Mesopotamian cylinder seals have been discovered at the Indus sites, and a few Indus seals have also turned up in Mesopotamia. Evidently, merchants traveled from one region to the other, carrying their seals with them to prove their ownership of sealed goods stashed away in a ship's hold. Since the style of Sumerian seals changed from century to century, it is possible to tell roughly when a particular seal was made.

In addition, the archaeological level at which an Indus seal was found in Sumer can help identify its approximate date. This sort of cross-dating shows that the two great Indus cities were well established by about 2500 B.C. and were destroyed about a thousand years later. Their destruction may have been caused by invasions from beyond the Himalaya Mountains that brought Aryan-speaking barbarians into India for the first time.

Harappa and Mohenjo-Daro were well-planned cities. Their exact geometrical layout and skillfully organized sanitation systems suggest that there was a strong central authority. Very likely the rulers were priests or priest-kings. But the doctrines of their religion and the methods by which they controlled and directed the common people are not known.

A surprising thing about Mohenjo-Daro and Harappa was that the archaeologists who dug them up were not able to notice much difference between successive layers. In Mesopotamia and elsewhere, changes in the ways things were made allow experts to date miscellaneous objects—even odd bits of broken pottery—quite accurately. Nothing similar was done at the Indus sites, partly because the men in charge of the excavation were in a hurry and did not record very carefully where they found things, but also because everything about the two cities seems to have remained remarkably unchanging for centuries. To be sure, floods often undermined the buildings; but, time and again, each damaged structure was carefully restored on exactly the same ground plan as before. Only toward the end did changes appear. Jerry-built structures replaced older buildings, perhaps because the rulers no longer had the means to keep the old traditions alive.

A few small statues were discovered amid the rubble of brick that constituted the bulk of the two Indus sites. No other works of high art were found. Other traces of ancient artisan skills had nearly all disappeared, so that we have scant material with which to judge the style and quality of ancient Indus workmanship. The statues were oddly different from one another, but full of charm and grace. Indus seal engraving was up to Mesopotamian standards. Indeed, the skills and knowledge attained by the Indus civilization were probably very similar to those familiar to the Egyptians and Mesopotamians of the same age. But we have too little information to be sure.

Numerous village sites dating from the Indus period have been uncovered. Several small towns along the seacoast are also known to have existed. Whether such communities were subordinated to the two main cities, and what was the nature and importance of relationships between the Indus peoples and their various neighbors remain completely obscure. A civilization as complex and wonderful in its own way as anything that the Egyptians or Mesopotamians achieved probably lies behind these puzzling traces. But without the access to men's deeds and thoughts that readable records allow, we must simply remain in ignorance.

CONCLUSION

The ancient Mesopotamians, Egyptians, and Indus peoples created the world's earliest civilizations. In the special environment of river flood-plains, they constructed societies rich enough to free a few persons from the task of producing their own food. Individuals set free from the need to spend their time producing food became specialists and developed a substantial range of new skills: writing, bronze-making, seal engraving, large-scale building, and many more.

To begin with, such skills were largely directed toward the service of the gods, conceived in Mesopotamia as invisible and immortal but in other respects very much like humans, whereas in Egypt the most important god was a man in all respects, the Pharaoh. As for the Indus civilization, we do not know what kinds of gods they may have worshiped; we do not even know for certain that the organizers and leaders of that society were priests, although archaeologists' discoveries do not contradict such an idea.

In Mesopotamia, from soon after 3000 B.C., when written records began, warfare became a second major consumer of the products of special skills mentioned above. This was not true in Egypt, where natural barriers to invasion were much greater than in Mesopotamia. Nothing in the remains from the Indus civilization suggests that military enterprise was particularly important there either. Yet these two civilizations did not escape militarization. Between 1750 and 1500 B.C. both were conquered (the Indus civilization was destroyed) by barbarians. The barbarians' style of fighting and military equipment had been developed through border warfare between the civilized cultivators of the Mesopotamian flood-plain and the dry land farmers and herders of the hills and steppelands surrounding the Tigris-Euphrates Valley. In the next chapter, therefore, we shall take up the interaction between civilized and barbarian peoples that resulted not only in these conquests but in the transfer of civilized skills and social organization to rain-watered land.

CHAPTER 3

The Rise of Civilizations on Rain-Watered Land

2000 to 1200 B.C.

In 3000 B.C. the complex kinds of societies which we call civilized could arise only on irrigated land in river floodplains. Elsewhere, farmers did not produce enough food, over and above what they needed for themselves, to be able to support specialists—whether soldiers, artisans, priests, or landlords. The invention of the plow removed what had previously been a limit upon agricultural production. With a plow and a team of oxen a family could easily raise more than enough grain for its needs on ordinary soil, as long as there was sufficient rainfall and a warm enough temperature to encourage plant growth. Hence, the special environment of river floodplains was no longer necessary for the support of civilized society.

This opened broad expanses of land in the temperate zones of the earth to civilization—but only potentially. The acquisition of varied skills and far-reaching changes in social structure were needed before simple Neolithic village communities could become civilized. By 2000 B.C. the necessary changes had been made throughout most of what we call the Middle East. During the following 500 years—between 2000 and 1500 B.C.— a series of dependent and derivative civilizations grew up on every side of the old centers of Mesopotamia. The ones we know most about are the Hittite society of Asia Minor and the Canaanite communities of Syria and Palestine, but others also arose to the east in Iran and in Armenia to the north of the Tigris-Euphrates Valley.

CIVILIZATION, BARBARISM, AND CULTURAL DIFFUSION

How did this transition from irrigated to nonirrigated land take place? In a general way, the answer is obvious enough. Some persons set themselves up over ordinary farming folk and made them plow and harvest more land than they needed for their own support. The surplus food was then used to support soldiers, priests, artisans, sailors, caravan folk, miners, loggers, and other specialists. As the skill and numbers of such groups increased, a society we recognize as civilized emerged.

To understand fully how simple villages—in which everybody did the same kind of work and lived very nearly in the same way—could give birth to the more complicated structure of civilized communities, we have to consider the nature of relationships between civilized and uncivilized peoples.

How Barbarians and Civilized Communities Differ

We may assume that most people wish to be able to enjoy or use anything new that seems to be an improvement on what they have already. Hence, civilized goods, produced by skillful artisans, and civilized ideas, worked out by full-time experts, usually impressed neighboring peoples favorably. These seemed better than anything they could do for themselves, because their societies lacked comparable specialization. When a whole people comes to realize that a distant neighbor is superior to themselves in important respects, they become, in the strict and proper sense of the word, barbarians. It is the awareness of the unequal relationship between a more complex and skilled society on the one hand and a simpler, less-skilled people on the other, that creates the gap between civilization and barbarism. Unaware of civilized superiorities, simple peoples may remain well satisfied with what they can do for and by themselves. As long as they know nothing of the existence of superior skills such peoples are not barbarians, but should be classified as "primitive," "savage," or "simple" societies.

The development of every civilization, obviously, created barbarisms by opening a gap between the skills of the people at the civilized center and others living round about; it also brought about a difficult love-hate relationship. The barbarians wanted to enjoy the fruits of civilization.

At the same time, they did not like to admit to being inferior. They often reacted by calling civilized ways corrupt. Civilized people, on the other hand, usually feared and despised their barbarian neighbors. Yet they sometimes admired barbarian hardihood, courage, and liberty, especially since civilized people were liable to lose faith in their own way of life whenever the injustices arising from social inequality became too sharp. In ancient times, all civilized societies were built upon social as well as economic inequality. Most of the people labored in the fields and were very poor. A few were rich, and some lived in luxury. By comparison, barbarian societies knew only slight differences of income and social status—slight, that is, until contact with civilized life changed their traditional ways.

Trade Relations
with Barbarian Communities

In the ancient Middle East, as elsewhere, the relationship between civilized and barbarian communities was always uneasy. Yet they could never leave one another alone for long. The cities of the floodplain needed to import timber, stone, and metal ores from barbarian areas. They could—and sometimes did—seize such commodities by force. More often they found it convenient to trade. Merchants and diplomatic agents from the Mesopotamian cities were usually eager to exchange artisan products—tools, cloth, trinkets—for raw materials that could not be found in the floodplain. But the task of gathering such commodities and preparing them for transport required changes in barbarian habits. Specialists inevitably arose whenever trade became regular and important. And such specialization within the barbarian community meant the beginning of inequality.

The new inequality arose between as well as within barbarian villages. Thus, for example, by 2000 B.C. trade relations had created a series of mining and logging communities in the higher hills of the Middle East. Such communities often had to import food. As human settlement reached beyond the geographical limits of local food supply, a new element of instability was introduced into the Middle Eastern scene. The livelihood of producers of raw material who lived high in the hills depended on delicate relations both with distant cities and with nearby villages which supplied their food. If war or natural disaster interrupted these relationships, miners and loggers faced starvation. They responded by raiding the villages at the foot of their hills and seizing the food they could not raise for themselves.

The result was that peaceful farmers of the Middle East increasingly found themselves boxed in between warlike pastoral nomads from the desert fringe to the south and raiding hillsmen from the north. Professional "protectors"—men who specialized in war and violence—wanted heavy rents and labor services in return for standing guard. But it might be safer and easier to pay such exactions regularly than to risk utter and unpredictable devastation. Between 3000 and 2000 B.C., this unpalatable choice confronted villages of the Middle Eastern plains more and more often.

War between Civilized and Barbarian Communities

War and violence played just as big a role in the relations between civilized and barbarian peoples as trade and peaceable contacts did. Organized armies, like those of Sargon of Akkad, could penetrate deep into barbarian territory. Everywhere civilized soldiers went they seized anything of value they could lay hands on. But barbarian countrysides offered rather slim pickings for such forces. Food supplies were scarce. Locally manufactured products hardly compared with civilized goods. Only new access to raw materials—which might better come by persuading barbarian manpower to dig the ore or prepare the timber—made such raiding by civilized armies worthwhile.

Barbarian war bands, however, had much to gain by penetrating civilized territory. Barbarian raiders could seize new and precious articles otherwise beyond their reach. If it was food they needed, civilized storehouses were likely to be larger than anything in their own country.

Barbarian raids had much the same effect on barbarian society as did trade: whenever raiding became successful and profitable, members of barbarian war bands made plunder a way of life. Civilized products spread. New tastes arose, and new knowledge about civilized customs seeped into barbarian society. The overall effect was to link the raiding and raided communities more closely than before; and as specialization and social differences spread among the barbarians, their own societies edged their way toward civilized complexity.

Frequently, of course, civilized rulers failed to check barbarian raids. In such cases, the raiders began to live among their victims and soon became a ruling class, extracting rents and services from everyone in sight. In return, such conquerors could be expected to try to defend the people under their control from further harassment. The most famous rulers of Mesopotamia, in fact, were often barbarian (or semibarbarian) conquerors of this kind. Sargon of Akkad, for example, started his ever-victorious career as an Akkadian chief on the borders of the civilized region of that age. Some 500 years later, Hammurabi consolidated his rule over all of Mesopotamia (c. 1700 B.C.) by leading a new people, the Amorites, from the desert fringes of the northwest into the heartland of Mesopotamia. Soon after Hammurabi's death, still another barbarian conquest took place, coming this time from the northeast and led by the people known as Kassites.

A definite political cycle thus established itself. One barbarian group after another conquered civilized peoples, but such rulers found it impossible to maintain themselves in power for more than a few generations. Either revolt, organized by heirs of the older civilization, overthrew them from within, or new barbarian bands started raiding again and worked up to a fresh takeover.

The dynasty of Ur III was the result of a successful revolt on the part of the old civilized population, as were the empires of Babylonia and Assyria that came after the Kassites. But civilized reactions against barbarian rulers were hard to organize, whereas barbarian war bands always had strong incentives to attack. The political history of the ancient Middle East was therefore dominated by successive waves of invasion from the barbarian fringe lands.

It is worth noting, however, that with the passage of time, those fringe lands got farther and farther away from the central heartland of Mesopotamian civilization, which always remained somewhere between the Tigris and Euphrates rivers. This reflects the fundamental fact that the complicated interactions between civilized and barbarian peoples steadily tended to spread civilized patterns of society to new ground. This is another way of saying that, in barbarian societies, specialization and a widening division between rich and poor were the usual consequences both of raiding and of trading with civilized communities.

Only after barbarian simplicity and equality had been undermined could the intellectual and artistic sides of civilized life find lodgment in formerly barbarian territory. At least a few persons had to have leisure and wealth before this aspect of civilized achievement could be appreciated or taken seriously.

The spread of civilization suffered many setbacks. Sometimes whole civilizations were wiped out, as we shall shortly see. But taking human history as a whole, it is clear that civilizations have always tended to spread to new ground, and did so from their earliest beginnings. There is nothing mysterious about such an overall trend. Civilized specialization and social inequality allowed people to command greater wealth and power than could be commanded in a simpler, less structured society. In ancient civilized communities farmers and artisans often suffered cruel exploitation, while rulers and priests always profited from work done for them by others. But civilized society as a whole exerted greater control over the environment than any simpler community could. When given a choice, most barbarians therefore preferred the way of civilization. Consequently the net result of contact between civilized and barbarian peoples was the borrowing of as much civilized skill and knowledge as the uncivilized partner was able to put to use in his particular social and physical environment. This meant an unending remodeling of barbarian societies along civilized lines, or, to look at the process from the other side, a persistent spread of civilization.

The Mesopotamian Sphere of Influence

We have already seen this process at work within the Tigris-Euphrates floodplain. Civilization began in the extreme south in Sumer. It moved upstream, first to include Akkad, then Babylonia and Assyria. Each time a new region or people entered into the circle of Mesopotamian civilization, minor changes were made in older styles of life. For example, when the center of political power shifted to Babylon in the time of Hammurabi, patriotic local priests revised the old Sumerian epic of creation to make their god, Marduk, the most important actor in the story. Marduk simply took over the role previously assigned to Enlil, god of storm and thunder.

At about the same time Babylonian priests also made important improvements in mathematics and astronomy. They learned how to measure and record the positions of the planets and of the sun and moon quite accurately, by using the same spherical grid (degrees, minutes, and seconds) used today. Accurate records of the movements of the sun, moon, and planets, in turn, allowed them to predict the location of these "movable lights of the firmament" at any particular time, whether in the future or in the past. Priest-astronomers also learned how to predict eclipses with considerable accuracy. All this required lengthy, complicated figuring, but the effort seemed worthwhile because everyone believed that the movements of the heavens foretold what would happen on earth. Careful observation of the positions of the sun, moon, and planets therefore allowed rulers to know the best times to start a war, build a palace, or sign a treaty. The mathematical breakthrough in Hammurabi's time permitted the priests to make more accurate and impressive predictions than their predecessors had been able to, but it did not lead to any fundamentally new concepts.

This illustrates the general fact that as long as irrigation agriculture remained the axis of life for the population of Mesopotamia, the ideas and techniques that had been first worked out by the ancient Sumerians remained generally satisfactory and were faithfully preserved as the center of political power moved northward. Akkadians, Babylonians, and then Assyrians, one after the other, gladly borrowed nearly everything they required from age-old temple rituals and traditional knowledge. They changed and elaborated only a few details.

THE SEARCH FOR NEW METALS   The influence of Mesopotamian civilization had never been limited to the floodplain. Even in early times, expeditions went into the mountains to cut timber, dig ores, and quarry building stone. The *Epic of Gilgamesh** describes such a venture, and we may be sure that trade in metals existed from the earliest beginning of Sumerian civilization. Civilized armies and military operations created an insatiable demand for tin and copper, from which bronze, the best metal for both weapons and armor, was made. To meet this demand, prospectors, miners, and smelters gradually became a distinct professional and social group, possessing craft secrets that marked them off from others. Such specialists operated throughout the mountain zone that lies in a great arc to the north of Mesopotamia. Soon sources of copper and tin were discovered farther afield, in the island of Cyprus, for example. Not long after 2000 B.C. copper was mined in Sardinia. The famous tin mines of Cornwall in England may have begun to feed tin into the Mediterranean market at about the same time.

Whenever the search for metals proved successful, links with the Mesopotamian market were established. Such links sometimes crossed long distances and involved several different intermediaries. An interesting proof of how far away the presence of Sumer made itself felt is provided by the shape of the favorite weapon used by a warrior people who lived (*c*. 2500 B.C.) in what is now southern Russia: their distinctive stone battle ax was modeled on a Sumerian bronze pattern!

SYRIA AND PALESTINE   Closer to the Tigris-Euphrates Valley, the influence of Mesopotamian models was stronger. Generally speaking, all of the peoples who lived in Syria and Palestine, together with people of the desert fringes of northern Arabia, fell under Mesopotamian influence to some degree. Nomad herders, to be sure, could not do much with civilized ways, although Babylonian stories about the beginning of the world, the great flood, and naïve descriptions of Mesopotamian temples— so high they seemed to touch the sky—were certainly told around the nomads' campfires. Our Bible preserves some of these tales as they were known among the Hebrews. Comparison with written Mesopotamian versions shows how persuasive the civilized myths seemed: the Hebrew story of Noah and the flood, for example, bears a close resemblance to the flood story in the *Epic of Gilgamesh*.

Where farming was established, it was possible to introduce far

---

* A long poem that tells the story of an early Sumerian king, Gilgamesh, and his heroic adventures in search of wealth and eternal life.

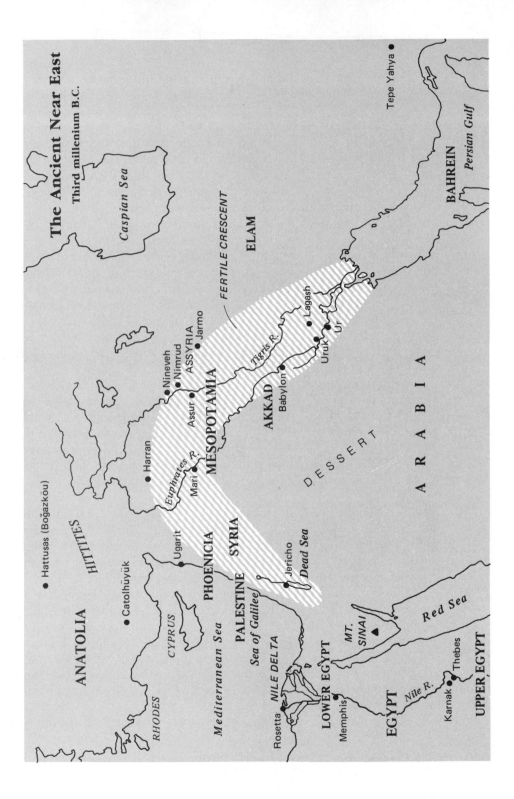

The Ancient Near East

Third millenium B.C.

more of the Mesopotamian way of life. Local chieftains, kings, or priests imitated the pomp and refinement of Mesopotamian courts and temples insofar as their resources allowed. Even a port like Byblos on the Mediterranean (near modern Beirut), where contact with Egypt by sea counterbalanced contact with Mesopotamia by land, took its style of writing and elements of religious myths from the land of the Two Rivers. Linguistic affinity was one reason for the influence Mesopotamian models of civilization exerted in all this region. The people of Syria and Palestine all spoke Semitic tongues, like the Akkadian which supplanted Sumerian to become the ordinary language of Mesopotamia by the time of Hammurabi.

IRAN, ANATOLIA, AND THE WESTERN STEPPE   Farther afield, Mesopotamian culture lacked the advantage of similarity of language. In Elam, and on the Plateau of Iran, different kinds of languages prevailed. But here, too, the Mesopotamian model of civilization colored the lives of all the peoples who settled down to an agricultural life. As we shall soon see, even distant herders of the Eurasian steppe, keepers of horses and cattle, borrowed and improved upon certain Mesopotamian skills. The same was true in Anatolia (modern Turkey). Archaeologists happen to have discovered a number of interesting letters written (c. 1900 B.C.) by merchants residing in small towns of Anatolia and addressed to their home base in the city of Ashur (later the capital of the Assyrian Empire) in northern Mesopotamia. These letters tell of a land divided between several different local princes, each of them eager for trade with Mesopotamia.

Soldiers, priests, and artisans gathered at these rulers' courts. They took the superiority of Mesopotamian goods, styles, and ideas for granted. As a result, no truly independent artistic or intellectual style took root among them. Even when a Hittite Empire arose and took control of most of Anatolia (c. 1800 B.C.), the court and capital at Hattushash remained a small town, by Mesopotamian standards. Hittite art, too, never rose above the level of a somewhat clumsy variation upon Mesopotamian styles. Local languages and local gods, different from those of Mesopotamia, persisted; but when it came to writing, even in that remote region scribes used cuneiform.

Farther away we have only indirect evidence of the influence of Mesopotamia. The same barbarians of the Russian steppe who shaped their battle axes to Sumerian patterns also remodeled their ideas about how the universe was governed, when they heard the Sumerian account of the way the gods managed things. Since these barbarians later overran Europe and gave their Indo-European languages to nearly all of that continent (as well as to most of India), the diffusion of Sumerian religious ideas among them had lasting consequences. Most of the pagan gods worshiped by the Greeks, Romans, Celts, and Germans, whose names and attributes enter into literary speech even today, had a distant connection with the Sumerian pantheon. (*Pantheon* comes from Greek and means "all the gods.") Thus, for example, Thor from Scandinavia, Zeus from Greece, Jupiter from Rome, as well as Indra from India, all began as country cousins of the ancient Sumerian Enlil, god of storm and thunder.

The Egyptian and Indus Spheres of Influence

Egypt's protective deserts reduced contacts between Egypt and barbarians. For that reason, Egypt did not develop as large a sphere of influence as ancient Mesopotamia did. But the Egyptian civilization was by no means without impact on outsiders. Westward along the Mediterranean coast lay Libya. That country, then as now only thinly inhabited, fell thoroughly under the spell of Egyptian culture; but the harsh desert environment did not permit much to be achieved.

We know far less about Egyptian influence upon peoples to the south. Fully developed Egyptian civilization never penetrated above the First Cataract of the Nile because the rapids stopped shipping. Yet rituals of chieftainship in the Great Lakes region of central Africa and in west Africa resembled the Pharaoh's role in Egypt. The question is: Did the Africans borrow ideas of divine kingship from ancient Egypt, or did the Egyptians, when they first began to farm the Nile Valley, bring the idea with them from an African hunting background which they shared with the peoples of central and west Africa? No one knows the answer.

MINOAN CIVILIZATION   Egypt's relation with the island of Crete to the north is much clearer. Trade between the two countries began very early. Precious objects made in Egypt have been found in Crete, dating from about 2500 B.C., but the goods probably got there on Cretan ships. Cretan society also carried a Mesopotamian imprint. Invaders from Asia Minor, who were indirectly in touch with the ideas and techniques of Mesopotamian civilization, seem to have reached the island before 2500 B.C.

The stimulus of contact with two differing civilizations led the Cretans to create their own distinctive type of civilization. The chief center was at Knossos on the north coast of the island. Here a vast palace-temple began to arise about 2100 B.C. The Cretans also invented a charming art style of their own, as well as a unique form of writing. We call their civilization Minoan, because, according to later Greek legends, King Minos ruled Crete and the surrounding seas before the Greeks themselves came

Ruins of ancient Crete: The palace of Minos at Knossos. (*Alison Frantz*)

on the scene. Like "Pharaoh," the term "Minos" probably referred to an office and was not a name.

The royal palace-temple at Knossos was several times rebuilt before suffering final destruction about 1400 B.C. Wall paintings of youths and maidens in ceremonial procession still survive, and they show how elegant Minoan court life became. Artisan skills also reached a very high level. Minoan painted pottery was delicate and lovely; and the naturalistic portrayal of octopi and other marine creatures reminds us of the importance of the sea to Cretan civilization.

The wealth that sustained the great palace-temple of Knossos probably did not come from rents and labor services extracted from peasants living in the immediate environs of the court. This was the only way the Hittite rulers and other inland monarchs could accumulate enough wealth to support soldiers, artisans, and other kinds of specialists. But the ruler of an island like Crete did not need many soldiers, nor did Minos need to hide behind heavy walls. Instead, he controlled the sea and profited from trade.

It is likely that Minoan Crete exported wine and olive oil, since grapevines and olive trees grew well in the climate of the island. Olive oil had many uses. As an element in the diet it supplied fats, which people who depended mainly on cereals often lacked. It could also be burned by means of a wick to provide artificial light at night. Finally, oil took the place of soap: small quantities rubbed on the skin helped to clean away sweat and grime. Wine was precious too. Drunken conviviality was an attraction no doubt. This, however, does not account for the importance of wine (and of beer) in ancient times. Most people were far too poor to be able to get drunk. But anyone who could possibly afford it put a little wine in his drinking water—and kept healthy as a result.

The reason for this was that alcohol from the wine poisoned many of the disease bacteria lurking in polluted water. Men in the ancient Mediterranean world of course did not know that alcohol destroyed bacteria. But they did know that drinking plain water, unmixed with wine, was often dangerous, to be avoided whenever possible.

The cultivation of grapes and olives required special skill; it also required farmers to wait several years between the time they planted and began to cultivate the vines and trees and the time of the first harvest. As a result, the cultivation of olive trees and of grapes spread rather slowly, and in Minoan times the Cretans may have had something close to a monopoly on these specially valued products. Almost anywhere along the Mediterranean coast they were, therefore, able to exchange them on very advantageous terms for grain or metal or any other valuable local product. Consequently, as long as Cretan soil produced oil and wine, Minoan ships could sail east or west and expect to return home laden with the assorted goods needed to keep the luxurious life of the palace-temple at Knossos well supplied. Such voyaging was aided by the establishment of more or less permanent shore stations on several of the Aegean Islands, on the Greek mainland, and as far away as Sardinia in the west and Syria in the east. Such trading posts extended the imprint of Minoan civilization over a very large part of the entire Mediterranean shoreline.

The style of life sustained by the profits of such trade was no mere backwoods version of Egyptian splendor. Unlike the Hittites and other peoples on the fringes of the Mesopotamian world, the Cretans built up their own unique style of civilization. They were only indirectly stimulated by the examples of the older civilized societies of the Middle East. The fact that the Minoans developed their own script is indicative of this independence. This fact, however, prevents modern scholars from understanding the inner structure and ideas of the society, since the script, known as "Linear A," cannot be read.*

The relation between Minoan and Egyptian civilization is like that

---

* A second script, "Linear B," came into use in later Minoan times. After World War II, it was deciphered using cryptographic methods developed during the war. It turned out to be an early form of Greek. But the only known surviving documents written in Linear B are inventories of palace storerooms, which do not tell us much.

between the earliest Egyptians and the Sumerians. When each civilization was beginning to develop, important ideas and new skills came by way of the sea. But the early Egyptians soon struck out on their own and began deliberately to reject borrowings from Sumer. Much the same occurred in Crete: stimulus from Egypt, important though it was, lasted only until the Minoans established their own style of life.

In both these cases, contacts by sea encouraged independent responses, whereas overland contacts between Mesopotamia and its neighbors failed to do so. It is worth asking why this was so. Communication by sea between civilized and barbarian peoples was sporadic. Every time a ship sailed away, contact was broken off, sometimes for years and nearly always for months at a time. This left lots of time for the weaker parties to think about what they had seen during the ship's visit to their shores. Ingenious local tinkerers might feel challenged to try to make for themselves some of the things that had been brought so dramatically to their attention by the visiting crew.

Overland contacts were different. Ordinarily it was rude frontier types, only semicivilized themselves, who took the risks of opening up communication with a previously isolated society. Such persons were often not much more skilled than the people they encountered. Moreover, they were more likely to rely on superior force than on superior goods. It was hard for the weaker community to borrow from people they feared and hated. Often they did not have time to think and experiment for themselves because the rude intruders refused to go away, but instead tried to collect rents or taxes, command labor for gathering raw materials, or in some other way set out to alter old habits and customs by issuing orders and making threats. Improvements in local skill that came from an outsider's initiative in this way obviously lacked spontaneous creativity.

The barbarian peoples who entered into the circle of civilization along this path only had to do what they were told, that is, to imitate, as best they could, the patterns of civilized craftsmanship and technique. The chance for sudden creative response under such circumstances was, quite understandably, far smaller than when contact with civilized ways first started by means of ships. Throughout history, therefore, seaborne contacts among peoples of varying cultures have played a different and often more creative role than the ruder collisions across land frontiers.

MEGALITHIC CULTURE   The special character of cultural stimuli that travel by the sea was well illustrated by the history of another high culture that spread through the western Mediterranean and along the Atlantic coast of Europe and Africa between about 2500 and 2000 B.C. We know of its existence because of stone graves and other structures, often called "megaliths" (Greek for "great stones"). Presumably what happened was that holy men, teaching a doctrine of life after death that probably derived from Egyptian ideas, traveled by sea and found welcome among simple farmers and fisherfolk. The doctrine must have been powerful enough to persuade local peoples to cut great hunks of stone and drag them into position to form the monumental graves that seem to have been essential to the faith.

Thus, just as Sumerian religious ideas were finding lodgment among the barbarians of the Russian steppe (as we saw earlier in this chapter), Egyptian—or at least partly Egyptian—religious ideas were also spreading among the farmers of westernmost Europe and north Africa. Soon after 2000 B.C. the two encountered each other. Warriors, whose ancestors had come from the steppe, reached the Atlantic coast of Europe and conquered the megalithic farmers and fisherfolk who lived there. The conquerors then put their new subjects' skill in handling big stones to use by compelling them to erect standing stone circles. Stonehenge in England is the most famous specimen of this kind of monument. These were versions in stone of tree-trunk circles which had presumably been the sort of sacred architecture the conquerors had previously known. The exact position of the stones was related to the rising and setting of the sun in such a way that sight lines from one pair of stones to another allowed the priests to keep an accurate calendar by checking the exact day when the sun and certain clock stars reached key points in their annual sweep through the skies.

Such precision is suggestive of Mesopotamian astronomical achievements, but the skill that quarried and carried the great stones to their resting places derived just as clearly from Egypt. In this remarkable way, the Egyptian and Mesopotamian spheres of influence met and mingled at Stonehenge (and similar structures existing elsewhere in the remote reaches of western Europe) about 1900 B.C.

INDIAN CULTURES   Many uncertainties arise when we try to trace the impact of Mesopotamian and Egyptian civilizations on surrounding peoples. But these are as nothing when compared to our ignorance about what sort of impact Indus civilization had upon its neighbors in India or elsewhere—for example, along the east coast of Africa. Without better archaeological evidence, it is foolish even to guess. Yet the impressiveness of the Indus cities at their height must have been borne in upon barbarian neighbors, just as much as the greatness of Mesopotamian cities impressed itself upon the neighbors of Sumer and Akkad. And since the Indus Valley lies open to overland contacts in much the same way that the Tigris-Euphrates Valley does, satellite communities of one sort or another presumably came into existence. There are scores of sites in southern and central India where traces of Indus civilization have been discovered;

but careful study is only beginning, and until it has been carried through no one can say anything definite about how Indus civilization spread.

THE CHARIOT REVOLUTION

Soon after 1700 B.C. a really basic change came to the balance of power between barbarians and civilized peoples. Barbarians, living on the distant flank of the Mesopotamian sphere of influence, invented or perfected a new instrument of war—the light, two-wheeled chariot.

How to Combine Speed and Firepower

The invention of the war chariot was a brilliant breakthrough in design. Four-wheeled wagons had been known in Sumer from before 3000 B.C. Wheels were fixed to the axle, which was strapped to the bottom of the wagon so that it turned against the wagon floor. This made it an extremely clumsy, slow-moving vehicle, but it was useful for carrying heavy loads overland. Turning was difficult, for the wagon could change direction only by slipping its wheels sideways.

War chariots differed from their clumsy predecessors in having only two wheels. This solved the problem of turning; a two-wheeled cart can turn easily and sharply by backing one wheel while the other rolls forward.

An ancient chariot: From an Assyrian monument depicting the siege and capture of the city of Hamanu in Elam. (Courtesy of British Museum)

In addition to this, a radically new wheel design gave strength and lightness to the chariot. Instead of being thick and solid, chariot wheels were constructed by combining separate pieces—hub, rim, and spokes. The axle was fixed to the chariot body and the hubs of the wheels turned around the ends of the axle, thus greatly reducing friction and making these vehicles comparatively easy to pull.

The two-wheeled design allowed the chariot to balance on its axle, so that little of the weight had to be carried directly by the team of horses. This permitted the horses to use all their strength to pull the vehicle over the ground as fast as they could gallop. The driver controlled his horses with reins attached to bits in the horses' mouths.

Once chariots had been perfected, two factors limited their use in warfare. The skills and materials needed for chariot construction made them very expensive; only a rich man could afford to have one. In particular, making good spoked wheels was difficult. Exact fitting of part to part was essential; and the problem of making a rim that was round and at the same time strong enough to stand up to the jounces and jolts that came from rolling rapidly across open country could only be solved by highly skilled, professional wheelwrights who knew how to steam wood, bend it into smoothly curving shapes and then bind all the pieces together with a tight-fitting tire.

Horses, too, were costly. These animals probably had not been domesticated much before 4000 B.C. At first they seemed inferior to cattle. Civilized people had no use for them; horsemeat was no better than beef, mare's milk was less abundant and less agreeable to humans than cow's milk; and because they lacked horns, horses could not be yoked for plowing. Only on the wide natural grasslands of the steppe, where herds of wild horses roamed freely, could anyone afford to keep such comparatively useless creatures!

When, however, horses became important in war, civilized peoples had to keep them too. In regions where natural grass was scarce—and that meant all of the civilized world in 1700 B.C.—horses had to eat grain. They thus competed directly with humans for food—and a single horse needed as much grain as six to eight persons could consume. This made horses very expensive, except on or near the steppe, where they could graze on natural herbage. But in the grasslands, where fodder for horses abounded, the artisan skills necessary for building chariots were ordinarily lacking.

Perhaps it was on the Iranian Plateau, not long after 1700 B.C., that the critical combination took place: barbarians who had long been accustomed to herding horses met artisans who could make good wheels. As a result, the first war chariots were designed and built. When that happened, barbarian horseherders suddenly found themselves in possession of a new master weapon.

TACTICS OF CHARIOT WARFARE   It may have taken some time for the first charioteers to realize what they could do with the mobility and firepower their chariots afforded. When tactics developed fully, each chariot carried a driver and an archer. As the array of chariots charged, archers launched arrows at the enemy. If the foe gave no signs of panic, the drivers made the chariots swerve sharply, as close as possible to the enemy front line. The archers continued to shoot while they galloped along the enemy front. Then the chariots would withdraw to a safe distance to give their horses a breather and to permit the archers to replenish their emptied quivers. The charge could then be repeated; or perhaps there would be a maneuver to take the foe from the rear. Under such harrassment sooner or later every enemy broke and fled. The charioteers could then pursue and hunt them down.

This tactic proved literally irresistible. Soldiers unfamiliar with horses were usually terrified at the mere sight of the charge, and even if they held their ground, the speed with which the chariots raced across the battlefield made it very difficult for foot soldiers to injure horse or charioteer. Walled cities were, of course, proof against chariot tactics. But if the countryside fell into the hands of an invading body of chariot warriors, even the strongest city would have to open its gates before long, since food had to come from outside the walls.

When dismounted, charioteers were vulnerable. To guard against surprise attack they soon learned to establish fortified camps, laid out on a regular quadrilateral plan with entry points in the middle of each side. This layout was used much later by Roman legions; it also provided the pattern for the ground plan of the city of Anyang, the Shang capital in China (c. 1300 B.C.). Such a range, all the way from China to Europe, reflects the chariot's power. Since no preexisting armies could resist the new tactics successfully, warriors with chariots could conquer whomever they chose. Wherever a sufficiently dense and skilled population tilled the soil, it was worth their while to make the cultivators into peasants by requiring them to pay rents and taxes. Where no such population existed, as in most of northern and western Europe, the chariot was used more to show a chief's prestige than as a practical weapon of war. Yet so high did the chariot's prestige become that remote chieftains in Sweden began to be buried with them (c. 1200 B.C.).

The Political Impact of Chariot Invasions

In different parts of the world the effect of the chariot invasions was very different. In far-off China, for example, chariot fighters of the Shang Dynasty (c. 1523–1028 B.C.) built the first Chinese empire along the middle reaches of the Yellow River (Hwang Ho) and began Chinese civilization by forcing the local farmers to support them in style. In India, on the contrary, the arrival of Aryan-speaking charioteers from the Iranian steppes (c. 1500 B.C.) was probably the blow that finally destroyed the Indus cities and inaugurated a "dark age" in India.

EFFECT ON MINOAN AND MYCENAEAN CIVILIZATIONS   In Crete the ancient Minoan civilization was snuffed out (c. 1400 B.C.) when an enormous volcanic explosion on nearby Thera (an island in the Aegean) created a devastating tidal wave and ash-fall. Perhaps invaders from the Greek mainland finished what nature had begun, leaving the palace-temple of Knossos plundered and abandoned. At any rate, control of the sea passed to Mycenae on the Greek mainland.

The fall of Knossos and the rise of Mycenae closely coincided with the appearance of charioteers in Greece. Indeed the power of the piratical kings of Mycenae may have rested almost as much on their horses and chariots as on their ships, although the report in Homer's poems seems to show that Mycenaeans did not know how to use their chariots effectively in battle.

According to Homer, Mycenaean warriors rode their chariots to the field of battle but then dismounted and fought on foot with spears. Perhaps the lords of Mycenae had developed their own style of spear fighting before they ever heard of chariots, and when they imported the new master weapon of the age—probably from Syria—continued to cling to their old-fashioned spears, despite the fact that spears could not be used in a chariot. The only other explanation of what Homer says is to suppose that the poet got everything about Mycenaean battle tactics wrong.

The civilization of Mycenae was closely akin to the Minoan. Greek-speaking rulers controlled Knossos in its last days, as we know from the decipherment of Linear B script. The rulers of Mycenae were also Greek-speaking, using the Achaean dialect. Art styles were very similar—so similar in fact that experts believe the decoration of the Mycenaean palaces was probably done by Cretan workmen. Perhaps the artists were enslaved, or captured in raids.

The great difference between Minoan and Mycenaean civilization was the increased importance of war. Heavy fortifications surrounded the palace at Mycenae; Knossos, by contrast, had no protective walls at all. We catch a glimpse of the warlikeness of Mycenaean society through Homer's poems. To be sure, Homer lived several centuries afterward and got a good many things about Mycenae mixed up. Still the poet did build upon an unbroken oral tradition coming down from the days when the high king, Agamemnon, sat in state at Mycenae and planned raids far and wide across the seas. There is no reason to doubt that a raiding expedition attacked Troy, as Homer says. Even the traditional date, 1184 B.C., fits everything modern scholars know. Troy was sacked and burned at about that time; but Homer's say-so is all that proves who did it. Mycenae's turn came soon afterward. Greeks speaking Dorian dialects came down from the north and destroyed Mycenae (*c.* 1100 B.C.). They brought a "dark age" to Greece like the Dark Age the Aryans had brought to India several centuries earlier.

THE CHARIOT EMPIRES OF THE NEAR EAST   Where the older and more massive Mesopotamian and Egyptian civilization held the ground, chariot conquerors did not inflict nearly so much damage. Kassite invaders brought the chariot into Mesopotamia soon after 1700 B.C. and ruled from Babylonia as Hammurabi had done before them. A little farther north a people called Mitanni ruled over Assyria and Syria. From them the Hittites in Anatolia (and, probably, the Mycenaeans in Greece, too) learned how to build and use chariots. With the stronger striking force chariots gave them, the Hittites soon created a large empire in Anatolia.

Egypt was ruled from 1730 to 1570 B.C. by another warrior band, known as Hyksos, who incorporated several different language groups into their ranks. During the latter part of their lordship over Egypt (and perhaps from the first) they, too, used chariots to overawe their restless subjects.

Yet in spite of their chariots, the Kassite, Mitanni, and Hyksos empires turned out to be fragile. The conquerors were few. They scattered out across the lands they seized, living as landowners. The income from each estate had to be large enough to allow its owner to maintain a chariot. But that kind of an income also allowed him to enjoy most of the luxuries of civilized life as well. After a few generations, descendants of the conquerors much preferred the comforts of their homes to the harshness of camp life and the risks of battle.

This made successful revolt easier to organize. Thus, for example, native Egyptians drove the Hyksos from their land about 1570 B.C. and founded the New Kingdom. The Pharaoh was no longer content to rule only Egypt. Perhaps it no longer seemed safe to have Palestine and Syria, where the Hyksos had come from, in foreign hands. At any rate, Egyptian chariots and armies crossed the desert and conquered the whole Mediterranean coastland as far north as the Taurus Mountains. Egypt's new imperial power also stretched southward, beyond the Nile cataracts, into Nubia. This was important, because the Pharaoh got gold from Nubia in rather large amounts, and used that gold to pay professional charioteers—mostly foreigners—who made up a standing army, ready at a moment's notice to sally out against an enemy. No other ruler had so much gold to keep so many soldiers at the ready. For a while, therefore, Egypt enjoyed military supremacy. Eventually, the Hittites far in the north became interested in Syria. In 1298 B.C. they fought a spectacular chariot battle against

HEINRICH SCHLIEMANN'S SUCCESS STORY

Heinrich Schliemann was the son of a German Lutheran pastor, so poor that he had to apprentice his son to a grocer. But young Heinrich was not willing to settle down to keeping shop and decided to seek his fortune overseas by signing on as a cabin boy on a ship bound for Venezuela. The venture had scarcely started when he suffered a shipwreck off the coast of Holland. He got a job with a Dutch merchant and did so well that at the age of twenty-four he was sent to St. Petersburg to act as the firm's agent in the Russian capital. Soon Schliemann set up an export-import business for himself, and quickly made a fortune.

By the time he was forty-one, Schliemann had made enough money to retire from business and do what he had dreamed of doing since he was a boy. In school he had studied Greek, and, having an excellent memory and a remarkable gift for learning languages, he memorized the whole text of the *Iliad* and *Odyssey*. He found Homer intoxicating. From that time on he dreamed of going to the places Homer had described in order to find whatever might remain from the times that Homer celebrated.

Such an idea seemed silly to the learned professors of the day. For fifty years they had argued about just how the Homeric poems had been put together out of earlier songs and stories. Most experts agreed that no one man had composed the Homeric poems. Absolutely no one supposed that the siege of Troy had really happened the way Homer said it did. To treat Homer as though he knew what he was talking about struck them as naive and foolish.

But Schliemann had enough money to make a fool of himself in his own way if he wanted to, so he proceeded to search for Troy, taking

the Egyptians at Kadesh in northern Syria. After the battle the Egyptians had to withdraw, although Pharaoh Ramses II, upon his return home, put up an inscription claiming victory.

A little before the Battle of Kadesh, the Mitanni were overthrown by Assyrians who, like the Egyptians, used the new chariots to defeat their old masters. Kassite rule in Babylon lingered until the Assyrians came south to "liberate" the rest of Mesopotamia from foreign rule; although, as it turned out, the Babylonians were not especially eager to be ruled by Assyrians either.

Homer's lines as his guide. By 1879 he decided that a mound of rubble, known locally as Hissarlik (situated in northwestern Asiatic Turkey, about four miles southeast of the mouth of the Dardanelles), fitted Homer's description. So he started to dig, finding Troy just where he said he would. Near the bottom of the mound, Schliemann discovered a hoard of buried treasure, and since Homer described Troy as rich in gold, Schliemann decided that this must be the level that corresponded to the city of which Homer had sung.

Schliemann dug at Hissarlik for three years. Then, when the Turkish government withdrew permission, he moved to Greece and began digging at Mycenae, where, according to Homer, Agamemnon once had ruled. Others had dug at Mycenae before him without finding anything much, but Schliemann decided to dig inside the vast walls. There he found a series of royal graves that had never been plundered and contained great amounts of gold and other precious objects. The richest, he decided, belonged to Agamemnon. It contained a death mask of thin gold, which allowed Schliemann to see, or at least so he thought, the actual features of Agamemnon's face.

Great was the confusion among the learned professors when Schliemann, by defying all their rules, found such treasures. Perhaps Homer's poems were not so unreliable as they had supposed. But how could a man like Schliemann—self-made, self-educated, and self-important—be right? In fact he was not right about details. He picked the wrong level at Troy for Homer's city and there is no reason, except sentiment, to think that the grave at Mycenae belonged to Agamemnon. Yet in a larger sense Schliemann was right and taught a valuable lesson to the dry-as-dust professors who had studied only the texts of ancient authors. For survey of local landscapes and digging, as Schliemann proved, may bring important new information and fresh understandings that could never come from study of the ancient texts themselves.

RELIGION, WRITING, AND ART IN THE CHARIOT AGE

The mixing of peoples and quickened communication that resulted from the chariot invasions called older religious beliefs into question. Gods who could not protect their faithful worshipers hardly seemed worth much.

Moreover, local traditions about how the world had been made and how the gods ruled over it conflicted with each other. If one were true, others had to be false. And if one were false, might not all of them be false?

TRADITIONAL FAITHS When merchant caravans, armies, and diplomats regularly traveled to and fro across the Middle East, it became hard to believe that a local god, worshipped in some small town in Syria, for example, could call the Egyptians from one end of the civilized world and the Assyrians from the other in order to punish the local inhabitants for not offering him the proper sacrifices. Yet that was how disasters were traditionally explained. But when what happened often depended on events far, far away, how could there not be one single divine control over the whole world?

Whatever logic might suggest, people could not readily bring themselves to reject established rituals and doctrines. Instead they believed less firmly than before, but went through the motions of traditional worship, partly from habit and partly just to be sure that the gods would not strike back if they were neglected. The world was ripe for monotheism, but old faiths cluttered the ground too much to permit a fresh start. All that could be done was to emphasize the greatness of one god at the expense of all others. Accordingly, among the Babylonians, priests of Marduk praised their god so much as to make all but him—the great god of Babylon—quite unnecessary.

Seeds of Monotheism: Atonism

These problems hit the Egyptians particularly hard. Before the Hyksos invasion, they had smugly disregarded everything that happened outside the Nile Valley. But when the Pharaoh came to rule an empire in Palestine and Syria, the world beyond the borders of Egypt could no longer be neglected. Nor was it easy to apply Egyptian political and religious ideas to lands where there was no Nile and where the local peoples had never even heard of the Pharaoh's divinity.

But the sun was everywhere, and no one who had ever crossed the desert between Egypt and Palestine was likely to forget its mighty power. Accordingly, a group of Egyptian religious reformers came to the conclusion that the sun-disk, Aton, was the only true god in nature and that all other gods were false. A young Pharaoh who came to the throne in 1380 B.C. accepted this idea. He renamed himself Akhnaton,* to honor

* Several variant spellings of these Egyptian names exist in English: *Akhnaton* as Ikhnaton, Akhenaten, or Akhenaton; *Aton* as Aten; and *Amon-Re* as Amen-Ra or Amon-Ra.

Aton, and proceeded to try to stamp out all other kinds of worship in Egypt. Since he claimed to be divine himself, Akhnaton's reform was not strictly monotheistic, that is, acknowledging only one god. But it was radical. Stonemasons were sent up and down Egypt with instructions to chisel the names of other gods out of every inscription they could find. The god Amon-Re of Thebes, whose priests led the resistance to Akhnaton, was the special target of this purge. The Pharaoh set up a new capital near the village known today as Tell el 'Amarna. There he tried to remake traditional Egyptian styles of art and architecture along lines pleasing to Aton. This meant an effort to be informal, true to the moment, and open in thought and deed. The contrast with the stiff postures and dignity of traditional Egyptian art could hardly be greater.

Akhnaton's revolutionary movement did not outlast him, however. Religious reaction set in immediately after his death. The capital was moved back to Thebes, and new bands of stonecutters were sent out to erase the name of Aton wherever they could find it. The priests of Amon-Re became more powerful and independent of the Pharaoh than they had been before. Nothing but a few broken fragments of the Aton cult remained, until modern scholars began digging at Akhnaton's abandoned capital. They were able to piece together a number of very interesting hymns to Aton and discovered a detailed file of diplomatic correspondence between the Pharaoh and distant rulers in Syria and Anatolia.

The Puzzle of Egyptian-Israelite Relations

The relationship between Egypt in its imperial period and the Israelites is a puzzling and unsolved problem. The Bible tells how Abraham left the Sumerian city of Ur (perhaps about 1950 B.C., toward the end of the Ur III period) and then wandered with his sheep and his human followers until they reached the land of Canaan. After Abraham's death, first Isaac and then Jacob (renamed *Israel* after wrestling with an angel) led the people. When famine struck, the aged Jacob with his sons and their followers fled into Egypt where grain was available. Meanwhile, according to the Bible story, Jacob's favorite son, Joseph, who, years before, had been sold into slavery by his jealous brothers, had become the Pharaoh's chief minister. He gave his father and brothers the grain they needed and then revealed himself to them. Great was Jacob's joy. He remained in Egypt until his death. His descendants also stayed on for many years until a Pharaoh "who knew not Joseph" began to oppress them. Then God raised up Moses to lead them back to the promised land. Moses obeyed, but died before the "children of Israel" reached their goal and began to settle in Canaan, where Abraham had pastured his herds long before.

Scholars have not been able to find anything in Egyptian records that corresponds to the Biblical account. Some have suggested that the story of Joseph and his brothers might be a folk memory of the Hyksos' invasion and their expulsion. But the dates do not fit, and the Hyksos did not come to Egypt as refugees from famine but as conquerors. Some scholars have thought that Moses (whose name is Egyptian) got the idea of monotheism from the worshipers of Aton. But this does not seem very likely, since Atonism was not strictly monotheistic, and Yahweh,* the God whom Moses worshiped, was not in the least like Akhnaton's Aton. In short, the records we have from Egypt and the records in the Bible do not match up in any satisfactory way. The puzzles cannot be solved unless new archaeological discoveries fill vital gaps in our information.

Simpler Forms of Writing

The mingling of men from many different backgrounds during the age of the chariot empires provoked the invention of a simpler form of writing. In Egypt and in Mesopotamia, well-established school systems for training scribes in the complexities of hieroglyphic and cuneiform continued to exist. As long as that was the case, no important changes could occur. But throughout the in-between zone, particularly in Syria and Palestine, confusion prevailed. In the town of Ugarit in Syria, for example, archaeologists found texts written in six different scripts. No school system could cope with the task of teaching so many complicated kinds of writing. As a result, intelligent but very badly trained scribes resorted to a radical simplification by inventing alphabetic writing.

THE EARLIEST ALPHABETS   Sometime between 1700 and 1500 B.C., and somewhere between Sinai and northern Syria, someone discovered that fewer than thirty signs could represent all the sounds used in speech. The secret was to neglect differences in vowel sounds. For example, a single symbol "b" could stand for *ba*, *be*, *bi*, *bo*, and *bu*. Since the Semitic languages used in Syria and Palestine always alternated consonant and vowel, it was not too difficult for a reader to supply the right vowel sound to go with the consonant. For example, *b-n-n* may not look like "banana," but if you try to say it, you will soon see that it cannot be

---

* *Yahweh* is used in this book to designate the God of the ancient Hebrews. Another way of translating the Hebrew word is "Jehovah."

read as anything else. Thus, what the scribes invented was in effect an *alphabet* in which only the consonants were recorded.

Such an invention made learning to write comparatively simple. To learn less than thirty signs was much, much easier than memorizing the thousands of symbols required by the older scripts. Indeed, as early as 1300 B.C. snatches of writing scratched onto bits of pottery prove that ordinary people had learned how to write. They sometimes recorded very trifling matters in this way.

Eventually, simpler writing made it possible to spread knowledge from specialists to common folk. But this result was slow to appear. Priests were not anxious to write down their sacred songs and stories for ordinary people to read. Indeed, the Egyptian and Mesopotamian priests and scribes clung faithfully to the old, complicated ways of writing until shortly before the Christian Era, when both hieroglyphic and cuneiform writing finally died out. Other kinds of knowledge were also likely to belong to a special group who saw no advantage in putting it into general circulation. Artisan skills, for example, were almost never described in writing. But legal records and government business offered wide scope for writing; private letters did also. Writing had been used for all these purposes before the invention of the alphabet. The fact that more people could read and write did not of itself make very much difference until a body of literature came into existence that opened new thought or made new types of information available. This occurred in a significant way only after 1000 B.C. (See Chapter 4.)

THE USE OF PAPYRUS AND PARCHMENT FOR WRITING   A second change in ways of writing is worth noticing. Instead of using the Mesopotamian clay tablet, which when baked became hard and all but indestructible, and instead of carving inscriptions in stone, as the Egyptians did, men began to write with pen and ink on a prepared smooth surface made from papyrus reeds. Papyrus sheets were usually prepared in long strips and then rolled up at each end on a stick. Writing was done in columns, running across the roll. Instead of turning a page, readers rolled up what they had read on one stick and unrolled the next column from the other stick. Sheets of papyrus resembled paper, though they were thicker and not so smooth as writing paper is today. The papyrus reed grew only in Egypt, where production of papyri (the prepared sheets) became an important business.

Many centuries later, parchment was invented as a substitute for papyrus. It was made by splitting sheepskins into thin layers and rubbing down the surfaces until they became smooth. Parchment was especially important in places where Egyptian papyrus could not be had easily.

THE USE OF PEN AND INK   Pens were made by splitting the stem of a reed partway up, so as to control the flow of ink by capillary action.

The use of pen and ink, however, required changes in the shapes of letters. A cursive (rounded, flowing) style of writing thus came in, related to more formal lettering just the way our written script is related to printed letters.

By 1200 B.C., therefore, when a fresh wave of invasion began a new period in Middle Eastern history, people had all the devices needed for making written learning really widespread. But the breakthrough came long afterward when the ancient Jews compiled their sacred scriptures.

Art and Society

Other facets of human life in the Middle East were not much affected by the chariot invasions. No important new principles of government administration or law were introduced by the conquerors. The Egyptian, Hittite, and First Assyrian empires made no improvements on Hammurabi's system of government. Economic relations were not fundamentally altered either. The great majority remained peasants, excluded from active participation in all the higher aspects of civilization. Commercial and military links between distant regions multiplied. But militarization brought destruction to peaceable (perhaps priest-managed) civilizations, like those of Crete and the Indus Valley, and made unsafe the peaceable sort of seafaring upon which the megalithic priests relied to spread their doctrine. Strangers, instead of being received as honored guests, were likely to be robbed and killed. Small boats could therefore no longer put in at night along an unfamiliar shore. Long-distance travel by sea had to be organized like a military expedition: sailors became part-time pirates, a fact Homer takes completely for granted.

No arresting new art styles arose either. Except for short-lived experiments under Akhnaton, Egyptian art remained almost unchanging. But Pharaohs like Ramses II were in a hurry to create vast new monuments. They therefore went in for shortcuts, and preferred size and bulk to elegance and perfection. Yet the extraordinary splendor of Pharaoh Tutankhamon's grave furnishings shows how excellent Egyptian craftsmanship was, and how rich Pharaoh's court must have been. Tutankhamon was the son-in-law of Akhnaton. He died while still a boy, after a reign of only a few years. Yet, when archaeologists discovered his previously untouched grave in 1922, they found an entire room crammed with furniture and precious objects, abounding in gold—a profusion that had only been dreamed of before.

In other parts of the civilized world, art, as always, reflected the age. Styles mixed and mingled all around the Mesopotamian center, but nowhere attained real distinction.

CONCLUSION

Between 2500 and 1200 B.C. people in the Middle East learned how to establish complicated, civilized societies on land that did not enjoy the special advantages of irrigation. Both trade and war tended to spread civilized complexity from the centers where such societies first arose into barbarian border lands. In addition, contacts by sea in the Mediterranean succeeded in stimulating the people of Crete to make a new civilization that was much more original than were any of the satellite civilizations that arose on the mainland.

The expansion of civilized societies suffered a setback after about 1700 B.C. when barbarians living on or near the steppe learned how to combine mobility and firepower by harnessing horses to light maneuverable chariots. Protected by the speed of their horses, charioteers could attack any foe without much risk to themselves. The new style of warfare was therefore quite literally irresistible. Chariot conquerors overran all of the Middle East, and the civilizations that had flourished in India and in Crete for centuries were destroyed. In the older and more deeply civilized regions of Egypt and Mesopotamia, however, the invaders merely set up new empires, and in time native peoples, having learned how to use chariots themselves, rose in revolt and overthrew them.

During and after the chariot invasions, widened contacts among distant and different peoples caused many Middle Easterners to doubt older religious ideas. Egypt, in particular, went through a religious revolution that tried to substitute the worship of Aton, the sun-disk, for all other gods. But reaction set in, and the old rituals and doctrines revived. Old, complicated ways of writing also were carefully preserved by the priests and scribes of Egypt and Mesopotamia; but in the regions in between, where schools for training scribes were not well established, a new, simplified alphabetic system for writing was invented by 1300 B.C. Our own alphabet and all the other alphabets used in the world today descend from this ancient invention.

The major importance of the Chariot Age and of the resulting rise and fall of empires lay not in any changes brought to the Middle East, for such changes were relatively modest. But during these same centuries, between 1700 and 1200 B.C., chariot conquerors in India, China, and Greece laid the basis for three new and distinct styles of civilization. Each of these civilizations was destined to play a great role in the world's history, and we will consider how each of them came into existence in later chapters. But first it seems best to continue with the history of the ancient Middle East until about 500 B.C., for both Greece and India drew important skills and knowledge from that part of the world during these centuries when they were shaping their own distinct styles of civilizations.

Dispersal of Agriculture

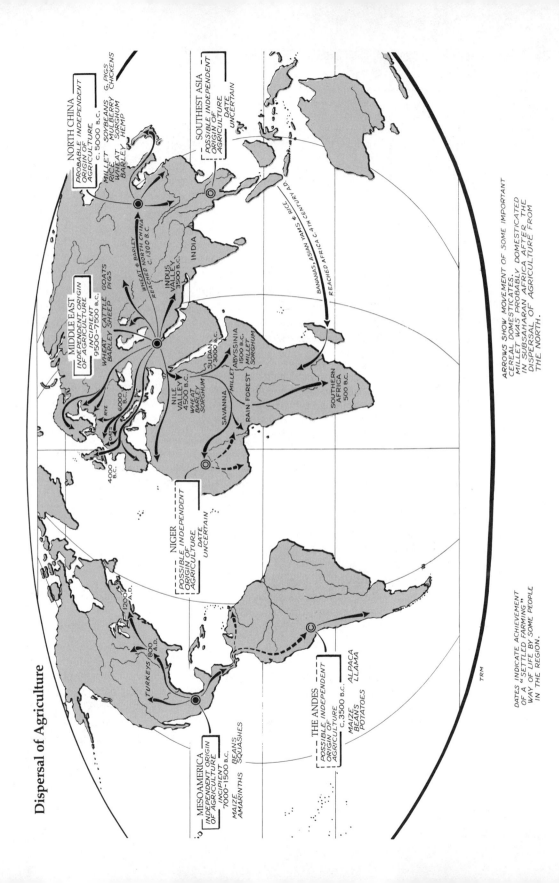

ARROWS SHOW MOVEMENT OF SOME IMPORTANT
CEREAL DOMESTICATES.
MILLET WAS PROBABLY DOMESTICATED
IN SUBSAHARAN AFRICA AFTER THE
DISPERSAL OF AGRICULTURE FROM
THE NORTH.

DATES INDICATE ACHIEVEMENT
OF A "SETTLED FARMING"
WAY OF LIFE BY SOME PEOPLE
IN THE REGION.

NORTH CHINA
PROBABLE INDEPENDENT
ORIGIN OF
AGRICULTURE
c. 5000 B.C.

MILLET
RICE
WHEAT
BARLEY

SOYBEANS
MULBERRY
SORGHUM
HEMP

G. PIGS
CHICKENS

SOUTHEST ASIA
POSSIBLE INDEPENDENT
ORIGIN OF
AGRICULTURE
DATE
UNCERTAIN

MIDDLE EAST
INDEPENDENT ORIGIN
OF AGRICULTURE
INCIPIENT
9500–7500 B.C.

WHEAT
BARLEY

CATTLE
SHEEP

GOATS
PIGS

WHEAT + BARLEY
REACHED NORTH CHINA
c. 1300 B.C.

INDIA

INDUS
VALLEY
3500 B.C.

BANANAS, ASIAN YAMS + RICE
REACHED AFRICA c. 4TH CENTURY A.D.

RYE
6000
B.C.

OATS
4000
B.C.

NILE
VALLEY
4500 B.C.
WHEAT,
BARLEY,
SORGHUM

SUDAN
3000 B.C.

ABYSSINIA
1500 B.C.
MILLET
SORGHUM

SAVANNA
MILLET

RAIN FOREST

SOUTHERN
AFRICA
500 B.C.

NIGER
POSSIBLE INDEPENDENT
ORIGIN OF
AGRICULTURE
DATE
UNCERTAIN

1200
A.D.

TURKEYS
800
A.D.

THE ANDES
POSSIBLE INDEPENDENT
ORIGIN OF
AGRICULTURE
c. 3500 B.C.

MAIZE
BEANS
POTATOES

ALPACA
LLAMA

MESOAMERICA
INDEPENDENT ORIGIN
OF AGRICULTURE
INCIPIENT
7000–1500 B.C.

MAIZE
AMARINTHS

BEANS
SQUASHES

TRM

THE USE OF PLANTS AND ANIMALS IN AGRICULTURE

Slash-and-Burn

For slash-and-burn farmers, leafy forests are the only kind of terrain suitable for farming. They slash the bark to kill the trees; a few years later they burn the dead tree trunks and branches and use the ashes as fertilizer. Slash-and-burn methods were first used in the Middle East before 7000 B.C.

1. For this kind of agriculture, farmers used land with thick and leafy forest growing on it. Such land produced a good grain crop.

2. To kill the trees, farmers slashed the bark all around the tree trunk. Sunlight reached the ground, filtering through the dead trunks.

3. Farmers raked away dried leaves to expose soft loam underneath. They scattered seeds on the loam and covered these with loose soil.

4. At first no competing plants existed in newly cleared forest patches, so only desired food-producing grasses could grow.

5. When the grain ripened, farmers harvested it with sickles and stored seeds in jars or baskets.

6. After a few years of cultivation in this way, farmers burned the dead tree trunks and scattered the ashes as fertilizer.

7. Each year more airborne seeds came onto the cleared land. These grew into plants that competed with planted seeds, so a satisfactory crop could no longer be raised.

8. Slash-and-burn farmers then moved on and found a new patch of forest land where they could repeat the whole cycle.

CROPS   Wild grain reseeds itself by allowing the ripe kernels to break off from the spike and fall to the ground. When people began to harvest grain, only kernels with tougher spikes could reach the storage area without being shaken to the ground and lost. And only kernels that reached the storage area were available for seed next season. This meant a very rapid seed selection for kernels that had tough spikes. New types of grain arose with spikes so tough that they could not seed themselves without human help. People, too, soon came to depend on these kinds of grains for food.

HIGHLIGHTS   The significance of slash-and-burn agriculture is that:

Human beings brought seed-bearing grasses into regions in which they did not naturally grow and eliminated the mixture of grasses and other plants found in nature.

Slash-and-burn farmers created food for themselves instead of finding or killing what grew naturally, as hunters did.

A new interdependence arose as human communities came to depend on plants, while the plants in question came to depend on human action for their biological existence.

Irrigation

Irrigation is the process of channeling water onto dry land to make arid soil fertile. This was the basis for Middle Eastern river valley civilizations along the Tigris-Euphrates, Nile, and Indus rivers, beginning 3500–2500 B.C.

1. Rivers, like the Tigris and Euphrates, that start in high mountains and flow through plains cut into the land in their upper reaches, but drop gravel, sand, and silt

as they flow more slowly across the plains.

2. In spring the river floods; and as it rises above its normal banks, it widens out, flows more slowly, and leaves large deposits at the edges of its usual bed. This creates natural levees.
3. When the flood subsides, the river returns to its bed, trapped between the levees. It continues to deposit gravel and sand. In time therefore it flows above the level of the surrounding plain.
4. When the flood subsides, stagnant water lies in shallow pools and swamps outside the levee on both sides of the river. As the year passes, these swampy pools evaporate until the annual flood comes to fill them again.
5. When the swamp water gets low, a channel cut through the natural levee can allow river water to reach the lower land lying on each side of the stream.
6. With construction of bigger channels, diked on each side to direct the flow of water, wide regions can be irrigated by following the contour of the land downstream. This is known as arterial irrigation.
7. Irrigation along the Nile differs. The lower Nile carries only fine silt which sinks too slowly to form natural levees.
8. The Nile flood comes slowly and gently, so that dikes can channel the flow of water onto the land and from field to field. This is called basin irrigation.

HIGHLIGHTS   The use of irrigation is important because:

As long as floods occurred, the same fields could be cultivated year after year. Comparatively large populations could then live in a relatively small space.

The operation of an arterial irrigation system required much human labor for construction and maintenance. Centralized control and planning were needed as canals became longer and deeper and irrigated more land.

Massed human labor, responding to centralized organization, created the material basis for the first civilizations.

Field and Fallow

Field and fallow is a method of farming in which a piece of land is plowed and sown with seed during one growing season, then plowed and allowed to remain idle during the next. It was probably first developed in Middle Eastern river valleys a little before 3000 B.C.

1. Field and fallow farmers used animals to pull a simple plow through the soil. This allowed them to cultivate more ground than when human muscles alone supplied digging power.
2. This method effectively kept down weeds by plowing the fallow field in summer time, killing competing plants before they formed seeds.
3. As a result, the fallow field had few weeds the next year to spoil the grain. The former grain field, left fallow, was cleared of weeds in turn by being plowed.
4. By plowing and planting the grain field at the start of the growing season, then plowing the fallow field, then harvesting

Slash and burn agriculture, Venezuela. (Tim Asch/ Anthro-Photo)

the ripened grain, labor was spread more evenly through the year.

CROPS AND DRAFT ANIMALS

The main crops of early field and fallow farming were the same as for slash-and-burn: wheat and barley. The big change was the use of animal power. Castrated bulls, called oxen, were used for plowing because of their strength and tameness, acquired at the expense of their normal biological power of reproduction. (Compare this to changes in domesticated grain crops.) Oxen also had horns to which it was easy to attach a simple plow.

The scratch plow had three essential parts: a beam or rope which attached the plow to the oxen, a share that dragged through the soil, and a handle which plowmen used to "steer" the share through the soil. The scratch plow had to be light enough for a man to steer, so it did not work well in heavy clay soil.

HIGHLIGHTS Field and fallow farming meant that:

Effective weed control and cultivation of more land allowed an ordinary farmer to harvest more grain than his family could eat.

This surplus grain could support a class which did not produce its own food but worked at other things. Such specialists created the earliest civilizations.

Farming had been women's work until the invention of the plow brought men into the fields with their animals. This made men, as in the hunting days, the main providers of food within families and assured male dominance in society at large.

Vegetative Root

In vegetative root farming, roots were cultivated for food, sometimes on flooded areas of land. Vegetative root agriculture probably began somewhere in southeast Asia. The date of origin is quite uncertain. It may have begun as early as 13,000–9000 B.C., before slash-and-burn agriculture got started.

1. Vegetative root farming probably started near the edge of rivers or lakes where fishermen had settled in permanent villages.
2. A live shoot from the parent plant was partly buried in the moist or flooded ground so that it would take root.
3. In tropical climates all stages of growth may be found on a single patch of land at any given time.

CROPS Many different kinds of crops were grown in vegetative root agriculture. Taros, yams, and manioc have large tuberous roots that store large amounts of starch. They were cultivated by primitive man because they were easy to use: a single root makes a meal for two or three people. Such roots can be fried, boiled, or baked. They can also be made into a soup, a paste, or a cake; and manioc is processed to produce tapioca.

HIGHLIGHTS Vegetative root farming is significant because:

Vegetative root agriculture solved the weed problem by raising a few individually large plants. Weeds could simply be pulled out by hand.

Since staple root crops provide mostly starch, fish or some other food source was necessary for the human diet.

This type of cultivation flourished mainly in tropical climates where plants can ripen at all times of the year, since the roots are not easily stored.

Rice Paddy

Rice paddy cultivation requires the land to be under water while the rice plants grow, but at harvest time fields are drained dry. This procedure causes competing plants to be either drowned or baked out, thus keeping weeds down. Rice paddy cultivation began somewhere in China or southeast Asia, perhaps about 3000–2500 B.C.

1. Since rice paddy land must be perfectly level, farmers have to cut down the higher portion and fill in lower parts of a field until water will stand at a uniform depth.
2. Only regulated amounts of water are wanted on the field. A rice paddy must therefore be surrounded by waterproof dikes with sluices and channels to control water flow.
3. After this preparation, fields are plowed and planted with seedlings sprouted in a special nursery. The water which flows gently into the fields prevents the growth of weeds that live on land, carries dissolved minerals, and supports a complex interaction of organisms that keep the soil fertile.
4. When the rice is ready to ripen, the farmer stops the water from flowing into the paddy, and it dries out. This kills weeds that flourish in water.
5. The rice is harvested with sickles; and if water remains available, a second crop of rice can be planted in the same growing season.

CROPS   Rice has the enormous advantage of producing more food per acre than any other crop, particularly when double-cropping is possible. This allows a very dense population to come into existence. The high food yield from rice paddies, in turn, supports the abundant labor force needed to construct and maintain paddy fields with the elaborate conduit system that brings water into fields and keeps it there as long as it is needed. The rice plant requires a mean temperature of 70° F., a good deal warmer than wheat.

HIGHLIGHTS The importance of the rice paddy is that:

The alternation between flooding and draining achieves both weed control and fertilization of the soil.

The labor required to build rice paddies ties the farmers to the land permanently. Nowhere else can they hope to secure as much food for their labor.

Dense population depending on rice paddy cultivation can be compelled to support distant governments, since farmers cannot leave the land nor hide harvest from tax collectors. This makes state-building easy.

Moldboard Plow

The moldboard plow turns the soil over in furrows instead of merely breaking it up into loose bits as the scratch plow does. The moldboard plow came into existence in the moist climate of northwestern Eu-

An Egyptian shadoof for irrigation. (*New York Public Library*)

Harvesting flax. (*Ronald Sheridan's Photo-Library*)

On a field plowed year after year in the same way, this builds up ridges in the centers and makes shallow ditches called balks on each side. The plow thus creates a drainage system on flat, water-logged fields.

HIGHLIGHTS   The moldboard plow changed farming methods because:

Moldboard plow agriculture opened the flat, abundantly watered plains of northwestern Europe to cultivation on a large scale for the first time.

With the moldboard plow, a rotating three-field system with winter crop, spring crop, and fallow could be used.

In northwestern Europe, the soil could be plowed with the moldboard plow at any time of the year. A single farmer could therefore cultivate more land and raise more food than in lands where plowing was seasonal. This helps to account for the rapid rise of Latin Christendom after A.D. 1000.

rope about A.D. 100; but it came into general use slowly, between A.D. 500 and 1000.

1. **Construction of the Moldboard Plow.** The moldboard plow has a share and a beam essentially the same as the scratch plow. (See Field and Fallow.)
   Two new parts were added to this. A colter that slices vertically through the earth from above runs just ahead of the tip of the share.
   A moldboard, lying behind the share, turns the furrow, cut from the earth by the combined action of the colter and plowshare. This exposes earth three to ten inches below the surface.

2. **Use of the Moldboard Plow.** Four to six oxen were needed to pull the moldboard plow, and such a team cannot turn quickly or easily. Long, narrow fields were, therefore, the only efficient shape for cultivation.
   The moldboard turns the furrow to one side only. As the plow comes and goes the length of the field, it turns the slices toward a center furrow, or ridge.

Elimination of Fallow

Between 1600 and 1750, Dutch and English farmers discovered that they could plant certain valuable new crops on land previously left fallow, and still keep down weeds or even increase and improve the soil's fertility. These new crops were used mainly for animal feed.

1. One way to use the fallow productively was to plant a fast-sprouting cover crop, like clover, alfalfa, or vetch, that can get started early in the growing season and smother competing plants.

2. A second way of using fallow was to plant crops in rows, and then cultivate between the rows often enough to destroy weeds.

3. Agricultural "improvers" used manure and other materials to fertilize their fields: chalk, lime, seaweed, ashes, even soot and sometimes sand were tried with good results.

Harvesting rice. (*United Nations*)

Scientific Agriculture

During the nineteenth century, the application of science and technology to agriculture became conscious and widespread. From western Europe and North America, scientific efforts to improve agriculture spread throughout the world.

CROPS AND FARMING METHODS Fertilizers and food additives supply chemicals needed for plant and animal growth. A German professor, Justus von Liebig (1803–1873) was the first to analyze plants chemically and experiment with artificial fertilizers. Scientific study of animal nutrition began only in the twentieth century with the discovery of vitamins.

Geneticists can alter plants and animals to suit human uses. Mendelian theories of inheritance (named after Gregor Mendel, whose ideas were published in 1866 but forgotten until 1900) enabled experimenters to create strains of hybrid corn in the 1920s that greatly increased U.S. farm yields. In the 1960s other experimenters invented new kinds of rice, giving Asians a chance to increase their food production very greatly.

Machinery allows farmers to plow, plant, and harvest large areas quickly. Farmers had always used simple machines, from the digging stick on up. But only with the industrial revolution could big, complicated, factory-made machinery come to the fields. The first practically successful farm machine was the McCormick reaper, patented in 1834.

Food storage and distribution were also altered by the application of science. Canning depends on heat to sterilize food and prevent decay. It was discovered in France in 1809, but came into common use in the United States only with the Civil

CROPS New crops came into use with the elimination of fallow. Nitrogen-fixing bacteria flourish in the roots of clover, alfalfa, and vetch. When the top part of these plants had been used for cattle food, the roots remained with extra nitrogen that the bacterial action had taken from the air and made into plant protein. This assured a noticeable improvement in the field's fertility. Turnips were the most important row crop; cabbages, beets, and later potatoes were also raised in this way.

HIGHLIGHTS The elimination of fallow meant that:

The new crops, suitable for fields formerly left fallow, were mainly used for animal feed. This allowed a vast increase in animal products with an improvement of the human diet.

The nitrogen-fixing crops incidentally improved fertility for grain raising, thus increasing cereal yields also.

With more and better fodder, farmers could develop specialized breeds of dairy, meat, and draft animals.

The moldboard plow at work. An illumination from the Duc de Berry's Book of Hours. *(Musee Conde Chantilly/Photographic Giraudan)*

War, 1861–1865. Freezing, another important method of preserving food, came in after World War I.

HIGHLIGHTS   The significance of scientific agriculture is that:

Fewer hands produce more food in less time. As a result, in the parts of the world where scientific agriculture has spread, most people eat food produced by others.

Until about 100 years ago, most human beings worked as farmers. Now most live in cities and work at other tasks.

American Crop Migration

With the opening of the world's oceans to shipping (1500–1600), the Old World received several important new food crops from recently discovered lands.

MAIZE   The center for early domestication was probably in Mexico and Central America. Corn was taken to Europe by Spanish explorers in the sixteenth century, and from there it reached the Middle East. The Portuguese are credited with introducing corn into Africa and India. Magellan is supposed to have brought it to the East Indies via the Pacific Ocean.

POTATOES   Potatoes were native to the Andes in South America and were first domesticated by the ancient Peruvians. They were introduced into Europe twice: first by Spanish sailors and a second time by Sir Francis Drake after his circumnavigation of the globe in 1580. From western Europe, potatoes were introduced to the North American colonies, central and eastern Europe, and the Middle East. As was the case with corn, the potato came to Africa with the Portuguese and to southeast Asia and China by way of the Pacific.

SWEET POTATOES   Sweet potatoes probably originated as a cultivated crop in the Caribbean region. Spanish explorers brought them back to Europe before white potatoes arrived from the more distant coasts of Peru. Sweet potatoes never became very important in Europe. But in southern China, the sweet potato, introduced across the Pacific in the six-

The Harvesters, *by Pieter Brueghel*. (*Metropolitan Museum of Art, Rogers Fund, 1919*)

teenth century, became a crop of basic importance. In parts of Africa, too, sweet potatoes rivaled corn in importance.

Eurasian Crop Migration

As food crops were introduced into Europe, Asia, and Africa from the New World, the crops and agricultural methods of the Old World also spread to the newly explored areas.

In many parts of the world, European settlers brought with them the equipment

Modern harvesting done by machine. (*USDA photo by John Shite*)

of agriculture that was familiar to them in their homelands. They simply displaced the peoples they found living there, as in most of North America and in Australia.

In some parts of the world, however, older forms of agriculture were little affected by the skills and knowledge that opening the oceans diffused around the world. This was the case with rice paddy cultivation, which continued unchanged and spread slowly in southeast Asia and to some Pacific islands.

In between were regions where new crops or domesticated animals radically altered older life-styles. An example was the rise of Plains Indian cultures in North America after they learned to use the horse, introduced by Spaniards.

The American and Eurasian crop migration had several effects:

Efficient crops and techniques of cultivation spread all around the globe into vast new regions climatically suited to them.

Human food supplies increased in amount; and in many places there was an improvement in quality as well.

The diffusion of agricultural techniques caused by regular oceanic movements of people, plants, and ideas tended to equalize the level of development within each climate zone all around the globe.

CHAPTER 4

Empire and Religion in the Middle East

1200 to 500 B.C.

Between 1200 and 500 B.C. the civilized regions of the Middle East went through a cycle of social and political change. At the beginning of this period, there were widespread invasions leading to the collapse of the old chariot empires. Chaldaeans, Aramaeans, Phrygians, Philistines, Hebrews, Medes, and other peoples, armed with iron weapons, took over. At first the newcomers divided into many small tribal groups, but rather rapidly large kingdoms and empires began to arise. By 750 B.C. most of the civilized parts of the Middle East had been united under a new Assyrian Empire. When the Assyrians in their turn suffered destruction, a Persian Empire soon took its place, uniting the whole Middle East and outlying regions into a single great state that lasted until 330 B.C. Arts of government already known in the age of Ur III and Hammurabi were improved and refined by the Assyrian and Persian rulers.

This political experience was accompanied by two fundamental changes, one in economic relations and one in religion. In economics, the use of iron for agricultural tools increased yields. Clay soils, that could hardly be cultivated with wooden plows and spades, became usable for the first time. In addition, peasant farmers now had to buy plowshares, scythes, sickles, and the like from smiths who knew the secrets of shaping iron into tools. They therefore entered the market more often than before, and for the first time began to gain a direct benefit from the specialization of skills upon which civilized society was based.

In religion, the centuries between 1200 and 500 B.C. saw the rise of a new pattern of belief. Instead of thinking that the world was controlled by innumerable and often rival gods, some thoughtful men came to believe that a single God ruled the entire universe, and ruled it justly. Sooner or later, they asserted, God would punish evildoers according to a great and wonderful plan laid down for all humankind. Such views are called *ethical monotheism*, "ethical" because God governs according to just or ethical principles, and "monotheism" (Greek: *mono*, one; *theos*, god) because a single God was believed to rule the world.

Older ideas lingered on, but were discredited. Men knew too much about the contradictions that existed among different religious myths. But only the Jews and a reforming sect among the Persians, led by the Prophet Zoroaster, took the radical, logical step to monotheism. And only the Jews fully developed the advantages that came from writing down sacred scriptures. By making sacred texts available to large numbers of quite ordinary folk, the whole Jewish people became able to shape their belief and behavior on models provided by the scriptures. A broadly based, popular religion, founded on extensive knowledge of sacred writings, was an entirely new phenomenon in human history.

This, together with the techniques for ruling empires, constituted the two most important achievements of ancient Middle Eastern society and civilization.

THE IRON AGE—
IMPORTANCE OF IRON

The use of metals was characteristic of civilized peoples, though some primitive societies also knew how to smelt copper and other ores. Most metals were used mainly for jewelry; only bronze was hard and tough enough to serve as a tool or weapon. But bronze was expensive, since the copper and tin ores that had to be combined to make bronze were rather scarce.

For a long time men were unable to use iron effectively. When iron was melted and poured into a mold—the way other metals were treated—it crystallized as it cooled and so became both very hard and very brittle. Any sharp blow simply shattered anything made of it. In addition, cast iron rusted easily and was not particularly handsome. Hence, even though iron ore was by far the commonest metal in the earth's crust, early smiths had no use for it.

About 1400 B.C., however, an entirely new technique for treating iron was discovered somewhere in eastern Anatolia. For a long time the ironworkers and their Hittite rulers kept the new methods secret. But after about 1200 B.C. the Hittite Empire broke up and the blacksmiths scattered in all directions. Knowledge of how to make useful tools and weapons out of common iron ore spread with them. As this happened, usable metal became vastly more abundant. New applications in ordinary everyday life became possible. Both farming and fighting were changed in fundamental ways. A new age dawned—the Iron Age. The Chariot Age, dominated by aristocratic warriors whose weapons were of bronze, faded into the past.

The secret of making iron into a useful metal was to mix small quantities of carbon into it. This changed the qualities of the metal in remarkable ways. Instead of the brittleness of cast iron, iron that had carbon mixed into it became flexible, yet hard and tough like bronze, and nearly as cheap as cast iron. Ancient smiths did not know that small quantities of carbon from the charcoal, on which they heated the iron, entered into the molten metal and changed its characteristics. What they knew was that if they took a piece of cast iron and heated it in a bed of burning charcoal until it became red hot and soft, it could then be hammered into any shape desired. Of course, this had to be done over and over again until the piece of metal had been beaten into what was needed—sword blade, helmet, plowshare, or whatever it might be. And if, after being hammered into shape, the metal was heated again and then suddenly plunged into a bath of cold water, a hard, tough, and strong end product would result. We call it "wrought iron." The one disadvantage of the new metal was that it rusted. No cure could be found for this, but the abundance of iron more than made up for this inferiority to bronze.

Iron Age Migrations

Because iron weapons and tools were very much easier to produce than bronze weapons had been, they were available to far larger numbers of people. This changed the balance of military strength between the civilized states of the Middle East and the peoples who lived in the deserts to the south and in the hills to the north. In the civilized part of the world, the political masters of the land did not dare to arm the rank and file of peasant farmers. They were subjects and rent payers, not warriors, anyway. With weapons in their hands, they might attack their masters rather than fighting against invading barbarians. Among the nomads of the desert and the tribes of the hills, however, every grown man was a potential soldier, eager for plunder and ready to obey his chief.

The result was the rapid overthrow of the charioteers' empires. The chariot lost most of its terror when shields and helmets of iron guarded foot soldiers against the charioteers' arrows. Infantry, of course, could not compete with chariot mobility. But a well-armored raiding party of foot soldiers, if properly disciplined, could keep the field against even the most furious chariot charge. And by catching such a force in a narrow valley or at some other disadvantageous place, foot soldiers might even be able to destroy the sort of chariot army that had once been irresistible.

Invaders of the Iron Age came both by sea and by land. The people known as Philistines, for example, came by ship from somewhere in Asia Minor or the Aegean. Their fleet may even have included some ships' crews from the shores of the Black Sea. After trying several times to invade Egypt, the remnant of the Philistine host settled in Palestine (c. 1190 B.C.). They conquered the Canaanite peasants of the land and ruled over them from fortified cities near the coast. At about the same time, Hebrews from the desert filtered in from the east and occupied the high ground overlooking the coastal plain of Palestine.

Farther north, along the Mediterranean coast, the Phoenicians remained little affected by the collapse of the Hittite Empire (1200 B.C.) and the decline of the Egyptian Empire, which began about 1100 B.C. They soon became the most active sea traders of the eastern Mediterranean, taking over the role formerly played by Cretan and then by Mycenaean ships. Inland, however, new tribes, from the desert, known as Aramaeans, occupied the land around Damascus, in Syria. They, too, became famous traders by operating caravans between Phoenicia on the coast and the cities of Mesopotamia. In southern Mesopotamia still a third group of tribesmen penetrated civilized ground, taking over the territory where Sumerian cities once had stood. These were the Chaldaeans, who, like the Hebrews and the Aramaeans, spoke a Semitic language.

In their native environment, these Semitic-speaking tribes from the north Arabian desert did not have easy access to iron or the fuel needed for smelting it. Iron weapons were therefore not an important factor when they first invaded civilized regions. All the same, their victories were made easier by the fact that the civilized empires were also being attacked by barbarians from the north—such as the Philistines—who did have iron. By and large, the invaders from the southern deserts learned about the new metal only after they had settled down in Palestine, Syria, and Mesopotamia.

The northern invaders spoke Indo-European languages. At least some of their ancestors had been warlike pastoral nomads on the steppelands between the Black Sea and the Aral Sea. Thus, nomadism and herding were still familiar to the Dorians who overran Greece between 1200 and 1000 B.C. The Medes, too, moved onto the plateau of Iran at about the same time, and at first continued to depend on herds of cattle and horses. Between these two flanks, the most important new peoples who appeared in the Middle East when the Iron Age invasions got under way were the Phrygians in Anatolia, who overthrew the Hittite Empire, and the Armenians, who settled south of the Caucasus Mountains around Lake Van.

Return to Civilized Patterns of Society

These movements of people tapered off after about 1000 B.C. Among the older states only Egypt and Assyria survived as independent kingdoms, but they ceased to be empires because they lost control of all their outlying territories where subject peoples had once obeyed them. The Hittite and Mycenaean empires disappeared entirely. Yet the memory of how to rule a great state did not entirely vanish; the bureaucratic principle was not forgotten completely. In due course new empires arose on the ruins of the old.

During and after the Iron Age invasions, however, rough, independent farmer-herders established themselves in many parts of the Middle East. Among these peoples, tribal ties and a strong sense of the equality of all fighting men remained near the surface; but before long, differences began to appear. Some families became rich and powerful, others stayed poor and became dependent on the rich. Rulers discovered again the advantages of standing armies and learned how to collect taxes in order to maintain professional soldiers. All the features of civilized society, in other words, speedily started to develop again, even among the most old-fashioned, equality-minded newcomers.

Trade, war, and population growth combined to produce this result. As the invaders settled down and became more numerous, they soon had to give up most of their animals and become crop farmers. With further population growth, some farmers found themselves in possession of too little good farmland for comfort. After a bad season they might have to borrow seed grain from a more fortunate or more prudent neighbor. If the borrower could not repay, he would first lose his land and then might have to become a slave simply in order to eat.

The prudent and ruthless lender soon grew into a landowner. He might then begin to use his extra wealth to trade with distant parts for various luxuries that could not be produced at home. A more luxurious style of life thus became possible. This, in turn, made it worthwhile to get hold of more and more land. As the rich got richer and the poor got poorer, it became easier for those who had large holdings to increase their possessions.

War had the same effect. Local chieftains needed bodyguards to be able to impose their will on others. Bodyguards in time grew into regular standing armies because of danger from neighbors and, sometimes, disloyalty at home among those who regretted the loss of the old tribal traditions of freedom and equality.

Obviously, an army required taxes; and taxes had to be collected from ordinary farmers—by force, if necessary. The whole development from tribal simplicity to full-blown bureaucratic government went very fast. Models lay close at hand in both Egypt and Mesopotamia where civilized techniques of government survived without interruption. As a result, by 900 B.C. even a rather backward kingdom like that of the Hebrews in Palestine had become civilized.

THE NEW RELATION
OF VILLAGE AND
COUNTRY COMMUNITIES

At first glance, therefore, it appears that the invasions of the Iron Age made almost no difference. But in fact this was not so. Even after landlords and tax collectors, standing armies, and bureaucratic government had once again established themselves all over the Middle East, the structure of society did not become exactly the same as in the Bronze Age, and this was so for several reasons.

First of all, iron plowshares, sickles, and scythes helped to extend cultivation. Clay soils that a wooden plow was unable to cultivate could be plowed with iron plowshares, and the labor of the harvest was much reduced by the use of iron sickles and scythes. This meant that more food could be produced. It also meant that every farmer had to go to the market from time to time to get new tools or to have his old ones repaired. The work of the blacksmith was too specialized for an ordinary farmer to learn; hence, he had to have his ironwork done by a professional.

This was a true landmark in history. Peasant farmers of earlier civilized communities ordinarily made their own implements. But, with the coming of iron tools, peasant farmers for the first time began to get a direct, practical benefit from the specialization of labor and the enlargement of human skills that had begun more than 2000 years earlier with the rise of the first cities and civilization.

Previously, only special classes of society—priests, soldiers, rulers, landlords—had reaped the benefits of such skills. The peasants at the bottom of the social ladder had worked in the fields and been forced to pay over part of their crop to somebody else. Now, however, with the coming of iron, every farmer had to have some of his tools made for him. This meant buying and selling, saving a little extra grain to trade for a bit of iron or for a fine new sickle. Once the idea that even the poorest cultivators could buy and sell got to be accepted all round, farmers who happened to have something left over when the season came to an end might buy other artisans' products too: a useful pot to put things in, or a pretty piece of cloth for a bride-to-be.

It is worth emphasizing the importance of this new relationship between artisans of the town and cultivators of the countryside. In earlier ages, if some military action wiped a town from the face of the earth, the local farmers felt no loss. On the contrary, they would find themselves freed—at least for a while—from having to pay rents and taxes to the cityfolk. The townspeople, in other words, were their natural enemies, not their friends.

This ever-present, half-suppressed hostility between town and country dwellers had meant that town life had always been fragile, insecure, and liable to drastic setbacks. This is why civilized life was so easily wiped out in Greece and India when rude invaders, who did not know or care much about city life, overran the towns and plundered everything they could lay hands on. The invaders then moved on, looking for fresh plunder, new pasture for their cattle, and fertile farmland for themselves.

When peasants began to depend on town artisans for essential supplies, however, a bond of mutual interest began to link the two classes together. Smiths, after all, needed metal, and metal came only by trade—at least in most places where mines and fuel supplies were not immediately at hand. Trade, in turn, required some sort of public order, which, in turn, required government, armies, and priests, too, for the gods could not safely be neglected. Such experts could only be maintained by the payment of rents and taxes. In short, for the peasant majority of mankind the price of iron was acceptance of the whole burden of civilization.

This does not mean that the peasants of the civilized world came to feel that paying rents and taxes was right or just. It does mean, though, that they began to have a stake in the survival of town life. When a town was destroyed, there were strong reasons for starting it up again, or for finding another town nearby where the services needed by the rural population could be provided.

Town life, therefore, became firmly rooted on rain-watered land in the Iron Age, not before. A new economic base level had been attained. Everybody, with the possible exception of nomad shepherds and herders, now had real interest in keeping town life—and therefore civilization—alive.

RESTORATION OF BUREAUCRATIC GOVERNMENT— THE HEBREW EXAMPLE

The speed with which the political structure of the Middle East returned to bureaucratic government between 1100 and 900 B.C. shows how stubborn the pressures toward civilized complexity were. We are particularly well informed about how this happened among the Hebrews, because the historical parts of the Old Testament deal in some detail with the conquest of Canaan and the campaigns of the earliest Hebrew kings.

When they first moved into Palestine, the Hebrews were organized loosely into tribes. The twelve tribes cooperated only on special occasions. Local problems were settled by "judges" whose authority rested on personal prestige and holiness. Soon, however, war with the Philistines required better organization. Accordingly, one of the judges, Samuel, called all of the tribes together and anointed a young man of unusual strength and stature as king. His name was Saul. The people all promised to obey him. This happened about 1020 B.C. For a while Saul was a successful war leader, but he quarreled with some of his best fighters, including a one-time shepherd boy, David, son of Jesse. In the end, King Saul met defeat and death in battle against the Philistines. His rival, David, succeeded to the kingship, decisively defeated the Philistines, and seized Jerusalem from a people called Jebusites, and made it his capital.

Under David, who ruled from about 1012 to 972 B.C., the kingdom became relatively stable. Taxes maintained a formidable standing army; diplomatic relations with neighboring kingdoms became important; commerce developed.

King Solomon, David's son, brought the Hebrew kingdom to its highest peak of prosperity. He imported workmen from Phoenicia to build a temple to Yahweh in Jerusalem, and he was famous both for the number of his wives and for the wisdom of his administration.

After Solomon's death the kingdom split into two halves: Israel in the north and Judah in the south. Israel was ruled from Samaria, Judah from Jerusalem. For nearly 200 years the two kingdoms fought one another from time to time and played a minor part in diplomatic and military maneuvers with greater powers. Then in 722 B.C. the Assyrians conquered the kingdom of Israel. They carried all the cityfolk of the kingdom off into captivity in Babylonia. Only peasants remained behind, subject to

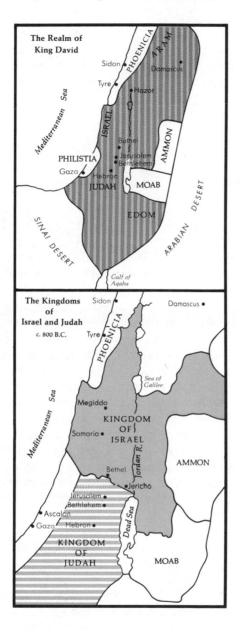

alien tax collectors and to governors appointed by the distant monarch of Assyria.

The Israelite upper class never returned. They made up the "ten lost tribes" of the kingdom of Israel. Presumably they simply merged into the general population of the Middle East. The peasants of Israel remaining behind were known to later Jews as "Samaritans" (so called after the capital city, Samaria). Their religion differed on some important points from later Jewish beliefs and ritual, a fact that horrified Jews who felt that the Samaritan religion was particularly dangerous because in most respects it was close to their own.

How to Rule an Empire: The Assyrian Example

The Assyrian kingdom that conquered Israel in 722 B.C. had barely survived the Iron Age invasions. The Assyrians were the cultural heirs of Babylonia located on an exposed frontier, where barbarism lapped up against the most northerly outpost of the ancient civilization of Mesopotamia. In such a position, the Assyrian kings were especially exposed to attack from the north, but had the advantages of superior numbers and wealth that came from irrigation agriculture. After a slow start, therefore, Assyrian power began to expand more and more rapidly. All of Mesopotamia and Syria had been conquered before the Assyrian armies attacked Israel. Thereafter, other campaigns extended Assyrian power still farther into Egypt, Armenia, and Iran. Such an empire was larger than any known before. It was also more systematically governed, but proved brittle because all the subject peoples hated Assyrian ruthlessness.

The Assyrians' success depended upon some important advances they made in military organization and government. In particular, the Assyrians seem to have been the first to organize an entire army into regular units of uniform size—tens, hundreds, and thousands—each with standard equipment and under commanders who could be promoted for success and bravery or demoted if they failed to perform as expected of them. The Assyrian army also had specialist troops: engineers for siege works, and cavalry and chariotry for pursuit and reconnaissance. Its backbone was a hardy infantry—spearthrowers and archers—commanded by a career officer corps.

All modern armies are built up on these principles. So were the later Persian and Roman imperial armies. The reason, of course, is that the system works. Ordinary men from very diverse backgrounds can be fitted into standardized army units and become effective and obedient soldiers, using the Assyrians' patterns of army administration. Promotion for demonstrated efficiency in the field made subordinate commanders into willing, even eager servants of the monarch. Anyone, if appointed by the king, could command any unit of the royal army. Because officers were often shifted around, their careers depended directly on the king. Their loyalty turned to him, too. No other ties—to locality, to a particular piece of property, or to a special body of troops—lasted more than a few years out of an officer's total career.

All this permitted (and still permits) control from the center to a degree otherwise impossible. Thousands upon thousands of men could be made to act together and cooperate effectively to win a victory and conduct an entire campaign. When a regular chain of command came into existence and was accepted by all from top to bottom of the army, generalship on the grand scale, with planned encirclements, ambushes, cross-country marches and other surprises, became possible. Over and over again Assyrian victories demonstrated the advantage of such a system of military administration in an age when opponents could not, or did not, equal it.

The Assyrians also built roads to facilitate the march of their armies toward threatened frontiers. They were wide enough to carry wheeled vehicles through difficult passes and across rough country. Such roads cut down the time needed for the king to arrive with his armies at any threatened point. A messenger system, using relay horses to carry news of any important event to the capital, also allowed the central government to react quickly to danger.

The elaborate Assyrian military system was supported by taxes and by a draft of able-bodied young men. Taxes were collected by governors who were appointed to administer provinces in the same way that the king appointed his military commanders. The Assyrians also had a code of laws which the governors seem to have applied throughout the area under their control. These principles were not new. Similar arrangements had prevailed under Hammurabi and earlier. Thus, the major breakthrough the Assyrians made was in military organization rather than in civil administration.

All the same, their victories did not produce obedient subjects. Both the Babylonians and the Egyptians found it hard to submit to upstarts, as they felt the Assyrians to be. Repeated revolts therefore took place; and Assyrian efforts to terrorize their subjects never checked rebellion for long. Endless campaigning cost a lot of Assyrian lives. Toward the end, the ranks of the Assyrian armies were filled with conscripts raised among their defeated enemies. Perhaps such soldiers did not fight as well as native Assyrians had once done.

Even so, it took attack from a new quarter and six years of war to overthrow the Assyrian Empire. Nineveh, the capital, was sacked in 612 B.C. By 605 B.C. the last organized Assyrian army had been destroyed, and the whole Assyrian nation with it. Three groups combined to destroy the Assyrians: Medes from the plateau of Iran to the east, Babylonian rebels from the south, and Scythians from the grasslands of southern Russia.

THE CAVALRY REVOLUTION   The appearance of the Scythians marked an important new epoch in Middle Eastern and world history. They were cavalrymen who exploited the speed of their horses and the accuracy of their arrows much the way charioteers had done, but without the elaborate and expensive equipment charioteers had needed.

Using horses for cavalry seems obvious now, but when humans first began to associate with horses, the idea of riding into combat seemed foolhardy. To shoot from horseback with a bow, a rider must let go of the reins. The horse is then on its own, and unless it is trained to respond either to the voice of the rider or to pressure from the rider's legs, there is no way to control it. With any sudden change of motion the rider will be pitched off onto the ground, bruised and helpless, perhaps at the very feet of his enemy.

Actually, the first records of the use of cavalry in battle come from the Assyrian army itself and date from about 875 B.C. Thus it appears that Assyrians who discovered they could train horses so well as to make it safe to ride them into battle paved the way for the eventual overthrow of their empire. For when the nomads of the steppe mastered this simple and cheap way to exploit the strength and speed of their horses, it gave them an enormous military advantage. Raiding parties of horsemen could rove far and wide, and could be gone before any defending infantry force could catch up with them. Only equally well-mounted defenders could hope to meet such raiders on more or less even terms. But, as we pointed out earlier horses were costly to keep where there was no natural grass for them to eat.

Of course, the steppe peoples had the permanent advantage of being able to raise horses cheaply and in such numbers that every man could easily possess two or three mounts. Bow and arrows and hit-and-run tactics did the rest. If cavalry raiders met serious opposition, they simply galloped off over the horizon and tried again somewhere else, after a day or two to rest their horses.

The Assyrian army was not prepared to cope with this kind of threat. Accordingly, the combination of Scythian tactics with mass rebellion in the rear brought the empire down. To be sure, the Scythians returned home after the sack of Nineveh in 612 B.C. Civilized lands did not have enough pasture for their horses, so they could not stay away from the steppe for very long. But neither the Medes nor the Babylonians—nor the Egyptians, who tried briefly once again to exert imperial power over Palestine—were able to prevent renewed raiding from the steppes.

Imperial Consolidation under the Persians

The overthrow of the Assyrian Empire and the departure of the Scythians created a power vacuum in the Middle East. The victorious rebels divided the spoils between themselves, but soon quarreled. The Babylonians wanted to control Palestine and Syria as the Assyrians had done; but the Egyptians wished to keep them at a safe distance and began trying to exert influence over the little kingdom of Judah. This persuaded Nebuchadnezzar, the Chaldaean ruler of Babylon, to attack Judah. The Egyptians were no help, so Nebuchadnezzar captured Jerusalem in 586 B.C., destroyed Solomon's Temple, and carried the cityfolk of Judah back to Babylon with him.

The shock to worshipers of Yahweh was tremendous, for after the destruction of Israel in 722 B.C. priests and religious reformers in Jerusalem had drawn the conclusion that their sister kingdom to the north had been punished for failing to obey God faithfully. They therefore set out energetically to reform religion and government in Judah, only to have a similar disaster visited upon them. Yet, as we shall soon see, the dismay of the exiles from Judah led only to a renewed and deepened effort to understand God's will—an effort that made Judaism into an enduring world religion.

The Jews who "wept beside the waters of Babylon" when they remembered Jerusalem did not have long to wait before their Babylonian masters' power was itself overthrown. In 539 B.C. Cyrus the Persian entered Babylon as a conqueror. He began life as a vassal of the Medes, but when he entered Babylon he had already conquered both the Medes' empire and the smaller kingdom of Lydia in Asia Minor. By the time of his death (530 B.C.), Cyrus was master of all the lands between the Aegean Sea on the west and the Amu Darya (Oxus River) on the east.

These amazing successes resulted from the fact that Cyrus had a hardy and warlike people under his command—the Persians who spoke an Indo-European language closely related to the language of the Aryans who had invaded India nearly a thousand years before his time. In addition, Cyrus was helped by fresh revolts that broke out in the ranks of his rivals for imperial power. He encouraged such revolts by giving special rights and privileges to everyone who would support him. Thus, for example, he allowed the Jews, whom Nebuchadnezzar had carried off to Babylon, to return to Judah. A few did; most, however, stayed behind amid the riches and wonders of the great city on the Euphrates.

The Persian Empire went from strength to strength. Cambyses, Cyrus' son and successor, conquered Egypt in 525 B.C. Darius the Great, the next Persian king, campaigned against the Scythians in southern Russia (512 B.C.) and extended his eastern boundary to the Indus River. He adapted Assyrian patterns of civil and military administration and improved upon the Assyrian example by organizing a navy. The Persians had considerable trouble along their northern frontier. Cyrus died fighting against a nomad tribe that lived near the Aral Sea; and Darius failed to win any kind of decisive victory when he invaded Scythia. The best solution Darius could find was to "hire a thief to catch a thief." By paying tribute to nomad tribes close by, others who lived farther off in the steppe could be kept away from the Persian frontiers.

The Persian Empire was also troubled by internal revolts, just as the Assyrian Empire had been, Nevertheless, even the pride of Egypt and of Babylonia gradually wore out in the face of repeated disasters. It took a fresh attack from outside, this time from Macedonia, to overthrow Persian power in 330 B.C. Until that time the vast Persian Empire kept all the peoples of the Middle East under a single political roof. The sheer size of the empire shows what a remarkable achievement this was.

THE RISE OF ETHICAL MONOTHEISM

In the age of the Assyrian and Persian empires, there was a great deal of mingling and borrowing among the peoples of the Middle East. Local peculiarities tended to wear away. Priests treasured ancient rituals and doctrines that had been inherited from Sumer and the Old Kingdom of Egypt. But much of that inheritance had become hollow and was no longer deeply believed in by anyone, not even by the priests who handed the old texts on from generation to generation. In secular life there had been great progress. The art of government and military administration had attained greater efficiency. Vast palaces and newly founded capital cities, like Nineveh in Assyria and Persepolis in Persia, allowed artists to express their rulers' greatness and glory. But in Egypt and Mesopotamia, religious thought and invention lagged. The weight of ancient tradition was too great.

In Palestine among the Hebrews and in eastern Iran among the Persians, conditions were different. In both these regions, prophets arose who taught that a single God ruled the entire universe, who was both good and just Himself and required that human beings try to be good and just in all their dealings with others. This sort of teaching is called 'ethical monotheism,' and marked a new era in the way civilized peoples understood the world and their place in it.

In particular, two new religions took shape: Zoroastrianism in the east and Judaism in the west. The ideas of Zoroaster and of the Hebrew prophets have shaped human lives ever since, and in very intimate and powerful ways. In the long run the impact of governments and armies, that demand submission but not belief, was trifling by comparison.

Zoroastrianism

Zoroaster was a Persian, and probably lived only a short time before Darius (ruled 521–486 B.C.) became king. Zoroaster lived far to the east, near the part of the Persian world bordering India. His ideas were radical, for he taught that all the traditional gods of the Persians were devils and should not be worshiped. Traditional rituals—blood sacrifices in particular—he also thought were wicked. In Zoroaster's lifetime the Persians, who had once lived as herders, were still adjusting to settled life as farmers. This was troublesome enough, but in addition they found themselves suddenly become rulers of a vast empire. As rulers, the Persians had to deal with all kinds of peoples who told various stories about how the world was made and governed. Each claimed to tell the truth, but nevertheless they all contradicted one another. What could anyone believe?

Zoroaster found an answer in inspiration. He believed that a supreme god, Ahura Mazda, communicated directly with him through supernatural spirits or angels. And what they told him he then repeated to all who would listen. His sayings took the form of poetry. Followers, believing the truth of Zoroaster's messages, memorized them. Later they were written down, and by accident or on purpose may have been altered. At any rate, the *Gathas*, as Zoroaster's verses are called, are hard for modern scholars to understand; and the modern Parsis of India, who still follow Zoroaster's religion and who believe the *Gathas* are divinely inspired scripture, do not entirely understand their meaning either.

All the same, the main ideas of Zoroaster's preaching are clear enough. Zoroaster taught that the world was the scene of a great struggle between Ahura Mazda, supreme god and champion of good, on the one hand, and Ahriman, the prince of darkness and of everything evil, on the other. Every human being had to choose sides in the struggle. Simple rituals built around the recitation of Zoroaster's poems, and good deeds based upon knowledge of the truth, were what Zoroaster asked of his followers. The good must join the fight, helping Ahura Mazda and the angels of light. They might have to face hardship, disappointment, and injustice but could do so without flinching because they knew, from Zoroaster's revelation, that Ahura Mazda would win the struggle in the end. Eventually the wicked would be burned in a vast fire, the world would cease to exist in its present mixed form in which good and evil were everywhere intertwined, and the good would live on forever in eternal bliss. Zoroaster believed that Ahura Mazda could not be seen by human eyes; but, though immaterial, his power extended over the entire world. Other gods were all false. Existing temples and religions were forms of devil worship. Only reverent acceptance of Zoroaster's revelation could save each and every person from religious error and fiery destruction at the end of time.

Zoroaster made converts in important places. King Darius himself used Zoroastrian language in some of his inscriptions; so did his son and successor, Xerxes (ruled 486–465 B.C.). Presumably a good many other important Persians also believed the prophet's teachings. But before long some of the things he had forbidden crept back into the religious practice of the Persian court.

No other peoples ever accepted the message. Zoroastrianism remained a Persian religion, but some of Zoroaster's ideas lived on among other peoples in a different form. Some Jews, for example, found Zoroaster's picture of a fiery end of the world very persuasive; later, Christians and Moslems also accepted the idea. The conception of angels in both Judaism and Christianity owes a good deal to Zoroaster's doctrine. Certainly the Christian idea of Satan, God's rival and enemy in trying to win men's souls, was strongly influenced by Zoroastrianism.

Three other points are worth noticing. First, Zoroaster taught that the supreme god who controlled everything that happened in the whole universe cared very much what individuals did and how each person behaved. Those who believed Zoroaster's revelation and obeyed Ahura Mazda's rules of life were saved, and those who rejected the prophet's message and instead "espoused the lie" were burned to a crisp. Reward and punishment for human behavior were postponed until the end of the world—an event not necessarily far away. In the meanwhile, if the wicked prospered, so much the worse for them. Righteous persons, even if wicked people made them suffer, knew that Ahura Mazda would sooner or later punish evildoers in a very painful way.

Such a doctrine made it easier to face the hardships and injustices of everyday life. With such beliefs, civilization became much easier to take, especially for those at the bottom of the social ladder, who often saw scant justice in the world around them, but could count upon God to set things right in the not-too-distant future.

Second, Zoroaster addressed his message to individual human beings everywhere. Anyone who listened to his words and understood them could join the ranks of Ahura Mazda's followers. Religion thus became separable from other circumstances of life. Anyone could earn salvation anywhere in the world, by knowing the truth. Not the tribe or the city

Masada, Israel (Israeli Government Tourist Office).

Jerusalem, west wall (Israeli Government Tourist Office).

or some other social group, but the individual human soul became the unit of religious action—known to God, and, perhaps, to his fellow believers, whoever they might be and wherever they might find themselves. Zoroastrianism, in other words, was a universal faith, intended to appeal to everyone, even though in fact only Persians accepted the prophet's words.

Last, Zoroastrianism was prophetic. The founder claimed to speak with supernatural authority, inspired directly by Ahura Mazda. Truth was in his words, and true religion depended on getting the meaning of the words right. Ancient tradition was false and utterly misleading. Truth came new-minted from Zoroaster's lips, its authenticity vouched for only by the prophet's own conviction and the persuasiveness of the inspired words themselves.

Judaism

By 500 B.C. Judaism, too, had become prophetic as well as ethical and monotheistic, and addressed its message to individual souls. The history of Judaism, however, was far more complicated than that of Zoroastrianism. The Hebrew prophets never rejected the past. They claimed always to be calling their hearers back to the original revelation God had made to Moses and to Abraham. Moreover, the prophets were counterbalanced by a priestly tradition fostered in Solomon's Temple at Jerusalem. This religious inheritance somehow had to be reconciled as far as possible with prophetic revelations, some of which were very hostile to certain priestly functions.

The reconciliation of priestly and prophetic traditions was achieved by gathering various writings about law, religion, and history into a carefully edited sacred scripture. The books into which these writings were divided became the only authentic revelations of God's will, according to Jews. Christians, however, believe that these books are only part of God's revelation—the Old Testament—which was later supplemented, and in some important ways altered, by the further revelation recorded in the books of the New Testament.

Even after the Jewish scriptures had been carefully gathered together, many seeming contradictions remained. This offered an unending series of problems for commentators to try to solve. Nothing could be more important, since the scriptures offered the only sure way to find out what God wanted human beings to do under varying circumstances. It was, therefore, every pious man's duty to study the pages of revealed truth with utmost care. Generation after generation of Jews have been shaped by this kind of study, down to the present. Christians usually left the task to priests and theologians, for whom, of course, the New Testament was more important than the parts of the Bible they shared with the Jews.

HISTORY ACCORDING TO THE OLD TESTAMENT   When the books of the Old Testament had all been assembled and recognized as sacred (a process not entirely completed before about 150 B.C.), a magnificent panorama of world history unrolled itself before believers. The Bible story of creation, the Flood, and the repeopling of the earth after the Flood closely resembled Mesopotamian religious myths. But beginning with the account of Abraham, Isaac, and Jacob, and the sojourn in Egypt, the Biblical story becomes unique.

According to the Bible, the God of Abraham did not fully reveal his special character until after the Exodus or journey of the Israelites out of Egypt. Whether or not we believe in the divine inspiration of Scripture, we can understand that when the people of Israel, under Moses' leadership, escaped from Egypt and gathered at the foot of Mount Sinai in the desert, they needed rules to govern their everyday actions. For generations they had lived in Egypt and had forgotten desert customs. Now that they were returning to the old style of nomad life again, they needed a written law just because their traditional unwritten custom had been lost. This was the situation Moses confronted when he ascended Mount Sinai, and, according to the Bible story, received the Ten Commandments from the hand of God. On Moses' return, he made the people promise to obey the Ten Commandments and accept the law of God. This Covenant (agreement) between the people and God was, at least as understood in later times, the real beginning of Judaism.

Nevertheless, there is some doubt as to the original meaning of the Covenant. Yahweh, the God whom Moses met on Mount Sinai, was certainly God of the Israelites. But it is not clear that the Israelites regarded him as supreme over all other peoples and all parts of the world. Some Biblical passages speak as though God merely protected his own people, while other gods protected other peoples and fought against Yahweh, as Yahweh also fought against them.

THE PROPHETIC TRADITION   In the days when the Hebrews settled the land of Canaan (c. 1300–1100 B.C.), they took over the fertility gods—the baals—of the Canaanites. Yahweh was a god of the desert and of battle; what did he know about making grain grow in the fields? Yet there were always some among the Hebrews who felt that honoring any god but Yahweh was wicked and would stir him to wrath against his people, sooner or later. These men sometimes gathered as bands of "prophets" and denounced the wickedness of baal worship and the greed of the rich.

GOD'S HAND IN HISTORY
II Kings 18:13; 19:9–36,
with elisions

Now in the fourteenth year of king Hezekiah* did Sennacherib, king of Assyria, come up against all the walled cities of Judah and took them. And he sent messengers unto Hezekiah, saying: "Let not thy God deceive thee, saying, Jerusalem shall not be delivered into the hand of the king of Assyria. Behold, thou hast heard what the kings of Assyria have done to all lands, by destroying them utterly, and shalt thou be delivered? Have the gods of the nations which my father destroyed delivered them?"

And Hezekiah went up into the house of the Lord, and spread the letter from the hands of the messengers before the Lord. And Hezekiah prayed before the Lord: "Lord, bow down thine ear and hear; open, Lord, thine eyes and see; and hear the words of Sennacherib. Of a truth, Lord, the kings of Assyria have destroyed the nations and their lands, and have cast their gods into the fire, for they were no gods, but the work of men's hands, wood and stone. Now therefore, O Lord our God, save thou us out of his hand, that all the kingdoms of the earth may know that thou art the Lord God, even thou only."

The prophet Isaiah,† the son of Amoz, sent to Hezekiah saying: "Thus saith the Lord God of Israel: 'That which thou hast prayed to me against Sennacherib, king of Assyria, I have heard. Therefore he shall not come into this city, nor shoot an arrow there, nor come before it with shield, nor cast a bank against it. For I will defend this City, to save it, for mine own sake, for my servant David's sake.' "

And it came to pass that night, that the angel of the Lord went out and smote in the camp of the Assyrians an hundred four score and five thousand; and when they arose early in the morning, behold, they were all dead corpses. So Sennacherib, king of Assyria, departed and returned to the city of Nineveh.

* In 701 B.C.
† Not the same Isaiah who prophesied in Babylon about 150 years later.

The balance between baal worship and the religion of Yahweh tipped decisively during the wars against the Philistines that led to the establishment of the Hebrew monarchy (c. 1028–973 B.C.). Yahweh was a god of battles. With his aid the Hebrews had conquered Canaan. Saul and David therefore again called on Yahweh's aid in fighting their wars, and made him their God to the exclusion of all others. But later, both David and Solomon were willing to allow foreign worship in their kingdom. Their successors followed a similar policy.

Nevertheless the old prophetic tradition never died away. Elijah, for example, led a great revival movement about 865 B.C. and temporarily drove out the worship of foreign gods. Israel and Judah thus became Yahweh's. To please him became the religious duty of all the people. When the fate of the kingdoms began clearly to depend less on what happened within the borders of the state itself than on wars and diplomatic dealings with Egypt, Assyria, and all the other powers of the Middle East, Yahweh's worshipers faced a new problem. They concluded that their God controlled all the world. His plans raised up the Assyrians and threw down the Egyptians. His purposes guided the feet of every living thing; nothing was too small and nothing too great for Yahweh to care for and control.

These ideas found expression in the poetry of a series of great prophets, beginning with the shepherd Amos, who preached about 750 B.C. His words were written down at the time of or very soon after his death. Other prophets followed Amos' example, and either wrote themselves or caused their words to be written down. In this way their thoughts and feelings were preserved for future generations. Like Zoroaster, the Hebrew prophets claimed to speak with the words of the only true God. Many of their hearers believed them. In time their poems were accepted as part of the sacred scripture, revealing the will of God for the benefit of everyone who was prepared to listen and understand.

The prophets' central message was simple. Unless his people stopped doing evil and began to obey God's will with all their heart and soul, God would become angry and punish them with some dreadful disaster. False gods were to be put aside. Moral conduct toward others and reverence for God—these were the things that mattered. God would punish those who disregarded the prophets' warnings, in a terrible Day of Yahweh, when all the injustices of the world would be set right.

Against such a background, the fall of Israel to the Assyrians in 722 B.C. seemed to be at least a partial fulfillment of the prophets' warnings. A reform party in the kingdom of Judah therefore set out to escape a similar fate by purifying religion in every way they could. Old manuscripts were consulted. With their help pious scholars put the record of God's dealing with humankind into an authoritative form. In this way many of the books of the Old Testament took something like their present form. The busy scholars discovered the entire Book of Deuteronomy and made so much of it that the movement is often referred to as the Deuteronomic reform.

Yet as we have seen, their efforts to reform religion did not ward off disaster. Nebuchadnezzar came and conquered; like the Assyrians, he carried off the educated population of Judah into exile (586 B.C.). What could the reformers do now? Their hope in God's help seemed to have failed. What more could Yahweh want?

Two great prophets, Ezekiel and Isaiah, answered this question. Ezekiel declared that God wanted an even more scrupulous personal holiness than the reformers of the Deuteronomic period had imagined. Precise rules for everyday conduct were required; and the Scripture lay ready for everyone to inquire into and find out exactly what God wanted them to do. If Jews would study the Word of God carefully and do exactly what it told them to do, then and only then would the kingdom be restored, glorious and united, as in the days of David and Solomon.

The second prophet, Isaiah, who was alive at the time when Cyrus conquered Babylon (539 B.C.), had an even grander vision of the future. Soon, he declared, God would come in glory and set the children of Israel in their rightful place at the head of all the nations. The despised exiles in Babylon would become rulers and governors, entrusted with the supreme task of guiding all people to knowledge of God's truths. Thus for Isaiah the Day of Yahweh, which the older prophets had treated as a dreadful time when evildoers (and who was not an evildoer in some degree?) would be punished, became a time of hope and expectation.

From this point of view, the more wickedness and oppression prospered, the sooner the longed-for Day of Judgment could be expected. With this belief Jews could endure any sort of disappointment or injustice and still keep alive their secret, burning hope. Relief was coming; the end of the world's wicked ways was not far off. Meanwhile, the task was to study carefully the sacred books so as to know God's will, and to wait in patience until his purpose might be fulfilled.

THE IMPORTANCE OF THE SYNAGOGUE   While they were in Babylon the exiled Jews created a new pattern of worship to go with their renewed hope. This was the *synagogue*—a meeting place where the faithful came together each week and read from Scripture, explained to one another the meaning of what they had read, and thus confirmed each other's faith. It was hard for everyone to be expert in the Scriptures. In time it became customary for each synagogue to have a teacher or rabbi who was specially trained, so as to be able to settle difficult points of scriptural interpretation. In essence, these same practices continue among Jews to this day.

A synagogue could be set up wherever Jews lived. (The legal minimum was later set at ten adult men.) In this way even scattered Jewish communities could and did keep their consciousness of being a special people, in Covenant with God. Instead of merging into the general population as similar small groups normally did, Jews henceforward were able to maintain their identity through good and bad times, among hostile and among hospitable peoples, and in almost every country of the world. The religion was no longer tied to the soil of Palestine, nor to the Temple in Jerusalem. It had become independent of all outward circumstances. It was a matter of belief and of learning, of obeying God's will as made known in the pages of Scripture, and waiting in hope for final deliverance from the evils of the world.

To be sure, when Cyrus permitted the Jewish exiles to return to Palestine, some of them did so and tried to rebuild the Temple and restore the old rituals. Some even sought to restore the kingdom of David by finding a descendant of the royal line and putting him on the throne; but the Persians would not permit that. The returned Jews had therefore to settle for a community built around the Temple. This did not affect the life of the synagogues, however. The Jews who remained in Babylon and those who took up residence in other cities of the Middle East continued to build their religious life around weekly meetings in the synagogues.

Today we take very much for granted the idea that religion is something personal and more or less private. It does not strike us as odd that groups of believers may worship God in any part of the world, each in its own way. Because these ideas seem so obvious now, it is hard to realize how surprising such ideas would have been before 600 B.C. Earlier peoples had always thought that their gods were tied to a particular place and had to be approached through a particular temple ritual. Zoroaster went part of the way, by making sacred words the heart of his religion; but he did not invent a meeting place like the synagogue, where the faithful could hand on the truths and make them come alive each week by reading and reflecting and hearing each other speak about them, the way the Jews did.

When Judaism emerged from the trial of the exile, therefore, it was a more flexible, stronger faith than ever before. The worship of Yahweh had begun with the Covenant in the desert. It had rallied the Hebrews in their wars. It had inspired the prophets to denounce unrighteousness. Such a religion could flourish and survive almost anywhere.

Judaism was particularly helpful to people trapped in the recesses of great cities, where no one much knew or cared what happened to neighbors. In such an environment, the fellowship of the synagogue and scriptural promises of a bright future, for those who studied and obeyed God's will, sustained individual believers in time of hardship as other religions of that age could not do.

Finally, Judaism became a religion of the Book. The beauty and grandeur of many passages of the Bible entered profoundly not only into Judaism but into Christianity as well. Stories, metaphors, heroes, villains, symbols, phrases, and—not least—the central idea that God rules the world, and cares about each and every human soul, all became fundamental elements in our Western civilization. No one foresaw such a history;

millions upon millions of Jews, Christians, and Moslems believe that God's will lies behind it.

CONCLUSION

With the full development of the techniques of empire and the matching development of ethical monotheism, the history of the ancient Middle East reached a logical fulfillment. No fundamental improvements have ever been made in the techniques of governing large numbers of people, living in different environments and speaking different languages, since the days of the Persian Empire. Modern means of communication and transportation, of course, make such government easier, shortening reaction to new developments, but the principles of imperial rule remain the same.

Monotheism, as developed by Zoroaster and by the Jews, went through greater changes. Yet here, too, the fundamental idea and the basic institutions by means of which believers might give expression to their religion had been invented by 500 B.C.

These were two great Middle Eastern contributions to the world. Other civilizations put their emphasis on other things, and it is time for us to turn to them now and see how the ancient Greeks, Indians, and Chinese worked out their own distinctive styles of civilized life.

CHAPTER 5

The Greek Style of Civilization

to 500 B.C.

In the mountainous land of Greece, the climate was much like that of the fertile parts of the Middle East. In summer the winds blew steadily from the northeast and the sun shone every day. In winter Greece came under the influence of westerly winds which brought in storms of rain or snow from the Atlantic. The Greek mountains were heavily wooded before slash-and-burn farmers cut the trees down; some of the flatter land had trees, too, and where less rain fell, there were some small grassy plains.

Neolithic farmers reached this land by about 4500 B.C., but for a long time the population remained too thin and scattered to make civilization possible. Shortly before 2000 B.C. Greek-speaking tribesmen began to filter into Greece from the northern Balkan Peninsula. Being warriors and herders, they soon made the earlier inhabitants submit to their rule. In time the Greek speech of the invaders became universal among the population as a whole, but some traces of pre-Greek life remained as late as 500 B.C.

With the rise of Minoan civilization (c. 2100 B.C.), familiarity with metal and other aspects of civilized accomplishments began to spread among the inhabitants of the Greek mainland. Mycenae and a few other strongholds became seats of civilization by about 1600 B.C. But local resources from surrounding farmland were never great enough to support the artisans, soldiers, servants, and courtiers that made Mycenae splendid.

Instead, the king and his warriors depended on booty gathered through pirate raids to keep their courts and capital cities going.

Civilization based on piracy was bound to be insecure. After a few unsuccessful expeditions the wealth and power of the king at Mycenae might simply evaporate. His followers would cease obeying if he led them to disaster. Something of the sort must have happened, but we do not know the details. We do know that, about 1100 B.C., Mycenae was burned and pillaged by a fresh wave of Greek-speaking invaders who came from the north. Thereafter, the great walls guarding the high king's palace remained a hollow shell. Yet the stones of which they were made were so large that later generations of Greeks told one another that they had been put in place by giants.

THE DARK AGE OF GREECE: 1100–600 B.C.

The tribesmen who destroyed the Mycenaean palace strongholds spoke a dialect of Greek called Dorian. They were simple herders, armed with iron weapons, more numerous and more primitive than the Greeks who had preceded them into Greece. With their arrival, courts and cities disappeared. By degrees, however, the newcomers settled down. Population began to increase, and because of a growing shortage of land, instead of cultivating a field for only a few years and then moving on, the Dorians began to plow the same fields year after year. All this paralleled what was happening at the same time in Palestine and other parts of the Middle East where Iron Age invaders had come in.

Aristocratic Government

The social consequences of settling down to fixed agriculture were also the same as in the Middle East. Chieftains and a few others became richer and richer, but many farmers became too poor to equip themselves as fighters and, after losing their land, some even had to sell themselves as slaves.

In the days of the Iron Age migrations, Greek society was tribal. When it seemed a good time to move on and look for new and better land, all able-bodied men gathered together to hear what their leaders—clan chieftains by heredity—recommended. If a move required military action, as usually it did, every arm was needed, and everyone had to know in a general way what the plan of campaign was going to be. Such plans were worked out in council meetings. The commander-in-chief or king consulted the clan chieftains first, and then the leaders informed all the male fighting force of the tribe what they proposed to do.

As the tribes settled down, there came to be fewer and fewer occasions on which the military manpower of the entire community had to be mobilized. Families scattered over the land, and each chieftain's household conducted its affairs more or less as it pleased. Under such circumstances, the authority and power of the king weakened. He became just one among equals, not much stronger or better off than clan chieftains.

Councils of the noble clan chieftains continued to meet from time to time, settling quarrels between families, arranging for worship of the gods, or planning defense against a hostile neighbor. But the common people were called in only in time of unusual emergency. Most matters could be handled by the nobles assembled together. Quite often, instead of trusting the king with too much authority, the council of nobles decided to assign special duties to one among themselves. The next step in dismantling the king's power was to appoint members of the noble council to handle public business for a year or for some other specified period of time. Kingship itself was sometimes made appointive. Authority thus fell into the hands of magistrates, chosen annually by the council of nobles from among its members.

This privileged political position was backed up by the nobles' new economic power. As large landowners they found it easy to lend grain to hungry farmers who needed seed for the next harvest. Debtors either had to repay such loans with interest or else give up their land and become servants or slaves of the person from whom they had borrowed.

Concentration of power in the hands of a noble class was also furthered by a change in military tactics. For the cavalry revolution that had come to the Middle East between 975 and 600 B.C. affected Greece, too. When Greeks learned to fight from horseback, superior mobility gave the cavalry a decisive advantage over mere foot soldiers. In Greece, however, pasture was sparse at best, and only the rich could afford to feed horses with grain. But, after the cavalry revolution, it was precisely those few who really counted in battle. The rest often became too poor to equip themselves with sword, spear, helmet, and shield. The development of cavalry tactics helped to consolidate the power of noble landowners.

The *Iliad* and the *Odyssey*

The ideas and values held dear by Greeks of the Dark Age found expression in poetry, some of which survived into later times. The greatest of the early poets, Homer, probably lived about 750 B.C., when life in mainland Greece was dominated by petty local clan chieftains. Homer took his themes from more ancient times, when the high king of Mycenae had ruled far and wide. The poet knew of these distant ages through an unbroken oral tradition. In Mycenaean times and later, warriors liked to listen to professional bards—poets and singers who recited tales of fighting and adventure. The Dorian invasions did not destroy the art, although perhaps it was only among those Greeks who claimed descent from the heroes of Mycenae that the bardic tradition survived.

In time new material crept into the songs, where it mingled with information about old genealogies, geography, battles, and feats of daring. Like other storytellers, the ancient Greek bards did not memorize their poems exactly. They had, however, a repertory of especially apt, fixed phrases that could be used to fill out a line or give the singer time to remember the next episode in his story.

From such materials the poet Homer fashioned the *Iliad*, one of the world's greatest literary masterpieces. Then a little later, the *Odyssey* was composed, either by the same man, as ancient tradition asserted, or by a different poet, as some modern scholars believe. The *Iliad* tells of the siege of Troy; the *Odyssey* is a tale of the strange adventures that one of the heroes of the siege of Troy experienced on his trip home to Ithaca in western Greece.

Actually, the *Iliad* tells only a tiny part of the whole story of the siege of Troy. Other poets, seeking to fill out the work of Homer, later wrote poems to explain how Agamemnon gathered his hosts to attack the Trojans because Paris, a prince of Troy, had run off with Helen, the wife of Agamemnon's brother. Legend held that only after ten long years of siege did Troy fall, and then by deception.

According to the old tale, Odysseus, the hero of the *Odyssey*, advised the Greeks to pretend to sail away, leaving an enormous statue of a wooden horse behind with a few Greek soldiers hidden inside. As Odysseus had hoped, the Trojans believed the horse was an offering to the gods. They hauled the horse into their city, on the theory that any benefit the Greeks might get from it would come to them if the horse entered the city. Then, after celebrating the end of the siege, the Trojans went to sleep, only to be wakened by the noise of the returning Greeks storming in through the gate, which their companions—emerging from their hiding place inside the hollow wooden horse—had opened for them in the night.

None of this is in the *Iliad*. It tells only of the wrath of Achilles, the greatest of Greek warriors. Achilles quarreled with Agamemnon over the distribution of booty taken from the Trojans. He swore he would fight no more for such an unjust king. The gods, sympathizing with Achilles, decided to let the Trojans win for a while. Soon, therefore, the Greeks found themselves driven back to their ships which were beached on the shore some miles from the walls of Troy.

Disaster loomed. In the emergency Achilles agreed to let his followers join the battle. They were led by his favorite and friend, Patroclus, who disguised himself by putting on Achilles' armor. But Hector, the greatest champion among the Trojans, killed Patroclus. This roused Achilles to furious anger. After getting a new set of armor by supernatural means, he hunted Hector down and killed him. Then Achilles fastened the slain Trojan's body to his chariot and dragged the fallen hero back to the Greek camp to show to gods and men how he had avenged Patroclus' death.

So ends the *Iliad*, a savage tale of pride and bloodthirsty violence. Yet this unpromising material comes to life in Homer's hands. In particular, the scene between Hector and his wife Andromache, just before he goes out to be killed by Achilles, is as poignant as any passage in literature. Hector foresaw death and disaster, yet went to meet his fate, brave and undaunted, because he was a hero, and heroes had to abide by the warrior code of conduct, come what might. Death was the end of it all; sooner or later it came to everyone. What mattered was to live heroically. Never quail; defend personal honor by always accepting battle, whatever the consequence; stand ready to meet death bravely when, decreed by fate, it finally arrived—these were the imperatives of the hero's career.

Measured against such an ideal, Homer's gods lacked heroic stature. They were immortal, by definition, and never had to pay the price of death for their escapades. Indeed, Homer's picture of the gods lacks all dignity. They quarreled over trifles and played favorites among the fighters in shameless fashion. Behind them all loomed Fate, something as much greater than the gods as the gods were greater than men and women. In some sense Fate was the will of Zeus, the most powerful of all the gods. But in another sense Fate loomed over and above the gods, in the same way that it loomed over even the greatest of heroes. For no matter what a person or god might will and hope and plan, Fate caused things to happen, often in ways neither the immortal gods nor any mere human being had foreseen or wished.

The *Odyssey* is a tale of magic and adventure. The hero, Odysseus, met with all sorts of strange experiences on his way back from Troy. He was blown off course, shipwrecked, and encountered giants and magicians. When he returned home he found that various noble suitors had been trying to persuade his faithful wife, Penelope, to marry one of them; so he appeared unannounced and slaughtered them all with his mighty bow in his own dining hall.

The travel tales woven into the *Odyssey* come from a much later time than the materials of the *Iliad*. Some scholars therefore think that the poem was composed later than the *Iliad* and by a different author. But ancient tradition always attributed both of the poems to Homer, and many modern students of the "Homeric question" think that the same man might have been able to produce a poem as different as the *Odyssey* is from the *Iliad* by turning to a new type of material.

THE INFLUENCE OF HOMER   We can be sure that both the *Iliad* and the *Odyssey* were recognized as masterpieces from the time they were first created. Homer probably composed orally, like his predecessors. Tradition held that he was blind. But not long after Homer's time the Greeks learned from the Phoenicians how to write, and put his famous poems into written form. Corrections and variations, of course, crept in. An official text was produced in Athens about 200 years after the time Homer lived, and was carefully handed down thereafter.

The importance of Homer's poems for later Greek life is difficult to exaggerate. They have been called the Greek "Bible," and with good reason. Boys memorized the poems in school. Everyone knew about Homer's heroes. Even today, references to Homer remain familiar in all Western lands.

In addition, Homer's ideas molded all later Greek thought. Priests could not reinterpret theological doctrine when Homer's words fixed his particular view of divine behavior in every Greek mind. Very soon, thoughtful men therefore rejected traditional religion completely. This opened the door for Greek philosophy.

Abstract ideas appealed to only a few, but Homer's ideal of the hero reached deep into classical Greek society and affected nearly everybody. Violence and self-assertion, courage and craftiness, shrewd counsel and naive joy in material gain—all these were aspects of heroic life as Homer defined it. These attitudes, admired across the centuries, gave Greek civilization much of its special tone. Above all, the effort to excel every rival took hold of Greek minds. Meekness, patience, and submission played no part in their catalogue of virtues, and for this Homer was largely responsible.

DEVELOPMENT OF THE GREEK POLIS

Homer had no counterpart in the Middle East; neither did the Greek city-state, or, to use the Greeks' word for it, the *polis*. The contrast with Middle Eastern developments was profound. Nothing like the bureaucratic, tax-collecting, royal government of Kings David and Solomon—much less the vast, imperial bureaucratic structure of the Assyrian and Persian empires—arose in Greece. Instead, Greek soil came to be divided among small city-states, in which a rather large proportion of the adult male population took a very active part in politics and in war.

In its fully developed form, each polis had a city and surrounding territory, within which its laws prevailed. Not everyone took part in governing the polis: women, children, slaves, and foreigners were always excluded. In many times and places poor men also were excluded, if they lacked a minimum amount of property or did not have ancestors who had been members of the polis.

Each polis had a center for public business. This was usually a particularly safe place, often on top of a hill made defensible by a supply of water which could allow defenders to stand days or weeks of siege. In time, such strong points became citadels with real cities spread beneath them. But in the beginning the polis was an administrative unit, not a center for artisans and traders.

The Ionian Example

Full-fledged *poleis* (plural for *polis*) arose first along the Aegean coast of Asia Minor among the so-called Ionians, who had fled from mainland Greece to escape invading Dorians. The tribal councils, dominated by nobles, that ruled in mainland Greece during the Dark Age, joined together to form poleis, too, but only after a working model of the new political structure had been established across the Aegean.

Tribal and other traditional ties were disrupted in crossing the sea to Ionia. The refugees probably came from different parts of Greece, and needed all the help they could get to survive on unfriendly shores. Hence, those who started the new settlements could not afford to be choosy about whom they made welcome.

Under these emergency conditions, the classical polis was born. The settlers agreed upon rules of law and procedures for choosing leaders, whom they promised to obey as long as the leaders commanded according to the rules. The customary discipline of the war band was a model for this sort of arrangement. But in this case not just the fighting men but whole families joined up, and the rules were laid down not for a campaign but forever. Instead of merely accepting temporary rules, the settlers agreed to submit to permanent laws. As a result, the community that came into being was not a mere war band but a political association— a polis. (The English word "political" comes, of course, from *polis*.)

THE ROLE OF LAW   Two or three centuries earlier, Moses and the Israelites had founded another political association. But in that case, the basis of agreement was different. Instead of agreeing among themselves as the Greeks of Ionia did, the Israelites had entered into a Covenant with God and promised to obey the laws of God which Moses brought down from Mount Sinai.

The early Greeks, too, did not think of their laws as something they made by themselves. Good laws, they believed, were eternal and could not be changed. But the Greeks could not find such laws by asking the gods to set them forth. Their gods were, after all, Homer's gods; and Homer's gods were spiteful, willful beings, quite ready to play dirty tricks on one another and on weak human beings. Instead of falling back on the gods, therefore, the Greeks believed that wise and good men could discover the law by using their own powers. When truly discovered, law fitted human nature and the nature of things. It also guided everyday thoughts and behavior, and thus defined real or true human nature. Good law made everything prosper and go well. Good law prevented unjust quarrels. It created harmony and established cooperation, not only on

The Phalanx illustrated on Greek pottery. (*Hirmer Fotoarchives, Munich*)

the human plane but also upward to include the gods and downward to include natural objects and forces as well.

On the Greek mainland, polis law and government did not replace tribal organization until a later date. The traditional authority of local chieftains made written law unnecessary for a long time. But when the poor complained loudly enough against what they felt were injustices done by wealthy landowners, magistrates found it wise to write down the customary law they proposed to enforce through judicial proceedings. In this way, by about 600 B.C., tribal communities on the Greek mainland began to catch up with the Ionian model. They turned into city-states, too, with magistrates, laws, and citizens who obeyed the laws—at least in principle—regardless of tribal and kinship connections or the personal whims of men in authority.

Not long thereafter, by about 560 B.C., the Ionian cities fell under the rule of Croesus, King of Lydia; and when Croesus was defeated by Cyrus the Persian, they became part of the vast Persian Empire. As such, the Greek cities of Asia Minor sent tribute to the Persian kings. Ionian workmen helped make the sculptures for the palace of the Persian King Darius I at Persepolis, and a Greek ship captain explored the Indus River at the command of the same Darius. The Ionian Greeks, in other words, seemed about to become one more bit in the mosaic of peoples that constituted the Persian Empire.

The Role of the Phalanx

Yet events on the other side of the Aegean Sea checked and eventually reversed this drift toward assimilating Greeks into the Middle Eastern style of civilization. A critical turn came about 670 B.C. when two cities on the island of Euboea, Chalcis and Eretria, started a long war for control of the plain that lay between them. During this war a new military formation was perfected. It was called the phalanx, and it had profound military as well as political consequences for the Greek world.

The idea of the phalanx was very simple. Heavily-armored men lined up eight ranks deep, standing so close to one another that each man's shield helped to protect the right side of the man standing next to him. Then at the command signal everyone started to run forward, keeping time with each footfall so that the ranks remained closed. When the massed weight of such a formation encountered an enemy, who was not organized in the same fashion, resistance was simply swept away before the momentum of the phalanx's charge. Horses could not penetrate a shield wall backed by seven following ranks of armored men. Since only a small area around the eyes and nose was not protected by iron armor, arrows were almost harmless. If a fighter did fall the man in the rank behind him was trained to move up at once to fill the vacant place.

When the Greeks discovered the superiority of a well-trained phalanx, the nature of their warfare changed. Nobles on horseback no longer dominated the battlefield. Cavalry still could chase a dispersed foe and turn a defeat into a catastrophe. And cavalry could also make trouble before and during a battle, if friendly horsemen were not on hand to guard the flanks and rear of the phalanx. But cavalry could no longer win battles or hold a battlefield. That was the prerogative of the phalanx of heavily armed infantry.

When a well-drilled phalanx became decisive in war, every able-bodied citizen who could afford to buy body armor, shield and spear—and this was not too difficult in the Iron Age—had to spend long hours in his youth practicing marching and running in step with his fellows. This created a quite unreasoning but nevertheless profound sense of belonging together. To learn to keep step, every young man had to go to a practice field, beginning at the age of eighteen. There all the youths of the polis formed into a long line and began shouting in rhythm—the Greeks called this "raising the paean"—until everyone was keeping time together. Then dressed in full armor they would run, sometimes at top speed, sometimes more slowly, for half a mile or more, keeping time, all the while, to the rhythmic sound of the shouted paean.

Anyone who has ever tried to keep step while walking down an aisle knows how hard it is to get a large number of persons to move in unison. Anyone who has danced with others to the sound of music will realize how strongly human beings respond to the experience of moving together in a common rhythm. Probably our first ancestors used to dance together after a successful hunt, and shouted their joy at a good meal in good company. And because it rouses echoes of these very ancient capacities for fellow-feeling that lurk in all of us, massed rhythmic motion has an extremely powerful effect upon the participants' innermost emotions. Those with whom a man has danced in such a fashion are his friends, his fellows, his own kind. Even in a modern army, close-order drill and the blare of marching bands have this effect. When a man's life and the welfare of his city depended on how well each and every individual kept the pace until the phalanx closed with the enemy, then the hypnotic effects of rhythmic motion were, presumably, much stronger than they can be today when marching is irrelevant to modern combat.

Moreover, the most primitive levels of human experience were directly evoked by the fierce, sharp, sudden muscular effort of combat, when the accurate timing of a thrust with sword or spear made the difference between life and death, victory and defeat. This form of combat was the skill of the ancient hunters brought up to date. Men who shared the dangers of such battles became close friends. Everyone's safety, as well as the common victory, depended on each man keeping his place and facing the foe valiantly until the enemy line broke and ran.

The emotional response to the phalanx soon overthrew the noble's political power in all the leading cities of Greece. Soldiers who fought in the phalanx could not be excluded from taking part in decisions affecting their lives. The rich could no longer be allowed, for example, to take a poor man's land if it meant that the impoverished citizen could no longer equip himself for the phalanx. A polis that let such things happen would soon have too small a phalanx to fight successfully against its neighbors, and that, plainly, was the way to disaster. The needs of defense thus created the strongest possible reason for checking the growth of inequality among the citizens. Such needs soon provoked drastic responses, and gave Greek life a characteristic stamp of its own, very different from anything known in the Middle East.

Sparta

The most extreme example of making society over to fit the phalanx occurred in Sparta, a leading city of the Peloponnese (the peninsula forming the southern part of Greece). About 610 B.C. the Spartans found themselves engaged in a desperate war with their Messenian neighbors. In order to defeat the Messenians, the Spartans introduced new laws that made every Spartan an "Equal." These laws required all children from the age of seven to leave home and enter on a rigorous training. At twenty years of age, males enrolled in special barracks, where they lived and ate and trained for battle when they were not actually on campaign. At age thirty they could go home and live with their wives; but until the age of sixty each man was subject to military service with the Spartan phalanx whenever called upon. The laws were later declared to be very ancient, the work of a mythical figure, Lycurgus.

The system worked. Sparta not only defeated the Messenians, but quickly became the most powerful city-state in Greece. Its phalanx was never equalled by less professionally expert troops. But the cost was high, for Spartan citizens had no time for anything but war and preparation for war. To feed themselves, they compelled the defeated Messenians—now called 'helots'—to cultivate the fields for them and hand over about half the harvest to their Spartan masters.

No further change in the Spartan constitution took place for many centuries. The citizens, trained for success in battle, held down the helots at home and established governments sympathetic to themselves in neighboring city-states. Sparta also set up a league among nearly all of the cities of the Peloponnese which required each member to send troops

THESEUS
AND THE
MINOTAUR

When the greatness of the ancient Cretan civilization reached its height, Athens paid tribute to King Minos. This tribute consisted, among other things, of young boys and girls who were sent to the temple-palace at Knossos to be trained as bull dancers. Few ever came back, for an unlucky fall or the unexpected swerve of the horns of a charging bull usually meant death.

Athenian folktale later transformed the bulls of Crete into the fierce Minotaur, a man-eating monster with a human body and the head of a bull. This creature lived, they said, in the secret depths of a maze or labyrinth (the many-chambered palace at Knossos, no doubt) so complicated that no one entering could find his way out again.

Whenever the tribute fell due, the youths of Athens assembled and drew lots to decide who would have to go and serve the Minotaur. One day the lot fell on Theseus, King Aegeus' son. Despite the king's anguish, he had to send his son off to Crete and probable death.

But on his arrival, King Minos' daughter, Ariadne, fell in love with Theseus and decided to save him from the Minotaur. Accordingly, when it was Theseus' turn to enter the dread labyrinth, Ariadne gave him a

---

to fight alongside the Spartan phalanx when called upon to do so. Otherwise, each city was left to its own devices.

Even so, the Spartans never got over the fear of helot revolt. In fact, the "Equals" became a professional army of occupation stationed in their own land. The stern discipline of the Spartan system of training suppressed all discontent. Spartans could never afford to quarrel too sharply among themselves lest they weaken their position against the helots.

Athens

In Athens, the other Greek state about which we have substantial information, the reaction to the phalanx was not as drastic, but it still made a great difference. As in other cities Athens' problem was that poorer citizens, if they fell into debt, might lose their land or become slaves and

sword and a spool of thread. Theseus entered, unwinding the thread as he advanced so as to be able to find his way out again. Presently he met the Minotaur and killed him. Then, before the guards could interfere, he rapidly retraced his steps with the help of Ariadne's thread. She was holding the other end at the entrance way, and the two fled together, embarking on the same ship that had brought Theseus from Athens. On the way back the ship put in at the island of Naxos where Ariadne went off to take part in a ceremony of religious purification: she had, after all, a good deal on her conscience, for the Minotaur was (or perhaps was only the spirit of) her own father.

Theseus, however, refused to wait, and set off to Athens without her. Yet his impatience to get home led to misfortune. Before the departure, King Aegeus had arranged that the ship should carry a white sail if, perchance, his son Theseus were still alive; but if the usual fate had befallen him, the sail would be the customary black. In his haste Theseus forgot to change sails. His father, seeing the black sail, hurled himself from the cliff and died on the rocks below. Theseus, therefore, succeeded to the kingship of Athens, having slain both the Minotaur and, indirectly, his own father.

As king of Athens, Theseus met many other adventures. Athenians later honored him as the founder of their polis, on the grounds that he was the first to compel all the inhabitants of Attica to make the city of Athens their political center.

could no longer equip themselves for service in the phalanx. This was too dangerous to be tolerated.

In 594 B.C., therefore, Solon was appointed *archon* (magistrate) with special powers to revise the laws. He canceled debts and made debt-slavery illegal. He classified the citizens according to the amount of grain and oil they harvested each year; and he defined the duties and rights of each class in war and in peace. All but the poorest class of citizens were allowed to vote for the magistrates, who, however, had to come from the wealthier classes. In addition, large juries of ordinary citizens were allowed to review and, if they wished, could reverse the judicial decisions made by magistrates.

Power within the Athenian polis thus shifted away from the nobles and men of wealth. Ordinary farmers, the soldiers of the phalanx, could now control the Athenian polis. These were the men upon whom the welfare and prosperity of the city had come to depend, for without a strong phalanx there could be no security or prosperity for anyone.

But Solon's reforms did not stop the Athenians from quarreling violently among themselves. The chief political figure in the next generation was a great noble, named Pisistratus. He first distinguished himself in the war with Megara that broke out over possession of the island of Salamis. The war ended (565 B.C.) in an Athenian victory. Soon thereafter, Pisistratus took personal control of Athens. He kept Solon's laws in force, or pretended to. He was content to rule from behind the scenes, by controlling elections to office.

Pisistratus favored the poorer citizens, who supported him against rival noble families. He distributed land to some of his followers and encouraged them to plant olive trees and grapevines by giving them loans, at low interest rates, to tide them over the long period between the planting and the first harvest. Finally, he took an active part in founding colonies to relieve overpopulation in Athens and to develop trade in the Black Sea region.

The Spirit of the Polis

Greek city-states were able to tap human energies to a degree seldom equaled before or since. An ordinary male citizen could and did feel that the polis was but an extension of himself. He was part of it and it of him. Men have seldom felt such an identity between the political community and their individual person. States have seldom demanded as much of their citizens' time, wealth, and service as the Greek city-states required. And men have seldom felt that, with good laws and by their own efforts, they could accomplish so much and remain so free as did the citizens of ancient Greece.

Manners soon changed to fit this spirit. To be too rich was no longer good form. Personal display of any sort was soon judged to be worthy only of a barbarian. The rich could use their wealth to make public religious celebrations more splendid, or to help with some other enterprise undertaken by the polis. But a rich person who used wealth for private purposes would be disgraced. For rich and poor alike the sphere of private life was narrowed by the demands for personal participation in polis affairs. The phalanx, the assembly of citizens, religious celebrations, and everyday gossip about what was going on—all demanded the attention of every male citizen. Women, on the other hand, were strictly excluded from public affairs. So were foreign-born slaves and strangers of every kind who lacked citizen rights.

Tyrants, Colonies, and Trade

However successful the phalanx training may have been in making farmers into enthusiastic citizens, Greeks still faced serious problems. Chief among these was a continued, rapid growth of population. A farmer with several children had no choice but to divide his land among his heirs; but a piece of land just large enough to support a family, and allow the head of the household to equip himself for the phalanx, obviously could not support three or four new families.

In Athens, as we saw, Pisistratus rose to power by rallying the support of the poorer citizens. Other cities, too, reacted by raising a single man to power. The Greeks called such upstarts tyrants; later the term came to mean a wicked or oppressive ruler. The tyrants could not do much to solve the economic problem, even when they seized lands belonging to their political rivals and redistributed them among their own followers, as happened in several cities. Continued population growth soon caught up with all such efforts at redistribution.

COLONIZATION   A second obvious response to the problem of too many mouths and not enough land was emigration. The cities of Ionia took the lead here, from about 750 B.C., by sending groups of colonists off to the Black Sea coast and to Sicily and southern Italy. Later on cities from the mainland did the same, until these coastal regions came to be lined with Greek colonies. Each colony became a new polis, and kept only sentimental ties with the mother city. Each had its own laws and government. Such communities were usually established near good farmland, for it was land that the Greek colonists wanted.

THE GROWTH OF TRADE   After a few years, if the settlement flourished, trade possibilities opened up. A prosperous colony could produce a surplus of grain and other products to exchange for wine and oil and manufactured goods. Greek colonies were also able to act as middlemen between Greece and various barbarian peoples who lived inland.

A sizable class of artisans began to develop in cities that were situated favorably for this kind of trade. Greek merchants also began to sail their ships to and fro across the Aegean Sea, the Black Sea, and throughout the Mediterranean.

Farmers had a stake in the development of trade, for the most important commodities the Greek cities could offer for export were wine and oil. As long before, in Minoan times, these precious products of Greek soil commanded a brisk market along the shores of the Mediterranean and Black seas. Local chieftains and landowners were eager to supply grain, fish, metal, timber, or other raw materials in exchange for wine and oil. Imported grain and fish fed the growing populations of Greece, and imported timber and metals supplied Greek shipwrights and artisan shops with materials needed to keep the trade going.

Such a pattern of exchange differed fundamentally from the economic patterns that prevailed in the Middle East. There peasant farmers entered only slightly and occasionally into the market. Middle Eastern cities got their food by taking rents and taxes from the countryside, but sent almost no goods back in exchange.

Sparta's helots found themselves in the same economic position that Middle Eastern peasants endured, but no such oppressed rural class existed in the commercially active parts of ancient Greece. Quite the contrary; the small landowning farmer became and long remained the ideal kind of polis citizen, even in times and places where such individuals were a minority. To own no land and have to depend on trade or, worse still, on artisan labor, was always looked down upon as beneath the true dignity of a citizen. Slaves did much of the hardest work; foreigners without rights of citizenship did most of the artisan tasks; citizens took such jobs only when poverty forced them to do so.

THE DECLINE OF COLONIZATION   As trade in oil and wine and the export of manufactures took hold in Greece, the movement overseas to new colonies slackened. This was partly because good farmland within easy reach of the sea, where local peoples were not well enough organized to resist Greek colonization, became difficult to find. In the western Mediterranean, for example, the Carthaginians, who lived in northern Africa, and the Etruscans, who lived in north-central Italy, joined forces in 535 B.C. to drive a newly established Greek colony out of Corsica. That defeat virtually stopped Greek colonization in the west. The conquest of Asia Minor, first by Lydia and then by Persia, had a similar effect in the Black Sea region. Under Darius, Persian forces gained control of the Dardanelles (ancient Hellespont), the passage between the Aegean and Black seas. Greeks therefore could no longer be sure of free and easy access, except on terms agreeable to the new masters of the straits.

At the same time, the need for new land decreased. More people could be fed at home, and more people were needed to perform all the tasks connected with the growing export trade. Ships had to be built and manned; oil and wine had to be produced, graded, stored, and shipped. Sails, ropes, oars, and ships had to be manufactured. Pots to hold oil and wine were needed in enormous quantities. Metalwork also flourished with the growth of trade and population.

All in all, the new trade patterns opened important new economic opportunities in Greece. In the active seacoast towns, merchants, artisans, and sailors became numerous and politically important. These new social groups began to alter the older, sharp class division between rich and poor, which had been based on ownership of land.

The Development
toward Democracy

In a few cities, chief among them Athens, the new social classes, depending directly or indirectly on the sea, became the force behind a surge toward political democracy. As long as seafarers played no military role in political affairs, however, such groups existed more or less on sufferance of the heavily armed infantrymen of the phalanx, who won battles and protected the city.

THE ATHENIAN FLEET   Shortly after 500 B.C., however, the Athenians decided to build a fleet of warships, especially designed for fast maneuverability. They were armed with beaks at their prows, projecting just below the waterline and intended to ram and sink enemy vessels. The design was not new, but the Athenians built more vessels of this type than any Greek or Phoenician city had ever built before. Citizen oarsmen manned the fleet. On command, they learned how to maneuver their ships as skillfully as any phalanx. As a result, in 480 B.C. the Athenian fleet (with help from other Greek cities) was able to defeat the might of Persia. In the years that followed, the oarsmen of the fleet built up an empire and made Athens more wealthy and powerful than any other Greek city.

As the greatness of Athens came to depend mainly upon naval victories, the rowers of the fleet assumed a dominating role in Athenian political life, just as members of the phalanx had done in Athens and other Greek cities a hundred or more years earlier. This involved a shift of power to the poorer citizen classes. An oarsman needed nothing but a strong back; the ship and its equipment were provided by the richest citizens, who were assigned the task as a special honor each year. Any citizen, sound of wind and limb, qualified as a rower. A free man who owned no land at all, or such a tiny parcel as to be insufficient for his maintenance, could still take a full and active part in Athenian political life in his capacity as an oarsman.

Pulling an oar was hard sweaty work, but the elements of rhythmic motion, shared danger, and shared excitement were similar to the experiences that welded men of the phalanx so strongly together. Hence the Athenian rowers, like the Athenian infantrymen, were schooled by their experience in war to become active, committed citizens. They developed a strong sense of their collective worth and dignity, and they stood ready to defend their stake in the polis against all comers.

THE SPECIAL CASE OF ATHENIAN DEMOCRACY   A thoroughgoing form of democracy, giving political power to the propertyless class of citizens, made sense for Athens, because the fleet became the backbone of Athens' power. Other cities did not go the way of Athens, except when under Athenian influence. Most Greek cities limited full citizenship rights to the moderately well-to-do, who were able to buy arms and armor and take their place in the phalanx.

Even though it was so exceptional, the Athenians' democratic adventure proved enormously successful and deeply impressive. Ordinary Athenians took part in deliberations of state. Every citizen was entitled to attend the assembly where all matters of importance were debated and decided by majority vote. Most Athenian citizens, in the course of a lifetime, must have served on one of the "committees of fifty" that took turns at presiding over public affairs. The members of these committees were chosen by lot. Each committee was charged with the conduct of state affairs for one month, and then handed over responsibility to a new committee.

The intensity of such involvement still commands wonder and amazement. The success with which the Athenians conducted their affairs between 510 B.C., when changes in rules for voting made Athens definitely democratic for the first time, and 431 B.C., when a destructive and (for Athens) disastrous war with Sparta broke out, is equally surprising.

Yet it is worth reminding ourselves that, at its height, the Athenian democracy never allowed more than about half the adult males living in the immediate surrounding territory of Attica to take part in public affairs. The disfranchised half were slaves and foreigners. Many of these, especially the foreigners, were well treated and lived in Athens by choice. Some, on the other hand, were miserably driven to work in the silver mines at Laurium—some thirty miles from Athens—under extremely inhumane conditions.

The polis always remained, in Greek eyes, a privileged body of free men. Women were completely excluded from political affairs. And the only issue between a democratic polis, such as Athens, and an undemocratic polis, such as Sparta, was the proportion of the male population that had the right to a voice in public affairs. The Greeks never thought that every man, regardless of where he had been born or who his parents were, should have full and equal part in the privileges of the polis. The right was almost always reserved for those born to citizenship.

THE CULTURE OF THE POLIS

The rights of citizenship were accompanied by duties, above all in war but also in peace. No citizen long escaped the tasks his status put upon him. It is not, therefore, surprising that the polis put its distinctive mark upon Greek religion, philosophy, and literature.

Greek Religion

The Greek inheritance in religion was confused. Gods whose origin extended back to Neolithic villagers, who spoke languages other than Greek, continued to be honored. Hades, Persephone, and Demeter were cases in point. Their special function was to assure the fertility of fields. But when Greek-speaking tribes first arrived in Greece, they brought their own quite different family of gods—Zeus, Poseidon, Hera, for example. These gods were said to inhabit the snowy heights of Mount Olympus in northern Greece, when not traveling abroad and making mischief among mortals. Finally, there arose a group of gods with mixed ancestry, including Apollo, Athena, and Dionysus.

Such a pantheon made no sense. The different gods' functions and powers overlapped hopelessly. Moreover, Homer's poems gave many of the leading gods an all-too-human character, both spiteful and petty. Since every educated Greek learned Homer in school, no later generation of priests or poets was able to come along and tidy up the system by assigning powers and duties (and a more respectable character) to the different gods.

Another factor that created confusion was that no single body of experts had the job of preserving or elaborating religious truths. Tribal chieftains, local kings, and heads of families all had religious functions to perform on special occasions. There were also priests and ritual experts at a number of especially holy places. Of these, by far the most important was the Temple of Apollo at Delphi, where an oracle gave advice to petitioners who wanted divine guidance in their affairs. Then there were wandering poets and soothsayers, who claimed to be inspired and might give advice on almost any issue, whether anyone asked their opinions or not.

Lastly, there were secret societies into which individuals could be initiated and thereby acquire religious knowledge, or could receive assurance of some other sort of religious benefit. Of these cults, the most famous was the Eleusinian Mysteries; but the most widespread was Orphism, connected with the worship of Dionysus, the god of wine.

What could anyone make of such a jungle of confusion? Not very much; the Greeks certainly never reduced their religion to a logical system. They settled instead for rule of thumb. The polis became the frame within which most religious ceremonies took place. Worship of gods of diverse origins and with the most diverse rituals went forward under public control, with magistrates in charge.

In Athens, for example, the worship of Athena was tied in with the Eleusinian Mysteries through a great ceremonial procession, the Panathenaea, which went from Eleusis to the Acropolis, where Athena's great temple stood. Similarly, the worship of Dionysus in Attica became the occasion for the presentation of dramas, sponsored by the state and paid for by private donors who were appointed to the job by state officials.

Other city-states made similar arrangements. No one tried to reconcile theoretical differences and contradictions. The persons in charge were politicians and magistrates, who could not get excited about such questions. Practical problems of getting the celebrations under way on time, and as magnificently as possible, were what they cared about. This approach worked very well. The great occasions and major festivals were managed by the polis. Older tribal and family rites could go on as before, but tended to fade before the magnificence and ritual elaboration of public religious celebrations.

THE CEREMONIAL GAMES   Among the more important religious ceremonies of ancient Greece were athletic contests. To honor the gods, naked young men ran races, wrestled, boxed, and competed in other tests of strength and skill. The winners were much admired; songs were composed in their honor; sometimes statues were erected to commemorate their success. Individual athletes from all over Greece came to the most famous of all these ceremonies, held in honor of Zeus at Olympia in the western part of the Peloponnese. The Olympic games were held every four years, beginning—if later records are correct—in 776 B.C. Other festivals. like that at Corinth, were almost as important for the ancients, but our modern international athletic competitions took the Olympic name when the tradition was revived in 1896.

Athletic games and the great oracles, like that at Delphi, helped to keep the Greeks together. Individuals from different cities could meet and talk freely at the important athletic festivals. The Greeks counted it a great crime to harm anyone on such occasions, even (or especially) an enemy. The Delphic oracle, by giving advice on important issues that arose between states, also played a large role in uniting the Greeks and keeping war and violence between cities within bounds.

Despite its logical flaws, Greek religion met human needs fairly well.

There were private and family ceremonies; there were public festivals for each city; and there were all-Greek ceremonies and institutions like the Olympic games and the Delphic oracle.

Greek Philosophy

Nevertheless, a small number of men in ancient Greece could not be satisfied with the theological confusion they had inherited. In early days, poets tried to bring some sort of order to traditions about the gods. Hesiod, for example, wrote a long poem, *Theogony*, in which he tried to explain which of the gods was descended from whom, and in what fashion. He lived two or three generations after Homer, when Greek life was still rural. Later, when trade opened up contact with other peoples, Greeks became aware that their religious traditions were both similar to and oddly different from those of other peoples. When authorities disagreed, who was right? Who, indeed, really knew anything at all about the gods? Thoughts like these led a few Ionians to turn away from religious speculation. They tried instead to explain the natural world in terms of law. Law, after all, ruled the polis; perhaps it also ruled the heavens, the seas, and the earth. At any rate the idea seemed worth exploring. Those who did so were called "philosophers," a word that means, literally, "lovers of knowledge."

The first philosopher, according to later tradition, was Thales of Miletus (the most important Ionian city), who lived about 636–546 B.C. He declared that the world was made from water. Water condensed to become earth, and became thinner to turn into air and the fiery substance of sun, stars, and planets. Thales had no proof for his theory; he just stated it. In choosing water as the originating substance, he borrowed an old Mesopotamian idea that creation had started with a primeval ocean. Indeed, from one point of view, all Thales did was omit the gods—whether those of Mesopotamia or those of Greece—from his account of how the world had come to be what it was.

But in another sense he broke fundamentally with all older ideas of how things happened in the world. For he suggested that the process that changed water into other things followed a regular pattern and needed no miracle-working power to explain it. Condensation and rarefaction were ordinary enough, and could be seen on a small scale every day. Thales had the bright idea that these processes, spread out over a long enough time and on a large enough scale, could explain how the world came to be.

Other philosophers, who came after Thales, tried to improve on his suggestion. One proposed that air was the primary substance; another preferred the theory of the primacy of the infinite or the unlimited—something a little like our idea of outer space. Later still, the notion that there were four primary substances—earth, air, fire, and water—gained widespread acceptance. Everything, including animals and plants, was believed to arise from different mixtures of these substances. Nothing was too complicated for these optimistic thinkers to try to explain.

In leaving out the gods and attributing everything in nature to the operation of regular laws, Thales and his successors were, in a sense, trying to analyze the inscrutable Fate which, according to Homer, presided over both gods and human beings. If Fate worked regularly, then it ought to be possible to say how it did so. The result would then be a law of nature. But Thales also had the model of polis law before him. The actions of his fellow citizens in Miletus were controlled and directed by the invisible bonds of laws that were declared in public and known to all. Free men, they were yet slaves to law. Could not nature be the same? The philosophers answered Yes. They therefore discarded the stories that poets told about the gods as mere fairy tales, and boldly tried to explain things by discovering natural laws.

Over the centuries, this stab in the dark turned out to be incredibly fruitful. Modern science is based on the assumption that natural laws exist and can be formulated in words or in mathematical symbols. Modern life would be inconceivable without science; its underlying basis is still, as it was for the Greeks, a belief in natural law.

In later Greek times Thales' basic idea continued to dominate philosophy. Later philosophers turned attention to a much wider range of questions: about our minds, about language and how we know; how we ought to behave; and how the polis should be run. But in asking these and yet other questions, philosophers always kept to the assumption that if they tried hard enough, natural laws could be discovered to answer these questions too.

The Middle Eastern peoples had come to a different conclusion. For them the basic assumption always remained that one or several gods controlled both natural and human actions. God's will, not natural law, was the ruling principle of the universe for them.

These two world views remain vigorously alive to the present. The problem of reconciling or combining them in a satisfactory fashion continues to be the central intellectual problem of Western civilization.

Greek Literature

Greek literature came into its own before the rich and noble found it necessary to conform to the modest norms of behavior established by the farmer-footsoldiers of the phalanx. Homer's heroes were egoists, pure and simple. They had absolutely nothing to do with the polis. Later poets, too, concentrated on exploring personal pursuit of glory, love, and honor.

To be sure, verse was used for all kinds of formal composition, because it was easier to remember. Thus Solon, the Athenian lawgiver, wrote poetry to set forth his political ideals, and the first philosophers wrote in verse too. In a long poem, *Works and Days*, Hesiod laid down rules for farming. Poems praising service in the phalanx have also survived. But in spite of these exceptions, the general fact holds: the major Greek poets stayed outside the polis framework and concentrated on exploring their own personal, private feelings.

Yet, paradoxically, the heroic ideal of conduct, so powerfully expressed in Homer's poems, entered the inmost fiber of Greek polis life. Citizens and soldiers, brought up on Homer, simply transferred to their city the heroic attributes that Homer and other poets had assigned to individual warriors. The Athenians felt about their city as Achilles or Hector felt about himself. The Spartans, Corinthians, Argives, and all the rest felt the same about their own particular city-state. Glory and greatness for the polis became ends in themselves, to be pursued at any cost. Cowardice was unforgivable; no human resource of strength or skill should be withheld, they felt, from the task of advancing the greatness of their particular polis.

It was not so much the polis that shaped Greek literature, therefore, as Greek literature that shaped the polis.

Greek Art

In art the relationship was reversed, for the polis gave rise to a distinctive art style and technique. Even though only a few, damaged statues survive, early Greek sculpture offers us a very sensitive indicator of how public purposes affected the way statues were made.

The earliest examples of Greek sculpture betray strong Egyptian influence. Several statues reproduce a stiff Egyptian posture as exactly as the imperfect skill of the Greek stonecutters then allowed. Once started, however, Greek techniques improved rapidly. Between 600 and 500 B.C. noble patrons commissioned statues, many of which have been recovered from the Acropolis in Athens. They portray rich, well-dressed women who seem to breathe an aristocratic atmosphere of luxury and display that was very different from the polis ideal that came to prevail later. Another type of statue portrayed naked athletes—winners in the Olympics or at some other famous games.

Then, from about 500 B.C., sculptors more and more used their skill to decorate public buildings, especially temples. For such purposes, portrait art was out of place. Statues of the gods required a more abstract, idealized sort of beauty. Sculptors learned how to achieve such an effect and, in doing so, created a classical style that has been admired and praised ever since.

Among the lesser arts, vase painting found an enlarged scope with the development of the export trade in oil and wine, for these products were shipped from Greece in handsomely painted pots, many of which have been dug up all over the Mediterranean world.

Because so many painted pots have been discovered, it is possible to observe how styles changed. In the Dark Age, vase decorations took geometric shapes. Next came a period when Greek vase painters borrowed heavily from the Middle East. Processions of animals and similar designs predominated. Then, about 600 B.C., an independent, new "Greek" style emerged, featuring human figures, sometimes drawn with exquisite skill. Often the painter illustrated a story from Homer or another poet. Battle and hunting scenes or gymnastic contests were common subjects; but unlike the Egyptian wall paintings, themes from everyday life rarely appeared. Thus, even in their relatively humble art, the Greek vase painters remained true to the heroic vision of humanity.

CONCLUSION

By 500 B.C. Greek polis had developed a style of civilization that was different in some very important respects from anything known elsewhere. This style of life was attractive enough, strong enough, and persuasive enough to stand comparison with the most highly developed Middle Eastern culture. The master institution of the polis, with its extreme demands upon all citizens, dominated nearly all aspects of Greek life. The master idea of natural law, which a handful of philosophers had begun to explore, rose out of and took nourishment from the polis environment, where citizens did in fact run their affairs according to law. The idea that all forms of human association and loyalty should be subordinated to the territorial state, and that such a state should be governed by its citizens, is one of the fundamental inheritances we and all the world take from the ancient Greeks. The modern concept of natural law no less descends from their speculations about how the world had come to be.

Middle Eastern administrative techniques and the idea of monotheism were different from, but just as vigorous as, the Greek polis and natural law. Therefore, when the Greeks began to build up their own distinctive way of life, it became inevitable that the new Greek way would both rival and interact with the older, more massive, and immensely deep-rooted civilization of the Middle East.

This enrichment of the human scene was matched by a similar development in India where, by 500 B.C. another great new civilization had taken an enduring form. We must see how it arose and study its characteristics in the next chapter.

CHAPTER 6

The Indian Style of Civilization

to 500 B.C.

The literature of ancient India that has come down to us is not much interested in wars and battles, nor in kings and empires. The authors were interested instead in what they felt were more important matters; for example, they believed that a hidden reality stood behind appearances and made all the pomp and ceremony of this world nothing but an empty show. It would be a mistake to assume that all Indians agreed with the people who composed the texts that have survived. There were plenty of kings and warriors in India, as well as merchants, dancing girls, and millions of peasants, for whom the ordinary everyday world surely mattered a great deal and whose interest in the world beyond may not have been particularly vivid. But we cannot know what they did and how they felt because priests and holy men, who made the record, left out everything that did not interest them.

The fact that Indian literature was oral also makes things difficult for historians. Works survived by being memorized. A master who had memorized a particular work taught it to his pupils, and they to theirs. But texts passed on in this fashion changed with the generations. Passages that did not seem to make much sense were forgotten; new explanations or stories to illustrate a point were put in; and language changed as old words faded out and new ones came into use. When such works eventually came to be written down, therefore, there was no way of telling what parts were very old and what parts had been added later. The "Homeric question" that troubles students of Greek literature arises from the oral tradition that lay behind Homer's poems. But Homer stands alone in Greece, whereas almost all of early Indian literature is the deposit of uncounted generations of oral learning. As a result, scholarly techniques for dating manuscripts, that proved very powerful in unscrambling the European historical record, simply will not work on Indian texts.

Archaeology is only beginning to fill some of the gaps. Moreover, the scraps and pieces of archaeological information that we have are hard to tie in with literary references. It is always hard to learn much about ideas or social structures by picking through ruins and rubbish heaps, which is what archaeologists must do; and it is particularly hard when the literary record itself says almost nothing about everyday tools and materials, and seldom even mentions governments or rulers.

Historians therefore find themselves handicapped when trying to write about ancient India. Main lines of change can only be guessed at.

INDIA'S DARK AGE

Before discussing what we know and can guess about India's early history, it is important to get a clear idea of the geographical conditions of India as they were before human activity changed the natural landscape. (See map, pp. 460–61.)

The Geography of Ancient India

The lower Indus Valley was a desert, quite like that surrounding the lower course of the Tigris-Euphrates rivers or the Nile. South and east of the Thar Desert, as it is called, increased rainfall supported grasslands, like those north of Arabia, with woods on some hillsides and along water-courses. All this closely resembled the conditions of the Middle East and of Greece, with the difference that India was a little hotter and lacked any season in which temperatures plunged below freezing.

Eastern and southern India had a very different climate and natural vegetation. Everything in that part of the country depended on the monsoon, a wind that blows off the land in winter and onto the land in summer.

In winter, when the monsoon winds come out of central Asia and blow across India from the north, little rain falls and vegetation dries up. In summer, when the winds reverse themselves and begin to blow in over the land from the Indian Ocean, they bring heavy rainfall. Where the rain-rich winds encounter the Himalaya Mountains, in northern Assam and Bengal, the result is one of the heaviest rainfalls in the world. Hills and mountains in other parts of India also affect rainfall and patterns of vegetation. In southern India, for example, the high central plateau—called the Deccan—is rather dry. Most of the moisture that comes in from the Arabian Sea and the Indian Ocean is squeezed out as the winds rise over the coastal ranges on either side. Lush, dense forests and swamplands therefore extend along the two coasts; but inland, thinner forest and grassland, or even semidesert, prevail.

The most fertile and important region of India is the Ganges Valley in the northeast. The Ganges River drains the towering Himalayas to the north, and though it is relatively short, it carries more water than does the other great river of India, the Indus. Also, the Ganges Valley gets the full benefit of the monsoon. Before men cleared the jungle away, it was heavily wooded and frequently swampy underfoot. Slash-and-burn cultivation did not work very well where the ground underneath was waterlogged. But on the flanks of the river floodplain, more lightly wooded and better-drained land in the Himalayan foothills offered primitive farmers really favorable ground, much like the hills where grain farming first started in the Middle East.

The Aryan Invasions

This, then, was the sort of country that the Aryan tribes found when they crossed the mountains and began to trickle into India about 1500 B.C. Except in the area where the Indus cities had organized irrigation farming, population was scant. As a result, after they had destroyed Harappa and Mohenjo-Daro, civilized skills disappeared from India for several centuries. Perhaps the irrigation works on which Indus civilization depended broke down, and no one knew how to put them in order fast enough to keep the farmers from either starving or fleeing into the forests to the south and east. In any event the Indus cities were abandoned.

Various references in Aryan sacred hymns to cattle and to an open-air, migratory existence, make it seem likely that the newcomers maintained, for a while, something like their old nomad way of life after reaching India. Natural grasslands were not lacking in northwestern India. These regions, in and near the Indus Valley, remained the main center of Aryan population for a long time. But eventually, Aryan-speaking peoples filtered south and east into forested regions, where they found peaceable slash-and-burn cultivators living side by side with peoples who were still hunters.

None of these communities could resist the Aryan warriors. Yet the Aryans could not force such peoples to pay rents or taxes. Slash-and-burn cultivators seldom had a food surplus. If strangers tried to collect rents from them, they could simply disappear into the forest and hide in some little clearing miles away, where it was hard to find them again. Hunters had still less that a conqueror could take away from them, for they ate what they killed as soon as they could. Aryan military superiority, therefore, did not lead immediately to state-building.

If this reconstruction is correct, the Aryan and the pre-Aryan peoples had relatively little to do with each other in the first phases of the Aryan penetration of the forested parts of India. Hunters had to learn not to attack the Aryans' herds of cattle. We may be sure that sudden and violent reprisal would follow the slaughter of a cow. Perhaps the Aryans discovered that they could force hunters to make arrows for them or that some of the forest peoples had priests and sorcerers who could cure disease or ward off disaster. Since they were stronger, Aryan tribesmen could demand such services under threat of violence—and probably got them.

FARMING   The Aryans knew how to raise wheat and barley before they crossed the mountains into India. Little by little, as in Europe and the Middle East, the newcomers settled down to farming. But the forests of India were broad, and slash-and-burn cultivation was an effective and cheap way to exploit that sort of environment. Hence, when they turned to farming, the Aryans took up the same style of cultivation that the pre-Aryan farming people used.

The spread of Aryan-speakers throughout nearly all of India (only in the extreme south did a different language, Tamil, become a carrier of literature) was a result of their search for new plots of forestland to be cropped and then abandoned.

WARFARE   In parts of India the Aryans created a barbaric, warlike society quite like that which prevailed, for example, in Mycenae. Noble charioteers fought one another in single combat. A few phrases in the Vedic hymns—almost certainly the oldest surviving Aryan literature—reflect this sort of violent, heroic life. If the stories of the *Mahabharata*—a long epic poem—are to be believed, they did not dismount as did Homer's heroes, but shot arrows at one another from galloping chariots. The whole poem is built around the story of armed struggle between two tribal families. But this heroic framework was crusted over with an enormous number of pious lessons and tales intended to point a moral or explain some local custom or religious practice. Priests and religious

Part of the ruins of Mohenjo-Daro, which, together with its twin city Harappa, was well-planned and laid out in rectangular blocks. Excavation has indicated that each city covered an area of approximately seven miles, with sufficient space for more than 20,000 people.

experts apparently took over from secular bards and then added various other matter to the original core. Still, there is no reason to deny that the *Mahabharata's* battle scenes probably reflect the kind of life that noble Aryans and chariot warriors did in fact know.

Sometime between 1200 and 800 B.C., iron reached India. Presumably, the impact of cheaper metal on Aryan society was much the same as among other peoples in the Middle East and Greece. New invasions may have taken place, bringing in other tribes from the Eurasian steppe who spoke languages closely related to the Aryan speech of the first arrivals. Or perhaps there were no new invasions, just a few wandering blacksmiths who brought the new metal to India and began to make weapons and tools for its inhabitants.

When iron became common, chariot warfare ceased to dominate battlefields, although chariots continued to have ceremonial importance for many centuries afterward. Cavalry was also introduced, but seems never to have been very important. Horses did not flourish in the hot

Indian climate, and in later times they usually had to be imported. This restricted the number of mounted warriors who could be maintained in India, since the road over the mountains from the north was long and hard, and shipping horses by sea was difficult and expensive.

The Rise of Monarchies

The big change that came to India was the rise of large, centralized monarchies in the Ganges Valley. How this happened, or even when statebuilding began, remains unknown. We can guess that iron tools made the tasks of clearing the jungle easier and opened new land to cultivation. We know, too, that the staple crop of the Ganges Valley was rice rather than wheat and barley, as in the Indus region.

Rice cultivation required irrigation and elaborate preparation of the ground. To be sure, the Ganges floodplain was well suited to rice cultivation, being both flat and very wet. A skillful layout of canals and dikes in such a landscape allowed the farmers to control the water supply at will. While the rice was growing, they kept the fields or paddies under a shallow sheet of water. When the rice ripened, they drained the water away to make harvesting easier. Once the necessary dikes and canals had been built, two crops a year could be produced.

Exactly how this intensive type of rice cultivation established itself in the Ganges Valley is unknown. It cannot have been very old; otherwise some trace of ancient cities in the region would surely have been found. Of course, some new archaeological discovery may yet prove these guesses wrong; but in the absence of evidence it seems best to assume that rice cultivation established itself soon after 1000 B.C., only a few generations before the rise of the Ganges states.

About 800 B.C. big, powerful monarchies, ruled by Aryan-speakers, started to thrive in the Ganges Valley. This, indeed, is the reason for supposing that rice farming had begun to take hold in that part of the world a few generations before we begin to hear of Magadha, Kosala, and similar kingdoms. Rice farmers were easy to tax. They could not afford to move away to escape tax collectors. Too much work went into making the fields ready for planting, since the cultivators had always to build suitable canals, dikes, and water sluices. At the same time, rice farmers could afford to part with a large proportion of their harvest. Paddies yielded abundantly, so that a hard-working family could produce a lot more than it needed for its own nourishment. With such a source of tax income, rulers, soldiers, administrators, artisans, and all of the other specialists associated with cities and civilized life could, therefore, come quickly into existence. This is what seems to have happened in the Ganges Valley.

The rise of cities and states in this part of India brought civilized life into a physical and social environment that was significantly different from that of the Indus Valley, where the Aryan as well as the ancient Indus culture had centered earlier. Some of the peculiarities of later Indian civilization reflected the special character of the monsoon environment. Disregard for time, for example, was natural enough in a part of the world where the monsoon determined the seasons, as it always does in the Ganges Valley. There was no particular problem about when to plant, as there always was in the Middle East. The monsoon climate probably encouraged the Indians to see the world as a theater for an endless return or repetition of fundamentally the same experience. Time and the particular moment seemed unimportant, whereas Middle Eastern farmers had always had to worry about just such questions.

THE DEVELOPMENT OF BUREAUCRATIC GOVERNMENT   We can only assume that the new Ganges kingdoms gradually built up the apparatus of a bureaucratic state—administrators, tax collectors, soldiers, and a train of merchants and artisans necessary to equip and feed the ruling classes. Sea trade between western India and Mesopotamia opened up on a more or less regular basis about 800 B.C. If the Ganges kings needed any help in figuring out how to extend their power by bureaucratic government, perhaps helpful hints came from traders who had visited the Middle East and knew something of the workings of government among the Babylonians and Assyrians.

Magadha was the most successful of the Ganges states, and eventually it became an empire that embraced nearly all of northern India. But before that came about, several other states, Kosala among them, divided the river valley and spread into adjacent regions. They fought one another and expanded their territory at the expense of less well-organized peoples who could not defend themselves successfully against the professional soldiery of the Ganges kings.

The Slow Pace of Change in Other Regions

Elsewhere in India no comparably rapid changes in society or politics occurred. The Indus Valley remained in the hands of Aryan tribes or tribal groupings who depended on shifting agriculture and herding. Nothing really is known about southern India. No very dense populations or

A wine jar from the 7th Century B.C. The relief depicts the Trojan horse on wheels (German Archaeological Institute, Athens).

powerful political units arose until much later, presumably because there was still enough land to allow herding and hunting and slash-and-burn cultivation to support whatever population there was in that part of the world.

Disease was a factor that may have delayed the peopling of India and kept back the level of development. In warm climates various disease organisms flourish, which cannot survive in regions where subfreezing temperatures prevail during part of the year. Animals and people moving from cooler to warmer climates are therefore always liable to meet diseases for which they have no immunity. If settlement becomes dense, new "tropical" diseases can wreak havoc with such populations. But as long as human communities remain very thin, infections are checked because there are fewer hosts in whose bodies infection can lodge, and fewer contacts among human beings that would allow the disease to pass from one person to another.

If, in fact, diseases were important in keeping India thinly populated in early times, then it is obvious that the rise of the Ganges kingdoms depended on the development of a population that was relatively immune to local infections and that could, therefore, survive even when living in densely settled communities. Perhaps pre-Aryan peoples had an advantage here, having been exposed to the special conditions of a monsoon climate much longer than the invading Aryans had been. Certainly, some of the aspects of historic Indian culture seem surprisingly at odds with the attitudes expressed in the earliest Aryan literature; and it is tempting to believe that these differences arose from the survival of pre-Aryan values and points of view in historic India. But since we do not know anything for sure about the pre-Aryans, we can only guess.

What we do know is that historic Indian society allowed numerous local groups to survive and maintain distinct ways of life. This was possible because Indian society as a whole was organized into castes, each marked off from the rest by special customs and rules. Since the whole notion of caste is strange to us, we need to define the concept carefully.

CASTE—THE MASTER INSTITUTION OF ANCIENT INDIA

In modern times, and as far back as records can take us, Indian society has been organized into castes. A person's caste was and is the most important thing about him or her. In any face-to-face encounter, the first thing that has to be established is to which caste does each person belong. With that information, everybody more or less knows how to behave, and the business in hand can then go forward with minimal confusion or friction. By comparison, the question of what state or kingdom a person belonged to was trivial. Nobody cared very much about that, except for the kings and tax collectors, who, of course, constituted their own castes.

An Indian caste today is a group of people who will eat together and who intermarry. They usually also refuse to marry or eat with anyone from outside the caste. Membership is therefore hereditary; and in most situations, each member carries some mark (usually on the forehead) that tells everyone which caste he or she belongs to. Caste is an extremely flexible thing. If a group of strangers appears, and everyone refuses to eat with them or to marry them, this group too, becomes a caste whether the individuals concerned wish to or not.

Most modern caste distinctions are related to occupation. If a new kind of job develops, such as the tasks of driving and maintaining automobiles, a new caste is likely to form among those who work around cars and know how to repair them. This is because other occupational caste

The persistence of caste in India: a Brahmin and his attendant, ca. 1890.

groups treat such persons as outsiders, who must, therefore, eat together and intermarry because no one else will eat with them or marry into their circle.

Another characteristic of the modern caste system is that rather exact rules define how the members of one caste are supposed to deal with the members of another. Thus, even indirect contact with a member of a lower caste "defiles" a member of an upper caste, and he has to wash, or perform some other ritual, to become "clean" again.

Some, but not all, castes have formal ways of disciplining their members. If a person disregards the caste rules, he or she can be excluded—lose caste—and have to face the world thereafter as an outcast, acceptable to nobody. This is a severe penalty in a village or small town, where everybody soon learns of what has happened. It is less meaningful in the impersonal environment of a big city, where many of the caste rules about defilement cannot be enforced anyway.

Early Records of Caste Society

Modern castes, of course, do not tell us anything about castes in the beginning of Indian history. The trouble is that nothing else tells us much about castes either, though a number of casual references make clear that something more or less like the modern caste system existed very long ago. About 300 B.C. a Greek ambassador to the court of Magadha, named Megasthenes, wrote a book about India in which he described seven hereditary classes into which, he said, Indian society was divided. And Buddhist stories and sermons, some of which were probably written earlier than 300 B.C., sometimes mention caste in a way that makes it seem entirely taken for granted.

THEORETICAL BASIS FOR CASTE   Even older than the Buddhist stories are texts called Brahmanas. These are commentaries on the Vedas, which are the most ancient and sacred Sanskrit writings. In the Brahmanas a theory of caste is set forth, according to which everyone is born either as Brahmans who pray; or as warriors who fight; or as farmers and artisans who work; or as Sudras, the lowest caste of all, who do ritually unclean jobs, like picking up the garbage or tanning leather. The first three castes, according to the Brahmanas, are Aryan; the fourth caste is reserved for non-Aryans. Later an additional group of "outcasts" or untouchables was added to the fourfold classification of the Brahmanas. The outcasts occupy the lowest positions in modern Indian society.

The Brahmanas also developed a theory to account for the differences of caste. Human beings, they say, do not start life with a clean slate. The soul of every newborn infant formerly inhabited some other body. Sometimes the soul came from another human being, sometimes from an animal. Wherever it had been before, it accumulated *karma*. Karma is a little like dust: it collects on the soul just through the process of living. Only a very wise and good individual, aided by ritual purification, can avoid accumulating a lot of it. Souls that in former lives had gathered a heavy load of karma, then, were born into babies of the lowest castes. Those who in former lives had accumulated only a little karma earned the right to be born as Brahmans; and those in between, of course, acquired an in-between caste status. Persons who lived well in whatever caste they had been born to could hope for rebirth higher on the scale. By the same principle, anyone who abused his position or failed to observe caste and religious rules of behavior would be reborn in a lower caste, or might even reappear as an animal or insect.

These ideas may seem strange, but one should never assume that something many millions of people have believed is absurd, however unfamiliar it may be on first acquaintance. Actually, the idea of reincarnation, as the doctrine of rebirth is called, explains sleep, birth, and death in a very convincing way—as long as one assumes that every living thing has a soul that can separate itself from the body at will. Since people had dreams, and could "see" things in their sleep, remembering strange and distant scenes and extraordinary experiences upon awakening, it seemed only reasonable to believe in a soul that could leave the body in sleep and return whenever it wished to wake the person up again. What then of death? Obviously it was due to the permanent departure of the soul. And where would the soul of a dead person or animal go? Reincarnation in a newborn body seemed a very reasonable answer to such a question—particularly since it explained why every newborn creature had a soul.

Once such ideas had been accepted, the doctrine of reincarnation had an additional advantage. It explained the inevitable injustices of life in a very neat way. Reward and punishment for good and bad actions did not have to wait for the end of the world, as Zoroastrians and Jews believed. Death and reincarnation was always close at hand. The poor and abused could therefore look forward, if they were patient and kept their assigned place in the caste system, to rebirth higher up the scale. Since civilization involved injustice, this idea helped everyone to endure the pains and sorrows of life more calmly. Civilized life became more stable as a result.

The Brahmanas, however, do not really tell us when or how the caste principle established itself in India. There never were just four castes, and a good deal of wishful thinking went into the classification of Brahman priests above warriors and rulers. In other words, we have here a theory rather than a description of what really existed.

Social and Psychological Bases of Caste

A search of the Vedas themselves for signs of caste yields no definite results. There are phrases distinguishing the color of Aryans from the color of the older inhabitants of India. Probably, when they first came into the country, the Aryans were white-skinned and very conscious of the difference between themselves and the dark-skinned peoples they encountered. This color line may have been an important factor in creating caste.

It would be wrong, however, to think that the caste principle arose only, or even mainly, because a group of Aryan conquerors wished to draw a barrier between themselves and those they had conquered. On the contrary, the strongest factor in caste organization was probably the preference that members of any group feel for doing things without interference from outside. Groups of hunters or slash-and-burn cultivators, finding themselves more and more closely surrounded by others who had different customs—and who, in many cases, spoke different languages—could get along by becoming a caste within Indian society. As a caste they could keep most of their own ways and inner values, and preserve private, family-level customs, while still spending their lives in close daily contact with all sorts of other people. Each such group occupied a niche in the larger society. Members of such groups could survive, more or less comfortably, as a part of Indian society as a whole, simply by finding out who stood above and who ranked below them in the caste system.

In point of fact it seems very likely that this was the way Indian society expanded. In modern times primitive parts of Assam have been edging into Indian society in just this fashion. Hill tribes, some of them still very primitive, become castes when their members, having come into contact with the outside world, take on special roles—as fishers or porters or something of the sort. What brought these groups into Indian society was the steady advance of settled agriculture. This, as in the Middle East or Europe, was in turn the consequence of population growth, making older ways of using the resources of the soil insufficient.

If this process extended back to the beginning of Indian history, it is likely that when cities began to arise on Indian soil, after about 800 B.C., the caste structure of society faced a crisis. In a city new possibilities opened up. People no longer knew one another from birth, as happened in the village. Strangers were everywhere, and a person could change caste without anyone who mattered knowing a thing about it.

This sort of pulling up of roots was what happened in the Middle East when a peasant made his way to town and began a new life as an artisan or porter or soldier. Sooner or later the newcomer left village ways behind and acquired new habits and new ways of looking at the world. Similar shifts certainly occurred in early Indian history. Some Buddhist stories, as a matter of fact, tell of changes in caste—a thing theoretically impossible. Perhaps this happened quite often during the first centuries of city life in the Ganges kingdoms.

Nevertheless, in the long run, caste prevailed. The religious idea of defilement from contact with persons of the wrong caste may have helped to produce this result. Religious literature certainly suggests that this was a major consideration. The number and variety of subgroups of peoples who inhabited India probably was another reason why caste survived. Over 200 languages are still spoken in India, and in times past the number may have been much larger. Forest hunters, who for all practical purposes are still in the Stone Age, survive today in a few secluded regions of India. In times past they were certainly more numerous.

When so many different peoples found themselves more and more closely entangled in the network of fields made by plowing farmers, what could they do? The Indian answer was: become a caste. Cities and towns therefore, in attracting peoples from far and near to perform the varied functions a large center of population requires, drew upon groups so different from one another that they formed a series of separate castes. These castes learned how to maintain their separateness even in an urban environment. Thus, instead of assimilating citizens to a more or less common pattern of life, as the Greek city-states set out to do, Indian society allowed maximum variety and freedom for all its different subgroups and peoples.

The Political and Cultural Consequences of Caste Organization

The organization of society into castes had far-ranging consequences. As long as people owed first allegiance to their caste, politics and the state remained superficial. Rulers could not make ordinary persons identify themselves with the state in the manner of the Greeks. What the government did or failed to do was its affair. Defeat or victory belonged to the soldiers and administrators, not to the ordinary folk in the field or in the shop. Life went on within the caste framework, while states and rulers might come and go, depending on who won the latest local battle. Ordinary people cared very little for such things, and learned persons did not even bother to record them. Enormous gaps in our knowledge of the political facts of India's history result. But then, politics and war, however complicated and full of sudden reversals and surprises, had little importance for most Indians.

In matters of culture, the caste organization of Indian society allowed very primitive ideas and magical practices to survive indefinitely. Any sort of ancestral religion (so far, at least, as it did not interfere with the lives of other groups of people) could be kept going generation after generation. Ideas and movements among an educated few had no particular impact on cult practices conducted within the privacy of the home, or in the semiprivacy of some humble caste gathering. On the other hand, these ideas and practices were always at hand, ready to be made use of by the educated classes, if it suited their purposes to fall back on primitive magic.

For society as a whole, the division into castes meant a certain rigidity. The caste structure reinforced the normal human habit of sticking to familiar and well-tried ways of doing things. If a person was born to be a garbage collector, there was small reason for him to do anything but collect garbage; and that put a rather narrow limit on his inventiveness. Other civilized societies, however, were not really very different, for in the Middle East, Greece, and China nearly everyone also did what he or she was born to do. Still, Indian castes, and the religious theory that went with them, made changes in an individual's social position that much more difficult.

On the other hand, caste had positive values. Otherwise it could scarcely have flourished so long as it has. First and foremost, it gave every person a definite group with which to identify. What the synagogue was for Jews living amid strangers, the caste was for any Indian who found himself also living among strangers, or, if not with strangers, at least with people whose habits and customs were very different from his own. In addition, the theory of reincarnation and of caste solved the problem of inequality in society more effectively than other doctrines were able to do. By doing what one was supposed to do, and staying in one's caste position, promotion in the social scale was to be expected. The Assyrian kings had used precisely the same reward to create a body of loyal and efficient officers for their army. It worked for the Assyrians, as it has for most armies that have tried the system since; and the prospect of promotion up a strictly graded scale of ranks in society worked with the same force among the Indian population as a whole. Taking reincarnation for granted, as something too obvious to be doubted, what else could a person do but try to rise (or at least avoid demotion) by carefully conforming to whatever local custom and caste rules prescribed?

On the negative side was the fact that caste weakened the military effectiveness of Indian society. States could not mobilize the emotions and loyalties of their subjects as Greek cities or even Middle Eastern empires could. India was, therefore, easily and repeatedly conquered by one wave of invaders after another. As long as the invaders came as barbarians, they soon accepted Indian civilization and faded quickly into the Indian social structure as one more caste. When conquerors arrived in India with civilizations of their own, however, the situation altered. From A.D. 1000 onward, first Moslems and then Europeans exercised political and military rule in India without becoming Indian in culture and outlook, though from an Indian viewpoint they did become a caste.

Conquest by Moslems and then by Europeans cramped the free development of India's own civilization. But this event was far in the future, when caste and the other dominant feature of India's civilization—transcendental religion—took form. For many centuries India's relatively protected position behind the Himalayas meant that fresh invasion merely brought another caste and a new set of barbarian masters to the Indian lands, who quickly assimilated Indian culture and thus only added one more strand to India's variegated scene.

Caste was India's master institution and molded Indian society, the way bureaucratic empire molded Middle Eastern society and the way the polis molded Greek society.

TRANSCENDENTAL RELIGION

Emphasis upon a realm of reality behind or beyond the world of our senses became characteristic of Indian religions. This is called "transcendentalism," because it transcends—that is, goes beyond—what ordinary people experience. Sights and sounds and all the everyday contacts we have with one another and with ordinary things make up the world of the senses, of appearances, of material things—in short, make up the usual, common, average world people live in. But Indian sages all agreed that this world was an illusion; reality was something else—spiritual, pure, perfect, hidden. How could they reach such a conclusion? What can be real, except experience?

The answer is that people do sometimes have unusual and extraordinary experiences—trances, dreams, ecstasies. Indian holy men came to treasure such experiences and learned how to bring them on by various kinds of bodily exercises. One easy way to have such experiences is to take various drugs, but the Indians did not do this very much. Instead, they held back their breathing until the oxygen supply in the blood stream got very low, and sometimes they also starved themselves or went thirsty for long periods of time. Such bodily rigors produced visions and other extraordinary experiences, as of course drugs can also do.

These experiences aroused intense emotions, and seemed to open the door upon a far more significant world than the world of everyday. Visions, in short, revealed a new level of reality—a spiritual truth—that lay behind and above ordinary sensory experiences; or so many millions of Indians, as well as Christians, Moslems, and Buddhists of later ages, came to believe.

The bodily discipline that leads to such visions is called "asceticism." The visionary experience itself is often called "mystical," and those who have such visions are referred to as "mystics."

Healthy young Americans may find it hard to take asceticism and mysticism seriously. It is all too easy to mock what other people hold dear simply because our own habits, values, and institutions make little room for such behavior or experience. The real task, though, is to try to understand the many different ways in which human beings have tried to cope with the complex world around them. Anyone who does so will soon realize that, however strange it may seem at first sight, Indian transcendentalism was and remains a very powerful and attractive way of looking at the world. In fact, it continues to appeal powerfully to some groups in American and European society, as the "hippie" movement of the 1960s showed.

Transcendental Religion and Caste

As might be expected, caste and transcendental religion tended to support one another. Since religion taught that everyday things were mere illusion, the pursuit of wealth, power, fame, and glory was obviously silly as well as futile. This did not mean that some Indians did not struggle for such things. But most Indians agreed that those who did so were less wise, good, and noble than the poor ascetics who withdrew from ordinary society in order to pursue holiness and religious truth. Such attitudes tended to weaken India's military and political organization, just as caste did.

In addition, the doctrine of reincarnation that justified caste distinctions fitted in well with transcendentalism. The realm of spiritual reality, approached through mystical visions, seemed to be the same as the world inhabited by souls when they were not tied to a particular body—for the mystic's soul, too, apparently left his body at the moment of visionary ecstasy. Thus, an overarching world view could and did arise, which made everyday life seem trifling and unimportant when compared to the spiritual world that was inhabited by souls, some of which were pure and free of material entanglements, and some of which were tied temporarily and, so to speak, by accident, to a particular body living in the material world of mere appearances.

How Transcendentalism Developed

Indian religion did not arrive at its distinctive transcendentalism all at once. The Aryan invasion of India brought a kind of religion into the country that had little or nothing in common with the religions of the peoples already there. Aryan gods were like those of other Indo-European peoples. Sun, air, sky, thunder, flame, and other natural forces were vaguely personified. Worship took place out of doors, at specially prepared places. But these altars, as befitted the life of a nomadic people, were abandoned after a single use and so could not easily become temples. Religious rituals centered around the slaughter of animals, as an offering to the gods, and the drinking of an intoxicant called *soma*, made from the juice of a plant which cannot be identified today. Priests prepared the sacrifice, and by voice and gesture they called upon the gods to accept the offering.

These statements are based upon the hymns of the *Rig-Veda* and the three other Vedas. The four books of the Vedas were gathered together in their present form by priests, who recited the Vedic hymns while preparing the altar and conducting the sacrifice. What purpose the Vedic poems may have served when first composed is unclear. Some of the surviving texts seem to have little or no connection with the ritual of sacrifice for which they were, nevertheless, used. How old the hymns may be is likewise unknown. Some may descend from the age of invasion itself.

Pre-Aryan Religion

About the other main element in Indian religion we are far less informed. The religious ideas of the Indus civilization are simply unknown. The fact that two or three seal engravings from Indus sites closely resemble the great god Shiva of later Hinduism certainly suggests continuities between the Indus cult and later Hinduism. Such continuity is entirely probable because villages continued to exist after the overthrow of Harappa and Mohenjo-Daro, where worship of the old gods may well have been carried on. It is tempting to believe that the Indus priests claimed very great magical power—power, in fact, to create and sustain the world anew each time they made sacrifice. It is tempting also to suppose that mystic visions were important to the pre-Aryan religion of India. But in truth we do not know. When these traits crop up later in Indian religious practice, they may have been fresh inventions rather than revivals of pre-Aryan ideas and customs.

Very likely the sharp departure from Vedic ideas, that shows up in later Indian religious texts, gathered headway when the Aryans abandoned their nomadic, warlike ways and became settled farmers.

Radical transformations were forwarded by special schools of religious learning. These had to exist to pass on orally the sacred tradition from one generation of priests to another. Unless the right words were said at the right time, and the right gestures performed when the ritual of sacrifice called for them, then the gods might be displeased and the whole ceremony fail. Worse than that, a badly performed sacrifice might

*The God Shiva, one of the three major deities whose
Attributes are discussed in the Vedas. Brahma is the
Creator, Shiva, the Destroyer, and Vishnu, the Preser-
ver. (Colombo Museum, Ceylon)*

even anger the gods. It became, therefore, a matter of the utmost importance to have priests who knew exactly what to do and what words to
say. This required taking instruction from a master who had committed
the sacred texts to memory, letter-perfect.

It is not known when this sort of school system arose, but when it
did the Vedas soon took a fixed form. Teachers who had mastered the
exact pronunciation of old and unfamiliar words insisted that accuracy
of that kind was the only way to please the gods. This, in turn, soon
made systematic study of the sacred language—Sanskrit—necessary,
since colloquial speech continued to alter, and the meaning of old words
and grammatical forms ceased to be obvious. But the priests of India
relied entirely upon oral memory for transmitting and preserving Sanskrit
literature and learning. The gods did not want to be read to; the sacred
words had to be memorized instead.

This bias against writing slowed the development of written texts.

Even after writing became an everyday matter in government administration, books were not used for religious purposes. The school system was built around memorization, and anything else was judged inferior, second-rate, not worth serious attention. This, incidentally, meant that nearly all forms of literature had to be put into verse, to facilitate memorization and to remind anyone reciting the work of what came next.

Mastery of Sanskrit grammar was not enough to make the sacred Vedic texts meaningful, particularly when verses that must have been composed for other purposes were recited as an accompaniment to the sacrifices. Some secret, inner meaning had to be extracted before such procedures made sense. This led learned priests and their pupils to invent explanations of the "real" meanings of old verses. These explanations became extremely fanciful and seem quite unconvincing to us. On the other hand, they allowed the priests to develop their own religious ideas freely, by explaining away the obvious, superficial meaning of the Vedas and treating them as symbols or hints of a deeper meaning that only the expert and educated could expect to understand.

THE BRAHMANAS   The texts in which such ideas were elaborated are called Brahmanas. The general drift of the Brahmanas was to exalt the power of the priests. The importance of the gods faded. In fact, the old gods of the Vedas became little more than puppets. If the sacrifice were performed in exactly the right way, the god to whom it was offered had no choice but to grant long life, abundant cattle, or whatever else the priest had asked for on behalf of the person who paid for the sacrifice. In its extreme form, the doctrine of the Brahmanas stated that priests created the world and the gods afresh each time they performed sacrifice. Everything, in short, depended on them, and their ability to make the sacrifice in exactly the right way. An ungenerous patron, who grudged paying the priests their full fee, might find that the priests turned a blessing into a disaster simply by slipping a word or two into the ritual in the wrong way.

ASCETICISM   Not everyone in India was satisfied with this sort of priest-ridden religion. A handful of ascetics fled from human company into the forest and there sought escape from the pains and frustrations of ordinary social life. Such persons often had little or nothing to eat, and they developed various bodily disciplines aimed at reducing all appetites to a minimum—or, ideally, extinguishing them entirely. Remarkable things can be achieved in this way. Ascetics have been able, for example, to control heartbeat and breathing and other "automatic" bodily processes, slowing them down until they almost come to a stop.

The basic idea behind Indian asceticism was that the body and its needs were bad, or at least troublesome, and interfered with the pursuit of truth, joy, and beauty. These supreme values the ascetics discovered through mystic trances, when for varying periods of time they lost normal consciousness and entered into rapturous communion with another, infinitely superior, reality. After a while, however, the rapture always faded and the mystic returned to the ordinary world of sense.

Mystics and holy men had special advantages in India. They were much admired, so that groups of disciples often formed around a particularly holy man, even if he lived far away in the forest. Such disciples, of course, tried to imitate their master and hoped above all to learn from him how to achieve the mystic vision. Thus, the relationship was not unlike the relationship between master and pupil in the Vedic schools where priests acquired their sacred knowledge. Before long, the words of especially holy men also became a subject for learning. Experiences and insights gained from a lifetime of asceticism could be put into literary form and memorized by admiring followers. In this way another body of literature, known as the Upanishads, came into existence.

THE UPANISHADS   The Upanishads, as one would expect from their origin, had no use for priests and rituals and ceremonies. They thus contrast sharply with the Brahmanas, though the two may have been composed at more or less the same time. The central teaching of the Upanishads is expressed in the phrase, "That art Thou." What this means is hard to express in English, since our words do not carry the meanings of the Sanskrit very exactly. But, roughly, what was meant is this: each human soul ("Thou") is really part of a universal spirit ("That"). Spirit is the only true reality. Matter and the body are illusions that hide the facts from ordinary individuals. By learning how to subdue the body and thus free the soul, mystic union with the universal spirit can be achieved. Those who have succeeded in entering into such a union, can then come back and tell others about it: and this is what the Upanishads set out to do.

Once the mystics had established the meaning of their strange experiences, by interpreting them along these lines, it was a matter of simple logic to extend their views to cover human life as a whole. No longer was it a good thing to try to secure the gift of wealth or long life from the gods—as the Vedas had assumed. Rather, the proper religious goal was to escape from life and allow one's soul to return to the great universal spirit from which it had come.

The doctrine of rebirth and karma fitted into this framework very easily. A person could now hope to rise so high in the scale of being as to shed the burden of karma altogether. In such a case a soul would no longer have to be reincarnated, but might rejoin the universal spirit, safely disentangled from connection with any sort of body, thus escaping all the pains and discomforts such entanglement involved.

Eternal bliss, therefore, came to be thought of as an escape from selfhood. It might require many incarnations before a silly or stupid person could rise to such heights. The wicked might even slip downward in successive reincarnations, and get farther from the ultimate goal of release from the pains of bodily existence. But the wise and good knew what to aim for, and knew how to get there faster—by imitating the ascetic practices and mystic trances of holy men.

Brahman priests soon agreed that this ideal was fine and fitting for old age. Earlier in life, however, family duties and the rituals of sacrifice and purification had to be attended to. Such a compromise made a good deal of sense in a poverty-stricken peasant society, where those too old and infirm to do their share of the work could become a heavy burden on the family. By going off into the forest and seeking holiness and release, such persons could hasten their time of death and relieve their relatives of the burden of feeding and caring for them. They could also die in hope of a more blessed future—whether reincarnated, or, perchance, escaping reincarnation and the pains of life entirely. Eventually, these ideas were combined with Vedic rituals and with new ideas of personal devotion to a particular god to create the religion of Hinduism.

BUDDHISM   In the long run, this compromise prevailed in India but it took many centuries for Hinduism to come clearly into focus, even though its elements were mostly present in India by 500 B.C. One reason for the gradualness with which Hinduism emerged was that another faith, Buddhism, came into existence in India just before 500 B.C., and seemed, for several centuries, to be destined to dominate India as well as most of the rest of Asia.

Buddhism arose because not everyone was willing to settle for a life divided between a period of ordinary activity and a period of ascetic withdrawal, as the Brahman priests recommended. There were young people who found the conditions of their everyday life so utterly unsatisfactory that they wished escape right away. One such person was Prince Gautama, the Buddha. (*Buddha* is a title, and it means the "Enlightened One.") The Buddha was born well before 500 B.C. and probably died about 485 B.C.

Guatama's personality and the moderation of his example may account for the impact his teaching came to have. But he had at least one mystic experience—The Enlightenment, as Buddhists call it. Sitting under a tree one day, he entered into a trance and saw in a flash all the fundamental truths of religion. Buddha's vision aimed at the same goal as the Upanishads: personal annihilation and escape from all the suffering due to incarnation. This was to be achieved by following the Noble Eightfold Path: Right Views, Right Aspirations, Right Speech, Right Conduct, Right

Siddharta Gautama, the Buddha, in contemplation. (Yale University Art Gallery, anonymous gift through Alfred R. Bellinger, 1917)

Livelihood, Right Effort, Right Mindedness, and, last but not least, Right Rapture.

All schools of Buddhist thought agree upon these formulas, but difficulties multiply when we try to spell out what each heading means. Presumably, what Buddha meant by these phrases was the sort of life he led himself. As followers gathered around him, they asked his opinions about how they should behave, and he settled such questions as they came up, in a common-sense sort of fashion. By degrees, a set of rules for the good life emerged from such decisions—but they applied only to those who took the pursuit of holiness very seriously and sought escape to Nirvana—as the Buddhists called the state of self-annihilation. Buddha's rules, therefore, applied only to religious athletes who wished to develop their spiritual power at the expense of everything else. We commonly call such persons "monks," although the term is, of course, Christian, and the organization and rules to which Buddhist monks submit are quite different in detail from those that bind Christian monks.

Buddhist monks, for example, do not usually take definite vows, and there is no single head or ruler of a Buddhist community. For particular purposes one of the monks may, indeed, take special responsibility, but each man is supposed to be his own master and to regulate his activity according to his own will and judgment. In Buddha's lifetime he had such prestige that everyone deferred to him in matters of importance. New members were admitted after an informal conversation designed to test their sincerity and purpose. Every so often the monks gathered to speak to one another about their spiritual experiences and to confess personal shortcomings.

Such an informal style of common life, with emphasis upon equality among all the members, may have been modeled on the aristocratic tribal community that Buddha had known in his youth. If so, one of the secrets of Buddha's success may have been that his community of monks preserved, in a new context, the personal freedom and independence which was becoming harder and harder to maintain in an age when great bureaucratic kingdoms like Magadha were growing more powerful every day.

For this reason, perhaps, and also because the daily round of religious life as Buddha outlined it had its own appeal, the company of followers who had gathered around him during his lifetime did not dissolve when Gautama died. Instead, the community continued to gather new members, and offshoots soon spread to other parts of India. As a result, about 200 years after Buddha's death it looked as though India would become a Buddhist country.

As communities of monks separated, their interpretation of Buddha's words and doctrines diverged, and new emphases crept in. The enormous doctrinal variation that exists among Buddhists today may therefore have begun quite early. What kept the movement together and gave it consistency was the rule of life and community organization that Buddha had laid down. Monastic communities always remained the organizational form of Buddhism. Here, more than in details of doctrine, lay the secret of its success.

But here also lay the great defect of Buddhism. It was not a religion for all occasions, even though ordinary persons soon began to find a place for themselves, giving food and other gifts to the monks and making pilgrimages to places where the ashes of a great saint had been preserved or where some sacred event, such as Buddha's Enlightenment, had taken place. This was satisfactory to all concerned; but what was not satisfactory was the lack of Buddhist rites and ceremonies with which to celebrate the ordinary crises of human life: birth, marriage, death. For these the Indian householder had to rely on Brahman priests. As a result India could never become an entirely Buddhist land. The Brahmans with their Vedic learning continued to have a necessary place in everyday life, and they kept their schools alive, in competition with Buddhist monasteries and with other, more extreme ascetic communities.

There was room in India for all. Any religious group that made

BUDDHA'S YOUTH

Siddhartha Gautama was born a prince, son of a king of the Sakya, close to Kapila. Kapila was located in the foothills of the Himalaya Mountains, between what is now the eastern end of Nepal and Sikkim. According to Buddhist legends, the young prince was very carefully raised. Servants supplied his every want, and since he had good health and was handsome and strong, he escaped all suffering. In due season he married a beautiful wife and began to look forward to becoming a king and father himself.

Then one day the young prince sallied forth from the palace gates and for the first time encountered the world of ordinary people. What he saw distressed him deeply. Other people did not enjoy the luxuries to which he had been accustomed. Many were sick and hungry. Animals and plants, too, suffered many injuries. Indeed, to live at all, people had to kill everything they ate; and even when they had killed enough to satisfy their hunger, they often went further, killing wantonly and even hurting and slaughtering one another. Suffering, in short, appeared to be the price of life. Being compassionate by nature, after such a revelation Prince Gautama could not longer enjoy his comfort as before. His knowledge of the world's suffering spoiled his joys. He was caught up in the pain of the world, whether he wanted to share in it or not.

As a result, the prince soon decided to abandon his former life. He left his wife, parents, and all the court behind, resolved to conquer suffering and free all living things from the pain of existence. He tried asceticism, but found that punishing his body did not destroy pain but merely increased it. He lived as a wanderer, depending on others' gifts for his daily food. Then one day, sitting in meditation under a Bo Tree at Buddh Gaya (in northeastern India), he suddenly experienced Enlightenment and became Buddha—that is, the Enlightened One. As Buddha he saw and followed the Noble Eightfold Path and taught others how to overcome suffering by doing so too.

special demands on its members could fit into the caste system by being treated like another caste. From the point of view of other Indians, Buddhist communities of monks were exactly that: honored for their holiness, perhaps, or feared for their magical powers, but in other respects a group apart, and treated for all practical purposes like another caste.

And just as separate castes adjusted their habits and customs to fit one with another, so also the Brahman priests, the Buddhist monks, and the ascetics of the forest retreats borrowed from one another and adjusted their ways to one another. They adjusted not by any plan or design but bit by bit, as a result of on-the-spot encounters. Before long Brahmans also accepted the other-worldly goals of religion which Buddhists and ascetics proclaimed. All varieties of Indian religion thus became transcendental. Sacrifices and rituals were reinterpreted as devices to help souls on their way toward release from the round of rebirths. The old, practical, material rewards for piety were played down. Religious attention was shifted away from this world. Every kind of holy man, priest, and ritual expert agreed that the proper thing to work for was escape from it all.

CONCLUSION

When Indian religions came to agreement on this point, soon after 500 B.C., one of the characteristic aspects of all later Indian civilization came fully into focus. More than any other part of the world, India has ever since remained the home of spirituality and transcendental aspirations.

Yet this side of Indian life constitutes only half the story. Side by side with playing down the values of the senses and of material goods, there was a luxurious, indulgent court life, which did not get praised in books and about which we know very little. Artisan skills and administrative skills also achieved high development. Many Indians cared very much about this world; and some of them explored the extremes of sense indulgence with almost as much energy as ascetics explored the extremes of self-denial.

It is perhaps true that the two extremes tended to support one another. That is, ascetics and sensualists may have existed partly in reaction to one another. Whether this is true or not, the sensuality of Indian life made a smaller impression on strangers from other civilizations than the ascetic, transcendental extreme did. In this sense—and because it was the religious tradition, not the courtly one, that entered the literary record which has come down to us—we are justified, perhaps, in taking it as the primary, most distinctive, and characteristic aspect of Indian civilization.

By 500 B.C., when Buddha was in mid-career, the special qualities of Indian civilization had become clear. At the same time another great teacher of mankind, Confucius, was active in China. We must turn our attention to that part of the world in the next chapter, to see how still a fourth civilization—comparable in scale, subtlety, and grandeur to those we have studied already—came into existence in the valley of the Yellow River.

CHAPTER 7

The Chinese Style of Civilization

Chinese civilization began in the region where the Yellow River (Chinese name: Hwang Ho) breaks through the last range of hills and starts across its floodplain toward the sea. Upriver lies a semidesert, known as Inner Mongolia, beyond which rise the snow-capped peaks where the river begins. The Yellow River can be considered the easternmost and largest of a series of streams that flow northward from the high mountains of central Asia. Most of these streams quickly peter out in the desert lands that lie at the foot of the mountain ranges. But before each stream dies in the desert sands, it creates an oasis, large or small, where irrigation farming can be successfully carried on. Stronger streams form interior seas, of which the Aral Sea and Lake Balkhash are the most extensive. Only the Yellow River breaks through to the ocean.

THE LANDSCAPE OF CHINA

The greater size and power of the Yellow River arise in part from the fact that its middle and lower course carry it through the northern fringes of the area of monsoon rains. In this part of the world rainfall is irregular.

Often it comes in sudden, heavy downpours, but there are seasons when the rains are weak, or fail to come at all. Just before reaching the floodplain, the Yellow River passes through a special kind of soil, called *loess*. This soil is made of finely powdered dust, deposited during the Ice Age by winds blowing from desert lands farther north. Loess, which also exists in smaller deposits elsewhere in the world, is a very fertile and easily worked soil, but liable to erosion. The Yellow River, in fact, gets its name because it carries such a heavy load of silt, picked up as it passes through the loess region.

On reaching the flat floodplain, the river's load of silt sinks to the bottom, with the result that the riverbed builds up until, from time to time, the whole stream shifts its course, just as the Euphrates River does. The waters from the melting snow of distant central Asian peaks sometimes reach the lower part of the river's length just as the first rains of the monsoon arrive. Disastrous floods result. The Yellow River thus deserves its nickname, "China's Sorrow." But it was also China's cradle, and learning how to farm successfully in so uncertain a climate shaped Chinese society fundamentally. People who could tame the Yellow River found other river valleys to the south comparatively easy to manage, thanks to the habits of hard work that were necessary to overcome the difficulties of farming in a region where flood and drought were both frequent visitors.

When Chinese settlers began to move southward into the valley of China's other great river, the Yangtze, the geographic differences all favored the newcomers. The waters of the Yangtze are cleared by passing through lakes that lie immediately below the famous gorge. Consequently, the lower portion of the river carries very little silt and does not usually flood. The Yangtze Valley also receives regular rainfall from the monsoons, so drought, too, is seldom a problem. In its natural state, the Yangtze Valley was heavily wooded. The floodplains must have been very wet. Still farther south, the Chinese landscape becomes hilly and mountainous. Since they are well watered, the slopes of south China were covered with dense jungle growth before being cleared by human hands.

The Chinese Style of Farming

Archaeological work in China is still very limited. For all practical purposes, nothing is known about the root and rice cultivators who must have been living along the riverbanks of south and central China by 2400 B.C. when rice was already a crop of some importance in the middle reaches of the Yellow River. But rice, which had to be grown in shallow

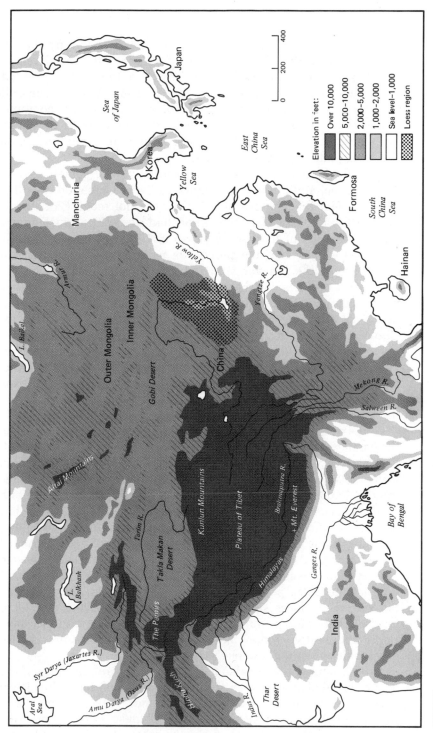

CHINA

fresh-water ponds or swampy land flooded in spring by the river, was not what the early farmers of China depended on. Their basic crop was millet, grown on the loess, without irrigation. In addition, they cultivated wheat and barley, the staple crops of western Asia. It looks, therefore, as though the Neolithic cultivators of northern China combined crops and techniques of farming that had originated far to the west (wheat and barley) with other crops and very different farming methods unique to China (millet and perhaps rice).

A fundamental difference between civilized society in the Middle East, Europe, and India, on the one hand, and China, on the other, arises from the fact that the use of the plow did not reach China until after a mature Chinese style of civilization had come into existence. The first definite records of the use of plows in China come very late indeed—after 400 B.C. Even if the plow was used somewhat earlier than that, which is possible, it never came to have the same importance for Chinese agriculture that it had in the rest of the civilized world. A Chinese peasant, even today, can get on, if he must, without use of animal power. Some farms are so small that the owners cannot afford to support an animal. Chinese farming, therefore, was, and is, akin to gardening; it depends on an enormous output of human labor and only secondarily upon animal power. By contrast, farming among the civilized peoples of the Middle East, Europe, and India depended on the plow, and on the exploitation of animal power, to allow farmers to cultivate enough land to support the various specialists upon whose skills civilization depended.

It is easy to see why the plow failed to reach China quickly. In the small, crowded oases that lay between the Middle East and the Yellow River valley, fertile land was limited in extent. Pioneer hoe-and-spade farmers had plenty of time to occupy all the available fertile land before they had ever heard of the plow. Once they had done so, they had absolutely no reason to start keeping big hungry animals, whose food could only be produced at the expense of food for humans. Hence plow agriculture could not easily spread across the oases of central Asia that lay between ancient China and the Middle East, where the plow was invented.

But how was it possible for the Chinese to create a civilization without the extra per capita food production that the plow permitted? For one thing, loess soil is unusually soft and easily dug. Therefore a hard-working peasant and his family could cultivate more square yards in the Yellow River valley than elsewhere. The loess soil was also unusually fertile when it got enough rain.

Another factor may also have been important. Because of the special geographical characteristics of the loess region of the Yellow River valley, early Chinese farmers may have been more easily taxed than farmers in most other regions. In other words, Chinese peasants may have been compelled to work harder and give up more of their crops to their social superiors than peasants in other geographical environments were compelled to do.

This was possible not because Chinese landlords and rulers were more ruthless than their counterparts in other places, but because it was probably more difficult for Chinese farmers to escape tax collectors by melting into the woods, as slash-and-burn cultivators could easily do in Europe and India. When farming first began in the Yellow River loess region, ground suitable for cultivation was probably quite limited in extent. Desert lay to the north and west, while the river floodplain was too wet to cultivate without first building elaborate drainage ditches. In between lay slopes and patches of well-drained loess soil, with enough rainfall, in most years, to raise a crop. Deeply eroded valleys separated one such area from another. Thus river swamps or slopes too steep to cultivate broke the landscape up into a series of "islands" of good farmland.

The farmers who established themselves on such islands found it hard to disappear when tax collectors came around. There was no place to go, no vast forest as in Europe and India, where a new clearing could be made with only a few weeks' work. It took many years of labor to dike and drain the waters of the Yellow River so that fields could begin to creep out into the flat floodplain itself. In time this vast task was carried through, so that a great carpet of fields engulfed the separate islands of loess cultivation where Chinese agriculture began. But this enormous engineering enterprise was organized by rulers and officials, though the work itself fell, of course, upon the peasant farmers.

A garden style of cultivation, demanding intensive human labor, gave an enduring stamp to Chinese civilization. During most historic ages the occupation of new territory by Chinese peasants was slow, because a great deal of labor had to be expended to tame new landscapes. But the human mass that was needed and could be sustained by the Chinese type of agriculture also meant that, when Chinese settlers moved into a new region, they—quite literally—dug themselves deeply into the landscape and utterly transformed earlier patterns of land use.

Chinese farmers in fact have moved across east Asia like a great glacier, beginning in a small way in the special environment of the loess regions of the Yellow River valley, about 2400 B.C., and spreading slowly but irresistibly eastward, southward, and, in recent times, also northward into Manchuria. Throughout this vast expansion, Chinese garden cultivators took possession of the land in a far more intimate sense than farmers with plows ever did. Each valley and hillside they brought under cultivation involved the use of human muscles to make the land over, yard by yard and foot by painful foot.

Enormous population density was one result. Relatively small surpluses from single families could become quite impressive when the number of families to be taxed was totaled. A civilization of a massive and extraordinarily stable character could and did arise on the basis of such surpluses. And at the bottom of the social scale, China's peasant farmers developed a capacity for work that no people dependent on animal power has ever equaled.

EMPIRE AND FAMILY IN ANCIENT CHINA

Our knowledge of ancient China depends largely on written histories. Unlike the Indians, the early Chinese valued history and compiled lengthy and elaborate records of past events. These records were arranged according to reigns and dynasties, and it is still customary to divide Chinese history along these lines, even when, as sometimes happened, the change from one ruling family or dynasty to another was not particularly significant.

One result of studying Chinese history in this way is to concentrate attention on court life and administration. Fundamental changes in the provinces, or gradual transformation of the structure of Chinese society as a whole, are often difficult to detect from the traditional Chinese dynastic histories. Nevertheless, these accounts at least define China's political past. From as early as 841 B.C. dates for emperors' reigns seem amazingly accurate, according to all the tests modern scholars can apply. Nothing remotely similar exists for Greece or the Middle East, much less for India; and we owe the scholars and historians of ancient China a great deal for keeping court records so carefully.

The Ruling Chinese Dynasties

According to tradition, China was first ruled by five Heavenly Emperors, who discovered or invented most of the useful arts. This, presumably, was myth, invented to explain the beginnings of civilized life. Next came the Hsia Dynasty, and after that the Shang Dynasty, which ruled from 1523 to 1028 B.C. Archaeologists have been unable to find sites that correspond to the Hsia period, but certain large Neolithic villages, distinguished by rather fine black pottery and stout earthen walls, may have recognized the leadership of that half-mythical dynasty.

When we come to the Shang Dynasty, archaeology becomes far more helpful. Their third and last capital, Anyang, was located and excavated in the late 1920s. The city of Anyang was the capital of the Shang

An oracle bone from the Shang Dynasty. (*Royal Ontario Museum*)

Empire from about 1300 B.C. to the end of the dynasty (1028 B.C.). It was laid out on a rectangular pattern, with entry gates in the middle of each side and two main streets that crossed in the center. This is the same pattern that charioteers in the Middle East used for their encampments. The Shang capital also had other characteristics that associate it with

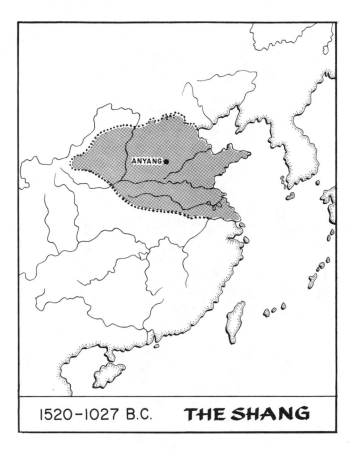

1520-1027 B.C.   **THE SHANG**

Middle Eastern charioteers: horses and chariots, bronze weapons, and a reinforced short type of bow suited for use in the cramped space of a chariot.

It therefore looks as though men who had somehow mastered the skills of chariot warfare overran China and founded the Shang Dynasty. One difficulty with this theory is that no definite connecting links between the Middle East and China have been discovered. It is a long distance, to be sure, and if charioteers did in fact travel from oasis to oasis through central Asia, one would expect to find traces of their passage. On the other hand, only very hasty surveys have as yet been made of the oases. Further digging is needed to reveal what lies hidden beneath the surface, before connecting links between China and western Asia can be expected to turn up.

SHANG WRITING   Whatever the relation with western Asia may have been, the civilization of Anyang was thoroughly Chinese. That is to say, styles of art and methods of writing, which continued to flourish in later Chinese times, were used by the Shang rulers of Anyang. Some Shang customs were later abandoned: human sacrifice, for example. The Chinese also gave up the Shang method of interrogating the spirits by heating a sheep's shoulder blade or a tortoise shell—on which questions had been written—until it cracked, and then "reading" the cracks according to a special lore that gave Yes or No answers to the questions. Hundreds of cracked shoulder blades and tortoise shells were discovered at Anyang, with writing sufficiently close to modern Chinese so that scholars were able, without much difficulty, to read the questions the ancient rulers of Anyang had put to the spirits.

Both modern Chinese and the ancient Anyang script are pictographic, that is, they are built upon hundreds of simplified little pictures. The pictures themselves, and the way several pictures may be put together to make a single "character," as each separate unit of the script is called, do not resemble any other known system of writing. It must have been invented in China, perhaps by men who had heard of the possibility of writing down words and sentences. The writing system discovered at Anyang was complete and could record any sentence or idea. No evidence of a gradual development, such as that which the Mesopotamians left behind, is known. But the archaeological record is so incomplete that we cannot be sure that Chinese writing was invented all at once, although it looks as though it might have been.

The discoveries at Anyang proved that the Yellow River valley had indeed become the site of a considerable empire by about 1300 B.C. The city was large and had special artisan quarters. Extraordinary skill was necessary to produce some of the objects found there. In particular, bronze pots, elaborately decorated with complex patterns, demonstrate a skill in bronze casting that has never been exceeded. Some of these pots, used for religious ceremonial, have shapes similar to earlier black pottery vessels. This suggests that there was some sort of religious continuity between the Hsia and Shang peoples.

SHANG RELIGION AND FAMILY LIFE   Reliable information about Shang religion comes to us only from the inscriptions used for interrogating the spirits. The traditional histories are misleading, since their authors assumed that later Chinese religious ideas were present from the beginning. But the tortoise-shell and shoulder blade inscriptions reveal only a fragment of the whole picture. Other practices and ideas simply escape our knowledge. From the inscriptions it is clear that the Shang peoples revered gods or spirits associated with various natural objects—hills, lakes, rivers, and the like. Ancestral spirits also commanded much attention, for the ancient Chinese expected them to protect their descendants from natural disasters and barbarian raids.

The importance of ancestral spirits in Shang religious attitudes reflected the vitality of the family in Chinese life. Every society has some kind of family organization, of course; otherwise children could not survive. But Chinese families are unusual and seem to have exerted an enormous influence upon their members from very ancient times. A Chinese family is not just a group of parents and children. Instead, it extends to innumerable generations. The living are only a small part of a much larger and more powerful community; for the spirits of the ancestors instruct, reward, help, and protect their descendants as long as their descendants respect and honor them. Without the aid of the ancestors, nothing can be expected to go well; with their aid, however, comes prosperity and good fortune.

Among the living, too, Chinese families enforce a strict pattern of good manners and duties. Age carries prestige and demands deference: husbands are superior to wives; elder brothers to younger; and between cousins, careful rules have been worked out to define exact precedence, depending on the relative ages both of the children and of their parents. Proper patterns of deference and authority are clearly understood by everyone concerned. Youth obeys, age commands; and the psychological strain of having to do what one is told, when one is a child, is made up for later by the satisfactions that come with age and the right to command the respectful attention and obedience of those lower down in the family order.

Obviously, not all Chinese families conform to this pattern. Bad-tempered wives and disobedient sons existed in China, too. But the ideal was clear, and its force in molding the conduct of young and old was and is very great. Proof of this force can be observed among Chinese living outside of China in modern times. Family discipline and manners survive among most Chinese, even in the United States. Open rebellion against a father's authority is extremely rare. The old customs continue for generation after generation, sustained by family custom and tradition.

The question that cannot be answered is when and how this pattern of family life arose in China. Was it present from Shang or even pre-Shang times? Shang inscriptions that refer to spirits of the ancestors suggest such a possibility. On the other hand, the cult of ancestors at first may have been limited to the upper classes. Peasants in historic times never lived in large households, as the wealthy generally did. Only the relatively well-to-do could afford time consuming rituals of politeness that day after day reaffirmed family ties among an extended circle of relatives. In early times, perhaps only noble families were expected to have ancestors who mattered. We simply do not know.

The importance of the family was reinforced by the fact that there seems to have been no distinct class of priests in ancient China. On all ordinary occasions, the head of the family acted as his own priest and dealt with the spiritual world—ancestors in particular—by means of traditional rites and ceremonies he had learned from his own father and which he would, in due time, pass on to his eldest son. The ancient Chinese seem to have sought supernatural help and protection mainly through family channels, not, as in other civilized societies, outside them. This enormously increased the father's power, for his role as link between ancestral spirits and the living generation meant that any disobedience to him might result in the ill will of the entire spiritual world.

Their priestly duties made it almost necessary for heads of families to be able to write. The reason was this: very early in their history, the Chinese decided that the best way to ask the ancestors questions was to write them a letter. As we have seen, in Shang times writing was done on tortoise shells and sheep shoulder blades. But this method was most likely reserved for royal or other high-ranking suppliants, since the supply of specially prepared bones and tortoise shells was not large enough to accommodate everyone. Later on, the usual method was to write out a question on a piece of paper and then burn it, thus "delivering" the letter to the spirit world by causing it to "die." Other perishable materials were probably used for writing such messages before the Chinese invented paper, but naturally nothing remains to show us how it was done.

Even today in China some heads of family cannot write, and in ancient times schooling was presumably much rarer. All the same, we know that as early as the Chou Dynasty (1028–221 B.C.) the sons of the chief nobles of the empire went to school in the royal palace, where they learned archery, manners and ritual, and how to write. In this way they prepared themselves for their future roles as heads of families and vassals of the emperor.

Such a linkage between literacy, priestly functions, military leadership, and the headship of families was unique to China. Warriors who could write were rare in other civilized societies, until quite modern times. Warriors who were also priests and experts in the supernatural were hard to find outside of China; and no other society ever developed a family system that required its heads to combine all of these roles as the Chinese pattern of family life did. This, more than anything else, shaped Chinese civilization from very early times almost to the present. The Chinese family, like caste in India and the polis in Greece, became a master institution that governed a great many aspects of human life.

Yet the available evidence does not really prove when or how the peculiar features of Chinese family organization came into existence. Unfortunately for historians, fundamental aspects of society are often taken so completely for granted that the persons who make records never bother to explain what everyone already knows. Yet despite gaps in the evidence, it seems probable that the family had an unusually wide range of functions in ancient China. If so, families must have shaped Chinese behavior more profoundly than families did in countries where religious and political affairs were carried on largely outside the frame of family life.

We can, perhaps, think of ancient Chinese society as a cluster of families, subordinated to the emperor who was himself, of course, the head of a family even larger and more important than that of any of his subjects. Family structure and the imperial structure were not really different. The emperor's relation to his subjects was like the relation of the family head to its living members. He was priest and father, leader, commander, protector—all of these at once. And just as everyone had his proper place within the family structure—above some and below others in rank and dignity—so also within the empire everyone had his proper place, and it was his duty to find it.

Nevertheless, the power of the emperor and his central government to some degree conflicted with the power of each separate family head; for the emperor's power was real only insofar as he could command obedience from the heads of families, who might not wish to obey him. Similar tensions arose within a family, as well, when the head commanded obedience from some junior member, who might not wish to obey him.

INTERACTION BETWEEN IMPERIAL AND FAMILY LOYALTIES

We really know nothing of how the Shang Empire was held together, and we have no direct evidence of family structure from that long ago. How far the empire's boundaries extended is unknown, as are the names and locations of subordinate tribes, peoples, families, provinces—or whatever else made up the empire.

With the establishment of the Chou Dynasty, more information becomes available. The Chou people came from the Wei Valley in the west, and when they first conquered Shang China they were classed as barbarians; that is, they were not Chinese. But the newcomers eagerly took on Chinese cultural traditions. Hence in art, literacy, and most other respects, the new dynasty did not bring any sharp break. Changes did come, however, and some important elaborations. The Chou, for example, brought the seven-day week to China, replacing a ten-day week used by the Shang. This change must have reflected some ultimate connection with Babylonia, where the seven-day week had its origin.

It may be worthwhile to pause a moment to ask why the seven-day week, which is so fundamental to our own life patterns, achieved

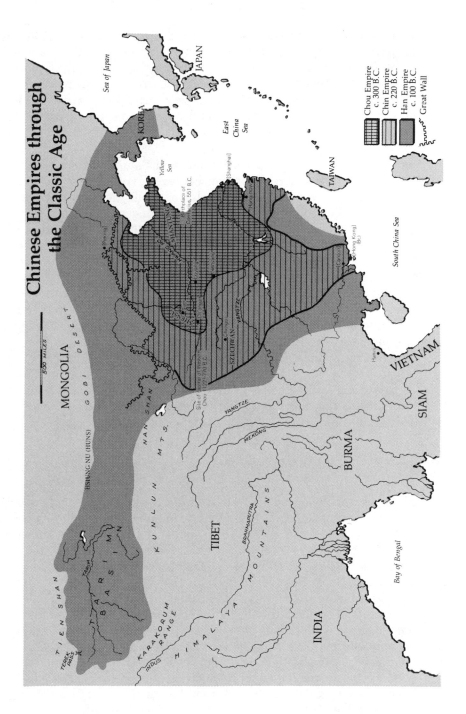

Chinese Empires through the Classic Age

500 MILES

Legend

Chou Empire
c. 300 B.C.

Chin Empire
c. 220 B.C.

Han Empire
c. 100 B.C.

Great Wall

MONGOLIA

GOBI DESERT

HSIUNG NU (HUNS)

TIEN SHAN

TARIM BASIN

TEREK PASS

KUNLUN MTS.

NAN SHAN

KARAKORUM RANGE

INDUS

HIMALAYA MOUNTAINS

TIBET

BRAHMAPUTRA

INDIA

BURMA

MEKONG

YANGTZE

SIAM

VIETNAM

[Hanoi]

Bay of Bengal

SZECHWAN

YANGTZE

Site of Capital of Western
Chou 1122-770 B.C.

Birthplace of
Confucius, 551 B.C.

Yellow
Sea

[Shanghai]

[Peking]

Loyang

[Hong Kong]
(Br.)

[Canton]

South China Sea

East
China
Sea

TAIWAN

KOREA

Sea of Japan

JAPAN

such universal acceptance, since Greeks and Indians as well as Chinese all followed such a calendar. It had two advantages. First, a seven-day week fitted into the cycle of the moon fairly well, since the moon takes only a little more than twenty-eight days to complete its circuit round the earth. The phases of the moon were by far the most conspicuous measure of time available to ancient peoples, and a calendar that matched the changing shape of the moon seemed obviously better than one that did not. Secondly, there were seven wandering "lights" in the sky: sun, moon, Mercury, Mars, Venus, Jupiter, and Saturn—one for each day of a seven-day week. Each of these bodies moved among the fixed stars in complicated ways. The planets, for example, seemed to advance and then go backward for a while before moving ahead again. Because of these irregular patterns, early observers of the sky concluded that the wandering lights must have special power or importance. A day dedicated to each seemed no more than prudent; and the fact that the result fitted the moon cycle seemed to prove the system.

In another and more important way, the Chou may have brought Babylonian ideas into China. The Babylonians believed that changes in the heavens were systematically related to changes on earth. Therefore, careful observation of the motions of the planets and sun and moon would enable men to forecast events and foresee dangers. The Chou, too, believed that events on earth corresponded to events in the skies. But instead of measuring and calculating the exact positions of the planets, as the Babylonians did, they contented themselves with a looser theory.

Chinese Theory of Government

Their central idea was that Heaven granted the right to rule on earth to a family of unusual merit. As long as members of that family continued to deserve it, Heaven's mandate remained with them. The emperor, Son of Heaven, was the connecting link between the world of men and the skies; and just as the entire sky turned around the polestar, so all things on earth ought to revolve around the emperor.

This theory of government became absolutely basic to all later Chinese political thought. It had several important logical consequences. For one thing, since there was only one Heaven and one polestar, there could be only one emperor. His authority ought to be universal, and if some distant barbarians failed to recognize his merit and submit to his rule, so much the worse for them. By such ignorance, they cut themselves off from Heaven's good graces and from the benefits that resulted from conformity to the proper, constituted order of civilized life.

In the second place, the theory justified any successful revolt. The fact that a dynasty fell proved that Heaven had withdrawn its favor. Various signs could always be found to show, at least *after* the event, that the mandate of the old ruling family had expired. Bad crops, unusual events, like the impact of a meteorite or the birth of a two-headed calf, might be signs of Heaven's displeasure. So might invasions and revolt. And an emperor, surrounded by such possibilities, always had to watch his step and be careful not to offend Heaven. If perchance he did so, he had to know the right way to make amends as quickly as possible, lest his dynasty be overthrown as a punishment. In practice this meant careful attention to traditional rituals of every sort.

One of the most dangerous things an emperor could do was to provoke the enmity of the ancestral spirits of any powerful and important family. Thus the emperor's power over his chief nobles was severely restricted. Any punishment that involved, for example, taking land away from a powerful family automatically offended the ancestors, who might be expected to make trouble with Heaven and thus endanger the emperor's position. Perhaps such religious scruples mirrored military realities.

To offend too many powerful families was certainly dangerous to the central power, for the Chou had parceled out their empire into a series of feudal holdings. Noble families that were granted lands were supposed to serve and obey the emperor. For a long time they did send their sons to school at the court. This practice may have helped to hold the empire together, since men who had spent their youth being trained at the imperial court were likely to retain a sense of deference toward the emperor all their lives.

Decline of the Chou Empire

Nevertheless, in time, the Chou Empire disintegrated. A significant blow came in 771 B.C., when barbarians from afar—perhaps raiders breaking in suddenly from the steppe—sacked the Chou capital in the Wei Valley and killed the reigning emperor. After this disaster another member of the family was set up as emperor, and reigned from the city of Loyang, thus establishing an Eastern Chou Dynasty in succession to the earlier Western Chou (1028–771 B.C.). But the prestige and practical power of the emperor never recovered. Local nobles soon became princely rulers in their own right, owing only nominal obedience to the Chou Dynasty. Princes struggled against one another and began to develop their own bureaucratic governments, standing armies, and tax systems to support their power.

This became possible, in part, through an increasingly rapid and successful reclamation of the river bottom lands. Availability of iron for

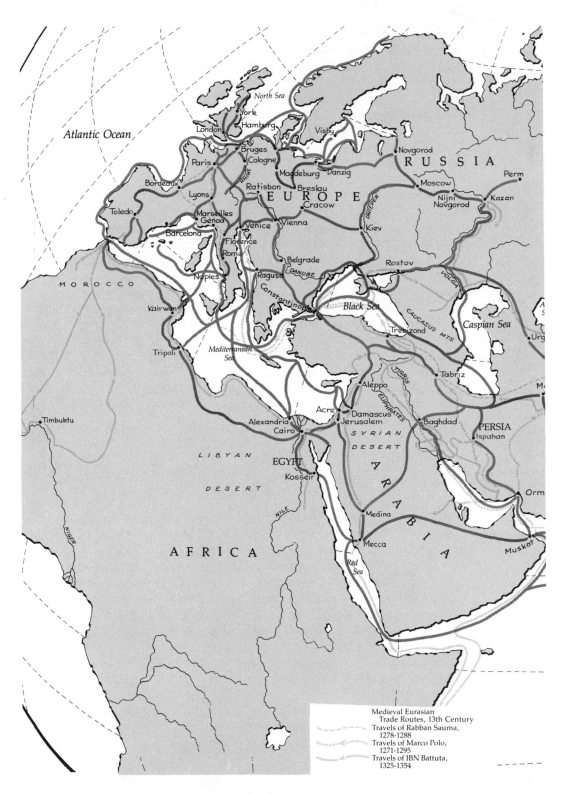

Medieval Eurasian
Trade Routes, 13th Century
Travels of Rabban Sauma,
1278-1288
Travels of Marco Polo,
1271-1295
Travels of IBN Battuta,
1325-1354

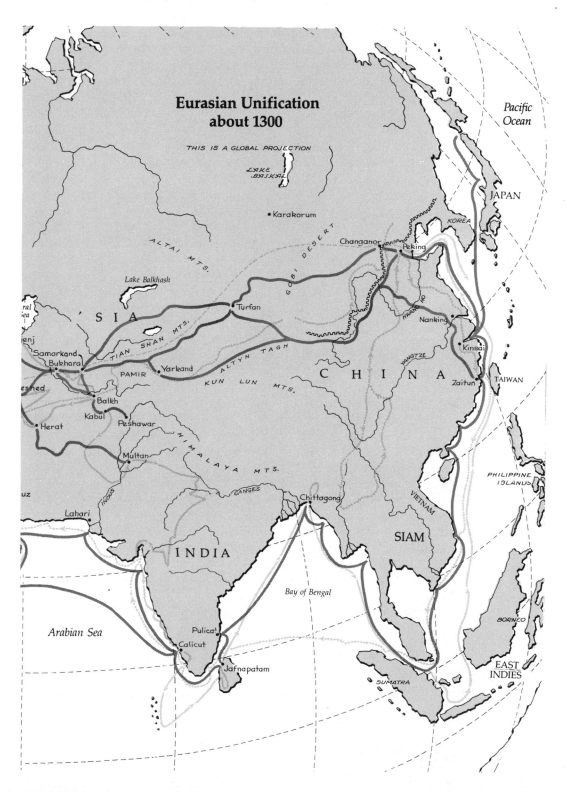

**Eurasian Unification
about 1300**

THIS IS A GLOBAL PROJECTION

tools may have helped to open the broad and fertile floodplains of the Yellow River to agriculture, though exactly when iron manufacture became important in China is not known. Large-scale diking and digging were needed to protect the bottom lands from flood. Noble or princely rulers organized the work. They then were able to get large rents from the land they had reclaimed from swamp. Before long the more successful landlords and princes began to seize weaker neighbors' lands, despite ancestral spirits and traditional rights and duties. War between neighboring princes hastened the consolidation of power in the hands of about a dozen rulers, and as the wealth and power of these rival princes increased, their wars became more ruthless. So severe did wars become that traditional Chinese historians called the last years of the Chou Dynasty, 403 to 221 B.C., the "Period of the Warring States."

An important by-product of these struggles was the expansion of the area of Chinese civilization. Thousands of individuals, finding themselves in danger, fled from the crowded center of the Chinese world, carrying with them various skills that neighboring peoples were often ready and eager to put to use. In addition, princes whose territory happened to lie along the boundaries of the civilized areas of north China were able to push their frontiers outward onto barbarian ground, and then by degrees brought the new lands to a fuller share in Chinese life. Systematic resettlement of peasant farmers was the most effective way of expanding Chinese territory; teaching former barbarians how to work and live like the Chinese was almost equally important.

Eastward this type of expansion extended to the peninsula of Shantung and the coastal region immediately north of that peninsula—a region that has ever since remained an extremely important part of China. Expansion southward toward the Yangtze River was equally significant. Chinese settlement and civilization took root in that river valley during the Eastern Chou period. However, because of the vastness of the region and the enormous amount of work involved in constructing fields throughout the Yangtze Valley, it took centuries for the potential wealth of this middle region of historic China to become a reality. Not until after the time of Christ, therefore, did the Yangtze Valley begin to rival and then surpass the Yellow River valley as a center of Chinese population and agricultural production.

Northward and westward the Chinese style of agriculture could not expand, because the water supply in Mongolia and the Gobi Desert was insufficient. Human occupation of these regions must, indeed, have been very sparse until shortly before 300 B.C., when Chinese records first mention horse-riding nomads along China's northwestern border. Thereafter, the problem of guarding China's peasant masses from parties of raiding cavalry became acute.

The border state of Ch'in, located in the Wei Valley, where the

Chou Dynasty had originated, bore the first brunt of the nomad attack. The princes of Ch'in finally solved the problem by developing a professional standing army of cavalrymen, who were equipped like the nomads with horses and bows and who were paid with taxes collected from the public at large. This cavalry army, tested and tempered by frequent campaigns against the nomads of Mongolia, proved itself superior to all other Chinese military forces. As a result, Shih Huang Ti, prince of Ch'in, conquered all China in 221 B.C. He declared himself Son of Heaven, thus bringing the long farce of Chou government to an end.

The new dynasty did not, however, last beyond the lifetime of Shih Huang Ti's son. Old loyalties to the princely states that the first Ch'in emperor had destroyed could not be rooted out all at once, and Shih Huang Ti's violent methods aroused general hostility. Hence, when he died (210 B.C.) revolts broke out all over China, and a fresh round of warfare began that continued even after Shih Huang Ti's son died (206 B.C.). Out of this confusion a new dynasty, the Han, emerged supreme over the whole of China in 202 B.C.

Under the Han Dynasty, a more or less effective balance was struck between the competing requirements of imperial unity and family loyalty. To gain a better understanding of how this balance was achieved, we must consider the Chinese intellectual and moral reactions to the confused and troubled time between 771 and 221 B.C., when the nominal authority of the Chou emperor in Loyang was increasingly disregarded, and a spiral of more and more ruthless wars kept the princely states in turmoil.

THREE SCHOOLS OF CHINESE THOUGHT

Respect for the spirits lay at the heart of Chinese family life, and this concept provided the ultimate explanation of why some persons should obey orders while others could command obedience. Refusal to conform could provoke supernatural punishment as well as social disapproval. But the conduct of the more successful rulers in the time of the Eastern Chou Dynasty (771–221 B.C.) flouted all such rules of conduct. They did not hesitate to dispossess a family from its ancestral lands if they were strong enough to do so. The wrath of ancestral spirits seemed ineffective. Moral conduct seemed only to lead to defeat and failure. The most deceitful double-crosser often won out, and a thoroughly pious and dutiful member of society might suffer all kinds of wrong without having the spirits come to his rescue.

The semi-legendary Lao-Tzu, alleged founder of Taoism.

Confucius (ca. 551–479 B.C.). His teachings exercized the greatest influence on the development of Chinese thought and culture of any of the philosophers of the Eastern Chou Dynasty. (Bettmann Archive)

Experiences of this sort were profoundly disturbing to Chinese minds. What could and should a wise and good person do under the circumstances? Many different answers were suggested to this question, and the writings of some of the men who attempted to solve the problem were read and respected throughout later Chinese history. The troubled time of the Eastern Chou period was thus the golden age of Chinese thought, when the enduring lines of the classical Chinese world view were first worked out.

It is enough here to sketch three different schools of thought, choosing them partly because they were influential later and partly because they expressed logically distinct and opposing ideas. Followers of these schools were known as Legalists, Taoists, and Confucians. Of the three, the Confucians became the most important in later times, though not until after they had adjusted their doctrines to make room for elements of both Legalist and Taoist thought.

LEGALISTS   The Legalists were closely associated with the state of Ch'in. They justified Shih Huang Ti's militaristic organization of power that allowed him to conquer the rest of China in 221 B.C. Their central doctrine was simple: The will of the ruler was law. Anything he commanded was morally right. Absolute obedience was a duty. The first and most important task was to create and maintain military strength. Only so could peace and security be attained, and from these prosperity would follow. Legalists paid no attention to the supernatural and left no room for the family. They had a low opinion of human character and argued that people had to be driven by force.

Legalists put no limit on the ruler's power to command or demand anything of his subjects. Censorship of books and close control of education were part of their program for making the state strong. Arbitrary conscription of labor for state projects was also taken for granted. Such ideas were not mere theories, for Shih Huang Ti conscripted Chinese peasants wholesale for his armies, for work on the famous Great Wall of China, and for building a no less remarkable system of military roads throughout the empire. He also censored books and suppressed all doctrines opposing his policies, including, among others Confucianism.

In sum: according to Legalist principles, the state and its ruler were everything and the family—not to mention the private individual—was nothing. Between the two poles of Chinese society, the Legalists chose exclusively and emphatically in favor of the state.

TAOISTS   Taoists utterly rejected all such ideas. They claimed Lao-tzu as their founder, whereas the Legalists had no single founder nor any one preeminent spokesman. The most distinguished Legalists were men of action, who served as administrators and generals and scorned mere theorists, which they considered the Taoists to be. Lao-tzu, according to tradition, had also served as a minister in one of the smaller states of ancient China not long after 600 B.C. But this may be myth, invented to give Lao-tzu a career like that of Confucius. As a matter of fact, modern scholars are not even sure that such a man as Lao-tzu ever lived.

What is sure is that a book attributed to him survives. It taught the doctrine of ruling by "nonaction." A good ruler, the Taoists claimed, did nothing. He simply let the grass grow and allowed the people complete freedom to do what came naturally. The good life required complete freedom from any kind of outward compulsion. In a world where force and violence were all too common, a wise and good person would always live for each moment, without fear or dread, freely and quietly.

Only so could human life accord with Tao. The word *Tao* is hard to translate: it means "the way," but this translation does not suggest the full range of its meanings. Tao was the way of the universe. It was not merely passive, for Tao could act. If people disregarded it, Tao eventually undid their deeds and destroyed their achievements. On the other hand, if people lived in accord with Tao, they prospered and things went well for them.

Tao, in other words, carried a supernatural as well as a natural meaning. It was the whole nature of things, and no one could ever escape it, however hard he or she might try. By understanding Tao, moreover, a person could acquire unusual powers. In particular, one could extend life perhaps indefinitely, and move from place to place at will. These magical aspects of Taoism were much elaborated among the Chinese in later times, although they were not emphasized in Lao-tzu's little book.

Taoism was essentially a personal and private doctrine. It completely disregarded all the obligations ordinary persons owed to their families or to the state. But, perhaps just because so much of Chinese life was hedged in by such duties, the appeal of Taoist ideas proved to be very strong. Throughout Chinese history, Taoism remained a significant school of thought. Many found the effort to attune themselves to nature and the Tao a pleasant change of pace from the usual round of patient restraint and dutiful deference to superiors! On vacation Taoism was fine, though in ordinary human situations most Chinese found some more specific guide to conduct was necessary. But between Legalism, with its ruthless pursuit of state power as an end in itself, and Taoism, which denied the effectiveness of deliberate human interference with Tao, there could be no compromise.

CONFUCIANS   The third school, Confucianism, traced its doctrine to the sage Confucius, who lived from about 551 to 479 B.C. He was a native of the state of Lu, near the center of the Chinese world, and came of noble family. As a young man, he was appointed minister, but failed to persuade the prince of Lu to follow his principles, and so left office to spend the rest of his life as a private citizen who "loved the ancients" and delighted to talk about them with anyone who shared his concerns. A group of admiring disciples gathered around Confucius. They recorded his sayings as well as stories about him in a book called the *Analects*.

Oddly enough, Confucius' reputation in later ages did not depend on anything he wrote or said himself. Instead, the Chinese revered him as the editor and complier of the five Classics, over which later generations of schoolboys were to labor. The Classics were a miscellaneous collection of poems, annals, histories, and handbooks of divination and of manners. When and for what purpose they were first gathered together is uncertain. Many modern scholars do not think that Confucius was the editor, though he may have been familiar with some or all of the books that later became the Five Classics.

In time these books, together with the *Analects* and some commentaries and independent works explaining the Confucian points of view,

HOW CONFUCIUS LEFT OFFICE

The following story, told by China's great historian, Ssŭ-ma Ch'ien, who lived about 300 years after Confucius, is probably an invention, intended to show what good manners required of a minister and of a ruler. This is the gist of the tale:

When Confucius was fifty-six years old, the prince of Lu appointed him first minister. Confucius' first act was to execute his predecessor, who had mismanaged the government. Within three months, prosperity and good order returned to Lu. Foreigners flocked in from neighboring states to bask under Lu's good government. A neighboring state, Ch'i, grew worried. If Confucius remained in office, Lu would continue to prosper, and even though it was only a small state, Lu might become able to dominate its neighbors.

The first minister of Ch'i decided to resort to stratagem. He collected eighty of the loveliest girls in the state of Ch'i, dressed them magnificently, and taught them to dance. He presented them, together with 120 beautiful horses, to the ruler of Lu. The prince was entranced. For days on end he watched the girls as they danced and the horses as they pranced, and forgot all about his official duties.

One of Confucius' disciples said: "When the ruler neglects his duties, it is time to resign." But Confucius replied: "Let us wait until the time for the Sacrifice to Heaven. If the prince remembers to send us the offerings due to his ministers, we will stay." But when the time for the Sacrifice to Heaven came around, the ruler of Lu was still too excited about the girls and horses to remember his official duties. Confucius therefore resigned and left the country.

formed a body of literature that every educated Chinese studied long and carefully. By reading these works and committing many passages to memory, the young Chinese learned to write and, at the same time, acquired an intimate familiarity with the code of values and manners that defined what it meant to be a well-educated, fully civilized Chinese.

No events during the lifetime of Confucius made such an outcome seem likely. He felt his life to be a failure, because he believed that a really good man could only exercise virtue to the full by ruling, or by serving as minister to one who rules. Indeed, Confucius claimed no originality. All he wanted was to reassert the ways of the ancestors, as he knew them through books. This required, of course, a united country, obedient to a single emperor, chosen by Heaven for the post. It required also well-ordered families, with sons obedient to their fathers, and fathers respectful toward the spirits. This side of Confucian teaching can be summed up in a word: decorum. If everyone knew his or her place and kept it, then, said Confucius, all would be well.

The first task, therefore, was to know what behavior was proper. That could best be found out by studying the ways of the ancients as recorded in the Classics. The second task was to behave properly in each situation as it arose. Confucius seems to have felt that this would follow more or less automatically if everyone knew what should be done in every human relationship. Knowledge, acquired by study, was therefore the key; and Confucians always put enormous value upon mastery of the Classics.

In emphasizing book learning in this fashion, Confucius altered older ideals without admitting or perhaps realizing it. At the court of the Western Chou, which Confucius took as his model, archery and military drill were part of the young nobleman's training. Confucius approved of archery. How could he do otherwise and be faithful to the ancients? But he abhorred war, thinking that the resort to violence was the result of a failure to observe decorum on someone's part—either a superior who had failed to exact obedience or an inferior who had refused to submit. Deliberate preparation for failure had few charms for the Confucians. They thought it better to avoid war by wisdom and good order. Hence a soldier's skills had a very low place in the Confucian ordering of virtues; as a consequence, in later ages educated Chinese, though eager for bureaucratic office, usually left military command to barbarian hired hands.

Confucius did not consider that nobility or virtue was necessarily inherited. By training and study a person could become virtuous, whatever his origins. This concept, too, was a significant departure from ancient practice. It had the effect, when Confucianism became official, of opening a career to talent. Any young man, having secured an education, who had been admitted to the bureaucracy, might rise as high as his abilities and the emperor's favor would carry him.

Finally, Confucius refused to speculate about supernatural forces. As long as it was so difficult to know how to conduct oneself, Confucius considered it fruitless to wonder about the world of the spirits. Approved old-fashioned ways of dealing with the supernatural had his complete support. But he did not think it useful to argue about the nature of the spirits which the ancestral rites somehow took care of.

The central thrust of Confucius' thought was a refusal to make any distinction between public and private life. Virtue was one and the same, whether a person occupied high office in the government or lived as a private citizen. Decorum was one and the same for those high and low in the social scale. The emperor stood at the top; all others ranged in proper order beneath him. Relations up and down this social pyramid seemed, to Confucius, no different from relations within a family. They were more complex, no doubt, requiring more careful learning of roles than was required within the bosom of a family. But the essentials of good order were the same in the two cases. The empire was the family writ large; and a state was well run insofar as it approached the patterns of family life. Ideally the ruler ruled without having to punish or threaten anyone, and all obeyed because each knew his or her place and accepted it.

If we compare the Confucian position with that of the Legalists and the Taoists, it is easy to understand why Confucianism prevailed in the end. For the Confucian way combined and reaffirmed the importance of both family and empire—the two central realities of ancient as well as of modern Chinese society. Confucians did not glorify tyranny as the Legalists did. The ruler had his duties and conventional role to play just as much as any of his subjects. But neither did Confucians despair of human society, as Taoists tended to do. The good life, for Confucius, could be led only in society, by fulfilling exactly and graciously the roles that fell to each individual human being, day by day, hour by hour, and even minute by minute, throughout life.

The Establishment of Confucianism as an Official Philosophy

In Confucius' lifetime, his disciples were not particularly influential. Nevertheless, Confucius' ideals continued to live among those who read the Classics and mulled over the *Analects*. The growth of bureaucratic government played into the Confucians' hands, for princes needed literate administrators, and literate men who accepted the values of the Classics were likely to be reliable and faithful servants.

Another important change in the texture of Chinese society was even more important in bringing the final triumph of Confucianism. The violent upheavals of the Period of the Warring States (403–221 B.C.) eliminated most of the old landowning nobility. This development did not, however, mean that peasant villages escaped the authority of landlords. Instead, a new class of landowners arose, men who laid no particular claim to noble birth or descent, but who nevertheless secured a right to collect rents and taxes from the peasants. Exactly how this "gentry" class arose is unclear. Moneylending and the amassing of landed property by richer and more prudent farmers may have raised some to the gentry. In other cases local tax collectors may have been allowed to keep part of what they gathered from the peasants for themselves, which then became a sort of rent.

The gentry were not as a rule military men. Posts in the administrative bureaucracy seemed to them the natural way to rise in the world. Such attitudes fitted Confucianism very well; or perhaps one should say that Confucianism expressed these attitudes, for Confucius himself and his first followers were mostly of gentry background.

Yet the unification of China by Shih Huang Ti in 221 B.C. at first seemed to be a serious setback for Confucianism. The new emperor was impatient with Confucian talk; he saw in the reverence for old ways, which constituted the core of Confucianism, an indirect expression of resistance to his rule. Accordingly, in 213 B.C., he ordered all Confucian books to be destroyed, except for a single set to be kept in the imperial archives, where only authorized persons could consult them. Extensive book-burnings apparently did take place.

Even more disruptive to the continuity of old, learned traditions was a simplification of the script, which Shih Huang Ti also decreed. At nearly the same time, the habit of writing with a brush, instead of with a sharp-pointed pen or stylus, was introduced. This brought about rapid change in the form of characters, which had now to be shaped to suit the strokes natural to a brush. As a result, within a short time, as the new and simpler kinds of writing caught on, old texts became almost unintelligible. Any copies of the Classics that had escaped Shih Huang Ti's book-burning, therefore, soon lost their meaning for any but extraordinarily learned scholars.

The Ch'in conqueror rode roughshod over the states he had conquered. Shih Huang Ti stationed troops at strategic places all over China and ruthlessly hunted down his enemies. He divided the land into provinces and districts and appointed officials over each unit. He standardized axle lengths so that carts would make only one set of ruts in his roads. He harassed members of the upper classes who failed to support him and ordered hundreds of thousands, if not millions, of peasants to work on roads and on the Great Wall. Only those members of the gentry class who were prepared to submit completely to his will, and who did not mind the military brutality of the Ch'in emperor, could serve him comfortably. Not many did, so when Shih Huang Ti died, resistance came out into the open and a fresh round of war broke out.

The new victor, who emerged as emperor of all China and founded the Han Dynasty in 202 B.C., owed part of his success to the courteous, open manner he had shown to all who crossed his path. A more or less conscious effort to woo the support of the gentry seems to have been part of his policy. And although many of the Ch'in practices were kept—the new script and the new provinces for example—the Han government allowed free circulation of books once more.

The tacit alliance between the gentry and the Han Dynasty elevated Confucianism to the rank of official doctrine by 136 B.C., when one of the most successful of the Han rulers, Emperor Wu Ti, decreed that anything not within the Confucian school of learning "should not be allowed to progress further."

By that time, however, official Confucianism had made extensive adjustment to practices that had first been approved by the Legalists. An emperor who commanded great armies and organized campaigns across all of China's borders scarcely conformed to the Confucianism pattern of a good ruler. Yet the emperor who made Confucianism official was nicknamed "The Martial Emperor," because he had done exactly these things. Only by accepting, therefore, some of the important changes brought by the Ch'in Dynasty and by the Legalists did Confucianism achieve official status.

Taoism and related schools of thought did not disappear, nor were their followers persecuted by Confucians, despite the wording of Emperor Wu Ti's decree. Rather, Taoism was allowed to flourish in private, among men out of office. Those who sought to serve the emperor and rise to positions of authority in the government were expected to be familiar with the Classics; and they were expected to have schooled themselves in the good manners and self-restraint that went with such learning. Official Confucianism and unofficial Taoism thus came to complement each other very effectively. The ever-present formal restraints of Confucian decorum may even have required the alternative that Taoism offered—an escape from tightly organized society into private communion with nature.

Thus, by absorbing elements from Legalism and by making room for Taoism, Confucianism finally became the official ideology of imperial China. From the time of the Han Dynasty until the twentieth century, Confucian scholars governed China. Generation after generation of schooling produced men remarkably uniform in outlook and style of life. They gave a conservative stability to China that no other civilization came close to equaling. Thousands of gentry families, scattered across the face of China, drawing rents and taxes from millions of peasants, aspired to serve the emperor in some appointive office. This became the human reality upon which Chinese civilization rested. The resulting reconciliation of family loyalty with the imperial ideal was so effective that any further basic changes seemed entirely unnecessary.

CONCLUSION

Chinese civilization arose in comparative isolation from the civilizations of Greece, India, and the Middle East. Labor intensive garden agriculture gave Chinese society a different economic base from that familiar in other parts of the civilized world. Even more fundamental was the special character of the Chinese family structure that provided a model for public as well as for private life throughout most of China's history.

A distinctive style of art and method of writing arose in China under the Shang Dynasty (traditional dates, 1523–1028 B.C.), but the classical definition of Chinese intellectual traditions occurred under the Chou Dynasty (1028–221 B.C.). Rival Chinese schools of thought all tried to answer questions about how men ought to behave. Legalism glorified the state and ruler at the expense of private life and family ties. Taoism, on the contrary, was individualistic and had nothing to say about public and family duties. Confucianism occupied a kind of middle ground, finding rules for proper behavior both in public and in private through careful study of ancient books and records.

Important changes came to Chinese society during the last centuries of the Chou Dynasty. After 771 B.C., the effective power of the emperor evaporated. Instead, rival princes built up bureaucratic governments and armies, and fought one another until the state of Ch'in conquered all the rest and unified China once more. The Ch'in conqueror, Shih Huang Ti, reorganized Chinese government along Legalist lines and carried through many reforms. Although fresh revolts and wars broke out, when a new conqueror founded the Han Dynasty in 202 B.C. he kept many of Shih Huang Ti's changes. Similarly, when a later Han emperor made Confucianism the official ideology of China, room was still found for Legalist and Taoist ideas within the official Confucian system.

The upshot of this evolution was to establish a conservative and stable style of civilization in China. The pattern of education that produced experts in Confucian learning also supplied the empire with loyal and capable officials. The landlords and peasants, who constituted the overwhelming majority of the population, found that the balance between imperial and family duties that the Confucians advocated fitted quite well with their own interests and needs. The result was a remarkable uniformity and stability across many centuries, even though China had become a vast and varied land by the time the Han Empire was founded and continued to extend contacts into new regions in the centuries that followed.

The secret of this stability and uniformity seems to have been the ability of Chinese families to mold their members to the roles tradition demanded of each of them, generation after generation, no matter where the family might find itself. The link between this "master institution" and the imperial system was close, for the whole empire was, ideally, a vast family that, at least in principle, ought to include all human beings.

DISEASES AND THEIR EFFECTS ON HUMAN SOCIETIES

Disease has played a very big part in human history. In all modern wars, more soldiers died of disease than from enemy action until World War II. Whole societies have sometimes been destroyed by epidemics. Unfamiliar diseases prevented successful European settlement in many tropical lands. Elsewhere European diseases, spreading like wildfire among local peoples, often cleared the way for settlers.

This essay explores the way people and diseases have altered their relationships across the ages. Lack of exact information means that we have to guess details; but there are some general principles—for example, the difference between endemic and epidemic disease—that go far to explain what happened.

The Case of the Vanishing American: 1519–1650

When Cortes invaded Mexico, the inhabitants of Montezuma's empire numbered more than 11 million persons. They lived close together in villages wherever good land for cornfields existed. They had never been exposed to Europe's "childhood" diseases: smallpox, chicken pox, measles, mumps, and whooping cough. One after another, these diseases spread among the Indians, killing adults as well as children. But the Spaniards, having almost always had such diseases in childhood, did not suffer. By 1650 the population of central Mexico, where Montezuma had once ruled, was about 1.5 million; at least 10 million persons had disappeared.

Why did so many Indians die of diseases the Spaniards and other Europeans did not find so very serious? The answer lies in the different disease history of the two populations. In Europe, smallpox, measles, and the rest had become *endemic*. This means that the disease was always around so that in the first years of life nearly everyone caught it. Natural immunities inherited from the parents made recovery more likely. Many children died all the same, but they were quickly replaced by new births. In Mexico and the rest of the Americas, the new diseases became *epidemic*. This means that old and young alike fell ill. Because they lacked any sort of inherited immunities, many died. When a large proportion of adults died, all activity began to fail.

HIGHLIGHTS The consequences of this disease pattern in the Americas were vast.

A handful of Spanish conquistadors and missionaries easily controlled large populations. Their resistance to diseases killing so many Indians seemed to prove that God was with them.

In Massachusetts and Virginia, weaker Indian communities simply disappeared, leaving empty land for English settlers.

Similar disease patterns often arose elsewhere. A population among whom a particular disease was endemic always had an advantage in any new encounter with another population among whom the disease was unknown.

How Europeans Acquired Their Childhood Diseases

Medical records are too vague to allow us to know exactly what disease hit when. But general considerations tell us a good deal. We assume that different diseases first broke out in different parts of the earth and among separate human communities. In any one area, a new disease begins as an *epidemic*. Either it kills everybody, and the disease germ itself disappears, or enough people survive the first epidemic to raise children who inherit some immunity to the disease. If enough of them survive childhood exposure to be able to reproduce themselves, after four or five generations the new disease will become *endemic*.

The spread of disease endemic in one human community to another where it is not endemic depends on how far and how often people travel between the two communities. Most major changes in disease distribution ought, therefore, to take place when people change the pattern of their travel and communication in some important way. (The arrival of the Spaniards in Mexico is such a case.)

Our question then becomes: When did people *first* venture upon important new kinds of travel and communication? About 100 B.C. to A.D. 200, caravans regularly traveled across Asia along what Eu-

The Bubonic plague in Europe, ca. 14th century.
(Bettmann Archive)

ropeans called the Silk Road. During this period ships also sailed the southern seas, connecting the east Mediterranean lands with south China via India and Malaya.

The disease consequences are clear. Severe epidemics hit both the Han Empire of China and the Roman Empire of Europe in the first Christian centuries. Serious depopulation resulted. Depopulation eventually made trade unprofitable, until regular movement along the caravan routes almost petered out. This was probably the time when most of our familiar childhood diseases became endemic among all the civilized populations of Eurasia.

HIGHLIGHTS

The distribution of infectious diseases depends on the patterns of movement and contact among human populations.

Important changes in human travel are likely to trigger new patterns of disease distribution.

The epidemic impact of new diseases upon a dense population without immunities may destroy the conditions needed to sustain the trade and travel that triggered the epidemic in the first place.

This natural cycle had much to do with the decline and fall of classical civilization of the Han and Roman empires, though military and other factors also played a part in the collapse.

The Black Death: A Different Disease Pattern

When infection passes direct from person to person, the transition from epidemic to endemic requires from four to five human generations. The pattern differs when there is another carrier for the disease. For example, the infectious organism for bubonic plague is carried by rats and is spread further by fleas. It is endemic among wild rats in parts of India and

China. From time to time, the disease takes hold as an epidemic among the dense rat populations of cities. When enough rats die off, their fleas may try to live on humans, thus spreading the epidemic to humankind, too. Immunities do not build up, for the disease disappears among humans when an epidemic is over, only to emerge again from the regions where it is endemic among wild rats.

Why then did bubonic plague cease in western Europe after 1718? Probably because changes in the ways Europeans got along with rats and fleas checked the spread of the disease. First, public quarantine of ships, houses, or whole cities where plague broke out made it illegal for anyone to leave the quarantined area until after a fixed time—usually forty days—had elapsed without fresh outbreaks of the disease. Second, improved cleanliness made it harder for fleas to take up residence on human bodies. Third, with better housing people encountered rats less often. What really stopped bubonic plague were the changes in European habits that made contacts between human beings on the one hand and rats and fleas on the other less common than before. In Asia and other parts of the world where no such changes took place, bubonic plague continues to threaten fresh epidemics.

HIGHLIGHTS

Some epidemic human diseases are endemic among animal population.

In such cases, the natural shift from epidemic to endemic forms of disease does not occur as far as humans are concerned.

One method of protecting ourselves from the diseases carried by animals is to reduce human contacts with the animal carrier.

The Impact of Scientific Medicine

During the past 150 years, scientists discovered how infectious diseases spread. With the identification of disease-causing bacteria and viruses, new methods of preventing disease became possible. Chief among them is inoculation with a weakened form of the disease-causing organism. This induces the human body to build up antibodies in the blood that make infection unlikely. In this way a long list of former killers, like yellow fever, smallpox, and infantile paralysis, have become unimportant.

In other cases, chemicals have been discovered that check the disease within the human body. In this way malaria, pneumonia, syphilis, and other diseases have been brought under control. These artificial immunities have extended hu-

An Aztec warrior striken with smallpox. (American Museum of Natural History)

mankind's freedom from infectious disease enormously, increasing the average length of life by many years.

Today scientific medicine allows control of most infectious diseases. This means that on top of the disappearance of epidemic disease as a major killer of humankind, many endemic diseases also have been (or are being) eliminated. An enormous improvement in the quality and dependability of human life results. Yet there is another side. Less infectious disease means longer life. Babies that would have died in infancy grow up to have children of their own; and their children do the same. Very rapid growth of population results. One of the most distinctive characteristics of modern times is the runaway population explosion.

Smallpox vaccination in 1870. (*Library of Congress*)

Growth of dense human populations created a fertile field for new infections, and several examples of recent disease transfers from animal populations to humans are known. Most of these were quickly eliminated by simple medical counter measures. But one new virus, which interferes with the immune reaction of human bodies, has not been brought under control. The Acquired Immune Deficiency Syndrome (AIDS) epidemic results. Increasing numbers of people began to die of AIDS in the 1980s, despite efforts by medical scientists to find a cure.

Because the causes of the bubonic plague were not fully understood, a variety of folk remedies were developed in an attempt to prevent infection. (*Bettman Archive*)

HIGHLIGHTS

Between about 1650 and 1850, epidemic diseases ceased to be important killers. Modern communications spread diseases around the world, and the epidemic-to-endemic shift occurred almost everywhere.

Since 1850 scientific medicine also brought the main endemic diseases under control.

Sustained population growth (about .1% per year) began about 1750 when epidemic diseases had been largely checked. Galloping population growth (up to 1.5% per year) took over as many of the important endemic diseases were also brought under control.

Disease and disease-control did not act alone. Increased quantity and quality of food supplies also contributed to modern population growth, and so did other changes in the condition of human life.

The State
of the World

The four civilizations that existed in 500 B.C. in the Middle East, Greece, India, and China occupied only a small part of the earth. Each was bordered by regions where barbarians had become aware of the charms of civilization, but there were still large parts of the world where the influence of civilizations had not been felt. Hunters, whose way of life had not altered noticeably in thousands of years, occupied all of Australia. South Africa also was inhabited by hunters, as were large regions of southeast Asia and the Indonesian Islands. The same was true of the Arctic shores and of large areas in both North and South America.

SPREAD OF AGRICULTURE

There was also a zone where agricultural or pastoral societies had come into existence but where full-scale civilizations had not yet emerged. It is difficult to see clearly what took place in this twilight zone, because there are no written records and archaeological study of such societies has only begun to scratch the surface. We may safely assume that agriculture continued to spread wherever suitable new ground could be found, but by 500 B.C. nearly all slash-and-burn cultivators had probably come up against various climatic obstacles. In Europe, for example, the wet climate of the Atlantic fringe made the great north European plain too waterlogged for wheat and barley. Only especially well-drained soils, on hill slopes, could be cultivated successfully with the methods known to these early farmers. The denser forests of the swampy plains were left to hunters and to cattle raisers, who fed their beasts on forest leaves. Too little is known elsewhere, but it seems likely that similar limits to territorial expansion had also checked the further spread of primitive grain farmers in Asia and Africa.

What, if anything, limited the advance of the root and rice growers of southeast Asia is altogether uncertain. Disease may have been a factor. Rice growing had caught on extensively in the Ganges and Yangtze flood-plains before 500 B.C. Elsewhere we have no sign of the dense populations rice cultivation might be expected to maintain. We do know that Indonesian root crops reached Africa by the time of Christ. As yams, bananas, and taro became established in what is now Nigeria, Ghana, and nearby regions, a populous agricultural society arose in the level grassland zone of west Africa.

SEA VOYAGING AND MIGRATIONS

This surprising plant migration underlines the importance of sea routes, even among quite primitive peoples. About the time of Christ, for example, the island of Madagascar, off the southeastern coast of Africa, was settled by people speaking Malagsy, an Indonesian language closely related to languages spoken today in Borneo. The transfer of this language implies that fairly large numbers of people crossed the breadth of the Indian Ocean. Since that ocean is relatively calm, such a voyage is not as surprising as at first it might seem. Monsoon winds blow half the year from one direction and half the year from a nearly opposite direction, making return voyages particularly easy. Moreover, coastal voyaging required only small, light boats that could be dragged ashore almost anywhere to cook a meal, to take on fresh water, or merely for a good night's sleep. As long as local populations did not attack the ships' crews—and the peoples living along the coast of the Indian Ocean appear to have been unwarlike—there was really no effective obstacle to traveling very long distances, once seaworthy boats, propelled by sails, had been invented.

There is strong reason to believe that seagoing vessels existed along the shores and rivers of southeast Asia from very ancient times. Chinese references to "longboats" coming from the south, and the undeniable fact of Indonesian settlement in Madagascar, are the principal evidence for this belief. Unfortunately, boats leave few archaeological traces. The shore villages and river mouths, from which such vessels presumably sailed, also do not make particularly impressive ruins. Hence, in this instance, archaeology does not help much.

On the other hand, archaeological finds at Dongson, in North Vietnam, reveal a people who used bronze and had horses from about 750 B.C. Horses in such an environment are surprising enough, for the horse was native to the Eurasian steppelands, far to the north. Even more puzzling is the fact that the bridle bits and other cavalry accessories found at Dongson closely resemble similar materials found north of the Black Sea in Scythian graves. A speculative theory explaining how such a linkage between southeastern Asia and southeastern Europe might have arisen runs like this: When cavalry tactics were new, Scythians living in and around the Altai Mountains of central Asia may have made a raid into China (the overthrow of the Western Chou, 771 B.C.?). A party of the raiders may then have proceeded south, until they reached Dongson, where they met a people who were already accustomed to sailing to and fro across the South China Sea and who had accumulated enough wealth to make it worthwhile for the raiding cavalrymen to set themselves up as rulers. Then, about a generation later, the main body of Scythians left their Altai homeland and migrated westward to the regions around the Black Sea. This meant breaking off further contacts with the Far East. The small party that had established itself at Dongson became isolated from the rest of the Scythian community. Migrations of such a kind are not impossible, but connecting links from Central Asia have not been found to confirm the theory.

Whatever the truth about such early cavalry raiding across the breadth of Asia may be, there is no doubt that the Dongson peoples, whoever they were, regularly voyaged across fairly long sea distances. Ships traveled from bases on the Asian mainland to the islands of Indonesia, and from island to island. It has even been suggested that Dongson boats (probably canoes hollowed out from big logs) may have crossed the vast expanse of the Pacific and made contact with Amerindian peoples in Mexico and Peru.

The reason for making such a surprising suggestion is that some of the bronze objects, which began to be manufactured in the Americas about 500 B.C., closely resemble objects manufactured along the south China coast. But most of the scholars who have studied American archaeology believe that the evolution of Amerindian cultures occurred in isolation from anything that was happening in Asia.

Speculation is really not very fruitful until more evidence has been discovered. For example, it seems obvious that the critical breakthrough for long-distance voyaging in the Pacific was the invention of outriggers to stabilize sailing canoes. With outriggers, there was small danger of a canoe tipping over, even in rough weather. Before these devices had been introduced, voyages across the open ocean probably occurred only by accident, when a canoe got blown off course and found itself out of sight of land. But with outriggers lashed firmly into place, trips of thousands of miles across open oceans became possible, as the Polynesians later proved. The difficulty is, however, that no one has a clue as to when outriggers were first invented. Without such information, guesses about the range and importance of early navigation in the Pacific and Indian oceans are not very profitable.

CHANGES IN THE CONTINENTAL INTERIORS

Practically nothing is known about the history of the world's continental interiors before 500 B.C., except in those regions where civilized peoples left written records. Yet changes were certainly afoot, and the pace of change probably tended to increase with time, as the consequences of increasing control over the natural environment were felt in more and more parts of the earth.

In Africa, for instance, agriculture increased in importance. The simple hunting style of life retreated southward and into the recesses of the Congo rain forest. But details are unknown, and even such an important matter as the establishment of Indonesian crops in west Africa cannot be dated exactly, nor are the routes by which yams and the other roots reached west Africa at all clear. Some think they were handed from one people to another across the interior of the continent, from east to west. Others believe that coastal voyaging may have carried the roots to western Africa by sea. We simply do not know. It does, however, seem sure that before 500 B.C. no African society south of the Sahara had yet attained a level of complexity to justify the term civilized.

The same was true of the Americas. Maize cultivation had become important in Mexico long before 500 B.C., but life remained at the village level, so far as we can tell, until after the time of Christ. The beginnings of bronze-making and the development of pottery manufacture did not lead immediately to the rise of civilization in the New World, because effective means for concentrating wealth and supporting specialists were not invented there until later.

In Asia, two interesting changes took place that altered human relationships in significant ways. After about 1000 B.C., the camel became

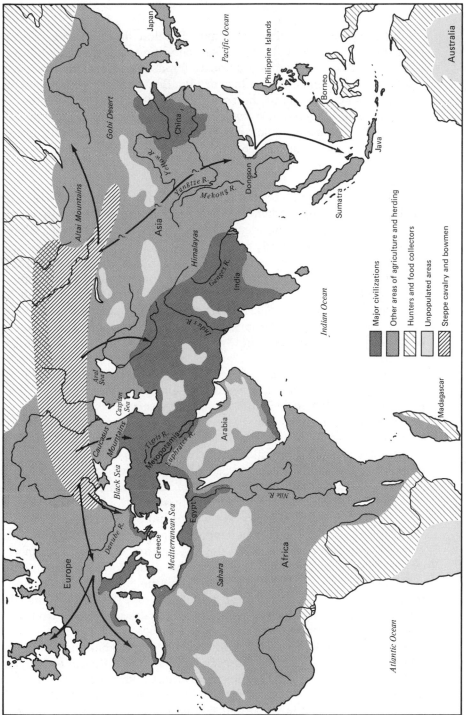

BALANCE OF OLD WORLD CULTURES 500 B.C.

Major civilizations

Other areas of agriculture and herding

Hunters and food collectors

Unpopulated areas

Steppe cavalry and bowmen

Japan

Pacific Ocean

Philippine Islands

Gobi Desert

China

Yellow R.

Borneo

Yangtze R.

Mekong R.

Dongson

Java

Altai Mountains

Asia

Sumatra

Himalayas

Ganges R.

India

Indus R.

Indian Ocean

Aral Sea

Caspian Sea

Caucasus Mountains

Tigris R.

Mesopotamia

Euphrates R.

Arabia

Madagascar

Black Sea

Danube R.

Nile R.

Greece

Mediterranean Sea

Europe

Egypt

Sahara

Africa

Atlantic Ocean

Australia

important as a domesticated animal. By that date, or soon thereafter, the camel's ability to withstand desert conditions allowed men to organize packtrains that could cross previously impassable desert barriers in Arabia and nearby lands. Soon afterward the Bactrian, or two-humped, camel was put to similar use in the cold deserts of central and eastern Asia. With camels, long-distance trade and movement throughout the desert zone of Asia became much easier than before. It was only gradually that the use of camels spread to north Africa. Caravans crossing the Sahara Desert were not organized on a regular basis until about the time of Christ.

We have already seen something of what happened farther north, on the grassy steppe, when men began to ride directly on their horses' backs. This way of using horses spread eastward by degrees along the grasslands of Asia. Shortly before 300 B.C., horse nomads appeared in Mongolia, the harshest part of the entire Eurasian steppe. Mongolia's cold winters and sparse rainfall made for poor pasture, and people who were used to living in that environment had to be as tough and hardy as their shaggy ponies. The farther west on the steppe one moved, the better the pasture and the milder the climate became. The richest part of the steppeland lay north and west of the Black Sea, in southern Russia and Romania.

As soon as the whole steppe came to be occupied by warlike horsemen, a tendency to migrate westward along the steepe asserted itself. No one wanted to go toward Mongolia; everyone wanted to move to better pastures. Hence, when there was any displacement, the conquerors or refugees usually headed west to see what they could find. Many must have met death and destruction at the hands of those already in possession of the pasture lands; but every so often the invaders were victorious. The net effect, therefore, was to create a westward drift of languages and peoples throughout the length of the steppe.

Forest hunters in the northern woods likewise tended to press southward into the grasslands, whenever a chance presented itself; and the steppe nomads, of course, were steadily attracted toward the rich lands of the civilized, agricultural peoples who lived south of them. Through most of recorded history, migration from the forest to the steppe and from the steppe to the cultivated land of China, the Middle East, India, and (less frequently) Europe competed with the movement from east to west along the steppe itself.

In Europe the discovery of how to ride a horse had important consequences. Riders established themselves in southern Russia about 700 B.C. The first horsemen of that region were called Cimmerians by the Greeks, but they were soon displaced by Scythians who came from central Asia, near the Altai Mountains. About 600 B.C., the Scythians set up a loose "empire" all around the north and west shores of the Black Sea. At about the same time, another people, the Celts, living in southern Germany and Bohemia, also learned how to ride. Their new mobility helped them to overrun most of northwestern Europe. Accordingly, Celtic tribes occupied northern Italy, all of France, and much of Spain, as well as the British Isles. In some of these places the Celtic conquerors encountered related peoples who had preceded them from the steppe. Elsewhere, in Spain for example, they met quite different and linguistically unrelated populations.

THE EXCHANGE OF IDEAS

The net effect of all these movements, and of improved patterns of communication, was to link all the parts of Asia and Europe more closely than at any previous time. South of the Sahara, Africa remained pretty well isolated from events in the north. The Americas remained apart, and Australia was unaffected. Yet by 500 B.C. a relatively extensive part of the world, inhabited by the great majority of humankind, had become a far more closely interacting whole than ever had happened before. No important new invention or discovery could fail to affect the lives of people throughout this wide zone—sooner or later, directly or indirectly. Invention meant change, upheaval, danger, and discomfort. No people could stay put for very long without having some new thing come up that required them to alter their customary ways. Historic change could nowhere be resisted or, indeed, really controlled. No one foresaw the consequences of a new idea or of a new technique. Innovations spread from place to place and from group to group, sometimes slowly, sometimes very quickly; and with each borrowing the idea or technique took a new twist from the way it fitted, or failed to fit, with the other things that the borrowers were familiar with or accustomed to.

As we have seen in Part One, within this interacting *ecumene*—a Greek word that means "inhabited world"—four main styles of civilized life had been defined by 500 B.C. Each was complete and self-sufficient. Problems could be answered, both practically and theoretically, by calling upon the ideas and techniques already worked out by the bearers of each of these civilizations. Hence, for the following 2000 years, each of these major civilizations went its own way, within the basic guidelines that had been laid down by 500 B.C.

Contact and communication did not cease; on the contrary they increased with the passage of time. More and more territory was brought into the circle of civilized society along every frontier. But this interaction among the separate civilizations, and between civilized and barbarian peoples, never upset the original fourfold balance of Old World cultures that had defined itself 500 years before the birth of Christ. This fundamental fact of human history is what Part One: Beginnings has tried to show.

CHAPTER 8

The Classical World and Its Expansion

500 B.C. to A.D. 200

By 500 B.C. distinct and different styles of civilization had taken form in China, in India, in the Middle East, and in Europe. During the 2000 years that followed, each of these civilizations continued to flourish and, despite some setbacks, tended to expand its territory by incorporating neighboring barbarians. In addition to this kind of interaction between the civilized centers and barbarian fringe lands, the four civilizations also acted and reacted on one another in different ways at different times.

First one and then another of the Eurasian civilizations attained a particularly brilliant flowering, and each was then able to export to the rest of the world some aspects of its achievement. The other peoples of the continent accepted what impressed them favorably and rejected the rest.

The first Eurasian civilization to pass through a special period of bloom—and thereby to influence its neighbors, both civilized and barbarian—was the civilization of Greece. This chapter will therefore describe the Greek achievement and trace how other peoples reacted to what they learned about classical Greek culture.

THE PERSIAN AND PELOPONNESIAN WARS

In 499 B.C. the Greek cities of Ionia revolted against their Persian rulers. Since local Persian forces were few and weak, the formidable Greek infantrymen met with initial success. The leagued rebellious cities even sent an expedition to capture Sardis, which was the former capital of Lydia and the provincial headquarters from which they had been governed.

The Great Persian War

It was not long, however, before the Persian monarch gathered his imperial armies and set out to punish the rebellious Greeks. One by one the cities were retaken, until Miletus alone remained. In 494 B.C., after a defeat at sea, it, too, was captured and sacked. The revolt had ended, but the wars between the Greeks and the Persians had only begun. During the revolt two obscure cities from across the Aegean Sea, Athens and Eretria, ventured to send a few ships to aid the Ionians. The Persians resolved to punish them for having dared to interfere.

The Persian general Mardonius, son-in-law of Darius the Great (Darius I), led the avenging army. He first restored Persian authority along the north shore of the Aegean Sea. Then he sent a small expeditionary force across the Aegean to attack Eretria and Athens (490 B.C.). He captured Eretria, after a week's siege, and transported all of its citizens to Susa, one of the empire's distant capitals. Mardonius turned next to Athens.

BATTLE OF MARATHON   The Persians, guided by an exiled Athenian, landed on the plain of Marathon, about twenty miles north of Athens, and waited for a faction within the city to open the gates. The Athenian army marched out to block the overland approach to their city, but did not dare to attack. Nothing happened. After a few days the Persians decided to board their ships in order to sail around the tip of Attica and land immediately in front of the city. When the Athenians saw what was happening, they formed their phalanx for the attack and charged across the plain of Marathon. The Persians were in confusion, trying to get on board their ships. The result was a great Athenian victory. The Persian army lost about 6000 men, while the Athenians lost only 190 men. The Persian fleet finally got under way, but by the time it rounded

Participants in the New York Marathon. The marathon race, now somewhat longer than originally, was created for the first Olympic games in 1896 in honor of the legendary Pheidippides, an Athenian soldier who supposedly ran from Marathon to Athens (approximately 25 miles), proclaimed the Athenian victory, and dropped dead from exhaustion. (Ken Karp)

the tip of Attica and approached the city, news of the battle had reached Athens. All chance of betrayal was gone, and Mardonius decided to withdraw his fleet. Athens had turned back the Persian forces singlehandedly. In later times the Athenians looked upon this as their finest hour. (See map, p. 217).

RENEWED PERSIAN ATTACK   The death of King Darius in 486 B.C. and a revolt in Egypt and Babylonia prevented Xerxes, Darius' son and successor, from taking up the Greek question until ten years after the Battle of Marathon. But by 480 B.C. the Persian king was ready to invade Greece with the full force of his imperial army and navy: more than 600 ships and perhaps as many as 150,000 men. Xerxes made careful preparations to speed the Persian attack. Stores of food were gathered along the route of march from Sardis. A bridge of boats was flung across the Hellespont (modern name: Dardanelles). Envoys were sent to all the

Greek cities, demanding that they submit to the Persians. So overwhelming did the Persian host appear that the oracle at Delphi, most respected of Greek shrines, advised all who consulted it to yield.

Nevertheless, a ragged coalition of thirty-two cities refused to give earth and water, which was a sign of submission, to the Persians. All leagued together under the leadership of Sparta. Athens' role, although subordinate, was most important, because of the Athenian fleet.

Athens' fleet came into existence as a by-product of bitter political rivalries within the city. The decisive turn came in 483 B.C. when a politician named Themistocles came to power in Athens through a remarkable device known as "ostracism." This was a procedure which called for a vote *against* a man rather than for him. It worked in the following way. Voters were asked to write the name of the citizen whom they considered most dangerous to the state on pieces of broken pottery or *ostraka*, from which the term ostracism derives. The names were counted, and the man with the highest total vote was then exiled for ten years. Through two such votes Themistocles' rivals were banished from the city, leaving him in control. Aware of the need for an Athenian navy with which to oppose the Persians, he persuaded the citizens to use income from newly discovered silver mines to build a fleet of warships. Thus 200 new Athenian triremes (ships rowed by oars so large it required three men to pull each of them) were ready to oppose the Persian attack. No other Greek city had more than a fraction of this number of ships to contribute to the allied fleet.

BATTLE OF THERMOPYLAE   When the Persian army invaded Greece in 480 B.C., the Spartans tried to check its advance at a narrow mountain pass called Thermopylae. The name means "Hot Springs." The Persians sent a select force over the mountains to attack the Greeks from the rear. Leonidas I, the Spartan king and commander, ordered all of the allies to withdraw, and with 300 Spartan "Equals" he held the narrow pass until they were all killed.

The opposing fleets, meanwhile, had fought three battles near Thermopylae, in the straits between the island of Euboea and the mainland. Once the Spartans had been overwhelmed, there was no point in holding such an advanced position any longer. The Greek fleet therefore withdrew to the Bay of Salamis. This left Athens exposed. The city was evacuated. When the Persians arrived, they destroyed the empty city.

By this time, the season was growing late. The main Greek fleet and armies had not been defeated. The Persian army was too large to subsist very long on local supplies of food, and bringing what was needed from Persian soil could not be done safely in winter, when storms interrupted navigation on the Aegean Sea. So Xerxes needed a decisive victory at once.

Within the Greek camp, there was great disagreement about how to conduct the war. Some wanted to retire to the south and defend the Peloponnese from behind a wall that had already been partially constructed across the Isthmus of Corinth. Themistocles, on the other hand, wanted a naval battle. He figured that in a general fight the Greek ships could destroy a large part of the Persian fleet. Then Xerxes' supply line across the Aegean would be endangered and he would have to withdraw.

BATTLE OF SALAMIS   To trap both Xerxes and his fellow Greeks into accepting his plan, Themistocles resorted to stratagem. He sent a message to the Persian king saying that the Greek ships were planning to slip away from the Bay of Salamis in the night, and suggested that if the Persian fleet were to attack, Greek resistance would crumble. Xerxes took the bait and ordered his ships to row in through the narrow straits between the island of Salamis and the mainland. He watched the fight from a throne specially set up on the steep bank. Great was Xerxes' dismay when the Persian ships ran afoul of one another in trying to crowd through the straits. This allowed the Greeks to ram and sink many vessels that were tangled, one with another, and unable to maneuver freely. As a result, the Greeks won a great victory. Nearly 200 Persian warships were sunk, while the Greeks lost only 40.

After the Battle of Salamis the Persian plan for subduing Greece became unworkable. Xerxes went home to Persia with most of his troops. Part of his army remained behind, however. The reduced Persian force, after spending the winter in Thessaly and Boeotia, once again moved south and devastated Attica, in the spring of 479 B.C.

BATTLE OF PLATAEA   The Greek strategy this time was to take the offensive by sea. A fleet crossed the Aegean to Ionia. Meanwhile the Spartan army, with the Athenian phalanx and all the other troops the leagued Greek cities could put into the field, marched against the Persians. They met at Plataea, where the Greeks won the only major land battle of the war—not so much by superior generalship as by the superior power and steadiness of their heavy-armed infantry. At the same time, the Greek fleet won a victory at Cape Mycale in Asia Minor. As the news spread, Greek cities along the coast of Asia Minor revolted against their Persian governors once again. The Greek fleet headed north to besiege the main Persian base at the Hellespont, which controlled the straits between the Black Sea and the Aegean. With the capture of Sestos, late in the winter, the retreat of the Persian troops was cut off. Only tattered remnants of Xerxes' proud host ever made it back.

It was a famous victory won by a handful of Greek cities against the might of the vast Persian Empire. A generation later it provided Herodotus with a truly epic theme for his history—the struggle of free men against the massed forces of Persian tyranny. And it presented the victors with a series of critical new problems: Should war continue? Should the struggle be broken off? What should be done with the Greek cities that had submitted to the Persians? What about the league of cities that had so successfully resisted the invasion? What was Athens' relation to Sparta going to be?

The Peloponnesian War

All these and other issues were decided by events rather than through any deliberate and judicious weighing of alternatives. The Spartans drew back; the Athenians, on the other hand, carried the war to the Persians by sending out naval expeditions year after year. Athens invited other Greek cities to send their fleets too; but the command always rested with an Athenian. Accordingly, until 448 B.C., the Athenians launched a naval expedition almost every year. In this way, they drove the Persians from the Aegean and Black Sea coasts entirely. They tangled indecisively with them along the south coast of Asia Minor. And they were badly defeated when they attacked the Persians in Egypt. Then, after an indecisive campaign on the island of Cyprus, peace was finally concluded (448 B.C.), leaving command of the seas firmly in Athenian hands.

THE RISE OF AN ATHENIAN EMPIRE   In the course of all these years of fighting, the free association of Greek cities, which had first carried the war to the Persians, was gradually converted into an Athenian Empire. In 467 B.C., when the threat from the Persians had diminished, the people of the island of Naxos, feeling that they had done enough, refused to send ships to join in further offensive operations. The Athenians regarded this as treason. They therefore attacked Naxos and compelled the Naxians to pay money tribute, instead of manning ships as before. Other Greek communities, voluntarily or by force, also began to pay tribute to the Athenians. Athens used this income to pay its citizens for rowing in the fleet. Hence, many poor Athenians came to depend on annual campaigns for their living. If there was no enemy to fight, they could not count on rowers' wages and the booty that came from a successful expedition.

The peace of 448 B.C. consequently threatened disaster for poor Athenians. A solution was found by using the tribute money for restoring the damage done by the Persians when they had occupied Athens in 480 B.C. The Parthenon—the great temple to Athena on the Acropolis—was built in this way, giving employment to many of the Athenians who could no longer count on a job each summer with the fleet.

This policy solved a critical problem at home, but it only made

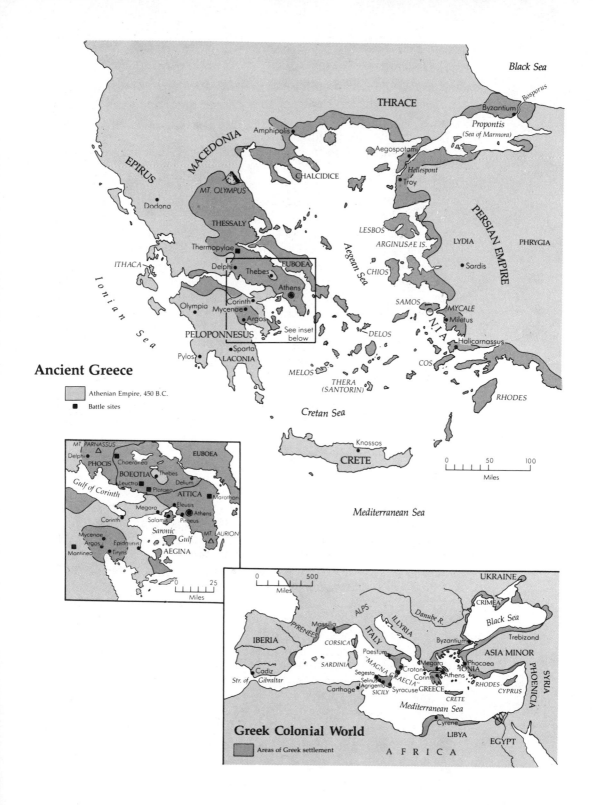

Ancient Greece

Athenian Empire, 450 B.C.

■ Battle sites

Black Sea

THRACE

Propontis (Sea of Marmora)

Byzantium

Bosporus

Amphipolis

Aegospotami

MACEDONIA

EPIRUS

CHALCIDICE

Hellespont

Troy

PERSIAN EMPIRE

Dodona

MT. OLYMPUS

THESSALY

LESBOS

ARGINUSAE IS.

LYDIA

PHRYGIA

Thermopylae

Aegean Sea

Sardis

ITHACA

Delphi

Thebes

EUBOEA

CHIOS

Athens

SAMOS

MYCALE

Olympia

Corinth

Mycenae

Argos

Miletus

I O N I A

DELOS

Halicarnassus

PELOPONNESUS

See inset below

Pylos

Sparta

LACONIA

MELOS

COS

THERA (SANTORIN)

RHODES

I o n i a n   S e a

Cretan Sea

Knossos

CRETE

0   50   100
Miles

Mediterranean Sea

MT. PARNASSUS △

Delphi

PHOCIS

Chaeronea

EUBOEA

BOEOTIA

Thebes

Gulf of Corinth

Leuctra

Delium

Plataea

ATTICA

Marathon

Megara

Eleusis

Corinth

Salamis

Athens

Piraeus

Saronic Gulf

MT. LAURION △

Mycenae

Argos

Epidaurus

Mantinea

Tiryns

AEGINA

0   25
Miles

Greek Colonial World

Areas of Greek settlement

0   500
Miles

UKRAINE

ALPS

Danube R.

CRIMEA

Massilia

PYRENEES

ITALY

ILLYRIA

Black Sea

Trebizond

IBERIA

CORSICA

Paestum

MAGNA GRAECIA

Byzantium

ASIA MINOR

Phocaea

IONIA

Cadiz

Str. of Gibraltar

SARDINIA

Segesta

Selinus

Croton

Megara

Corinth

Athens

GREECE

RHODES

CYPRUS

SYRIA

PHOENICIA

Carthage

Agrigento

SICILY

Syracuse

CRETE

Mediterranean Sea

Cyrene

LIBYA

EGYPT

A F R I C A

217

Athens' reputation with other Greek cities worse than before. The Greeks, after all, had fought the Persians to preserve their freedom. But a city that had to pay tribute to Athens was not free. Moreover, the Athenians often interfered in the political struggles of other Greek cities, helping their friends and trying to prevent their enemies from coming to power.

SPARTA'S REACTION   At first the Spartans did nothing. They continued to direct the "Peloponnesian League" of cities in the southernmost part of Greece and to watch, with growing alarm, the rise of Athens' power. In 460 B.C. some of Sparta's allies went to war with Athens. Spartans eventually joined in, but only halfheartedly, and they made peace at the first opportunity. But the Athenians did not remain quiet for very long. Soon they were busy extending their empire along the north shore of the Aegean; and they began also to reach out toward Sicily and southern Italy, where prosperous Greek cities, quarreling among themselves, were eager to invite the formidable Athenian fleet to join in their struggles.

Athens had already become supreme in the Aegean and Black Sea regions. The further possibility that Athenian naval power might fasten itself upon the western part of the Greek world threatened the economic prosperity of some of the Peloponnesian cities. In such case they would find their exports and imports completely at the mercy of the Athenian navy.

WAR BETWEEN ATHENS AND SPARTA   Such a threat stirred the reluctant Spartans into action. War broke out in 431 B.C. A long and bitter struggle lasted until 404 B.C. and is usually called the Peloponnesian War, although from the Spartan point of view it was surely the *Athenian* war. Its history was written by Thucydides (*c*. 471–400 B.C.), an Athenian who lived through it and personally took part in its beginning phases. At first the Athenians were able to prevail, even though they could not prevent the Spartan army from invading Attica and burning their farms. But in 415 B.C. the restless Athenians overreached themselves by sending a large fleet to Sicily, in hope of conquering that island. The whole expedition perished; then the Persians entered the war against Athens and supplied the Spartans with money for hiring rowers to man a fleet. Eventually, after several dramatic reversals on the sea, the Spartans destroyed Athens' last fleet, whereupon the city was compelled to surrender.

Sparta's victory in 404 B.C marked the end of the "Golden Age" of Greece; for amidst so much war and turmoil, the Athenians, with some help from other Greek cities, created classical Greek art and literature. Philosophy and science flourished also, though those branches of learning reached their high point later. Classical Greek culture became a model for later generations and still influences us today. It therefore deserves closer consideration.

CLASSICAL GREEK SOCIETY AND CULTURE

Athenian Society

As Athens became an imperial city, the trade and tribute of the Aegean and Black Sea coasts began to flow toward the city's harbor, Piraeus. Strangers from all over the Greek world came, too. On the eve of the Peloponnesian War the population of the city and its surrounding farmland was about 300,000, of whom nearly half were slaves and foreigners without political rights. Adult male Athenian citizens numbered not more than 50,000 men; yet they held an empire in their hands and governed themselves in a democratic way. Some 30,000 citizens were able to equip themselves to serve in the phalanx as heavy-armed infantry. Many of them were farmers, with small, family-sized plots of land in the countryside, who came into the city only on special occasions. Others had little or no land and depended on wages gained by rowing in the fleet. These citizens, when the fleet was idle, had lots of time to attend meetings of the assembly. They therefore tended to dominate its decisions, unless some unusual emergency called the farmers in from their fields.

Clearly the citizens who depended on booty and on wages gained by rowing in the fleet could not afford to stop annual campaigns. This was the reason for Athens' aggressive foreign policy. As long as it brought victories and new wealth, the more conservative countrymen were willing enough to go along with this democratic-imperialist policy. Pericles, who dominated Athenian counsels from about 461 until his death in 429 B.C., was the main architect of this coalition between the rowers of the fleet and the soldiers of the Athenian phalanx.

After Pericles' death, under the pressures of the Peloponnesian War, the two parties found their interests diverging. For a while the landless, urban element prevailed. Cleon was their chief spokesman in the assembly. Pericles' nephew, Alcibiades, attempted to revive the alliance of interests that had sustained his uncle's policy, but the conservative farmers distrusted Alcibiades' overweening personal ambition. He was driven from office just when his most dangerous project, the expedition to Sicily, got under way. Real trust and mutual collaboration between the two elements in Athenian society was never restored.

Similar social fissures opened among the citizens of most other Greek cities. By the time the Peloponnesian War had run its course, democrats who had been in alliance with Athens were discredited nearly everywhere. Thereafter oligarchies—government by the richer citizens—prevailed. Even in Athens, where democracy was restored, the old energy evaporated. Poor citizens no longer rowed in the fleet. They preferred to collect fees, if possible, for sitting on juries or attending the meetings of the assembly and left soldiering to hired mercenaries from the poorer parts of the Greek world.

Literature, Art, Science, and Philosophy

The fifty years between the defeat of the Persian invasion and the outbreak of the Peloponnesian War spanned a time when everything seemed possible to the Athenians. Dedicated to the greatness and glory of their polis, as almost all the citizens were, the Athenians constituted an unusually responsive, and at the same time critical, audience both for political speeches and for the public religious festivals that created Greek drama.

THE GREEK DRAMA   These festivals evolved from ceremonies honoring Dionysus, the god of wine. Rude songs and dances, performed by a chorus, first developed into a dialogue between a leader of the chorus and the rest of the dancers. Then a story line was introduced; and soon the story line required two or three actors to appear at the same time, so that they could talk to one another as well as to the chorus. Thus tragedy and comedy were born from a common root.

At the yearly festivals, the Athenians awarded a prize for the best poet as well as for the best-equipped and best-trained chorus. Under the stimulus of popular acclaim, three great tragedians arose in succession to test their poetry against the taste of the Athenians: Aeschylus (525–456 B.C.), Sophocles (495–405 B.C), and Euripides (480–406 B.C.). Each of them took old stories about gods and heroes—stories the Greeks thought of as ancient history—and put them in dramatic form. In addition to the magnificence of their verbal music—the poetry—the Greek tragedies were also serious efforts to express the truth, as each playwright saw it, about relations between human beings, the gods, fate, and the nature of things. Finally, song and dance, costumes, and painted scenery added their effect to the original performances.

We cannot share nor accurately recreate these ancient spectacles, but the dramatic texts that survive continue to command admiration. The ancients agreed; and next only to Homer, an apt quotation from one of the three Athenian tragedians became, throughout Greek and Roman antiquity, the mark of an educated man.

The Greek tragedians' view of the human condition was a modification of Homer's ideal. Their heroes were great and admirable persons, but proud and unwilling to submit to ordinary limitations upon human knowledge and power. Such pride brought its due punishment, either directly from the gods or through some natural and inevitable interlocking of cause and effect. Heroism, in other words, was treated as something admirable, but dangerous. Wisdom required submission to the human norm. Such a conclusion sat well with a city that demanded so much from its citizens both in war and in peace.

The gods, however, presented the dramatists with unresolved problems. Traditional stories, such as those enshrined in Homer, could not be reconciled with the moral standards of the age. Thoughtful Athenians found it harder and harder to respect gods who behaved like spoiled children. Yet few were ready to doubt the existence of the gods. When so many things happened in defiance of human purposes, it seemed obvious that stronger wills than their own were at work in the world.

Comedy had a very different character. It was topical, funny, and bawdy. Aristophanes (448–385 B.C.), the only comedian whose works survive, wrote during the Peloponnesian War and made fun of everyone of note, with absolutely no holds barred.

ART AND ARCHITECTURE   Art also achieved a new perfection. The greatest monuments of the age were the buildings on the Athenian Acropolis, dominated by Athena's temple, the Parthenon. Simplicity of line and exquisite refinement of detail made it, and the other buildings of the Acropolis, a standard for all later ages. Their ruins still remain—solid evidence of how skillfully the ancient Greeks designed and constructed public ceremonial buildings.

The outside of the Parthenon was richly decorated with sculpture, but the admiration of the ancients was especially reserved for the great gold and ivory statue of Athena that stood inside the temple. Its creator, Phidias (500–431 B.C.), was also entrusted with the construction at Olympia of a similar and equally famous statue of Zeus, who was known as "father of all the gods." Both of these statues have long since disappeared, but some of the surviving Parthenon friezes suggest the calm, aloof dignity with which Phidias endowed the gods' images.

THE GREEK HISTORIANS   No less impressive was the work of the two great historians of ancient Greece, Herodotus (c. 484–428 B.C.) and Thucydides (c. 471–400 B.C.). Herodotus was born at Halicarnassus, in Asia Minor, and traveled widely in Egypt and Asia. He probably spent little time in Athens. Nevertheless, he made that city the hero of his story of the Persian Wars. Thucydides did so as well, though with a tragic sense, when telling the story of the Peloponnesian War. His skill in analyzing motives and the interplay of forces within the Greek world during the war set a standard for historical writing that has seldom been

The Acropolis. The Parthenon is to the right. (D. A. Harrissiadis, Athens)

equaled since. Both historians were also great writers. Indeed, it was their literary style which later generations of Greeks and Romans valued most of all.

THE PRACTICE OF MEDICINE   Like the earliest Ionian philosophers, Herodotus and Thucydides kept the gods out of their histories. This same cast of mind, applied to the practice of medicine, created the Hippocratic school, named for Hippocrates of Cos, who lived about 400 B.C. Books attributed to Hippocrates or, more vaguely, to his school, carefully describe the symptoms and stages of various diseases. Hippocratic texts regarded diseases as natural and prescribed rest and quiet as cures.

Medical school graduates today often take the "Hippocratic oath." This oath required doctors to use their skills only to help their patients. It thus established an ideal of professional conduct that still stands.

THE GREEK PHILOSOPHERS   Even though Hippocrates and his school gave up the idea that disease was caused by some kind of alien "spirit" entering into a person's body, the ancient Greek doctors did not really get very far in their effort to understand natural bodily processes. The same was true of philosophers. Yet they did hit on some remarkably fertile ideas—for example, the atomic theory—and kept on bringing up new questions to wonder about. The philosopher Empedocles (c. 444 B.C.) tried to explain physical and biological changes as the result of combinations and recombinations of elements. Another philosopher, Anaxagoras, was banished from Athens about 440 B.C. for trying to explain the nature of the heavenly bodies by comparing them with red-hot stones.

A second line of development made logic the key to solving all problems. The founder of this school was Parmenides (*c*. 480 B.C.). He proved—at least to his own satisfaction—that all change was an illusion. He said that a thing either was or was not. If a thing really was—really had *being*—then it could never turn into its opposite, *non-being*. That would be a logical contradiction. Hence he concluded that whatever was, simply *was* and could not change.

Parmenides' logical puzzles provoked Democritus of Abdera (*c*. 440 B.C.) to suggest that the world was made up of atoms, so small as to be invisible but each of them unchangeable in itself—just like the unchangeable *being* that Parmenides had described. Democritus explained growth and decay as the result of the coming together and breaking up of clusters of atoms. To account for their movement he had, of course, to assume a void for them to move about in.

Other philosophers boldly set out to apply logic to human affairs. They were known as "Sophists," and they undertook to instruct young men in all they should know to enter public life. This meant, in a democratic city like Athens, teaching their pupils how to speak and argue a case in public in a way that would seem convincing. Some of the Sophists really thought that skillful manipulation of words could solve any problem. Like Parmenides, they assumed that words naturally or necessarily corresponded to *things*. Hence if a man got his words into order, so that one followed logically from the other, he would know all there was to know about the natural world and about human beings as well.

Other Sophists felt that truth did not really matter. Practical persons did not need to worry about whether words really corresponded to things in some ultimate sense. Words were merely tools for convincing other people. For the Sophists who thought in this way, right and justice and all the other moral standards to which politicians appealed were no more than useful devices for persuading the common people to accept one opinion or another.

Such ideas challenged the very basis of polis loyalty. If the world were nothing but a place where clever politicians attained power by deceiving their followers, then the willing dedication to common enterprises that had held Athenians together in war and peace was based on nothing but delusion. A real man would follow his own interests, regardless of appeals for self-sacrifice.

The disasters of the Peloponnesian War encouraged such attitudes. Sophistry, however, also provoked a powerful and important reaction. Socrates (469–399 B.C.) and his pupil Plato (427–347 B.C.) were the key figures. They sought to find a basis for truth and justice in the nature of things. Socrates never wrote anything, and we know of his thought mainly through dialogues in which Plato later recorded his own version of what Socrates had stood for. Plato also wrote dialogues to explain his own ideas, and sometimes he put words in Socrates' mouth that the real Socrates probably would never have used.

We can be sure, nevertheless, that Socrates spent his time in the streets and public places of Athens, talking with all comers and asking them difficult questions about truth and knowledge, the good life, and how people ought to behave. Socrates' questions swiftly showed how flimsy most common opinions really were. For himself, he claimed only to be aware of his own ignorance.

Socrates performed the duties of a citizen, fighting as an ordinary soldier during the Peloponnesian War, and serving on the council when elected to that post by lot. He never violated his own sense of justice and right. But some of the bright young men who listened with relish while Socrates deflated democratic politicians and would-be politicians took part in coups d'état against Athens' democratic government during the later stages of the Peloponnesian War.

When the democracy was restored after the war, therefore, Socrates was accused of corrupting the youth of the city. He was tried and condemned to die by drinking poison. Although his friends urged him to flee, he refused, arguing that he could not defy the laws of the city which had nourished him and protected him all his life. Before sorrowing friends, one of whom was Plato, Socrates drank the poison and died quietly in 399 B.C.

Plato became a philosopher through his association with Socrates. Like his teacher, Plato was always mainly concerned with how one ought to behave. To know how to behave properly, he felt, a person had to know what was good, true, and beautiful. All the different things commonly thought to be good or true or beautiful, he argued, must have something in common, just as all tables have something in common that make them into tables. A philosopher, therefore, ought to be able to find out exactly what it was that all similar things had in common. With enough study, a person might catch a glimpse of the changeless and immaterial essences (Plato called them ideas) that lie behind every particular example of any class of objects. Then he would know how to behave. Anything less, Plato felt, was just an opinion, not necessarily better than its opposite.

Plato developed this theory in a famous dialogue, *The Republic*. Yet he was never altogether satisfied with such an answer to his main problem. How could he really prove the existence of pure and unchanging ideas? And even if they did exist, how did things "participate" in them to become good, or true, or whatever? Since he was unable to solve such problems, Plato left to later generations a series of questions rather than definite answers. But Plato's questions defined most of the issues about which Western philosophers still concern themselves: Above all,

A bust of Plato (427–347 B.C.). He and his pupil Aristotle (384–322 B.C.) exercised a profound influence upon the development of Greek and Western thought. (The Vatican Museums)

how do we know? And how do words and ideas correspond to things? Plato's great pupil Aristotle (384–322 B.C.) had answers. He undertook the mastery of all the knowledge of his day and classified it into neat, logical parts. Nothing escaped him—or almost nothing. He perfected a method for arguing according to rules of logic, and he applied those rules to all the questions Plato had asked as well as to matters we call science, physics, biology, and even the weather. In fact, many of the distinctions we still take for granted—for example, between politics and economics—were first formulated by Aristotle.

Plato founded a school which Aristotle attended for many years before establishing his own separate lecture hall. After the two philosophers' deaths, their pupils kept the rival institutions going. Plato's Academy, in fact, lasted nearly 900 years, longer than any university yet has done. Other philosophic schools were set up later in Athens, and similar institutions arose in other cities. Athens, however, remained the most famous "university town" of the ancient world. There wealthy young men continued to come from all over the Greek and Roman world to sow their wild oats and learn enough philosophy to keep them out of mischief. As a result, little by little, philosophy as well as other aspects of Greek culture gradually turned into a code of conduct for well-to-do gentlemen.

Such a change could be carried through only after the city-state framework, which had raised Greek civilization so high, itself broke down. We must next consider how this happened.

THE RISE OF MACEDON AND THE EXPANSION OF HELLENISM EASTWARD

Conquest from the north, at the hands of a semibarbarous kingdom of Macedon, ended Greek political independence in 338 B.C. But before the Macedonians were able to transform the political basis of Greek life in this way, far-reaching changes had first to occur within the kingdom of Macedon itself.

Macedonian Empire

When the Persians marched into Greece in 480 B.C., they passed through Macedonia without meeting any resistance. Later the Athenians treated the kings of Macedon as a kind of dependent ally. Then under King Philip, who reigned from 359–336 B.C., Macedonian power grew very rapidly. Philip was able for the first time to get the Macedonian nobles to stop weakening the country with bitter feuds.

The secret of his success was to bring young noblemen to court, where they became accustomed to the luxuries and refinements of the Greek style of life. After spending some years at court, few of them cared to return to the backwoods. Instead they stayed to serve the king as administrators and army officers. This quickly allowed King Philip to mobilize the full resources of his kingdom for war. By comparison with any of the Greek states, the kingdom of Macedon was enormous. Hence, when the Macedonians stopped fighting among themselves and learned how to put an efficient phalanx into the field, superior numbers began to tell.

As for the Greeks, they found it impossible to unite. After Athens'

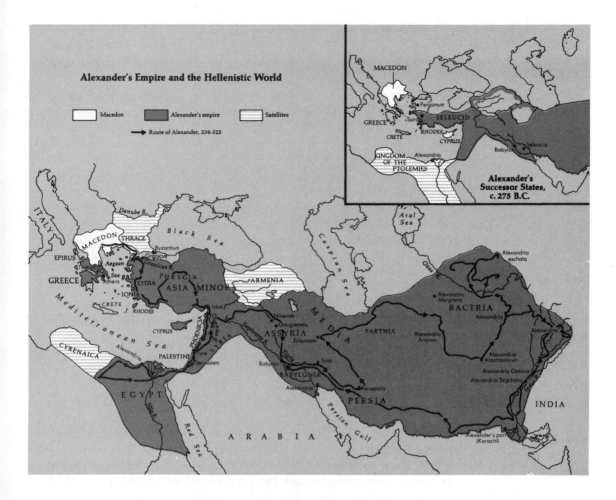

defeat in 404 B.C., for a while the Spartans were by far the strongest power in Greece. But they quickly antagonized all the other Greek cities and were overthrown by a coalition led by Thebes, a former Spartan ally. The Thebans, in turn, soon saw their allies against Sparta turn into enemies. They were, therefore, defeated easily enough by King Philip at the Battle of Chaeronea in 338 B.C.

ALEXANDER'S DAZZLING CAREER   King Philip made himself president of a league of all the Greek cities. His plan was to lead the Greeks in a war of "revenge" against Persia. But Philip was assassinated in 336 B.C., before he could start. His son, Alexander, was then only twenty years of age. The Thebans rose in revolt; so did barbarian Thracians to the north who had also been conquered by King Philip's armies. The youthful Alexander proved his mettle by the speed with which he checked both of these threats to his power. Thebes having been captured and destroyed, the rest of the Greek cities quickly submitted. Alexander then took up his father's project for an attack on Persia.

The great adventure began in 334 B.C. King Alexander won battle after battle as he moved deeper into Persian territory. In 333 B.C. he met and defeated the full muster of the Persian field army at Issus, in the southeast corner of Asia Minor. Then he marched his army into Egypt, where he founded the city of Alexandria before returning to face the Persian king Darius III again, defeating him this time at Gaugamela (331 B.C.) in northern Mesopotamia.

In the following year Darius III was murdered by his own followers. Alexander thereupon claimed to be the legitimate successor to the Persian throne. He had to campaign hard in the eastern parts of the Persian Empire to enforce his claim. Then he crossed the mountains into India, but when he tried to press ahead into the Ganges Valley his troops mutinied and he had to turn back. But Alexander did not return by the way he had come. Instead he followed the Indus River to its mouth and then marched through a barren desert, along the shores of the Persian Gulf, until his weary troops finally arrived in Mesopotamia. Soon afterward, in 323 B.C., Alexander died in Babylon at the age of thirty-three.

Such a career dazzled everyone. The young Alexander had set out to rival Achilles, hero of the *Iliad*; he more than succeeded. While in Egypt, priests of Amon-Re greeted him as a god, as they had greeted every ruler of Egypt from the days of the Old Kingdom. Alexander himself may have half-believed it (and many of his new subjects certainly did), but the idea shocked most Greeks and Macedonians.

He left an empire in confusion. Nevertheless, his reckless daring and vast conquests, all crowded into the space of eleven years, had changed the course of history. Alexander's importance lay not so much in his astounding military exploits and personal actions as in the way he spread Hellenism (Greek culture) everywhere he went. He founded numerous cities in the conquered lands. These became centers of Greek and Macedonian population. And wherever they settled, the conquerors brought their customs and institutions with them. As a result, in the centuries that followed, local peoples of the Middle East, northern India, and central Asia had ample opportunity to take over whatever they felt was worthwhile in the Greek cultural inheritance. The blending of Greek and Oriental civilization that resulted we call "Hellenistic" because, at least to begin with, the Hellenic element tended to dominate.

Alexander apparently wished to rule the empire he had conquered by uniting the Greek, Macedonian, and Persian peoples. He even arranged a mass marriage of his soldiers to Persian women, and he himself married a Persian princess. But when he died, this policy died with him.

HELLENISTIC MONARCHIES   His successors, hard-bitten Macedonian generals, despised both Greeks and Orientals. They had to depend on the loyalty of their Macedonian soldiers to maintain power. Soon the generals quarreled, and the great empire split apart. Egypt passed to the family of Ptolemy. Most of Asia fell into the hands of Seleucus I and his heirs. Macedonia itself eventually passed to the family of Antigonus I (Antigonus Cyclops).

Greece became independent again, but the separate cities were no more than playthings for the vast new Hellenistic monarchies. Efforts to form leagues that might withstand the new empires met with limited success, but Greece as a whole could never unite. The leading cities shifted back and forth between alliance with the Ptolemies, who had a powerful fleet, and with the Antigonids, who had a strong army. Never again did the Greek city-states really matter militarily. But the Greeks became very important to the new rulers of Asia and Egypt, who could not trust the native population and who badly needed well-trained soldiers and administrators. A great emigration therefore took place. Parts of Greece became depopulated. Farming passed into the hands of slaves or of poor strangers who had no voice in city politics.

Within Greek cities, political rights more and more were limited to the wealthy. In other words, the pattern of Greek society came to resemble the more ancient civilized society of the Middle East. At the same time, the Middle Eastern peoples eagerly took on many of the traits of Hellenic culture. Peoples farther east, in India and central Asia, also learned to admire and imitate aspects of the Greek achievement.

Cultural Blending in the Hellenistic East

The cultural interaction that resulted from Alexander's conquests was very complex. Babylonia and Egypt resisted Greek ways, as did the Jews. In Syria and Asia Minor, on the other hand, Greek dress, speech, and manners slowly seeped down the social scale until most city residents spoke, and in a certain sense were, Greek. Oddly enough, the Greek influence was also felt far to the east, where Alexander had founded a lot of garrison cities near the frontier. Persians and others living in those parts found Greek civilization more impressive than any they had known before. Even when a Parthian empire rose in Iran, the court and cities continued to prize Greek culture. Still farther to the east a Greek kingdom of Bactria (c. 250 B.C.) arose and flourished for about two centuries, straddling the mountain divide between India and central Asia.

Before Alexander the Great reached India, artists had never made representations of Buddha. When sculptured figures like this bodhisattva, first appeared, the influence of classical Greek sculpture was evident in the treatment of the hair and flowing robes. (The Bettmann Archive)

From Bactria, in turn, Greek influences passed into India and also spread farther east along trade routes toward China. Sculptural style is the main surviving evidence of this movement. But the sculptors of India and those of China were not copyists; they altered and transformed the

Greek models, just as, long before, the Greek sculptors of the Archaic Age (650–500 B.C.) had borrowed and transformed Egyptian models while developing their own art style.

About other matters we know far less. Some ideas in astronomy seem to have traveled from the Aegean to India, and perhaps to China. The idea of world empire may have entered Indian political theory by imitation of Persian or Hellenistic examples. But Greek impact in such distant parts remained always fragmentary, weak, and superficial.

Westward, however, things were different. The peoples of Italy and western Europe were still barbarians when classical Greek civilization reached its height. As familiarity with Greek culture spread, those who could afford it eagerly absorbed all they could of the Greek style of life and luxury. We shall consider this great movement next.

THE RISE OF ROME AND THE EXPANSION OF HELLENISM WESTWARD

Greece was conquered by the Romans but, as the Roman poet Horace expressed it, the captive Greeks revenged themselves by captivating their conquerors. But that is only part of the truth. Long before they allowed themselves to be captivated by Greek high culture, the Romans had a well-worked-out life-style of their own. This was a blending of native Latin ways with other cultural strands. In particular, the Etruscans contributed much to Roman life. The Etruscans were a semicivilized people who invaded northern and central Italy about 900 B.C. They probably came from Asia Minor, but no one is sure. Some of their skills and customs that became important in Rome—for example, the art of divination—seem closely connected with ancient Mesopotamian traditions. In addition, contact with both Greek and Phoenician traders, who carried goods up and down the coasts of Italy, added to the knowledge and skills of early Rome.

The Early Republic

According to legend, Rome was founded in 753 B.C. by two brothers, Romulus and Remus. The city began to grow into a center of some importance when a few Etruscans captured the place and made Rome their headquarters. Then about 509 B.C., through a revolt, the Etruscan king, Tarquin, was overthrown and a republic was established. The Romans now found themselves between two worlds: the world of city-state civilization—Etruscan, Greek, or Phoenician—on the one hand, and the old Latin world of loosely federated villages and tribes on the other. In the years that followed, the Romans managed to combine these two principles of political organization. For themselves they kept the city-state form which they had inherited from the Etruscan kings; but they also maintained a "Latin league" with simpler rural communities living nearby.

ROMAN SOCIETY   Warfare broke out practically every summer as soon as the harvest was in. For a long time the Romans' simple rural life made it hard for them to keep the better-equipped Etruscans at bay. Eventually, however, the Romans began to prevail. Rome's great advantage lay in numbers, for even the poorest Romans were ready to fight—especially when victory might mean new land for them to settle on and cultivate. The rulers of the Etruscan and Greek cities of Italy lived mostly on rents. They could not easily mobilize their rent-paying subjects, who often spoke a different language and were reluctant to fight in their masters' wars.

Roman society, too, was divided sharply between privileged patricians and the common folk, or plebs (plebeians). The plebs often quarreled with the patricians, demanding and in time securing a greater share of political power. But when outside danger threatened, the Romans managed to check their domestic strife and could therefore offer a united front to the outside world. No other city of Italy had this history. No other ruling clique could call upon the fighting manpower of the countryside in the way the Romans did. The result was first a slow and then a very rapid expansion of Roman power over Italy.

Roman manners long remained conservative. Traditional religious rites were strictly maintained; luxury and display of private wealth were frowned upon. Most citizens remained simple farmers. In the early days, even the patricians sometimes worked in the fields, as shown in the famous story of how Cincinnatus was called from the plow to become temporary dictator of Rome. As long as that pattern lasted, sympathy between the various social classes of Rome remained strong enough to allow the state to overcome all rivals in Italy.

FIRST CONQUESTS   The first important success for Roman arms came in 396 B.C. with the capture of the Etruscan city of Veii. The Romans destroyed the town and divided up the conquered land among themselves. This policy gave the plebs a solid stake in military enterprise. Success in battle meant land for the poor. Yet scarcely had this victory been won when Roman power suffered a severe setback. A raiding band of Gauls came down from the north and sacked the city in 390 B.C. Only the fortified capitol held out. Nevertheless, Rome recovered quickly and in the next fifty years conquered much new territory, becoming one of the "Great Powers" of the Italian peninsula. Seventy-five years later, after still further warfare, the Romans became supreme in all of Italy south of the Apennines (265 B.C.).

THE CONSTITUTION OF THE REPUBLIC   The Roman constitution was extremely complicated. Three different kinds of assemblies had different and at times overlapping powers. The *Comitia Curiata*, organized by "tribes," voted on laws. Election of magistrates, who exercised executive power, rested with the *Comitia centuriata*. This was a citizen body in military array; those with better equipment had a larger number of votes than the poor and ill-equipped. To counterbalance this distribution of power by wealth, the plebs created their own assembly, called the *Concilium plebis*. This body of plebeians elected tribunes of the people who had the power to veto any action undertaken by any magistrate.

In addition to the popular assemblies there was a Senate. This body originally admitted only patricians, but in 367 B.C. (when plebs were permitted to stand for election as magistrates), ex-magistrates of plebeian birth also were admitted to the Senate. Its influence was very great, largely because nearly all of the most active and individually powerful citizens of the state were members of the Senate. They usually tried to settle things quietly among themselves before bringing any important question before one or other of the assemblies.

ROMAN MILITARY ORGANIZATION   Rome's military organization differed from the phalanx of the Greeks. In the course of difficult wars in the hill country of central and southern Italy, the Romans discovered that the long, unbroken line of the phalanx was ineffective. Instead they divided their army into tactical units of 200 to 300 men, each of which could maneuver independently, suiting its line of march to the terrain. In flat open country the separate *maniples*, as these units were called, could form a solid battle line, like that which the Greeks worked so hard to maintain. In rough country each maniple could act on its own, keeping only loose contact with other units on its flanks. Maniples were grouped into larger units called legions, numbering, usually, about 6000 men. Special units of cavalry and light-armed troops supplemented the legions, but the strength of Roman armies rested always, as it had with the Greeks, on heavy-armed infantry. The great superiority of the Roman legions was their ability to fight in rough country as well as on open plains—a superiority which soon made them masters of the entire Mediterranean Basin.

THE FEDERAL PRINCIPLE   Another factor of critical importance was the use of the federal principle to bind subject allies to the Roman state. At strategic locations, the Romans established colonies of Roman citizens on conquered land. Such colonists continued to enjoy full citizens' rights, but they could vote only by coming to Rome. There were not nearly enough Roman citizens to occupy all of Italy, so in most cases the Romans simply concluded a treaty with a conquered town or tribe. Such treaties required the signatory "to have the same friends and enemies as the Roman people" and to send troops whenever and wherever called upon to do so. Everything else was left to local custom and initiative. The net effect of these arrangements was to allow the Roman city-state to organize the male population of all Italy for common military enterprises. By 265 B.C. no other state in the entire Mediterranean area could call on such large military resources.

Roman Conquest of the Western and Eastern Mediterranean

THE PUNIC WARS   The greatest test of Roman power took the form of a long struggle with Carthage, a Phoenician colony in north Africa. The Romans referred to the conflict as the Punic Wars ("Punic" being derived from *Poeni* which is Latin for Phoenicians).

While the Romans had been welding Italy together, the Carthaginians had also built an empire that in some ways resembled the Roman confederation. Carthaginian power, like Rome's, rested on collaboration between a city-state government and native manpower—in this case Numidian manpower in what is now Tunis and Algeria. Later, the Carthaginians added recruits from Spain (Iberia) and southern France to their armies. But Carthage differed from Rome in being first and foremost a naval and trading city. There was no great reservoir of countryfolk, sharing the ideas and attitudes of the state's leaders and backing up Carthaginian policy. Rome had such a reservoir; and in this, fundamentally, lay the Romans' decisive advantage.

War broke out over Sicily in 264 B.C. Before winning decisive victory, the Romans had to create their first fleet. Despite heavy losses, they persisted until Carthage ceded the island to them in 241 B.C. This victory presented the Romans with a new problem: How were they to govern an overseas territory which was inhabited by Phoenicians, Greeks, and various native peoples? Their decision was to put Sicily under a Roman governor, since it seemed impossible to trust the various local communities to govern themselves in alliance with Rome, as had been done so successfully in Italy.

The Carthaginians did not accept defeat passively. Instead, under the leadership of the Barca family, Carthage built a new empire along the coast of Spain. The Barcas created a formidable army by enlisting native Celts and Iberians under their personal command. They used this force to capture new territory and extend their power, much as the Romans

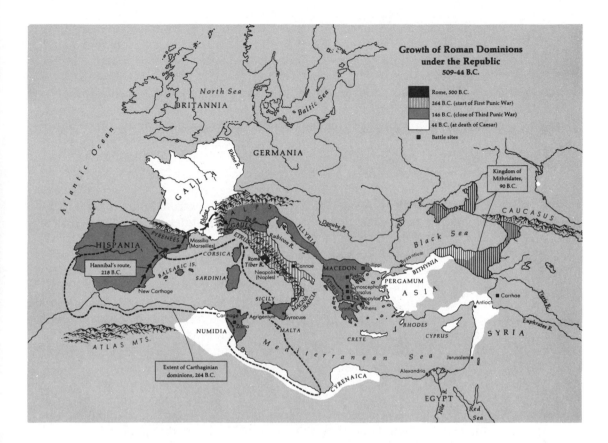

had done in Italy. This aroused Roman fears. Hence, when Saguntum (modern name: Sagunto)—a small Greek city situated along the Spanish coast south of the Ebro River—asked Rome for an alliance against the Carthaginians, the Romans agreed. In effect this act said to Carthaginian empire-builders, "So far and no further."

Hannibal, who had just succeeded his father in command of Carthaginian forces in Spain, was not willing to submit to this kind of limitation. He therefore attacked and captured Saguntum in 219 B.C. The Romans declared war. Hannibal promptly marched from Iberia (Spain) through southern Gaul (France) and over the Alps, bringing his war elephants with him. In northern Italy he met and defeated Roman armies in two major battles. Victory seemed to be in his hands.

Yet the Romans stubbornly refused to make peace. After another costly defeat at Cannae in southern Italy (216 B.C.), they decided to fight no more battles against Hannibal. Instead they sent out armies year after year to shadow Hannibal's every move, cut off stragglers, and in general make life difficult for the invaders. Cities that had broken their treaties with Rome and opened their gates to Hannibal, whether voluntarily or by force, were besieged by still other Roman armies. Hannibal could not match Roman numbers; little by little the balance in Italy turned against him.

Carthage and Rome spared no effort in this great war. It eventually turned into a "world war" involving the entire Mediterranean region. Carthage, for example, made an alliance with the king of Macedonia, who, however, contributed little to the struggle. Rome countered by sending an expeditionary force to Spain and making an alliance with the king of western Numidia (modern Algeria) against Carthage.

Carthage eventually broke under the strain. In 207 B.C. the Romans defeated reinforcements which had come to Italy from Spain to help Hannibal. The next year, Scipio, a Roman general later nicknamed "Africanus," drove the Carthaginians out of Spain. Scipio also made a secret alliance with the king of eastern Numidia, who had long been an ally of Carthage. In 204 B.C., therefore, when he led a Roman army into Africa, all the Numidians went over to his side. This threatened Carthage's position in north Africa even more seriously than Hannibal's presence in Italy threatened Roman power. The Carthaginians had to call their great general home. Accordingly, in 202 B.C. Hannibal fought the last battle of the war at Zama in north Africa, not far from Carthage itself. There for the first time he met defeat. Carthage had to sue for peace.

The Romans wanted to be sure that the Carthaginians could never again endanger them. Spain became a Roman province. The Numidians were declared free. The Carthaginians agreed to pay a war indemnity, to destroy their fleet of warships, and "to have the same friends and enemies as the Roman people," that is, to become Rome's subject allies.

Within a generation Carthaginian trade revived. This excited alarm in Rome, where the memory of Hannibal's invasion remained fresh. A party of old Romans kept demanding the utter destruction of their former rival. In 149 B.C. a quarrel arose between the Carthaginians and the Numidians. Rome sent an army. The Carthaginians tried to make peace again, but the Romans would not agree. Instead they sacked and destroyed the city and, according to legend, sowed the area with salt so that Carthage could never rise again. The region around the former city was made into a province; the rest of north Africa was handed over to the Numidians. Rome was now absolute master of the western Mediterranean.

Hannibal's years in Italy led to great changes there. His soldiers lived off the country. Year after year the small farmers of Italy were called to serve in the Roman armies. The land became desolate. Many army veterans felt no wish to go back to the hard, quiet life of the farm. To start again without tools or animals, or even a house, was difficult at best. To loiter in the city and see what might turn up seemed far more attractive to a great many discharged veterans. Supplies of grain coming from Sicily as tribute made such an existence possible. If, in addition, booty from new campaigns continued to roll in, city life seemed obviously more attractive than rustic poverty.

ROME'S CONQUEST OF THE EASTERN MEDITERRANEAN   Rome had reason enough to quarrel with the powers of the eastern Mediterranean. In 215 B.C., when Hannibal was at Rome's gates, the Macedonians had made an alliance with Carthage. After Carthage had been defeated, the Romans were therefore ready to respond when Greek cities appealed to them for aid against the Macedonian king. Rome sent an army into Greece in 197 B.C. and defeated the Macedonian phalanx at Cynoscephalae (Dog's Head). The Romans then demanded that the Macedonians pay an indemnity, reduce their army to 5000 men, and make war only with Roman approval. As for the Greeks, like the Numidians, they were declared free.

No such settlement could last. All sorts of quarrels among the Greeks were appealed to Rome, and though some Romans resisted involvement, others were very ready to intervene, since soldiers and commanders alike found the rich booty and easy victories of campaigning in the east too attractive to give up. In 148 B.C., therefore, after another campaign, Macedonia also was made into a province. Rome was now able to dominate the eastern as well as the western Mediterranean.

Changes in the Economic and Political Life of the Romans

By this time the old simplicity of Roman life had gone by the boards. Land-grabbing senators had taken possession of large estates in southern and central Italy, where Hannibal's devastation had emptied the countryside. Slaves cultivated those lands or tended sheep and cattle on them. A new class of traders and financiers had grown wealthy by organizing the collection of tribute from the provinces. Rome, in other words, evolved very rapidly into a society sharply divided between rich and poor, free and slave, citizen and noncitizen, soldier and civilian. A rash of civil wars and upheavals resulted, including a spectacular slave revolt led by Spartacus, a Thracian gladiator.

Efforts at reform got nowhere. Tiberius Gracchus in 133 B.C. tried to use his power as tribune of the people to break up the great estates and divide the land among the city poor. He was murdered in an election riot; and when his brother, Gaius Gracchus, tried to renew and extend Tiberius' program in 123 B.C., he, too, was killed by his political opponents. Street gangs of thugs began to play an important part in electioneering, but this kind of violence was soon eclipsed by the soldiers, who in the end overturned the civilian game of politics.

Roman armies became increasingly professional, especially after property qualifications for serving in the ranks were waived in 106 B.C. This meant that the old idea of sending soldiers back home to the farm when a campaign was over could not work any longer. Veterans had no home to return to. If they could not be reenlisted for another war almost at once, land had to be found for them. The return of a victorious army thus created a crisis for Romans at home. This became painfully clear in 100 B.C., when Gaius Marius, after victories in northern Africa and in southern France, acquired land for his soldiers by executing his political opponents among the Senatorial party and seizing their possessions. His example was soon followed by Sulla (83–79 B.C.), who tried to restore the old government by violently suppressing the so-called "Popular" party that Marius had helped to establish.

POMPEY AND CAESAR: RIVALS FOR POLITICAL POWER   The feud between rival cliques continued in the next generation. Pompey the Great (Gnaeus Pompeius Magnus) and Julius Caesar became the two chief figures. Pompey conquered the East, putting Syria and most of Asia Minor under Roman governors and setting up client kings in Palestine and elsewhere (65–62 B.C.). Caesar conquered Gaul as far as the Rhine (58–51 B.C.) and made a brief invasion of Britain. In 60 B.C. Caesar, Pompey, and Marcus Licinius Crassus (a Roman financier and politician) entered into a political alliance that allowed them to control the Roman state.

The First Triumvirate, as this arrangement was called, lasted until 53 B.C. when Crassus met his death in an attempt to conquer Parthia to the east.

Not long afterward Pompey and Caesar quarreled, and civil war broke out. Caesar prevailed; but not until 45 B.C. was he able to bring the entire Roman world under his single military control. Caesar thereupon returned to Rome, where he faced the task of somehow putting the government in order.

Caesar probably wished to control Roman politics from behind the scenes, but his enemies accused him of wishing to be king. A clique of conspirators decided that the only way to preserve the Republic was to kill him. They therefore slew Caesar on the steps of the Senate house in 44 B.C.

Civil war broke out again. Caesar's friends rallied to defeat the armies raised by his assassins. Then they set out to divide the Mediterranean world between them. Mark Antony, Caesar's most ambitious general, took the East. He expected to win great victories against the Parthians and to return, as Caesar had done, in triumph to Rome, where he could dictate his own terms to his rivals. Octavian, Caesar's adopted son and heir, was assigned the difficult task of trying to bring peace and order to Italy. He had to share power with another of Caesar's generals, Marcus Lepidus.

This so-called Second Triumvirate lasted from 43 B.C. until 32 B.C., when open war broke out between Antony and Octavian. Octavian's fleet won a great battle at Actium (31 B.C.) and Antony fled to his headquarters in Egypt. There he committed suicide. His ally and mistress, Cleopatra, did the same when it became clear that she could not captivate the victorious Octavian as she had captivated first Caesar himself and then Antony.

The Beginning of the Roman Empire

By 30 B.C., therefore, the entire Mediterranean basin was once again under the military control of a single man, Octavian, or, as he is more commonly called, "Augustus"—an honorific title meaning "great and holy one." The new ruler of the Roman world proceeded cautiously. He personally kept command of most of the Roman armies. He stationed the troops along the frontiers, where they could keep barbarians at bay and had less temptation to intervene in politics. As *imperator* (commander) of the soldiers, Augustus' power remained supreme.

Yet Augustus deliberately disguised the military basis of his power. In 27 B.C. he "restored the Republic"—at least in name. What he restored were the procedures of electing magistrates and of consulting the Senate on matters of importance. Augustus also organized police and fire services for the city of Rome and took charge of supplying the city with grain.

In general, a far more orderly life set in, free from the fierce destructiveness of the period of civil wars. As *princeps* (first citizen) of the Senate and imperator of the soldiers, Augustus exercised firm control in the city and provinces, although in theory the Senate and people of Rome once more ruled themselves according to the old Republican constitution. The difference was that only men whom Augustus had approved could expect to be elected to office. All the zest went out of politics. But few grumbled. Civil war and disorder were too high a price to pay for the old Republican liberties.

THE PAX ROMANA   The principate, as the system of government Augustus established is usually called, lasted more than 200 years. During most of that period of time, the peoples of the Roman Empire enjoyed unbroken public peace. To be sure, there was plenty of fighting along the frontiers against barbarian tribes; two bitter Jewish revolts devastated

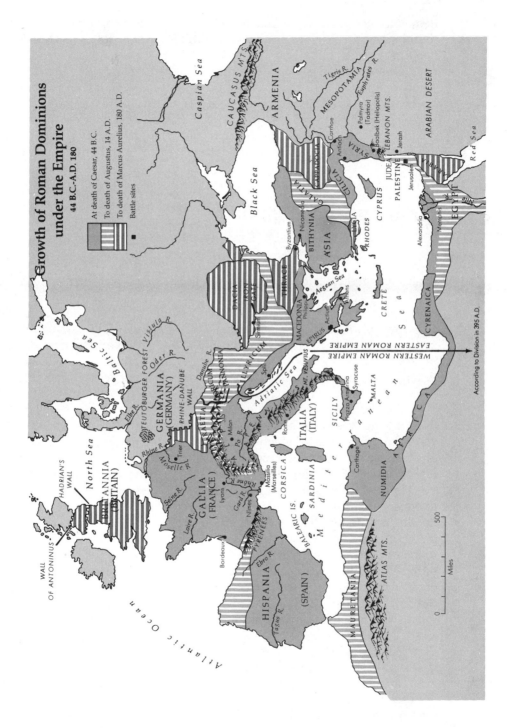

Growth of Roman Dominions under the Empire
44 B.C.–A.D. 180

At death of Caesar, 44 B.C.
To death of Augustus, 14 A.D.
To death of Marcus Aurelius, 180 A.D.
■ Battle sites

Caspian Sea

CAUCASUS MTS.

ARMENIA

Tigris R.

MESOPOTAMIA

Carrhoe

•Palmyra (Tadmor)
•Baalbek (Heliopolis)
LEBANON MTS.
•Jerash

ARABIAN DESERT

CAPPADOCIA

GALATIA

CILICIA

SYRIA
•Antioch

Red Sea

Black Sea

Byzantium

Nicomedia•

BITHYNIA

ASIA

CYPRUS

JUDEA
PALESTINE
Jerusalem•

EGYPT

Nile R.

Memphis•

Alexandria•

LYCIA

RHODES

CYRENAICA

•Ephesus
•Athens

Aegean Sea

MACEDONIA
Philippi•

CRETE

Mediterranean Sea

EPIRUS
•Actium

THRACE

DACIA
IRON
GATE

ILLYRICUM

Sirmium•

Danube R.
PANNONIA
RAETIA
NORICUM
•Split

Vistula R.

Oder R.

TEUTOBURGER FOREST

GERMANIA
(GERMANY)

Elbe R.

RHINE-DANUBE
WALL

Rhine R.
•Trier

Moselle R.

Baltic Sea

North Sea

BRITANNIA
(BRITAIN)

HADRIAN'S
WALL

WALL
OF ANTONINUS

Atlantic Ocean

GALLIA
(FRANCE)

Seine R.

Loire R.

Bordeaux•

Garonne R.

PYRENEES

Ebro R.

HISPANIA
(SPAIN)

Tagus R.

Lyons•
Rhône R.

Massilia
(Marseilles)•

Nîmes•

BALEARIC IS.

CORSICA

SARDINIA

Po R.
•Milan

ITALIA
(ITALY)
MT. VESUVIUS
•Rome
•Piazza Armerina

MALTA

SICILY
•Syracuse

Carthage•

NUMIDIA

MAURETANIA

ATLAS MTS.

A F R I C A

Adriatic Sea

WESTERN ROMAN EMPIRE

EASTERN ROMAN EMPIRE

According to Division in 395 A.D.

0   500
Miles

Palestine; and twice the Roman legions deserted their posts on the frontiers to take part in civil war to determine who should succeed to the imperial purple. But never before or afterward in European history did so many people—some 60 million according to one estimate—enjoy peace for so long a period of time. Memory of *Pax Romana*—the Roman peace—lasted for centuries.

A weakness of the principate was uncertainty over succession to the imperial position. In theory the office was freely conferred by the Senate and people of Rome. In practice each reigning emperor was at pains to choose his successor—often a son or other relative. Memories of the old Republican freedom, when elections were real and no single person controlled the state, lingered for a long time. Not until the Roman noble families died out, and new provincial landholders took their place as the principal supporters of the Roman Empire, did these memories fade away. This occurred by about A.D. 100, when a series of "good" emperors came to power, beginning with Nerva in A.D. 96 and ending with Marcus Aurelius, who died in A.D. 180.

Greco-Roman Culture

As long as Roman society was composed of small farmers and conservative patricians, Rome offered small scope for the arts and refinements of civilization. With the very rapid change that came to Roman society during and after the Punic Wars, however, a few wealthy Romans developed an interest in Greek art, literature, and thought. A far larger number of the Mediterranean world's new masters became interested in fancy cooking, popular music, and party manners. The new wealth also allowed the Romans to develop their own customs in new ways. For example, gladiatorial combat, which had once been performed as a religious ritual at dead heroes' graves, was revived and made into a spectator sport. Men fought against men or were pitted against wild beasts, as the Roman people howled with excitement. One of the best ways for an aspiring politician to win votes was to put on a particularly lavish display of gladiatorial games. Later, under the principate, this became the responsibility of the emperor.

CICERO   Romans were not philosophic. They found suitable ideas ready and waiting among the Greeks, where philosophy had already become a school of good manners for the leisured class. But to be available to the Roman world, Greek ideas had to be translated into Latin. This task was vigorously undertaken by the famous orator, Cicero (Marcus Tullius Cicero, 106–43 B.C.). Cicero sometimes had to invent new words to carry

Marcus Tullius Cicero, 106–43 B.C.
(*New York Public Library Picture
Collection*)

new meanings into Latin, and in doing so he made it a more flexible, sophisticated tongue. His orations and private letters, published after his death, made it possible for us to know him, both as a private and public figure, more intimately than any other man of classical antiquity. His use of Latin became standard in Renaissance Europe and is still taught in our schools. His writings became the model for western Europe's medieval and early modern men of letters.

PLAYWRIGHTS AND HISTORIANS   Plautus (*c*. 254–184 B.C.) and Terence (*c*. 190–159 B.C.) are the only significant Roman playwrights whose work survives. They wrote comedies of manners, borrowing heavily from Greek comedy writers of the Hellenistic period. The two greatest Roman historians were Livy and Tacitus. Livy (59 B.C.–A.D. 17) wrote a very long history of the Roman Republic, of which only a small part has survived. He was full of regret for the decay of the old Roman simplicity and virtue, which he held to be responsible for the breakdown of Republican government. Tacitus (A.D. 55–118) wrote of the empire, full of bitterness at the loss of liberty that Augustus and his successors had inflicted upon Rome.

THE ROMAN POETS   Next to Cicero, the greatest literary figures of the Roman world were poets. Lyric whimsy, eager explanation of why there was nothing to fear from the gods, reflection on the joys of private life, and epic accounts of the foundation and destiny of Rome all found a place in Latin poetry. Vergil (70–19 B.C.) was the most famous and influential. He modeled his great epic poem, *The Aeneid*, on Homer, intending to give the Romans as respectable an origin as the Greeks could claim. Vergil traced the wanderings of Aeneas, a Trojan prince, from Troy to Italy where his descendants, in due course, established the city of Rome. In his great poem, Vergil defined Rome's role: not to rival Greece as the home of art and literature, but to rule the world and put down the proud.

BIOGRAPHICAL, PHILOSOPHICAL, AND SCIENTIFIC WRITINGS
About A.D. 100 Greek writing revived. Plutarch (A.D. 46–120) wrote a popular series of parallel lives of the Greeks and Romans. Marcus Aurelius, the Roman emperor (who reigned A.D. 161–180), wrote his *Meditations* in Greek. Galen (*c*. A.D. 130–200), a doctor, and Ptolemy (*c*. A.D. 85–165), a mathematician, geographer, and astronomer, each wrote extremely influential handbooks of science. Galen's work became a standard for medical practitioners of both the Islamic and Christian worlds until after 1700. Ptolemy's authority was overthrown only by the great European explorations after 1500 and by the astronomical advances associated with the names of Copernicus and Galileo.

ROMAN LAW   Roman law, the other great inheritance passed on from the ancient world to medieval Europe, matured later. Its development began in the early days of the Republic, when *Praetors* (the principal judicial magistrates) adopted the custom, at the beginning of their term of office, of publishing the laws they intended to enforce. Under the empire this practice continued, and the praetors' edicts assumed a more or less standard form.

Changes came as Roman law had to be applied more and more widely to citizens who were scattered all over the empire. This caused jurists to wonder about the relationships between natural law, which some Hellenistic philosophers had emphasized, and the actual laws magistrates were prepared to enforce. Simple but radical principles, such as recognizing one—and only one—owner with full rights of use or sale for each piece of property, thus evolved. Law so conceived could be applied to private relationships everywhere and anywhere in the world. Such laws made relationships among strangers far more predictable, flexible, and precise.

Lasting formulations of the Roman law, however, did not occur until after A.D. 200, and the definitive code was drawn up only under Emperor Justinian (who reigned A.D. 527–565).

In A.D. 180 the law was still growing. Little else in the cultural world of upper-class Romans was. Great artists, writers, philosophers, or scientists failed to appear. Polite education and the luxuries of civilized life became very widely available to landlords in all the provinces of the

Roman Empire. Everywhere the Greek model, as modified and adjusted to Latin tastes in the period of the later Republic and early empire, prevailed. But the trouble was that no one cared very much any longer.

Statues and handsome public buildings sprang up all over Spain, Gaul, and the other parts of western Europe that were brought under Roman rule. (Augustus had conquered the lands south of the Danube; his successors added Britain and Dacia; for a short time they also controlled Mesopotamia.) Orators delivered elaborate speeches about unimportant subjects, and provincial towns put on gladiatorial shows modeled on those that made Rome famous.

All things that had made life exciting in the times when Athens fought for survival, or when Rome first built the empire, seemed to have gone. The lower classes were not interested in their masters' philosophy and art; nor were the masters deeply committed. Human aspiration had turned away from the classical forms of expression, seeking instead a predominantly religious outlet. In the next chapter we shall try to see the ways in which this happened.

CONCLUSION

The classical civilization of ancient Greece and Rome attained an enormous success between 500 B.C. and A.D. 200. The Greeks, an unruly little people on the fringes of the great Persian Empire in 500 B.C., turned the tables completely. The whole Middle Eastern region felt the impact of their culture after Alexander's conquests; even distant India and China found aspects and elements of the Greek achievement interesting. Westward, too, Greek ideas, art, and styles of life spread widely after the Romans had conquered Greece itself along with all the rest of the Mediterranean world.

What was the essence of this Greco-Roman classical civilization? In Athens' greatest days, active and eager participation by all citizens in the public life and culture of the city was a hallmark that later generations never forgot, and never lived up to. Rome, too, in its early days involved its citizens in war and politics far more deeply than most rival states ever tried to do. The ancients themselves believed that political freedom—the right of every citizen to take part in public debate and decision-making according to some recognized rules of law—was at the heart of their greatness. Though power was, *in fact*, often concentrated in the hands of a few men or even of a single person, as in the days of the Roman Empire, the ideal of free participation in political affairs always remained a distinguishing mark of the ancient classical world.

Classical art and thought, too, had their own distinctive characteristics. Sculptors made their works resemble real human beings, even down to such details as showing veins in arms and legs. Most classical thinkers relied on their powers of reason and argument, and accepted nothing on the strength of sacred revelation. These ideals, too, were not fully maintained, especially in the eastern parts of the Greek world. But people never forgot them either, even when it was perfectly clear that reason and argument would not permit citizens to agree about very much.

Political liberty, naturalistic art, and rationalistic thought—these perhaps made up the essence of classical civilization. These values were enshrined in the pages of the great classical writers, and through them have continued to be a living force down to the present. The heights of heroism and despair described in the works of Aeschylus, Herodotus, Thucydides, Plato, Aristotle, Cicero, and Vergil—to name only the most illustrious—have provided models and examples for later generations of Europeans and their descendants overseas. In this fashion the influence of deeds done long ago at Marathon and Salamis, Zama and Actium, looms large even today. For the ancient Greeks and Romans are a pivotal part of our past; and like all human beings everywhere, we are to some degree prisoners of our past.

CHAPTER 9

Civilized Religions and Barbarian Invasions

220 B.C. to A.D. 600

Between about 100 B.C. and A.D. 200, the civilized peoples of Eurasia organized caravan and sea trade far more effectively than ever before. The result was a mingling of goods, diseases, and ideas across the whole breadth of Eurasia, from the British islands on the west to the Japanese islands on the east, and embracing India and the islands of Indonesia as well as parts of east and west Africa.

Population losses, resulting in large part from the ravages of new and unfamiliar diseases, helped to break off regular and close contact across such long distances after A.D. 200. In addition, barbarian raiding and conquests, issuing mainly from the steppe regions of Eurasia, tended to break up peaceful trade.

But before the separate civilizations of Eurasia fell back upon their own local resources, the mixing and blending of traditions, which traders did so much to carry forward, stimulated the creation of three new world religions: Mahayana Buddhism, Christianity, and Hinduism. In later centuries, each of these faiths spread widely, in part through conscious missionary efforts, and provided a lasting cultural mold for a large part of civilized humanity. The barbarian migrations that assumed a new scale after A.D. 200 established language and cultural boundaries that have lasted until the present in many parts of Europe and, to a lesser extent, also in Asia.

The rise of new faiths and the migration of peoples are thus the dominant themes of this phase of world history.

TRADE ROUTES
AND EMPIRES OF EURASIA

The rise of the Roman Empire around the Mediterranean Sea in the Eurasian Far West closely paralleled the establishment of a united China in the Far East. Indeed, the foundation of the Han Dynasty in 202 B.C. came in the year of Hannibal's defeat at Zama in north Africa—the event that established Rome's supremacy in the entire Mediterranean area. The fall of the Han Dynasty in A.D. 220, more than 400 years later, came at a time when the Roman Empire was also suffering from serious barbarian invasions and seemed near collapse. These parallel events were not entirely unrelated. The two great empires were in contact with each other indirectly through trade. In addition, both of them bordered on the Eurasian steppe, where barbarian nomads acted upon each other and upon their civilized neighbors in important ways. In this chapter we shall first consider the influences that passed between the different civilizations of Europe and Asia along the trade routes, and then see how the barbarians of the steppe, by their conquests and migrations, changed the course of civilized history between about 200 B.C. and A.D. 600.

When China was first united by Shih Huang Ti (221 B.C.), the Far East was still isolated from western Asia by the desert region of the Tarim basin. In 102 B.C., however, the Chinese emperor, Wu Ti, sent an army westward to Fergana in west-central Asia. This opened regular contact between China and the civilized peoples of the Middle East for the first time. More than 200 years before, the conquests of Alexander of Macedonia in India had reestablished a connection between the Middle East and India. His successors in Asia, the Seleucids, maintained diplomatic and trade relations with India, where soon after Alexander's time the king of Magadha conquered all of the Ganges and Indus valleys and founded the Maurya Empire. The civilized region of the Middle East therefore was already in regular touch with both the Greek and Indian worlds when the Chinese showed up in Fergana and joined the circle of interacting Old World civilizations.

Increase of Trade

In the course of the next 100 years, regular caravan trade was organized between China and the eastern end of the Mediterranean Sea. This required a great deal of effort. To organize, supply, and protect a caravan was as complicated as equipping a ship for distant voyaging. Local authori-

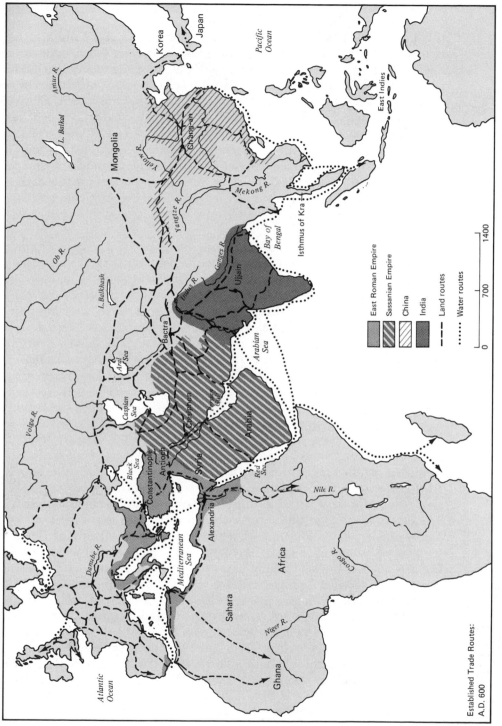

Established Trade Routes:
A.D. 600

Established Trade Routes: A.D. 600

ties had to establish safe resting places (caravansaries). They also had to learn that they could not tax traveling merchants so heavily as to destroy their profit. Means of financing trade and methods of distributing goods at both ends of the caravan route also had to be found before trade could become important. In ways we know nothing about, all these things were done. As a result, what the Romans called the "Silk Road" came into existence by about A.D. 1. It ran from the Wei Valley in China through central Asia to Mesopotamia, and ended at Antioch on the Orontes River in Syria. Thousands of men and animals began to move back and forth along nearly 4000 miles of tracks rubbed smooth by camels' feet. Goods and ideas, as well as diseases, traveled with the caravans. Their combined impact on the civilized societies along the way was very great.

At about the same time, the sea routes between the Mediterranean area and India gained new importance. About 120 B.C. a ship captain sailing from the Red Sea discovered that he could steer his ship by the stars, far from land, and travel directly from the Straits of Aden to southern India. Such a trip took a much shorter time than when vessels skirted the coast and stayed within sight of land. Moreover, there were no tolls to pay or pirates to fear far out at sea. And by waiting for the monsoon wind to reverse itself, the return voyage became just as easy. This discovery soon gave employment to a fleet of vessels sailing between Egypt and India. Venturesome captains soon explored the Bay of Bengal; and not long after A.D. 180, at least one traveler portaged across the Isthmus of Kra, took ship again on the eastern side, and arrived in southern China, where he claimed to be an ambassador sent by the Roman emperor, Marcus Aurelius. In this fashion, therefore, the seafaring peoples of southeast Asia made firm contact with the seafarers of the Mediterranean. All the southern seas became a single trade network.

Many different sorts of things traveled along these trade routes. The first Chinese expedition to Fergana brought back grapevines, alfalfa, and warhorses. Later they imported metals, glass, and silver. The Romans wanted silk above all else, for this fabric became extremely fashionable. Chinese silk cloth was actually unraveled in Antioch and then rewoven into a much thinner, semitransparent fabric. From India came perfumes and spices. Alexandria sent many sorts of manufactured goods, including mass-produced statuettes of Greek gods, to India. In addition, coined money was exported to India from Roman territory.

Other trade routes connected barbarian peoples, living both north and south, with the belt of civilized territory that had come into existence across the middle of Eurasia. An "amber route," for example, ran from the Baltic Sea to the Black Sea, following the river courses. Camel caravans also began to cross the Sahara, thereby linking west Africa with Roman north Africa. Along this route gold from the Niger River area was exchanged for salt and other products. India's trade relations with southeast Asia and Indonesia became quite important. China, similarly, traded with the nomads of Mongolia and opened up political and commercial relations with both Korea and Japan before A.D. 600. Altogether, the range of civilized influence was clearly expanding along every open frontier.

Spread of Diseases

But with goods came new diseases, some of which proved very damaging to densely settled civilized populations. Exactly what kind of germs caused ancient plagues and epidemics cannot now be discovered. Records are incomplete and usually do not describe symptoms in a way that would permit modern doctors to know what the disease was. Yet we do know this: in modern times, childhood diseases—measles, mumps, chicken pox, and even the common cold—can be killers when they reach a population that has never before been exposed to them. At some time in history, civilized peoples must have acquired their present levels of immunity to these diseases. The centuries between 100 B.C. and A.D. 300 were probably the time when at least some of them first entered into general circulation. Long-distance trade in Eurasia and Africa was more regular than ever before; and diseases, too, could therefore spread farther and faster than ever before. We have references to unusually severe epidemics, especially in Roman and Chinese sources; and much evidence shows that both the Roman and Han Empires suffered from serious depopulation beginning soon after A.D. 100.

It is worth noting that when the ravages of a disease became sufficiently serious, the situation tended to correct itself. As population became thinner, infections passed less often from one person to another because close contacts became fewer. In addition, severe epidemics interrupted long-distance trade and travel. Depopulation meant less wealth; less wealth made trade unprofitable; and as trade became unprofitable, strangers who might accidentally bring in some new disease stopped coming. Moreover, those who survived developed various kinds of biological immunity to each disease. When enough people in a given population become immune, epidemics cease. The disease does not disappear entirely; instead it may become a childhood disease, not very likely to kill anyone because children inherit partial immunities from their parents.

A natural cycle of this kind probably took place in the ancient world. New diseases spread, especially in Europe and China, and at first killed off large numbers of people. Then, in the course of three or four centuries, rising immunities and greater isolation combined to check the spread of infection. But before that occurred, both the Roman and the Chinese empires had collapsed. Depopulation due to disease probably played a part in weakening both these great empires. But with records as imperfect as they are, this explanation is no more than a good guess—not an established fact.

Exchange of Ideas

Exchange of ideas along the trade routes of the Old World was even more important for later history than the exchange of goods and diseases.

The most significant of these ideas were religious, although some were (or pretended to be) scientific. Thus, for example, what Europe later knew as alchemy seems to have started among Chinese Taoists, who tried to concoct a magic drink to prolong life. As alchemy spread westward, its sister "science," astrology, traveled eastward to India and China from Alexandria in Egypt, where it originated from a combination of Greek and Babylonian ideas about the heavens.

Alchemy and astrology were always more or less secret sciences and much mixed with magic. New religious ideas, on the contrary, were public and affected everyone. Three new world religions—Mahayana Buddhism, Hinduism, and Christianity—arose between 200 B.C. and A.D. 200. And, in the next country, Manichaeism (founded in A.D. 241 by a Persian prophet named Mani), almost succeeded in becoming a fourth world faith. Each of these religions expressed a similar central idea: every believer could attain salvation through a close relationship with a savior who was at one and the same time both human and divine. For all of them, the world of eternity beyond the grave was more important than the ordinary, everyday world. Common to all three of the major religions was the belief that women, too, had souls to be saved, and they were therefore expected to take an equal part in religious observances with men. These are important resemblances, but the differences were also very great.

MAHAYANA BUDDHISM

Mahayana Buddhism shifted emphasis away from self-annihilation, which earlier Buddhism had declared to be the supreme religious goal. Instead, Mahayana Buddhists believed that the souls of good persons entered any of a number of "heavens" where they might live happily until, at last, every single soul in the universe was freed from the suffering of incarnation. At that far-off time, all the souls of the world would complete the cosmic cycle by entering Nirvana together. But until that time, it was the function of saved souls to help others up the ladder of existence, until they too could escape reincarnation and enter heaven. Souls that had purified themselves and reached heaven were called "bodhisattvas." They closely resembled Christian saints.

From a practical point of view, an ordinary person might help his or her soul along by praying to a bodhisattva or by honoring him in some other way. The bodhisattva might then be expected to take particular care of the soul of the person who had called upon his aid. Buddha ceased to be a historical figure for the monks who speculated along these lines. They argued that there had been innumerable Buddhas who took on a visible body in order to explain salvation to souls who needed help; and since there had also been innumerable worlds, created and destroyed over and over again, innumerable Buddhas were none too many to keep the true doctrine alive.

Fusion of Indian and Greek Ideas

Statues representing bodhisattvas and Buddhas were very much a part of the Mahayana faith. Making such a statue was a good thing in itself and might help others along the path to salvation. Caves and temples richly decorated with statues were built as centers of worship and prayer.

Mahayana art bears an unmistakable relation to Greco-Roman art. Some of the details of Buddha statues were borrowed from standard Greco-Roman statues of Apollo. To be sure, Buddhist art soon left the Greek model behind. It developed along its own lines in India, in China, and in Japan.

The fusion of Greek and Indian ideas in Mahayana Buddhist art gives visible form to a more general mingling of Indian with Greek ideas. The bodhisattvas who were both divine and human resemble Greek ideas as developed in the centuries after Alexander, when the monarchs of Egypt and Syria all claimed to be divine and sometimes called themselves "savior." At courts and caravanserais, people from the Greek world had plenty of opportunity to argue about religion and reality with travellers from the Indian world. Just as the Buddhist sculptors borrowed some features from mass-produced Greek statues, it seems possible that the monks who developed the Mahayana doctrine may have accepted some of the ideas coming to them from the eastern Mediterranean through Greek-speaking traders. Since no one kept records of such conversations, we can never be sure.

The Spread of Mahayana Buddhism

By A.D. 200 Mahayana doctrines began to spread along the trade routes of central Asia into China. By A.D. 400 Buddhism in China had assumed a form of its own, derived mainly from the Mahayana. By A.D. 600 Chinese forms of Buddhism had been firmly planted in Korea and had made an initial impact upon Japan as well. In these two countries, conversion to Buddhism was a very important step toward civilization. Local courts and rulers welcomed the monks, who brought literacy and part of the learning of the Chinese world with them. Even when, during the T'ang Dynasty, the Chinese government began to persecute Buddhists, the Koreans and Japanese remained attached to the faith that had come to them through China from India.

The expansion of Buddhism north of the Himalaya Mountains is one of the tremendously significant facts of history. China, India, and Japan support more than half the human race, and insofar as they to this day share a common background it is because of their common experience of Buddhism. To be sure, Buddhism did not remain the dominant faith in either India or China. It survived mainly along the fringes of Asia, in Korea and Japan, and in southeast Asia and Ceylon. Buddhist missionaries reached southeast Asia by sea sometimes before the time of Christ. Most of them taught the older form of Buddhism, so that Mahayana doctrines were (and are) unimportant in such countries as Ceylon, Burma, Siam, and Vietnam.

HINDUISM

The part of India where Mahayana Buddhism flourished most was in the extreme northwest, not far from where the routes leading across the mountains into India met the Silk Road. At almost the same time, however, another important religious development was taking place in southern India. There Brahmanism developed into Hinduism. Brahmanism is a name for the rules and rituals that were developed by Brahman priests. It was based partly on the old Vedas, partly on a great variety of local religious customs. Hinduism continued to honor the Vedas and accepted all of the rules and rituals that the Brahmans had devised. The difference was that Hinduism concentrated attention on two great gods, Vishnu and Shiva. Ordinary Hindus devoted their religious observances to one of these two deities, believing that, if properly worshiped, the god would assure them of reincarnation at a higher level on the ladder of souls. Indeed, if devotion to Vishnu or Shiva were intense enough, it might even permit the worshiper to merge his or her soul with the soul of the great god himself.

Once again, the idea of a savior god was central to the faith. The Hindu myths, however, treated the incarnation of Vishnu and of Shiva as something that happened often. It might occur at any moment and at any place. The god might appear in almost any form: as a magnificent animal, as a simple herdboy, or radiating a blinding splendor. Devout worshipers might meet him walking down the street or find him through mystic ecstasy; or they might never see the god at all. The important thing was to trust in Vishnu or Shiva. The god and his worshiper were lovers who had been separated by the accident of birth. Through love, expressed in private devotions and through public ceremonies, salvation could be attained.

The Changing Balance between Hinduism and Buddhism

Elaborate temples, built around a statue of the god, became the centers of Hindu worship. Hindu art does not show Greek influence in the way Mahayana art does. Moreover, the adventures attributed to the two high gods seem closer to peasant life than to the city life of the traders who came to southern India, by sea, from Egypt. Hinduism, far more than Mahayana Buddhism, smacks of the soil. Perhaps it was for that reason that it prevailed over Buddhism in the end.

The changing balance between the two religions in India is hard to trace. About 250 B.C., when the emperor Asoka ruled nearly all of India, it looked as though Buddhism were going to become the official religion of the entire country. Asoka was an enthusiastic convert to Buddhism, and he tried to spread the doctrine throughout his domains and beyond. One way he chose to do this was to erect pillars in far-distant parts of his empire, on which he inscribed religious instruction for all to read. Several of these pillars still exist; they give us practically all of the definite information we have about Asoka's reign. After his time, information fades away again. The empire broke up; Indian life went on.

Hinduism was not a missionary religion. Some of the courts of Indonesia and southeast Asia became Hindu, or at least took on Indian culture in a Hindu form. But the worship of Shiva, by far the most popular

Hindu god in "Greater India," was probably built upon older cults which were practiced in those parts of the world before Indian courtly civilization ever reached Java, Cambodia, and regions located in between.

The Mixed Culture of the Gupta Dynasty

Five hundred years passed before northern India was once again united into an extensive empire. This new state was created by the Gupta Dynasty that ruled from about A.D. 320 to about 535. The Gupta kings were Hindus, but so far as we can tell they did not take religion too seriously. Their court became the center of an unusually elegant and luxurious life. Kalidasa (c. A.D. 400–455), the greatest of Sanskrit poets, lived at the Gupta court. His plays and lyric poems reflect an exquisite refinement of life.

During this same period of time, India's two great epics, the *Mahabharata* and the *Ramayana*, reached something like their present form. The first of these, like the *Iliad*, is a story of heroic chariot combat, but priests later added so much other material that the original story was nearly buried. Folktales, religious instruction, incantations, philosophical discourses—all were put in. As a result, the entire poem is longer than the Bible, with which it should also be compared since the Hindus regard the *Mahabharata* as a book of religious instruction. The *Ramayana* is much shorter and better organized. It tells the story of the wonderful adventures of Rama. Once again religion became central, for Rama was an incarnation of Vishnu, one of the two great gods of Hinduism.

The Indian epics had a long evolution before the Gupta period, and a few additional passages may have been added later. But in the age of the Guptas, Indians adopted the practice of writing down works of literature instead of preserving texts by transmitting them orally. This was a borrowing from the Greeks, as we know from the fact that the technical terms connected with books are of Greek origin. Written literature required professional copyists who worked mechanically and were less likely to add new material or alter old passages, as those who memorized orally were tempted to do each time they recited. Hence as book writing and copying spread to India in the Gupta Age, the two epics as well as such complicated texts as those from the pen of Kalidasa assumed a stable, lasting form.

Ever since then, the Gupta Age has been considered India's classical high point. We know it almost entirely through literature; its surviving art is mostly Buddhist. This points up the fact that Hindus and Buddhists lived quite peacefully side by side, just as the different kinds of Buddhists did. No one in India thought that persecution over differences in religion made sense. The drift away from Buddhism toward Hinduism in India therefore left almost no traces. Buddhist monasteries continued to exist until Moslem raiders destroyed them after A.D. 1000. But once destroyed, nobody cared enough about the monks' way of holiness to restore them. The search for salvation had found new ways of expressing itself. Buddhist monasteries simply had become unnecessary.

CHRISTIANITY

Christianity began in Palestine among the Jews. It later spread among Greek-speaking peoples of the eastern Mediterranean. From this center it then expanded rapidly in almost every direction—eastward along the Asian trade routes, south into India and Ethiopia, and west throughout the Roman Empire. Not until after A.D. 600 did Christianity win important territory north of the old Roman borders. Between A.D. 600 and 1000, however, practically all of northern Europe was converted to the Christian faith. Despite such successes, Christianity, like Buddhism, was eventually pushed out of its land of origin. Islam, the faith of Mohammed, surged up from the Arabian desert, beginning in A.D. 634. Hence, while Christianity was winning converts among Slavs and Germans in the European north, Islam conquered Palestine and Syria—Christianity's cradleland—and all of the rest of the Middle East and north Africa.

Jewish Background

Christianity built upon Judaism. The later Hebrew prophets had proclaimed a Messiah, an anointed King and Savior, who would restore the Kingdom of David and remedy injustice. By the time of Christ, differences of opinion arose among pious Jews as to how to interpret the words of the prophets. Some expected a supernatural end of the world, when the skies would open to reveal God in splendor, and the Messiah would come down from God's right hand to reward and punish individuals for their good and bad deeds. Others thought the Messiah would be a man like King David, sent by God to restore justice and defend true religion.

The Jews expected the Messiah with mounting intensity because times were very hard in Palestine. Wicked rulers and brutal taxgatherers seemed to be tempting God's forbearance and inviting His punishment. Nearly two centuries before the time of Christ, the Seleucid monarch, Antiochus IV Epiphanes (reigned 175–163 B.C.) had tested the faith of

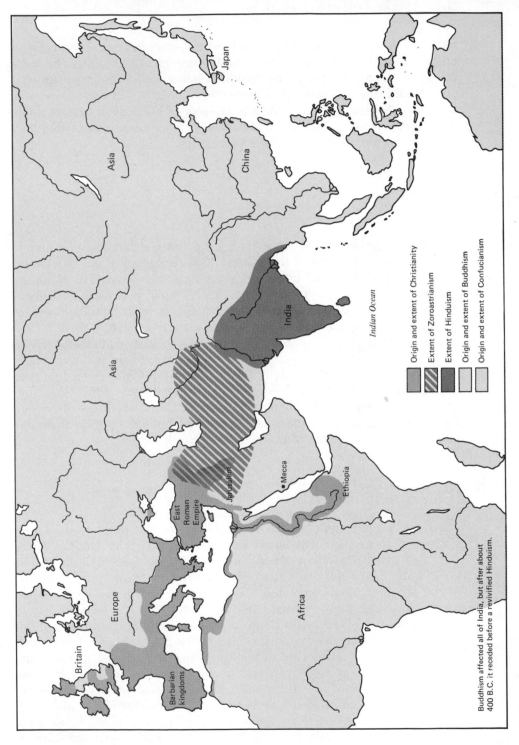

Major Religions: A.D. 600

Origin and extent of Christianity

Extent of Zoroastrianism

Extent of Hinduism

Origin and extent of Buddhism

Origin and extent of Confucianism

Buddhism affected all of India, but after about 400 B.C. it receded before a revivified Hinduism.

the Jews by requiring them to honor him as a god. But the Jews refused to commit idolatry and rose in revolt. Under the leadership of Judas Maccabaeus, Jewish forces were victorious. This seemed clear proof of God's help; but to the distress of pious Jews, the kingdom that Judas Maccabaeus established soon fell into the hands of rulers who were more interested in pagan Greek culture and in getting along with the Romans than in observing God's law or governing justly.

In 64 B.C. the Romans established a protectorate over Palestine and put a new dynasty on the throne. Herod the Great (reigned 37–4 B.C.) was the last of the line to rule a sizable kingdom, for on his death the lands he had ruled were divided among his four sons. Then in A.D. 6 the eldest died, and the two central provinces of Herod's kingdom, Judaea and Samaria, were put under direct Roman administration. About A.D. 30 a minor Roman official, Pontius Pilate, was in charge. As procurator of Judaea and representative of the emperor Tiberius, he authorized the crucifixion of Jesus of Nazereth because his followers recognized him as the long-awaited Messiah, God's Son, who had been sent to redeem the world. Crowds in Jerusalem had hailed him as "King of the Jews."

Most Jews were not convinced that Jesus was the Messiah. His career on earth did not correspond to their expectations. They therefore continued to wait. In A.D. 66 many Jews thought that the time for the Messiah's coming was finally at hand and revolted against Roman rule. Fighting lasted until A.D. 70. After a siege, the Romans captured Jerusalem and destroyed the Temple. It was never rebuilt. The war also scattered the little Christian community that had remained in Jerusalem after the crucifixion. From that time on, Christianity left its Jewish origin farther and farther behind. When still another revolt broke out in Palestine in A.D. 132, Christians were not directly affected. This time, however, the Romans took extreme action. They devastated the rebel territory and destroyed almost the entire Jewish community of Jerusalem and Judaea. Only Jews who lived in other places, mostly in cities among strangers, survived. The Jewish hope for the Messiah remained; but military uprisings of the sort that had occurred repeatedly from the time of Judas Maccabaeus ceased.

The Teachings of Jesus of Nazareth

This was the background for Jesus' ministry and teaching. He spent his active years in Galilee, far to the north of Jerusalem, where he preached among the poor peasants and fishermen of the region. His central theme was, "Repent, for the Kingdom of Heaven is at hand"; and he urged his listeners to observe a very strict moral discipline without, however, worry-ing too much about all the rules for ceremonial purification that had be-come important to Judaism. Jesus' preaching aroused great excitement. Miraculous, or seemingly miraculous, healing convinced many of those who gathered to listen to him that Jesus did indeed possess supernatural power. When he started toward Jerusalem for the Passover feast, his closest followers, the Twelve Apostles, expected that God would reveal the fact that Jesus was the long-awaited Messiah. Such talk frightened the priests of the Temple. They therefore arrested Jesus, convicted him for claiming to be "King of the Jews," and handed him over to the Roman authorities for punishment.

Jesus' death on the cross was a terrible shock to his disciples. Simon Peter, chief among the Apostles, three times denied any connection with Jesus. Yet soon afterward, gathered in an upstairs room, some of the Apostles suddenly felt their Master's presence. The Holy Spirit descended among them; joy and excitement replaced their disappointment and fear. In the next few days, several of his most devoted followers reported that Jesus had shown himself to them, still very much alive, despite his death on the cross. Here, they felt, was the final proof that Jesus was the Messiah: he had risen from the grave, victorious over death itself, and would soon come back in glory to establish the Kingdom of Heaven.

The good news could not be kept bottled up among the handful of disciples and their friends. They began to preach in the streets of Jerusa-lem. Soon missionaries appeared in other cities where Jewish synagogues existed. In some of these communities, the everyday language was Greek. The Hebrew word "Messiah"—the Anointed One—was translated into Greek as "Christ." Believers in Christ were first called "Christians" in Antioch, one of the great centers of Hellenistic culture and commerce and also the former capital of the Seleucid Empire.

The first generations of Christians lived in daily expectation of the Second Coming of Christ. They tried to prove to unbelieving Jews that Jesus was in fact the Messiah, by showing how his first appearance on earth had already fulfilled prophecy in many details. A critical question soon arose: Were the provisions of the Jewish law, as they had been laid down in what Christians came to call the Old Testament, still binding? Or had Christ's authority repealed the old law? This question was impor-tant for the Jews; it was even more important for persons who were not Jews, but who, listening to the Christian message, were attracted to the faith. The man who gave a decisive answer to this question was Paul.

Born a Jew and a Roman citizen in the Greek-speaking city of Tarsus on the coast of Asia Minor, Paul was a highly educated man, unlike the simple Galileans who had first responded to Jesus' message. At first, Paul took an active part in persecuting the Christians in Jerusalem. Then he started for Damascus to warn the Jews there against the new doctrine. However, Paul met a strange experience on the road. He had a blinding vision of Christ. His blindness lasted only a few days; on recovery he became a fervent Christian.

On the basis of his personal experience of the risen Christ, St. Paul emphasized the idea that faith in Christ was what mattered. Whoever believed in the Resurrection and the Second Coming of Jesus Christ would be ready for the Last Judgment. For them death had no terrors; a blessed life beyond the grave in the presence and enjoyment of God Himself was assured. Everything else was secondary, and in particular observing the rituals of Jewish law did not matter. Before Christ's coming the law had been needed to lead people to God, but it was beyond human power to live up to the law in every detail. Salvation by the law was impossible. Therefore, Christ had come to show another way to eternal life. He would soon return; in the meanwhile, all that a Christian needed to assure salvation was faith in Christ and a warm, mutual, loving care for the welfare of every member of the community of the faithful.

Christianity as interpreted by St. Paul soon took root and flourished in the Greek-speaking cities of the eastern Mediterranean. When arguments broke out, he wrote letters to explain disputed points. These letters, together with the four Gospels—parallel accounts of Christ's life and ministry on earth—were later gathered together to form the core of the New Testament. A few other apostolic writings were also added; chief among them were the Revelations of St. John, which described in detail Christ's return and the expected end of the world.

St. Peter, the chief of the Apostles, and St. Paul both got into trouble with the Roman authorities. Preaching the end of the world sounded like revolution, and religious arguments between Jews and Christians provoked riots. The emperor Nero authorized the first organized persecution of Christians in A.D. 64. Both St. Peter and St. Paul were probably martyred on this occasion.

Usually the Roman government paid little attention to Christians. Most of them were poor people who met, more or less secretly, to hear the gospel story once again and to share a ritual meal. Like the Jews, they refused to offer sacrifices to the emperor's statue, arguing that this was idolatry. But Roman authorities were usually willing to overlook this stiff-necked behavior as long as Christians offered no open threat to public order.

Another kind of problem arose for the Christians, however. What did Christian good news really mean? What was the true relationship between Jesus Christ and God? What was the Holy Spirit that had inspired the prophets of old and that sometimes descended upon Christian congregations, inspiring new (often very surprising) prophecies, excited and unintelligible speech, and other unusual behavior? Learned Greeks, trained in philosophical argument, were not satisfied with the simple text of the New Testament. What did Holy Scripture mean?

For a long time these matters could be left for the Second Coming to decide. But the urge to present a logical defense of Christian faith was hard to resist, especially when critics began to argue against it. Between A.D. 200 and 300, therefore, Christian theologians began to define and defend a Trinitarian doctrine, according to which God the Father and Christ his Son shared a single and undivided Godhead with the Holy Spirit. By degrees, the method and much of the vocabulary of Greek philosophy entered the Christian tradition through such discussion.

Christianity's Effect on Political and Social Life

After the death of Marcus Aurelius (A.D. 180), the Roman Empire met with hard times. Civil wars and barbarian attacks troubled the peace. Plagues depopulated many parts of the empire. Taxes were harder and harder to collect, and without taxes it was impossible to maintain a strong army to guard the frontiers. Many Christians believed these disasters proved that the end of the world was at hand. Increasing numbers of pagans agreed—and accepted the new faith. Others accused the Christians of being responsible for the bad times. Accordingly, a few of the emperors launched widespread persecutions. These reached their climax under the emperor Diocletian (reigned A.D. 284–305), who reunited the empire after fifty years of confusion and then tried to root out and destroy what he viewed as the Christian conspiracy. However, in the end it was Christianity that prevailed.

This occurred when Constantine came to power after new civil wars. While marching toward Rome in A.D. 312, he saw a brilliant cross of light in the sky, which he interpreted as the first two letters of Christ's name. Constantine concluded that Christ was on his side. When, therefore, his troops won a victory at the Milvian Bridge just outside Rome, Constantine believed that he owed his success to Christ's help. Consequently he stopped official persecution of the Christian communities in the territory which he controlled and, instead, began to favor them. Imperial favor soon turned to support. By A.D. 395 the emperor Theodosius forbade all pagan worship. Rome thus became Christian exclusively, officially, and enduringly.

This great victory quickly created a new problem, however. As long as Christians had been a persecuted minority, they got along with one another, in spite of differences of opinion about doctrine. To be sure, even in early days, extremes of behavior and belief had to be ruled out.

Some of St. Paul's letters addressed themselves to such problems. There were always routine matters to be decided; for example, procedure at meetings, or how to distribute gifts for the poor. From the very beginning the Apostles helped to decide such matters. When they died, successors, called bishops, inherited the responsibility of managing Christian affairs. In early times, each city where there was a Christian community or church had its own bishop. Bishops of larger cities, where richer and better-educated Christian communities arose, naturally had greater prestige. It was for these reasons that Alexandria in Egypt and, later, Constantinople on the Bosporus exercised religious leadership over wide territories. On the other hand, churches which had been personally founded by one of the Apostles claimed to have superior knowledge of true doctrine because of their origin. The Church of Rome had special prestige on both grounds. Rome after all was the traditional capital of the Roman Empire; in addition, the Roman Church traced its establishment to St. Peter, the chief of the Apostles.

These claims did not, in themselves, solve the problems that arose when rival theologians began to denounce one another as teachers of false doctrines. Constantine tried to settle such disputes by summoning all Christian bishops to a meeting or council. The first such general council took place at Nicaea in A.D. 325. It prepared the Nicene Creed. Creeds had been used for a long time among Christians in ordinary services of worship and especially at baptism, when new members were formally admitted to the Church. But the Nicene Creed was the first official effort to define the exact relationship between God and the Father and God the Son, in a brief but authoritative way.

The Council of Nicaea, however, failed to end quarrels. Christians found it impossible to agree on any of the definitions of the exact relationship among the persons of the Trinity. After more than a century of bitter debate, Christians of Syria and Egypt, most of whom spoke the local Syriac and Coptic languages, refused to accept the creed as defined by Greek-speaking Christians; and they set up their own independent churches.

Difficulties also arose between Latin- and Greek-speaking Christians. The issue was not theological doctrine, however, so much as the question of how the Christian church should be governed. As successors to St. Peter, the bishops of Rome claimed authority over all Christian churches; but bishops of the Greek-speaking East refused to agree. They argued that the whole body of bishops inherited the authority over the Church that Christ had conferred upon the Apostles.

After A.D. 378, as we shall soon see, barbarian invasions destroyed Roman government in the Latin-speaking parts of the empire. This meant that most Latin-speaking Christians were no longer effectively under the control of the Roman emperor, who continued to reign from

Constantinople. Each Christian community of the Latin West simply had to do the best it could under very uncertain conditions. This often meant giving wider and wider powers to bishops, who took over functions formerly reserved for local governors and judges. For example, the bishop of Rome, or pope as he is usually called, became the effective ruler of the city and its immediate environs. But in the troubled and disturbed times that followed the barbarian invasions, the pope usually could not make his authority felt very far away.

The Teaching of St. Augustine of Hippo

The collapse of the Roman Empire in the West led some remaining pagans to blame the disaster on Christianity. St. Augustine of Hippo (354–430) set out to answer this accusation in a book called *The City of God.* Writing in Latin, Augustine developed a Christian view of history on the basis of the Old and New Testaments. According to his vision of humanity's experience on earth, the barbarian attack on Rome in A.D. 410 was a trifling event, of no significance when compared with God's plan for human salvation. God had begun to reveal His plan in the days of Abraham and Moses; it had been fully revealed by Christ and would be fulfilled by the Second Coming, when God would bring the great drama to its appointed close. In the meanwhile, the world was divided into two parts—or, as Augustine called them, cities: the City of God, or Heaven, and the City of Earth.

The church was the great link between the two parts of creation. By means of the church, people could hope to pass from the evils of earth to the glory of Heaven, for it was through the church that God had chosen to dispense His grace to sinful humankind. This assigned a far more important role to the Church than early Christians had usually done. The end of the world and Christ's Second Coming, which had been so eagerly awaited by the first Christians, became, for Augustine, a matter that would come to pass when God willed, at the end of time. But for the present, and indefinitely into the future, Christ had established the Church to shepherd the souls God had chosen for salvation toward their eternal home, the City of God.

Augustine's vision of the human condition shaped all later Latin Christianity. His view of the Church, of sin and salvation, and his interpretations of biblical passages all played a central role in later theological discussion. In addition, our consciousness of time as a fundamental dimension of reality can in large part be attributed to Augustine.

After Augustine's death the heat of theological controversy slowly died down. The Greeks defined Orthodox doctrine, in a lasting way, at the Council of Chalcedon in A.D. 451. They accepted a creed formulated by Pope Leo the Great. This kept Latin and Greek Christians in agreement on doctrine for a while longer. After Chalcedon, the Copts in Egypt and the Syriac Christians in Asia defined their own creeds in opposition to the Greeks. When each of these major segments of the Christian community had defined its position with an official creed, further controversy was controlled by the care each church took to stay within its own particular definition of the truth.

By A.D. 600, therefore, when Christianity was about to face a fresh challenge from the followers of Mohammed, the Church had changed very much from its early days. Expectation of the Second Coming did not cease; but day-to-day prayer, rituals, and the routine of administration usurped ordinary attention. For those who were not content with such practical compromises, special monastic communities developed. These started as loose gatherings of hermits and ascetics, who swarmed into the Egyptian and Syrian deserts after about A.D. 250. Later on, more strictly organized communities were established. The most influential of these in the Greek church were governed by the rule of St. Basil (A.D. 330–379), while in the Latin-speaking world the rule of St. Benedict of Nursia (c. A.D. 529) became standard.

THE IMPACT OF BARBARIAN INVASIONS

The rise and spread of Mahayana Buddhism, Hinduism, and Christianity changed the aspect of civilized communities throughout Eurasia. People expected more from an afterlife and less from life on earth. This is not so surprising, since most of them found little ease or comfort in their daily experience of the world. One reason was that wave after wave of destructive barbarian invasion inundated civilized lands. Even when the invaders did not conquer, they strained civilized defenses to the limit. This often meant heavier taxes for common folk to pay in order to escape the burning and looting of everything they possessed.

If we try to view the military problem facing all the civilized states of Eurasia—from the Roman Empire in the west to the Chinese Empire in the east—a common factor at once appears. They all had to protect themselves against bands of raiders coming from the grassy steppes extending across almost the entire continent—from Hungary, Romania, and southern Russia in eastern Europe, to Mongolia and Manchuria in eastern Asia. Nomad horse-riding peoples had first occupied the steppe regions

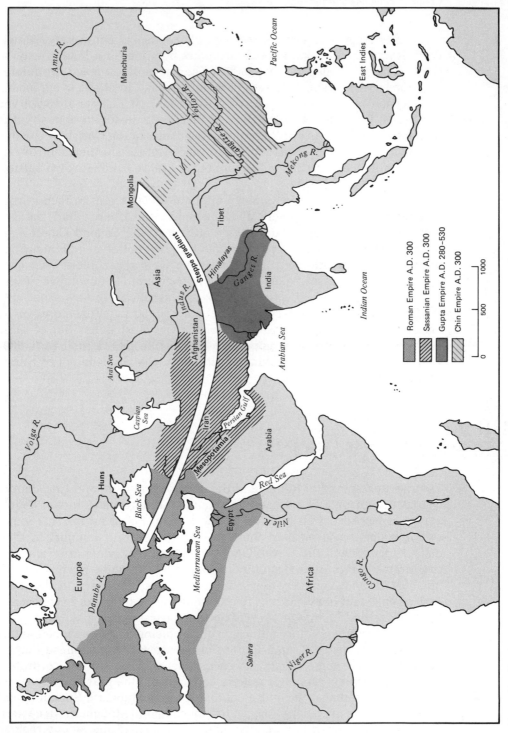

Map labels:

Amur R.
Manchuria
Pacific Ocean
East Indies
Yellow R.
Yangtze R.
Mekong R.
Mongolia
Tibet
Steppe gradient
Himalayas
Ganges R.
India
Indian Ocean
Asia
Indus R.
Afghanistan
Aral Sea
Caspian Sea
Iran
Persian Gulf
Arabian Sea
Arabia
Volga R.
Huns
Black Sea
Mesopotamia
Red Sea
Egypt
Nile R.
Europe
Danube R.
Mediterranean Sea
Africa
Congo R.
Sahara
Niger R.

Legend:
Roman Empire A.D. 300
Sassanian Empire A.D. 300
Gupta Empire A.D. 280–530
Chin Empire A.D. 300

0   500   1000

Eurasian Steppe

(moving from west to east) between about 800 and 300 B.C. These nomads were great traders. Possessing numerous animals and being accustomed to moving to and fro in search of pasture, they provided personnel as well as animals for the caravans that had tied Eurasia's civilizations together since about 100 B.C.

Raids were an ever present alternative to trade. The nomads' quickest way to wealth was to make a successful raid on someone else's herds. Success was greatly admired. Fighting, in short, was essential to the way nomads lived—and died. Their weapon was the bow; they rode to war on the backs of hardy ponies that could survive on the natural grasses of the steppe. Speed and surprise gave them an enormous advantage over slower-moving forces. On the other hand, steppe cavalry seldom could capture a fortified town. In particular, a long siege was almost always beyond their capacity. After a few weeks of staying in one place, pasture for their horses was sure to run short, so they would have to move on to keep their mounts in good condition.

Yet farms and villages exposed to nomad raiding suffered great damage. City dwellers, depending on the flow of food from the surrounding countryside, might suffer almost as much as the plundered farmers. How to stop nomad raids therefore became a critical problem for Eurasia's settled agricultural populations from the time when the steppe came to be occupied by tribes of nomad cavalrymen.

We have already seen some of the earliest consequences of this confrontation. The first massive raids by steppe cavalry accompanied the overthrow of the Assyrian Empire (605 B.C.). Nearly four centuries later, the unification of China (221 B.C.) was another example of the impact of steppe warfare on civilized society, for the Ch'in armies that conquered China had learned their skill through long border strife and, as a matter of fact, had borrowed the nomads' style of cavalry warfare themselves.

As soon as the Eurasian steppe had been fully occupied by nomad warriors, major events in any region of the steppe echoed throughout its length. If one group of people were driven from traditional pasturelands by some neighboring tribe, they had either to find a new home by driving others away from their traditional pastures or else perish. Thus, for example, when the Hsiung-nu formed a powerful confederation in Mongolia about 200 B.C., they were able to drive away other people who had formerly lived on the borders of China. The defeated nomads fled westward along the steppe. One branch of these refugees later established the Kushan Empire in what is now Afghanistan. At about the same time, Parthian tribes left the central regions of the steppe and overran Iran and Mesopotamia.

A few generations later another people, the Sarmatians, pushed into southern Russia, the lower Danube region, and eventually reached Hungary, where they collided with the Roman defenses soon after A.D. 150.

Civilized Countermeasures

Shortly before the time of Christ, however, civilized peoples perfected a new style of warfare that went a long way toward stopping nomad raids and making the agricultural villages and fields of the countryside safe for farming. The Parthians, who controlled Iran and Mesopotamia from about 141 B.C. to A.D. 226, played a particularly important part in this development. They discovered that by feeding horses with alfalfa and hay during the winter when natural forage was scarce, a far bigger and stronger breed could be maintained. Such a great horse could carry heavy armor itself and bear the additional weight of an armored rider, without ceasing to be mobile. Such heavily armored cavalry could withstand nomad attacks very successfully, since nearly all the raiders' arrows would simply shatter or glance off harmlessly. At the same time, skilled horse archers, astride their great horses, could pick off a fair share of any unarmored steppe cavalrymen who dared to approach them. This meant that a body of properly equipped and trained cavalrymen could defend any locality against the hit-and-run tactics of steppe warfare. On the other hand, this type of warrior could not take the strategic offensive against nomad enemies, because the big horses could not find adequate food by grazing on the open steppe.

The great problem with this sort of cavalry was how to pay for it. It required years of practice to become a really effective horse archer. The rider had to be able to hit a target from a moving horse, while also controlling his mount without holding the reins. Moreover, food and armor for the big horses were very expensive. The Parthian solution was to scatter the cavalrymen out among the villages and let them collect rents from local peasants. This had the advantage of keeping skilled and effective defenders always at hand. Its disadvantage was that the central government could not control such warriors. When the king called on them for a campaign, he could never be sure how many would show up, or, having shown up, whether they would follow him where he chose to lead.

The Chinese government was never willing to adopt the Parthian style of local self-defense against nomad raiding. The big horses proved too expensive. Instead, the Chinese preferred to hire warriors who rode and fought like the Hsiung-nu whom they opposed. Or, by sending gifts (or tribute) to the Hsiung-nu, the Chinese could hope to keep them quiet. The Roman government, too, long refused to make use of the Parthian pattern of local self-defense. The Romans were therefore ill-prepared for the next wave of barbarian attacks that developed abruptly after A.D. 374, when a people known as Huns broke into southern Russia from

Germanic Invasion Routes 371-568 A.D.

North Sea

NORTHUMBRIA

MERCIA

WESSEX

Baltic Sea

JUTES

ANGLES

5TH C.

SAXONS   BURGUNDIANS

Vistula R.

FRANKS

Rhine R.

Seine R.

Paris

Loire R.

420

Troyes

451

443

406

HUNS

LOMBARDS

VANDALS

Dniester R.

Dnieper R.

455

375

HUNS

Atlantic Ocean

AQUITAINE

Garonne R.

SUEVI

VANDALS

Ebro R.

PYRENEES

Toulouse

412

Tagus R.

411

VISIGOTHS

Straits of Gibraltar

429

Saône R.

ALAMANNI

ALPS

568

Rhône R.

493

410

Rome

455

OSTROGOTHS

Danube R.

397

445

VISIGOTHS

GEPIDES

378

Adrianople

SCIRAE

Black Sea

Constantinople

Athens

VANDALS

Carthage

439

Mediterranean Sea

■ Battle sites

0   500

Miles

the east, conquered the Ostrogoths, who had set themselves up there a
short time before, and spread terror far and wide.

In the next year, the Visigoths fled before the Huns into Roman
territory. There they soon quarreled with Roman officials. When an imperial army went to subdue them, they defeated the army and killed the
emperor Valens in the Battle of Adrianople (A.D. 378). The Visigoths were
never driven from Roman soil again. They plundered the Balkans thoroughly before going to Italy, where they sacked Rome in A.D. 410, and
then went on to Spain. Other German tribes soon followed, fleeing from
the terrible Huns, who had meanwhile established their headquarters
in Hungary and were raiding deep into Roman territory year after year.

Sassanian Persia

While devastation thus spread through much of the Roman world, the central portion of the civilized front against the steppe held firm. To be sure, in A.D. 226 the Parthian kings were replaced by a new Sassanian Dynasty. Their empire is often called the New Persian Empire (226–651 A.D.), because the Sassanians took the empire of Darius and Xerxes as their model. Realities, however, had changed, and the Sassanians depended even more completely than their predecessors upon the heavy-armored cavalry of the Iranian countryside.

The Sassanian government tried a number of interesting religious experiments. One king patronized the prophet Mani (lived c. A.D. 215–273) who tried to create a new religion by bringing together the "true" teachings of Zoroastrianism, Judaism, and Christianity. But official favor did not last. When his royal protector died, Mani was arrested and actually died in prison. Nevertheless, his followers met with considerable missionary success. They penetrated both Roman and Chinese territory as well as regions along the trade routes in between. In Roman lands, Mani's doctrines rivaled Christianity for a while. St. Augustine, for example, became a Manichaean in his youth, as he tells us in his *Confessions*. But when Christianity became the official faith of the Roman state, Manichaeism was outlawed and the combined forces of church and state soon eliminated it from Roman soil. The faith lasted much longer in central Asia and China; but there, too, Manichaeism ceased to have a numerically significant following after about A.D. 900.

The long-range failure of Mani's faith to establish itself among the great world religions did not affect the ability of the Sassanian Empire to hold neighboring barbarians at bay. On the contrary, rural landholders, trained from childhood to ride and shoot—and ready at a moment's notice to don their armor and ride forth to defend the locality from which they drew their rents—proved very effective in discouraging raiders from the steppe. Because of their geographical position, the Sassanian warriors also protected India, where, as we saw above, the Gupta Empire flourished through a long period of peace.

China's Recovery

But the fact that the Sassanian frontier guard, in the middle portions of the steppe frontier, was so successful tended to concentrate nomad harassment of civilized peoples at the two extremes, east and west. China, for example, suffered a long series of raids as the Han Dynasty approached its final collapse (A.D. 220). During the following three and a half centuries, China was divided into a varying number of rival states, many of which were ruled by barbarian invaders. This was also the time when Buddhism won its major successes in China. Then in 589 a new dynasty, the Sui, was able to unite the whole country once more, and launched vigorous military expansion into Korea and Vietnam.

In A.D. 605 the Sui opened the Grand Canal that connected the Yangtze River with the Yellow River. This canal allowed cheap and easy transport between the two great river valleys of China for the first time. It became possible to deliver rice and other commodities produced near navigable water anywhere in the Yangtze Basin to the imperial capital at Loyang, far in the north. The Grand Canal therefore doubled or more than doubled the income at the disposal of the imperial court. Always before, the Chinese emperors could expect to have only the tax yield from the Yellow River valley available for feeding the capital and supplying the armies needed to stand guard against the nomads in the north. But after the canal came into operation, the surplus products of the vast Yangtze Valley could be carried north and used for these same purposes. An enormous strengthening of the Chinese imperial government therefore resulted. Rapid development of the Yangtze region and a southward shift of China's center of wealth and population were other consequences of the opening of the Grand Canal.

China's reunification was long-lasting and launched the Chinese upon a new phase in their history. As long as China's vast resources were united under one command, it was not too difficult to keep the nomads at a safe distance from Chinese soil. Even when another powerful steppe confederation arose, the Juan-juan, China remained secure. Nomad peoples, defeated by the Juan-juan, started westward, and headed toward the European steppe. There, as we shall see, new migrations of peoples broke through the frontiers of the East Roman or Byzantine Empire and changed the linguistic map of Europe in far-reaching ways.

Emergence of Byzantium

While these events were taking place in China, Europe went through a similar cycle of barbarian invasion and recovery. The barbarian invasions that followed the overthrow of the Han Dynasty in A.D. 220 were like the Hunnic and German invasions that brought down the Roman Empire in the west after A.D. 375. But in A.D. 454 the Hun's confederacy broke up after the death of their greatest leader, Attila. Thereafter, flights and migrations slacked off. Fairly stable governments, ruled by German tribal chieftains or kings, emerged on what had formerly been Roman soil. The

Vandal kingdom in north Africa, the Visigothic kingdom in Spain and southern Gaul, and the Ostrogothic kingdom in Italy were the most important of these states (see maps, pp. 269 and 275).

As pressure from the steppe frontier decreased, Roman power in the eastern half of the empire recovered. Under the emperor Justinian (reigned A.D. 527–565), the empire launched a systematic effort to regain control of the lost western provinces. Justinian was in fact able to recover north Africa from the Vandals, and Italy from the Ostrogoths. He also won control of part of Spain from the Visigoths. The East Roman or Byzantine Empire won these victories with a combination of sea power and heavy-armored cavalry, equipped and trained on the Sassanian model but supported by the imperial treasury and not by land grants as was the custom among the Persians.

Only in remote Britain, and along the Rhine and Danube frontiers of the Roman Empire, did German advances remain unchallenged. In Britain, Saxons and Angles, who had their homes near the German coast of the North Sea, invaded Britain, beginning about A.D. 420, and gradually drove back the older Celtic and Latin-speaking inhabitants. Similarly, along the Rhine and Danube frontiers, tribes of German farmers—Franks in the west and Bavarians, Burgundians, and others along the upper Danube—steadily advanced their line of settlement by clearing new fields in the vast forests that covered these regions.

Toward the end of Justinian's reign it looked, therefore, as though the reunification of at least the Mediterranean parts of the Roman Empire could be carried through successfully. On the surface, this recovery resembled the reunification of China by the Sui Dynasty that occurred only a little afterward. But in reality, there was a great difference. Thanks to the Grand Canal, the Sui were able to tap new revenues that made the restored imperial government in China stable and secure. The East Roman or Byzantine government was not able to do anything of this sort. On the contrary, when dangers from the steppe frontier in the north once more became acute, the Byzantine authorities lacked the armies and material resources required to hold the invaders back. As a result, in Justinian's last days and throughout the half century that followed his death, a new avalanche of barbarian migration set in.

The driving force behind these movements was the appearance of a new steppe people, the Avars. Like the Huns before them, they set up their raiding headquarters on the grassy plain of Hungary, and plundered far and wide. A German tribe known as Lombards ("Long Beards") fled from the Avars and invaded Italy. The Byzantine armies that had been able to overthrow the Ostrogoths were too few to hold the Lombards at bay. In the Balkans, Slavic tribes filtered southward in great numbers. Farther west, Franks and neighboring Germanic peoples continued to advance their settlements at the expense of Latin-speaking inhabitants; and

THE EMPRESS THEODORA

Theodora was an actress—slender, vivacious, popular. She was born into the theater, for her father exhibited trained bears in the circus at Constantinople. Yet from this disreputable origin, at the age of twenty-four Theodora became the reigning empress of Byzantium, sharing power with her husband, the famous emperor Justinian.

Before they could legally marry, an old law forbidding men of high rank to marry actresses had to be repealed. The bitter opposition of the imperial family had also to be overcome. Indeed, not until after the death of Justinian's aunt could the emperor Justin, who preceded Justinian on the throne, be persuaded to agree to the marriage.

As empress, Theodora took an active part in the government of the empire. Her most fateful act came in 532, when the populace of Byzantium broke out in fierce riots. For many years the Byzantines had been passionately interested in chariot racing. The races were held between two factions, the Greens and the Blues, and practically everyone in the city belonged to one or the other faction—betting on and hoping and praying for the victory of one side or the other.

Feeling ran so high in 532 that the rival factions came to blows in the great circus, where the people had gathered for the race. When Emperor Justinian tried to check the rioting by ordering his soldiers to clear the circus, the crowd turned against the imperial couple, then only five years on the throne. So fierce were the crowds and so uncertain the loyalty of Justinian's soldiers that the emperor, after several days of wild rioting had occurred, decided to flee from the city in hope of saving his life by giving up the throne. But Theodora, who had risen so high so surprisingly, refused to flee. "The purple makes a handsome winding-sheet," she said, as she persuaded her husband to renew the battle. Within a few hours the fighting spirit of the crowds melted away, the soldiers' discipline held, and peace returned to the capital. After 532 Justinian never forgot that he owed his throne to Theodora, as she had owed her throne to him before that time.

across the English Channel, the Anglo-Saxons did the same. These movements permanently changed the language map of Europe. Franks and Anglo-Saxons in the west and Slavs in the east made the land their own by settling on it as farmers. The language boundaries that resulted from these migrations remain almost unchanged to the present day.

One reason the Byzantines failed to resist these barbarian pressures from the north was that their eastern frontier was also threatened. The Sassanian heavy cavalry, so effective against nomad raiders, could also be mobilized against the Byzantines. Byzantine armies, generally speaking, were too few in numbers to stop such attacks. On the other hand, the Byzantines always kept command of the sea. This allowed the emperors to use ships to outflank any force that raided so far into Asia Minor as to threaten the capital of Constantinople itself.

In A.D. 634, just after the conclusion of a long and costly struggle between the Sassanian and Byzantine empires, a new and revolutionary force appeared in the Middle East. In that year, Arabs from the southern desert, united by the new religion of Islam, attacked the exhausted Byzantine and Sassanian empires. In an amazingly short period of time, they overran Byzantium's richest provinces and utterly destroyed the Sassanian state. By doing so, the Arabs inaugurated a new period of world history which we will consider in the next chapter.

THE FRINGES OF
THE CIVILIZED WORLD

The rise of three new world religions and all these raids, invasions, and migrations of peoples had the overall effect of blurring the boundaries between civilized and barbarian territory. The Hsiung-nu and Juan-juan, in the periods of their strength, enjoyed a rich supply of goods sent from China as tribute. Obviously, the tastes of at least the upper classes among them came to be attuned to the Chinese style of living. The same was true of the Germans who invaded Roman territory. As Roman civilization coarsened with the destruction of the class of landowners who had shared the ancient classical culture, it became easier for the barbarians to take full part in what remained. Accordingly, the Ostrogoths of Italy and the Visigoths of Spain soon came fully abreast of the level of culture that existed among their Roman subjects. But the fact that these German tribes had accepted a form of Christianity that the Latin Christians viewed as heretical kept them and their subjects apart.

Beyond the old Roman frontiers, only by slow degrees did rude, rural, and warlike Slavs and Germans find anything of interest in the Greek or Roman brands of Christian civilization. In distant Ireland, however, Christianity was introduced about A.D. 430 by St. Patrick, a native of Wales. The Irish quickly agreed that Christianity was an improvement on druidry, which had existed there before. The druids were priests whose doctrines may have descended, at least in part, from the old megalithic religion. At any rate, the special character of the Irish Christian monasteries resembled druid practices. The special love of learning shown by the Irish monks may have been a Christian version of a pagan custom that required each generation of druids to memorize lengthy texts in order to perform traditional sacred ceremonies. Their apprenticeship to Christian learning was so successful that, by A.D. 600, Irish monks far surpassed anything known in England, or anywhere else in western Europe.

Along the southern flank of the Roman world, new civilizations, or the beginnings of new civilizations, came into existence during these same centuries. In west Africa, for example, the first evidence of an organized state, known as the kingdom of Ghana, dates from about A.D. 300. Peasants raising crops that had originated in distant Indonesia provided a valuable source of income for the rulers. In addition, they profited from

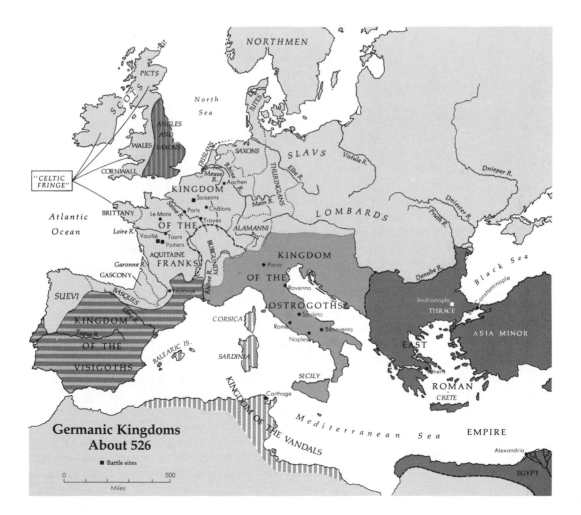

Germanic Kingdoms About 526

■ Battle sites

0   500
Miles

caravan trade that crossed the Sahara and connected Ghana with Roman north Africa. Little is known of Ghana's court life or high culture, since no written documents from that ancient African Empire have survived (see map, p. 278).

Farther east in Africa, the kingdom of Abyssinia also rose to prominence and, for a short while, extended its power across the Straits of Aden into Arabia. The wealth of Abyssinia rested in large part on taxes levied upon the trade passing through the Red Sea. When the Abyssinians raised their tolls too high, overland caravan trade, up and down the length of Arabia, became a practicable way of bypassing the tolls. Sea trade between Egypt and India thus died away. It was partially counterbalanced by the rise of Arabian caravan trade upon which the city of Mecca, where Mohammed was born, prospered.

In Asia, also, new border states and regions attained a level of organization we recognize as civilized. Beginning about the time of Christ, a series of kingdoms in southeast Asia and Indonesia imported their court culture from India, either in a Buddhist or in a Hindu form. Trade, missionary work, and peaceful penetration were the methods of Indian expansion. War and violence played a very small role. Tibet, to the north, and such mountain regions as Kashmir also came within the circle of Indian culture between A.D. 200 and 600.

China added Korea and Japan to its sphere of influence in the same centuries. South and west, in Vietnam and in central Asia, just before A.D. 600, the Chinese began to penetrate regions that were already in touch with Indian culture. Thus the expansion of the zones of influence around these two great Asian civilizations almost closed the geographical gap that had formerly separated them from one another. Pockets of wild country remained in southeast Asia, where primitive hunters and slash-and-burn cultivators lived as their ancestors had done for uncounted centuries; but along the rivers and wherever transport was easy, the impact of higher civilizations made itself felt.

Farther south, Australia and south Africa as yet showed no signs of reacting to the changes under way in the civilized world. In the Congo rain forest, however, the arrival of Indonesian plants, suited to cultivation in such an environment, allowed the development of agricultural communities throughout central Africa. Exactly when this type of cultivation began to spread in Africa is not known; but it was probably well established by A.D. 300.

In the New World, also, civilization had appeared by A.D. 600. Elaborate temples and cult centers began to arise in the highlands of Guatemala and the adjacent part of Mexico soon after the time of Christ. At about the same time, other temple communities arose in the central Mexican plateau to the north, and very similar developments also took place far to the south along the coast of Peru and high aloft in Andean valleys.

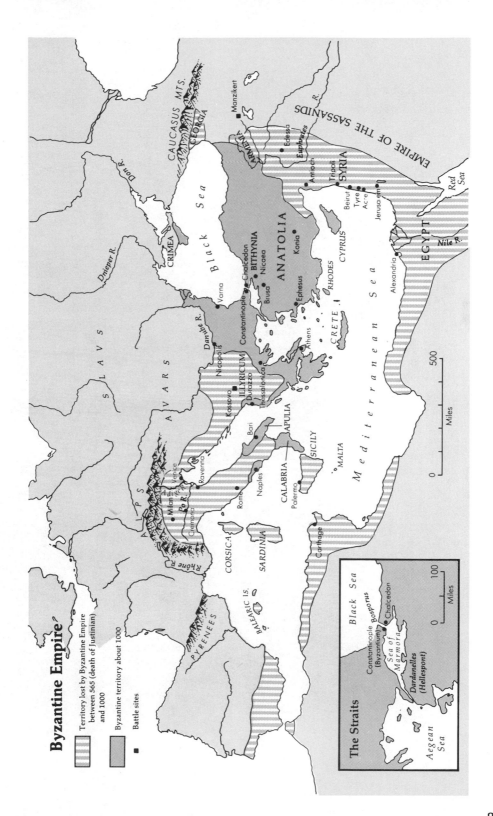

Byzantine Empire

Territory lost by Byzantine Empire between 565 (death of Justinian) and 1000

Byzantine territory about 1000

■ Battle sites

CAUCASUS MTS.

Don R.

GEORGIA

ARMENIA

Manzikert

EMPIRE OF THE SASSANIDS

Edessa

Euphrates R.

Antioch

Tripoli

SYRIA

Beirut

Tyre

Acre

Jerusalem

Red Sea

EGYPT

Nile R.

Alexandria

CRIMEA

Dnieper R.

Black Sea

Varna

ANATOLIA

BITHYNIA

Chalcedon

Constantinople

Nicaea

Brusa

Konia

Ephesus

CYPRUS

RHODES

CRETE

Athens

Mediterranean Sea

SLAVS

AVARS

Danube R.

Nicopolis

Kossovo

ILLYRICUM

Durazzo

Thessalonica

Bari

APULIA

SICILY

MALTA

Calabria

Palermo

Naples

Rome

Ravenna

PO R.

Milan

Venice

Adriatic

Cremona

ALPS

Rhône R.

CORSICA

SARDINIA

Carthage

BALEARIC IS.

PYRENEES

500

Miles

0

The Straits

Black Sea

Bosporus

Chalcedon

Constantinople (Byzantium)

Sea of Marmora

Dardanelles (Hellespont)

Aegean Sea

100

Miles

0

277

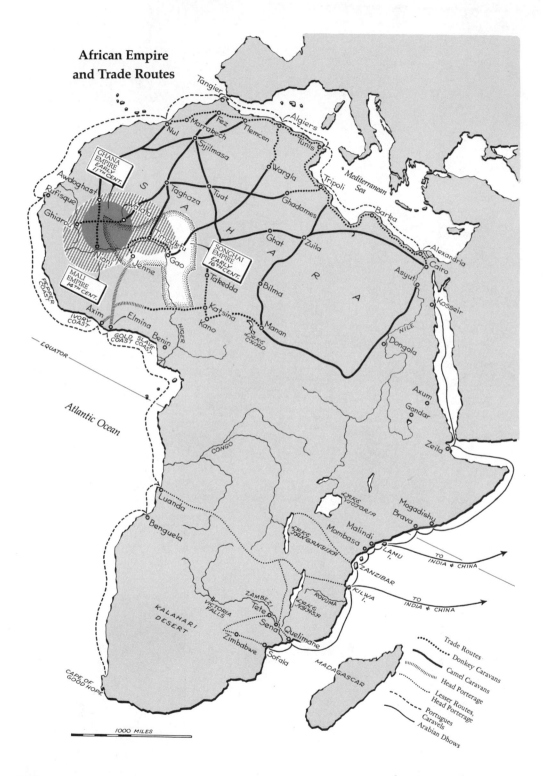

**African Empire
and Trade Routes**

Tangier

Nul
Fez
Marrakech
Tlemcen
Algiers
Tunis

Sijilmasa
Wargla
Tripoli
Mediterranean
Sea

GHANA
EMPIRE
EARLY
11TH CENT.

Awdoghast
S
Taghaza
Tuat
Ghadames
Barka

Rufisque
A
H

Ghiarou
Walata
A
Ghat
Zuila
Alexandria

Timbuktu
SONGHAI
EMPIRE
EARLY
16TH CENT.
Asyut
Cairo

Niani
Jenne
Gao
R
Kosseir

MALI
EMPIRE
14TH CENT.
Takedda
Bilma
A
NILE

PEPPER COAST
Axim
Elmina
Katsina
Manan
Dongola

IVORY COAST
NIGER
Kano
LAKE CHAD

GOLD COAST
SLAVE COAST
Benin

EQUATOR

Axum
Gondar

Atlantic Ocean

CONGO
Zeila

Luanda
LAKE VICTORIA
Mogadishu
Brava

Benguela
LAKE TANGANYIKA
Malindi
Mombasa
LAMU I.
TO INDIA & CHINA

ZANZIBAR

ROVUMA
KILWA
TO INDIA & CHINA

KALAHARI
DESERT
ZAMBEZI
VICTORIA FALLS
Tete
LAKE NYASSA

Sena
Quelimane

Zimbabwe
Sofala

MADAGASCAR

Trade Routes
Donkey Caravans
Camel Caravans
Head Porterage
Lesser Routes,
Head Porterage
Portugues
Caravels
Arabian Dhows

CAPE OF
GOOD HOPE

1000 MILES

In many respects these new civilizations resembled the early phases of Sumerian civilization. Priests seem to have been the organizers. They persuaded the farmers to deliver part of their crop to temple authorities, who then used the temple income to support professional stone carvers, architects, calendar makers, and ritual experts.

The Mayan cities in Guatemala and southern Mexico kept in touch, and the various temple centers in these places resembled one another closely. The Mayans invented an elementary kind of writing based on pictographs. Modern scholars are able to decipher this writing in part and can read dates which the Mayans recorded with exact precision. The earliest Mayan date yet deciphered is equivalent to April 9, A.D. 328. In central Mexico and in Peru archaeologists lack this means of knowing exactly how old their discoveries are. Uncertainty prevails as to whether these regions were behind the Mayans, or kept abreast of them in the development of monumental building, metal working, writing, and other skills mastered by Mayan priests and artisans.

Peruvian cultures differed in several important respects from those of the Mayan and Mexican regions. The river valleys that plunge from the high Andes to the Pacific are separated from one another by barren and utterly inhospitable deserts. Hence Peruvian agriculture depended on irrigation, whereas Mayan farming relied on rain. Different crops were apparently first cultivated in Peru, but maize, the great staple of the north, soon became important in Peru, too. The ancient Peruvians did less stone carving but elaborated their pottery more than the Mayans ever did. Moreover, each of the short river valleys that became the seat of irrigation agriculture developed its own style of art. Nothing like the cohesion of the separate Mayan cult centers can be discovered in Peru until long after A.D. 600. These differences suggest, perhaps, that the development of civilizations in Peru may have been independent of what was going on in the Mayan and Mexican areas, although long before the time of Columbus the two regions had entered into more or less regular contact.

Even though the world was thus beginninig to fill up with civilized and semicivilized societies, the commercial links that had united the Mediterranean world with China and India at the time of Christ tended to break off in the centuries of barbarian invasion. Each civilization was more inclined than before to fall back upon its own devices. A period of withdrawal and comparative isolation therefore succeeded the extensive exchanges and migrations of people and of ideas that had been so prominent in the centuries between 200 B.C. and A.D. 600.

CONCLUSION

A cycle of advance, retreat, and partial recovery can be detected behind all the confusing detail of events dealt with in this chapter. First, the different civilized regions of Eurasia came closer together than ever before as a result of organizing regular trade connections. Caravans linked China with the Mediterranean shore and moved southward into India as well. Sea trade between the Mediterranean and India was equally or more important, and a few merchants got as far as southern China.

These enlarged contacts allowed new religious ideas to spread widely among civilized populations. In particular, Mahayana Buddhism and Christianity won enormous numbers of adherents, and Hinduism was not far behind. All three of these faiths offered their followers a hope for salvation and a future heavenly existence. Moreover, salvation in each case was believed to be possible because of a special link between each individual believer, no matter how humble, and a divine yet manlike savior. In detail, of course, the teachings of each religion differed from the others, and each faith developed its own kind of religious organization—church, monastery, or temple, as the case might be.

The three new religions continued to prosper and spread even when, after about A.D. 200, the complicated arrangements needed to sustain long-distance caravan and sea trade began to break down. At the two extremes of the civilized world, in Europe and in China, local self-sufficiency became more common. Trade did not cease, but the scale and regularity of movement to and fro across long distances declined sharply as the wealth and political stability of both Rome and China suffered serious decay.

Exactly what caused the decline of the Roman Empire—and the no less disastrous decline of the Han Empire in China—has long been a theme for scholarly debate. Depopulation, resulting from exposure to unfamiliar diseases that had been spread throughout Eurasia and parts of Africa by traders, was probably one important factor. Weakened and impoverished governments, in turn, found it impossible to prevent barbarians from overrunning wide territories in Europe and China. China recovered after A.D. 589, when the Sui Dynasty united the Yellow River valley and the Yangtze River valley under their sway, and proceeded to link the two parts of China securely together by building the Grand Canal.

In the Far West, civilized government could not be restored so quickly. To be sure, the East Roman or Byzantine Empire did indeed regain much lost ground in the age of Justinian (527–565). But no new resources like those that became available to the Chinese emperors allowed the rulers of Byzantium to fasten their power securely over the full extent of the Old Roman Empire.

The decline and recovery of the Roman and Chinese empires at the two extremes of the civilized world of Eurasia had no parallel in Iran, Mesopotamia, and India. There, on the contrary, barbarian raiders were kept at bay by heavy-armored cavalry, perfected, apparently, by Parthians about 100 B.C. The solid success of the Parthians and of their Persian successors in keeping the steppe peoples from invading the Middle East also protected India, which reached its classical peak under the Gupta at a time when both China and Rome were in the throes of barbarian invasion and civil wars.

Thus the cycle of expansion, contraction, and then at least partial recovery made itself felt mainly at the extremes of the civilized world— that is, in Europe and in China. The Middle Eastern regions, where danger from the steppe was most immediate, suffered less because local institutions and defense establishments were better fitted for holding the steppe peoples at bay. Yet in the centuries that followed the Middle East proved vulnerable to a new kind of nomad attack, issuing this time from the Arabian desert to the south and inspired by a new religious faith, Islam.

The surge of Islam, sudden and successful in surprising degree, sharply altered the pattern of relations among the world's civilizations and marked a new era in the history of Eurasia. This will be the subject of the next chapter.

CHAPTER 10

Islam
and India

600 to 1200

The prophet Mohammed (A.D. 570–632*) established a new world religion, Islam, that transformed relationships among the peoples of western Asia within an amazingly short period of time. Mohammed's new revelation united the Arabs as never before. They then set out to conquer and subdue the peoples of the world, beginning with those nearest at hand in Syria, Egypt, Mesopotamia, and Iran. Many of the inhabitants of these regions were quite willing to submit. Ever since the time of Alexander the Great (330–323 B.C.), Semitic-speaking peoples of the Middle East had been subjected to rulers who drew their culture from Greek sources. Just before Mohammed's time, Syrians and Egyptians had proved their growing self-consciousness by breaking away from the Greek form of Christianity. Farther east, in Mesopotamia, the successors to the ancient Babylonians had shown their dislike of Persian (Sassanian) rule by espousing still another form of Christianity—Nestorianism.

The Arab conquests brought all these peoples back under a single political roof, for the first time since the overthrow of the old Persian Empire. By extending their power across north Africa and into Spain, the Moslems (as followers of Mohammed's faith are often called) added to their domains the territories that had once belonged to the empire of Carthage.

* Henceforth all dates are A.D. unless otherwise specified.

This was a remarkable achievement. Even more remarkable was the fact that the power of Islam quickly created what amounted to a new civilization within this broad territory. The new Moslem civilization carried forward and developed some aspects of the Greek and ancient Near Eastern heritages. But in many ways it was unique, built around religion and the fresh revelation of God's will that, as all Moslems believed, had inspired the prophet Mohammed.

The rise of a strong and self-conscious civilization in the Middle East created new problems for neighboring peoples. Even the distant Chinese were affected by it, for the collapse of the T'ang Empire in central Asia began with military defeat suffered in 751 at Moslem hands. Living much nearer the centers of Moslem power, Christian rulers of Europe found themselves hard pressed to hold back the Moslem advance. India, on the other flank of the Middle East, entirely lacked the military organization needed to resist the warriors of Islam successfully, particularly when Moslem armies were reinforced by Turks from the central portions of the Eurasian steppe. As a result, between 1000 and 1200, Islamic invaders conquered all of northern India, and Hindu religion and culture had to adjust to the loss of state support throughout the broad territories that passed into Moslem hands.

In a worldly sense, such a record was a tremendous success story. Throughout the first six centuries of their history, Moslems never stopped adding new territories to the realm of Islam. All rivals had to withdraw or submit. In a deeper sense, however, as military successes followed one after the other, the original aspiration of the community of the faithful failed dismally. To understand this seeming contradiction, we must look more closely at the faith Mohammed preached.

MOHAMMED'S LIFE AND HIS MESSAGE

Mohammed was born in the trading city of Mecca in the west-central part of Arabia. Until he was about forty years of age he led an ordinary, undistinguished life. In youth he traveled north with caravans carrying goods to Palestine, which was under Byzantine rule. Later on he married a wealthy woman and could afford to stay at home while others trudged with the camels. By local standards, this was a successful career. However, Mohammed was troubled by voices and visions. After several years of distress and uncertainty, he came to the conclusion that he, Mohammed, had been chosen to deliver new and compelling revelations from God.

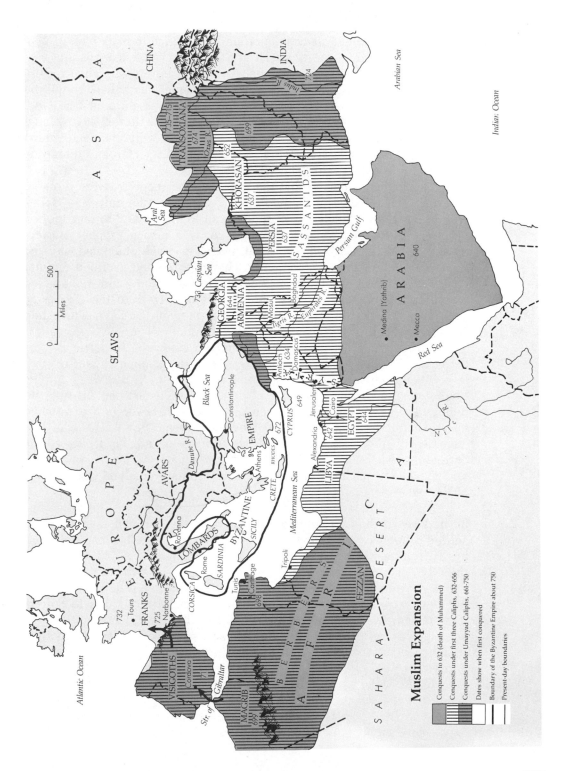

Muslim Expansion

Conquests to 632 (death of Muhammed)

Conquests under first three Caliphs, 632–656

Conquests under Umayyad Caliphs, 661–750

Dates show when first conquered

Boundary of the Byzantine Empire about 750

Present-day boundaries

285

With nothing but his conviction and eloquence to back him up, Mohammed therefore began to preach in the streets of Mecca. His message was direct and simple: the established local worship was abhorred by God. The idols of the Kaaba, as the local temple was called, should be destroyed at once and give way to the worship of the one true God, Allah. In addition, Mohammed threatened scoffers with the Day of Judgment, when God would raise the dead and judge everyone, condemning sinners and unbelievers to eternal torment in a fiery Hell and admitting the faithful to a cool and delicious Paradise.

Mohammed believed that the messages he received were dictated to him by the Angel Gabriel and came from God—the only true God—who had revealed himself to Abraham and to Moses and to the Hebrew prophets. Jesus, according to Mohammed, was also a prophet, a mere man like Mohammed himself. Here, according to Mohammed, lay the fundamental mistake of Christianity. Human error had ascribed divinity to Christ, whereas in fact there was no God but God—and Mohammed was his prophet, sent expressly to correct the errors of the Christians and Jews. As for the latter, their great error was the Law, which had come not from God but from human invention.

At first, few Meccans took Mohammed seriously. In particular, his denunciation of the traditional local religion aroused opposition. Nonetheless, the old faiths of Arabia were no longer able to inspire deep convictions. Bedouin tribes, who lived as nomads, could rest content with ill-defined local gods and observances that expressed reverence for unusual natural features, such as springs, rocks, or trees. But Arabs who had become city dwellers, living as oasis farmers or on the profits of the caravan trade, found these old faiths inadequate. Many became Jews, and some became Christians; but Mecca itself had remained a stronghold of the older paganism.

Mohammed was acquainted with stories from the Bible. Perhaps he had heard them around campfires when the caravan reached more settled country on the fringes of Palestine. At any rate, his inspired utterances repeat several of the episodes familiar to Jews and Christians from the Old Testament, with some variations. Certainly Mohammed did not know very much about either Judaism or Christianity. If he had, he could not have expected Jews and Christians to accept his efforts to correct their religion; yet at first this was exactly what he did expect. Was he not a prophet of God, sent for the precise purpose of correcting doctrine that had been corrupted through the centuries by human carelessness and vice?

In 622 Mohammed left Mecca and went to a nearby oasis city, Medina. He departed secretly, fearing that his enemies in Mecca might waylay him on the road. His withdrawal to Medina was afterward referred to as the Hegira (Arabic for "flight"), and it is from that event that the

Moslems date the establishment of their religion. To this day in Moslem countries, dates are counted from the year of the Hegira, so that 1990, for example, overlaps the Moslem years 1368–1369.

In Medina, Mohammed entered upon a new life. The oasis in which Medina was situated was in the throes of civil strife. Some of the inhabitants were Jews, while others had remained pagan. Tribal relationships had weakened and the community badly needed a lawgiver to declare and enforce rules that would fit the conditions of agricultural and urban life. A faction among the people of Medina had invited Mohammed to play this role. On his arrival he energetically took up the new task. With Allah's help, Mohammed prescribed a set of rules for everyday behavior.

A handful of followers accompanied Mohammed to Medina. Soon the Prophet's lawgiving won over most of the pagans of Medina, but the Jews stubbornly refused to admit the truth of Mohammed's revelations. A trickle of new recruits drifted in from Mecca and elsewhere, as news of the new faith spread.

This created a serious economic problem, for the fertile land of the oasis of Medina was limited, and the newcomers had no means of support. Mohammed met this problem by taking the offensive. He sent out war parties to intercept Meccan caravans; and when the angry Meccans attempted to revenge themselves by attacking Medina, the little army Mohammed sent against them won a victory. Mohammed hailed this success as a miracle, a clear sign of God's will. His critics had long demanded a miracle to prove the genuineness of his mission. Now God had given them a miracle—or so Mohammed and his supporters believed.

In addition, Mohammed drove the Jews from Medina and seized their property. He promptly divided their fields among his followers; but the size of the community continued to grow, so that the oasis of Medina soon became insufficient to support them all. Mohammed therefore launched an attack upon another oasis, some distance away, which was also inhabited by Jews. This time he did not drive them out, but instead required that they pay a head tax as a sign of their submission to the community of the faithful.

Perhaps Mohammed made this arrangement because he did not want to split up his followers. It was to have enormous importance later, for Mohammed's policy toward these Arabian Jews set the pattern for all subsequent Moslem policy toward "People of the Book," as Mohammed termed both Christians and Jews. Mohammed's view of the proper relation between his own followers and their Jewish and Christian fellows was simple: Jews and Christians should be allowed to keep their own religion, but ought to submit to the Moslems and pay a head tax to the Moslem community as a sign of their subjection.

As the community of the faithful grew, Mohammed defined what was expected of a Moslem believer, partly through revealed utterances, and partly by quite casual acts and everyday decisions. These, too, in later time, became binding upon Moslems. The fundamental aim of everything Mohammed did was to try to obey God completely. He called his faith *Islam*, which means "submission"—submission, that is, to God's will.

As interpreted by Mohammed, God's will did not impose very complicated obligations. The faithful prayed together five times daily. This was the chief ritual. It consisted of the repetition of set phrases of praise and of bowing down to the ground before God's majesty. As long as it was possible for the entire community of the faithful to assemble in one place, Mohammed led them in prayer. When a portion of the community was sent off on some military expedition, however, their commander took over the role of prayer leader in the absence of Mohammed.

In other words, civil and religious authority were one and the same. Nothing like an organized church, distinct from society as a whole, ever grew up within Islam. The idea of separating religious duty from other affairs would have seemed absolutely incomprehensible to Mohammed and his early followers. God's will was just as important in deciding how to eat or fight or marry as it was in choosing how to pray.

In addition to daily prayer Mohammed imposed four other religious duties. Good Moslems should give aid to the poor when they could afford it; they should fast from sunrise to sunset during the month of Ramadan each year; they should not eat pork or drink wine; and, after his triumphal return to Mecca (630), Mohammed also required Moslems to make a pilgrimage to Mecca. Other rules, such as how to divide booty taken from the Meccan caravans or how many wives a man could marry (the answer was four), became of importance later, but they did not rank as religious duties in the same way as the five "pillars of Islam."

During his years in Medina, Mohammed gathered a tightly knit and extremely well-disciplined community around himself. Believing as they did that Mohammed spoke the word of God, the followers obeyed him unquestioningly. Daily prayers had a psychological effect similar to that which had been achieved among the soldiers of the phalanx during the classical age of Greece. Hundreds and soon thousands of men, praying together and making the same ritual motions together, learned to think and feel together. This in turn allowed them to act together with an energy and conviction that made Moslem raiding parties extremely successful.

Many Meccans were not sure that it was right to oppose Mohammed. Every success he won seemed to prove that God was really on his side. Opposition therefore crumbled, and in 630 the Prophet was able to return in triumph to his native city. Other Arab tribes then had the choice of either recognizing the religion of Islam and accepting Mohammed's leadership or facing fanatical Moslem attack. One by one the Arab chieftains came to terms with Mohammed and joined the Moslem community by publicly reciting the creed of Islam: "There is no God but God and Mohammed is his Prophet."

The First Caliphs

The unification of Arabia was barely complete when Mohammed died (632). Many of the Arab chieftains assumed that their only obligation was to Mohammed himself; they therefore withdrew from the Islamic community. This presented Mohammed's closest associates and followers with a difficult choice. How, first of all, could the community continue without the Prophet to instruct them in God's will? And what should be done to prevent the community from breaking up, now that Mohammed was no longer there to lead them?

ABU-BAKR   Mohammed's closest followers met soon after his death and decided to recognize Abu-Bakr as caliph. The term *caliph* means "successor"—successor, that is, to the Prophet. Abu-Bakr was one of Mohammed's earliest converts and came from a prominent Meccan family. He was also older than most of the other important Moslems. As Mohammed's successor, however, Abu-Bakr did not claim to be a prophet himself. The community would have to get along on the basis of the revelations already received through Mohammed. But pious Moslems consoled themselves with the thought that God, being just, would not take the Prophet away until all the truths they needed had been revealed.

Abu-Bakr decided that anyone who had accepted Islam could not withdraw from the community. So he attacked the tribes that had fallen away from the faith. After two hard campaigns, the Moslems were victorious everywhere. At the time Abu-Bakr died (634), Arabia was therefore united once again.

OMAR   The next caliph was Omar, a much younger man, who possessed both unusual energy and an absolute religious conviction. As caliph, Omar launched the fighting manpower of all Arabia against the Byzantine and Persian empires. Success came at once. In 636 a Byzantine army was defeated near the river Jordan (Battle of Yarmuk). The emperors in Constantinople never reasserted their power in Palestine and Syria. The next year Omar turned the Arab army against Mesopotamia and captured that rich province from the Persians. Egypt fell in 642 and the Sassanian Empire collapsed entirely in 651, opening all of Iran and the borderlands north and east of Iran to the Moslems.

Thus in fifteen years the Moslems overran the entire Middle East, with the exception of Asia Minor which remained in Byzantine hands. Nothing in Moslem military equipment or tactics can account for this success. The heavy-armored cavalry of the Persian and Byzantine armies should have been as effective against Arab troops as they had always been against steppe nomads from the north. The new factor was religious: the conviction that God was with the Moslems gained force with every victory. Friend and foe alike could scarcely doubt that God's hand lay behind the Moslems' amazing successes. Moreover, years of campaigning, the habit of victory, and the discipline of Islam all reinforced one another to make the Arabs irresistible.

Omar had to decide how to manage the wide lands that fell into his hands. He had only Mohammed's precepts to follow, and follow them he did. He preferred to keep the Moslems together in communities, so that the pattern of life Mohammed had prescribed for them might continue. This meant that the new conquerors could not follow the Sassanian pattern of stationing warriors on country estates for local defense. Instead, Omar set up special garrison cities to control each important new province. Whenever possible, these were located on the edge of the desert, so that the Arabs stationed there could remain in touch with their old form of life. The conquered peoples paid taxes as always. Omar simply kept the Byzantine and Persian tax system in force. He even reappointed the same officials as tax collectors. The yield from the taxes was distributed among the garrisons, so that each Moslem soldier received something similar to a dividend each year, representing his share of the booty and of tax income that Moslem victories had made available for distribution to the faithful.

The Arabs continued to belong to tribes. A chief and his followers simply settled down in one of the new garrison cities where other tribes were also quartered. Except for conduct prescribed by Islam, tribal manners and customs remained in force. Islam made a difference, of course; Mohammed's rules for settling quarrels prohibited the old blood feud, for example. But the different tribes remembered past enmities among themselves as well as their more recent victories over their new Christian, Zoroastrian, and Jewish subjects.

OTHMAN   Omar did not live to see the final victory over Persia, since he was assassinated in 644. His successor in the office of caliph was Othman, head of another important Meccan family, the Omayyad. Othman did not command universal respect among Moslems as Abu-Bakr and Omar had done. Naturally, he tried to reinforce his position by appointing members of his own family to key positions, making them commanders of the principal Arab armies and favoring them in other ways as well. Other families, not unnaturally, were jealous.

THE KORAN   Othman also faced opposition from those who felt that he was not a strict and reliable guardian of Mohammed's revelation.

Mecca. (*Saudi Arabia Public Relations Bureau*)

Since it no longer seemed enough to trust the memory and judgment of the caliph, a group of those who had known Mohammed closely went to great pains during Othman's caliphate (term of office) to establish the correct text of the Prophet's inspired utterances. They did this by comparing their personal memories of what Mohammed had said. They set each separate revelation apart as a chapter or *sura* (117 in all) and then arranged them according to length, starting with the longest and ending with the shortest.

This carefully authenticated text of God's revelation to Mohammed was known as the Koran. It has since remained absolutely central to Islam. In principle, Moslems took it for granted that everything they needed to know of God's purposes was recorded there. The beginning of piety and wisdom, therefore, was to memorize the Koran word for word. Since the entire book is only about a quarter of the length of the Christian Bible, this was not an impossible task. Nearly all Moslems memorize large parts of it; scholars pore over its every phrase with utmost reverence, for to them it is the *Word* of God in the exact and literal sense of the term.

The importance of the Koran was magnified by the fact that Islam rejected the Jewish and Christian scriptures on the ground that careless, ignorant, or unscrupulous interpreters had confused God's revelation by mingling their own words with those that were authentically God's. Special precautions were needed to prevent anything similar happening to Mohammed's revelation. As a result, an overriding concern for the exact text of the Koran has remained absolutely central to all later Moslem learning.

Since the words and phrases of the Koran came to bear such tremendous significance, it soon became important to find out what shades of meaning a particular expression or word carried in its Koranic context. This called for study of the Arabic language and of how rare words were used in different passages of the Koran. An elaborate linguistic science thus arose, which continues to demand careful attention of Moslem scholars today.

THE PROBLEM OF SUCCESSION TO THE CALIPHATE   The Koran, recited weekly or more often before gatherings of true believers, and the discipline of prayer, five times each day, standardized and defined the Moslem faith. But when Arabs from different tribes were stationed for years at a time in widely scattered garrison cities, it was impossible to maintain the unquestioning subordination to the caliph that had been possible when the whole company of the faithful constituted a single community in the small oasis of Medina. This situation became all too obvious when Othman was murdered in 656. Omar had been assassinated by a lone individual; Othman was murdered by a group of unruly warriors who accused him, justifiably, of favoring his own family. His death brought to a head the problem of succession. With armies scattered far and wide there was, in fact, no way of agreeing on a suitable caliph. The community of the faithful could not assemble in any one place; and if the attempt had been made, they could not have agreed. No one of the stature of Omar or Abu-Bakr was known to all Moslems and respected by them all.

Two conflicting principles were advanced to meet this crisis. Some argued that the rightful succession must belong to members of Mohammed's family. The Prophet had no surviving sons. His closest male relative was Ali (Ali ibn-abi-Tālib), son of Mohammed's uncle and the husband of his daughter Fatima. Accordingly, after Othman's assassination Ali claimed to be the legitimate caliph. Some Moslems, especially the garrison of Mesopotamia (or Iraq, as the Arabs called that land), supported him. On the other hand, members of Othman's family argued that the succession belonged to them by virtue of tribal custom that defined how chieftainship should pass from one generation to the next.

Only force could decide between these rival claims. But the Moslem rank and file were not eager to fight against one another. Preliminary maneuvers, therefore, did not lead to much bloodshed. The problem

The Dome of the Rock in Jerusalem (built, ca. A.D. 661–691). Islamic tradition holds that Mohammed ascended into heaven from this spot. It is also the place, according to Judeo-Christian tradition, where Abraham prepared his son Isaac for sacrifice. (Israel Government Tourist Office)

seemed solved when Ali was murdered by one of his followers. Muawiyah, head of the Omayyad family, forestalled Ali's son, Husain, who attempted to take command of the forces stationed in Iraq. The military base for Muawiyah's strength lay in Syria; part of the struggle between the rivals, therefore, was a contest for leadership of the new Moslem state between forces based on ex-Byzantine territory and those stationed on ex-Persian territory. Tribal differences also entered into the struggle for power.

The lasting importance of this strife was that it provoked the first irremediable split in Islam. Some of Ali's supporters were religious enthusiasts who held that only a perfectly pious man could be a true caliph. This created an impossible standard against which to measure any real man and ruler; and as long as Ali and his son, Husain, lived, the doctrine did not take firm hold. But after Husain had been killed in battle while trying to make good his claim to leadership over the Moslem community, the situation altered. A group of pious and enthusiastic Moslems then asserted that the true caliph was in fact hiding, because the times were too corrupt for him to emerge and take his rightful place as head of the community of the faithful. At some future time, they believed, the "Hidden Imam"—the secret true head of God's faithful servants—would emerge; and until then it was necessary to wait patiently, mourn Husain's death, and be ready for the Imam's eventual appearance.

This represented one sectarian extreme. There were those who believed that, after Husain's death, legitimate succession to the Prophet passed to other descendants of Ali. One group recognized a line that ran for seven generations; another group preferred a line that ran for twelve. But all these groups agreed on this: the existing leaders of the Islamic community were usurpers, who should not be honored as true successors to the Prophet. Such dissenters were known as Shia, in contrast to the majority who came to be known as Sunni Moslems.

The Omayyad Caliphate

From 661, when Muawiyah made good his claim to be the caliph, until 750, the realm of Islam was governed by the Omayyad family. It was a time of continued territorial expansion. Moslem armies moved across north Africa and entered Spain in 711, where they speedily overthrew the Visigothic kingdom and made themselves masters of that country. By 705, on the opposite flank, other Moslem armies reached India and overran the province of Sind, along the lower Indus River. In central Asia, north of the Himalayas, still other Moslem troops collided with the Chinese and defeated them in a battle at the river Talas in 751. As a result of such successes, the caliph controlled a territory that covered almost exactly the same ground that the old Persian and Carthaginian empires once had governed.

On one front, however, the Moslems met with failure. After several minor thrusts against Byzantium, the caliph sent his brother to lead an assault upon the capital of the East Roman or Byzantine Empire in 717. The siege lasted a year, and both sides used naval as well as land forces. The siege failed. This was a serious setback to the Moslems, materially as well as psychologically. For the first time, when large forces had been engaged, God had not crowned Moslem arms with victory.

The failure before the walls of Byzantium put other strains upon Moslem society. As long as new territories opened up rapidly, any individual or group that found itself defeated or snubbed at the seat of power in Damascus, where the Omayyads established their capital, could drift toward the frontier and there carve out a satisfying career. When, however, expansion onto ground where there was anything worth conquering came to a halt, discontented tribesmen were tempted to fight things out near the center of the caliph's domains and try to seize by main force what the caliph's administrators had awarded to someone else.

Armed clashes had not been wanting in the first years of Omayyad rule; but after the failure before the walls of Constantinople in 718, the scale of fighting among Arab tribes and factions increased markedly. Radical sects rose in revolt; tribal intrigues flourished. The upshot was the overthrow of the Omayyads in 750 and the transfer of the caliphate to the Abbasid family, which held that office until 1258.

Another important source of discontent that weakened the Omayyads was the rising friction between Arab and non-Arab Moslems. The Arab conquerors were not very eager to spread Islam among their subjects. First of all, conversion to Islam excused a convert from paying taxes, and that reduced the revenues upon which so many Arabs had come to depend. In the second place, as long as tribal organization survived among the Arabs, there was no way to fit a convert into the Islamic community without undermining the traditional structure of Arab society. Converts could, indeed, be classed as "wanderers." This status, inherited from desert days, meant that the person in question was under the protection of the tribe but was not a member, since a tribe by definition was supposed to be based on common descent and blood relationship.

Nothing in Mohammed's revelations, however, said anything about tribes. Believers were all equal, animated by an immortal soul entrusted to him or her by God. And if someone accepted the truths of Islam and professed them in public, then the convert became a Moslem and should, in logic at least, have the same rights and status as any other Moslem. Naturally, converts were inclined to take Mohammed's revelation seriously and wished to be treated like other Moslems, not as inferiors. They therefore reinforced the groups among the Arabs who felt that the Omayyad caliphs were unworthy of their position.

THE HADITH   The underlying fact was that, as the size of the Moslem community increased, the original identity between secular and religious leadership could not be maintained. Mohammed, Abu-Bakr, and Omar had been able to fill both roles, but the Omayyads were more like tribal chiefs presiding over an uneasy confederation of other tribal chiefs. There were Moslems who kept to the original idea of living a life pleasing to God in every detail. They studied the Koran, of course. And when questions arose which were not covered by any passage of the Koran, they fell back upon the memories of what the Prophet and his close companions had done in similar circumstances. These memories were carefully gathered and then checked, as far as possible, by listing who had heard the story from whom, all the way back to an eyewitness. The Hadith, as these records were called, became second only to the Koran as authoritative guides to conduct.

THE SHARIA   Yet the system was not complete. In the environment of the Middle Eastern cities, amid alien peoples, Moslems encountered new situations to which neither the Koran nor the Hadith applied. Experts in Islam worked from analogy to answer such problems; and if analogy

Santa Sophia. (*Hirmer Fotoarchiv*)

failed, they fell back on the general opinion of the faithful, arguing that God would not in fact permit the community to err on any important question.

On the basis of these four kinds of authority, a group of learned Moslems busily set out to create a complete set of rules for conduct according to God's declared will. The result was the Moslem Sacred Law or Sharia. The class of religious experts who worked it out were called ulama. (The word *ulama* means "learned" in Arabic.) At first, the ulama gathered mainly in Medina, where memories of Mohammed's life were most vivid. Later experts in the Sacred Law scattered all over the Moslem world, ready to give advice to ordinary persons about how to obey God's will in any unusual or difficult case.

RELIGIOUS EXERCISES   Conduct of the common prayer also passed into the hands of specialists, whose main qualifications were a loud, clear voice and good standing as a Moslem. At each of the appointed hours of the day, these men called the faithful to prayer. The summons caused all to interrupt whatever they were doing in order to kneel on the ground and pray, their faces turned toward Mecca. On Fridays, special services took place at specially designated spots—an open square, for example. There, prayer and recitation from the Koran reminded the faithful of their obligations to God. Sometimes the Moslems took possession of a Christian church for these services. That was the case in Damascus, for example, where the Omayyad caliphs seized the largest Christian church for Moslem use. In other cases, new structures were built, usually leaving the interior wide open to the sky. The enclosed mosque, with slender minarets and a high-domed roof, remained quite unknown until much later than the time we are here considering.

CULTURAL RELATIONS BETWEEN MOSLEMS AND THEIR SUBJECT PEOPLES   The first Moslem generations generally tried to hold themselves apart from the peoples they had conquered. Secretly and in private an Omayyad caliph might hire a painter to decorate his bedroom walls in Hellenistic style. Several such damaged frescoes survive from the period. In addition, the bureaucratic machine remained in Christian and Zoroastrian hands. The Omayyad caliphs were more concerned with adjusting frictions among tribal leaders of the Arab community than with details of how taxes should be collected.

As for the Christians, they regarded Islam as a form of heresy. Most of the inhabitants of Syria and Egypt felt no loyalty to Byzantium. They had quarreled with the Byzantine authorities over the proper definition of the relation between the divine and human natures of Christ, and had formed their own churches—Syriac in Syria and Coptic in Egypt. Hence when the Moslems first arrived, most Christians in Syria and Egypt felt that they were simply exchanging one kind of heretical rule for another. This, of course, aided the Moslem conquest enormously. In many cities the Arabs were welcomed as liberators; nowhere were they vigorously opposed by the local inhabitants.

Through the centuries, the inhabitants of Syria, Egypt, and Mesopotamia had become used to foreign rule. They had known Greek, Roman, Parthian, or Persian domination for nearly a thousand years when the Arabs appeared on the scene. Passive withdrawal and careful preservation of what they valued worked just as well under the Arabs as under their predecessors. As a result, in the first Moslem centuries far less cultural interchange occurred than the geographical mixing of Arabs and Christians would lead one to expect.

In Persia proper this was less true. The Persians submitted to Islam with some enthusiasm; their ancestral Zoroastrianism and the Manichaean effort to update Zoroastrianism somehow failed to hold their affection. As a warrior people—and the Persian gentry of the eastern frontier lands were above all warriors—they respected the Moslems: clearly God was with them and sensible people did not fight against God. Hence the Persian nation, as a whole, rapidly went over to Islam, keeping its own language intact. Eager study of the Koran and of Moslem traditions led many Persians to forget their national past; but memories lingered and the knowledge that their ancestors had once ruled the whole Middle East was never entirely forgotten.

The Abbasid Caliphate

The Abbasid family, another Meccan clan, claimed distant relationship to Ali. This lineage attracted the Shia groups in the population. In 750 the head of the family, Abu-al-Abbas, was governor of Khorasan, one of the easternmost of the Persian provinces, and the troops that carried him to power were nearly all Persian. Persian Moslems did not really mind fighting the Arabs upon whose military supremacy the Omayyad caliphs had based their power. Moreover, when the Arab troops had been defeated, the victors took away the tax revenue that had supported the Arab garrisons ever since Omar's day. Loss of this privileged status had the effect of rapidly breaking up the old tribal structure. In the settled environment of the Middle East, tribal ties had already weakened. Many Arabs had married local women; some had acquired land. When the tribe members lost the privilege of sharing the tax income of the state, chiefs lost their power. Individuals simply scattered out among the rest of the population and soon forgot their tribal identity.

SEPARATION OF SACRED FROM CIVIL AUTHORITY   As a result, the former barrier between Arab Moslems and other Moslems disappeared, and a much more widespread and intimate interaction between Arab and non-Arab peoples set in. The Koran tied Islam to the Arabic language absolutely. This assured the ultimate linguistic dominance of the Arabs. On the other hand, the superior sophistication of the Syrian and Persian populations meant that many aspects of the new Moslem civilization that emerged under the Abbasids were more Syrian and Persian than Arabic.

This was particularly evident in the pattern of Abbasid administration. The new rulers established their capital at Baghdad in Mesopotamia on the Tigris River. The manners of the court were modeled on Persian royal etiquette. The sovereign lived in private and seldom appeared before the eyes of his subjects. Day-by-day power rested in the hands of a minister, the vizier (literal meaning, burden bearer), appointed by the caliph. Military force was represented by a royal bodyguard; but when a major campaign had to be fought, landholders from the country were required to join the royal army. All this corresponded exactly to the way the Sassanian kings had ruled.

Obviously such a government did not satisfy the pious Moslems who wanted to see the original purity of the community of the faithful revived. The Abbasid family's claim to rule was no better than that of the Omayyads. Instead of being more than life-sized Arab chiefs, as the Omayyad caliphs had been, the Abbasid caliphs behaved like Persian kings who happened to be Moslems.

Such a failure to restore the original purity of Islam caused some of those who had supported Abu-al-Abbas in his struggle against the Omayyads to turn against him when he came to power. On the other hand, most Moslems were prepared to accept the sort of informal compromise that the Abbasid government made with the learned and pious ulama, inviting the experts who had memorized the Koran and mastered the Sacred Law to instruct ordinary Moslems in what they should do to please God. All that the Abbasids reserved for themselves was the collection of taxes and the defense of the community of the faithful from foreign or domestic enemies.

Clearly such an arrangement fell short of the high hopes of religious fanatics. The caliph was not a model of piety. His fitness for office rested on descent, not on his religious perfection. But most serious Moslems were willing to accept half a loaf. After all, the Abbasid religious compromise allowed pious men to lead the community in everything that mattered. The ulama, sitting in the marketplace, could pass judgment on all points of conscience brought before them. Private life could therefore be thoroughly Moslem, conducted in perfect conformity to the will of God as defined by the Sacred Law. And if public life fell short of such perfection, then it was the rulers and their ministers that would suffer the consequences when God's Day of Judgment came at last.

THE ROLE OF SCIENCE   A similar compromise allowed limited scope for science and even for philosophy. The Abbasids needed doctors to look after their health and astrologers to foretell the future. Experts able to serve in these capacities had to know Galen, who had summarized Greek medicine, and Ptolemy, who had summarized astronomy. As Arabic became more and more firmly established as the common tongue of all the peoples inhabiting the Middle East, the Greek texts had to be translated. And, of course, not all useful knowledge was to be found within the pages of Galen and Ptolemy. The Caliph al-Mamun (reigned 813–833) therefore organized a "house of wisdom," where translations from Greek, Persian, and Indian languages were systematically made. Much of what we know of Greek science today was preserved through these translations, since in the Christian world of the time no one was very interested in pagan notions.

Among the Moslems, however, translations soon stimulated more original work. Commentaries upon the ancient Greek texts were a first step; presently Moslem authors began to confront Greek learning with ideas and data that reached them from India and China. The best example of how important this could be is the history of what Europeans later learned to call "Arabic" numbers. The Greeks had used the letters of the alphabet to symbolize numbers, and the Romans had used an even more clumsy system of tally marks and letters. Such methods of notation made ordinary arithmetic very difficult and prevented calculations involving large numbers.

The ancient Babylonians sometimes used a place value notation for numbers, but without any sign for zero. This defect deprived the system of its main usefulness. In India, however, religious speculation about the reality of nothingness may have made it easier to treat zero as something real. At any rate, Indian mathematicians invented a place value notation with a symbol for zero. The system was in use as early as 269, but since nearly all early Indian writings have perished, we cannot tell how much use Indians made of this perfected notation for a decimal number system. Moslems picked up the idea from India in Caliph al-Mansur's time (reigned 745–775). Less than a generation later a famous mathematician, al-Khwarizmi (from Khiva, in central Asia, now part of the Soviet Union), began to use the new notation to solve the problems called, from his name, algorithms—a form of algebra.

The Abbasid example made patronage of scholars part of rulership. Hence when the political unity of the Moslem world began to break up, after about 950, the effect at first was only to increase the number of places at which scholars could find employment. The height of Arab science therefore came after the greatest days of the Abbasid caliphate had passed. Special scientific centers of activity tended to arise at the extremes of the Moslem world. Independent rulers in Spain, far to the west, and in Bokhara, in central Asia, were particularly anxious to prove their sophistication by patronizing men of science.

In general, the Moslem scientists kept within the framework of knowledge they had inherited from the Greeks. Galen's medicine and Ptolemy's astronomy always remained fundamental. In due time the Moslems produced famous summaries and handbooks of their own. In medicine the greatest textbook writer was ibn-Sina (980–1037), known as Avicenna by the doctors of the Latin West. His work did not so much replace Galen as add new cures and additional information to the body of observation and theory that Galen had offered. Such filling out of detail, rather than any fundamentally new theories, characterized nearly all Arabic sciences.

PHILOSOPHY AND RELIGION   Study of the material world did not strike most Moslems as particularly worthwhile. Those who interested themselves in such things were religiously suspect because they studied texts other than the Koran which, according to pious Moslems, contained everything anyone needed to know.

Some who were attracted to Greek philosophy became so entangled in the charms of logic that they, perhaps, deserved the reproaches that pious Moslems made against them. Al-Farabi (d. *c*. 950), for example, had little use for revealed truth of any sort and thought it more important to try to combine Plato's doctrines with those of Aristotle into a perfect, rational system that would owe nothing to revelation. Later on, another famous philosopher, ibn-Rushd—or, as the Christians called him, Averröes (1126–1198)—argued that revealed truth and the truth knowable by reasoning were two quite separate realms. Rational and revealed knowledge might even be contradictory on such a question as whether the world was created or whether it had existed from the beginning of time. Most Moslems felt that this kind of speculation was plainly contrary to religion, because it set up another kind of authority—mere human logic—against the Koran and God's revelation. Arabic philosophers, in short, were too much like Greeks to fit easily into the Moslem scheme of things.

On the other hand, the elaboration of the Sacred Law did not satisfy religious aspiration for long. By 800 or so, four orthodox schools of law had defined themselves. Thereafter, application of established rules to new cases became a more and more mechanical affair, requiring the expert only to find a suitable precedent or parallel case. How could that sort of dry-as-dust legal reasoning satisfy personal yearnings for God?

Islam prohibited monasteries, so this refuge for religiously troubled souls was not available. Mohammed had also denounced unauthorized prophets who pretended to converse with God. This meant that mystical religion was deeply suspect, since mystics claimed to see God, or to merge themselves in God, or in some other way to experience the presence of God. Yet in spite of the emphatic disapproval of the experts in Moslem law, mystical religion could not be held back. Moslems, too, began to experience God directly, bypassing the Koran and the Sacred Law.

At first, all mystics were regarded as heretics. Moslem mystics therefore remained underground. Mystical sects and brotherhoods became channels for the expression of social and political resentments. Many artisans joined these underground societies, which served some of the

A beautifully detailed miniature from the epic poem Shah Namah *by the Persian poet Firdausi.* (*The Metropolitan Museum of Art, Gift of Alexander Smith Coderan, 1913*)

same functions that guilds did in western Europe. Official disapproval and occasional persecutions could not prevent mystics from following their own way. So, eventually, the upholders of the Sacred Law reconciled themselves to allowing Moslems to seek God along this unorthodox path.

THE COLLAPSE OF POLITICAL UNITY   Before mysticism triumphed, however, the Abbasid caliphate had become a hollow shell. The decay resulted from its military policy. The caliph al-Mutasim (ruled 833–842) surrounded himself with a bodyguard of Turkish slave soldiers. At first, these barbarians may have been more obedient and dependable than the Persian bodyguard his predecessors had relied on. But the Turks soon realized how easy it was to take advantage of their position and began to treat the caliph as a puppet.

Such abuse of the caliph's power provoked some outlying regions of the empire to break away. As a matter of fact, Spain had never recognized Abbasid rule, because members of the Omayyad family were able to hold onto power there after the rest of the dynasty had been overthrown. As the Turkish soldiery at the Abbasid court in Baghdad became oppressive, other families asserted independent authority in other regions. Until 909, however, no one had claimed the title of caliph—successor to the Prophet—except the Abbasids. Then a family descended from Mohammed's daughter, Fatima, took power in north Africa and Egypt. According to Shia doctrine, they claimed to be the only rightful caliphs. Soon afterward the Omayyads in Spain made the same claim. Thus the political unity of Islam was broken forever, not only in practice (that had been common enough even in the Omayyad period) but also in theory.

THE IMPACT OF ISLAM ON INDIA

Moslems regarded Hindus and Buddhists as idolaters because they made images of their gods and built temples around such images. Of all crimes against the majesty of God, this, according to Moslem ideas, was the most serious. The toleration accorded to Jews and Christians, "People of the Book," was therefore not extended to Hindus and Buddhists—at least, not in theory. In practice, when Moslem conquerors brought substantial numbers of Indians under their rule, they found ways to live together.

The rise of Islam, however, did put the Indian world on the defensive. Moslems cut off the road to China north of the mountains almost at once. Moslem ships began to sail from the Persian Gulf and from the Red Sea into the Indian Ocean, and soon cut Indians off from regular contact with southeast Asia and Indonesia, where flourishing courts had previously imported Indian culture wholesale. Only on the northeast did the Moslems leave India an open frontier. Here the old patterns of expansion continued. The royal courts of Nepal and Tibet became Indianized before 1000, and the slow process of taming the jungles in eastern Bengal and Assam continued as peasants laboriously built new fields.

Between 600 and 1000, India was divided among many rulers. Dynasties rose and fell, apparently without making much difference. Hinduism developed in two seemingly contradictory directions. On the one hand, a school of philosophers tried to reduce Hindu belief to a system. They explained that all of the different gods and rituals that had found a place in Hindu worship were mere images and suggestions of abstract truth.

Their function was to lead simple and uneducated people toward a level of holiness that would permit them eventually to penetrate the veil of illusion. But this would require many incarnations. At any one time, only a few souls could be expected to rise above the world of ordinary appearances and know that God—infinite, eternal, impersonal—alone was real. Shankara, who lived about 800, was the most famous Hindu philosopher who argued in this way.

At the same time, other Hindus came to the conclusion that magic rites could give them supernatural powers. Instead of studying sacred texts or subjecting the body to painful ascetic discipline, as India's holy men had previously done, a school of Tantrism arose that offered the same results by means of magic. Buddhists as well as Hindus were attracted to this idea; but insofar as people believed such promises, there was no longer any reason for becoming a monk. Tantric magical rites emerged from the villages and among the submerged castes, where very primitive religious practices had survived. Tantric speculation centered much upon sex. Rites that may once have been expected to assure the fertility of crops were freely reinterpreted as means for securing enhanced personal vigor. Yet the extremely crude superstition of Tantrism and the highly sophisticated thought of Shankara all fitted into the Hindu scene: each to his or her taste, with something for everyone.

Beginning in the year 1000, however, Moslem raiders began to affect Indian society and culture. The raiders systematically destroyed temples and monasteries, which to them were seats of idolatry and also offered rich plunder. Soon the Buddhist monasteries of northern India were all destroyed and no one cared to rebuild them. Hinduism proved more durable. Even without great state-supported temples, private rites and village observances continued. Temple services were replaced by open-air ceremonies at which singing and dancing and general excitement prevailed— an excitement that reinforced the fellow-feeling of all the participants and made them uninterested in the legal formalism of Islam.

All the same, the destruction of Hindu temples and the overthrow of Hindu rulers in northern India hurt Hindu civilization. Secular culture, which had reached such a high level at the Gupta court, faded away. The Moslem newcomers brought with them a Persian style of courtly life that accepted almost nothing from Indian tradition. Secular learning withered, too, for the Moslems also brought their own languages (Arabic, Persian, and Turkish), literature, and professional experts with them.

As partial compensation, in the southern parts of India the Tamil language achieved literary form between 600 and 1000. Tamil is not an Aryan language and is, therefore, not related either to ancient Sanskrit or to modern Hindi, the popular speech of northern India which descends from Sanskrit.

The most important forms of Tamil literature were short religious poems or hymns and romantic epics that emphasized love more than war and piety more than heroism. Many Hindu temples in the south escaped Moslem destruction, so temple rituals survived and flourished in Tamil country. This, together with the profound difference of language, gave the cultural scene of southern India a very different character from that created by the Hindu-Moslem collision in northern India.

THE TRANSFORMATION OF ISLAM, 1000–1200

When even the pretense of political unity had to be abandoned, Moslems confronted a new crisis. The Abbasid compromise, which left military affairs and taxes to the government and religious matters to the learned ulama, had broken down. Moreover, the political history of the centuries that followed made it harder and harder to believe that rulers could possibly be instruments chosen by God. Swarms of Turkish adventurers overran the heartland of Islam. Sometimes they kept their tribal organization and were able to create relatively stable states. This was the case with the Seljuk Sultanate, for example, which lasted from 1037 to 1092. But often the Turks came to power only after breaking away from their tribal order. In such cases, they became rootless, ruthless predators who owed loyalty to no one but themselves and served only those who paid them well or promised richer booty than the next man.

The Role of the Turks

The Turks, as they drifted in from Asian steppes, were willing enough to accept Islam, but they took it lightly. Making the effort needed to seek God's will through careful study of the Koran never seemed really vital to them. The Turks did not abandon their own language, which a really energetic search for religious truth would have required. Instead they remained soldiers and masters of older populations—Moslems in outward things but, above all else, eager to make their fortunes.

These tough and greedy warriors kept the political life of Islam in uproar. Abbasid rulers continued to sit on the throne at Baghdad, but were only insignificant figureheads. Utter confusion prevailed. Yet by allowing Turkish fighters to crowd into Islamic lands, the Moslems acquired new and effective, if also disorderly, troops. Like Arabs in the first decades of the Omayyad caliphate, those who failed to rise to the top in the old centers of Islamic life tended to drift toward the frontiers.

SOHRAB AND RUSTUM

The Persian poet Firdausi (c. 940–1020) told the following tale in a famous epic, *Shah Namah* (Book of Kings):

Rustum was the greatest Persian frontier fighter against the Turks. One day he mounted his no-less-famous horse, Rakush, to go hunting, and spent the day pursuing wild asses across the open steppeland. Toward evening he made a kill. He ate and, feeling weary, fell asleep, loosing his horse to let it graze. Some traveling Turks passed by while Rustum slept, captured Rakush, and rode on with their booty to the nearby town of Samengan. When he awoke, Rustum searched vainly for Rakush. Finding hoofprints nearby, he followed them until he came to Samengan, full of fury at what had happened.

The Turkish ruler of the town sought to appease him by entertaining him in his own house, while promising to make every effort to find the stolen horse. It took several days to chase down the horse thieves. While waiting for Rakush to show up, Rustum married his host's daughter, who, having heard of his fame as a fighter, had fallen in love with him. But presently Rakush was returned, and Rustum mounted and set off for Persia.

Nine months later a son was born to the Turkish princess. She named him Sohrab. He grew to man's estate so fast that by the time he was ten years old he could defeat everyone in tests of strength. Sohrab therefore demanded of his mother who his father might be. She told him and

This was approved of by Moslems; fighting against unbelievers was an honorable duty, and rulers and people of the Islamic heartland always agreed that locally troublesome Turks ought to take up the sword against Hindus or Christians, instead of making life difficult for good Moslems.

CONQUEST OF INDIA   This situation fed the raiding armies that began to overrun India after 1000. By 1200 all of northern India had been conquered, and in 1206 a relatively stable Moslem government emerged. It lasted until 1526 and is referred to as the Slave Sultanate of Delhi, because Turkish slaves were the rulers and their capital was at Delhi. Since Turkish (and Persian) recruits from the north were always relatively few in number, the slave kings had to come to terms with the various local Hindu rulers and landlords, admitting them to military service and, in general, softening the official dividing line that Islam drew between idolaters and true believers. The fact that Turks were usually not religious fanatics made such accommodation easier.

gave him the jeweled armband that Rustum had left behind as a keepsake. Full of excitement at the news of his descent from so famous a fighter, Sohrab decided to go and find his father. To do so, he organized a raiding party against Persia.

When news of the raiders' approach reached the shah of Persia, he called on Rustum to help turn back the foe. Rustum responded reluctantly. But when the Turkish force drew near, he went forth as befitted a champion and accepted Sohrab's challenge to single combat. He refused, however, to identify himself, thinking that Sohrab and his Turks would then suppose that some still mightier champion lurked in the Persian ranks.

Long and hard they fought, breaking off at nightfall, until on the third day Rustum succeeded in casting Sohrab down from his horse and breaking his back. Dying, Sohrab boasted that his conqueror would yet feel the weight of his father Rustum's revenging arm. Rustum saw what he had done when he drew off the boy's armor and recognized the jeweled armband he had left behind ten years before with the Turkish princess. But it was too late. Sohrab died, and after mourning mightily Rustum built him a tomb in the shape of a horse's hoof. As for the Turks, their leader dead, they withdrew and mourned alike for Rustum, who had slain his son, and for Sohrab, who had been slain.

Matthew Arnold made the story famous in the English-speaking world with a poem, "Sohrab and Rustum," published in 1853; but he changed some details of Firdausi's story to suit his own purposes.

This in turn allowed extensive interaction and interchange between Indian and Moslem elements in the population. Some Indians became Moslem, particularly those who stood near the bottom of the caste system. The equality of all believers, preached by Islam, had an obvious appeal to such persons. As a result, the Moslem community in India came to be sharply divided between an upper class of rulers and warriors and a poor class of people at or near the very bottom of society. Relatively few Hindus from the middle and upper castes were attracted by Islam, although the courtly culture and Persian language of the Moslem rulers did make some impact upon the Hindu princes who served under the Moslem slave sultans.

CONFLICTS WITH CHRISTENDOM Along the frontier between Islam and Christendom, the arrival of the Turks also had important effects. In 1071, at the Battle of Manzikert, the Seljuk sultans defeated a Byzantine army and captured the emperor himself. In the following period, the whole

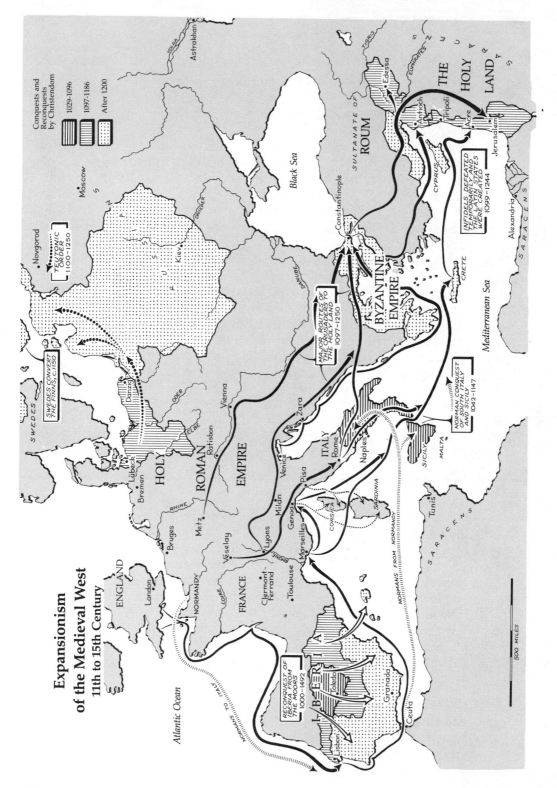

Expansionism
of the Medieval West
11th to 15th Century

Conquests and
Reconquests
by Christendom

1029-1096 1097-1186 After 1200

SWEDES CONVERT
THE FINNS, c.1150

TEUTONIC
ORDER
1100-1250

MAJOR ROUTES OF
THE CRUSADERS TO
THE HOLY LAND
1097-1250

NORMAN CONQUEST
OF SOUTH ITALY
AND SICILY
1042-1147

RECONQUEST OF
IBERIA FROM
THE MOORS
1000-1492

INFIDELS DEFEATED
TEMPORARILY AND
THE LATIN STATES
WERE CREATED
1099-1244

THE
HOLY
LAND

SULTANATE OF
ROUM

BYZANTINE
EMPIRE

HOLY
ROMAN
EMPIRE

ITALY

SICILY

MALTA

IBERIA

FRANCE

ENGLAND

SWEDES

Atlantic Ocean

Black Sea

Mediterranean Sea

SARACENS

NORMANS TO ITALY

NORMANS FROM NORMANDY

Moscow
Novgorod
Kiev
Astrakhan
Constantinople
Edessa
Antioch
Tripoli
Acre
Jerusalem
Alexandria
Cyprus
Crete
Danzig
Lübeck
Bremen
Ratisbon
Metz
Vienna
Zara
Venice
Milan
Genoa
Pisa
Lyons
Vézelay
Marseilles
Toulouse
Clermont-
Ferrand
London
Bruges
Rome
Naples
Tunis
Ceuta
Granada
Toledo
Lisbon
Sardinia
Corsica
Malta

VOLGA
DNIEPER
DANUBE
ODER
ELBE
RHINE
RHONE
LOIRE
TIGRIS
EUPHRATES

NORMANDY

500 MILES

central part of Asia Minor passed into Turkish hands. Danger from the Turks persuaded the emperor of Byzantium to appeal to the pope in Rome for help in pushing them back.

Accordingly, in 1096, Pope Urban II proclaimed a crusade against the Turks. The goal Pope Urban set was liberation of Jerusalem and the Holy Land from the Moslems., The response in western Europe surprised both Byzantines and Turks. Armies from France, Germany, and Italy made their way through the Balkans to Constantinople and then crossed into Asia Minor. After many difficulties, the crusaders captured the great city of Antioch on the Orontes River, and then continued south to take Jerusalem in 1099. The victorious crusaders set up a series of little states along the eastern coast of the Mediterranean, leaving the great hinterland to the Moslems.

The success of the First Crusade depended in large part on Moslem political disarray. When stronger Moslem rulers emerged, the Second Crusade was organized (1147–1149), but this time the crusaders never reached the Holy Land, meeting defeat in Asia Minor instead. The situation became more critical for the Christians when Saladin (ruled 1169–1193) built up a strong kingdom in Syria and Egypt. In 1187 he captured Jerusalem and wiped out what remained of the crusading states, except for the single city of Acre on the coast. The pope responded by proclaiming the Third Crusade. But even though the kings of England, France, and Germany joined forces, this effort also failed. Saladin and the Moslems remained in control of the Holy Land, and nearly all of Asia Minor also remained under Turkish rule.

EXPANSION ON OTHER FRONTS   Along other fronts, too, Islam demonstrated a new expansive energy in the centuries after A.D. 1000. Moslem towns and traders spread far down the east coast of Africa. In west Africa, Moslems from north of the Sahara destroyed the pagan kingdom of Ghana in 1076. Thereafter, various Moslem states and empires dominated the African farming peoples of that region.

Throughout the western and central steppes of Eurasia, Moslem missionaries also met with widespread success. Turks and other nomadic or partially nomadic peoples accepted Islam at various times, tribe by tribe, not because they were conquered but because traveling holy men and merchants from the cities of the Middle East converted them. Even in distant China, substantial Moslem communities came into existence in the western regions of that country.

As a result, the territory of Islam almost doubled between 1000 and 1200. This tremendous success was less dramatic than the first burst of Moslem expansion had been, but it was scarcely less significant for world history.

Only in Spain did Moslem power retreat. Frontier fighting between

Moslems and Christians in the Iberian Peninsula never stopped for long. At first the advantage lay with the Moslems, who reached their high point in 732 when a raiding party advanced as far as Tours in central France before meeting defeat. Later, the Moslems withdrew behind the Pyrenees, and their domain kept on shrinking southward as Christian knights pressed the attack. In 1212 the Christians won a great victory at the Battle of Las Navas de Tolosa. Thereafter Moslem power was restricted to the principality of Granada in the extreme south of Spain. But on a world scale, this failure was small compared to Islamic advances elsewhere. Retreat in Spain seemed trifling in the overall balance between Islam and its rivals.

The Role of Sufism

The secret of Islam's new energy was not entirely military. The strong arm of Turkish adventurers was powerfully assisted by the preaching and example of enthusiastic missionaries. These missionaries were often merchants or wandering artisans, humble people who had no particular claim to knowledge of the Moslem Sacred Law. But they were mystics, who experienced God or knew others who had done so, and were eager to talk about it. Moslem mystics were referred to generally as "Sufi."

All levels of involvement were possible. Some Sufi were full-time holy men, who lived only for God and communion with Him, but most were ordinary laymen. An unusually holy mystic often gathered disciples and admirers. His followers might go their separate ways on their master's death, but sometimes they chose to remain together and continued to follow their founder's rules of holiness. Men who followed such a way of life were called dervishes. Their ways of entering into communion with God varied widely. Some danced and chanted; some smoked hashish (a drug that induces a trance); some suppressed normal breathing; some simply lived a quiet, regular life of meditation and prayer.

Sufis played a role in Islam much like that which friars played in Christendom. But there was one important difference. Mohammed had expressly prohibited monasteries, and set up no separate clergy to minister to the religious needs of his followers. Hence Moslem mystics could not withdraw so sharply from ordinary life as was customary in Christian communities. Instead, Sufi holy men normally continued to earn a living like everyone else. Lay and religious organizations, therefore, tended to merge. Dervish associations became particularly important in towns, and developed most strongly among artisan groups.

The contrast between Sufi mysticism and the legal approach to holiness, that had dominated the first centuries of Islam, is startling. Like some vast tide, Sufism rose up through the older form of Moslem faith. The Sacred Law and the Koran were not rejected. Sufis honored experts in the Sacred Law; the ulama somewhat grudgingly accepted the direct experience of God through mystical experience as part of orthodox Islam.

The key figure in arriving at this compromise was a learned and religiously intense man named al-Ghazali (1058–1111). He started his career by becoming a professor at Baghdad, teaching the Sacred Law. But the brilliant young professor began to suffer doubts about religion. He left his position and for several years led an agonized life. Then he found relief in mysticism. Having seen God, his doubts were stilled. He returned to writing and teaching but preached the Sufi message: argument and reasoning were in vain; only faith and mystic communion with God mattered.

After the time of al-Ghazali, a bulky Sufi literature developed, describing in great detail the steps and stages of the path to God. This literature supplemented the old commentaries on the Koran and the Sacred Law; between them, they came to define Islamic learning.

The new energy and respectability of Sufism meant that strangers did not have to subscribe to the entire code of the Sacred Law before they could become Moslems. Instead, reverence for a holy man, participation in mystical exercises, and listening respectfully to stories about the heroes of Islam—from Mohammed on down—was enough to start a person along the path to becoming a Moslem. Later, the Sacred Law and the more formal apparatus of Moslem life might follow.

CONCLUSION

Islam, then, passed through two phases between 622, when the faith was founded, and about 1200. The first phase spread Arab power across the map of Asia, Africa, and Europe, from Spain and Morocco in the west to the Indus and Oxus rivers in the east. Within this vast domain a new Moslem civilization came quickly into existence, centered around the effort to follow in every detail the revelation of God's will that had been given to all humanity through Mohammed. Compromises proved necessary, but as long as the political unity of the realm of Islam could be maintained—at least in form—the effort to make human life and society match the ideal of the early Moslem community at Medina seemed worthwhile.

After about 1000, the inroads of Turkish adventurers and the political chaos they brought to the Moslem heartland inaugurated a second phase of Moslem history. Islam both suffered and profited from the Turkish invasions. The military energy of the Turks carried Islamic power deep into the Hindu and Christian lands. Simultaneously, the inner patterns of the faith were altered in such a way as to make the spread of Islam among barbarous peoples of Asia and Africa much easier than before. The result was to double or more than double the realm of Islam within about two centuries.

Yet, in another sense, Islam suffered a crippling defeat. The hope of the first days—to make a community totally pleasing to God—had to be abandoned. The political ideal of the early caliphate, when all Moslems were supposed to stand together against the infidels, had become a farce. By accepting mysticism, Islamic thinkers turned their backs upon science and philosophy. Instead of following up new experiments and theories, Moslem doctors more and more felt satisfied with manuals already available. Astronomy became astrology again, as suitable handbooks simplified the casting of horoscopes. Philosophy and abstract reasoning fell under too much suspicion to flourish.

Moslem intellectual energy, in short, turned almost entirely to mystical exercises at the very time when the universities of western Europe were beginning to foster an eager interest in their intellectual heritages from Latin, Greek, and Moslem writers. By contrast, Moslem scholars almost ceased to concern themselves with anything foreign, fearing that novelty would upset the faith. Even when the Mongols brought them into much closer contact with the Chinese than before, Moslems took little interest in Chinese knowledge and skills. The Europeans, on the other hand, felt no compunction about seizing upon anything that interested them and might be useful. Printing, for example, had almost no impact in the Moslem lands, because the ulama forbade the use of that great Chinese invention for anything more intellectual than the manufacture of playing cards. They feared that God's Word would be defiled if reproduced by machine.

Yet we should not scoff. Their wisdom was, perhaps, demonstrated by the fact that in Europe the religious upheaval of the Reformation was largely created by the use of printing presses to spread new doctrines and controversies. That sort of upheaval, challenging fundamental convictions, was exactly what learned Moslems wished to avoid; and avoid it they did, but at the cost of falling behind their Chinese and Christian contemporaries.

But before that could happen, western Europe and China had to recover from the barbarian invasions that had overthrown both the Roman and the Han empires. China recovered before Europe was able to do so and, after about 1000, began to outstrip the realm of Islam in some important respects. How that happened will be the theme of the next chapter.

TRANSPORTATION AND COMMUNICATION

To those who lack long-range means of travel and communication, walking is the only way to go and talking face to face the only way to communicate. The people to get along with, guard against, trade with, and pay attention to are those living nearby; and such people are referred to as neighbors.

Through most of history this was the case, although from the beginning of civilization, ships and pack animals gave some people a longer reach. Writing, wagons, and mounted messengers came later; but by 500 B.C. transportation and communication reached a limit that lasted for about 2000 years. Using relays of horses or simple sailing vessels, a person could travel about 100 miles a day, whether by land or by sea.

Then, beginning about 500 years ago, a series of new inventions transformed transportation and communication. Greater speed changed the definition of "neighbor," until today all of us have become neighbors throughout the habitable globe.

Breaking the Ocean Barriers

Between 1400 and 1500, Europeans learned how to make ships that could travel safely across stormy seas and in waters where tides ran swift and high. Strongly built hulls, a big rudder, and multiple masts with sails that could be put up or down, according to the strength of the wind, all played their part in making ships safer and more maneuverable.

With such vessels, long voyages across the oceans became easy. But how to get back? This required new methods of navigation, which would allow a ship to find its position by observing the sun or the stars. European sailors—especially the Portuguese—worked out this problem, too, by 1500.

Finally, how to protect oneself against strangers, whether on sea or land? The answer was to put cannon on board ship. Strong hulls, built to hold up against heavy waves, could also withstand the recoil of heavy guns.

HIGHLIGHTS

When all these things came together, travel across the oceans lost most of its terror.

Within less than thirty years (1492–1521), European seafarers broke through the vast ocean barriers that had previously divided humanity into separate continental blocks.

The North Atlantic is a stormy ocean. When European sailors learned to master its waves and currents, no sea was difficult for them.

The opening of the oceans by European ships started new kinds of interaction among the peoples of the world. Trade, migration, and exchange both of diseases and of new food crops all took new paths.

Printing

Printing from wooden blocks was invented by the Chinese before A.D. 800. Since Chinese writing uses thousands of different signs or characters, it was easier to carve a whole page at a time than to assemble separate bits of type made in advance.

In Korea and in Europe, however, alphabetic writing required only a small number of different signs. Therefore it made sense to cast type for each letter in multiple copies ahead of time, and then to assemble the movable type into words.

In Europe the first book printed in this manner was made in Germany by Johann Gutenberg in 1454.

HIGHLIGHTS

Printing made it possible to produce large numbers of copies of a text cheaply and accurately. This had revolutionary effects in Europe but a conservative effect in China.

In China, printing was used to reproduce the Confucian classics and commentaries upon them. Wider familiarity with these texts simply strengthened Confucian ideas and attitudes.

Among Europeans, an intensified interaction of old and new ideas and information shook established beliefs. Printing spread the Protestant Reformation. It also spread information that came pouring in after the opening of the oceans. Europeans also used printing to reproduce Christian and pagan classics, making them more easily available.

Inland Transport

Since the invention of ships, water transportation had always been much cheaper than land transport, and often faster as well. Canals could extend the advantages of water transportation inland, even where natural riverways were absent. Locks allowed barges to travel up over a watershed, crossing from one river basin to another. In northwestern Europe, canal-building became important for inland transportation between 1750 and 1850. Canals could carry heavy loads cheaply once they were built; but in many cases construction and maintenance were costly.

Roads used by wheeled vehicles must have some kind of drainage; otherwise the rain softens the surface, mudholes develop, and the road soon turns into a quagmire. The Romans built narrow roads of paving stones. After 1700, Europe-

An illustration of a Viking ship. (*Library of Congress*)

ans discovered a much cheaper way of making durable roads by scattering gravel on the roadbed so that rain could drain away without leaving mudholes behind. Smooth roads allowed higher speed, so stagecoaches carried goods and passengers as much as 100 miles a day, reaching the old limit civilized peoples had known ever since they tamed the horse.

HIGHLIGHTS

Cheaper movement of heavy goods by water and faster movement of goods and passengers by land intensified interaction across longer distances.

Rapid economic development resulted, with remarkable growth of both industry and agriculture.

Nationwide solidarity and cooperation set in more intensively than before.

As a result, national wealth and power increased, especially in the states of northwestern Europe, England, France, and the Netherlands.

Popular Press

Early presses were worked by men using their own muscles to press a sheet of paper against a bed of ink-covered type. Even with the help of carefully designed levers this went rather slowly. A few hundred printed sheets per hour was all that could be printed, as long as the press worked by moving back and forth, toward and away from the typeface.

Faster printing came by making the type fit onto a curved, cylindrical surface. Such a cylinder could print by spinning around while a long sheet of paper rolled past. Cylinder presses made on this principle could print many thousands of sheets in an hour.

HIGHLIGHTS

High-speed printing gave birth to mass circulation newspapers and magazines.

Newspapers and magazines read by millions created a new kind of interaction between the government and the public.

Mass circulation newspapers often appealed to crude and ill-educated readers by simplifying problems, distorting facts, rousing emotions.

But government action supported by the aroused will of a whole people attained much greater force than had been possible before and used greater resources, both human and material, to carry through common purposes.

Steam Railroad

Railroads reduce friction between wheels and the ground by concentrating comparatively large weights on very narrow, hard rails. This principle was first used mainly in hauling coal, both inside the mines and on the surface. Men or children and animals could drag heavy coal wagons along wooden or metal rails.

The railroad came into its own when steam power was set to work moving whole trains of cars along metal rails. More powerful locomotives and carefully prepared roadbeds allowed the trains to reach speeds up to 100 miles per hour.

HIGHLIGHTS

Railroads could carry people and goods overland faster than ever before and often more cheaply than by other methods of overland transport.

Railroads linked up with ocean-going steamships to deliver cheap grain to European ports from America and Australia. This damaged European agriculture and forced millions of European peasant farmers to emigrate to America.

The rise of Germany and of the United States as great powers depended on the development of the continental interiors of Europe and North America. Railroads opened up these interiors between 1850 and 1914.

Global Communication

Smoke signals and fire beacons spread alarms in very ancient times. Semaphore

A Chinese war junk, ca. 19th century. (Illustrated London News, *March 21, 1857*)

CHINESE WAR JUNKS OF THE OLD STYLE.   SEE PAGE 293.

A 19th century printing press. (Library of Congress)

A modern high-speed printing press. (Laimute Druskis)

flag stations carried more complicated messages during the Napoleonic wars. But from the 1830s the electric telegraph offered a far superior way of sending messages over long distances.

By interrupting an electric current according to a prearranged code, messages could be transmitted instantly wherever a copper wire could reach. Waterproof cables, laid across the ocean beds, soon linked continent with continent. Key points in the world came into instantaneous contact with one another.

After 1876, telephone communication speeded up the process, since words can be spoken faster than a telegraph operator can send letters by code. Over long distances, however, background noise often made spoken words unclear when telegraph signals could get through.

HIGHLIGHTS

Telegraph and telephone extended the range of human communication enormously, by linking up the globe into a single communications network.

Person-to-person interaction became possible anywhere on the earth where telegraph wires reached.

Orders for purchase and sale could reach around the world. This created a world market for standard bulk commodities like wheat.

Central command and precise control, both in peacetime diplomacy and in war, became possible for the first time.

Mass Communication

Wireless communication uses electromagnetic waves to transmit messages at the speed of light. Complicated transmitters and simpler radio and television receivers allow massive communication at low cost. The only important limitation is that electromagnetic waves travel in straight lines and, unless bounced off reflecting layers of the atmosphere, soon leave the earth. Sending stations can be connected by wires, however, to relay a given signal.

HIGHLIGHTS

Radio and television stations create a new form of mass communication, since the same messages can be sent into millions of homes at small cost to the sender.

Political propaganda by radio and television exercise a strong influence, especially in countries where the government maintains control of sending stations.

Radio and television tend to reduce class and regional differences within the radius of the broadcast.

Air and Space Travel

Flying changed patterns of long-distance travel fundamentally. Old barriers fell. Mountains, deserts, and valleys ceased to

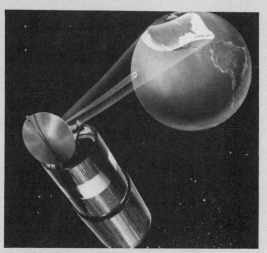

An illustration of the Westar IV communication satellite. (Western Union Corporation)

matter much for overland travel; harbors, tides, and shoals ceased to affect travel overseas. For long flights earth became a sphere, making the Arctic a particularly strategic region. This is because major population concentrations are in the northern hemisphere; and the shortest air routes between distant population centers always follow the bulge of the earth northward toward the Arctic. The earth became still smaller when rocket propulsion opened the possibility of escape from earth's gravity and exploration of the solar system.

HIGHLIGHTS

Air and space travel changed transport routes and shortened time of travel between distant portions of the globe.

In case of a war, air and space travel mean that every state's borders are in danger.

Humanity's exploration of the earth and space beyond the earth continues with consequences—psychological, political, economic, and ecological—still unknown and unknowable.

CHAPTER 11

The Far East
and the
Americas

600 to 1200

The establishment of Islam in the Middle East encouraged trade, for the Arabs were accustomed to caravans and respected merchants. But Islam was a dogmatic religion, like Judaism and Christianity. Very quickly, Mohammed's followers worked out a Sacred Law which, like the Jewish law, told the faithful followers of Islam how to conduct themselves in most situations. This, in turn, meant that everyone had either to conform to the Sacred Law, and be a Moslem, or else reject it. No halfway house was acceptable. Mingling and compromise of different cultural traditions under these circumstances still could occur, but only in matters that did not come within the scope of religion. In everything concerned with faith and revelation, the boundary lines between cultures became sharp and clear.

The rise of Islam in the Middle East put the Moslems astride the lines of communication between the civilizations of Eurasia. By A.D. 750 they had reached the frontiers of India and China and had rolled back the boundaries of Christendom to the Taurus Mountains in Asia Minor and the Pyrenees in Spain. Across each of these frontiers, believers in Islam confronted enemies of the faith of Mohammed. A far more sharply divided world resulted.

Of the separate compartments into which the civilized world broke up, the Far Eastern area was by far the most populous. Between 600 and 1200 it also became the seat of a commercial transformation that increased China's wealth enormously by permitting more efficient use of resources. Artisan skills soon surpassed the level of other civilizations, and cities flourished as never before. Expansion of agriculture kept pace with the elaboration of urban life, however, so that the dominance of the rural landowners, or gentry, which had begun in Han times, was never seriously questioned. This gave a fundamental stability to Chinese civilization and set a limit to its growth. Nothing that really disturbed the interests or ideals of the bureaucracy and gentry could get very far without provoking official action to check the danger.

In the same centuries between about A.D. 600 and 1200 Chinese artists and writers filled out the older cultural framework. The ingrained political and moral ideas of Confucian thought were never repudiated, but Buddhism added important new strands to Chinese art and thought. Even after the imperial government officially repudiated Buddhism, its influence was shown by the way in which Neo-Confucian philosophers enlarged the range of Confucian thought. They asked new and, in part, Buddhist-inspired questions of the old classic texts—and consequently came up with new answers.

The style of life suitable to a Chinese gentleman also enlarged its scope. Painting and poetry became gentlemanly accomplishments; and where thousands dabbled, scores of truly great masters emerged. Life was also enriched by the development of public restaurants, featuring fine food and professional entertainers.

The lower classes were, of course, too poor to share in such elegance, but the Chinese gentry always accepted newcomers without question. A really bright young man, with aptitude for literary study, could rise as far on the ladder of imperial office as luck and his own talents allowed. Wealth that could be passed on to his sons and other relatives came with high office, and there were no hereditary bars to this kind of personal advancement. Humble peasant families sometimes pooled resources to send an unusually promising boy to school, hoping to profit from his later successes.

The peoples within the reach of Chinese culture all tried to acquire for themselves as much of the Chinese way of life as they could; and at the very beginning of the period we are considering, both Korea and Japan entered the Far Eastern circle of civilized nations with a rush. In later centuries, both nations modified the borrowed Chinese skills and ideas to suit local tastes and circumstances.

This Far Eastern circle of nations was relatively self-sufficient and indifferent to things happening far away. As educated Chinese saw the world, everything that mattered was concentrated in the "Middle Kingdom," as they called their own country. Round the imposing bulk of China proper were ranged various sorts of barbarians, each of whom shared to some degree the benefits of subordination to, and communication with, the "Son of Heaven"—who sat on the imperial throne of China and kept peace and order at home, while holding even the most unruly barbarians in awe. This, of course, was exactly as things should be, according to Confucian principles.

Nevertheless, across the Pacific, far beyond the ken of Confucian sages, new civilizations—Mayan, Mexican, and Peruvian—entered their classic phases in Central and South America about the year 600. They then gave way to a more militarized age of empires some 300 or 400 years later.

The civilizations of the Americas were not related directly to the civilization of China. Yet we can be almost certain that accidental voyaging sometimes carried boats all the way across the Pacific, allowing occasional contact between Asia and America. The distribution of certain useful plants among the Pacific islands, as noted by the first European explorers of that ocean, can only be explained by assuming that both Asian and American plants had arrived, from time to time, in different assortments on different islands. Certain striking resemblances between Chinese and Amerindian art also suggest that bits of Chinese pottery or bronze work had somehow crossed the ocean, giving Amerindian stone-cutters and metalworkers a model for some of their own designs.

THE GROWTH OF CHINESE CIVILIZATION

China's Political History

Three major dynasties ruled China in the centuries with which we are now concerned: the Sui, A.D. 589–618; the T'ang, 618–907; and the Sung, 960–1279. This traditional organization of Chinese history hides more than it reveals. The Sui Dynasty, which reunited China for the first time since the fall of the Han in A.D. 220, followed an aggressive military policy on every border. The first T'ang emperors followed the same policy. The change of ruling family that took place in 618 therefore was not crucial. But from 751 onward a series of military disasters struck the Chinese Empire. Defeat at the hands of the Moslems in central Asia was followed by defeat in Korea. Far more serious was a widespread revolt in 755 that paralyzed imperial power. The dynasty was rescued by barbarian intervention, but from that time on the T'ang emperors depended on foreign protectors and paid heavily in the form of tribute.

The remaining centuries of T'ang dynastic rule, consequently, were politically very different from the dynasty's first century of vigorous expansion and military energy. Instead, the emperor's real power eroded bit by bit, because he lacked an army capable of imposing the will of the central government. Local warlords sprang up, often fighting among themselves and paying scant obedience to the distant T'ang ruler. The end of the dynasty in 907 therefore made no real difference.

The rise of the Sung, on the other hand, did mark a return to centralized and effective bureaucratic government within the part of China which the dynasty was able to control. But the Sung never ruled the whole country. A tier of northern provinces remained in the hands of various barbarian rulers; Sung administration was never secure north of the Yellow River, and after 1127 the area it controlled shrank back toward the Yangtze.

THE SUI, T'ANG, AND SUNG DYNASTIES   Under the Sui and early T'ang dynasties, when China's government was strong and aggressive, Chinese armies were recruited from the sons of free peasants who had established themselves throughout most of north China during the barbarian invasions and the wars that followed the collapse of the Han Dynasty. These troops were both hardy and numerous, and they carried T'ang arms deep into central Asia. Tribes located as far away as the Caspian Sea recognized Chinese authority, and for a brief moment the Chinese even claimed control over Kashmir on the southern slopes of the Himalaya Mountains.

But campaigns on distant frontiers required professional standing armies. Peasants could not leave their farms for long periods of time and remain peasants. By 750 the T'ang armies were therefore recruited almost entirely among barbarians and were even commanded by barbarian generals. The change in army recruitment had dramatic consequences when a series of defeats in the field set off a large-scale revolt in 755. The troops attempted to seize power on behalf of their commander, who was a barbarian. They were defeated only after many years of warfare, when a more cohesive barbarian force, led by Turkish-speaking Uighurs, rode in from the west and propped the helpless T'ang emperors up on their ancestral throne once more.

Thenceforward, the relation between the Chinese and the barbarians was reversed. Instead of trying to secure Chinese rule over the wide borderlands lying north and west of China, the emperors abandoned these regions to local barbarian tribes and kingdoms. Judicious distribution of tribute, and diplomatic intrigues among the rival chieftains, allowed considerable room for maneuver as long as the Chinese government was able to gather large resources through its tax-collecting system. But little by little the tax system broke down, too. Local upstarts intercepted the central government's tax income and built small domains for themselves.

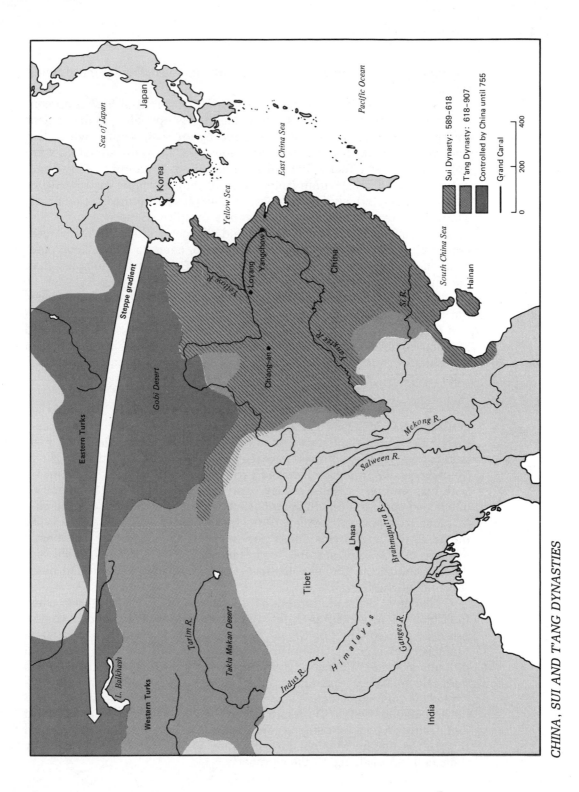

CHINA, SUI AND T'ANG DYNASTIES

Barbarian intervention and raiding naturally increased under these conditions.

The decay of imperial government and the threat of barbarian conquest ran against the grain of Chinese feeling. By appealing to the ancient traditions and standards of the past, and by arousing antiforeign feeling that was never far from Chinese consciousness, the Sung emperors were able to rebuild an effective central administration. A standing professional army, recruited from within China, was an indispensable instrument for the Sung rulers. But what held things together was a reformed bureaucracy. The reform was thoroughly conservative in spirit. Sung emperors consciously harked back to Confucius and the good old days. New men, recruited mainly from the southern provinces, came to office. They managed the Sung government more nearly on Confucius' principles than had ever been done before.

Yet Confucian principles failed to unite all of China. The provinces north of the Yellow River, including territory where Chinese civilization had originated, were ruled by various barbarians—Turks, Mongols, and Manchus. The most notable such state, known as the Chin Dynasty to the Chinese, came from Manchuria, and ruled a large part of northern China between 1122 and 1234, when the advancing Mongols destroyed it.

FOREIGN RELATIONS   As long as the Sui and T'ang armies were strong, the Chinese kept their doors wide open to strangers. Traders and merchants from the West brought new religions with them. Christianity, Islam, Manichaeism, Zoroastrianism, and various forms of Buddhism all mingled with one another in China's busy caravan cities. Buddhism soon gained official support, and Buddhist monasteries grew wealthy through the gifts of pious or repentant laymen. With these foreign religions came other things as well: art styles, ideas pertaining to astrology and astronomy, and the decimal system. But these innovations did not take hold and flourish among the Chinese. Instead, antiforeign sentiment gained fierce force under the Sung.

The most dramatic turning point came in the period 843–846, when the Chinese government prohibited foreign religions. This policy was triggered by the collapse of Uighur power in 840. The Uighurs had made Manichaeism their official faith after 763, and they became the special protectors of that religion in China. Since the Chinese disliked the Uighurs intensely for their repeated exaction of tribute, Manichaeans who accepted the Uighur protection also became the objects of widespread popular and official dislike. Therefore, when the Uighur Empire was attacked and destroyed by a new steppe confederation in 840, the Chinese revenged themselves on the Manichaeans dwelling in their midst by prohibiting their faith and seizing all their property.

This thoroughly popular measure only whetted the government's appetite. One by one the other foreign faiths suffered the same fate, including Buddhism, which by this time had many wealthy monasteries in various parts of China. The official T'ang history, in fact, records that 44,600 monasteries and nunneries were suppressed, and more than 400,000 monks and nuns were either enslaved or put back on the tax lists.

From that time onward, the Chinese allowed their distrust of all things foreign to blind them even to such useful devices as the decimal notation system for numbers. This set a ceiling upon the development of Chinese civilization that turned out to be very costly in the long run; but at the time and for centuries to follow, Chinese attainments were in fact so high that they had ample excuse for believing that there was nothing of value or importance they could learn from foreigners.

Social and Economic Evolution of China

THE SPREAD OF RICE FARMING   The basic fact about Chinese society was its dense population. Hard-working peasants, tilling small plots of land with skills that had been perfected through generations, constituted the solid base of Chinese civilization. Tiny farms, having high yields per acre but relatively small surpluses per agricultural worker, made Chinese farming different from that of Europe and western Asia, where animal power allowed peasants to till more land and raise a larger surplus per head, but at the expense of a lower yield per acre. Year by year and generation after generation, the area under cultivation in China increased. New fields were built farther and farther up hill slopes, where more and more labor was required to carve out a level patch of cultivable ground.

A change in the center of gravity of Chinese rural life took place as the Yangtze Valley came under intense cultivation. This process began very early, long before the time of the Han Dynasty; but it was not until the Sui Dynasty opened the Grand Canal in A.D. 605 that the full economic and political importance of the agricultural exploitation of the Yangtze Valley was felt. Doubling and more than doubling the tax income at the disposal of the Chinese imperial court was important enough; but in addition, the climatic conditions of the Yangtze basin encouraged a shift toward rice farming and away from the cultivation of wheat, barley, millet, and other dry-land crops that had been the staples of early Chinese cultivation in the Yellow River valley.

Rice had one enormous advantage: far more calories could be harvested from a well-cultivated rice field than any other cereal crop could

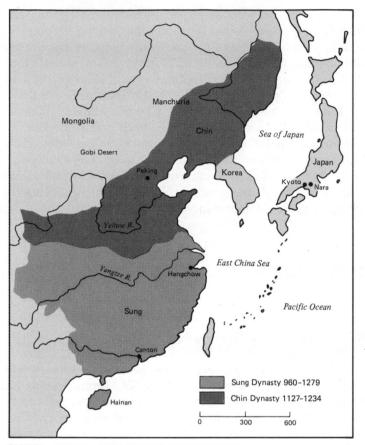

CHINA, SUNG AND CHINA DYNASTIES

produce on the same amount of land. There was a corresponding disadvantage: the labor of preparing fields for rice and of planting and harvesting was enormous. First of all, the soil had to be leveled and channels prepared through which water might flow onto the field. Dikes or low walls had to be built to retain this water, since rice plants prosper only when a few inches of standing water keep their roots well soaked. When the field was ready, rice seed had to be set out to sprout in special beds. Then each seedling had to be transplanted by hand into the field where it would grow. Only when the rice began to ripen could the water be allowed to drain off the fields, so that at harvest time the reapers might have the convenience of dry land beneath their feet.

It requires a stretch of the imagination to conceive how much human labor is required for successful paddy rice growing, as this kind of cultivation is called. The agricultural year consists of innumerable hours spent digging and trenching the fields, followed by backbreaking days required to transplant the seedlings and the scarcely less difficult task of harvesting the ripe rice with sickles.

No one knows when and where paddy rice cultivation first developed. Rice growing was already part of China's agricultural practice in Shang times, but it was only when the fertile, well-watered, and vast expanses of the Yangtze Valley came under cultivation that the rice paddy style of farming became *the* standard form of Chinese agriculture.

No records allow us to follow exactly the steps of the process whereby a carpet of paddy fields spread from river edges and the margins of lakes up the slopes of valleys and along the contour lines of the hills, until almost every available patch of land that human labor and ingenious water engineering could make productive had been brought under cultivation.

The entire process may be compared to the way a glacier moves across the earth's surface, altering the landscape profoundly as it advances and engulfing all the obstacles that it may meet. The numerical mass of the Chinese peasantry throughout historic time advanced like a glacier, taking over new regions, enfolding the remnants of other peoples, absorbing conquerors, and changing the natural landscape far more thoroughly than most other human communities have done. Only in Korea, Japan, Java, and some parts of southeast Asia—where rice paddy cultivation also became the dominant form of agriculture—have equally dense, disciplined, and hard-working rural populations ever arisen.

An important improvement came to Chinese farming during the centuries with which we are concerned. About A.D. 1000 a new kind of early-ripening rice was discovered or, perhaps, imported from southeast Asia. This kind of rice allowed peasants to harvest two crops a year on well-watered land. In addition, places where water was not available for more than a few weeks of the year became potential paddy land, since with the early-ripening rice it was not necessary to keep standing water on the ground for more than thirty to forty days. The result was a very substantial increase in total food production, for in many parts of China, especially inland, the spring run-off left dry, empty stream beds through most of the year. Such land could now grow rice. Accordingly, many interior regions that had previously lacked enough water were opened up to the Chinese style of agriculture for the first time.

THE GROWTH OF TRADE   But it was not the indefinite multiplication of peasant village communities that made Chinese civilization prosper. The village surpluses had to be concentrated and used to support artisans, scholars, soldiers, and other specialists. Here, too, important improvements came into play during the Sui and T'ang periods. First of all, the opening of the Grand Canal meant that bulky and comparatively cheap commodities could move back and forth between the Yangtze basin and the valley of the Yellow River. A single barge, hauled by human muscles or by an animal, could easily carry a cargo of several tons. Long-distance overland transport thus became cheap enough to tie the richest and most productive lands of central and northern China into a single network.

By about 750, the construction of feeder canals and connecting waterways had advanced so far that the court no longer needed all of the produce that could be delivered. Instructions were therefore sent to local tax officials to sell portions of the foodstuffs and other coarse goods they had collected in their warehouses and buy fine artisan products instead. These were more valuable, and the court quickly developed an insatiable appetite for fine lacquer ware, porcelain, or embroidered cloth—whatever it might be that local skills or resources could produce. The effect of such a policy was to stimulate local artisan trades. Regional specialization became possible on a substantial scale. Wealth increased, population grew, and China's skills began to surpass anything known elsewhere.

The court and capital were the main beneficiaries of the new wealth, but others shared in it, too. Private trading grew up beside and around official transactions. Wealthy Buddhist monasteries may have played an important role in this development. After all, merchants and men of affairs had brought Buddhism into China from the trading cities of central Asia; and as a result, the commercial spirit was thoroughly familiar to the monks.

The development of private trade meant a much wider use of money than had formerly been common in China. This in turn allowed the government to collect more of its income in cash and to rely upon purchases from private suppliers to provide many of the goods the government needed or wanted. Scattered statistics show, for example, that in 749 only 3.9 percent of the imperial tax income took the form of coined money, whereas in 1065 the proportion had risen to 51.6 percent. The flexibility of a market economy thus came to China. Wider use of money and improved and cheaper transportation, together with enlarged scope for private trade, all combined to allow the Chinese to distribute and develop their resources more efficiently than had been possible before, when taxes in kind were liable to yield too much of one kind of commodity and not enough of another.

The rise of local warlords in the later T'ang period did not seriously check these developments. If anything, it spurred them on. For instead of having a single great capital to which tax monies flowed, the rise of independent provincial rulers meant that their residence cities began to attract tax income that had previously gone to the distant imperial capital in the north. This stimulated the development of provincial cities, particularly in the south.

In the Sung period the commercialization of Chinese society went into high gear. Even poor peasants began to enter the market, buying and selling food and other commodities. By specializing on raising whatever sold best, they could increase their productivity, just as urban populations had done for centuries. But as the peasant majority began to respond to market prices and increased their productivity, the wealth of the country as a whole shot upward.

Everything depended on cheap and reliable transport, provided by canal boats. These could move to and fro along the canal network that the Chinese had constructed initially to made sure their rice paddies got enough water each year.

Intensified trade within China and rising productivity soon spread beyond the limits of the two great river valleys where the canal system already existed. In particular, seafaring began to play a more significant role than before. Coastal cities in the extreme south began to trade with southeast Asian and Indonesian ports, thus opening another source of wealth. Important improvements in the design of ships made this development possible: cotton sails instead of bamboo slats that had been used earlier, a centerboard keel that could be raised in shallow waters, and a larger, sturdier hull were key inventions. In addition, by 1100 Chinese sailors began to use the magnetic compass for navigation at sea.

The value of the compass may need a little explanation. What it did was allow a ship to travel long distances across the sea without losing a sense of direction, even in cloudy weather when the stars could not be seen. Distant ports were comparatively easy to find if the ship's captain could steer along a compass line and know that he would fetch up within a few miles of the expected landfall. But in the monsoon climate that dominated the seas adjacent to the south China coast, the compass was not usually necessary. Clear weather prevailed most of the time, and sighting the stars could always provide a practiced mariner with the necessary sense of direction. In northern seas, where clouds might linger for weeks on end, the magnetic compass was of far greater importance, as European navigators discovered some three centuries after Chinese sailors first learned the advantages of having a compass on board ship.

The commercialization of the Chinese economy meant the rise of large, busy cities. The largest of them far surpassed anything known elsewhere. The hardheaded Venetian merchant and traveler, Marco Polo, left an account of his experiences in China (A.D. 1275–1292), in which he explained with awe exactly how vast the Chinese capital was and how large and prosperous other Chinese cities appeared when compared with those of other parts of the earth.

By Marco Polo's time, China's lead over the rest of the world was unquestionable. Yet there were limitations built into China's economic and social system that eventually allowed western Europeans to catch up and surpass Chinese accomplishments. First of all, the social leadership of the landed gentry class was never seriously challenged by any of the new groups called into being by the commercial transformation of the country. Confucian doctrine viewed merchants as social parasites, who added nothing to the value of the goods they handled but unjustly marked up the price of what they sold. Together with soldiers, they were classed as necessary evils. Individuals who gained a fortune in trade were therefore strongly tempted to become respectable by buying land, sending their sons to school, and making them into gentlemen or even into officials. Merchants, in other words, lacked any sort of independent spirit. How could they challenge the gentry when each of them had the ambition of becoming a man of property, leisure, and education, if possible?

The predominant position of landlords in Chinese society was, of course, sustained by the growth in agricultural production referred to previously. In addition, the artisan trades were devoted largely to meeting the needs and pleasing the tastes of the gentry, since they were the class with money to spare for such purchases. Since they were naturally eager to please their best customers, artisans, too, found it hard to challenge the gentry in any effective way.

THE DEVELOPMENT OF TECHNICAL SKILLS   The tastes of the gentry and of the court put a premium on luxury craftsmanship. Chinese artisans, consequently, developed unexcelled skills. Only a few examples of their handicraft survive from T'ang and Sung times—mainly porcelains and other kinds of pottery. But literary records make clear that more perishable objects of silk, wood, and metal were also produced with the greatest refinement of detail and workmanship. In Sung times, north China also developed a large-scale iron industry, using coke as fuel. Not until the eighteenth century did Europe begin to do likewise. Yet, oddly enough, when barbarian invaders sacked the capital and overran the region where the iron furnaces were located, the industry was not revived.

Perhaps the most instructive example of how Chinese social structure and ideas channeled technical development along certain lines and checked its progress in other directions is the history of gunpowder. The first Chinese record of the use of explosives in warfare dates from the year 1000, when an inventive officer filled lengths of bamboo with some kind of chemical mixture and then used this sort of primitive "bomb" to blow open a city gate. The Chinese recognized the military value of this invention—and continued to fill bamboo with explosives! They also had the idea of putting explosive powder in a metal pot and setting a projectile on top of it before setting off the explosion. They used this kind of primitive gun to bombard enemies from a distance. But the Chinese refrained from developing the military use of gunpowder further. They preferred to use their invention for firecrackers, to scare unfriendly spirits away on festive occasions.

Several good reasons can be suggested for why the Chinese did not invent heavy artillery, as Europeans did almost as soon as they learned of the explosive properties of gunpowder. For one thing, the enemies that the Chinese had to fear were steppe cavalrymen; and gunpowder was hard to use against so elusive a target as a galloping horseman. In addition, warfare was fundamentally felt to be an unworthy activity—a result of political failure, not a sign of energy and success, as Europeans often felt it to be. Hence the Chinese government was not inclined to devote serious thought and resources to discovering new ways of fighting. Better, they felt, to cultivate virtue as Confucius had taught, and hope that the barbarians could be won over by gifts and diplomacy.

In a time when the hydrogen bomb threatens us all with extinction, we should not be too ready to scorn the old Chinese attitude toward warfare. Less effort and ingenuity spent on inventing weapons might make the world's problems a good deal simpler today. Certainly, in the situation that the Sung rulers faced, their policy of not developing the military uses of gunpowder very far worked well enough. Traditional dangers along the northern frontiers were met in traditional ways: tribute missions and diplomatic intrigues alternated with occasional bouts of war against the barbarians, in which light cavalry in Chinese pay played the decisive part.

The Filling Out of China's Cultural Life

The T'ang and Sung dynasties saw China's greatest flowering in thought, art, and literature. Chinese in later centuries took the writings and paintings of this age as models for their own work, and felt themselves inferior to the old masters whom they so admired. Modern scholars agree with this judgment, even though many famous masterpieces of Sung painting are known only through copies made by later generations of artists.

Perhaps the reason T'ang and Sung art and literature attained such heights was that under those two dynasties the Chinese absorbed and made their own the mass of foreign ideas that had flooded into the country during the troubled centuries after the fall of the Han, when the divided land of China was repeatedly overrun by barbarians. This meant, first and foremost, coming to terms with the art and thought of Buddhism, which itself combined Indian, Greek, and central Asian cultural strands. Only after the Chinese had adjusted and transformed their thought and art along Buddhist lines did they begin to repudiate the fascinating foreign faith. So even after 846, when Buddhist monasteries were suppressed by the government, Buddhist influence lived on in China, disguised in Confucian and Taoist dress.

T'ang and Sung China and Gupta India occupy a similar place in the cultural history of their respective civilizations. Each was an age of synthesis, richer and more complex than anything known in earlier centuries; each was luxurious, courtly, and refined. Each developed a school of poetry that concerned itself with the complexities of love and the ebb and flow of feeling that make up individual inner consciousness. Each has ever since been greatly admired.

Resemblances do not stop there, for both in India and China the high development of abstract thought came several centuries after artistic expression achieved its most admired perfection. Thus, Neo-Confucian philosophy flowered in the Sung period, especially toward its close, whereas in India, Hindu philosophy reached its full development three or four centuries after the court poetry of Kalidasa had scaled the heights of Hindu imaginative literature.

These parallels, like the parallels between the early river valley civilizations in the Old World and the development of the American civilizations in the Americas, may prove that there are norms in human history resulting from some kind of natural pattern of development that people fall into if left undisturbed for a sufficient length of time. On the other hand, these parallels may be only the result of paying attention to some aspects of the human past while overlooking others. The study of society is so inexact and the historical record is so patchy that we cannot really be certain.

THE BUDDHIST INFLUENCE   Whatever the truth may be about resemblances in the histories of different civilizations, the manner in which the Chinese reacted to the Buddhist stimulus is easy to understand in a general way, even if the details were far from simple.

The first thing to understand is that even when they were in highest favor at court, Buddhists never tried to persecute Confucian scholars or others whose views differed from their own. This attitude was not shared by conservative Confucians. They looked upon the Buddhists with active distrust. The otherworldly Buddhist ideal, after all, took people away from their duties to family and ruler; of this a good Confucian could never approve. On the other hand, Buddhist writings raised many questions with which Confucians had never dealt. To refute all the elaborate doctrines Buddhist monks brought from India required Confucian scholars to work out their own views on these questions. Confucius' blank refusal to talk about the spirit world was no longer enough.

Yet a well-trained Confucian scholar could not feel comfortable with arguments that rested on nothing but their own merits. This was the way of the Greeks, the way of philosophy. Confucius had claimed that

THE GREAT ANCESTOR
OF THE T'ANG

T'ai Tsung was the second son of a Chinese general in the service of the Sui Dynasty. Yet at the age of eighteen it was he who counseled his father to revolt and lay claim to the title "Son of Heaven." More than anyone else, he steered the way to success and made his father the first emperor of the new T'ang Dynasty (618).

His brothers became profoundly jealous, and attempted to poison him at a banquet. But T'ai Tsung had immunized himself to poisons by taking small doses, and therefore he recovered. Next, his brothers laid an ambush for him outside the palace gate. But T'ai Tsung heard of it and laid a counterambush of his own. In the ensuing fight both his elder and younger brothers were killed. His father, grief stricken, abdicated, and T'ai Tsung succeeded him on the throne as the second T'ang emperor.

Early in his reign the Turks of the steppeland north of China broke off the alliance they had made with T'ai Tsung and marched on his capital at Ch'ang-an. T'ai Tsung hastened to meet them. Coming in sight of the Turkish troops, he rode out in front and, using the Turkish language, challenged the khan to single combat. The Chinese were appalled, but the Turks were impressed, for they deeply admired personal prowess.

In the end no battle occurred. The Turks withdrew; and not long thereafter the khan, discredited in the eyes of his followers, was overthrown by agents of the T'ang court working within the Turkish community itself.

By these completely un-Confucian methods, T'ai Tsung extended his empire over almost half the Eurasian steppe and earned the honorific title, "Great Ancestor."

he invented nothing and merely passed on what the ancients had taught. A good Confucian had to do the same. The solution scholars found to this dilemma was to borrow from Buddhist thinkers a new way of reading the old classic texts. Buddhists were accustomed to finding hidden truths in old writings and stories by interpreting them symbolically. A person or a thing, they believed, might stand for something else—often an abstract idea. Thus, for example, the actual human being, Gautama Buddha, stood for a whole host of Buddha traits. He had become a symbol for cosmic principles, and the symbol was obviously more important than the actual man.

This method of reading and interpreting texts made it easy to discover new meanings in the Chinese classics. Confucian scholars could now argue from the authority of the ancients that the world of sense was not mere illusion, as Buddhists claimed. The men who developed Confucian thought in these ways are known as Neo-Confucians. The greatest of them was Chu Hsi (1130–1200) whose teachings offered convincing answers to all the questions that had been raised by the discussions between Buddhists and Confucians during the preceding 300 or 400 years.

Taoists also learned something from the Buddhists. Taoist doctrine borrowed little, so far as we can tell; but the Buddhist monastic pattern of organization did show Taoists how to pass their ideas on to larger numbers of persons in a more coherent fashion. Presently Taoists organized a monastic way of life similar to the Buddhists'. From that time onward, as experts on the spirit world, Taoist monks offered their services to ordinary Chinese peasants and townspeople who needed to find out how the spiritual forces would react to the building of a new house, or why a child was sick, or whether a particular marriage offer should be accepted.

After the destruction of Buddhist monasteries in 846, surviving Buddhists competed with Taoists in performing services of this sort. They were active mainly near the fringes of the Chinese Empire, where the authority of the central government was not so effectively enforced as in the areas closer to the capital. Buddhism tended to benefit as well as suffer from falling out of favor with officialdom. Peasants and unsuccessful scholars, if they felt rebellious, were likely to find Buddhism especially attractive just because it was outlawed. This, in turn, powerfully affected the further development of Buddhism in China. It became an unofficial, intellectual opposition to prevailing Confucian and Neo-Confucian ideals. For example, the Chan sect, which became the principal Buddhist group in China, emphasized the futility of study and relied entirely on instantaneous "enlightenment." The challenge to Confucian emphasis upon study and perpetual self-control could not have been more direct. This sort of Buddhism had little in common with Indian ideas. In the Chinese environment, in other words, what had begun as an alien faith and pattern of life survived by becoming Chinese.

THE INCREASE OF LITERACY   A balance between official Confucianism, private Taoism, and suspect Buddhism emerged in China by 1200 and remained quite stable thereafter, though the doctrines of each group continued to alter in detail. The invention of paper and printing (first recorded in A.D. 756) confirmed and strengthened this balance. Books and tracts of each of these schools of thought became common. Cheaper books allowed a larger proportion of the population to read. City dwellers thus became able to share the literary heritage of the past more fully than before. Gentleman scholars were no longer the sole guardians of book learning, as had tended to be the case in Han times, when books were expensive and had to be copied by hand.

Printing may have developed from Buddhist efforts to waft innumerable prayers to the countless array of bodhisattvas (Buddhist saints). Very ancient Chinese custom had known how to communicate with the spirit world by writing a question on some perishable material and then burning it. Buddhists in China adopted this method of delivering prayers to the bodhisattvas. Shortly before 756, it occurred to someone that if he first painted the characters of his prayer on a flat piece of wood—and chiseled out all the spaces in between—he could then reproduce the prayer over and over again by inking the smooth wood surface that remained and then pressing silk or paper (invented in the time of the Han Dynasty) against the wood block. This seems to have been the first use to which printing was put in China. Later the same technique, using either stone or wood blocks, was used to print texts for human consumption. In particular, the Buddhist and Confucian classics were reproduced in large numbers. The first official printing of the classics took place at the T'ang capital between 932 and 953. Printed paper currency was also put into circulation, to the utter amazement of foreign visitors like Marco Polo.

The Chinese long continued to use block printing even when the possibility of printing with movable type had become thoroughly familiar to them. This was not due to mere conservatism, for the number of separate characters needed to write Chinese made it almost as easy to carve a whole page at a time as to have to assemble a page from thousands of different pieces of precast type. Only when printing passed to Korea, where an alphabetic script already existed, did movable type come into its own. Korean movable type was in use by about 1400. European printing with movable type began in 1456.

Printing made many kinds of Chinese literature available to larger audiences than could be reached with handwritten manuscripts. Histories, encyclopedias, essays, even poetry circulated widely. Each of these forms of literature flourished vigorously in T'ang and Sung times. The sheer bulk of Chinese literary output far exceeded anything known from other civilizations; and despite extensive losses that have since occurred, an impressive amount of T'ang and Sung writing still survives.

THE REFINEMENT OF POETRY AND ART   In China, painting and poetry overlapped. Both were the work of the brush and both became genteel accomplishments. A painting might include a few words that added to the painting's effect, in much the same way that skillful brushwork in writing the characters added to the impact of a poem by giving it an artistic appearance on the page. The poems of Li Po (701–762) and Tu Fu (712–770) provided the main model for later poets. Li Po in particular

The exquisite detail of this illustration is characteristic of the work of Sung artists. (The Metropolitan Museum of Art, gift of John M. Crawford, Jr., 1984)

took verse forms from the popular songs of the streets; indeed, if his autobiographical references are to be believed, he led a semidisreputable life by the standards of a Confucian scholar. But he expressed new feelings: love, longing, despair, self-disgust. Always he was acutely self-conscious in a way that earlier Chinese writers seem not to have been. So powerful was the impact of his poetry that the styles and verse forms he used were later made part of the imperial examinations. As a result, every scholar who wanted official position in the government had to learn to write passable verse in Li Po's manner. An enormous outpouring of polished but uninspired verse resulted.

Painting reached its peak under the Sung Dynasty, when several famous masters developed the styles we think of as typically Chinese. It was an art of ink and paper, with little reliance on color. The Buddhist technique of using figures and scenes to tell a story became part of this style of art; in addition, the great Sung masters learned to portray three-dimensional space in their landscapes. Long vistas and mighty mountains sprang from the paper as the result of the few brushstrokes.

Despite the limits inherent in brush and ink, great variations of techniques proved possible, and quite different effects could be produced. Painters learned how to present haziness and mist; but they could also command clarity of line. Some went in for detail—there were painters who painted nothing but bamboo leaves; others painted panoramic views stretching toward infinity on a scroll only a few inches wide. The simplicity of their materials did not prevent endless variation. Because the variables were few, the greatest attention and skill could be concentrated upon making much out of little. The Sung painters succeeded as few artists have ever succeeded. They created the Chinese style of painting that lasted almost unaltered until the twentieth century.

CHINA'S ASIAN NEIGHBORS

China moved south with the Sung. Chinese painting reflects the Yangtze rather than the Yellow River scenery. The northern tier of provinces that had been ruled by Han and T'ang emperors were never brought under the Sung Dynasty's regular administration, although various barbarian rulers and chieftains who controlled these regions sometimes recognized the Sung imperial title in return for an appropriate gift or tribute payment.

Chinese records disguise the barbarian element in these northern states. Writers gave barbarian rulers and peoples Chinese names and tried to fit the facts to Confucian ideals as much as possible. Any trader or ambassador was described, therefore, as a bringer of tribute, eager to honor the Son of Heaven. Desperate efforts to buy off some threatened attack entered the records as gracious imperial gifts, delivered as a gesture of courtesy in return for the barbarian's deferential and polite behavior toward the emperor.

In reality, not all the barbarians who had important dealings with China were eager to become Chinese. The Uighurs, for example, became Manichaeans a few years after they assumed a dominant role in Chinese imperial politics. The effect was to mark themselves off from the Chinese more sharply than before. Tibetans, too, built up a considerable empire in central Asia after 751. But they did not hurry to become Chinese. Instead, they took their religion, a form of Buddhism, from India and combined it with local rites to produce a faith called Lamaism.

Farther east, China's neighbors could not so easily draw upon another civilized tradition to bolster their cultural independence. Inhabitants of Manchuria and nearby regions lived too far away from the central Asian trade routes to be able to find any foreign style of civilized religion to pit against Chinese ideas. Yet some of these peoples, when they conquered China's northern fringes, resisted assimilation into the Chinese body politic by setting up special political arrangements, leaving civil administration to the Chinese and keeping military affairs strictly in their own hands. The system worked for a few generations. But in time even the proudest barbarians found the attractions of Chinese civilization too much to resist.

The Koreans

Korea had a similar problem. Independent organized kingdoms arose there about 300 B.C.; but the great Han emperor, Wu Ti, conquered most of the Korean peninsula in 108 B.C. Similar events had led to the incorporation of one province after another into China. Yet Korea, in the end, remained separate, in spite of the immediate presence of China to the west. Exactly why this happened is hard to say. Fresh barbarian invaders came to Korea, as well as to China, with the end of the Han Dynasty; and the new Korean kingdoms that emerged in T'ang times were tougher and far more military than earlier Korean states had been. The Sui emperors tried vainly to conquer Korea; the T'ang, too, fought hard to subdue them. In the end, when the Koreans admitted Chinese overlordship in 668, it was only nominal.

Two features of Korean life kept the country separate from China thereafter. One was the Korean language, which differed completely from Chinese and could not easily be written in Chinese characters. Soon after 600, Koreans began to write little marks in the margins beside Chinese characters to stand for grammatical endings and other parts of speech that were needed to make the meaning clear. In time this sytem evolved into a Korean script that differed from Chinese. Korea therefore developed a literary tradition of its own and preserved its separate language.

The other great distinguishing feature between Chinese and Korean civilization was Buddhism. When the Chinese turned against Buddhism, the Koreans clung to it all the more strongly. Korea thus became a Buddhist land. This meant that the study of Confucian classics and the eager imitation of the latest Chinese styles of dress or manners could never turn Korea into a mere province of China. To be sure, the Chinese chose to regard trade missions as tribute missions; but in fact Korea remained effectively independent, though often divided into rival kingdoms.

The Japanese

Japan was far enough away from China not to have to fear cultural absorption. Japanese tradition holds that the emperor who reigns today descends in an unbroken line from the first emperor, Jimmu; and that Jimmu, in turn, descended from the Sun Goddess, who created the Japanese islands first and then went on to make all the other lands of the earth. Jimmu's traditional date, 660 B.C., does not have much greater claim to accuracy than the Japanese story of creation.

Chinese and Korean records show that, in the early centuries of the Christian era, the Japanese islands were divided among warlike clans or tribal groups, of which the imperial clan was only one. Not until A.D. 552, when Buddhism was first introduced into Japan, did the country come closely into touch with the civilization of China. In A.D. 607 the first of several official missions went from Japan to the Chinese court. These Japanese missions carefully studied Chinese ways in order to take back useful information. Each mission involved several score of persons, who remained in China for months or even years at a time. Hence, the Japanese—as later in the nineteenth century when they set out to learn about European civilization—were nothing if not systematic.

The result was spectacular. The Japanese court found Chinese ways attractive, if only because the Chinese attributed so great a role to the emperor—a role the emperor of Japan was eager to play among the warlike and insubordinate clans of his native land. A wholesale importation of T'ang courtly culture, therefore, took place. This era is known as the Nara period of Japanese history, because the imperial court was then located at Nara (A.D. 710–784). Literature, art, and manners were brought in from China and developed brilliantly. In 838 the twelfth and last official embassy went to China. Thereafter, the Japanese decided that they had nothing more to learn from the decadent T'ang emperors. Official relations were accordingly broken off.

The realities of Japanese clan life never fitted smoothly into the forms of bureaucratic imperial administration imported from China. Instead, rival clans continued to struggle for power and influence, much as before. The imperial court appointed successful warriors as provincial governors with due Confucian rituals; but the effective authority of such governors rested on fighting clansmen, who obeyed not because the emperor had appointed them to office (as bureaucratic theory required) but because they were born to chieftainship or had risen to clan leadership in some other traditional fashion.

The hold of clan organization on Japan was steadily reinforced by the fact that the northern and eastern parts of the Japanese islands were a wild frontier region, where warrior clans steadily carved out new territories for themselves at the expense of earlier inhabitants known as Ainu. As a matter of fact, the military clans remained so important in Japan that one or more of them were often able to control the imperial court from behind the scenes, manipulating appointments and the award of dignities to suit the clan's interests.

In 794 the capital of Japan was relocated at Kyoto, inaugurating the so-called Heian period (794–1185). Life at the new imperial capital was less completely modeled on Chinese patterns. Distinctive Japanese art and literature made their appearance. In particular, about 1020, a lady-in-waiting at the court, Murasaki Shikibu, wrote a delightful prose romance, *The Tale of Genji*. A lively love story and one of the masterpieces of world literature, it owes little or nothing to Chinese literary models and everything to Lady Murasaki's keen observation of human nature and the manners of court life in Japan.

Buddhism, rather than the official Confucianism of the imperial court, took root among the rough warrior clans of the Japanese countryside. So close was their association with the rural and military classes that Japanese Buddhist monks often took sword in hand to defend the interests of their monastery in a fashion that other Buddhist communities never thought of doing. Successful monasteries, in fact, behaved very much like successful clans. Monastic discipline had its counterpart in clan discipline that marked off the way of the warrior or samurai class from peasant ways of life. And just as a man could become a monk by accepting the prescribed pattern of monastic life, so too at least some of the Japanese military clans admitted promising warriors to their ranks. This happened most freely in the zone of the frontier, where additional fighters were often much in demand.

At the bottom of society, of course, were peasants who learned to cultivate the soil as skillfully as the Chinese peasants did. How and by what steps paddy rice fields spread through the mountainous landscape of Japan is not known. We may assume that the laborious leveling of fields and the channeling of water occurred slowly, advancing into new districts as the Ainu were forced back, step by step, toward the harsh and forbidding climate of the northernmost island, Hokkaido, where rice would not grow.

The imperial court appointed officials to collect taxes from the peasants. Obviously, taxes were collected; otherwise the luxury of the Nara and Heian periods could not have been achieved. Yet perhaps from the beginning and increasingly as time went on, lands were granted tax free to military clans. Such warrior groups had the right to collect rice for their own support directly from the villagers. As this became more and more common, a feudal system arose in Japan that resembled the contemporary feudalism of western Europe quite closely. The emperor's theoretical supremacy was never called into question. But with the consolidation of Japanese feudalism, the imperial court's power and wealth decayed rapidly. Indeed, during the so-called Kamakura period (1185–1333) the emperor became no more than a puppet figure. Real power was concentrated instead in the hands of one particular clan that controlled the emperor and his court. As the imperial court became poorer, the courtly level of learning, art, and manners—modeled on the Chinese—decayed.

Instead, a cruder, more popular style of thought and feeling began to emerge.

Thus Japan too, by 1200 or so, had discarded the borrowed finery of Chinese civilization in favor of a simpler and more authentically Japanese type of culture and politics. Yet the civilizations of Japan, Korea, Tibet, and the less stable cultural styles of Uighurs and other central Asian peoples, would have been unthinkable had they not had the Chinese model against which to react and from which to borrow. China remained the Middle Kingdom, the central lodestone of the entire Far Eastern scene. Nothing within the vast expanse could really rival the dignity, wealth, splendor, and power of imperial China.

THE PACIFIC AND THE AMERICAS

The Polynesians

Beyond the outermost fringe of China's sphere of influence, Polynesians began their extraordinary spread sometime about A.D. 600. Perhaps the key invention that allowed them to move so freely across the wide Pacific was the outrigger canoe. By attaching buoyant outrigger to the gunwales, a canoe hollowed out from a single tree trunk became a seaworthy vessel, able to travel on the ocean with safety. Such vessels, driven by sails and guided by a steering paddle, allowed the Polynesians to establish themselves on islands scattered thousands of miles apart. Hawaii and New Zealand represent extremes of their expansion north and south; Easter Island, which lies not very far from the coast of South America, became the Polynesians' easternmost outpost.

The Polynesians were root growers and did not know about rice. They may have had some connection with the Indonesian seafarers who settled on Madagascar some 600 or 700 years before the Polynesians began moving eastward through the Pacific. Both may, in turn, have been related to seagoing peoples of the southeast Asian mainland. But origins are unclear; and for that matter the stages and dates of the Polynesian migration through the central Pacific cannot be reconstructed with certainty.

Occasional boatloads of Polynesian voyagers must have arrived on the shores of the American continent. Some of them (or perhaps other voyagers) also returned to the islands of the Pacific. The evidence for these voyages is that various plants native to the Americas were growing in Hawaii and other islands when Europeans first visited them. These plants must have been carried there by human travelers.

The Amerindians

Such contacts may account for otherwise surprising resemblances that occasionally crop up between Asian art forms and some Amerindian work. But contacts of this sort probably made little difference to the way the inhabitants of Mexico and Peru developed their civilizations. About A.D. 600 the so-called "classical" period began in the Mayan region of Guatemala and Mexico; soon thereafter, or perhaps at the same time, Peruvian cultures and the civilization of central Mexico also entered their "classical" phase. The word "classic" in this connection simply means that, about A.D. 600, temples and other monumental works of art attained a scale and excellence of workmanship that surpassed anything that had been done before and was not equaled later.

In the Mayan temple-cities, for example, scholars can observe changes of sculptural style very exactly, because the Mayans had the custom of erecting carved slabs of stone, called stelae, on special occasions, and dating them with symbols that can now be read. Archaeologists cannot tell what persuaded the Mayan farmers to support the priests and professional sculptors who carved these elaborate stelae and other decorations on the temple walls and approaches. Presumably some doctrine that made the temple necessary to assure the fertility of the fields lay behind the erection of such impressive monuments.

Then, beginning about 850, the Mayan cult centers were abandoned one after the other, and the jungle reclaimed them. No signs of violence suggest conquest. Perhaps all that happened was that Mayan peasants discovered new rites that made the crops grow without the service of the priests and their temple rituals. When the Spaniards arrived in the region, Mayans lived in simple village communities much as they had in the days of the temples, but they had forgotten about the great monuments buried in the jungle.

Farther north, in central Mexico, temple centers seem to have been overrun by warrior peoples at about the same time that the Mayan temples were abandoned. New and far more bloodthirsty religious ceremonies were introduced by these conquerors. Human sacrifice, sometimes on a mass scale, became central to temple rituals. In Yucatan a new center arose at Chichen Itza. The temple carvings there show a mingling of the older Mayan styles with motifs derived from the warrior cults of central Mexico. It looks as though conquerors had come down from the

Mayan architecture: The Pyramid of the Sorcerer, ca. 900–1100 A.D., Yucatan, Mexico. (Laimute E. Druskis)

north, overrun some of the Mayans, and set up a new religious center in Yucatan, several hundred miles away from the older Mayan cult centers in Guatemala and nearby parts of southern Mexico.

In South America, also, the classic period of the different cultures of the west coast was followed by an Age of Empire. At any rate, this is a good way to interpret the fact that after each separate river valley of the coast had developed its local art style to a peak of refinement, a new and uniform type of art spread throughout the area. This "imperial" art style is associated particularly with Tiahuanaco, a great temple complex situated high in the Andes. Perhaps it was only a new religious cult that spread throughout Peru; but military conquest seems likely.

As at Chichen Itza, the monumental building of the Age of Empire in Peru and also in central Mexico was less carefully done than in the classic period. This succession, from a temple-centered social system to a more militarized form of rule, resembled the change that came to Mesopotamian society about 3000 B.C. when written records first became available. We seem to be confronted with a standard pattern in human history.

**Amerindian Empires
on the Eve of the Spanish Conquest**

Gulf of Mexico

Atlantic Ocean

Querétaro
Oxitipan
Tuxpan
Tenochtitlán
TLAXCALA
Coatza-
coalco
TARASCANS
Petlatlán
Acapulco
Oaxaca
Mitla
Chiapa
Comitán
Ayotlán
MAYAS
Chichén Itzá
Uxmal
Tikal
Copan
*INDEFINITE
EASTERN
FRONTIER*

APPROXIMATE
AREA OF THE
AZTEC
EMPIRE

Caribbean Sea

THE
CHIBCHAS
Orinoco R.

- EQUATOR -

Pasto
Manta
Quito
Tumbez
Moyobamba
Cajamarca
Chimu
Huanuco
CHINCHAS
INCAS
Machu Picchu
Cuzco
L. TITICACA
Tiahuanaco
Cochabamba
Arequipa
Amazon R.
SOUTH AMERICA

APPROXIMATE
AREA OF THE
INCA
EMPIRE

Pacific Ocean

Iquique
Atacama
Tarija
Copiapó
Tucumán
Catamarca
Coquimpu
*MAULE
R.*
ARAUCANIANS

1000 MILES

344

Perhaps the wealth a society can create through specialization and division of labor under priestly management makes it worthwhile for warlike barbarian neighbors to conquer and subdue the pioneers of civilized life. And military conquest is likely to coarsen monumental building, if only because the fine details of workmanship, intended to please the gods, seem less necessary when one is serving an alien (and perhaps hated) foreign master.

The civilization of Mexico and Peru affected neighboring peoples just as the rise of Sumerian civilization touched the lives of people living within range of ancient Mesopotamia. Before 1200, for example, fairly elaborate cult centers were beginning to develop in what is now the southeastern part of the United States. Amerindians of Colombia, in the northernmost part of South America, living between the Mayan and Peruvian area, had also acquired many of the skills of their civilized neighbors. They had, for instance, begun to manufacture fine gold ornaments. We can safely assume that agriculture was spreading through the woodlands of North America and into the southern parts of South America as well. But, as in the Old World, the rain forest was a difficult environment for primitive farmers, so that no noteworthy development seems to have occurred in the vast Amazon basin.

The Amerindians lacked several elementary devices which were of basic importance to Eurasian civilizations. They never used wheeled vehicles, for example, and knew nothing of iron metallurgy. Except for the dog, they also lacked the domestic animals of the Old World—and the llama of the high Andes was a poor substitute for cattle, sheep, horses, camels, donkeys, goats, chickens, and pigs that expanded the resources of the peoples of Eurasia so greatly.

Finally, Amerindian civilization got started late in comparison to the civilizations of Asia—about 3500 years late, if we take Sumerian temple communities as roughly equivalent to the Mayan temple centers of the New World. This was a handicap the Amerindians never overcame. By comparison with the developments of Asia and Europe, they remained far behind—weaker and vulnerable to the superior skills and knowledge Spanish conquerors were able to bring from Europe after 1500.

CONCLUSION

This survey of the Far Eastern, Pacific, and American parts of the world between about A.D. 600 and 1200 reveals the very great contrasts that had developed within this vast region. Primitive hunters continued to populate Australia, large portions of America, and the northern parts of Asia. A few regions of southeast Asia also harbored similarly simple peoples. At the other extreme was the rice paddy style of cultivation that remodeled the landscape of China, Japan, Korea, and some parts of southeast Asia, and provided the principal economic basis for Chinese civilization and for the related high cultures of surrounding lands.

As compared to the situation in Europe, India, and the Middle East, the thing that stands out about the Far Eastern and Pacific area is the sharpness of the contrast that resulted from such different ways of exploiting the geographical environment. The wealth, skill, cultivation, and learning of China were immense. By any quantitative standard China surpassed the achievements of all other civilizations of the age. Population was greater, cities larger; more goods were exchanged and carried longer distances; more books were printed, read, and discussed; education was better organized and more energetically pursued; more people painted pictures and wrote more poems with more refined skills. In these respects and in many others, China stood preeminent in all the world. The Middle Kingdom was even more overpowering within the circle of the Far East itself, where the real and different achievements of the other great civilizations of the world remained almost unknown. China was like a vast sun, radiating skill, knowledge, and power. Other east Asian peoples were like planets, revolving around the Chinese sun. Beyond their planetary orbits, where Chinese influence was not felt directly, the achievements of the more distant peoples of the Americas and Oceania could not begin to compare with what the Chinese had accomplished.

The sharpness of the contrasts between the civilized and uncivilized regions of the Far East arose from the special nature of rice paddy agriculture. Where that kind of cultivation dug into the landscape, dense populations, intensive agricultural production, and the human basis for high civilization existed. Where paddies were absent, it was simply impossible to approach, much less to achieve, Chinese levels of civilization. The best proof of this is the fact that the nomads of Mongolia and Manchuria, although they maintained close relations with the Chinese from 300 B.C. if not before, only knew Chinese civilization through the silks and other luxuries sent as tribute. They could not make Chinese artisan skills their own, and never even tried to do so.

In the western half of Asia and in Europe, no such sharp boundaries arose. Civilized agriculture was not so intensive. Social skills shaded off more gradually from regions of the highest complexity toward the fringes of the habitable world. In short, in Europe and western Asia the gap between civilization and barbarism was smaller, cultural boundaries were fuzzier, and sharply contrasting ways of life less often existed side by side than in the Far Eastern and Pacific regions, where the geographic limits of civilizations built upon rice paddies were as clear and definite as the dikes that enclosed the rice fields to keep the water from running off.

CHAPTER 12

Europe

500 to 1200

In Greek and Roman times, the civilized life of Europe centered on the Mediterranean; but between A.D. 500 and 1000, Europeans learned how to exploit the resources of regions further north far more effectively than before. As a result, Europe's medieval civilization extended into parts of Europe that had always before been desolate forest and swampy wilderness. To understand how this happened requires a grasp of Europe's geography and of how the natural regions of that continent limited early agricultural efforts.

The Mediterranean zone of Europe is defined by the annual shift of the trade winds, north in summer and south in winter. In summer, when the Mediterranean lands fall within the trade-wind zone, no rain falls. In winter, when the trade winds shift southward, the Mediterranean lands come under the influence of the cyclonic storms that move from west to east all round the globe. With these storms come clouds and rain and snow. The limiting factor in such a climate is moisture. Crops must be planted in the fall with the first rains. Grain sprouts in the fall and ripens in the spring after the last rains have fallen. Only deep-rooted plants, like olives and vines, can survive the summer drought by tapping groundwater that runs far below the surface of the soil. The Mediterranean type of climate exists in southern California but nowhere else in the United States.

To the north of a line drawn approximately along the Loire River in the west and just south of Constantinople in the east, the desiccating influence of the trade winds is never felt. Instead, the zone of prevailing westerlies lasts all through the year, so that rain may fall at any season; and storms occur every three or four days, more severe in winter and somewhat less frequent in summer. This is the climate that prevails over most of the United States.

Surprising as it may seem, this type of climate was not favorable to early farming. Grain, after all, was a plant naturally adapted to semiarid conditions like those of the Mediterranean lands. If puddles of water remain on the surface of the land for any length of time, grain plants drown. This is exactly what happened every spring in the flat plains of northwestern Europe. Especially in March and April, when the rainfall was at its highest point in the year, the flat landscape got thoroughly waterlogged, and could therefore not be used for grainfields.

Only hill slopes, especially those with chalk or loess underneath— where drainage was especially good—made suitable fields for Europe's early farmers. Obviously, as long as farming had to be concentrated in these relatively small regions, there was little possibility of establishing a flourishing civilization in northwestern Europe. As a result, all through Roman times and until after 500 this region remained a vast forest, only broken by a few isolated clearings.

Wetness was greatest near the Atlantic. As the storms moved across Europe, from west to east, dropping their rain as they went, precipitation gradually diminished. In addition, the mild winter temperature resulting from the warming of the Atlantic waters by the Gulf Stream—a phenomenon so strong that dwarf palm trees grow in western Scotland!—faded out as distance from the Atlantic increased. Eastward of the Elbe River, the oak and beech forests that grew luxuriantly in northwestern Europe gave way to birch and conifers, and sandy soils became more common. This region extended all the way to the Urals, fading off in northern Russia into tundra—a zone where the subsoil remains perpetually frozen and only scrub trees and mosses can grow.

Waterlogged soil was not usually a problem in this eastern forest zone. What limited early farmers there was the shortness of the growing season. Wheat and barley often could not ripen before frosts came to cut them down. Rye, a plant that probably originated as a weed in wheat fields, matured faster and became the staple crop of this region. But it produced far less grain per acre than wheat, and required about the same amount of seed. As a result, farmers who raised rye had a much smaller margin between what they harvested and what they needed for next year's seed than was usual in regions where wheat and barley could be raised. This in turn meant that rye cultivators could support far fewer landlords and townspeople.

Civilization, in other words, could not flourish easily on such poor agricultural land. In fact, it did not begin to arise in the northeastern forest zone of Europe until after 900.

Another factor that delayed the development of civilized patterns of life in northeastern Europe was that the grasslands of the western steppe separated it from the Mediterranean centers of civilization. As we have seen, this landscape came to be occupied by warlike cavalrymen, beginning about 700 B.C.; and long before then it had supported nomads who depended on herds of cattle and horses for their livelihood, and looked upon farmers as fair game for robbery and plunder. For many centuries, the fact that barbarian nomads separated the northern forests of eastern Europe from the Mediterranean lands hindered the spread of civilization northward.

By A.D. 1000 Europeans had worked a fundamental change in the way they farmed. New techniques, suited to the wet conditions of the northwestern parts of Europe, had spread across the formerly waterlogged plain between the Loire and Elbe rivers. As this occurred, the fertility of the soil, the abundance of rainfall, and the ease with which boats could move along the slow-moving rivers of northwestern Europe created conditions for the rapid and spectacular rise of medieval European civilization.

To understand how this happened, we need to look at the political history and migrations of peoples that came to Europe during the first part of the Middle Ages, between 450 and 900. This period is often called the Dark Ages, because so little was written during this time that survives for modern scholars to study. Yet however low the level to which literacy sank (and in that age very few people in western Europe could read or write), and however dangerous life became when one barbarian invader after another swarmed across the country—burning and looting as they went—these same Dark Ages were also a time of fundamental agricultural advance, when northern Europe's farmers laid the basis for all subsequent western European civilization.

BARBARIAN INVASIONS AND MIGRATIONS

The German tribes that fled before the Huns (375) to Roman soil were only the first of a long line of invaders who, in the course of the following 600 years, profoundly changed Europe's ethnic patterns. We have already seen how the Visigoths, Ostrogoths, and Vandals set up kingdoms in

Spain, Italy, and north Africa, and how Justinian, emperor of Byzantium*
(527–565), restored imperial administration in Italy and north Africa.

While these changes were taking place in the Mediterranean parts
of western Europe, less spectacular but more important migrations also
occurred in the north. Large numbers of German settlers crossed the Rhine
into northern Gaul and pushed back the Latin-speaking population to
about the line that still divides French and German speakers today. Britain
also became English as Angles, from what is now Denmark, and Saxons,
from the coastal regions of Germany, crossed the North Sea and started
to settle the southern and eastern parts of what we can now begin to
call England (that is, Angle-land).

These movements may seem trifling compared to the migrations of
the Visigoths and Vandals, who traveled thousands of miles before settling
down in their respective kingdoms. But the Anglo-Saxons in England and
the Germans in the Rhinelands, who called themselves Franks (that is,
the Free), took possession of their new lands in a very different way
from the way of the Visigoths, Vandals, and Ostrogoths. As conquerors
had done innumerable times before, the Visigoths, Vandals, and Ostrogoths set themselves up as landlords and rulers but left the hard work
of the fields to the people already on the spot, most of whom spoke
Latin or languages derived from Latin. Not so in the north, where the
newcomers came in as settlers and cleared the forests to set up their
fields in land which, for the most part, had never been cultivated before.

New Techniques of Farming

Obviously, the Franks and Anglo-Saxons knew how to farm land that
had before been too wet to produce a crop. Their secret was a new
kind of plow, of a design fundamentally the same as that which is still
commonly used today. It is called the moldboard plow to distinguish it
from the scratch plow, which had been used by Middle Eastern and Mediterranean farmers from the time when plows were first invented. A scratch
plow, as the name implies, simply scratches the soil, breaking the surface
into loose clods. A moldboard plow is more elaborate. In addition to
the horizontal plowshare, that goes through the ground just like the share
of the scratch plow, there was a colter to cut the soil vertically and an

---

* Byzantium is the Greek name for the ancient city which was renamed Constantinople
in 330, when Constantine made it his capital. The Turks, after capturing Constantinople
in 1453, called it Istanbul. Oddly enough, scholars commonly call the period from Justinian
to 1453 the Byzantine Empire, though the rulers called themselves Roman emperors and
their subjects (most of whom spoke Greek) called themselves Romans. During all this period
the official name of the capital city was Constantinople.

"ear" or moldboard attached on one side of the plow. This moldboard was curved in such a fashion that it turned the soil over in a long furrow as the plow drove through the earth. For illustrations see the essay on Agriculture, pp. 84–91.

In itself this may not seem like an important change. Turning the soil all the way over, instead of just breaking it up, took extra force so that plow teams pulling a moldboard plow had to have four, six, or even eight oxen instead of the pair of animals that sufficed for a scratch plow. The plow itself also had to be much bigger and stronger; it used more metal and was in every way more expensive. To make up for these disadvantages, such a plow could be dragged through "heavier" soils—that is, soils with more clay in them—than the light scratch plow could penetrate. Many of the soils of northwestern Europe are clayey; so this at once made it possible to cultivate wide areas of low-lying plain that before had been useless for farming.

But there was a second and less obvious advantage to the moldboard plow. The plow turned the furrow to one side only. To plow a field, it was necessary to go first in one direction and then back again in the opposite direction, throwing the furrow to the opposite side as one did so. If fields were laid out in the same way each year, the effect of such cultivation was to pile the soil in toward the center of each "plowland" and to create shallow trenches between one plowland and the next. This made an efficient drainage system for flat, waterlogged land. Plowlands were laid out to take advantage of whatever natural slope there might be. Furrows all running parallel to one another down even a very slight slope and grouped into raised plowlands—with shallow trenches or "balks" every sixteen yards or so separating one plowland from the next—sufficed to make most of the flat, waterlogged plainlands of western Europe fit for farming.

No one knows when and where the moldboard plow and the "Long Acre" system of cultivation (as it is called) were first invented. It must have developed some time before 450, when the Frankish and Anglo-Saxon migrations got started. Pioneer German settlers used this kind of cultivation from the time of their arrival on formerly Roman soil. Obviously they brought the moldboard plow with them.

Heavy plows with "ears" may have been known for a considerable time in the flatlands between the Rhine and Elbe rivers. But it was not easy to assemble a plow team to pull such a heavy instrument through the soil. Possibly the most stubborn obstacle to the spread of the moldboard plow was the difficulty of establishing a workable pattern of cooperative tillage. Unless a group of farmers were ready to pool the oxen at their disposal to make up a single plow team, and then could agree on how to divide up rights to the land they had plowed, the heavy plow was not much good. No one family was likely to own the necessary four, six, or eight oxen and such an expensive piece of machinery as a moldboard plow—at least not among the free barbarians of the forests, where social inequality had yet to establish itself.

The way in which this problem was eventually solved seems to have been this: a group of six or more cultivators got together and each contributed an ox to the plow team. At the end of each day's work in the fields, the soil that had been made ready for planting on that day was assigned to one of the partners who then had to wait for his *next* piece of land until everybody else had his turn. Eventually a day's plowing was standardized as an acre, 220 yards long and 16 yards wide, which was in fact about what a team could get done by working from dawn to dark. But before any kind of written records were made, which would allow us to understand how moldboard cultivation worked, permanent property rights to particular acres of cultivated land had been assigned to individual families, so that only traces can be found of the system that may have allowed cooperative tillage to get started.

The whole history of how cooperative tillage started and spread among the west Germans is therefore speculative. Perhaps this kind of cultivation was easiest to establish in a new settlement, where there were no preexisting property rights to land and where the pioneers had to help one another anyway to make a go of their venture. It is not unlikely, therefore, that the moldboard plow and cooperative tillage really got started on a large and significant scale only at the time when the Franks and Anglo-Saxons began to colonize former Roman territory along the Rhine and in Britain. At any rate, the field layouts of these settlements are the earliest known examples of the typical Long Acre field, which the moldboard plow made necessary because it was so awkward to turn.

The Frankish and Anglo-Saxon Kingdoms

As we might expect, the establishment of a new and productive style of agriculture in northwestern Europe soon resulted in the rise of new and more powerful states. At first, the Franks, as their name implied, were free from obligations to any sort of central authority. They did, however, recognize traditional clan or tribal leaders. Scattered about through their forest clearings, they lacked any sort of common government until the time of Clovis (reigned 481–511). Clovis started life as a petty chieftain of one of the Frankish tribes, but very early in his career he eliminated all rival chieftains among the so-called Salian (that is, "salty," living near the sea) Franks. He then began to use the fighting capability of his comparatively numerous subjects to extend Frankish power in every direction. By the end of his life, the Frankish kingdom extended over almost all of Gaul, and his sons conquered additional territory to the east, in the valleys of the Rhone and upper Rhine.

Frankish power in these conquered regions was like that exercised earlier by Visigoths and Vandals. A thin layer of landowners and military governors represented the Frankish king, but the work of cultivating the soil was performed, as before, by people who as yet knew nothing of the moldboard plow and spoke a language derived from Latin and ancestral to French. Relations between the Frankish ruling class and the "Roman" population were more cordial than in the Visigothic kingdom of Spain. This was because in 496 Clovis accepted the papal form of Christianity and thus ranked as orthodox in the eyes of his new subjects, whereas the Visigoths and Ostrogoths had both accepted what their subjects rejected as a heretical form of the Christian faith, known as Arianism.

Across the channel in England, the Anglo-Saxon settlers did not unite into a single kingdom until after 900, when raiding Danes forced them to do so. Instead, seven small kingdoms divided control over southern and eastern England, and by degrees pushed the Britons back into Cornwall, Wales, and the highlands of Scotland. Christianity reached England from Ireland, where St. Patrick had established a flourishing church about 432. In 597, however, a missionary from Rome, named St. Augustine (not the famous author of *The City of God*), arrived in Kent and converted the kingdom of the Angles to Christianity. He made Canterbury, the Kentish capital, his headquarters.

Irish Christianity differed from the practices of the Roman church in several respects. Controversy centered around the question of how the date of Easter ought to be calculated. In 664 a meeting of leading representatives of the English churches took place at Whitby, and it was decided that the papal method of setting the date of Easter was correct. This decision led to the withdrawal of Irish missionaries from England and brought the Anglo-Saxons firmly within the circle of Latin Christendom.

RENEWED BARBARIAN INVASIONS

The rise of the Frankish kingdom on the continent and the conversion of England to Christianity, together with the resurgence of Byzantine power in Mediterranean Europe in Justinian's time (527–565), did nothing to stabilize the situation in eastern Europe. In Justinian's last years, the arrival in Hungary of a new steppe people, the Avars, led to widespread raids climaxing in an unsuccessful siege of Constantinople in 626. Half a century later still another steppe people, the Bulgars, set up headquarters along the lower Danube and added their depredations to those of the Avars.

Balkan farmers could not survive such harassment. Land fell vacant, and the Avars and Bulgars allowed (or sometimes may have driven) Slavic-speaking tribes to move southward, from the spruce and pine forests of the north into the richer farmland of the Balkan Peninsula. The Bulgars, in fact, soon became Slavs themselves by intermarrying with Slavic women and taking the language of their subjects. When Slavic manpower was combined with the Bulgar war band organization, a strong new state came into existence that several times threatened to overwhelm Byzantium.

Arab, Avar, and Bulgar Assaults on Byzantium

The Avar and Bulgar attack on Byzantium came at the same time that the Arabs were threatening from the south. As we have seen, the emperors of Constantinople lost their richest provinces in Syria, Egypt, and north Africa to the Arabs and had to fight hard to keep command of the sea. After the great siege of 717–718, however, the Moslems, for the time being, ceased trying to rival the Byzantine fleet. Indeed, after 750 the Abbasids were entirely willing to leave the Mediterranean and Black seas in Byzantine hands and developed a flourishing trade with Constantinople.

Farther west, the Avars drove the Lombards into Italy, where those rough German barbarians divided control of the countryside with Byzantine garrisons still stationed in important cities. In Frankland, too, a new wave of Germanic invasion took place. Clovis' descendants, known as Merovingians, had divided the old Frankish kingdom into two separate halves: Austrasia in the east, where Germanic-speaking peoples lived, and Neustria (New Lands) in the west and south, where the former subjects of the Roman Empire still spoke a form of Latin. Effective power, however, had shifted from the Merovingian kings to officials known as "mayors of the palace" who conducted the actual tasks of government.

Pepin II of Heristal inherited the post of mayor of the palace in Austrasia from his father. In 687 he led his followers into Neustria and made himself mayor of the palace in that kingdom, too, thus in effect reuniting the two parts of the Frankish state. To secure his power in

Neustria, Pepin then granted Neustrian lands to his Austrasian followers. The result was a new Germanic invasion, for the rude Austrasians had little use for the somewhat more civilized Latin-speaking Neustrians.

Then another invasion came from the south, for in 711 Moslems swarmed into Spain from north Africa, crossing at the Strait of Gibraltar. The Visigothic kingdom quickly collapsed, and the Moslems drove northward across the Pyrenees and along the Mediterranean coast of what is now France. This brought them into direct contact with the Frankish state. At first the advantage lay with the Moslems, but in 732 Charles Martel, Pepin's son and successor as Frankish mayor of the palace, met and defeated a Moslem raiding party near Tours. In the border wars that continued to rage thereafter, the Franks usually had the upper hand. The Moslem frontier therefore shrank back southward toward the Ebro River, south of the Pyrenees, where a more nearly stable border defined itself by about 800.

Byzantine Recovery

We have seen how the Byzantine capital survived the Arab siege of 717–718. The emperor, Leo the Isaurian (reigned 717–741), who came to the throne at the moment of crisis, was able to push the Moslems back to the Taurus Mountains in eastern Asia Minor, thus regaining important territories for his empire.

After his victory, Emperor Leo tried to change the religious habits of his subjects by prohibiting the use of images in churches. Perhaps he felt that ignorant people were worshiping statues and paintings of the saints instead of God. But many monks resisted the emperor's effort to alter Christian custom, and the common people of Constantinople (and elsewhere in the empire) objected to having their holy images destroyed. Who besides the emperor supported the destruction of images is not known for sure; perhaps his soldiers attributed Moslem victories to Mohammed's rejection of images, and so favored the reform.

In the end, the iconoclasts (as the people who wanted to destroy images were called) failed. Decoration of Christian churches with paintings of the saints became again an important part of Greek Orthodox culture. Statues, however, never really came back to favor, being too similar to pagan statues of the gods. The result of the quarrel over images was to restore Christian customs nearly to what they had been before. The monks and the people had prevailed against the emperor and his armies.

The Rise
of the Carolingian
Monarchy

In the West, however, the iconoclastic controversy provoked fundamental realignments. First of all, the pope in Rome was among those who resisted the Byzantine emperor's efforts to change Christian worship. But Rome was, at least in theory, still part of the Byzantine Empire. The pope felt the need of a new protector. He looked northward where Pepin III, known as Pepin the Short—a grandson of Pepin of Heristal—had succeeded Charles Martel as mayor of the palace. Pepin the Short wished to displace the figurehead Merovingian rulers and become king himself. But overthrowing Clovis' heirs was risky. The upstart Carolingians, as Pepin's family is called, needed papal blessing and support to get away with their usurpation. In return, the pope needed Pepin's military aid in Italy against both Lombards and Byzantines.

The alliance was sealed in 754 when Pope Stephen II traveled north to anoint Pepin as king of the Franks. In return, Pepin marched into Italy and rescued Rome from the Lombards. A second campaign in Italy was necessary before the Lombards, at Pepin's dictation, handed control over a belt of territory in central Italy to the papacy. In this way the "papal states" came into existence. They lasted, with many shifts of boundary, from 756 to 1870.

CHARLEMAGNE   The alliance between the Carolingian rulers of Frankland and the popes was of the greatest importance for European history. Under Pepin's son and successor, Charles the Great, or Charlemagne (reigned 768–814), the military strength of the Frankish state and the moral and religious prestige of the papacy worked hand in hand to unify most of western Europe. The geographical base for all later western European civilization emerged for the first time as a result of this collaboration.

On the military side, Charlemagne led his armies nearly every year to fight against some enemy. He annexed the Lombard kingdom of Italy in 774. Later he conquered German tribes and dukedoms that lay to the east of Frankish territory. The Bavarians in the south submitted without too much resistance; but the Saxons in the north proved extremely stubborn foes. No sooner were they defeated in one campaign than they revolted again. Thirty years of fighting were required to break their resistance. Still farther east, in 796 Charlemagne destroyed the Avar power, based in Hungary, and forced a fringe of Slavic tribes and kingdoms to recognize his authority.

On the religious side, Pepin and Charlemagne supported and encour-

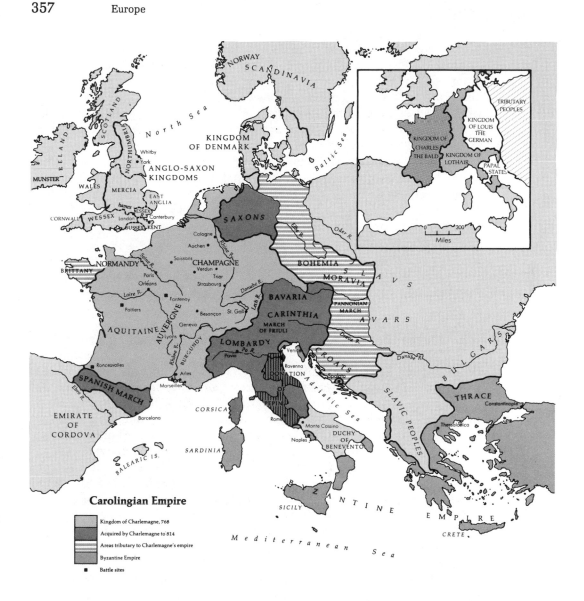

Carolingian Empire

Kingdom of Charlemagne, 768

Acquired by Charlemagne to 814

Areas tributary to Charlemagne's empire

Byzantine Empire

■ Battle sites

aged Christian efforts to convert those Germans and Slavs who were still pagan. The most successful missionary was St. Boniface (d. 755). Boniface was born in England, where Christianity had made rapid progress. There the stimulus of Irish learning had created a much better-educated clergy than survived anywhere in Frankland. St. Boniface and others, therefore, went among the pagan Germans, establishing monasteries, bishoprics, and schools for training priests.

Everywhere they destroyed idols, forbade heathen sacrifice, and tried to persuade the chiefs and warriors of the truth of Christianity.

Except among the Saxons, who clung to paganism as part of their struggle against the Franks, resistance to Christianity was small. The prestige of Rome and of the pope, as well as the prestige and military strength of the Franks, backed up the missionary efforts. In addition, German chiefs and rulers could see the usefulness of literacy and law; and only the Church could bring them these advantages, for there was no educated class except the clergy.

The alliance between the Carolingian kings and the pope achieved its final form on Christmas Day, 800, when the pope crowned Charlemagne emperor of the Romans. The title of emperor had not been used in the West since 476, when a boy emperor, Romulus Augustulus, had been forced to abdicate and send the badges of supreme office back to Constantinople. The Byzantine rulers, of course, continued to call themselves Roman emperors, and at first refused to recognize Charlemagne's new title. Later, however, in return for some territory in the western Balkans, Constantinople recognized Charlemagne's imperial rank.

THE FIRST MEDIEVAL KNIGHTS   Two other changes occurred during the Carolingian Age that were fundamental for later European history. The first of these was the emergence of a new kind of cavalry warrior: the European knight. Knights were protected by helmets, shields, and chain mail to begin with; later plate armor, cunningly fitted to the contours of the body, replaced the leather jerkins covered with overlapping rings of iron that protected the first knights. Armored cavalrymen were nothing new: Byzantine and Persian armies had introduced the big horses needed to carry armored men into battle centuries before. What was new in western Europe after A.D. 732 was the way heavy-armored cavalrymen fought. Earlier, their principal weapon had been the bow; but European knights preferred the lance. Instead of attacking the foe with arrows at a distance, European knights charged at a gallop, with lances fixed under their arms and using stirrups to brace themselves against the shock of contact. In this way the momentum of horse and man could be put behind the lance head, producing an immense force. Nothing could stand against such a force except another mounted man riding at equal speed in the opposite direction, in which case one or both of the charging knights might be knocked completely out of the saddle. Sometimes the lance shafts shattered instead. This simple tactic created a superior force against which troops differently equipped and trained were nearly helpless. Eventually, infantry tactics were invented that proved capable of checking charging knights. But that took a long time. For about 300 years, therefore, European knights dominated the battlefields of western Europe, and exercised social and political as well as military leadership over the whole of western Christendom.

At first, the number of knights that could be maintained in the Caro-

French knights jousting in full plate armor, ca. fifteenth century. Heavy armor was utilized during the later Middle Ages. In earlier centuries, the knight wore only a long chain mail shirt and a helmet. (Courtesy of British Museum)

lingian lands remained very small. A knight's warhorse, weapons, and armor were expensive, and it took years of special training to learn to exploit the possibilities of lance warfare to the full. But the need for knights to guard local communities against raiding strangers, whether they came like the Vikings by boat or like the Magyars by land, was very great. The second great invention of Carolingian times, the manorial system of agriculture, eventually solved that problem by providing the means for supporting relatively large numbers of knights. As a result, after about 1000, western Europe ceased to suffer invasion and began instead to expand its frontiers in every direction.

THE MANORIAL SYSTEM   The second important change that occurred in the Carolingian Age was the growth of the manorial system. A manor was a big farm, cultivated by the inhabitants of a village partly for themselves and partly on behalf of a lord or owner. Exact arrangements differed: sometimes the lord held part of the land "in demesne." This meant that he owned part of the land personally and had the legal right to require the peasants to cultivate it for him. The peasants lived on what they could produce from what remained. In other cases, the lord got part of what every peasant raised and did not keep any part of the land under his own direct management.

This was nothing particularly new in the parts of the Frankish kingdom that had formerly been Roman territory. In those regions landlords had for centuries divided the produce of the soil with the peasants who did the actual tillage. Among the Germans, however, no such inequality prevailed; as a result, during Carolingian times there were only a few manors in the purely German hands.

But, as we have seen, the Germans already had the moldboard plow and knew how to cultivate low-lying land. When the German technique of plowing was joined with the Roman system of making peasants work for a lord, the medieval manorial system came fully into existence. All the elements were present in Carolingian times, but there were deep resistances that had to be overcome before the combination of German and Roman elements could be welded together into a new system of society.

Landlords of the former Roman lands were not always eager to serve as knights, preferring to live an easier kind of life. And German farmers, even more definitely, disliked the thought of submitting to a lord, even if he were a very good knight. Not until 900, when still another round of barbarian invasions had made it clear to all concerned that Europe vitally needed a numerous body of knights—ready at a moment's notice to ride off in any direction to drive dangerous invaders away—did these resistances collapse so that a new, enormously successful pattern of European society could finally emerge.

THE MAGYAR AND VIKING ASSAULT

Fleeing from a defeat they had suffered on the Russian steppe, the Magyars crossed into Hungary in 895. From this base they soon began to raid western Europe, just as the Huns and Avars had done before them. German foot soldiers, however brave, could not oppose the mobile Magyar riders effectively. It became painfully obvious that to drive them off the Germanic peoples would have to find ways of maintaining cavalry themselves. Raids from the sea matched these new attacks from the steppe. In the eastern Mediterranean, Arab seapower revived soon after 800. Not long afterward, a new danger appeared, this time from the north. River pirates, coming from Scandinavia, having traveled along the Russian rivers, appeared before Constantinople in 860. The Black Sea, where Byzantine vessels had always sailed unhindered, was no longer safe.

The appearance of Scandinavian river pirates before the walls of Constantinople was one extreme wing of a general Viking assault upon civilized Europe. Even in Charlemagne's lifetime, a few Viking ships appeared off the coasts of his domain; but there were easier pickings for these pagan warriors farther west in Ireland and Scotland, where undefended monasteries had accumulated considerable wealth. A few successful raids of this sort encouraged other Scandinavians to build ships and go looking for a fortune too. Hence the number of Viking boats increased rapidly; and since the boats could travel much faster than any opposing land forces, it was easy for them to coast along until they found an undefended place, then go ashore and seize anything that seemed worth taking. The Viking ships had a shallow draft—about three feet—and so could go long distances up the rivers that flowed slowly across the north European plain. Thus a large part of the continent came within their reach. Where the Vikings did not penetrate, the Magyars usually did.

The foot soldiers of the Carolingian army were utterly unable to cope with these new threats. They could not move fast enough: the emperor had to wait weeks on end before his troops assembled; and by the time they were ready, the raiders were gone.

The Peak of Byzantine Power

The Byzantines did better. A new dynasty, the Macedonian, came to power in 867. It remained in control of the Byzantine Empire until 1054. Most of the Macedonian emperors were energetic and capable generals. Basil I, who founded the dynasty, built up the navy and was able to push back Arab and Scandinavian marauders. He and his successors also created a strong army by allowing local magnates to create large households of professional cavalrymen. Of course the emperor's household was greatest of them all, and when they all joined together, the Byzantine state was able to field a strong army.

The result was rapid territorial expansion. By now the Moslems were divided and politically weak. Hence the Macedonian emperors were able to recover Armenia and other lands to the east. But the most strenuous fighting and the greatest territorial gains came in Europe, where after long wars with the Bulgarians the Byzantine emperor, Basil II (reigned 976–1025), destroyed the Bulgarian state entirely and annexed its territory as far as the Danube. The Byzantines were also able to recover possession of southern and eastern Italy. Never since the days of Justinian had the Eastern Roman Empire extended so far.

Byzantium's reach was reinforced by missionary activity. In 865 the Bulgarians accepted Christianity in its Orthodox form. Long before Basil II destroyed their kingdom, the Bulgarians translated prayer books and other religious books into Slavic. A new literary language, Church Slavonic, thus came into existence. When in due course the Russians also

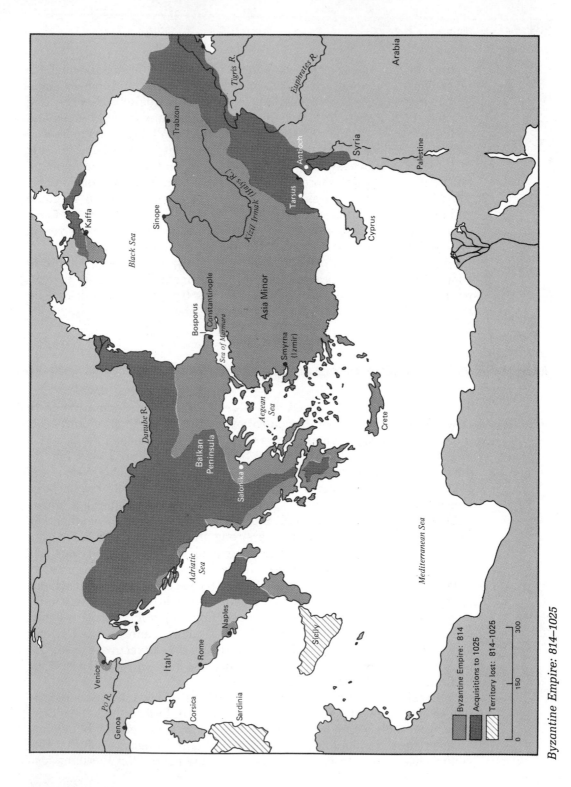

Byzantine Empire: 814–1025

Byzantine Empire: 814
Acquisitions to 1025
Territory lost: 814–1025

Arabia

Tigris R.

Euphrates R.

Syria

Palestine

Antioch

Tarsus

Cyprus

Trabzon

Kizil Irmak

Tigris (?)

Asia Minor

Smyrna (Izmir)

Kaffa

Sinope

Black Sea

Bosporus

Constantinople

Sea of Marmara

Aegean Sea

Crete

Danube R.

Balkan Peninsula

Salonika

Adriatic Sea

Mediterranean Sea

Venice

Po R.

Genoa

Italy

Rome

Naples

Corsica

Sardinia

Sicily

0   150   300

became Christian, they took over their ritual language from the Bulgarians. This happened after 989, when St. Vladimir of Kiev ordered his warriors to throw the old pagan idols into the Dnieper River and accept Christian baptism.

The Russian state, like the Bulgarian, combined Slavic manpower with foreign political organization. In the case of the Bulgarians, the military framework had been provided by steppe nomads. In the Russian case it was river pirates, moving down from Scandinavia, who created the political umbrella under which the Russian peoples first united.

There is a reason why the Slavs entered history without forming large political units of their own. As we saw, agricultural conditions in the eastern spruce and pine forests, where they lived, were not nearly as favorable as elsewhere in Europe. Rye, instead of wheat or barley, was the only grain that would grow well, and the yield from rye was much lower than from wheat. Hence, only a poor, thinly scattered population could exist in the eastern forest lands of Europe. Such communities could not support great states or large war federations like those familiar among the steppe peoples, or those possible among the Germans, as their wealth and numbers increased with the spread of moldboard plow cultivation.

The Germans, too, had lived as poor and scattered tribes until the moldboard plow came into use. As wealth and population density increased, we have seen how new German war federations—the Franks (meaning "free men") or the Alemanni (meaning "all men"), for example—took form. Comparable political federations established themselves among the Slavs, not through their own action but as a by-product of conquest or invasion by strangers. This did not mean that the Slavs were any less warlike. It did mean that they had not time and wealth enough to develop large military units of their own until the Bulgars and Rus—as the Scandinavian pirates were called—did it for them.

The Decline of the Carolingian Empire

While the Byzantine Empire was responding victoriously to barbarian and Moslem pressures, the Carolingian Empire fell to pieces. Viking and Magyar raids, year after year, met with no effective response from Charlemagne's successors. The western European rulers were helpless. Local authorities and self-made men had to do the best they could to pick up the pieces left behind after raiders had passed through. They had to take steps to be better prepared next time, if possible. Nobody cared too much about property rights or formal law. What was needed was defense—local, dependable, and effective.

The answer, of course, was the knight, living on the spot as lord of a manor—ready at a moment's notice to put on his armor, mount his horse, and go off after Vikings or Magyars as the case might be. If every village could have a knight in residence (and villages could flourish close together on the fertile north European plain), then a considerable number of extremely effective fighting men could gather, literally overnight, from a radius of only a few miles to attack dismounted Viking ships' crews with devastating effect. Instead of being nearly a sure thing, raiding then became extremely dangerous. Under these circumstances Viking ships soon stopped coming. The barbarian attack had been turned back, not as in the east by a reinvigorated empire, but by a host of armed men whose roots were local and whose obedience to any theoretical political superior was, to say the least, unpredictable.

Northern France was the center for the development of knighthood and of the manorial system that made it possible to maintain large numbers of knights. In Germany society changed more slowly. After the Carolingians had been thoroughly discredited by their ineffectiveness, a new ruler, Otto I, the Great, claimed the imperial title in 962. He did so after defeating the Magyars in a great battle at Lechfeld in 955. His army was partly composed of old-fashioned foot soldiers like those Charlemagne had commanded. But Otto and his successors also had increasing numbers of knights under their command. They were mostly supported, on the Byzantine pattern, as the rulers' own household followers rather than as lords of manors in the French fashion.

Nevertheless, the spread of knighthood, both in its French and in its German forms, not only turned back the last wave of barbarian attack but soon allowed European knights to take the offensive. As a result from about 900, western Europeans began to expand their domain in every direction. The conversion of Poland in 966, and of both Hungary and Scandinavia in the year 1000, to the papal form of Christianity showed how attractive the new style of life emerging in western Europe had become.

Losses, of course, were real. Barbarian freedom and equality ceased to distinguish German society from that of more civilized parts of Europe. Moreover, Irish civilization, which had blossomed so remarkably for a few centuries, had been killed off by the Vikings. The Anglo-Saxons also suffered severely from raiding Northmen. The monasteries, in which scholars such as "the Venerable Bede" (d. 735) had lived, were all destroyed.

The effort of fighting off the Vikings had, however, created a single kingdom of England. Alfred the Great (ruled 871–901) was the hero of this struggle. But when his heirs proved ineffective, the Saxons handed the crown to the Danish king, Canute II (1016). It looked for a while as though England might become part of a Scandinavian empire of the north, of which Scotland, Norway, Ireland, and Denmark would all be part. But when King Canute died in 1035, the separate parts of his empire-in-the-making broke apart again.

The net effect of all the barbarian invasions and of the recovery Christendom made each time was to bring the northern parts of Europe fully into the circle of civilization for the first time. The Russian rivers and Scandinavia as far as the Arctic Circle had become active components of the military, political, commercial, and religious history of Europe. The westernmost portion of the steppe in Hungary had been Christianized too. The center of gravity of the continent for the first time shifted north of the Alps to the fertile plains of northern Europe, where new methods of farming supported a new military class of knights and, before long, also made it possible to feed a growing population of townspeople.

THE RISE OF TOWNS AND TRADE

Until after the year 1000, Byzantium remained by far the biggest and richest city of Christendom. The splendors of the capital on the Bosporus dazzled the crusaders who passed through in 1097 on their way to Jerusalem. Nothing in the West came close to rivaling the seat of the Byzantine emperors. For 500 years, from the time of Justinian, the Byzantine state had profited from the special and peculiar geographical position of the capital city. The people of the city ran the empire. Trade brought goods from all the coastlands of the Black and Aegean seas to the city wharves. The interiors of the Balkan Peninsula and of Asia Minor were only sometimes controlled by Byzantium; but coastal Italy, especially in the south, was usually under Byzantine control. The empire of Byzantium, in other words, was built around a network of port cities connected with one another by the sea. In this, as in so many other respects, the Byzantine Empire was more the heir of the Greeks than of the Romans.

Under the Macedonian emperors, however, social predominance within the Byzantine Empire shifted away from cities by the sea. Great landed estates in the interior of Asia Minor became important military units. Frontier defense far inland became necessary to hold what Basil II and his predecessors had conquered. Cities and seaborne commerce took second place to the rough military men, who now ruled the empire. Simultaneously, Byzantine trade passed into the hands of upstart Italians. Circulation of money and goods between Constantinople and the provinces weakened as Italian merchants skimmed off the profits from the carrying trade. A period of commercial weakness set in, exactly when the commercial energies of western Europe were rising to new heights.

Mediterranean versus Northern Towns

In the west there was a basic contrast between the Mediterranean zone, where towns had been thickly established in Roman times, and the more northern regions, where Roman towns were few and where, beyond the Rhine and Danube, they did not exist at all. Revival of trade and town activity began in Italy and southern France even before 900. Venice, for example, was founded about 500, when refugees from the mainland fled to a cluster of mudbanks located at the head of the Adriatic Sea. The city began to be an important trade center after about 800. In 1082 the Venetian Republic got special trading rights in Byzantine ports and soon captured a large part of Byzantine trade. The Venetians helped the First Crusade and got special privileges in all the cities the crusaders captured. Soon the only rivals that the Venetians had to fear in the eastern Mediterranean were other Italian cities, chief among them Genoa, located on the western side of the peninsula.

The climax of Italian commercial dominance over the Byzantine lands came in 1204. Knights who set out from Venice to go to the Holy Land on a Fourth Crusade stopped off at Constantinople and, after quarreling with the Byzantine emperor, besieged and captured his capital. A Latin empire was then established in which the Venetians—who had been the financial and diplomatic wirepullers behind the whole assault on Constantinople—enjoyed an even more privileged position than before.

As for the Holy Land, the crusaders never got there, but either stayed in former Byzantine lands as rulers or returned home to western Europe. The crusading idea was widely discredited by this attack on a fellow-Christian state. Many efforts to revive the ideal were made; but none of them met with much success. The commercial spirit, so clearly expressed by the Venetians and other Italian trading cities, did not fit well with the crusaders' simple faith.

North of the Alps, in Germanic territory, towns were mostly new foundations. Even when the Romans had built a town at a place that later became important—London or Paris, for example—almost no urban society survived the barbarian invasions. After the Viking raids stopped, however, town life revived. Even in the Viking age, trade existed. The raiders never found just the booty they needed, and so they had to exchange their plunder for swords and sails, or for the raw material to

An example of Caroline or Carolingian minuscule. (*Trustees of the Pierpont Morgan Library*)

make them. Typically, a ship's company started out in the spring—ready for either raiding or trading, depending on what they met. When raiding became unsafe, because there were too many knights scattered about the landscape, even the most bloodthirsty pirates had to settle for trading.

Before long, ships' companies found it convenient to settle down at a convenient place and make it a permanent headquarters. In this way towns began, or took on a new life. Often such a town was formed around a fortress, controlled by a bishop or by some other lord. The relations between the merchants and the lord were usually cool. The merchants, with their hangers-on, were accustomed to defending themselves and did not wish to be treated like peasants, or made to pay tributes or perform labor services. But the local lord did not like to have other people running affairs in territory that belonged to him.

Compromise was possible, though, if the trading community would agree to pay a lump sum to the lord in return for the right to be left alone. As trade and artisan production increased in volume, the sums a lord could acquire from a flourishing town that had grown up on his land became quite large. By 1200, lords even began to found new towns, offering generous "liberties" to merchants and artisans who would settle there, for they knew how prosperous a flourishing town could make them.

In the Mediterranean zone, towns also had some difficulty fitting themselves into the political pattern of the countryside. Often the towns-people admitted or invited local noble landowners to come into the city

COEUR DE LION'S
MINSTRELSY

In 1192 Richard, Coeur de Lion, King of England and lord of broad dominions in France, started home from the Third Crusade. He was in a hurry
to get back, for his brother John and the French king were both trying
to take over his possessions. But Richard had a problem: enemies controlled the convenient homeward routes. He decided, therefore, to disguise
himself as an ordinary traveler, in hope of sneaking past their guard.
Instead, he was captured by the duke of Austria, himself recently back
from the crusade, where Richard had personally insulted him.

For a long time no one in England knew what had happened to
the venturesome king. In the next century, minstrels invented a story of
how he was discovered, as follows:

Blondel, King Richard's court minstrel and personal friend, set out
in search of the king. To avoid imprisonment himself, he dared not ask
questions that might betray his mission. Instead he relied upon music.
Visiting castles where the king might be imprisoned, Blondel casually
seated himself beneath their walls and sang, as traveling minstrels were
supposed to do. But the song he sang was one King Richard himself had
composed. After several vain attempts, one day Blondel approached the
castle of Durenstein, started his song, and to his delight heard the answer-
ing voice of King Richard rising from within and joining in the strains
of his own familiar song. Having thus discovered the king's whereabouts,
Blondel was able to inform the English authorities, who soon arranged
for his release.

So goes the story; but although Blondel may have gone searching
for King Richard, and although the king was certainly a lover of music
and a minstrel in his own right, his captors were never interested in
keeping his whereabouts secret. On the contrary, they wanted what they
got: a large ransom in cash, payable upon the king's release.

and become citizens. This, after all, was the ancient, classical pattern.
But merchants and artisans kept a more important place in town affairs
than they had in ancient times. They organized guilds for each particular
trade or business, to protect their interests. Town politics therefore usually
became a struggle for power among rival guilds and a struggle conducted
by all the guilds against demands made by local territorial lords.

The Decay of Serfdom

Peasants soon began to benefit from the impact of towns upon the country-side. From late Roman times, peasants had been legally enserfed, that is, fixed to the land, so that a peasant could not leave the place where he or she was born without breaking the law. Towns, however, welcomed newcomers from wherever they came. No questions were asked; and lords had to admit the rule, "town air makes free." This was generally interpreted to mean that if a runaway lived for a year and a day without being challenged, then he or she could stay forever. Serfs sometimes did run away; and those who stayed behind soon found themselves in a good position to improve their status. They could buy freedom from tradi-tional services owed to the lord, since they could now earn money by selling foodstuffs in town. They could also demand better treatment, and the lord might think it well to agree, lest he lose his labor force.

By 1200, as a result, in the parts of Europe where town life had developed most strongly—in northern France and the Rhinelands, south-eastern England and northern Italy—most peasants were free, in the sense that they did not owe compulsory services to their lord. The economic level of life in the countryside had quite perceptibly improved. Towns prospered by supplying ordinary peasants with such things as iron tools, smoked herring, and coarse wool cloth, as well as through luxury trades. Lords prospered on rents and tolls charged on trade. Peasants prospered from selling extra foodstuffs and raw material to the towns. In short, northwestern Europe entered upon a boom period that reached a peak between 1200 and 1300. Military expansion across every frontier was matched by rapid internal economic expansion. New fields were cleared until forest land became scant. Trade intensified; population grew; every-thing prospered.

Structure of Medieval Towns

Medieval town life organized in this way differed fundamentally from the town life of Greek and Roman times. In early Greece and Rome, citizens had been farmers. Traders and artisans were marginal people who had been squeezed off the land and had to make a living somehow. In later classical times, citizen rights in towns of the Roman Empire were nearly always limited to landowners whose income depended on rents paid by those who tilled the fields. But in northern Europe, knightly land-lords remained mostly in the country.

The commercial and artisan classes of western Europe that began to flourish shortly before 1000 felt no need to bow low before the knightly landlord class. They were used to defending themselves, and made alliances and fought wars more or less at their own discretion. The local lord was a natural enemy. A distant lord, especially when he was a king or some other kind of superior to the local lord, was a natural ally. And if the townspeople became powerful enough to defend themselves against all comers, then complete independence could be, and often was, attained.

No other part of the world gave birth to a merchant and artisan class like this. Among other civilized peoples, merchants and artisans knew their place; they catered to the tastes and submitted to the control of their social betters, which meant soldiers, officials, and landlords. Self-government and aggressive self-assertion were not part of the merchants' stock-in-trade anywhere except in Europe and, a little later, also in Japan. The whole character and growth pattern of western European civilization depended on this fact. For towns became the primary seat of civilized activity in Europe, as they were elsewhere. The habits and expectations of the townspeople therefore played a particularly important part in defining the spirit of all later European civilization.

CHURCH AND STATE

The importance of towns in medieval Europe after about 1000 showed up at once in politics. The comparative simplicity of the Carolingian Age was gone. Instead of one great empire, cooperating with the Church to extend and defend Christendom, western Europe divided up into an extremely large number of more or less independent political units.

In theory, imperial unity lingered on. In 1000, Otto III of Germany had the title of emperor, but his power was very limited. Charlemagne's empire had been divided among three grandsons in 843. Separate kingdoms of France and of Germany emerged from this division; and the middle zone, containing Italy and the Rhinelands, became a bone of contention between Germany and France—a bone of contention that remained critical as recently as World War I. When the pope conferred the imperial title, Holy Roman Emperor, on the German king, the rulers of France never admitted his superiority. The kings of England, Scotland, Denmark, Norway, Sweden, Poland, and Hungary also asserted independence (although some of them at times entered into special relations with the German emperor and admitted his claim to be supreme ruler of Christendom—or at least of its western half).

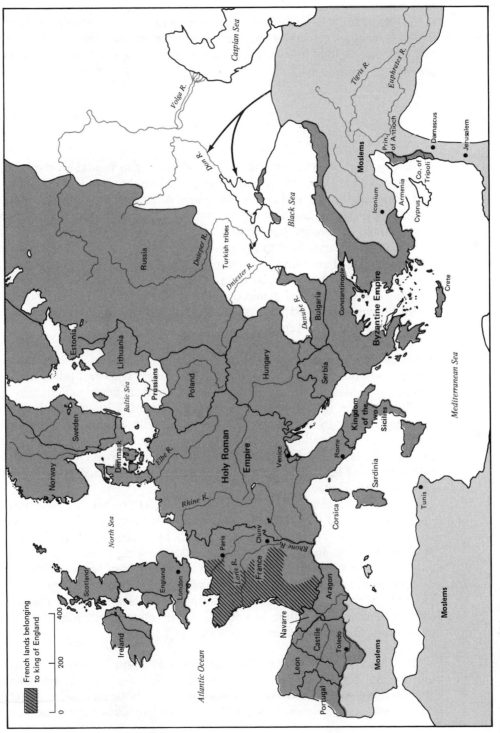

Europe, Late Twelfth Century

The papacy also claimed to have a vague sort of superior authority over all bishops, monasteries, and other church establishments. But the papacy was as unable as the emperor to enforce its claims to universal power.

Feudalism

In theory, Europe was organized according to the feudal system. This meant that every nobleman had a lord to whom he owed certain duties and from whom he received a fief in return. A fief was any kind of income-producing property, usually, of course, land. According to legal theory, God granted sovereign power to His chosen agent, the king. The king in turn granted large fiefs to his principal men, or vassals. They granted smaller fiefs to their subvassals; and their subvassals might in turn grant still smaller fiefs to sub-subvassals. At the bottom of the system was the single knight, lord of a manor whose peasants had to work for him, while he was supposed to protect them and serve his lord in battle or in council when called upon to do so.

At each level of the feudal system, duties and obligations bound superior and inferior one to another. A formal oath of homage sealed the contract between lord and vassal. The vassal who had taken an oath of homage to his lord was then honor-bound to come when called, bringing his fighting men with him. If a vassal failed to fulfill his duties, he could be judged guilty by his peers, that is, by his fellow vassals at the lord's court, and they would take steps to punish him. If a lord violated his duties, the vassals could band together to resist him. Everywhere, political relations were looked upon as contracts willingly entered into by men of honor and of war.

In practice things were never so tidy. First of all, a single knight might find himself the vassal of more than one lord; and if the two lords should quarrel, he could not obey them both. Moreover, many lords refused to obey the king. Indeed, in the year 1000, the king of France was only one of a dozen equally powerful men in the kingdom of France. His claims to sovereignty over such a mighty vassal as the duke of Normandy, for example, were entirely empty. Sometimes counts and dukes could not control their vassals either, in which case effective public administration broke up into very small units indeed.

THE RISE OF PAPAL POWER   In this confusion, towns fitted awkwardly. So did the Church. In all parts of Europe, the Church owned considerable amounts of land. Bishops and abbots controlled most of it; but unlike other great vassals, they could not pass their lands on to their sons, for the clergy did not marry. From the point of view of the German emperor, therefore, the most important power he had was to appoint most of the bishops and many of the abbots of his kingdom. He could put his own men in such posts and could count on their aid in his struggles with other lords, whose positions were hereditary. In France the king had no such power. Appointment to the key offices of the Church had fallen for the most part into the hands of counts and dukes.

According to the law of the Church, bishops were supposed to be chosen by the people and the clergy of their dioceses, not by a king or secular lord. Abbots were supposed to be chosen by the monks of the monastery. The Church, in short, was supposed to be independent of secular government. But these rules were seldom followed. Ever since Constantine had made Christianity an official religion, the emperor of Byzantium had claimed extensive powers over the Church. Charlemagne, too, had taken his right to appoint a new pope more or less for granted. On the other hand, Pope Stephen had crowned him emperor in 800, and so it became possible to claim that the imperial power was a gift of God conferred on the emperor by the pope.

Such problems became acute after 1054, because a vigorous reform movement won control of the papacy. The reform began in 910, when the duke of Aquitaine founded a new monastery at Cluny. Cluny quickly became a center of piety and learning; and soon daughter monasteries, established by monks from Cluny, spread widely through Latin Christendom. The principle upon which the Cluniac monasteries insisted, above all others, was complete independence of any control from lay rulers. To help protect each separate monastery, new ones remained in close association with the monastery of Cluny. Soon the monks began to claim that the rest of the Church should have the same independence from outside interference. In particular, they felt, the appointment of the pope should no longer depend on the whim of a few powerful Roman families.

In 1054 Cluniac reformers captured the papacy. Five years later the proper way to choose a pope was spelled out by listing the clergymen of Rome who had the right to elect the next pope. These were the cardinals; and each pope had the right to appoint new cardinals to keep the number at a proper size. Since the pope was bishop of Rome, each cardinal had to have charge of a parish in Rome—a custom that continues to this day whenever a new cardinal is appointed.

STRUGGLES BETWEEN EMPIRE AND PAPACY   At first the emperor (Henry IV at the time) sympathized with the Cluniac reformers. But the cardinals interpreted their power to mean that they ought to elect a pope without consulting the emperor, and this provoked quarrels. When a simple peasant's son, the monk Hildebrand, became Pope Gregory VII in

1073, dispute flared up fiercely. Gregory demanded that the German bishops should be chosen, as he had been, without lay interference.

Pope Gregory's reform required Emperor Henry IV to confront the prospect of seeing the strongest support of his government crumble away. He denounced Gregory; Gregory denounced him. After excommunicating Henry (1076), Gregory made an alliance with Norman adventurers in southern Italy and with towns in northern Italy that resented the efforts which the imperial government was making to bring them under control. Gregory also allied himself with the nobles of Germany who feared the emperor's power.

In 1077 Emperor Henry IV found himself so weakened by the foes the papacy had raised against him that he had to come to Canossa, in northern Italy, and there submit to all of Pope Gregory's demands. But when Henry's German opponents elected another "king" to oppose him, Henry attacked them and was again excommunicated (1080). He then marched on Rome and imprisoned the pope in Castel Sant'Angelo. Pope Gregory's Norman allies rescued him, but sacked Rome so thoroughly that Gregory dared not return to the city. He therefore died—an exile from Rome—with the struggle undecided.

A compromise was reached between the papal and the imperial claims in 1122. According to this agreement, if a bishop were properly chosen by the clergy of his diocese and approved by the people, then the emperor might give him power over the lands assigned to the bishopric (the so-called "regalia") in a separate ceremony. But it proved impossible to make this plan work. Further struggles ended only when the imperial power north of the Alps had been utterly destroyed. Germany came to be divided into a large number of princely- and city-states, some of them ruled by bishops or abbots. The imperial title remained nominally in existence until 1254; but after 1197 the emperor had no real power in Germany.

CHURCH REFORM IN FRANCE AND ENGLAND   Papal efforts at Church reform in France and England had no such disruptive effects. Reform in France mainly meant taking control over the appointment of bishops and abbots out of the hands of the great feudal lords, who were not usually obedient to the French king. The king was glad enough to see this change occur, and the papacy was glad to have royal help in carrying through the reform.

In England the situation was still different. There, in 1066, William the Conqueror, duke of Normandy, made good a very dubious claim to the English throne by invading with a force of about 5000 knights. He distributed the land of England among his principal followers. William and his successors kept a tight control over the kingdom. Because of this, from 1066 onward England was a far more united kingdom than France or Germany

With royal control of the nobles of England as secure as it was under the first Norman kings, control over Church appointments could be lodged in the hands of the archbishop of Canterbury without in the least endangering royal power. Hence, so long as the archbishop of Canterbury checked with the king on all important matters before taking action, the Norman kings found it fairly easy to get along with the reform movement that was running so strongly in the Church.

The strength of that movement and the enhanced authority it brought to the papacy were influenced directly by the growth of towns. Townsmen served in various capacities in the Church. A man of ability could rise through the Church all the way to the top, as the career of Hildebrand (Pope Gregory VII) showed. Restless and ambitious men of lowly birth therefore found a career in the Church particularly attractive.

Such men systematized and extended Church law on the principle that anything affecting a sacrament—baptism, confirmation, marriage, ordination, mass, confession, extreme unction—came within the scope of Church courts. They organized the collection of Church revenues. They preached to and fed the poor. They taught law and theology to aspiring clergy. They built cathedrals, developed Church music, put on plays, and wrote histories. They constituted, in short, the most active and adventurous segment of society—and made medieval civilization and the activities of the Church almost equivalent to one another.

LAGGING DEVELOPMENT OF EASTERN EUROPE   Farther east in Europe, the new life and energy pouring into the Church—and to a lesser degree into civil governments and other secular activities—did not show itself. Moldboard plow agriculture did not extend much beyond the frontier of German settlement. This meant that the countryside was less productive, and town life failed to develop so rapidly and powerfully as in the western parts of Europe. In 1054 the last powerful ruler of Kiev died, and the Russian state broke up into a dozen or so smaller principalities. When a new wave of Turkish-speaking steppe invaders showed up, the Russian princes were not able to drive them back or to convert them to Christianity. Instead, the newcomers became Moslem and cut Russia off from easy communication with Byzantium.

Byzantium also fell on hard times. Seljuk Turks filtered into Asia Minor and, after the Battle of Manzikert (1071), pushed the Byzantine frontier back nearly to Constantinople. At almost the same time, a small company of free-lance adventurers from Normandy seized control of the Byzantine portions of Italy, founding the Norman kingdom of Italy and Sicily that played such a key role in the struggle between pope and emperor. In 1054, also, a final quarrel between the patriarch of Constantinople and the pope led to a lasting estrangement between the Greek Orthodox and the Roman Catholic churches. Bad feeling was not reduced when

Italian traders took over most of the Byzantine trade or when crusading knights captured Constantinople in 1204.

Inland in the Balkan Peninsula, an independent Serbia and a second Bulgarian Empire came into existence on the territory Emperor Basil II had once controlled. Only fragments of the Byzantine Empire remained. Thus the relationship between eastern and western Europe had been startlingly reversed. By 1200 the once backward and barbarous Latin West had become richer, stronger, and infinitely more venturesome in art and thought, as well as in war and trade, than the broken and impoverished Greek East.

CULTURAL LIFE

In Europe's Dark Ages, Byzantium preserved far greater knowledge of ancient learning than did the Latin West. Byzantine scholars never entirely forgot pagan Greek writings. Roman law continued to live in Byzantium when it had been forgotten in the West. And early Christian literature counted for even more among the Byzantines. Anything they were able to make anew for themselves seemed poor and weak by comparison.

In art, however, the Byzantines were remarkably creative. In Justinian's day a great new church, St. Sophia, was erected in Constantinople. It embodied new principles of construction which made it possible to build a great central dome over a square space in the middle of the church. This type of construction may have been borrowed from the Persians or Armenians; but the Byzantines brought it to mature perfection. Mosaics, composed of many small fragments of stone or glass, sometimes coated with a thin layer of gold, shimmered on the walls. So successful was St. Sophia that, ever since, most Byzantine and other Orthodox churches have been modeled after it. No art style has had a longer or more distinguished history.

The Dark Age and the Revival of Learning in the Latin West

At the time when Justinian's architects were building his famous church, the West was poverty-stricken and ignorant. Monasteries dotted the landscape where monks spent part of their time reading books or teaching boys to read. In Ireland and England a higher level of knowledge and scholarship existed; but on the continent, even in Italy itself, the Dark Age was very dark indeed. In Charlemagne's time a few scholars and teachers gathered at his court, many of them coming over from England. They made one very important change in European learning by introducing a tidier way of shaping letters. Our familiar small letters descend directly from the "Carolingian minuscule," as this style of handwriting is called.

After the breakup of the Carolingian Empire, learning once more fell upon hard times. Then with the reform of the Church, beginning with the establishment of Cluny in 910 and reaching full force 150 years later, scholarly and literary activity began to revive all over western Europe. Bishops developed schools to train clergymen; from these the medieval universities evolved after about 1150.

The universities of southern Europe formed around schools of law or, in some cases, of medicine. The University of Paris, which became the model for universities in northern Europe, formed around schools of theology. Law and theology remained overwhelmingly important for the Church. Church law was based on decisions at councils, on writings of the Church Fathers, and on the Bible. Papal decisions and decrees also added to it. It never became a closed system like the Sacred Law of Islam. Things changed too fast. New problems continued to appear. And the bases of Church law were too complex and full of contradiction to allow anyone to create a single code that could harden into permanent form, as had happened among the Moslems.

Interest in Church law soon led to the discovery of the Roman law, which had remained continuously alive in Byzantium. Study of Justinian's Code offered a way of strengthening civil government. It made relations among strangers more predictable and flexible, easing transfer of property and defining all sorts of contract rights more clearly than the different kinds of local customary law could ever do. Roman law therefore found vigorous application within the Church and on every level of secular government, from the emperor downward.

Theological learning took on new life when men began to ask what some of the old books, that had been handed down in monastic libraries from ancient times, really meant. A work by Boethius (d. 524), for example, discussed the "universals," that is, terms such as "human" or "tree" that stand for a whole class of particular objects. Did such things really exist? If not, how could Christ redeem everyone? How did each particular person share in the universal class of "humanity" so that each individual soul might be saved by Christ?

When difficulties appeared in finding clear answers to questions such as this, seekers after theological truth first looked more energetically into what Scripture and the Church Fathers had to say. But this only produced more and more conflicting opinions. One famous teacher, Abelard (d. 1142), systematically listed the many points on which established authorities disagreed. He called his book *Sic et Non*—"Yes and No."

How could men solve such questions? The answer Abelard and others gave was to use human reason. Some 1800 years earlier, the Ionian philosophers of Greece had arrived at the same answer when they saw how contradictory traditional stories were about the power of the gods and the nature of things. Shortly before A.D. 1200, keen-minded men in and around Paris, having come to the same conclusion, were therefore eager and ready to welcome Greek philosophy, which opened to them the answers pagan thinking had arrived at centuries before.

But to be useful to them, pagan science and philosophy had to be translated from Arabic or Greek into Latin. When scholars of the Latin West became aware of what treasures of ancient knowledge the Greeks and Arabs had preserved, they therefore organized systematic translation centers in Spain and Italy. As a result, the Latin-speaking world soon had at its disposal almost all of the science, philosophy, and miscellaneous learning of the ancients that the Arabs and the Greeks could pass on to them. The recovery of this store of learning set the stage for the monumental task of thirteenth-century Scholastic philosophy: the reconciliation of pagan thought with Christian theology in such a way as not to sacrifice either human reason or Christian faith.

Canterbury Catheral in England, an example of late English Gothic architecture. (Courtesy of British Information Services)

Art and Architecture

In art, western Europe proved equally creative. The best Charlemagne could do when he wanted to build a fine church was to imitate the Byzantine style on a much reduced scale. But the crying need to create defenses against Viking and Magyar raiders soon compelled western Europeans to learn how to build with stone. By 1000, therefore, Europe was studded with stone castles. Towns, too, needed and got strong stone walls for protection. Then as wealth increased, men were able to use their skills in stonemasonry to build monumental churches. The earliest of them were built in a style called Romanesque. It is distinguished by the use of round arches. Walls were mostly of solid masonry and, as a consequence, the interiors were dark.

About 1150 a new "Gothic" style of architecture was invented. By using pointed arches and ribs, it became possible to concentrate the weight of the roof at certain points, where great piers of stone could then support the whole structure. This allowed the space between the piers to become

An example of Romanesque architecture, the basilica of St. Ambrose in Milan, Italy (ca. 8th–9th century). (Alinari, Art Resource)

great windows; and when the windows were filled with colored glass, a new and even more glowing sort of mosaic decoration became possible. Stained-glass windows, together with the lofty roofs and slender curved ribbing, made the interior of a Gothic church equal to anything the Byzantines had achieved. Sculptural decoration over church doors and on the outside of the edifice added another dimension to the Gothic structures, whereas, after the iconoclastic controversy, the Byzantines stayed away from sculpture as being too close to idolatry.

CONCLUSION

The long succession of barbarian invasions that brought Germans and Slavs into territory formerly part of the Roman Empire had the result of equalizing conditions between Mediterranean Europe and the northern forest regions in both eastern and western Europe. The gap that once existed between Roman culture and barbarian illiteracy was reduced, both by lowering the level of civilization within Roman boundaries (the Dark Ages) and by Christian missionaries who established the first glimmerings of literate culture among the Slavs and Germans of the north. In this fashion, a boundary that had always before limited the northern range of civilized life in Europe was broken through. Consequently, by the year 1000, the groundwork for the rise of northern and especially of northwestern European civilization had been laid.

These same Dark Ages saw, too, the establishment and spread of a new type of agriculture built around the moldboard plow, which was well suited to the wet conditions of the north European plain. Also by 1000 a social organization, the manorial system—that allowed European peasants to make effective use of the new type of plow—had established itself widely in northwestern Europe. Thus the agricultural basis for western Europe's very rapid development in the following centuries was well and truly laid during the first turbulent centuries of the medieval period.

Finally, from 732 onward, European fighting men developed a knightly style of warfare that made both horse and rider into a single missile. These violent **shock** tactics made defense of western Europe secure as soon as means were found to support enough of these newfangled cavalrymen or knights. The manorial system served this purpose admirably by concentrating the rents from each village in the hands of a resident knight, whose function was to protect the community from raiding strangers.

As soon as these elements had been brought together, western Europe became too dangerous for barbarians to attack successfully. Raiding stopped and was replaced by trade. Towns sprang into existence. In northern Europe they began as temporary settlements around some strong place where ships' crews—part traders, part pirates—spent the winter season. From such beginnings, self-governing and self-assertive town corporations speedily developed, ready to defend themselves against all comers and capable of effective self-government.

After about 900, the new forms of wealth that agricultural progress and the rise of trade and towns brought to western Europe allowed the development of more stable and effective government. The pope was the first ruler to take advantage of the new possibilities. Beginning in 1054, a series of reforming popes created a regularly administered Church government that extended all across western Europe and gave religious and legal cohesion to Latin Christendom for the first time. Within the framework of the Church a new artistic and intellectual life also began to flourish, rising toward a peak of energy and perfection by 1200, when what is often called the High Middle Ages may be said to have started.

Eastern Europe failed to share in these developments. The moldboard plow did not exist there; manorial arrangements were uncommon; knighthood failed to take root. Until 1200, however, Byzantium remained by far the biggest city of Europe and it was, by most standards, still the seat of a more sophisticated civilization than anything known in the Latin West. Yet Byzantium's great days were already past, whereas the flowering of west European civilization was only beginning.

Nothing in the history of Europe itself really justifies breaking off our story at this point in time. Only when one considers the state of the entire civilized world does the date 1200 have much significance, for it represents the horizon at which the Mongol Empire, uniting China, most of the Middle East, and eastern Europe into a single vast state, burst upon the world's scene, starting a new round of interaction between China and the rest of Eurasia.

It seems best, therefore, to break off the story of Europe's development at this point to pay some attention to the remarkable career of the Mongol conquerors and the consequences of their extraordinary victories for world history.

Chapter 13

Steppe Peoples and the Civilizations of Eurasia

1200 to 1500

Between 1200 and 1500 two main developments altered the balance of civilizations in Eurasia. Neither of these developments was exactly new, but each of them attained a scale and force much greater than in any earlier age. It therefore seems wise to treat 1200 as a bench mark in the history of Eurasia, even though (or just because) it intersects European history at the point when medieval civilization was rising to its most brilliant peak.

The two developments in question were: (1) the Mongol conquest of China, central Asia, eastern Europe, and most of the Middle East; and (2) the maturation of independent, vigorous civilizations in the easternmost temperate part of Asia (that is, in Japan) and in the westernmost part of Europe (that is, in Italy, Spain, France, Germany, and England).

We will study these developments in turn, first taking up the Mongol explosion and its consequences for the old, established high cultures of Eurasia, because it was so sudden and dramatic and because it defined a new era in Asian history. In this connection, we will also touch upon the rise of the Japanese version of civilization in the Far East. Then, in the next chapter, we will return to the story of medieval Europe to see how the brilliant first phase of western European civilization laid the groundwork for the expansion of European influence all round the world— the expansion that began with the great explorations just before and just after 1500.

THE GREAT
MONGOL CONQUESTS

While Turks from the central steppe were filtering into Islam in ever growing numbers after 1000 and changing the political climate of that civilization fundamentally, China, too, had constant trouble with its nomad neighbors. The Sung Dynasty (ruled 960–1279) was never able to control the northern provinces of China. Instead, these lands were ruled by nomad confederations that collected taxes from the Chinese peasants with the help of Chinese officials. In other respects these nomad rulers generally left their Chinese subjects alone.

The reason for such a policy was that the nomads wanted to keep their own political-military organization separate from the Chinese tax-collecting bureaucracy. In practice the barbarian rulers had to try to maintain their traditional way of life, even when living among Chinese peasants. If they failed to maintain military habits and an abundant supply of horses, they became easy prey for new tribes of conquerors, fresh from the rigors of life on the steppes.

Nomad Rulers of China
before the Mongols

The first lasting empire built on this dual system was ruled by Khitans, known in Chinese history as the Liao Dynasty. This dynasty ruled northernmost China and a broad stretch of steppe country in Mongolia and Manchuria from 907 to 1123. What the Liao rulers commanded was a tribal confederation, including peoples of several different language groups. The secret of their leadership, to a large degree, depended on receiving tax income from their Chinese subjects, which allowed them to distribute gifts and favors among lesser nomad chiefs in suitably generous fashion. As long as handsome gifts kept coming from the court, most local chiefs remained loyal, and their overlords had nothing to fear.

A leading principle of Khitan government was to keep the nomads separated from the Chinese. If they came too close, local nomad chiefs might discover that they could extort taxes and gifts from the Chinese directly, without having to depend on gifts from the Khitan ruler. Moreover, if nomad warriors were allowed to spread over the Chinese countryside and make particular villages tributary, the ruler would find it hard to get them to assemble when he wanted them to rally for a campaign. It was much better, the Khitan rulers decided, to keep the nomads as *nomads,* ready to follow their chiefs into battle on short notice—leaving women, children, and animals behind to await their return.

The capital of the Khitan Empire was Peking, close to the zone where the grasslands of the steppe abutted on cultivated fields. Such a location was very strategic, as Peking's later history proved. Canals connected the city with the Yellow River, and through it with the system of waterways that had been constructed since the days of the T'ang Dynasty (618–907) to allow rulers to bring tax income from all China to their place of residence. Yet at the same time, Peking lay within easy reach of the open steppe to the north and west, whence came Khitan military strength.

It was not too difficult to keep the Chinese and Mongol peoples apart. Most of the Mongols lived north of the Gobi Desert, in what is today Outer Mongolia. The desert region separating them from China could not be cultivated and, therefore, provided a form of natural insulation between the two communities. Moreover, the Mongols were in touch with the oases peoples of central Asia and with tribes living on the open steppe to the westward. Here they learned of civilizations other than the Chinese; in particular they had contact with the Uighur Turks, who kept Manichaeism alive in some of the oases of the Tarim River basin. Buddhism, Tibetan Lamaism, and Nestorian Christianity had followers in central Asia too. Hence Chinese civilization was not the only kind of civilization the Mongols knew; and they were less eager, therefore, to accept Chinese models than they might have been if no alternatives had existed.

In Manchuria, to the east, however, geographical circumstances were different. In that direction no desert barrier separated the grasslands from Chinese fields. The soil was better watered; farming was possible. The tribes who lived in this region spoke a group of languages called Tungusic, and they knew only Chinese civilization. These conditions paved the way for a much closer and more intimate interaction between Chinese and Tungusic peoples than ever took place between Chinese and Mongols.

This difference became important when the Khitan Empire was overthrown in 1123 by a new ruling tribe, the Jurchens. They came from Manchuria and were not content to remain on the northern fringes of the Chinese lands as the Khitans had done. Instead the Jurchens drove on south approximately to the line of the Yangtze River. Nearly half of China thus came under their rule, together with much of Manchuria. The Jurchens, or Chin Dynasty to give them their Chinese name, ruled until 1234. They allowed a more extensive intermingling between their own people and the Chinese than the Khitan rulers had done. Thus the Jurchens became thoroughly Chinese in culture.

Mongol Life

Meanwhile, the Mongols were thrown back on the meager resources of their homeland. Hunting and herding in the harsh climate of Mongolia offered a hard life at best, and it was made harder by constant struggles among rival clans and tribes for rights to the scant pastures of the region. Nevertheless, people (and horses) capable of surviving in such an environment were unusually hardy. They made excellent soldiers, being accustomed to outdoor living; but as long as the Mongols continued to be divided into small kinship groups, energies were spent fighting among themselves.

Yet in a sense, they already knew better. The Mongols had centuries of contact with China behind them, and in the days of the Khitan control of north China they had shared in the wealth that came from Chinese taxpayers. The trouble was that Mongolian pastures were so thin that the Mongols had to break up into very small groups—often as few as fifteen or twenty families—in order to find enough forage for their herds; and such scattered groups regularly quarreled with their neighbors over possession of animals and pasture rights.

About 1162, however, a son was born to a petty Mongol chieftain who was destined to unite all the Mongols and most of the Eurasian steppe into a vast new empire. His name was Temujin, but he is usually known by the honorific title he assumed when his victories had made him famous: Genghis Khan, that is, "Ruler of all within the seas."

The Secret of Genghis Khan's Success

What Genghis Khan did was simple but radical. He entirely disregarded clan and kinship ties in building the army that made his name so widely feared. Instead of relying on traditional kinship groupings, he organized his followers bureaucratically. In the early days when his forces were still small, each squad of 10 men was put under the command of a leader personally chosen by Temujin for his abilities, and without regard for family ties or traditional social rank. Ten squads were in turn grouped into a company, commanded by a man who had demonstrated his capacities in battle. Later, when larger units of 1000 and of 10,000 men were organized on the same lines, senior officers had the authority to appoint squad and company commanders. But the bureaucratic principle, according to which a man's rank depended not on birth but on appointment to office, always remained in force.

The Mongols raid into Hungary (ca. A.D. 1241), from a woodcut of 1488. (The Metropolitan Museum of Art, gift of A. W. Bahr, 1947)

By choosing his commanders shrewdly and promoting those who did well, Temujin quickly created a formidable fighting force. His followers soon overcame all opposition among the Mongols. Each victory meant new recruits for Temujin's army, since he promptly folded the manpower of his defeated enemies into the command structure he had created. This had the additional advantage of guaranteeing rapid promotion among his own followers, so that capable men found ample scope for their ambitions within the system Temujin had created.

When all the fighting manpower of the Mongol people had been organized in this way, they were in a position to strike with devastating effect against other steppe peoples. This soon brought Turkish and Tungusic-speaking peoples into the Mongol army. But they were treated in the same way as the Mongols themselves. Since the number of nomad Turks was far greater than the number of Mongols, the so-called Mongol armies, especially those operating in western Asia and eastern Europe, were in fact composed mainly of Turkish-speaking soldiers. Topmost command, however, remained in Mongol hands.

Genghis' nomad army could also turn its energies against the settled agricultural peoples who lived southward of the steppe. In central Asia, his troops found it relatively easy to overrun the isolated oases with their mixed population of Uighurs, Persians, and other peoples. From the cities Genghis recruited a class of scribes and record keepers, who began to be needed as the size of the Mongol forces grew.

Expansion southward into China was a tougher proposition. The Jurchens were good fighters and had the vast resources of all north China at their disposal. New military problems arose when the Mongol cavalry came up against city walls and had to face the sophisticated weaponry—including gunpowder. But the Mongol cavalry was able to overpower the Jurchens in open country. Genghis could therefore raid deeply into China, more or less at will. Moreover, the Mongols soon learned how to break through city walls with the aid of catapults and gunpowder

EUROPE

RUSSIAN
STATES

HUN-
GARY

Vladimir

Kiev

G R E A T   S I B E R I A N   P L A I N

Karakorum

Shangtu

Khanbaligh

KHANATE OF
KIPCHAK

GOLDEN HORDE

Sarai

KHANATE OF
THE GREAT KHAN

Constantinople

KHANATE OF
CHAGHADAI

Samarkand

Kashgar

CHINA

Foochow

Baghdad

Balkh

KHANATE OF
PERSIA

ILKHAN

TIBET

ARABIA

Mecca

Red
Sea

INDIA

Arabian Sea

AFRICA

Indian Ocean

**Mongol Empire
at the Death of Kublai Khan
1294**

bombs. These weapons were designed and produced by Chinese artisans, who were as willing to serve the Mongols as they were to work for the Jurchens. When, therefore, Mongol armies encountered walled cities in western Asia and eastern Europe, they were already equipped with all the skills of Chinese siegecraft, and, as a matter of fact, were probably responsible for bringing gunpowder to the attention of Europeans for the first time.

As long as Genghis Khan lived, he alternated the main thrust of his campaigns at will. Some years he went southward into China; other years he turned his horses' heads westward along the steppe. Everywhere his armies proved victorious, but they behaved as raiders and plunderers rather than as rulers. By 1227, when Genghis Khan died, his forces had raided as far west as southern Russia and had almost destroyed the Jurchen Empire over north China. Central Asian oases were firmly tributary too. But the fundamental new fact was this: for the first and last time in history, the fighting manpower of the entire Asian steppe, all the way from Manchuria to the Urals, stood ready and organized for further campaigns under the capable and experienced command of the Mongol generals that Genghis Khan had created around himself.

Alexander the Great of Macedon is the only man who can rank beside Genghis Khan as a conqueror. Both died undefeated, and through their victories both of them altered preexisting relationships among the civilized populations of Europe and Asia in lasting and significant ways.

GENGHIS KHAN'S SUCCESSORS According to Mongol custom, Genghis divided his possessions among his four sons. One of them died before Genghis did, so his share passed directly to Genghis' grandson, Batu. To keep effective unity among the separate "hordes"—as each part of the Mongol domain was called—Genghis arranged to transfer the Mongol part of the army to one of his sons, Ogadai (ruled 1229–1241). This made the others dependent on Ogadai, for even a son of Genghis Khan was helpless without Mongol officers and a Mongol bodyguard to overawe the Turkish, Chinese, and other peoples who had been portioned out to them as heirs of the great conqueror. In this way, then, the unity of the Mongol Empire was maintained for a century.

Under Ogadai's leadership, Mongol victories continued as before. In 1234 the last of the Jurchen rulers was hunted down. The Mongols now had all of north China to exploit. They decided to restore the Chinese style of administration, using officials trained in the Confucian mold to collect taxes and run local affairs. Thereafter, Mongol rule made little difference to ordinary Chinese peasants or townspeople. Raiding horsemen from the steppe continued to travel across China from time to time, since the southern part of the country was not finally subdued until 1279. Even after that date, the Mongols organized expeditions against Burma

(1287) and Siam (1289) by marching their forces across China. Nevertheless, on a day-to-day basis the Mongol overlords were not much in evidence. The availability of competent Confucians to staff the administrative machine meant that China continued to be governed, except at the highest levels, by Chinese.

Expansion westward matched the continued Mongol expansion southward. Between 1237 and 1241 all the Russian princes and cities, except Novgorod, in the far northwest, were subdued. The rich steppe country of southern Russia became the base for the "Golden Horde" that ruled from a headquarters at Kazan on the Volga.

The Mongols demanded tribute payments from the Russians just as they did from the Chinese. Indeed, it seems clear that the Mongols took their experience in China as the pattern for their government of the rest of the empire. To begin with, the Russians had no ready-made system for collecting tribute. The Mongols, therefore, entrusted the task to merchant firms of central Asians—the same sort of people who kept Genghis' records for him. This did not produce very good results, however, so when the Russian princes offered their services as tax collectors, the Mongol overlords agreed. This required (or allowed) the Russian princes to build up a body of tax-collecting officials whose loyalty and obedience was to the prince who appointed them rather than to the distant and alien Mongol khan. The germs of the later Russian state thus came into existence.

A third great territory came into the Mongol orbit after 1256, when Mongol armies overran Persia, Mesopotamia, and Syria—the heartland of Islam. Baghdad was sacked (1258) and the last Abbasid caliph perished in the confusion. Moslems could no longer even pretend that the Prophet Mohammed had a worthy successor on earth. The original basis of Moslem political life had finally been swept away—a fact later Moslems never forgot or forgave.

In the Moslem world the Mongols applied the same pattern of administration as in China and in Russia. The trouble was that most Moslems were unwilling to cooperate by taxing themselves for the benefit of the Mongols. Christians who had lived for centuries under Moslem rule did not mind working for the new masters of the Middle East. But these formerly oppressed peoples were a weak reed for the Mongols to lean upon. The Moslems hated them as traitors, and the Christians had been submissive for so long that they could not easily become effective administrators.

Another weakness of the Mongol position in the Middle East was that most of the soldiers available to the Il-khans, as this branch of the Mongol ruling dynasty was called, were Turks. They had much in common with the Moslemized Turks who had preceded them from the steppe into that part of the world. Accordingly, in 1295 the Il-khans found it natural and wise to become Moslem themselves and to conform to age-old patterns of Moslem, Turkish, and Middle Eastern imperial government. More than a generation earlier, in 1257, the rulers of the Golden Horde in Russia had taken the same step.

MONGOL POWER AND UNITY UNDER KUBLAI KHAN   As both these western khanates or territories became Moslem, the Turkish element in the Mongol armies and ruling class came to the surface. Correspondingly, the influence of the Far East receded. Yet before that happened, the Mongol Empire reached a peak of power and unity under Kublai Khan (ruled 1260–1294). Kublai succeeded his brother who had been in supreme charge of the empire from 1251 to 1259; and between them they ruled for nearly half a century over an empire that extended from the Pacific Ocean to Poland and that combined eastern Europe, most of the Middle East, all of China, and the intervening territory in a single great empire.

The Great Khan's power rested on command of the Mongol army proper. Only small detachments of Mongols were assigned to the other khanates. A remarkable efficient postal system maintained communication between the Great Khan's headquarters and the other khans' courts. Horses and riders were kept ready at stations some twenty to thirty miles apart. When a message came through, it was carried at a gallop from station to station until it reached its destination. The same method had been used by the ancient Assyrians and Persians, but the speed and regularity of the Mongol postal system had never been equaled before.

The Mongols were also good at spying. Sometimes they used merchants and other seemingly innocent agents to get information; sometimes they sent scouts as much as 200 miles ahead of the main force. When the Mongol army advanced, messengers, dispatched daily, kept separate columns in touch with each other. This allowed the columns to come together in time to attack an enemy or, as the case might be, to go around some defended place and take their less mobile foe in the flank and rear.

Traders and merchants enjoyed a high standing among the Mongols. The Venetian, Marco Polo, for example, served Kublai Khan in a number of important posts, although at home he was only a trader in jewels. Indeed, skilled strangers of all kinds were welcome at the Great Khan's court. The Mongol rulers always needed people with civilized skills—reading and writing, if nothing else—whom they could trust. Outsiders assigned a responsible job and a high salary were unlikely to disobey, if only because they owed their position entirely to the khan who had appointed them. This was the same principle that had made the army so effective; and it worked when applied to civil administration too. Local tax collecting could be left to local leaders; but central records and positions around the person of the ruler, where high policy had to be decided, were entrusted to strangers. Mongols were illiterate soldiers, incapable of keeping records. Men from nowhere, like Marco Polo, had to be used instead.

At court, there was a great commingling. Individuals from all parts of Europe and Asia drifted first to Karakorum, Genghis' capital, and later to Cambaluc, just outside Peking, the capital that Kublai built for himself in 1264. Practically every religion was represented among the crowd that assembled around these imperial capitals. This fitted Mongol policy perfectly. Genghis and his heirs took the line that there must be something true in every religion—or at least there might be. Therefore it seemed sound policy to have experts from every faith on hand to help guard the khan against divine anger.

The Christians of Europe entirely misunderstood Mongol religious attitudes. When they discovered that the Great Khan admitted Christians to his court and sometimes entrusted them with important tasks, the pope and all Christendom assumed that the Mongol khan was about to become Christian. Repeated efforts were, in fact, made to send missionaries to assure his conversion. Two of them actually reached the Great Khan's court. They were listened to politely—and the khan continued the same religious policy as before. Kublai perhaps favored Lamaism over other faiths as a matter of personal worship; but the religious intolerance that Moslems and Christians took for granted had no place in his world view.

BREAKUP OF THE MONGOL EMPIRE

Mere distance set limits to the Mongol armies' triumphs. In 1241, for example, after subduing Russia, the Mongols started toward central Europe, where they defeated a Polish and German force in Silesia and overran all of Hungary. But the death of Ogadai called them home to Mongolia to take part in the choice of a successor. By the time the quarrels that this stirred up had been settled, there were other campaigns to be fought, and the Mongols never returned to Hungary.

Much the same was true in Syria and India. The main Mongol field army was called back from the Middle East by another succession crisis in 1259 and never returned. Egypt therefore remained unconquered. It was ruled by slaves, called Mamlukes, after Saladin's dynasty died out in 1250. These slaves came mostly from the Caucasus mountains at the east end of the Black Sea. As young men they were shipped to Egypt by slave traders, and served there as soldiers. A few became commanders by promotion in the ranks; and the top military commanders ruled Egypt until 1798. The Mamlukes were formidable fighters and recovered Syria from the Il-khans in 1260.

As for India, the main Mongol armies never tried to invade. The Il-khans did launch several small raids into India between 1285 and 1303, but the Himalayan barrier was formidable, and the Mongol rulers of the Middle East needed their troops nearer home.

Setbacks in central Europe, Syria, and India were trifling, since the Mongols did not really try to enforce their power in these regions. On the other hand, their failure to conquer Japan in 1281 was a serious check—the first the Mongols had ever met. Kublai sent a large invading force, but the Japanese prepared special defenses; and a typhoon destroyed much of the shipping upon which the Mongol army depended for its supplies. The remnant of the invading host therefore had to withdraw in disarray. Kublai never gave up planning to do something about this failure; but other naval expeditions—undertaken in part to practice the art of landing on a hostile shore (one went as far as Java in 1292–1293)—never had sufficiently brilliant results to make another attempt on Japan seem feasible. After his death, in 1294, Kublai's heirs gave up the project, having enough to do trying to keep peace within the empire already under their control.

Three factors combined, after Kublai's death, to weaken and, in the end, to destroy the Mongol Empire. One was the wearing-out of the Mongol manpower. Losses in battle and from disease must have been severe; moreover, the victors enjoyed an easier, more luxurious life than their ancestors had known on the harsh Mongolian steppes. As a result, the supply of hardy soldiery became too small to keep the Mongol armies at their original strength. Men who could not ride day and night for a week or longer, without stopping for food or sleep, were not like the Mongols that Genghis Khan had led across the world. Without the ability to endure extreme hardship and fatigue, the extraordinary mobility that had made the Mongol conquests possible ceased to exist.

The second factor was the weakening of effective central power over the empire as a whole. If the Mongol field army could no longer come streaking across Asia in a matter of weeks, then the Il-khans and the khans of the Golden Horde had nothing to fear from the distant Great Khan. After Kublai's death, they discovered this to be true. Therefore, the real unity of the empire vanished.

The third factor was the growing divergences between the Mongol forces stationed in each of the three main agricultural areas that the Mongols had overrun. As the soldiers and administrators around Kublai Khan became more familiar with Chinese things, they lost touch with central Asian and Moslem civilization. The Golden Horde and the Il-khans moved in the opposite direction, becoming more and more part of the Moslem world and being less and less in touch with the Chinese style of life that was seeping into the Great Khan's court.

By 1300, therefore, the administrative and military unity of the empire had disappeared, although close diplomatic and commercial ties continued to operate across all of Asia for another half century. The rulers of China, for example, usually cooperated with the Golden Horde against the two intervening khanates. As late as 1332 a bodyguard of Russians existed at Peking, specially recruited by the Golden Horde for the protection of the Great Khan's person. Not until 1368, when the Mongols were driven out of China by a new Chinese dynasty, the Ming (ruled 1368–1644), did the memory of Mongol unity fade.

Before that time, the Il-khans had lost control of Persia to a swarm

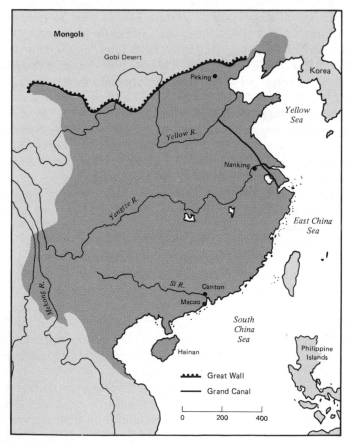

Chinese Empire under Ming Dynasty: 1368–1644

of quarreling upstarts, most of whom claimed descent from Genghis Khan—although they were Turks in language, Moslem in religion, and resembled Genghis only in their ruthlessness. The Golden Horde lasted longer. Indeed, its last fragment was wiped from the map of Europe only in 1783, when Catherine II of Russia annexed the Crimea. But the power of the Golden Horde over the Russian lands had been broken by 1480.

Crowded back into Mongolia itself, the surviving Mongols remembered the great Genghis but were quite unable to equal his deeds. This was the case largely because the Chinese viewed every move toward unification among the Mongolian tribes with the most intense suspicion, and they took prompt steps to break up any new center of power by every means they could command—bribery, diplomacy, trade boycott, and in case of necessity, direct military action. Chinese diplomats and rulers had learned their lesson well, and resolved never to permit the Mongols to unite again. Moreover, they were so concerned with the danger from the steppe that the Chinese court utterly failed to recognize the new opportunities and dangers that came in the following centuries by way of the sea.

Measured against the whole span of human history, the Mongol Empire was a short-lived affair. But its influence and impact lingered on long after it had broken up. Memories of the Mongol assault affected the behavior and policy of both the Chinese and Japanese governments very strongly. The Mongol Empire also had an impact, although less important, upon Islam and Europe. In the rest of this chapter we shall, therefore, look at each of these regions to see the different ways in which these peoples reacted to their collision with the Mongol conquerors.

The Ming Reaction in China

After the death of Kublai Khan in 1294, the Mongol control of China began to falter, but it was not until 1368 that the Chinese succeeded in uniting behind an ex-Buddhist monk who was able to drive the hated foreigners out of the country. The Ming Dynasty, which he founded, ruled China from 1368 to 1644.

The overriding thought behind everything the Ming rulers did was to keep China free from a new invasion. They moved their capital to Peking in 1421 to be able to guard against any renewal of invasion from the steppe. Systematically the Ming officials set out to erase all signs of the Mongol period. Faithful and exact imitation of the old ways was the obvious path; and they did their best to follow it. Merchants, who had enjoyed unaccustomed prestige in the time of the Mongols, were once again put firmly in their place near the bottom of the social scale. The old social order of China was restored, as exactly as human will and intention could do so.

Some changes remained in spite of everything. For example, the use of gunpowder in war had become a lot more important under the Mongols, who were most eager to adopt anything new in the way of weapons. It is not certain that the Mongols ever used siege guns, though, like the Chinese before them, they did fill hollow lengths of bamboo with gunpowder and exploded such "bombs" under city gates with good success. But by 1393 the Ming court ordered that each ship setting off for the Indian Ocean should carry four guns with "muzzles the size of rice bowls." Such large weapons were very effective against city walls and gates, and the threat they posed made it much more difficult than before for a local governor or upstart warlord to defy the central government. Even if it took several months to bring artillery from imperial headquarters to the rebel stronghold, a few such guns could destroy the walls of any stronghold in short order. The effect of gunpowder and heavy artillery was therefore to strengthen the central authority. In other words, the new weapons had the effect of reinforcing the old imperial ideal. The Ming regime accepted and approved that novelty.

MING VOYAGES OF DISCOVERY   When, however, new developments did not serve to strengthen old ways and values, the Ming emperors set out to check the source of disturbance. One of the strangest "might have beens" of history turns upon what the Ming court did about naval expansion. Under Kublai, the Mongols had experimented with combined sea and land operations. The invasion of Japan in 1281 was the most famous of these, as well as the least successful. To support such ventures overseas, Chinese shipbuilders and merchants created a large and seaworthy merchant fleet. In doing so they had the full support of the imperial court. Kublai, after all, never gave up his intention of conquering Japan, and for that he required a very large fleet indeed.

The Ming policy was to put officials in charge of seafaring. Seven times between 1403 and 1433 a court official, named Cheng Ho, gathered a great fleet in south China and sailed into the Indian Ocean. He returned successfully, bringing with him the king of Ceylon, the prince of Sumatra, and tribute (including a giraffe from east Africa) from no fewer than sixteen rulers at whose ports the Chinese ships had put in. The Ming emperors were in a position to create a naval empire in the Indian Ocean, like the one that the Portuguese actually established a century later. But the court decided to draw back. In 1424 further voyages were forbidden; and although that order was later modified to permit Cheng Ho to undertake a final voyage in 1431–1433, the Chinese never followed up their initial expansion. Instead, the Ming emperors actually prohibited the construction of large ships for travel on the oceans and made it a crime for any Chinese to leave the country by sea.

Exactly why the Ming emperors made this decision is unknown. Perhaps it was mainly the result of a court intrigue, pitting one group of advisers against another. Cheng Ho, after all, was a eunuch and this made him suspect in the eyes of Confucian scholars. Moreover, fitting out naval expeditions took manpower and resources that could be used to strengthen defenses against the Mongols. This was no mere theoretical problem, for in 1449 the reigning Ming emperor was actually taken prisoner when he took the field against a new confederation of Mongol tribes.

But what made the policy stick was surely the fact that the only people who seemed to benefit from such enterprises were merchants and other riffraff, for whom Confucian scholars had only the greatest contempt. Or, to put it another way, the merchants and other social groups who profited from seafaring were quite unable to make their interests felt at court. Classified as social parasites by Confucian doctrine, Chinese merchants lacked habits of self-assertion against their betters, the scholar-officials. Hence what the court decreed was in fact enforced. China deliberately threw away the strategic position in the Indian Ocean which Cheng Ho's voyages had won.

This was only the most dramatic example of China's overall course. For by settling back toward tried and true patterns of behavior, the Ming emperors and officials allowed the rest of the world to catch up with China. In 1400, as in 1200, China outclassed the rest of the world in numbers, skills, and habits of hard work. Chinese learning and art were exquisitely refined. A strong army and a vigilant emperor with well-trained officials kept the country secure, even against the Mongol danger. When the emperor was captured in 1449, for instance, his brother took the throne and the government went on as before. Holding fast to the way of the ancients was exactly what Confucius had recommended. It was what the Ming Dynasty did. It worked.

In the long run, to be sure, such a reactionary policy allowed Europeans to catch up and eventually leave the Chinese behind. But it is quite unfair to judge Ming policy by what happened 400 years later. At the time and within the world they knew, they did well. Order, security, and civilization were maintained; the hateful barbarian lordship had been overcome. What more could any reasonable person ask or expect?

JAPAN'S COMING OF AGE

Until 1200, Japan's civilization had copied China's, always falling short of the model because Japanese society differed from Chinese society in some important ways. The most obvious differences were that Japanese warriors and landowners kept a clan organization and habits of violence that the Chinese upper classes entirely lacked. The warlike clans of Japan fought one another frequently; but they turned their practice in war to good use when the Mongols landed and tried to conquer the country in 1281.

The fact that they defeated the mighty Kublai Khan, when everyone else in the whole world had been unable to stand against the Mongol assault, gave a great fillip to Japanese self-confidence and pride. China did not seem so impressive to warriors who had turned back China's masters.

JAPANESE TOWNS AND THE SAMURAI CLASS   This independent spirit was fed by the increasing importance of towns and of sea-roving in Japanese life. As long as the Japanese court was the only place where people had the leisure or the wealth for civilized pursuits, it was natural to imitate China. The rough border barons and feudal lords, who had taken nearly all practical power away from the court, were too busy fighting to bother much with culture. But as towns became larger and wealthier after about 1200, they began to provide a new setting in which a privileged few could read, paint, and amuse themselves in other ways. In such an environment Japanese culture took on the color of the local scene and ceased to be a mere copy of Chinese achievements.

Japanese towns housed artisans who made things for the warrior, or samurai, class. In particular, Japanese smiths learned to produce sword blades of specially treated steel that were the best in the entire world. The secrets of Japanese sword manufacture are not entirely understood today!

But Japanese towns also served as headquarters for merchant-pirates who operated overseas. Many of these men were of samurai origin. Driven away from control over rice-producing villages by some stronger clan, defeated groups of samurai took to the sea—and soon discovered that their military skills paid off handsomely in dealings with less warlike peoples of southeast Asia. New wealth, derived from piracy supplemented by trade, began to pour into Japanese ports, especially in the southern and western parts of the islands. Population grew, and there began to emerge an urban upper class that was ready and able to support a more distinctly Japanese and less Chinese form of high culture.

The importance of seafaring for Japanese town life made the urban classes largely independent of the masters of the countryside. A spirit of self-assertion and a readiness to resort to violence in pursuit of their own interests prevailed in the towns, just as they did among the samurai. Instead of catering politely to the demands of the warrior class, Japanese townpeople tended to deal with them sometimes as rivals, sometimes as allies, and always as equals.

*In this illustration, Japanese soldiers attack and board some of the
Mongol ships which survived the typhoon. (The Bettmann Archive)*

To be sure, by far the majority of the Japanese population remained
on the land and lived in rice-growing villages, controlled by the members
of a samurai clan. This remained the norm. Towns began to grow to a
new size and importance only by becoming havens for those who had
failed to make good in the countryside—that is, for poor runaway peasants
as well as for defeated samurai. But when these refugees began to prosper
on the proceeds of their overseas ventures, the lords of the rural villages
had to confront a new kind of rival for dominance within Japanese society
as a whole.

Buddhist monasteries created a third center of power and wealth
in Japan. These monasteries owned important rice lands, and the monks
defended them—when need be, sword in hand—against samurai clans
that tried to take over rights the monks claimed as their own. Some monasteries (mainly of the Zen sect) accepted monks primarily from the samurai
class. Such communities simply maintained their warlike habits despite
their monkish robes. Some, however (the so-called "Pure Land" sect),
seem to have opened their doors to ordinary peasants, and therefore
represented a more democratic element in Japanese political and social
life. Little armies of monks from both these sects entered into the armed
struggles for power among the samurai clans from time to time, and held
their own quite successfully.

Presiding over this unruly political scene was the emperor. The imperial office remained hereditary in a single family. According to myth,
the imperial family descended directly from the Sun Goddess through

The Divine Wind

Early in his reign Kublai Khan sent a message to the Japanese demanding that they should recognize his greatness with appropriate submission. The Japanese authorities refused reply. Six years later, in 1274, Kublai sent an expedition of about 15,000 Mongol soldiers to enforce his demands. But the Japanese met force with force, and after a single day's battle, the Mongols reembarked and returned home. For the next five years, Kublai was busy in southern China, snuffing out the last traces of the Sung Dynasty. He completed this task in 1279. The Great Khan was now free to turn his full forces against the rude and warlike Japanese.

The shogun of Japan and his followers kept themselves informed of what was afoot in China and made elaborate preparations for resistance. They built a wall around the harbor where they expected the Mongol fleet to land; they mustered all the fighters of the islands; they prayed to all the gods of Japan. Even the sacred person of the emperor was mobilized: he vowed to launch 300,000 prayers heavenward, and did so by dividing the task among his courtiers, each undertaking his numerical share.

In June 1281, the test came. A Mongol army of about 50,000 men headed toward Japan from Korean ports, and a much larger expedition (about 100,000) sailed from southern China. The landing took place on June 23, and hard fighting lasted about fifty days. The Mongols had supe-

Emperor Jimmu. But the emperor was powerless, despite the fact that all Japanese clans accepted the fiction of subordination to his authority. Central control—so far as it existed at all—was in the hands of an official known as the "shogun."

The shogun was himself head of a clan and leader of a coalition of clans sufficiently strong to control the emperor, who was the only person who could appoint a shogun. This made control of the imperial court worth fighting over. Rivalries among the different clans never ceased to alter the lineup of groups supporting the shogun. To maintain his position, the shogun always had to maneuver among his friends and enemies, seeking support and sometimes fighting regular campaigns against some rival coalition. And sometimes a shogun met defeat and had to yield to a rival. One such overturn took place in 1338, when the Ashikaga clan seized the shogunate (that is, the office of the shogun). Members of this clan remained in office until 1568, and gave their name to the entire epoch of Japanese history.

rior discipline, superior missiles (both arrows and gunpowder projectiles), and the habit of victory. The Japanese had superior swords and home ground beneath their feet.

Details of the struggle cannot be reconstructed. Desperate courage was plentiful on both sides. But the Mongols never were able to get their cavalry loose to launch long-distance raids across country, as they were accustomed to doing. Instead they remained cooped up in a narrow bridgehead through the summer, until the season of typhoons came on.

Early in August 1281, the first typhoon of the season struck and came with unusual force. Trees were uprooted on land; and on the sea the Mongol fleet suffered destruction. The Japanese claimed that of 4000 ships only 200 escaped, and that of the invading forces less than a fifth ever got back to the Chinese mainland.

It was a stunning victory. The whole affair paralleled the story of the Persian invasions of Greece that preceded Athens' Golden Age. But there was one great difference. The Greeks won the Battle of Salamis through human guile and their own seamanship; the Japanese attributed their victory to the gods who had so clearly demonstrated their special attachment to Japan by sending a "Divine Wind" when the human defenders of the islands were hardest pressed.

Memories of the Mongol invasions and their failures revived in World War II, especially when another August typhoon delayed the ceremony of surrender until September 1945, and postponed the arrival of the first American troops in Japan by several days.

CULTURAL LIFE   In matters cultural, the Japanese continued to be able to imitate Chinese painting and literature very skillfully. The court circles, where this had been done for centuries, continued to foster such activity. Sometimes the Japanese attained great excellence, particularly in painting. But in addition, new traditions emerged in the Ashikaga period. Cartoons and caricatures, for example, would have been beneath the dignity of a Chinese scholar-painter. In Japan, however, painters had a lower social status and often belonged to the artisan class. This allowed them not only to copy Chinese styles with utmost skill but also, when they felt like it, to express their own points of view.

Japanese literature also developed new forms. Noh drama was the most important. This was a ritualized performance by masked actors and a chorus, in which music played a large part. Great precision of movement and refinement of voice and posture made Noh performances into a dance and song recital as well as a drama. It appealed especially to the samurai. Other arts for which Japan is famous seem to date from the same period; for example, flower arrangement and the so-called tea ceremony. The tea ceremony was another ritual art: every step in the making and drinking of tea had to be done in a particular way so that those who took part could admire the grace and beauty, the taste and rhythms, with which the host and his guests carried through the performance.

Japanese priests of the Sun Goddess, from whom the imperial family claimed descent, began to make her worship into an organized cult. This religion is known as Shinto. Shinto did not become generally important in Japan until later. In the beginning it was more like the Confucian cult of the ancestors, conducted by the imperial family for its own benefit and the benefit of the imperial household. But the ideas and rituals that later were thrown open to the Japanese public at large took form in this period, when Shinto priests borrowed rituals and ideas from Buddhism as well as from Confucianism.

The rise of towns in Japan, the samurai lordship over villages, and the militaristic spirit of the country all resembled western Europe of the same age. The parallels were indeed real and important; yet there were two differences that are worth emphasizing.

First, the Japanese did not build their society upon any radically new technique, as did the Europeans. Moldboard plow agriculture and the manorial system provided western Europe with something new that changed daily experience at the very bottom of society. The Japanese had only rice paddies, familiar for centuries. With enough hard work, more and more land could be brought under paddy cultivation; and with Japan's abundant rainfall, it was possible to push the paddy fields quite high up the mountain slopes. But the routine of life for the peasant majority remained fixed as before. In medieval Europe, on the contrary, from about 900, peasants had new techniques to exploit and new horizons of the possible to explore. This made European society more changeable, even at the bottom of the social scale, than Japanese society.

In the second place, the Japanese, like the Chinese, were handicapped by shortages of metal, at least as compared to the supply available to western Europe. Why this was so is not easy to say. Shortage of ores may have been a factor; but the weak development of mining and prospecting techniques is a more likely explanation for Japan's and China's restricted supply of metals. But whatever the reasons, the fact remained that in some key respects—particularly the casting of heavy artillery pieces—the Japanese (and Chinese) could not keep up with Europeans when the two peoples finally came into touch with each other.

Such differences between medieval Japan and medieval Europe were matched, of course, by the complete difference of cultural forms and social tradition that made the two civilizations what they were. Each was unique; each had recently played second fiddle to an older and more sophisticated civilization. And by about 1200, the world as a whole was richer both for western Europe's rise and for Japan's coming of age as an independent civilization.

RESPONSE OF ISLAM

The Mongol conquest came as a great disaster to Islam. The caliphate ended in crushing defeat at the hands of pagans. God seemed to have deserted the Moslem cause, and their Christian subjects proved disloyal. Yet a half century later Islam had recovered its balance and self-confidence. The Mongol-Turkish conquerors had been converted to the faith of Mohammed; and as soon as they found themselves back in the driver's seat, the Moslems made life so uncomfortable for their Christian subjects that nearly all of them accepted Islam in order to escape persecution. For the first time, therefore, the overwhelming majority of the inhabitants of Syria, Mesopotamia, and Persia became Moslem. In Egypt and Asia Minor, where the Mongols never established their power, important Christian subject populations remained in existence. In India the great majority remained Hindu. Only where the Mongols had threatened Moslem political and social dominance did the religious minorities disappear.

To be sure, the old question of how the Moslem community ought to find a worthy successor to the Prophet was not solved. Political life in the heartland of Islam remained chaotic and violent. Turkish-speaking war captains, claiming descent from Genghis Khan, struggled against one another. The most successful of them was Timur the Lame, sometimes called Tamerlane (ruled 1360–1405). Timur build a vast empire along the lines of the empire of Genghis Khan. From his capital at Samarkand, he led victorious raids in every direction throughout central Asia and the middle steppe—to Persia and Mesopotamia, Asia Minor and southern Russia, and into northern India. At the moment of his death, he was preparing a great expedition against China. But after he died the empire fell apart, for Timur had no solid core of fellow tribesmen upon whom to build, in the way Genghis Khan's successors could depend on the Mongol hordes.

Continual disorders and sudden reversals of fortune kept a stream of Turkish adventurers moving toward the frontiers of Islam. If unsuccessful in the center of the realm, a warrior might still hope to find fortune in India, or in the west, fighting against Christendom. Accordingly, a flow of Turkish fighting men kept moving in from the central steppe and then either south into India or westward into Asia Minor. The state that benefited most from this pattern of migration was the Ottoman Empire.

The Ottoman Empire started in obscurity, along the borderland be-

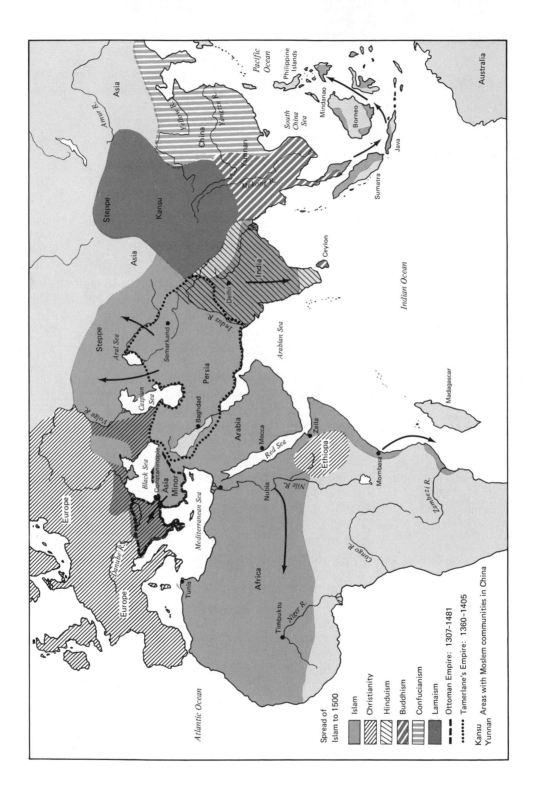

Spread of
Islam to 1500

Islam
Christianity
Hinduism
Buddhism
Confucianism
Lamaism
Ottoman Empire: 1307–1481
Tamerlane's Empire: 1360–1405

Kansu
Yunnan   Areas with Moslem communities in China

tween Christian and Moslem territory in Asia Minor. It got its name from Osman, or Othman (1290–1326), a Turkish warrior who carved out a small principality in northwestern Asia Minor at the expense of the Byzantine Empire. His heirs and successors enlarged the state steadily. In 1354 they crossed into Europe and took possession of the Gallipoli Peninsula. From there they spread rapidly through the Balkans. After defeating the Serbian army in a famous battle at Kosovo in 1389, the Ottoman sultan, as the head of the state was called, emerged as by far the most powerful ruler in the Balkans.

Constantinople remained in the hands of a Greek ruler who claimed to carry on the ancient Byzantine tradition, although continuity had been broken by the Fourth Crusade, when knights from the west captured the city (1204). Greek power was restored at Constantinople in 1261, but the empire that had made Byzantium great could never be regained. Instead, the Turks took control of the Balkan interior and seemed about to close in on the old capital when Tamerlane appeared from the East, defeated the sultan, and took him prisoner (1402). The great city therefore enjoyed a respite from Ottoman pressure until the Turks recovered themselves. Then in 1453, Sultan Mohammed II, the Conqueror, besieged it both by land and sea. After a three-months' siege he captured Constantinople, which then became the Ottoman capital.

The Ottoman state was, first and foremost, the creation of religiously dedicated warriors who believed God had sent them to extend the area under Moslem control at the expense of Christendom. The rise of the Ottoman Empire was thus the Moslem equivalent of a crusade, lasting hundreds of years. Many of the most fanatical fighters for the Turks were themselves converted Christians; but the Turkish element in the empire was also steadily reinforced by the arrival of newcomers from the east.

But a stable empire could not be built upon religious enthusiasm alone. Heresies easily took root among the rude warriors of the Moslem frontier. They particularly favored Sufi mystical teachers. But personal experience of God in moments of ecstasy made Sufis quite unwilling to obey any lesser authority—such as a mere sultan—in case of any conflict between their religious impulses and their worldly obligations.

Hence the Ottoman sultans fell back upon the learned experts in the Sacred Law of Islam to bring greater order and regularity into the religious life of their subjects. They chose the Sunni form of orthodoxy and soon made the Ottoman Empire the strongest supporter of that form of Islam in all the world.

The sultans also used their personal household, staffed by slaves, to conduct much of the business of government. Like other Moslem rulers, they organized a corps of slave soldiers, the Janissaries, who acted as a vast bodyguard and elite corps, always ready to obey any command the sultan might issue. With such troops at his disposal, the Ottoman sultan could counterbalance and control the disorderliness of the frontier warriors, upon whose religious enthusiasm and individual prowess the state still fundamentally depended for its continued victories against the Christians.

The sultan also used slaves to govern provinces and to run the central offices of his administration. Special palace schools for training young slaves in the necessary skills had to be invented. The result was a career open to talent. A simple village boy, seized as a slave in his youth, might end up as grand vizier—the real ruler, on a day-to-day basis, of the Ottoman Empire. For many years, this slave system produced efficient and hard-working administrators who made the sultan's will effective throughout Ottoman territory. The unruliness of Turkish warriors and the strength of the innumerable local ties and interests among the sultan's subjects were counterbalanced by the absolute dependence of all the members of the slave household upon the sultan—for their posts, promotion, income, and for life itself.

At first the sultan's slave household was recruited mainly through capture in war. When the supply of captives proved too small to staff the Janissary corps and all the posts in the sultan's administration, the Turks began to seize children from remote mountain villages of the western Balkans. These villages were generally too poor to be able to pay much in the way of taxes. But strong and healthy village boys, taken between the ages of twelve and twenty, could, with appropriate training, be made into splendid Janissaries and even more splendid grand viziers.

Thus, by a remarkable reversal of roles, the Ottoman Empire came to be governed by ex-Christian village boys, aided by freeborn Moslem experts in the Sacred Law of Islam. Turkish warriors continued to provide the bulk of the army. Each of them was assigned a village or two for his maintenance; but throughout the summer months, he was required to go off to fight on some far frontier. Moreover, the goods and services which the Turkish warriors could demand from the villagers were carefully defined by the sultan's regulations.

This meant, in practice, that the Turks demanded less from the Christian peasants of the Balkans than Christian lords had formerly been accustomed to squeeze out of them. Hence the Turks were popular among the peasants and could afford to leave each village to run its own affairs while the Turkish armed forces were far away, fighting under the sultan's command. Security in the rear allowed the Turks to concentrate their whole fighting force on the frontier, with the result that victories continued to come, almost every year, and Ottoman territory continued to increase until long after 1500.

ISLAMIC EXPANSION ELSEWHERE   On other fronts, too, Islam regained the initiative after 1300. In China important Moslem communities arose in Yunnan, to the southwest, and in Kansu to the northwest of China proper. Missionaries also won new successes in southeast Asia. Moslem communities arose in all important trading cities and gradually extended control inland. Java, for example, became a Moslem land by 1526, when coastal princes combined to overthrow the Hindu Empire of the interior. Mindanao, in the Philippines, and Borneo, in Indonesia, also became Moslem outposts by 1500 or before; while along the east coast of Africa, Moslem towns extended as far south as the mouth of the Zambezi River.

In Africa the Moslems won an important strategic victory when they overwhelmed the Christian kingdom of Nubia (c. 1400). This allowed nomadic Moslem tribes to move westward through Africa from the region near the Red Sea all the way to the Niger River. The arrival of nomad tribes in west Africa actually caused some retreat of agricultural settlement in that region, for the newcomers were accustomed to rob and plunder. But they brought west Africa more fully into contact with the rest of the world than before, when caravans across the Sahara had been the main link.

Moslem Culture

With such a record of success on every front, the Mongol setback soon ceased to seem important. As Islam expanded into one new region after another, however, the rather narrow mold into which religious ideals had pressed early Islamic culture broke apart. A wide variety of new, or newly perfected, art forms arose. The principal surviving works of Moslem architecture, for example, mostly date from the period after 1300. Handsome mosques for public worship made the dome and slender minaret standard architecture throughout the Persian, Arab, and Turkish lands. In addition, vast and handsome palaces and pleasure gardens were constructed according to a more distinctively Persian architectural tradition. Fewer of these survive for modern inspection.

Persian miniature painting was another high art that began to flourish after the Mongol period. The Persian painters owed a great deal to the Chinese, whose art had come west with the Mongols. But their use of bright colors was entirely different. From Persia the art of miniature painting spread into India, where instead of illustrating Persian books of poetry and romance, artists often represented episodes from Hindu myths.

Persian miniature painting was, in fact, developed to illustrate books of poetry. And throughout the Moslem world Persian poetry became, next only to the Koran, the most important aspect of genteel education. Turks, Persians, and Arabs alike, if they wished to count as cultivated, had to learn at least a few tags from the great Persian poets.

Firdausi (d. 1020) started the revival of Persian as a language for poetry by writing an epic account of Persian history. But Persia's supreme poetic achievement took the form of lyrical verses in praise of love. Three great poets rang the changes on this theme. The earliest of them, named Rumi (d. 1273), was a Sufi mystic. His poems celebrated God's love for human beings in very sensuous terms. The slightly shocking effect of comparing human love with the relation between believers and their God was carried much further by the other two great Persian poets, Sadi (d. 1291) and Hafiz (d. 1390). By hovering on the edge of sacrilege, they achieved a particularly powerful effect. The poems of Rumi, Sadi, and Hafiz gave the Sufi mystical movement within Islam a suitably ambiguous body of inspired texts, for the Sufi holy men, like the poets, hovered always on the edge of heresy—at least in the opinion of orthodox Sunni Moslems.

In the realm of thought, Islam did not return to philosophy or science. But geographers and travelers described the widening world with gusto and considerable accuracy. And a north African, ibn-Khaldun (d. 1406), wrote a remarkable history of the world. He saw a repetitive pattern in politics based upon fixed differences between nomads and cultivators. Herder-conquerors, he said, always lost their military strength and discipline after three generations of ruling over cultivators, thus preparing the way for a repetition of the cycle of conquest and decay.

Islam was thus in a flourishing condition between 1200 and 1500,

A court yard in the Alhambra, a palace and fortress built by Moorish kings in Granada, Spain in the later 13th Century. (Eugene Gordon)

having recovered brilliantly from the Mongol disaster. To be sure, economic life in the old centers of the Moslem world did not thrive. In both Egypt and Mesopotamia, the irrigated area decreased and population must have declined. In Spain, too, the last Moslem ruler was overthrown by the Spaniards in 1492. But Asia Minor and the Balkans seem to have prospered under the Ottoman government, and cities grew up in the region of the central steppe and in eastern Iran where there had not been cities before.

If anyone had been able to survey the world in 1475, before the European voyages of discovery changed the shape of things, it would have seemed obvious that the future belonged to Islam. Under the Ming, China withdrew from the Indian Ocean; Islam, on the contrary, was expanding. Traders, holy men, and warriors fresh from the central steppes were spreading the faith of Mohammed at a rapid rate in Europe, Africa, and Asia. And the geographical position of Islam gave Moslem faith and culture the strategic advantage that came from control of all the main lines of communication among the different civilizations of Eurasia.

BALKAN AND RUSSIAN CHRISTIANS

Whenever they were offered a choice, Balkan Christians preferred to submit to the Turks rather than to their fellow Christians from the west. The reason was twofold. As we just saw, Christian rulers squeezed the Balkan peasants and artisans harder than the Turks did. Then, in the second place, whenever western Christians achieved political power in the Balkans, they forced their subjects to change their religion to make it conform to their own kind of papal Christianity. Greek Orthodox populations resented this policy deeply, for they felt that their Christianity had a better claim to being true and correct than anything championed by Latin-speaking priests from the west.

The Greek Orthodox church underwent a vital rebirth about 1350. Monkish enthusiasts and mystics, supported by mobs in the streets, made it a rule that only monks could become bishops or archbishops. This rule was aimed at a party in the Greek church who had tried to negotiate with the pope in hope of getting military and financial help from the west. The reform movement did not prevent representatives of the Orthodox patriarch from agreeing to accept a papal definition of Christian doctrine at the Council of Florence in 1439. But this decision was extremely unpopular in Constantinople and did not last.

When Mohammed II conquered the city, he promptly appointed a new Orthodox patriarch and entrusted him with responsibility for looking after the Christians in the whole of the Ottoman Empire. Armenian Christians and Jews were given a similar organization; so was the Moslem community, a little bit later. In this way the church became for Orthodox Balkan Christians a sort of state within a state. Lawsuits between Christians could not come before Moslem judges, who applied the Sacred Law of Islam. They were therefore settled by church officials, or else by informal agreement and custom of the local Christian community.

Conversion from Christianity to Islam never entirely stopped, but it became much less common when the Moslem missionary enthusiasm of the earliest Ottoman times wore itself out. Only in frontier regions, where prolonged warfare between Moslems and Christians continued, did conversions occur on a mass scale after 1400. Thus the Balkans remained overwhelmingly Christian. The Turks were only a ruling stratum, except in a few towns where an artisan population of Moslems also came into existence.

Far to the north, amid the Russian forests, another group of Orthodox Christians also found itself under Moslem rule from the moment the khan of the Golden Horde accepted Islam (1257). Under the Mongols, however, both the native Russian princes and the Russian Orthodox church were allowed to conduct their affairs with no day-to-day interference from their distant overlords—so long, that is, as tribute payments were made regularly. The demands for tribute may have forced Russians to produce more; at any rate, agriculture and trade both increased in the Mongol period, and a powerful new administrative machine gradually took form under the control of the grand duke of Moscow. The grand duke owed his position to the fact that he became chief tribute collector for the khan of the Golden Horde. Anything extra he kept for himself; and in some years it even seemed safe to keep back all of the tribute, since the Mongols began to suffer from dynastic quarrels and internal splits after about 1419.

The decay of the Golden Horde's power was dramatically demonstrated in 1480, when Grank Duke Ivan III (reigned 1462–1505) announced that he was not going to pay tribute any longer. The only response was an ineffectual raid. Thereafter Muscovy (the territory ruled from Moscow), which comprised most, but not yet all, of the Russian lands, was independent again. It emerged from the Mongol domination as a strongly centralized state supported by a tough-minded tax-collecting bureaucracy and a pious, obedient church.

If they had to choose between foreign overlords, the Russians—like their fellow Christians of the Balkans—clearly preferred the Moslem khans to western Christians. The choice often presented itself, because after the crusading states in Palestine collapsed crusading orders of German knights set themselves up along the coast of the Baltic Sea. From this base they pushed inland, subjugating Latvian and Estonian peasants and completely destroying a stubbornly pagan community of Prussians.

Giovanni Arnolfini and his wife, by Jan Van Eyck (1434), a realistic portrayal of a representative of the newly emerging merchant class. (National Gallery, London)

(Prussia was then resettled by Germans who, however, kept the Prussian name.) When these Christian crusading orders came up against the borders of the Russian lands, they tried to force the Russians to accept the Latin form of Christianity. Russian princes and peasants agreed in rejecting this course and fought effectively, on several occasions, against the threat to their own faith and way of life that the western (mostly German) knights presented.

The widespread Russian distrust and dislike of the West found expression in the doctrine of the Third Rome. The idea was this: Rome had fallen to the barbarians because of its paganism. Constantine's New Rome on the Bosporus, Constantinople, also had fallen to the Moslem Turks because the Byzantine government had betrayed true Christian doctrine at the Council of Florence by accepting papal errors. Thus there remained only one haven of true Christianity: Moscow, the Third and last Rome, which would never betray Orthodox religion and would therefore endure until Judgment Day. The belief that they guarded a precious truth, destined to save the whole world, remained a deep conviction among the Russian people from that time even to the present—although under Lenin, Russia began to guard a very different kind of faith.

Indian Inaction

Since the Mongols failed to penetrate India, Indian life and society were not affected by the great political storm that raged north of the Himalayas. Nevertheless, the centuries from 1200 to 1500 were full of political upheaval in India. Moslem rulers controlled most of the land, although a large Hindu kingdom of Vijayanagar arose in the south about 1335 and lasted until 1565. But Vijayanagar employed Moslem soldiers sometimes, just as Moslem rulers often employed Hindus as soldiers and administrators. Religious hostility was not important. The old zeal against idolatry that had inspired the first Moslem invaders, or at least had given them a good excuse for plundering Hindu temples and Buddhist monasteries, was gone.

With time, however, interaction between Islam and Hinduism began to make a difference to both communities. Among Hindus, some religious teachers began to argue that Hinduism and Islam had fundamentally the same message—a simple, monotheistic, and basically mystic faith. The most influential person who talked in this way was Kabir (lived about 1450), whom the Sikhs today regard as the founder of their religion.

Among Indian Moslems, the Indian environment encouraged the rise of a great variety of holy men, some of whom developed wildly heretical views. One sect, for example, held that Mohammed's son-in-law, Ali, was an incarnation of the Hindu god Vishnu. Moslem rulers were usually too insecure on their thrones to try to enforce any sort of religious uniformity. Even in the heartland of Islam all sorts of sects taught different doctrines and yet got along with one another somehow. The range of toleration in India was even wider, for the Moslems could not usually afford to offend Hindu feeling too sharply, and in Hinduism everything was possible.

India, therefore, saw no great changes. Life went on, while holy men, as they had done for centuries, looked beyond the varied everyday scene to the real world of transcendent truth—where suffering and luxury, victory and defeat, shrank to nothingness.

CONCLUSION

The dramatic rise of the Mongol Empire and its later breakup made less difference to the peoples of Asia than might be expected. This was because the Mongols, after an initial period of paganism, accepted the civilization and religious traditions of the peoples they had conquered. Some mingling of cultural traditions occurred as a result of the improved communications that held the Mongol Empire together. But they were limited to matters of small importance—Chinese motifs in Persian miniature paintings, for example. Each of the great Asian civilizations—Chinese, Moslem, and Indian—had worked out traditions and techniques of its own so well that even when novelties appeared they were usually judged unnecessary.

Deliberate rejection of new techniques and ideas went very far. The Moslems, for example, repudiated printing, although they learned of it from contacts with China long before Europeans did. The reason was that Moslem teachers felt it would be irreverent, even sacrilegious, to reproduce the Koran, God's own Word, by mechanical means. To prevent such a possibility, they prohibited printing entirely.

Such conservatism was fully matched elsewhere. When people felt that all important problems had already been solved, new ideas or methods of making things met with great resistance. Novelties from foreign lands were usually not worth the trouble they caused. As a result, the Mongol unification of northern Asia left few lasting traces behind. Ming rulers of China, where the Mongol imprint had been by far the strongest, tried systematically to erase everything they felt to be of foreign origin. Hindus and Moslems behaved in an essentially similar fashion, preferring to develop and carry forward—within their own civilizations—trends that had already been under way before the Mongol conquests.

Japan, however, reacted to victory over the Mongols by cutting loose from the Chinese leading strings that had previously dominated Japanese higher culture. At the other extreme of the Eurasian continent, western Europeans found themselves in a similar position. They never had to face the Mongol storm, yet took advantage of what they could learn from distant China, as well as from nearer regions and places, with reckless energy. And because Europeans were able to respond to new possibilities, they laid the basis for their later expansion around the world during the centuries 1200–1500, when the rest of the civilized world (except in the Americas) suffered from and reacted against the Mongol conquests.

In the next chapter we will therefore study the changes that came to western Europe in these years.

CHAPTER 14

Western Europe

1200 to 1500

Western Europe, between 1200 and 1500, went through a period when all the diverse elements of the western inheritance seemed to come together into a balanced, internally coherent pattern, and then found that balance toppling over as new ideas and techniques called into question various aspects of the earliest synthesis.

During the initial period of bloom, the Church played a central part throughout Latin Christendom. Church officials controlled art and learning as well as many aspects of daily life. Secular rulers, landlords, craft guilds, and village communities also had their place; but the special and peculiar stamp of medieval civilization came always from the Church.

The breakup of this "medieval synthesis" therefore meant a weakening of the power of the Church. Royal governments, for example, clearly proved their superiority to the international administration of the papacy when matters came to a head in 1303. On the level of theory, critics arose who challenged the clergy's right to worldly power. Others undermined the position of the Church by turning to the study of ancient pagan authors with a new enthusiasm that left less room for Christian theology. Art also ceased to be wholly in the service of the Church.

The Church was, of course, not the only victim of Europe's continuing upheaval. Knighthood suffered from the rise of disciplined infantry and the multiplication of walled towns. Craft guilds and even the manorial system, upon which the remarkable upswing of medieval Europe had rested, also began to alter in fundamental ways when a class of cotters—who were part-time artisans, part-time cultivators—became numerous in the most developed parts of the European countryside.

What was challenged and in doubt could be defined easily enough by 1500. Not until long after that time did anything like a new pattern promising some sort of stability begin to emerge in western Europe. Nevertheless, 1500 is a good date at which to break off the story of how Europe changed and kept on changing, because it marks the approximate time when European ship captains opened all the oceans of the earth to their voyaging.

THE MEDIEVAL SYNTHESIS

Between about 1200 and 1275 the medieval Church brought the entire civilization of western Europe into unusually sharp focus. Christian and pagan, as well as Roman and barbarian inheritances from the past, blended into a new and vigorous style of life. The different groups and classes of society quarreled often enough, yet the energies of townspeople, clergymen, great lords, and common peasants nevertheless combined more effectively in these decades than they did earlier or later. Historians often refer to this period as the High Middle Ages. Another name, which draws attention to the way in which quite different elements were brought together harmoniously during this time, is the "medieval synthesis."

By 1200 the poverty, ignorance, and local self-sufficiency of Europe's Dark Ages already lay behind. The rise of towns, the increase of communication through trade and travel, the crusades and pilgrimages to especially holy shrines, all meant that people knew a lot more about the world and about what others did and thought than had been possible before. This offered a challenge to the Church and to Christianity, since local variations in religion and many new thoughts could (and did) spread. It was not enough to say, "It is so because it is so." But priests and teachers met the challenges successfully and were able to balance religious and secular ideals, one against the other.

The Meaning of the Medieval Church

To understand the medieval civilization, it is important to have a clear idea of what the Church was and how it affected ordinary people's lives. According to medieval theologians, the Church was the "channel of grace" through which God made salvation available to human beings. *Grace* was forgiveness of sins. Only God could grant that; and the way He did it was through the sacraments of the Church.

There were seven sacraments. Four of them were usually administered only once in a person's life: baptism, came soon after birth and wiped away the child's original sin; confirmation, came in youth and signified the individual's conscious acceptance of membership in the community of Christians that had already been symbolized by baptism; marriage, which needs no explanation here; and extreme unction, administered on the deathbed, which wiped away any remaining sins.

Two of the sacraments could be repeated as often as needed. They were the Eucharist or sacrifice of the Mass that constituted the central act of Christian worship; and penance (or confession) which, in conjunction with the Eucharist, wiped away sins committed since the prior confession. The last of the sacraments was ordination, which made priests different from ordinary people by conferring upon them the power to administer the other sacraments. Without the sacraments, administered by a properly ordained priest, natural impulses were sure to lead human beings into sin; and sin, if not forgiven by God's grace, caused the soul's damnation to eternal suffering in Hell.

Careful attention to religious duties as defined by the Church was, therefore, the only way a person could expect to attain salvation. This meant obedience to priests, and priests were supposed to obey the bishops who ordained them. The authority of bishops, in turn, descended directly from the Apostles (whose successors they were); and the Apostles received their authority from Christ himself. Among the bishops, the bishop of Rome, or pope, was preeminent. Papal power rested on the doctrine that the bishop of Rome was successor to St. Peter, the chief of the Apostles. An old and probably correct tradition held that St. Peter had been martyred in Rome under the emperor Nero. This gave the popes ground for claiming to be his successor, endowed with all the powers that Christ had assigned to Peter.

But the popes also claimed to have superior authority to all secular rulers in matters of ordinary government. This claim was based in part upon a document known as the "Donation of Constantine." According to this text, when the emperor Constantine moved his capital to Constantinople he transferred the government of the western provinces of the Roman Empire to the pope. As early as 1450, a famous scholar, Lorenzo Valla, proved that this was a forgery; but in the Middle Ages, the text was generally believed to be authentic.

The pope's claims to superior authority over secular rulers did not rest entirely on the Donation of Constantine however. There was also the Bible, which says that when Christ was about to be arrested by Roman soldiers in the Garden of Gethsemane, the Apostles pulled out two swords.

Medieval readers assumed that the two swords mentioned in the Gospel symbolized the sacred power of the Church and the secular power of the state. And since both swords were in the hands of the Apostles, it followed that the pope—as heir to Peter, the chief of the Apostles—also inherited supreme power over both Church and state.

Church Government

Such arguments, of course, could only be meaningful if the popes were, in fact, able to build up a system of government that could make papal decisions hold, even when some local ruler opposed them. This had been the real issue in the great struggle with the German emperors that began in 1076, for if the emperors controlled the bishops and abbots of Germany and Italy, then the pope could not make his government effective. By 1200, as we have seen, the power of the emperor had been thoroughly broken and the bishops and abbots of Germany and Italy were, more or less, ready to obey the pope. Elsewhere the popes achieved nearly the same results without quarreling openly with kings and princes.

The whole of western Europe, wherever the pope's power was recognized, was divided into archdioceses, with an archbishop in charge of each. Archdioceses were divided into dioceses, each with its bishop; and the dioceses were in turn divided into parishes, where a priest had charge of all the souls living there. Parish priests might be appointed in various ways. Usually some local landowner had the right to choose a candidate. But only a bishop could ordain a priest. This usually allowed bishops to veto any bad appointment.

Much the same system prevailed in appointing bishops. Nomination had to come from the clergy of the cathedral, but the archbishop and pope both had the right to examine the way in which the election had been made, and they were in fact often consulted in advance. The pope, ever since the reform of 1059, was chosen by the cardinal clergy of Rome; and a reigning pope had the right to appoint cardinals.

Bishops were the key administrators of the Church. Many bishops controlled much property and enjoyed handsome incomes from their landholdings. They were responsible for all the affairs of the Church within their diocese; and the Church had many concerns. Building cathedrals and arranging for religious services constituted only a small part of the bishops' duties. Collecting rents and other income and administering Church properties took much attention. In addition, Church law covered any dispute in which the sacraments played a part. This meant, in effect, that practically any lawsuit could be brought before a Church court and tried according to Church law. However, local rulers never accepted this broad interpretation of the Church's power. Various deals were made, according to which some types of cases went to Church courts and other kinds of cases came before the king's or some lesser nobles' courts.

The question of what courts should have the right to try particular cases was of the highest importance in medieval government. Fees and fines brought income to the court that tried the cases; moreover, when possession of property was at stake, as was often the case, who it was that judged the case often affected the verdict. The Church, for example, often acquired property as gifts from repentant individuals on the point of death. The dying did not always have time to complete all legal formalities. Even when the intention of the deceased person was clear, heirs might not accept proofs offered by church officials who were also beneficiaries of the will. In such a case, it mattered a good deal whether the quarrel came before the king's court or a bishop's court.

THE ENFORCEMENT OF PAPAL AUTHORITY   The pope tried to make all the bishops cooperate. Letters and more formal instructions were fundamental means for doing so. In addition, when something important was in the wind, the pope might appoint a legate with special authority to act in his place. Also, the pope might call a council, either of all bishops or of those in a selected part of Christendom, and give them instructions or ask their support and advice about particular problems. Thus, Pope Innocent III (reigned 1198–1216) called the Fourth Lateran Council in 1215. This council settled various questions of doctrine and declared that every Christian ought to accept the sacrament of confession and do penance as prescribed by his or her parish priest at least once a year.

The magnificence of church services, the force of Christian doctrine as preached and taught by the learned men of Europe, and the threat of hellfire caused most people to honor and obey the Church, in principle at least. The great majority, of course, fell short of their Christian duties and failed to live up to Christian virtues in some degree or other. But the sacraments were always available to wash away sins. Some pious souls were not content with such an easy way of assuring salvation. For them, monasteries offered a stricter life of worship and an opportunity to do holy works. The monks lived according to rules—in Latin, *regula*— and so are called "regular clergy," whereas priests and bishops are called "secular clergy." Because the regular clergy were particularly holy, they often became wealthy. Elderly people who felt the weight of their sins frequently gave property to a monastery, in return for which the monks promised to pray for the donor's soul even after he or she had died. Such gifts, of course, made the monks rich, and rich monasteries tended to relax the pursuit of holiness. This situation called for reform; but re-

St. Thomas Aquinas (*1225–1274*).
(*New York Public Library*)

formed monasteries by their fierce dedication to holiness, regularly became wealthy, too, and so prepared the way for a new wave of rigorous reform.

CHALLENGES BEFORE THE CHURCH   From the time of the First Crusade (1096–1099) onward, the Church made considerable progress in Christianizing knighthood. The fierce, strong-armed fighters who answered Pope Urban II's call for the crusade were serving the Church and Christendom, as well as looking for new lands to conquer for themselves. The idea that a knight should fight only in good causes, should protect the weak, and should remedy injustices became a theme of poetry. Courts and castles began to echo to the tales of King Arthur and his knights, Charlemagne and Roland, Parsifal, the Nibelungs, and others. These stories illustrated Christian ideals of *noblesse oblige*, that is, the duty of the strong to help others. Boys of noble and knightly rank, brought up to familiarity with these stories, acquired a code of manners softened, though by no means completely controlled, by Christian ideals.

The towns offered a more complicated challenge to the Church. Urban populations often opposed the bishop who, as chief local landlord, wanted to rule the town, or at least tried to restrict local self-government. In addition, townspeople often criticized ignorant, greedy, or immoral priests. Heresies began to spread, especially in northern Italy and southern France. The most radical was a form of Manichaeism, commonly called the Albigensian heresy because the town of Albi in southern France became a hotbed of the faith. The Albigensians, like most other heretics, demanded a more rigorous moral and religious example than most parish priests were able to give.

Pope Innocent III found a solution to the challenge of disaffection in the towns of Christendom when he authorized the informal brotherhood that St. Francis of Assisi (1182–1226) had gathered around himself. St. Francis was a layman, a mystic, and a man totally given over to religion. He preached, helped the sick and the poor, and above all else set an example of joyous selflessness. He and his followers strove to imitate Christ and the Apostles in a simple, literal fashion. Giving up all possessions, they lived from hand-to-mouth on charity and did good in every way they knew.

Here were people whose practical example came up to the demands of even the most critical towndwellers. But from the point of view of priests and bishops, the friars—from Latin *fratres* meaning "brothers"—offered an embarrassing kind of competition. Bishops, after all, were the official successors to the Apostles. What right had mere laymen to imitate Christ and the Apostles, especially when their mode of life, modeled on the Gospel account, differed so much from the pomp that surrounded the pope and other rulers of the Church?

Pope Innocent III, therefore, hesitated before approving St. Francis' order and insisted that the friars must have a definite organization. St. Francis was not fond of administrative regularity. He retired from the headship of the order shortly before his death, because Church authorities wanted his followers to set up houses, each with its duly appointed head. This meant acquiring property, which St. Francis thought would spoil the whole idea behind his order. On the other hand, he always emphasized obedience to the pope; and on this issue, as on others, he submitted reluctantly.

St. Francis' obedience and Pope Innocent III's statesmanship thus allowed the explosive energy that gathered around the Franciscan movement to operate within the framework of the Church. Franciscan friars tapped feelings that had previously poured into heretical channels, and they made Christian idealism a living reality in the towns of western Europe.

St. Dominic (1170–1221) also organized a brotherhood of friars. St. Dominic wanted to supply preachers who would convert Albigensians and other heretics by arguing the truths of Christian doctrine with greater knowledge and conviction than parish priests were usually able to muster. This required special training, and almost at once the Dominicans became prominent in university life. It also required organization; and the representative system that St. Dominic invented for the government of the Dominican order became a model for the reorganization of the Franciscan order after St. Francis' death. It also influenced later development of parliamentary representation in royal governments.

Trinity Church, chartered by King William III in 1697. (N.Y. Convention & Visitors Bureau)

The Church's Influence on Culture

The influence of the Church was strong on all forms of cultural life. The music, hymns, and splendid robes of church services, together with the vaulted architecture of the new Gothic churches that arose all over Europe, were great achievements in themselves. An abundant literature of saints' lives reinforced Christian teachings. "Miracle plays" reenacted sacred stories. Even the most irreverent tales, especially popular among towns-folk, often paid priests the backhanded compliment of holding their failings up to ridicule.

The Church controlled almost all formal education. Elementary schools taught Latin—not the language of Cicero, but a living Church Latin that was used in everyday speech by the learned of all western Europe. It contained many words unknown to the ancients, and used simplified grammar. In addition, schoolboys got a smattering of the liberal arts as handed down from antiquity. These were classified as grammar, rhetoric, logic, arithmetic, geometry, music, and astronomy. Above that level came university work for those who wished to qualify for profes-sional careers. Medieval universities offered training in law, medicine, and theology. Medicine was studied with the help of the works of Galen and the Moslem Avicenna, both translated into Latin. Law meant study of Justinian's Code of the ancient Roman law, or the study of contemporary Church law. When, as in England, a body of royal law came into existence, it was not studied at universities, which were Church organizations, but in separate institutions, the so-called Inns of Court.

SCHOLASTICISM   Theology held first place among the subjects studied at medieval universities. Theologians undertook to explain Christian teachings about God and to make sense of everything on earth as well. Soon after 1200 the works of Aristotle were translated into Latin from Greek and Arabic. This presented Christian thinkers with what was to them a brand-new world view, complete and balanced, reasonable, and carefully worked out.

Some felt that Aristotle's writings should be left strictly alone be-cause they were pagan. But unlike the Moslems, most of whom took this position, leading Christian theologians boldly set out to use Aristotle's logical method to show how the doctrines of the Church fitted in with truths knowable by human reasoning. The University of Paris became the main center of this enterprise. Those who carried it through are known as Scholastics, because they taught in schools; and their ideas and method of arguing are called Scholasticism.

The greatest of the Scholastics was St. Thomas Aquinas (1225–1274). His main work was entitled *Summa Theologica*, that is, *Summary of Theology*. It consists of a series of questions, each answered by presenting various opinions pro and con, followed by Aquinas' own answer, with reasons for it, and ending with a refutation or reinterpretation of the opinions disagreeing with the position Aquinas had taken. In this book St. Thomas Aquinas took up almost every dispute that had been raised among theologians in his time; and he provided reasonable and moderate answers to all of them. He was both admired and attacked in his lifetime—for he trusted reason very far, believing that it could demonstrate all but a very few of the revealed truths upon which human salvation depended.

DANTE'S *DIVINE COMEDY*   A second great literary monument to the medieval world view was created by the poet Dante Alighieri (1265–1321). Dante was born in Florence, Italy, but in 1302 his political enemies exiled him. These enemies were allies of the pope. This made Dante fiercely antipapal. Yet he was also profoundly Christian.

His great poem, the *Divine Comedy*, put everyone and everything in its proper place. He did this by sending his soul on an imaginary trip through Hell, Purgatory, and Heaven and describing what he encountered. Pope Boniface VIII, for example, Dante assigned to Hell; others found their places in Purgatory and Heaven. The poet also made clear in each case *why* each soul was in bliss or torment. The result, therefore, was a vivid poetic statement of the medieval conception of the human condition, teetering precariously between an eternal home in Heaven or in Hell.

Dante was one of the earliest poets to write in Italian. He used the dialect of Florence, which through his work, and that of others, became standard for all of Italy. In other parts of western Europe, other vernaculars began to emerge as literary languages a bit later. Geoffrey Chaucer (1340–1400), for example, wrote his *Canterbury Tales* in London dialect, and thereby helped to shape the mixture of Anglo-Saxon, French, and Latin spoken in London into the language we know as English.

THE RISE OF NATIONAL MONARCHIES

The importance of the papacy between 1200 and 1275 and the unity in diversity that the Church was able to create in western Europe depended in part on the weakness of other political units.

Central and Eastern Europe

Emperor Frederick II (reigned 1212–1250) gave up trying to rule Germany and concentrated only on making his power over Sicily and southern Italy secure. This decision aroused papal opposition. Soon after Frederick's death in 1250, the imperial office became vacant. Not until 1273 did a new emperor take office. He was Rudolph of Hapsburg, a minor German nobleman, chosen largely because he had no hope of dominating Germany and Italy on the strength of his personal power or private possessions. Rudolph did not try. Instead, he founded his family's fortunes by taking for himself the first attractive landholding that became vacant, which happened to be Austria. His descendants remained rulers there until 1918.

All of central Europe, therefore, from the Baltic to Sicily, broke up into small states of various kinds. There were city-states, such as Florence, run by a republican government. There were princely states; states governed by bishops; and minor kingdoms, such as Sicily or Bohemia. In addition, a swarm of "imperial knights" recognized no superior except the distant and powerless emperor, were, consequently, effectively sovereign—at least in their own backyard.

Around Europe's rim, however, larger kingdoms took form. In the east, Poland and Hungary stood guard against the steppe. Like the Scandinavian kingdoms, they were relatively poor and thinly inhabited. The Polish kings saw the need for towns and trade, and encouraged Jews from Germany to come to their kingdom in order to build up these activities. The Jews, living in small communities in many European towns, suffered serious persecutions during the crusades. Christian soldiers, en route to their wars against the Moslems, often attacked them as unbelievers. This made many Jews glad to flee eastward, with the result that Poland became the main center of Jewish population in Europe by about 1400. Most of the functions carried out by townsfolk in the west were performed by Jews in Poland. The Poles thus acquired a relatively well developed town life and began to export grain, timber, and other raw materials to the more crowded lands of western Europe.

The Scandinavian kingdoms in the north were barely strong enough to resist the German trading cities of the Baltic, for with the end of Viking raids, the kings of Denmark and Sweden (Norway was usually combined with one or the other) had little income with which to maintain any kind of strong government.

The Kingdoms of France and England

The kingdom of France to the west was far more important, for it was the main center of knighthood, of manorial agriculture, of the Gothic style of architecture, of scholasticism—in short, of everything most distinctive in Europe's civilization. But France was divided into dozens of feudal states, and the king of France was only first among equals.

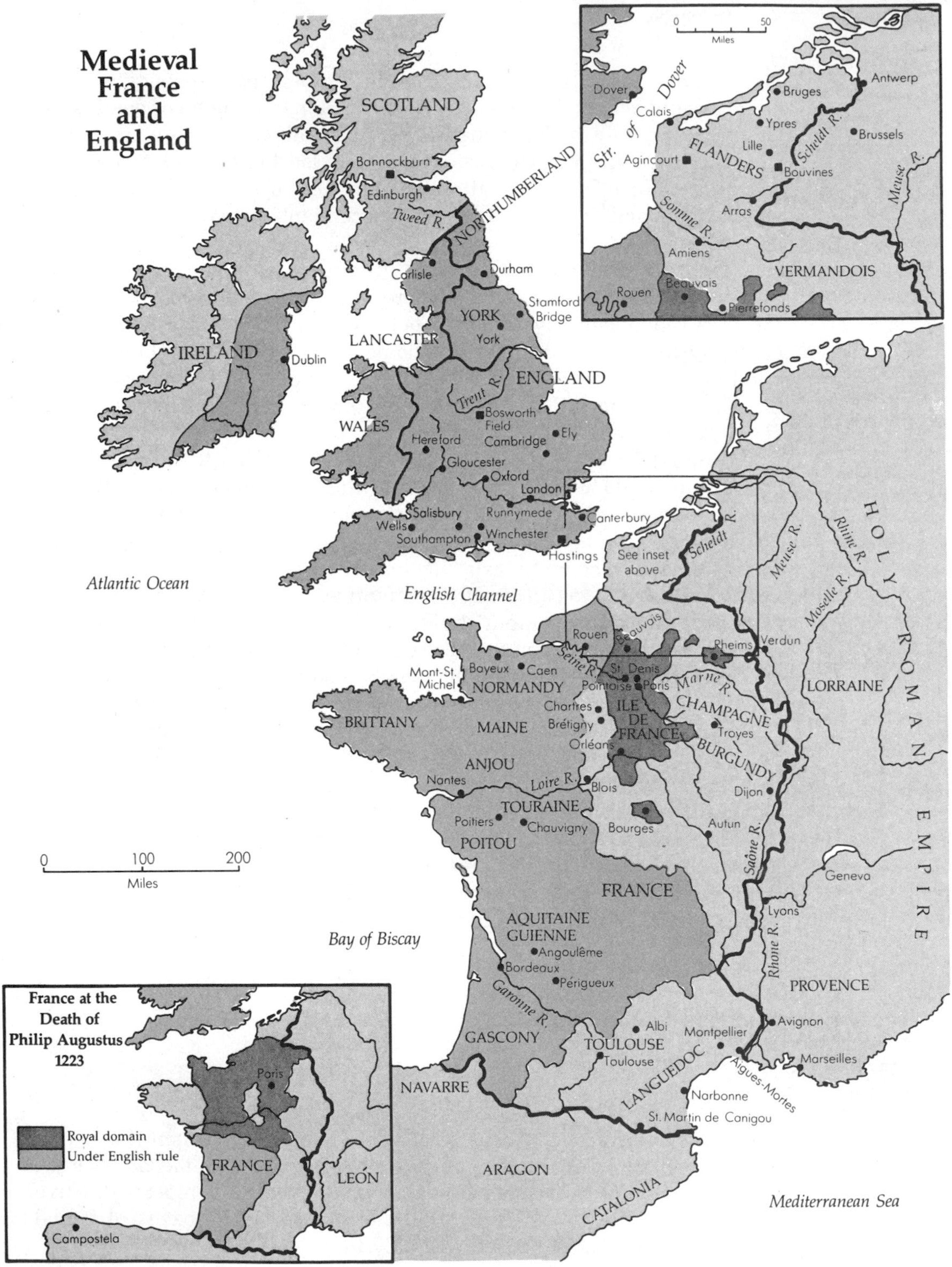
Medieval France and England
SCOTLAND
Bannockburn
Edinburgh
Tweed R.
NORTHUMBERLAND
Carlisle
Durham
Stamford Bridge
YORK
York
LANCASTER
IRELAND
Dublin
ENGLAND
Trent R.
Bosworth Field
WALES
Hereford
Cambridge
Ely
Gloucester
Oxford
London
Salisbury
Runnymede
Canterbury
Wells
Southampton
Winchester
Hastings
See inset above
Atlantic Ocean
English Channel
Scheldt R.
Meuse R.
Rhine R.
Moselle R.
HOLY ROMAN EMPIRE
Rouen
Beauvais
Rheims
Verdun
Mont-St. Michel
Bayeux
Caen
Seine R.
St. Denis
Pointoise
Paris
Marne R.
NORMANDY
LORRAINE
Chartres
Brétigny
ILE DE FRANCE
CHAMPAGNE
Troyes
BRITTANY
MAINE
Orléans
BURGUNDY
ANJOU
Nantes
Loire R.
Blois
Dijon
TOURAINE
Poitiers
Chauvigny
Bourges
Autun
POITOU
Saône R.
0 100 200
Miles
FRANCE
Geneva
Lyons
AQUITAINE GUIENNE
Angoulême
Bay of Biscay
Bordeaux
Périgueux
Rhone R.
PROVENCE
Garonne R.
GASCONY
Albi
Avignon
TOULOUSE
Montpellier
Toulouse
Marseilles
LANGUEDOC
Aigues-Mortes
NAVARRE
Narbonne
St. Martin de Canigou
ARAGON
CATALONIA
Mediterranean Sea
0 50
Miles
Dover
Str. of Dover
Calais
Bruges
Antwerp
Ypres
Brussels
Lille
FLANDERS
Agincourt
Bouvines
Meuse R.
Arras
Somme R.
Amiens
VERMANDOIS
Rouen
Beauvais
Pierrefonds
France at the Death of Philip Augustus 1223
Paris
Royal domain
Under English rule
FRANCE
LEÓN
Campostela

From the time of Hugh Capet (reigned 987–996) the kings of France ruled the Île-de-France, that is, a territory lying between the Seine and the Loire rivers, including both Paris, in the north, and Orléans, in the south. But this principality was no greater in extent or wealth than half a dozen others in France. Such states as the duchy of Normandy, established in 911 by Northmen or Normans who settled in the lower valley of the Seine, or the county of Flanders, where the cloth trade developed early, were nominally part of France. Their rulers held their land, in theory, as fiefs from the king of France. But in fact the duke of Normandy and the count of Flanders drew a good deal more income from their lands than the king enjoyed from the Île-de-France. They were correspondingly more powerful than their nominal sovereign.

This gap between theory and practice increased after 1066, when the duke of Normandy (William the Conqueror) seized England and became king of England as well as duke of Normandy. During the next century a series of marriages produced an even more lopsided situation, for Henry II, king of England (reigned 1154–1189), was also count of Anjou, duke of Aquitaine, duke of Normandy, and lord of still other French fiefs. He, in fact, controlled more than half of France and was a far more powerful ruler than the French king.

Nevertheless, legal forms sometimes mattered. In 1202 Henry's youngest son, John, was king of England. The king of France, Philip Augustus (reigned 1180–1223), stirred up trouble between John and some of his subordinate vassals, and then summoned King John to come to court in order to try the case. This was entirely in accord with feudal law; and when King John refused to attend the court of his liege lord, the king of France, Philip Augustus declared all his fiefs forfeit. This, too, was perfectly legal. The surprising thing was that King Philip was able to enforce the legal decision. He was helped by the fact that King John was also in trouble with the pope because of a dispute over the election of the archbishop of Canterbury. Philip was, therefore, able to march in and take over John's French fiefs, adding them to his own domain.

King John then decided to divide his enemies by making peace with the pope. Pope Innocent III required him to surrender his kingdom to the papacy, and then granted it back to him as a fief. From John's point of view, this maneuver was intended to assure papal support against Philip; but John's effort to get revenge failed in 1214, when his troops were defeated at the Battle of Bouvines.

This failure, in turn, encouraged the barons of England to revolt and demand that King John stop trying to wring more taxes from them and the whole kingdom, without their consent. John, once again, was helpless and had to submit to his vassals' demands by signing the Magna Carta at Runnymede, outside of London, in 1215. Magna Carta listed all the things King John and his agents had done against the will or interests of the barons and promised that the king would stop all such practices. The pope later declared that John did not have to obey an oath taken under threat of violence; but John's son, Henry III (reigned 1216–1272), reaffirmed Magna Carta early in his reign. It thus became a basic charter of English liberties to which opponents of royal power always appealed.

After this great success, the French monarchy went from strength to strength. The son of Philip Augustus led a crusade against the Albigensians and annexed the county of Toulouse, where heresy had been particularly widespread. The result was that between 1202 and 1216 the territory directly under royal administration in France increased about eight times. The French king had suddenly become the strongest ruler in Christendom.

Louis IX (reigned 1226–1270), later canonized St. Louis, finally made peace with the defeated kings of England. He allowed the separate duchies and counties of France to remain as they were when his predecessors annexed them. That is to say, separate administrations with different tax systems and local variations in law continued to operate as before. The difference was that the French king now received the income formerly collected by the local count or duke. The king appointed bailiffs to make sure that the proper revenues were paid on time. This created the beginnings of a central administration—but only the beginnings.

In England, from the time of the Viking invasions, a far more systematic central administration existed. William the Conqueror kept the division of the kingdom into shires, each headed by a sheriff appointed by the king. In addition, a national system of royal justice developed. The king sent traveling judges on circuit (that is, on trips to certain places) to hear cases brought before them by aggrieved persons who were willing and able to pay the high fees required before the judges would hear a case. The decisions of the king's traveling judges soon built up what came to be called the common law, that is, a body of law common to the whole kingdom. The procedure had the advantage of allowing low-ranking people to get justice against even a great nobleman, if they had both a good case and enough money to pay the necessary fees.

When the king of England lost his French possessions, the two kingdoms started to grow apart. Norman French gradually ceased to be the language of the English court, and a new language—English—developed from a merger between the Anglo-Saxon speech of the common people and the French and Latin formerly spoken by the governing class. A new nation likewise arose, as the nobility lost its French consciousness. In France, no such unification occurred. Differences between the old feudal principalities usually seemed more important than anything shared by all the subjects of the French king.

The Spanish Kingdoms

The Spanish peninsula was divided into five separate Christian kingdoms, of which Portugal, Castile, and Aragon were the most important. Aragon closely resembled southern France, but elsewhere in Spain there were important differences. For example, Moslems and Jews had a leading position especially in the towns. This drove a wedge between the kings and the townspeople, for the Spanish rulers kept alive the crusading idea as long as part of the peninsula remained under Moslem control. The crusading outlook, in turn, tended to maintain close ties between the class of noble fighting men and the various kings of the Spanish peninsula, whereas in other parts of western Europe, kings often aligned themselves with the towns and against the nobles.

BREAKDOWN OF THE MEDIEVAL SYNTHESIS

St. Louis of France died in 1270; Henry III of England followed him to the grave two years later. They were succeeded by less pious and more aggressive kings who were not content to leave the pope with such wide powers as Louis and Henry had done. At about the same time, the growth of towns slowed down. Friction between the poor and the rich became serious; guilds split between masters and wageworkers, and political power in the towns tended to concentrate in the hands of a relatively small number of influential men and powerful guilds, squeezing out the poorer classes. The open flexibility of the years between 1200 and 1275, when townspeople, rulers, and clergy all worked together without sharp conflict, came to an end.

The Decline of Papal Power

The most dramatic sign of the new age was the disruption of papal leadership. Pope Boniface VIII (reigned 1294–1303) quarreled with Philip IV, king of France (reigned 1285–1314), over the question of whether the king had the right to tax the clergy who lived in France. Boniface prohibited such taxation; but King Philip defied the pope, and felt the issue was so important that he called together representatives of all the influential classes of France—clergy, nobility, and townspeople—in order to explain to them what the quarrel was about and to seek their support. This was the first meeting of the Estates-General, which later French kings summoned from time to time when they wanted special taxes or some other sign of support from the country at large. It corresponded closely to the English Parliament that had emerged as a regular feature of English government a generation earlier.

Having assured himself of support at home, Philip sent a small detachment of troops into Italy and kidnaped the pope, who was staying in the little town of Anagni. Pope Boniface was outraged; Christendom was aghast; and Philip himself scarcely knew what to do with the pope once he had seized him. The French soon released their captive; but the events at Anagni in 1303 quickly became a symbol of the papacy's fall, just as the humiliation of Emperor Henry IV at Canossa in 1077 had symbolized the rise of papal power.

The papacy's fall was as dramatic as the fall of the empire had been. Pope Boniface died a few months after his release. The cardinals then selected as pope a Frenchman, Clement V, who made peace with King Philip by giving in on all disputed points. The new pope did not go to Rome, but set up headquarters at Avignon, a town on the Rhone River just outside the borders of the kingdom of France. For more than seventy years the popes remained at Avignon and governed the Church by working closely in harmony with the kings of France. King and pope, in effect, agreed to tax the lower clergy more and more heavily—and to divide the proceeds between them. A similar deal was made with the king of England, though cooperation was never so close. Elsewhere in Europe, too, the Avignon popes developed more and more ways of bringing income to the papal court. Their methods often dismayed religious persons.

Some Franciscans felt that this kind of Church betrayed Christian truth. They remembered St. Francis' praise of poverty and declared that the only way to follow Christ and the Apostles was to give up all property and depend on charity. These Franciscans were called "Spirituals." Their praise of poverty implied criticism of the pope and of all other rich clergy. The popes responded by declaring the doctrine that the Apostles had not owned any property to be heretical. When some of the Franciscans refused to change their opinions, they were burned.

But no sooner did one heresy disappear under threat of persecution than another appeared. John Wycliffe (d. 1384), a professor at Oxford, for example, began to develop radical views that won wide following in England. From England, Wycliffe's movement passed to Bohemia, where John Huss (burned at the stake in 1415) found himself in sympathy with some of Wycliffe's ideas.

Obviously, the link that Pope Innocent III and St. Francis had estab-

Battle scene during the Hundred Years' War.
(Art Resource)

lished between the official Church, with all its pomp, ceremony, riches, and splendor on the one hand, and the intense religious enthusiasm of those who sought holiness at any cost, on the other, was seriously strained. Both sides suffered from the break, for neither hunted heretics nor harassed administrators could do what they really wanted to do as long as each had to fight against the other.

The Hundred Years' War

The French monarchy, which had seemed so strong and victorious in collision with the papacy, also fell on evil days later in the century. In 1328 the last of the Capetian kings of France died; succession passed to a new family, the Valois. Ten years later, however, Edward III of England chose to challenge the legal principle according to which the Valois had claimed the French throne, and sent an invading army to enforce his own claims to the French crown. This began the misnamed Hundred Years' War, for the struggle between France and England lasted on and off, with long periods of truce and military inactivity, from 1338 until 1453, a total of 115 years.

Long years of warfare brought severe devastation to France. The English king had to hire mercenaries to fight in France. The French king also found it useful to hire professional archers and other specialized troops to support the by now old-fashioned knights, who at the beginning of this long war constituted the main force at the king's command. Both kings found it hard to pay their soldiers and discharged them at the end of each campaigning season, often withholding their promised wages. The discharged soldiers stuck together and lived by plundering until someone offered to hire them to fight once again.

As aggressors, through most of the Hundred Years' War the English had the advantage of being able to choose the time and place for attack. They also profited from deep and long-standing divisions among the different provinces of France. In particular, the dukes of Burgundy often collaborated with the English against the French king, for they hoped to build an independent kingdom of their own along the length of the Rhine between France and Germany. Yet in time, the presence of English troops on French soil roused a sense of common identity among the French. Provincial differences began to seem less important as the French came to feel a common hatred of the invaders.

The French cause reached a low point when a vigorous English king, Henry V (reigned 1413–1422), put fresh energies into attacking France. Recovery began with the remarkable career of Joan of Arc. Initial successes were quickly followed by her capture and execution (1431); but nevertheless the tide of battle continued to favor the French thereafter. In 1439 the Estates-General granted the French king the right to collect taxes at his discretion and without time limit, in order to get enough money to pay an army that could drive the English finally and forever from French soil. When peace came in 1453, the French had all but achieved this goal; only the town of Calais remained in English hands. Moreover, the French king emerged from the struggle with a tax-collecting machine at his disposal that made him far richer and stronger than any other ruler in Christendom.

The Black Death

Early in the Hundred Years' War, western Europe was ravaged by the Black Death, a form of bubonic plague. For two years, 1347–1349, the plague raged in city and town. Half to a third of the entire population of some districts died. The infection probably came overland from China, but ship's rats spread it through Europe, for the lice that transmitted the infection to humans were carried by rats. At the time, of course, people did not know how the disease spread and felt sure it was a divine judgment for their sins.

The Black Death had long-lasting effects on Europe's economy. The disease reappeared at intervals after its first arrival in Europe. Each time the plague broke out, as many as a quarter or a fifth of the people living in the locality where it was raging would die. Exact figures are beyond recovery, but it is probable that the total population of western Europe did not recover to the level it had reached in 1346 until after 1500. This represented a serious setback to Europe's prosperity. Economic life slowed down, wages rose, and all traditional economic relationships were thrown askew. The boom that had prevailed from about 900 until 1300 gave way to much harder and more uncertain times, worsened by conflicts between rich and poor in the towns, and by the long-drawn-out agony of the Hundred Years' War.

New Forms
of Economic Organization

Yet hard times had the effect of forwarding some new kinds of economic organization that were to play an important part in later ages. For example, in the manufacture of woolen cloth, guilds were supplemented by what is called the "domestic" or "putting out" system. According to this system, spinners and weavers lived in cottages out in the country where town guilds had no jurisdiction. They sometimes worked at farming part time, and the rest of the time spun or wove materials provided to them by a capitalist or middleman. The spinners and weavers did not own the wool they worked with; sometimes they did not even own the spinning wheels and looms they used, but had these provided to them also by their employer. They were paid piece rates, so much for each yard of cloth or hank of yarn they produced.

Moreover, the middlemen who put the wool out to be processed were themselves only small cogs in the bigger machine. However rich and powerful in the eyes of poor spinners and weavers, such persons were usually mere agents for some big businessman operating from Flanders or Florence across half of Europe, buying and selling raw materials and the finished cloth in wholesale quantities. Greater efficiency and specialization could be achieved by such a system. But when the livelihood of poor weavers depended on market conditions in cities hundreds of miles away, there was also a new element of risk and uncertainty. Hard times hit hard, for the poor had no cushion against unemployment.

Mining also became big business in the late Middle Ages. In central and southern Germany, miners learned how to dig deeper and how to pump water out of mines. Prospectors opened up new bodies of ore in Bohemia and in Hungary. Silver was most sought after, but with mining skills as highly developed as they were, Europe never suffered serious shortage of any metal, and at all times had an abundant and comparatively cheap supply of iron.

Great financiers, operating from Italy and southern Germany, managed most of Europe's mining enterprises. This was a by-product of dealings with kings and emperors, who always needed loans. One of the best kinds of security for a loan that a ruler could give was the right to exploit subsoil minerals. Roman law made subsoil rights the property of the sovereign; and Europe's rulers gladly took over that right since it allowed them to borrow larger sums from moneylenders. When, as often happened, the loan was not repaid, mining rights passed to the lender, who had to try to get his money back by organizing efficient, large-scale mining.

Other industries that remained within the older guild organization often stagnated or even went downhill. Along the Baltic coast, however, prosperity continued to prevail. In that region German towns developed commercial relations with Swedes, Russians, and Poles, bringing those northern regions into close touch with western Europe for the first time. The herring catch in the North Sea and the Baltic Sea also increased. Better fishing boats and nets helped, but the development of a system for preserving herring in brine and shipping them to all of Europe was the critical innovation. This, too, employed comparatively large amounts of capital for salt (mostly brought from the Mediterranean), barrels, and ships.

The difficulties in Europe's towns after about 1300 did not, therefore, stop economic development entirely. Capitalistic organization of the wool, food, and mining industries allowed greater regional specialization than before. But this tended to widen the gap between rich and poor and made the Church's rules for economic behavior more and more irrelevant to what was going on. The Church, for example, forbade taking interest on loans. Yet Europe's big business rested on such loans; and nearly all of Europe's rulers, including the pope, were up to their ears in debt to the same bankers who financed large-scale industry and charged interest on every loan they made—regardless of what the Bible said.

Such wickedness fed the anger of the "Spiritual Franciscans" and other heretics against the rich rulers of Church and state. Those same rulers, sometimes not without twinges of conscience, felt compelled to suppress their critics by force. The "medieval synthesis" of earlier times had clearly broken apart.

RESPONSES TO THE BREAKUP OF THE MEDIEVAL SYNTHESIS

People, of course, did not merely sit idly by and complain, although many did complain loud and long. Three different responses had a more positive ring to them and became important enough to alter the life of Europe. These were (1) an effort to develop representative government as a way of checking abuses in both Church and state; (2) religious mysticism; and (3) humanism. Each of these needs some explanation.

Representative Government

CONCILIARISM IN THE CHURCH   Representative government had its greatest stronghold in the Church, where no one could simply inherit a position. According to the law of the Church, bishops were supposed to be elected by the clergy of their cathedrals and the selection then ratified by the people. Similarly, abbots were supposed to be elected by the monks of the monastery. Many other important decisions were taken by vote at meetings of bishops and other clerics. The Franciscans and Dominicans developed a precisely defined system of representative government, according to which delegates from each house gathered in a general meeting to discuss overall policy and elect the head of the order.

The tradition of papal monarchy was, of course, very strong, buttressed by the forged Donation of Constantine and by time-hallowed interpretations of biblical passages that made St. Peter chief of the Apostles. But there was a conciliar tradition, too. In the emperor Constantine's time (d. A.D. 337) and for two or three centuries after, major issues had been settled at a council of all the bishops; and in those days the pope had been no more than bishop of Rome, on a plane of equality with other bishops, even though his claim to be the successor to St. Peter assured him a degree of deference.

The pope's enemies had long been accustomed to emphasize the authority of a general council of the Church. Philip IV of France, in tangling with Pope Boniface VIII, had done so, for example. Such thinking gathered headway throughout the years when the popes stayed at Avignon (1305–1378). In 1326, for example, Marsiglio of Padua, a professor at the University of Paris, published a famous book, *Defensor Pacis* (Defender of the

Peace), in which he argued that all legitimate political power came from the people and that the Church should be governed by councils and have nothing to do with the affairs of secular government.

Others criticized the popes for staying away from their proper post at Rome. Finally, one of the Avignon popes did return to Rome and died there in 1378. The cardinals met, and elected a new pope under pressure from angry mobs who wanted the pope back in Rome. Then the cardinals withdrew and met again, choosing a second pope who took up his residence at Avignon. Each promptly denounced the other as a false pope. Europe was presented with the spectacle of two angry rivals, each claiming to be the earthly head of the Church. The Great Schism, as it is known, lasted until 1417.

It seemed obvious that the only way the quarrel could be solved was to call a general council. The professors of the University of Paris championed this solution, but the first effort misfired. Cardinals from each of the rival camps called a council at Pisa in 1409 and elected still a third claimant to the papal office; but the two others continued to exist. Finally, in 1414 another council met at Constance. Emperor Sigismund (1410–1437) joined forces with the pope chosen at Pisa to summon this council, and it was well attended.

The Council of Constance set out to reform the Church, combat heresy, and end the schism. Fortunately the assembled bishops succeeded in persuading two of the three popes to resign. The third lost all support, so that when a new pope was chosen by the council in 1417, all of Latin Christendom recognized him. The council combated heresy by declaring some of John Wycliffe's views to be false and by burning the Bohemian heretic, John Huss, who made the mistake of attending the council on the strength of Emperor Sigismund's promise of safe conduct.

Church reform was more difficult. The University of Paris professors hoped that councils would be called regularly in the future, to deal with important issues as they arose. They arranged for a new council that met at Basel in 1431. But the pope was unwilling to allow councils to cut into his authority, and the leaders of the Council of Basel, having quarreled with the pope, made the mistake of proposing to elect a rival pope. This roused general revulsion: the prospect of dividing the Church once again between two popes seemed too much of a risk.

The pope took advantage of this situation by calling a rival council at Florence in 1439, which won what seemed like a great victory: acceptance by representatives from Constantinople of the pope's definition of Christian faith. The Council of Basel simply petered out, meeting for the last time in 1449.

With its failure to reform the Church in any important way, the conciliar movement ended in defeat. Papal monarchy had been restored; and in the ensuing years the popes plunged eagerly into the busy world

PETRARCH ON MOUNT VENTOUX

The Italian poet and scholar, Francesco Petrarch (1304–1374), has been called the first modern man. What this means is that his enthusiasm for classical Latin authors and for some of the pagan values—a desire for fame, above all—offers the earliest clear example of an intellectual movement known as *humanism*. But Petrarch was also a priest, and he looked back toward the Middle Ages as much as he looked forward to anything new or modern.

His own account of how he climbed Mount Ventoux, near Avignon in France, symbolizes the doubleness of Petrarch's life. He tells us that after some hours of climbing he reached the top and looked around to enjoy the view spread out magnificently below. The bridge across the Rhone River and the city of Avignon lay spread out before his eyes. Around and beyond these works of human hands stretched the surrounding hills and mountains, with glimpses of the Rhone sparkling in between.

But while contemplating how the grand works of humanity were dwarfed by the still grander works of God in the landscape below, Petrarch's mind suddenly turned inward. Overwhelmed with a sense of his folly at climbing a mountain simply to look at the view, he drew a copy of St. Augustine's *The City of God* from his pocket and began to read and meditate upon his own sinfulness. After a while he started down, careful to watch where he put his feet, but never raising his eyes to the view lest he lose sight of the state of his soul by enjoying the sights of the world.

---

of Italian politics, where they were merely one among other princes and rulers. Less and less attention was paid by the popes to the religious concerns of believers who were not willing to settle for routine administration of the sacraments by the Church—a Church preoccupied with raising and spending money for wars and diplomacy, erecting churches, and maintaining hospitals, schools, monasteries, and bishops' palaces.

PARLIAMENTARIANISM IN SECULAR GOVERNMENT   The idea and ideal of representative government had smaller scope in most royal governments. In France, for example, the Estates-General ceased to be important after 1439 when it voted to give the king the right to assess and collect taxes as needed. Nevertheless it did meet occasionally, at the king's command, until 1614.

In England, however, the Hundred Years' War had just the opposite effect. The king was always in need of more money for the wars in France, but the lords and commons of England were none too eager to give it to him. They made their feelings known through Parliament. Parliament developed from the custom of calling vassals to the lord's court at frequent intervals for consultation, feasting, and the settlement of any judicial business that might have arisen since the last meeting. In the time of Henry III, who reigned from 1216 to 1272, the circle of men whom the king of England consulted on such occasions was enlarged to include representatives of the towns and of smaller landholders from the shires.

In 1295 a parliament met that became the model for later ones. Its membership was made up of two representatives from each shire and the same number from each town that had a royal charter. These made up the House of Commons, which met separately from the House of Lords, where the great nobles, bishops, and abbots of the kingdom gathered, each invited individually by the king.

Throughout the Hundred Years' War, parliaments continued to meet. The House of Commons began to go slow in approving new taxes or renewing old ones until after the king had promised to "redress grievances." These were listed in bills which the king had to agree to before the Commons would approve new taxes. The effect of such a procedure was to limit the powers of the king, especially in matters of taxation, at a time when the French king's powers were being enlarged. It also meant that the royal government had to pay close attention to the wishes and interests of the propertied men of the kingdom represented in Parliament.

The House of Commons, however, was by no means proof against control by great landed nobles. During the Wars of the Roses (1455–1485), for example, Parliament almost ceased to function. Rival cliques of nobles fought one another in an effort to put their candidate on the throne. Many noble families were killed off in these wars before Henry Tudor emerged victorious in 1485. After he was crowned as Henry VII, he was able to establish a nearly absolute monarchy in England. Parliament nevertheless continued to meet, even though it usually accepted Henry's orders obediently.

In other parts of Europe, representative government also suffered setbacks. Generally speaking, princes and kings got stronger, and checks upon their power from representative assemblies—called Estates or Diets—became weaker. In Germany, however, it was not the central administration of the empire, but princes of the second rank—dukes, margraves, and bishops—that consolidated their authority. Each emperor's power depended on the family possessions he happened to have. This put the emperors more or less on the same level as other German princes, although they never entirely gave up the effort to revive some of the old imperial rights.

In northern and central Italy, town governments controlled most of the countryside. Until 1250 or later most of these towns were governed by some sort of coalition among the guilds; but as time passed, republican forms of government broke down more and more often. Harsh conflicts between rich and poor were part of the problem. A growing unwillingness of citizens to drop their other activities and fight as common soldiers created an even more critical weakness. For when military affairs came to be entrusted to hired bands of professional soldiers, sudden coups d'état could put the commander of such a band in charge of the city he was supposed to defend. But what one coup created, another could undo. Hence plot and counterplot produced innumerable sudden political shifts. Complicated alliances and factions racked the political life of almost all the cities of Italy.

The three most brilliant and important cities (except for Rome, where the popes remained political masters) were Venice, Milan, and Florence. Each followed a different political path. Venice came into the hands of a small group of patrician families after 1297. Milan, on the other hand, fell under the despotic rule of the Visconti (1277–1447) and then of the Sforza (1450–1535) families. Florence was at first more democratic, permitting lesser guilds to take part in city government; but from 1434, a wealthy banking family, the Medici, took control by acting as political bosses from behind the scenes, while leaving the republican forms of government unchanged.

In some remote and backward parts of Europe, monarchies remained weak, and local chieftains, of whatever kind, retained correspondingly greater importance. This was true in such lands as Scotland and Poland, for example. Free villages and associations of villages also survived in the Alps and in parts of Sweden and Norway. Taking western Europe as a whole, however, one must conclude that the effort to reform Church and state through representative forms of government clearly failed. The idea took fresh life in later times, to be sure, but in 1500 representative institutions looked like no more than outworn forms from a disorderly and half-barbarous past.

Religious Mysticism

Religious mysticism and doubt about the powers of human reason tended to replace the optimistic effort of the earlier age to fuse Aristotle and Christianity into a single, logical whole. William of Ockham (1300–1349), for example, was not convinced that Thomas Aquinas had really proved so much of Christian doctrine by reasoning. Ockham argued that faith and reason really had little to do with one another.

The more positive side of this kind of doubt was seen in personalities like Meister Eckhart (c. 1260–1327) and Thomas a Kempis (c. 1380–1471), who, as mystics, withdrew from the world of everyday in an effort to find God. *The Imitation of Christ*, a book of private devotions compiled by Thomas a Kempis, became and still remains a best seller. By searching within the individual soul and cultivating private virtues, this school of piety simply bypassed the tangled problem of how to reform the Church and human society. It found its main response in the Low Countries near the mouth of the Rhine.

Humanism and the Renaissance

Humanism looked to ancient Greek and Roman authors for inspiration in somewhat the same way that the mystics looked within themselves. The term "humanism" was invented to distinguish the study of humankind and humanity's affairs from theological study of God and God's relation to humanity. First Latin and then Greek authors were eagerly seized upon by scholars who found the moral code of Cicero, for example, or of Livy helpful in defining an ideal of conduct for themselves. Some scholars, especially in Florence, hoped to create a kind of public virtue that would sustain republican government; but most humanists were hangers-on at princely courts or attached themselves to the papacy. Their humanism offered a pattern for private life and gentility.

The poet and essayist Francesco Petrarch (1304–1374), a Florentine who served in a minor capacity at the papal court in Avignon for most of his life, was one of the first to express the humanist ideal. Others after him became great scholars. They combed through monastery librar-ies in search of forgotten classical texts. They discovered how to correct errors that had crept into ancient books as one copyist after another made blunders, and they found excitement and value in the labors of scholarship, which became an end in itself. A limited circle of wealthy patrons shared their enthusiasm and supported them.

When these scholarly skills were turned upon sacred texts and medi-eval charters, problems arose. Lorenzo Valla (1406–1457), you will remem-ber, took a careful look at the Donation of Constantine and was able to prove beyond all reasonable doubt that it was a forgery. This did not help the papal cause. The text of the Bible itself offered interesting problems also. But Italian humanists were too busy with pagan texts (and perhaps also too prudent) to try tampering with Holy Scripture. The first great scholar who attempted to purge errors from the text of the Bible was a Dutchman, Desiderius Erasmus (1466–1536).

Still another result of humanist activity was to discredit the living Latin of the Church. Cicero's diction and style were so extravagantly admired that some scholars felt *no* Latin word should be used that Cicero had not employed. This ruled out a vast vocabulary that had grown up in European learned circles. Not everyone accepted Ciceronian Latin as the only proper standard; but in proportion as this ideal did take hold, it choked off Latin as a living language.

Humanists believed they were reviving the glory of ancient literature and thought. They viewed their age as a kind of rebirth, or renaissance, of Latin literature, and invented the term "Middle Ages" to mark their own new age off from the dark ignorance of earlier centuries. Their choice of terms still dominates our view of Europe's history, even though we no longer think that the earlier years of the Middle Ages were so dark— and historians have applied the term "Renaissance" not simply to the rebirth of Latin literature but to a whole age, starting in Italy sometime about 1300, but spreading north of the Alps mainly after 1500.

Humanism and mysticism therefore, each in its own way, changed the texture of European thought and feeling; yet neither was entirely successful in coping with the problems of the age. The two movements represented opposite poles within the spectrum of European thought and feeling—the one emphasizing God almost to the exclusion of everything else; the other reversing matters and almost omitting God. Neither extreme could win general consent; the tension between them expressed the restlessness and dissatisfaction of the age.

The Mirror of the Age In Art

The two centuries from 1300 to 1500 were the time when western Europeans discovered a style of painting as powerful and original as the Gothic architecture of the period from 1150 to 1300 had been. The main centers of artistic development were Italy, especially Florence, and Flanders. Flemish art grew out of medieval manuscript illustration and always retained the rich colors and minute detail appropriate to illustrations. The greatest master was Jan van Eyck (1370–1440), whose realistic portraits and harmonious composition reflected the comfort and taste of upper-class life.

Italian painting developed out of Byzantine art styles. The need to decorate the walls of churches and other religious buildings gave a painter like Giotto (1276–1337) his main employment. A strain toward realism and accuracy of detail was apparent in Italian painting, just as in painting north of the Alps. The otherworldly effect attained by Byzantine elongation and other distortions of human figures did not satisfy western European tastes.

Methods for suggesting the roundness of limbs by skillful shading, for example, were invented by Masaccio (about 1401–1428); a few years later Leon Battista Alberti (1404–1472) discovered the geometrical rules for linear perspective. The trick was to make all parallel lines converge upon a disappearing point, located anywhere on the surface of the painting or, as was discovered later, even off the painting. By drawing figures and buildings to fit the differing scale thus established, an illusion of three-dimensional space could be created.

When painters first learned to construct their works of art on these principles, the effect was entrancing and delightful. It all looked so "real," as though the viewer could walk in among the figures and scenes of the picture! We are so accustomed to photographs that we can hardly imagine how exciting the new art was to eyes that had never before seen three dimensions accurately plotted on a two-dimensional surface.

The effort to achieve perfect accuracy and realism called forth further refinements: so-called aerial perspective, which changes colors with distance; and the use of living models for figures of saints and mythological figures. The subject matter of painting broadened to include pagan and historical themes. Sandro Botticelli's (1444–1510) *Birth of Venus* shows how far painting could go in a secular direction. Leonardo da Vinci's (1452–1519) *Virgin of the Rocks* shows how far a religious theme could be humanized.

Renaissance painting was matched by changes in sculpture and architecture. Roman remains were plentiful in Italy, and the humanist enthusiasm for things ancient spread also among architects and sculptors, who assumed that what the Romans had done must be superior. Accordingly, Donatello (1386–1466) introduced free-standing nude statues again in imitation of classical works. Michelangelo (1475–1564) brought the Renaissance sculptural tradition to its climax just a century later.

Architecture was too closely tied to everyday wants and to the requirements of church services to imitate the ancient models exactly. But Renaissance architecture freely borrowed decorative details, such as columns and "egg and dart" design moldings. Grand and harmonious effects were sometimes achieved, the most famous example being St. Peter's Church in Rome, built between 1445 and 1626.

In painting and sculpture, as well as in architecture, tension between sacred and secular attitudes can be seen almost everywhere. Realism and interest in visual detail suggest the joys of ordinary human existence;

yet the subject matter was more often than not religious. How to keep the two in harness was the great unsolved question people faced all over western Europe. It remained critical throughout the following century.

CONCLUSION

About 1450 western Europe seemed to be in real trouble. The bloom of the High Middle Ages was definitely a thing of the past. Internal struggles had hardened lines almost everywhere. Alternative ideals for reform and a new start seemed to be getting nowhere. Certainly neither representative government nor humanism was providing a solution to the quarrels that racked European society; and mystical religion did not even try to do so. The Turkish capture of Constantinople in 1453 showed that Islam was again on the march. No state of Christian Europe was in a position to meet the Turks on anything like even terms. Art of the Italian Renaissance was lovely, but quite unable to resolve social tensions.

Yet in fact Europe was on the verge of its most dramatic expansion. After the event, it is possible to see some of the things that were at work in European society, which made possible the extraordinary age of exploration and self-transformation that came to Euorpe between 1500 and 1650.

First, Europe's economy activated a larger proportion of the whole population than commonly happened elsewhere. Coarse and common articles came regularly into the market for sale and purchase: wool, fish, timber, plowshares. This meant that relatively large numbers of people benefited and suffered from the ups and downs of prices. Responses to price changes drove workers into some lines of activity and out of others. This made Europe's economy flexible. Even fixed agricultural routines were less unchanging than elsewhere in the civilized world. When opportunity offered, labor and resources could be mobilized for new projects on a greater scale than was possible in more custom-bound societies.

This was Europe's first strength. It was the reverse side of the economic frictions and uncertainty that fomented struggles between rich and poor. The absence of any single, controlling center meant, also, that no distant imperial order could turn off sea ventures, for example, as had happened in China when the Ming emperors called all seagoing vessels home.

A second element in Europe's life that proved advantageous in the long run, though also very costly, was the warlikeness that ran all the way through European society. Peasants and townspeople were in the habit of defending themselves; they did not meekly submit to their social superiors. And the nobles of Europe were specialists in war. Only the Japanese were as ready to resort to violence, or as dedicated to a code of personal heroism. In China the rulers of society were more pacific. In Islam peasants and townspeople knew their place and usually did not try to fight back.

A third element was Europe's acquaintance with three new techniques whose potentialities had only begun to be explored in 1500. These were (1) printing with movable type and the more rapid and exact diffusion of knowledge that printing permitted; (2) the compass and other improvements in shipbuilding and navigation that made it reasonably safe to sail across even the roughest oceans of the world; and (3) gunpowder and artillery techniques that made bombardment even of strongly defended places very effective.

Finally, there was in Europe's habit of mind an ingrained recklessness that allowed adventurers to carry any new project or idea to its extreme limits. The old Greek motto, "Nothing too much," was the exact opposite of this spirit. Europe's motto might better have been, "Overdo it, please!"

For all these reasons, and perhaps for others we are not wise enough to recognize, the fraying out of Europe's medieval synthesis did not lead to deadlock. Instead, it proved to be the preface to new and world-shaking changes within Europe and among the civilizations and barbarian cultures of the entire world.

BREAKTHROUGHS IN THE USE OF ENERGY AND FUEL

Muscles came first: arm, leg, and tongue. Then were tamed a few big animals strong enough to carry heavy loads or pull great weights. The horse, ox, camel, and water buffalo were the most important of these sources of power; and until two hundred years ago they remained, with human muscles, the most important sources of power humans knew.

Yet from very early times people also tapped inanimate forms of power. Fire, for example, unlocked chemical energy—and from Paleolithic times, hunters used fire to warm themselves and to cook. Later civilized peoples made fire to bake pottery and smelt metals as well.

This was only the beginning. Wind, water, coal, electricity, and most recently nuclear energy have all been put to work for men's purposes with consequences— good and bad, foreseen and unforeseen— that have entirely transformed our natural environment.

Natural Power of Water and Wind

The Romans made the swift-flowing river Tiber grind grain into flour to feed the swollen populace of their city in the first century B.C. The principle was simple: a paddle wheel half in and half out of the river revolved as the flowing water pressed against each paddle.

Windmills worked on a similar principle but were invented later. The earliest known came from central Asia, where Buddhists used them to launch prayers to heaven. Later, windmills were put to more material uses—for grinding grain, pumping water, and driving other machines.

HIGHLIGHTS

Wind and watermills provided a new source of mechanical power that could be put to many uses.

The great advantage was that, once a mill had been built, the power cost nothing and it could be put to work whenever the water flowed or the wind blew.

The main disadvantage was that, for many centuries, no one had a steady flow of grain to be ground or wood to be sawed. The superior work capacity of water and wind was wasted.

Since it was expensive to build mills initially, they were not much used until the sixteenth and seventeenth centuries in Europe, when improvements in transportation did make it possible to keep water and windmills steadily at work.

Explosive Power of Gunpowder

Gunpowder is a chemical mixture that does not need to take oxygen from the air in order to "burn." When ignited almost all of it turns into gas. The effect, in an enclosed chamber, is explosive.

The Chinese discovered gunpowder about A.D. 1000. They used it first to blow up fortified gates by filling hollow chambers of bamboo with the explosive mixture and pushing them under the closed gates. Soon afterward the Chinese began experimenting with hollow metal pots, filled with gunpowder and open at one end, which they used as primitive guns.

Europeans started similar experiments in the thirteenth century, having learned about gunpowder probably from China via the Mongol Empire. By 1500, Europeans excelled in the manufacture of big guns, perhaps because they already had a highly developed metallurgy. Peaceful

A water mill constructed in the 19th century.
(*Virginia State Travel Service*)

uses for explosives, as in mining for instance, came later, mainly in the nineteenth and twentieth centuries.

HIGHLIGHTS   Gunpowder altered warfare and government in far-reaching ways all over the world.

> Big guns were expensive, and only a few rulers could pay for them. Those who did could knock down their rivals' castle walls. Large terrritorial states could be built with the help of big guns.
>
> Handguns became important in warfare only in the seventeenth century. Infantry armed with guns overcame the age-old superiority of steppe cavalry. This allowed the Russian and Chinese empires, in the eighteenth century, to divide the steppelands of Eurasia between them.

Expansive Power of Steam

Modern steam engines let steam under pressure flow into a cylinder, closed at one end by a close-fitting piston. Steam pressure then makes the piston move. There were different ways of bringing the piston back again. The earliest type of engine in common use allowed the steam to condense, so that atmospheric pressure

pushed the piston back. James Watt in 1776 improved upon this method by using valves to let the steam both into and out of the cylinder. A heavy balance wheel carried the piston back, expelling the old steam and readying the cylinder for the next rush of high-pressure steam.

The steam engine was soon put to work at many different tasks, like pumping, driving trains, and activating machinery in factories.

HIGHLIGHTS   Steam engines could be set up where fuel was easily found.

> Since coal fires were the easiest way to produce steam, available coal beds became the prime factor controlling the location of heavy industry after 1850, when the steam engine came into its own.
>
> Because the steam engine was invented in Great Britain, the British achieved a head start over all other peoples in exploiting the potential of the new, cheap, and flexible source of power.
>
> The many possibilities opened by the use of steam power between 1776 and 1850 made this the era of the Industrial Revolution in Britain and western Europe.

Gunpowder was invented by the Chinese, who used it in the manufacture of fireworks and weapons. (*Library of Congress*)

An electrical storm. (*NOAA, National Oceanic and Atmospheric Administration*)

Electricity as a source of power is clean, and it can be precisely controlled.

In time, electricity opens the possibility of modulating power at short intervals. This allows refinements in manufacture otherwise unattainable.

In space, electrical power can reach down to the level of individual molecules and atoms by ionizing them. This opens the possibility for new kinds of processes, like silver-plating.

Electrical power also allows worldwide instantaneous communication, making precise information readily available to government, business, and other decision-makers.

Enormous Power of the Atom

All humanity's earlier adventures in harnessing diverse forms of energy have been

A French musketeer. (*Library of Congress*)

Instantaneous Power of Electricity

Lightning and static electricity awed and puzzled humankind from earliest times, but not until the nineteenth century did anyone begin to learn how to control the power of electrical currents. Electric motors on a toy scale were known as early as 1831, but it was the 1880s when engineers began to conceive of building large-scale dynamos to supply electric current to large numbers of customers.

Electric power was first used for interior lighting. But in the twentieth century more uses for electricity in industry have been found, with the result that heavy cables have largely replaced steam engines as energy sources in modern factories.

dwarfed by the most recent breakthrough: the controlled release of nuclear energy. The first successful experiment took place in Chicago in 1942, and atomic energy was initially used for making the bombs dropped on Nagasaki and Hiroshima at the close of World War II. Peaceful uses of atomic energy include the generation of electricity and underground blasting.

Atomic energy was developed by highly-trained scientists acting on extremely abstract mathematical theory. Theory and practice had been closely linked in the development of electrical power too, but not as deliberately and consciously or on such a scale as in this case.

HIGHLIGHTS

By converting matter itself into energy, atomic power offers an almost limitless supply of energy.

Such a storehouse of potential energy can be used for any and all of the peaceful purposes to which electrical and other forms of power have been put.

At the same time, atomic energy has the potential for destroying all higher forms of life.

Systematic application of scientific theory to the improvement of techniques was carried through successfully in unlocking atomic energy. The development of new products and manufacturing processes is faster than ever.

Costs of Power Over Nature

Humanity's enormous triumphs in using power for its own purposes involve unexpected and unwished-for costs. Too rapid changes in machinery strained modern society by asking people to alter their habits too fast; too reckless a use of power in manufacturing products has upset the natural environment in ways we do not fully understand.

The use of nuclear reactors to produce electricity, while not without risks, has facilitated the production of generally low-cost energy. (American Electric Power Service Corporation)

Still, some of the risks are clear. Carbon dioxide added to the atmosphere by burning coal and other fuels alters the way sunlight reaches the earth. A "greenhouse effect" may melt glaciers, raise sea levels, and alter climates.

The risks of nuclear radiation are more obvious and sure. Disposal of radioactive wastes from nuclear power plants is difficult, and the risks of accidental disaster are immensely dangerous, as the Russians found out in 1986 at Chernobyl. Nuclear warheads, fired in anger, threaten to destroy all human life by disrupting the balances of nature irremediably.

The State
of the World,
1500

Let us pause now to survey the world on the eve of Europe's oceanic discoveries and compare it with the state of the world 2000 years before. The four styles of civilization that had appeared by 500 B.C. were still much in evidence in A.D. 1500. China, India, the Middle East, and Europe each continued to support a civilization of its own; and in many ways the basic structures of each civilization were unchanged from what had been there 2000 years before in each of the areas concerned. Innumerable changes had come in detail. Ideas and skills had passed from one end of the civilized world to another. But still the European emphasis upon territorial states, the Middle Eastern concern with monotheism, the Indian caste system, and the Chinese familial form of government and social order continued to shape the lives of everyone belonging to each of these civilizations.

The territory on which civilized life flourished had increased so much that by 1500 an almost continuous belt of civilized land ran across Europe and Asia from the Atlantic to the Pacific Ocean; and important new off-shoots had developed to the north and south of the four main civilizations. The rise of medieval Europe meant a shift northward from the Mediterranean Sea to a focus in the drainage area of the North Sea and English Channel. The conversion of Russia involved an even greater northward displacement of the center of gravity for the Orthodox Christian world from Constantinople to Moscow.

(*Library of Congress*)

Moreover, in 500 B.C. Greek civilization had been a very new, small, and sharply focused pattern of life, planted around the Aegean Sea. By A.D. 1500 its heirs and successors had taken in so much from the barbarian world of the north, and from the Middle and Far Eastern civilizations, that the sharp definition of the early days was gone. Instead, the Greeks' European heirs had created two branches of Christendom—Greek, Orthodox and Roman Catholic—that were so different from each other as to justify counting them as separate civilizations.

ASIAN CIVILIZATIONS

A similar development had taken place along China's northeastern borderlands; for, as we have seen, by 1500 Japanese civilization had become different from Chinese patterns of life. It should, therefore, be counted as a separate civilization, too. Finally, the Moslem world had penetrated all of the western and central steppe region of Asia. It would not be wise to count the culture of the Golden Horde or of the other nomadic confederations as new civilizations. The way of the nomad could never sustain the range of specialisms we expect of a civilization. Yet the steppe peoples were deeply tinged with Islamic civilization and distinct in their ways of life from their settled neighbors. Let us say, therefore, that a semicivilization or high barbarism had arisen on the western and central steppes, related to Islam in the way that the new northern civilizations of Japan and Europe were related to ancient Chinese and ancient Mediterranean civilizations.

To the south, the expansion of civilization created a more diverse pattern. In southeast Asia, for example, those living in Sumatra and Java and mainland peoples living in what is today Thailand (formerly Siam), Cambodia, and Vietnam had come into touch with Indian civilization about the time of Christ; but by 600 they all began to develop independent art styles of their own. Fusion between local fertility cults and Buddhist and Hindu ideas produced a series of court cultures of great splendor. They are known to us mainly through the ruins of massive temples and palaces. But creating the social and political organization required to build such monuments was itself a great feat; and these cultures deserve the term "civilization" just as much as do the achievements of the Sumerian, Inca, or Aztec peoples. The comparison is, indeed, hard to avoid. Like the ancient river valley civilizations and the Amerindian civilizations, each of the civilizations of southeast Asia consisted of a great temple-palace and court set in the midst of simple peasant villages, with very little in between.

In Java and Sumatra, civilization was sustained by shipping; on the mainland, each big river valley provided the setting for a local court civilization. Each river valley was more or less self-contained, with fertile rice fields and only limited trade or other contacts with the outside world. The Indian imprint was strong everywhere, but it always mingled with differing native customs. After about 800 the region was also influenced by Moslems, who dominated the sea trade and eventually (1520s) conquered Java and Sumatra. The inland valleys, however, escaped Moslem control. Their rulers simply cut off most contact with the outside by preventing strangers from coming upriver. This policy left the landward, northern borders unguarded.

Thus, for example, the Khmers in the Mekong Valley built enormous temple-palaces at Angkor Wat and Angkor Thom. But by 1431 invaders from the north—the Thais—broke up their empire and established a more warlike state of their own based on the neighboring Menam Valley. The Burmans came down from the north at about the same time as the Thais. Both of these groups were dislodged by Chinese expansion. The newcomers preferred Buddhism to the mixed Hindu-Buddhism of the earlier em-

Wood carvings from the Yoruba tribe in Nigeria, ca. late 15th century. The Yorubas became very skilled in sculpture and carving in wood, ivory, and bronze. (American Museum of Natural History)

pires; they were more military, less withdrawn, but did not create such vast and impressive architectural monuments as the Khmers had done.

AFRICAN CIVILIZATIONS

In Africa, too, a cluster of court civilizations came into existence, not only in the Islamic portions of east and west Africa, but also much deeper in the continent. In the Congo basin, for example, a pagan kingdom of Kongo existed when the Portuguese first appeared along the coast. Farther south a similar empire of Monomotapa centered on the east coast between the Zambezi and Limpopo rivers.

These relatively large states were created by Bantu-speaking peoples who had begun to spread through central and southern Africa soon after the time of Christ, starting out from a region around the Bight of Benin, where the west African coast turns southward toward the Cape of Good Hope. The spread of the Bantu peoples probably started when Indonesian food crops, suited to cultivation in the heavy rain forest of the Congo basin, reached them. At an unknown later date some Bantu tribes acquired cattle, perhaps from Nubia. A much more rapid movement down the highland spine of east Africa then began, as cattle herders drifted south looking for new pastures for their animals. Hottentot and Pygmy hunters retreated south before the advancing Bantus or withdrew into the shadows of the dense Congo rain forests.

Trade with Moslems brought a large part of Africa into touch with the rest of the world. Caravans regularly crossed the Sahara from north to south, connecting the cities and kingdoms of west Africa with the Mediterranean. In addition, traders and raiders moved east-west through the grassy savanna country that lay south of the Sahara.

By both these routes west Africa came into close touch with Islam. A series of imperial states arose after the overthrow of Ghana (1076) that united large areas of west Africa under a single monarch. The rulers and their courts all professed Islam and drew a major part of their income from trade. The most important of these states were the Mali Empire, which reached its peak soon after 1300, and the Songhai Empire, which ruled most of the Niger River region (and beyond) by 1500.

The fact that rulers and traders were Moslem did not make the common people into followers of Mohammed. Many villages in west Africa remained loyal to older, "pagan" forms of religion. They were little affected by the rise of the new empires, except when someone came from the capital and made the villagers perform some labor service (for example, carrying heavy goods to market) or forced them to give up part of their crop as a form of tax.

The imperial courts, however, like those of southeast Asia, were splendid indeed. Gold dust was abundant in the Niger and its tributaries. Rulers organized the search for gold and took possession of what was found. This made the monarchs of Mali and Songhai very rich. Merchants from all parts of the Moslem world were eager to exchange luxuries of every sort for African gold and ivory.

A trade in slaves also existed in parts of Africa, mainly along the east coast. But this way of exploiting African manpower was not nearly as important as it became later, after the discovery of America.

All in all, Africa remained on the margins of the civilized world up to 1500. Powerful states and grand courts had come into existence in several parts of the continent; agriculture and herding were expanding southward quite fast; and a large part of the entire continent had entered

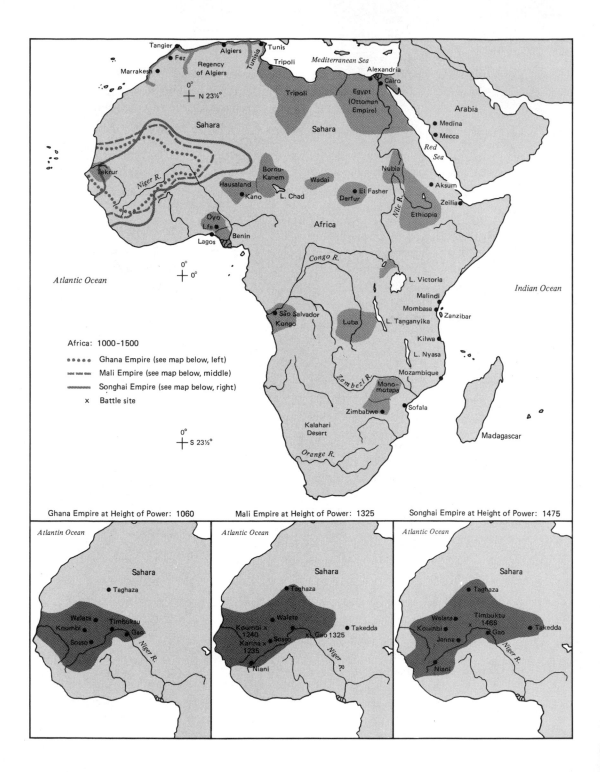

Ghana Empire at Height of Power: 1060   Mali Empire at Height of Power: 1325   Songhai Empire at Height of Power: 1475

into trade relations with the outside world. But due to tropical diseases and to the fact that all the African rivers (except the Nile) have falls near their mouths, it was hard for strangers to penetrate deeply; and the Africans themselves mostly lived in small, self-sufficient villages and had only a few contacts with anyone outside their own immediate community.

Specialized skills, elaborate social organization, and other hallmarks of civilized life were definitely present in Africa. But they were concentrated at a few courtly centers. Moreover, these centers were vulnerable, like the temple-palaces of southeast Asia and of the Americas, because the common people shared scarcely at all in the benefits of civilization. Instead, they had to pay taxes and perform labor services for the rulers, and we may assume they did not like it. The early civilizations of the Middle East and of all other parts of the world had been just the same and suffered from the same basic weakness. Africa, like the Americas and southeast Asia, was simply at an earlier stage of development at the time when the opening of the world's oceans to European shipping fundamentally changed relations among all the world's civilizations.

NEW WORLD CIVILIZATIONS

Across the ocean in the Americas, the "imperial" period, which seems to have begun about 1000, moved toward recorded history when the Aztecs began to build an empire in Mexico (c. 1400) and the Incas extended their power over all of Peru (c. 1438) and Ecuador (c. 1500). The Inca Empire was a tightly administered, bureaucratic regime. The Aztec state, however, exerted only a loose control over surrounding peoples. The Aztecs, in fact, spent much effort on raids required to round up the large numbers of captives that were needed to appease the Aztec gods, who fed on human hearts. No strong and stable empire could arise on the basis of such a relation between the Aztecs and their neighbors.

Tenochtitlan, the Aztec capital, was nonetheless a large and splendid city. It was situated on islands in a shallow lake, connected to the mainland by narrow causeways.

Vast temples, great marketplaces thronged by buyers and sellers, and stately palace rituals disguised the inherent frailty of Aztec society. Elsewhere in Mexico other palace and temple centers had evolved into genuine cities as well. To the north, in what is now the United States, many different agricultural and hunting peoples existed. Some of them were organized to support large ceremonial centers, vaguely modeled on the more splendid civilizations of Mexico. The Mayas, on the other

The Bayon, a gigantic temple at Angkor Thom containing many reliefs which illustrate various aspects of Khmer civilization. (*Laimute E. Druskis*)

hand, who had once supported temples and priests, relapsed towards simple peasant village life after about 1400, when their last imperial center in Yucatan somehow lost its hold on the surrounding countryside.

Peru, too, supported a series of impressive cities, some of them defended by enormous walls of stone. Roads and irrigation works were more elaborate than anything known in Mexico; and Inca rulers kept records by means of an ingenious arrangement of knots in fringed leather. Forms of picture writing also existed among the Aztecs; and calendrical calculations continued to play an important part in religious ceremonies, as they had among the ancient Maya.

Altogether, then, Amerindian civilizations, like those of Africa and southeast Asia, were in a flourishing condition in 1500, even though their skills and level of organization never caught up with the major centers of the Old World.

THE BALANCE OF WORLD CIVILIZATIONS

Obviously, the civilizations of southeast Asia, of sub-Saharan Africa, and of America were of a different magnitude from the four great "main stems" of Europe and Asia. Far more people shared Chinese, Indian, Islamic, and European styles of civilization than took part in any of these temple-palace civilizations. No single blow could disrupt one of the great civilizations. Devastation of a single center was not enough to destroy the tradition of skill, learning, and taste that made each civilization what it was. By contrast, devastation of a single center or of a few separate centers could easily destroy the weaker civilizations of the Americas, as the Spaniards soon proved. Southeast Asian civilizations were nearly as fragile. Moslem conquest of Java, for example, exterminated the Hindu court culture of that island, and the Thais did the same to the Khmers in Cambodia.

If temple-palace civilizations were so fragile when exposed to sudden, brutal contact with the outside world, how much more defenseless were the remaining primitive peoples of the earth! All the warlike populations of Eurasia had shouldered their way into the circle of recorded history by the time of the Mongol Empire. But farther from the centers of civilized life, peaceable hunters still survived. Such tribes occupied Australia and southern Africa; and Eskimo hunters had recently spread all the way round the Arctic coastline, preying upon seals and walrus that lived on the ice. But, by and large, only refuge zones remained. Primitive life was being pushed to the far corners of the earth.

In 1500 the four main stem civilizations of Europe and Asia were still more or less equal to one another in their skills and attainments. Europe had metals, ships, and guns, but was far behind the other great civilizations in refinement of artisan skills. China was by far the most populous, but after the experience of the Mongol conquest the Chinese deliberately decided to retire from the sea in order to concentrate on defense against the threat from the steppes. Islam, of all the great civilizations, seemed the strongest and most successful in expanding its frontiers. In particular, a majority of the steppe nomads had been won over to the service of Islam. This imparted a tremendous military drive to the Moslem world, for it was the steppe nomads who had harassed and invaded civilized lands of Eurasia, time after time after time, for a full 2000 years. India, of the four civilizations, seemed the weakest, lying passive under the political domination of Islam. But India's greatest successes in influencing other peoples had never depended on military or economic strength; and one can argue that the rise of Sufi mysticism within Islam was yet another demonstration of the quiet, subtle power of Indian influences. Certainly the Sufi path and the piety of Indian holy men had much in common; and in suffering Moslem conquest, Hindu India had by no means lost the ability to convert their conquerors to traditional Indian ways of thinking.

Western Europe, therefore, was only one of four civilizations and, at least on the surface, not the most promising, strongest, or most successful of the four. Yet Europe's readiness to learn and experiment, to change its own habits in the light of new experiences, and, above all, never to flinch from the next confrontation meant that in three and a half centuries, between 1500 and 1850, a fundamental reversal of balance took place. Europe ceased, in that time, to be one among equals. It became instead the center of by far the strongest and most skillful civilization in the world.

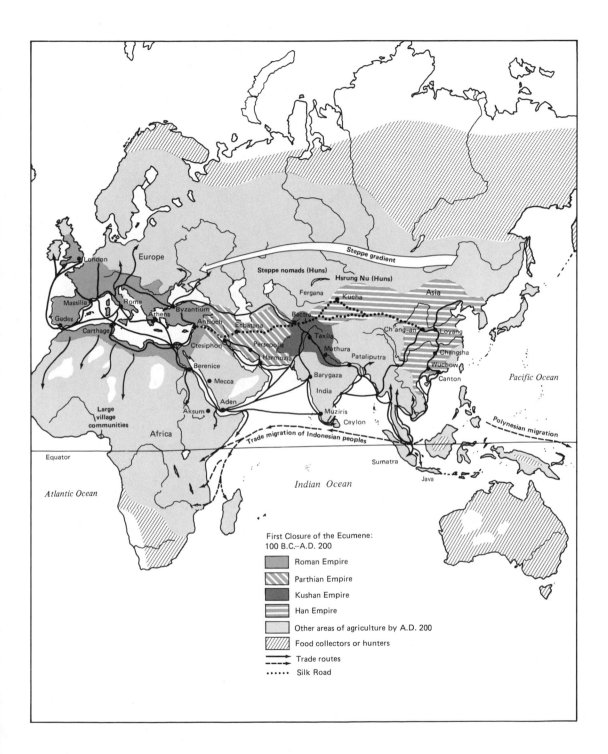

London

Europe

Massilia

Rome

Gades

Athens   Byzantium

Carthage

Antioch

Ecbatana

Ctesiphon

Persepolis

Harmozia

Berenice

Mecca

Aden

Aksum

Large village communities

Africa

Atlantic Ocean

Equator

Indian Ocean

Steppe gradient

Steppe nomads (Huns)

Hsrung Nu (Huns)

Fergana

Kucha

Asia

Bactra

Taxila

Mathura

Pataliputra

Barygaza

India

Muziris

Ceylon

Ch'ang-an

Loyang

Changsha

Wuchow

Canton

Pacific Ocean

Polynesian migration

Trade migration of Indonesian peoples

Sumatra

Java

First Closure of the Ecumene:
100 B.C.--A.D. 200

Roman Empire

Parthian Empire

Kushan Empire

Han Empire

Other areas of agriculture by A.D. 200

Food collectors or hunters

Trade routes

Silk Road

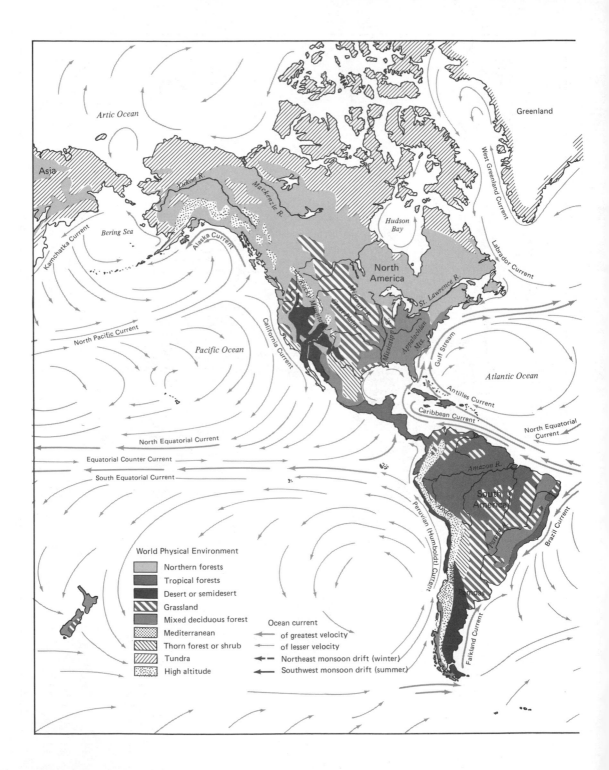

Arctic Ocean

Greenland

Asia

Kamchatka Current

Bering Sea

Yukon R.

Mackenzie R.

Alaska Current

Hudson Bay

North America

West Greenland Current

Labrador Current

North Pacific Current

Pacific Ocean

California Current

Rocky Mountains

Missouri R.

Great Plains

Mississippi R.

St. Lawrence R.

Appalachian Mts.

Gulf Stream

Atlantic Ocean

North Equatorial Current

Antilles Current

Caribbean Current

North Equatorial Current

Equatorial Counter Current

South Equatorial Current

Amazon R.

South America

World Physical Environment

- Northern forests
- Tropical forests
- Desert or semidesert
- Grassland
- Mixed deciduous forest
- Mediterranean
- Thorn forest or shrub
- Tundra
- High altitude

Ocean current

← of greatest velocity
← of lesser velocity
◄-- Northeast monsoon drift (winter)
◄━ Southwest monsoon drift (summer)

Peruvian (Humboldt) Current

Andes

Paraná R.

Pampas

Brazil Current

Falkland Current

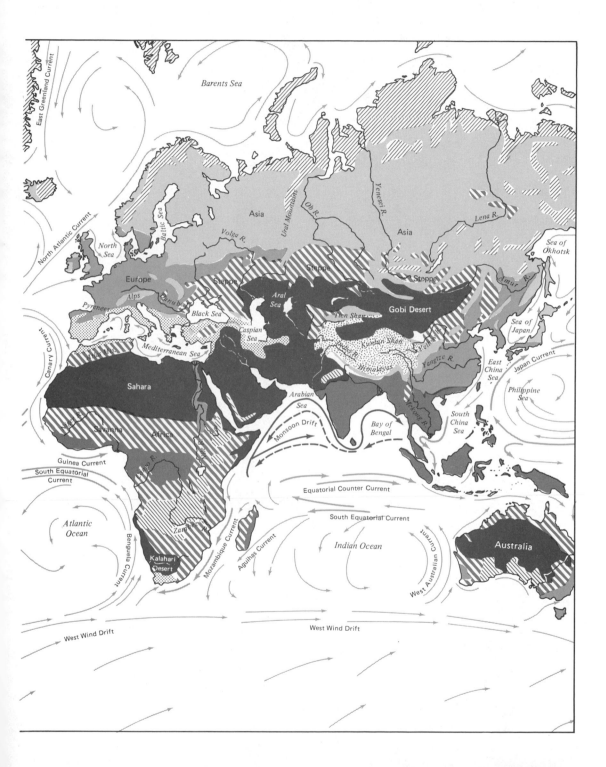

461

Volume II

A HISTORY OF THE HUMAN COMMUNITY

1500 to the Present

CHAPTER 1

The
Great European
Discoveries

1480 to 1550

In our modern age when radio and telephone enable us to maintain instantaneous contact all round the world, it takes an act of imagination to think what it was like to live in a world bounded on every side by the gray shadow of regions utterly unknown, and at a time when news of great happenings in the more distant parts of the known world might take months to reach even the best-informed persons. Yet this was the sort of world in which everyone lived 500 years ago. Of course some people knew more than others about other lands. The immense majority were peasants, who seldom knew or cared anything about regions more than twenty or perhaps fifty miles from where they labored in the fields. Merchants knew more. Some of them traveled thousands of miles to and fro along caravan routes or by sea during all of their active lives. Many such adventurers wandered off the beaten track once in a while; but unless they found something new they could use in trade, they would seldom go back a second time, and whatever they reported about their explorations soon faded from the memories of other merchants and travelers. Merchants' lore about routes and markets, wars and famines, passed almost always by word of mouth and was seldom written down. Even such a remarkable adventure as that of Marco Polo was recorded by merest chance. In later life, Marco Polo found himself in prison with a fellow prisoner who could write and who chose to write down the strange tale Marco Polo had to tell. Except for these unusual circumstances, we would know absolutely nothing of his adventures at the court of Kublai Khan.

Side by side with the flow of gossip exchanged by long distance travelers was another and usually quite separate tradition of knowledge about the geography of the earth based on books. From the time of the ancient Greeks, learned Europeans all knew that the earth was spherical. They even had a map of the world based on one drawn up about A.D. 150 by the astronomer and geographer, Ptolemy of Alexandria. Moslems shared this Greek inheritance and added to it a substantial body of travelers' reports about remote regions of the Eurasian world. The learned classes of other civilizations were less influenced by the mathematical calculations made by Ptolemy and his predecessors. The Chinese, for instance, took the view that their own land was the center of everything and measured all others by their distance from the "Middle Kingdom." Hindu tradition located a great mountain (the Himalayas?) at the center of the earth. Other people had still different traditional maps of the world's geography. But even the most learned, just like merchants and like simple peasants, always faced a limit beyond which the layout of the earth's surface was a blank.

In the half century between 1492 when Columbus discovered America and 1542 or 1543 when a Portuguese ship first visited Japan, European seafarers went far to fill in the blanks that had existed for so long in western Europeans' knowledge of the geography of the earth. Discoveries were pushed inland by missionaries who set out to convert Asians and Amerindians to Christianity, and by military men who overwhelmed the Aztec and Inca empires in the Americas and probed other less-developed regions of the Americas, Africa, and the Spice Islands (the Moluccas) of Indonesia.

It took a long time before other civilized people heard of these great European discoveries; but within Europe itself the news of the American and Asian worlds spread speedily, even among very humble people. Europeans broke down the old separations between learned tradition and the experience of travelers. News of fresh discoveries got into print. Books of exploration found ready sale, as stay-at-homes eagerly read about the wonders of far places. Map makers, too, set out to chart the new discoveries and arranged all the newly discovered lands in their proper places according to mathematical methods for projecting a curved surface onto the flat surface of a map.

New knowledge of the world's geography was not the only lasting consequence of the European discoveries. For when the habitable seacoasts of all the earth had been linked together more closely than ever before by European shipping, trade began to follow new routes. Exchanges of goods also attained greater volume than before in many parts of the globe. New crops and new diseases spread widely. Enlarged food supplies and heavier death rates from hitherto unknown diseases resulted.

Reactions in the different parts of the world differed sharply. Western Europe profited most directly. New products, new techniques, new ideas, and a new perspective on the world as a whole all swarmed in upon the nations that had initiated the new patterns of contact among the peoples of the earth. They were free to pick and choose among all the new things that competed for their attention, with no sense of being threatened or endangered by novelty, since it was they and they alone who had started it all in the first place. This openness to change put a special energy behind Europe's self-transformation throughout early modern times.

Eventually, Europe's willingness to experiment with new techniques and ideas put European or western civilization ahead of all the other civilizations of the world in some very important ways. But for a long time, Europe's superiority was not very obvious. Both the Moslems and Far Easterners preferred their own well-worn habits and customs to anything that Europeans had to offer. The strength and skill these people had at their command, together with the distances that separated them from the European center, allowed them to follow their own paths for centuries.

Nevertheless, a new era of world history dawned when the Americas entered for the first time into the interacting circle of civilized humanity and when Europe's restless probing and self-revolution launched a force upon the world with which the rest of humanity, sooner or later, had to cope. The Eurasian Far West, previously at one extreme edge of the civilized world, therefore became central to the subsequent history of all humankind. When that happened, modern history began.

PROBLEMS OF SEAFARING

The seas and oceans of the world are by no means uniform. Winds, tides, and currents all make an enormous difference, especially to ships that do not have powerful motors to drive them through the water. Only when seafarers learned how to make their ships sail upwind as well as downwind could they hope to travel safely in the stormy, tidal waters of the North Atlantic that touch Europe's western shores. On the other hand, abundant fish life provided a constant lure, for anyone who could sail those stormy seas in safety could make a living by catching fish.

A late Medieval European ship illustrated in religious art. Note the high fore and after castles and the heavy masts. (*Art Resource*)

Other seas are not as dangerous as the North Atlantic. In the Mediterranean Sea, for example, for about half the year the trade winds blow steadily from the northeast, and storms do not occur. This was the season when Greek and Roman mariners sailed. A voyage late in the year was considered very risky, for then storms might blow the ship ashore on a rocky coast. Oars could help guide the ship into harbor or out again; but on the open sea sails were essential, even for war galleys with hundreds of rowers. The Romans never mastered the northern seas where storms might occur at any season. Even crossing the channel from France to Britain was a risky enterprise. Longer voyages were rarely attempted.

In the Indian Ocean, however, the monsoons made seafaring comparatively simple. Half the year the winds blew from one direction at almost an even pace; half the year they reversed themselves, so that return voyages were particularly easy. The broad trade-wind zones of the Pacific and Atlantic oceans were like the Mediterranean during the summer months. Throughout these zones a steady northeast wind in the Northern Hemisphere, or a southeast wind in the Southern Hemisphere, could propel sailing ships through bright, cool, clear air every day in the year. Near the American and Asian continents, to be sure, tropical storms could interrupt the regularity of the trade winds. But they occur only during a well-defined season (August to October) and affect the weather for only a few days of the year.

In the tropical zone between the two trade-wind belts the air is often dead calm. Winds are local and usually die away after a few hours. In this region the air is thinned as the sun warms it and then gets pushed aloft by the inrushing denser and cooler air from more northerly and more southerly latitudes. It is this that creates the trade winds, which push toward the tropics to take the place of the thinned and heated air of that region.

Navigation of the tropic zone offered a problem to sailing ships, since light and variable winds might leave a vessel becalmed for weeks on end. Still, there was no great danger in lying becalmed, and ocean currents might allow a skilled captain to travel even without wind in the direction he desired. Conversely, if he had planned his course without due regard for winds and currents, he might find himself traveling backward, willy-nilly. Experiences of this sort quickly taught European navigators where favorable and unfavorable winds and currents could be expected; and as that knowledge spread, voyaging across the vast distances of the oceans became quite easy. Anywhere in the trade-wind zones— and they occupied a large part of the entire ocean area of the earth—a sailing ship could move at least a hundred miles a day. These regions, therefore, became the throughways of the age of the sail.

As soon as European sailors learned how to navigate successfully in the stormy North Atlantic, the trade-wind and tropic zones of the oceans offered no serious dangers. On the contrary, sailing in such gentle waters was easy by comparison with the problems sailors had to solve in the coastal waters of northern Europe.

European Shipbuilding and Navigation

Throughout the Middle Ages, European shipbuilders and sailors made progress in mastering the dangers of the North Atlantic. But not until shortly before 1500 were all the technical and financial problems worked out successfully. The reason was that European mariners decided, from early in the Middle Ages, to try something radically new, building a ship big enough and strong enough to cut through the waves instead of riding upon them, as smaller and lighter vessels did.

Long before the developments of the Middle Ages, a different solution to the problems of navigating on the stormy seas of the North Atlantic had been tried, quite successfully, by early navigators. Small, saucer-shaped craft, made of wickerwork and covered with watertight animal skins, could only carry a few persons—usually no more than three or four. But such *coracles* (to give them their proper name) could sail before the wind across very rough seas, rising and falling with the waves like a cork. Vessels such as these carried Irish missionaries as far as Iceland in the early Middle Ages; and similar craft carried the ancient megalithic folk to and fro along the Atlantic shores of Europe and Africa, beginning about 2000 B.C. Coracles were light enough to be picked up and taken safely ashore by two or three persons; and they were small enough to be rowed or paddled for short distances against the wind. They were, in short, quite seaworthy so long as they stayed close to shore where refuge against headwinds could be found. Coracles actually remained in use for fishing off the shores of Ireland until about 1900.

By A.D. 900 the Vikings put an end to long-distance travel by coracles. The Viking ships were far bigger and carried crews of forty to a hundred men. Coracles were easy prey for such ships; and when travel in unprotected vessels ceased to be safe, sailors soon lost the skills needed for long-distance coracle navigation.

Viking ships were superior to coracles in having a keel, and a steering oar attached at the back of the ship. When the wind blew at an angle to the ship's desired course, the rudder and keel checked the ship's sidewise slip through the water. But, like coracles, Viking ships could not sail against the wind, and had to wait on shore until the wind blew from a suitable direction. Since the seas in which the Vikings sailed were in the zone of prevailing westerlies, where cyclonic storms succeeded one another week after week throughout the year, they never had to wait long before the wind changed direction.

THE DEVELOPMENT OF RIGID HULLS AND MULTIPLE MASTS   Medieval shipbuilders made two major advances over the level attained by the Vikings. First, they made the hull of their ships stronger and more rigid. This was done by enlarging everything about the Viking hull structure: heavier keel, stouter ribs, double planking attached inside and outside the ribs, and a deck to add strength and keep out water splashed over the gunwales. Medieval shipbuilders eventually learned how to make a hull strong enough to stand the strain of being picked up by two great waves at the bow and stern, leaving little or no water to sustain the weight of the middle portion of the ship. These, then, were the large, stout ships that could safely cut through the waves instead of bouncing about on top of them as light, small vessels had to do.

European sailors also learned that a much safer and more maneuverable ship could be created by substituting rudders for steering oars. Rudders, being larger and attached directly to the rear end of the ship, could exert more force to steer the ship in any desired direction. A second major improvement was to make it easy to adjust sails according to the force and direction of the wind. This was done by planting several masts on the same vessel and dividing the sails on each mast into several different pieces of canvas. If the wind blew very hard, most of the sails could be taken down. By displaying only small storm sails of heavy canvas to the gale, a captain could keep his ship moving through the water fast enough to give the rudder steerage way and thus maintain his course even in stormy weather. With light winds, extra canvas could be spread to make the most of the slightest breath of air.

Sturdy and maneuverable ships built along these lines had another advantage that came by accident. For when European gunsmiths began to make large cannons, the ships which European shipbuilders had learned how to design proved able to withstand the recoil of a heavy gun as easily as they could withstand the buffetings of wind and wave. Lighter and less rigidly constructed ships could and did sail safely in Mediterranean waters and in the Indian Ocean or South China Sea. But such vessels could not carry heavy artillery: the recoil would simply shake them apart. Hence, vessels built for rough seas of the North Atlantic enjoyed an additional and critically important advantage in being able to carry heavier armament than ships of any other design could bear up under.

Multiple masts, rigid hulls, and heavy guns came together in the century between 1400 and 1500. The Portuguese took the lead in developing ship and sail designs. From 1418 on, Prince Henry the Navigator set out systematically to improve the sailing quality of ships with which he wished to explore the Atlantic coast of Africa. Until Prince Henry's death in 1460, Portuguese ships sailed southward almost every year. On his return each captain reported what lands he had found and how his ship had performed. These reports were studied and compared; and when it came time to rig out a new expedition, the practical lessons of preceding years were acted upon. In this way, reliable knowledge of winds, currents, reefs, and harbors accumulated rapidly. The same spirit when applied to ship design led to rapid improvements in the seaworthiness and maneuverability of Portuguese "caravels," as these new oceangoing ships were called.

DEVELOPMENT OF CANNON   Big guns had a different history. When the Mongols invaded central Europe in 1240–1241, they brought Chinese explosives with them, and European artisans probably learned more about Chinese gunpowder and guns during the century that followed. The first important use of guns in European wars took place at the Battle of Crécy in 1346, where the noise of the explosion scared the horses but did little real damage. The development of guns was closely tied to the mining and metal industries in which Europeans already excelled as early as

1300. Comparatively abundant supplies of metal, in turn, allowed Europeans to outdistance others in the manufacture of artillery by about 1450. For example, the Turkish sultan Mohammed II, when he besieged Constantinople in 1453, employed European artisans to cast enormous guns on the spot, with which they then battered the city's walls on behalf of the Turks.

THE PROGRESS OF NAVIGATION   The combination of stout hulls, maneuverability, and heavy guns made European ships clearly superior to all others. Yet before the exploration of the oceans could proceed, sailors had also to learn how to find their way across the trackless sea and get back home again. This called for skill in navigation. Here, too, Prince Henry of Portugal played a critical role. European sailors had long been accustomed to sighting the North Star and measuring its angle above the horizon in order to tell how far north or south they were. But as soon as a ship crossed the equator this method failed. There was no prominent star near the southern pole that could be used as the North Star was used in the Northern Hemisphere. To meet this problem, therefore, Prince Henry employed expert astronomers and mathematicians to make tables that would show how high the sun stood above the horizon at noon of each day in the year at different latitudes. Then a sea captain could estimate how far north or south of the equator he was by sighting the sun at its highest point in the sky and measuring the angle between the sun and the horizon.

Prince Henry's captains, as soon as they discovered some new cape or estuary along the African coast, put ashore and took careful measurement of the sun's altitude, thus establishing the latitude fairly accurately. This in turn meant that a ship could head for a particular place by sailing far out to sea, safe from the dangers of shoals and rocks, until it reached the right latitude, and then head east until the African coast appeared. Landfalls within thirty to forty miles of the intended goal could regularly be achieved by this method.

Measuring longitude was a different matter. No solution to this problem was discovered until 1761, when John Harrison designed a marine clock that could keep accurate time, even on a pitching ship and for long periods at a stretch. The clock kept Greenwich time; and by noting exactly when the sun reached its noon time height, it became possible to know how far the observer was east or west of the Greenwich meridian. Hours and minutes and seconds, east or west of the Greenwich meridian, could then easily be translated into actual distances (which varied with latitude) by use of tables.

At the time of the great European discoveries, however, ships' captains had no way of telling exactly how far east or west they might be, and, as a result, sometimes blundered far off course. Brazil, in fact, was

An astrolabe from the Middle East, ca. 13th century. Such devices had been used since ancient times to measure the position of celestial bodies. The astrolabe, a forerunner of the sextant, was made considerably more accurate by the 16th century Portuguese mathematician and cosmographer Pedro Nunes. (The Metropolitan Museum of Art, bequest of Edward C. Moore 1891)

discovered in this way in 1500, when a Portuguese expedition heading for India went farther west than was necessary to clear the coast of west Africa and ran into South America.

But for most purposes, informed guesswork quite adequately took the place of accurate measurement of longitude. This required knowing the ship's speed through the water and then correcting for the speed and direction of ocean currents. The ship's speed through the water was measured by an interesting method. A slender rope with knots tied in it at regular intervals was attached to a "sea anchor" made of canvas and designed to offer so much resistance to being dragged through the water that it would remain almost still while the rope was paid out over the side of the ship. By counting the number of knots that went overboard in a given period of time, the captain would have a fairly acurate measure of how fast his ship was sailing through the water.

Detection of ocean currents was impossible by direct measurement. Instead, captains kept logs in which they entered the estimated distance traveled each day. Then when some large error showed up (for example, when the ship reached land either sooner or later than would be expected by adding up each day's mileage), the difference could be attributed to some current in the ocean. And by comparing records made by many different ships traveling along different courses, the direction and speed of the ocean currents could be defined with reasonable accuracy. The Portuguese became expert in this kind of rule-of-thumb calculation, before other Europeans knew much about oceanic navigation.

The idea that the earth was flat and that if a ship sailed too far it might fall of the edge of the world and never come back may have frightened sailors. But European navigators and scholars knew better. To be sure, Columbus seriously underestimated the size of the earth. But measurements of latitude along the coast of Africa had given the Portuguese an accurate idea of how big the earth was, since the curvature north-south was, of course, the same as the curvature east-west, if the earth were a sphere. Therefore, when Columbus came to the Portuguese court with his plan for sailing westward to China and the Indies, the experts in Lisbon knew that the Indies were much further away than Columbus believed. They had their own plan for reaching the Indies by sailing around Africa and, quite correctly, decided that Columbus' route was far longer than the one they proposed to take. From the Portuguese point of view, there was absolutely no point in bringing in an ignorant stranger who wanted full rights for himself in anything he might discover. And so they turned Columbus down!

THE VALUE OF NAVIGATION SECRETS   The Portuguese court treated information about the African coast and ocean navigation as secrets of state. The idea was to keep the trade along the coast for Portuguese ships exclusively. Exactly how much the Portuguese captains and navigators knew about the Atlantic Ocean, before Columbus and the other great explorers opened up knowledge of the New World to all of Europe, is still debated. Perhaps the Portuguese already knew of the existence of Brazil and of the Americas. Or perhaps the store of myths and sailors' yarns about a beautiful land in the west, where the souls of the dead went—an idea as old as Egypt and the megalithic sailors—was all that lay behind the scattered hints about lands beyond the Atlantic that survive in medieval records for modern scholars to read and wonder about.

The Vikings had certainly reached North America from Greenland, where a colony existed until the 1340s. Reports of Leif Ericson's "Vinland" (first visited c. 1000) were known in northern Europe; but Viking settlements in the New World did not take root and flourish, though one of them was recently identified and excavated in northern Newfoundland.

A generation or more before Columbus' time, humble fishermen had also begun to sail far out into the Atlantic, and there is some reason to think that Basque and Breton fishermen from the Bay of Biscay may have sailed after cod all the way across the North Atlantic. But fishermen, like members of the Portuguese court, kept their secrets to themselves and certainly did not write books about where the best fishing grounds were to be found!

Problems of Organizing Exploration

Whatever the exact facts were, it is clear that by 1480 European seafarers and shipbuilders had solved the problem of navigating the stormy ocean waters of the North Atlantic so well that no other seas were difficult for them to sail upon. The remaining problem was one of money and organization. Who would pay for long voyages to unknown destinations, and how would newfound lands be treated? Spain and Portugal, the two nations that pioneered Europe's ocean contacts with the rest of the world, found two quite different answers to these questions. Under the leadership of Prince Henry the Navigator, Portugal started ocean voyaging and exploration in 1418. At first Prince Henry had to operate on a very modest scale. Funds came from the income of a crusading Order, of which Prince Henry was head. The Order was supposed to devote its resources to fighting the Moslems, and Prince Henry conceived his explorations as part of a grand plan for outflanking the entire Moslem world. Rumor had reached Europe of a great Christian ruler named Prester (that is, Presbyter or Priest) John, whose kingdom was located somewhere in Asia, or perhaps, in east Africa. Prince Henry hoped to be able to find a way to Prester John's kingdom by sailing around Africa. Then, he thought, a combined assault on the Moslem world might lead to final victory over Christendom's traditional enemy.

The existence of Christians in Ethiopia, of Christians in India (said to have been converted by St. Thomas), and of smiliar small communities of Nestorian Christians in central Asia provided the basis in fact for the stories of Prester John. But when a Portuguese diplomat named Pedro de Covilhão actually reached Ethiopia in 1487, what he found was disappointing. The Ethiopian royal court was not ready or indeed able to help against the Moslems who surrounded their kingdom. The emperor of Ethiopia was interested in getting guns and other weapons from the Portuguese and did actually import some cannons when Portuguese ships reached the Indian Ocean after 1497.

Dependence on Prester John therefore proved a flimsy hope, and the resources of Prince Henry's Order soon became inadequate to pay for fitting out ships year after year. Borrowing was the next step. Bankers

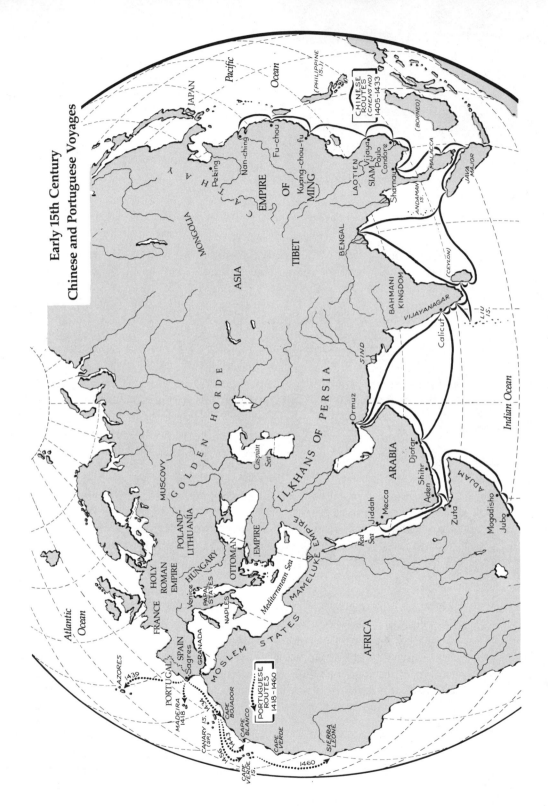

**Early 15th Century
Chinese and Portuguese Voyages**

Atlantic
Ocean

AZORES
1439

PORTUGAL
Sagres
SPAIN
MADEIRA
1418
GRANADA
CANARY IS.
(SP.)
1445
CAPE
BOJADOR
CAPE
BLANCO

PORTUGUESE
ROUTES
1418-1460

CAPE
VERDE

CAPE
VERDE
IS.

1460

SIERRA
LEONE

AFRICA

FRANCE

HOLY
ROMAN
EMPIRE

MUSCOVY

POLAND-
LITHUANIA

HUNGARY
Venice
PAPAL
STATES
NAPLES
OTTOMAN
EMPIRE
Mediterranean Sea

MOSLEM STATES

MAMELUKE EMPIRE

Red
Sea
Jiddah
Mecca

ARABIA
Shihr
Djofar
Aden

Zufa

Mogadisho
Jubo

AJUA

Caspian
Sea

GOLDEN HORDE

ILKHANS OF PERSIA

Ormuz

SIND

BAHMANI
KINGDOM

VIJAYANAGAR

Calicut

(CEYLON)

LIU
IS.

Indian Ocean

ASIA

MONGOLIA

TIBET

BENGAL

EMPIRE
OF
MING

Peking
Nan-ching
Fu-chou
Kuang-chou-fu

LAOTIEN
SIAM
Vijaya
Poulo
Condore
Sharnau

ANDAMAN
IS.

MALACCA

(BORNEO)

JAVA
MAJOR

(PHILIPPINE
IS.)

JAPAN

Pacific
Ocean

CHINESE
ROUTES
(CHENG HO)
1405-1433

12

were quite accustomed to lending money to kings for wars and other royal undertakings. They were ready enough to finance the rulers of Portugal, if proper security for the loans could be found. At first this was difficult, for Portugal was not a rich country. But when Prince Henry's ships passed the barren Saharan coast and reached as far south as the Senegal River (1444), a lively trade with the local peoples began to develop. Slaves, gold, and ivory were the main products the Africans offered the Portuguese. Tools, weapons, and knickknacks, offered in exchange, made a trade that seemed advantageous to both sides. This sort of business the bankers of Italy and southern Germany understood. They were ready enough to finance such ventures, making loans and advances against a share in the profits to be expected from each voyage.

PORTUGUESE TRADE AND EMPIRE EXPLORATION

Trade with the African coast sustained the costs of continued exploration, and new exploration added to the extent of trade. The process, in short, became self-sustaining, and the pace of Portuguese discovery picked up accordingly. New and better ships, together with a growing body of experienced crews and captains, could be supplied year by year since the voyages paid off and new financing was comparatively easy to find.

A few examples will show how rapidly progress was made once these operational problems were solved. When Prince Henry died in 1460, Portuguese ships had worked their way as far south as the Gambia River and the Cape Verde Islands. Twelve years later (1472) Fernando Po reached the island that still bears his name, located near the big bend where the African coast turns south again. Ten years later Diogo Cão discovered the mouth of the Congo River (1482). Five years thereafter Bartholomeu Dias rounded the Cape of Good Hope (1487).

The pace of exploration was interrupted briefly by quarrels with Spain arising from Columbus' discovery in 1492. But progress around Africa was resumed when Vasco da Gama (1497) sailed south through the mid-Atlantic to the latitude of the Cape of Good Hope, then turned eastward until the coast of Africa appeared, after ninety-seven days at sea without sight of land. After coasting along the east shore of Africa, da Gama arrived in Mombasa, where he picked up a pilot who guided him across the Indian Ocean to Calicut in southern India. There the Portuguese were able to load their ships with valuable cargo, and returned in triumph to Portugal (1499). Africa had been rounded at last! The way to the Indies had been discovered in sober fact.

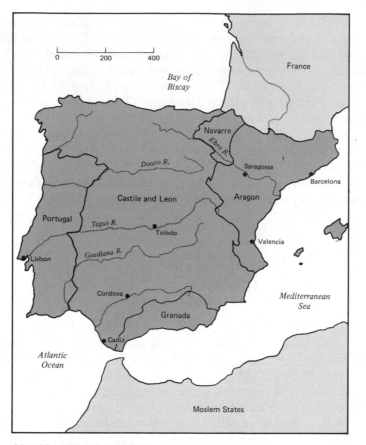

SPAIN AND PORTUGAL, 1492

THE SPICE TRADE   The Portuguese set out energetically to develop the possibilities of trade in the Indian Ocean. "Spices" were especially in demand in Europe. Spices meant almost anything that came from the Indian Ocean coastlands and adjacent islands that could be used to flavor food or as a medicine or dye. But the familiar spices of the modern kitchen were always the most important: pepper, cinnamon, cloves. From medieval times, rich Europeans had become accustomed to consuming surprisingly large quantities of these spices. The reason for this was that without refrigeration the meat they ate was nearly always spoiled. Used in large enough quantities, pepper and other spices disguised the taste and smell of decaying meat and were valued accordingly. Spices were also believed to have medicinal effects, and because they were expensive, they also had show-off value.

Different spices came from different parts of the Indian Ocean area. Before da Gama appeared, spices had been gathered by Moslem merchants and shipped from southern India or southern Arabia up the Red Sea to Egypt. From Egypt the spices were forwarded to Venice and other Italian cities and then distributed over western Europe. This trade route involved many exchanges and a fancy price markup with each exchange. Taxes and tolls at each end of the Red Sea also added to the cost of the spices as delivered in Europe. Vasco da Gama interfered with this route by collecting spices in Southern India and carrying them in a single, unbroken voyage to Lisbon. This made Lisbon, instead of Venice, the main port for delivery of spices to Europe.

The Portuguese quickly followed up da Gama's successful voyage by sending out a fleet in 1500 (the same fleet that, incidentally, discovered Brazil on its way to India). Other fleets followed. This new route around Africa obviously threatened the Moslem merchants who had been accustomed to making a living by sending spices via the Red Sea route; but the Moslems were not able to stop the Portuguese from doing anything they wanted to do on the high seas. Portuguese ships had guns that could sink enemy vessels at a distance of 100 yards or more. The lightly constructed ships used on the Indian Ocean could not arm themselves to match the Portuguese since the recoil of heavy guns was almost as damaging as cannonballs. Hence, when the Moslems assembled a great fleet in 1509, the handful of Portuguese ships that sailed against them had no difficulty in winning a decisive battle off the port of Diu in northwestern India.

This battle marked a drastic revolution in naval tactics as far as the Moslem sea powers of the Indian Ocean were concerned. For at least 2000 years, ramming and boarding had been the methods of fighting at sea in both Mediterranean and Indian Ocean waters. But these close-in tactics became suicidal when cannon fire could sink an approaching vessel before it came close enough even to touch its enemy. In face of such catastrophic change in old patterns of naval warfare, the seafaring peoples of the Indian Ocean did not even try to borrow Portuguese techniques. They submitted instead to paying tolls or risking capture at Portuguese hands.

PORTUGUESE LAND BASES OVERSEAS   Having demonstrated their command of the seas in such a convincing fashion in 1509, the next problem for the Portuguese was to seize strategic points on land for the control of trade. The port of Goa on the western coast of India (captured 1510) became their headquarters. Ports and naval stations at the mouth of the Persian Gulf (captured 1515) and at Malacca, in the straits between Sumatra and the mainland (captured 1511), made naval control of the whole Indian Ocean possible. Links with home were secured by means of a series of African coastal stations. Still farther east lay the Spice Islands

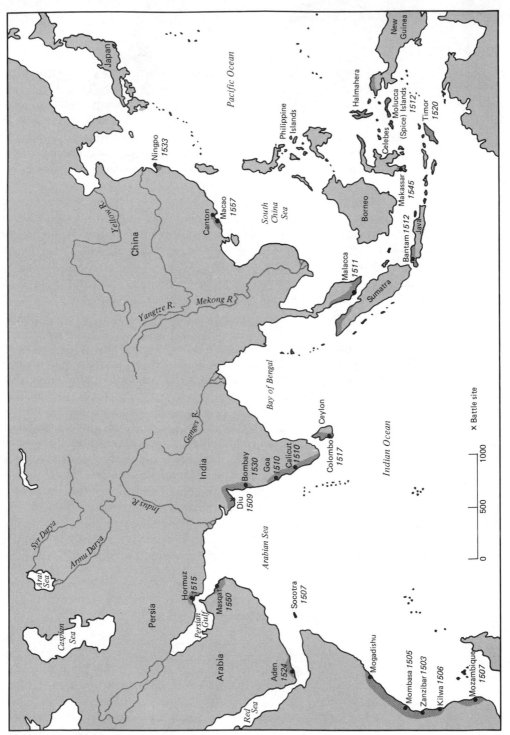

PORTUGUESE TRADE BASES

16

themselves—that is, the Moluccas—and China. A Portuguese explorer reached the south coast of China as early as 1513, and by 1557 the Portuguese had founded a permanent colony at Macao, near Canton. Japan was visited first in 1542.

All these naval operations cost large sums of money. At first, the Portuguese king had no trouble raising the sums needed to build and equip the fleets that sailed to the Indies. Individual voyages came home with cargoes that paid the total costs two or three times over when the spices had been sold in Europe. But windfalls of this sort soon disappeared. The Moslems reorganized themselves to compete once more with the Portuguese. After all, the route around Africa was at least three times as long as the route through the Red Sea, and the costs of building and maintaining the stout oceangoing ships used by the Portuguese were greater than costs that had to be met by the flimsier ships of the Indian Ocean. Thus by lowering tolls and taxes and reducing the markup at each change of hands along the route, it was possible for the old pattern of the spice trade to catch up with Portuguese competition within about twenty years.

This in turn meant that the financing of the Portuguese enterprises in the Indian Ocean became more difficult. Local garrisons had to find ways of paying for themselves. Supplies from home came more rarely and in smaller quantity. The first great burst of energy died away, and the Portuguese began to fit into the Indian Ocean scene simply as one set of traders operating in competition with others, with special advantages in the strength of their vessels but with handicaps too—above all, the difficulty of supplying themselves adequately from a distant and by no means wealthy homeland.

In some places, nevertheless, the Portuguese continued to prosper. They carried on trade between Japan and China for nearly a century, for example, and reaped the usual middleman's profits from this trade. Macao thrived on such a role, without any particular support from home. Local merchants could afford to buy the supplies they needed and to equip their ships from their profits. This was a special case, however, made possible by the fact that the Chinese government treated all Japanese merchants as pirates and prohibited dealings with them, but allowed the Portuguese (who were not, to begin with, much less piratical) to act as go-betweens.

In the Spice Islands, too, the Portuguese were able to extract cloves and other trade goods by demanding them from local rulers as the price for being left in charge of a particular town or island. Since Portuguese ships and crews were equipped with weapons far superior to those that the local people had access to, it was relatively easy for the Portuguese to punish disobedience with sudden catastrophic violence. After a few such acts, local chiefs and princes found it wise to do what was demanded of them and required their people to work for the Portuguese by gathering cloves or whatever other products the island could produce.

VARIATIONS IN LOCAL TRADE PATTERNS   Various local trade patterns arose elsewhere. The export of Asian goods to the African coast and exchanges between different regions of the Indian Ocean area offered some trade possibilities. But in general, local traders were in a better position than the Portuguese to develop these commercial relations, since they knew languages, market conditions, and local political relationships better than European intruders. The Portuguese could demand protection money from the ships engaged in such trade, by virtue of their superior armament—and did so with considerable success.

The enduring handicap that the Portuguese faced in the Indian Ocean area and in the Far East was that there were almost no European products that anyone in Asia seemed to want. European manufactured goods were generally coarse and unattractive to Indian, Chinese, or Japanese consumers. Even in Africa, Asian goods were cheaper and better adapted to African use. Metal and guns interested the Japanese from the start. Elsewhere even these had little market. In any case, it was obviously unwise to sell too many guns to people who might use them to drive the Portuguese away.

A second problem, almost as difficult, was that the king in Portugal had no effective way of controlling his agents in Africa, India, and distant China. The king financed the major expeditions and claimed to rule the forts that had been set up along the trade routes. As early as 1505 a governor went out to India to represent the king. Governors continued to be sent to Goa until 1961, when Portugal finally lost control of that city. But the governors could not easily control the activities of agents scattered over thousands of miles. It was a standing temptation for official representatives of the king of Portugal to trade on their own account. Under these circumstances, profitable undertakings tended to pass into private hands; and dealings that lost money or returned little profit tended to stay on the king's accounts. The result, therefore, was that the king of Portugal seldom had anything to show for his imperial venture in the Indian Ocean. Soon he could not get loans to keep up his forts and ships abroad. Local enterprises, particularly in Macao, did not suffer; but after about 1520 nourishment from home began to slacken, and new ventures into still more distant seas came to a halt. Individuals still might profit handsomely; but the king and the great bankers who had financed the king, in the beginning stages of Portuguese exploration, were not receiving a return on their investment. Accordingly, they stopped advancing money for further ventures.

GROWTH OF SPAIN'S OVERSEAS EMPIRE

The Spaniards came into the business of overseas empire by the back door. Indeed, in 1492 there was no such thing as a kingdom of Spain, for even after the marriage of Ferdinand of Aragon to Isabella of Castile (1469) the two kingdoms retained separate governments. Since it was Isabella who financed Columbus' voyage, her kingdom of Castile fell heir to the Americas. But Castile was an inland kingdom, concerned, over the centuries, with crusading wars against the Moslems. Castile's crusade against Islam reached a climax in 1492, when the last remaining Moslem state in the Spanish peninsula, the kingdom of Granada, was finally conquered. Ferdinand and Isabella followed up this victory by expelling from their kingdoms all Jews (1492) and Moslems (1502) who refused to become converts to Christianity. In this way the crusade was carried through to its logical conclusion at the very moment when a vast new field of missionary endeavor opened up in the Americas before the astonished eyes of the Spanish rulers.

The Voyages of Columbus

The fact that Isabella took Columbus seriously was itself an indication of how little experience the Spaniards had in overseas operations. As we just saw, the Portuguese knew better and turned him down cold. But Isabella was impressed by his piety and energy; and when Granada fell she decided that she could afford the cost of outfitting the three little ships Columbus used on his famous voyage to the "Indies." Moreover, Isabella agreed to make Columbus "Admiral of the Ocean Sea," with wide rights to any new lands that he might discover. The pattern she had in mind, presumably, was the familiar one of lord and vassal. Anything Columbus might find could be treated as another fief of the kingdom of Castile.

Columbus sailed from Spain in August, 1492, and headed south to the Canary Islands, which had belonged to Castile since 1344. Then he headed west and sighted one of the Bahama Islands after only thirty-six days out of sight of land. Since the Canaries lie in the trade-wind zone, Columbus simply let the northeast trades blow his ships across

Conquests in the New World

<del>→</del> Cortes' conquest of Mexico: 1519–1531
◄•• Pizarro's conquest of Peru: 1531
◄••• Coronado's explorations: 1540–1543
← DeSoto's explorations: 1539–1542
Dates indicate year of conquest by Spain

the ocean. For the return, he headed north until he reached the zone of prevailing westerlies, and then turned east toward Spain. Columbus was a skilled navigator and knew before he started how to take full advantage of these favoring oceanic wind patterns. From a technical point of view, in fact, his famous voyage was not in the least difficult. Its significance lay in the fact that he opened regular contact between Europe and the Americas for the first time.

Ironically enough, Columbus refused until his dying day to admit that he had discovered a new continent. He believed instead that he had found islands lying somewhere off the coast of Asia. Before his death in 1506 he made three more voyages, discovering Santo Domingo, Cuba, and other islands of the Caribbean Sea, and touching also upon the coast of South America in the region near the Orinoco River. He found small amounts of gold in Santo Domingo. Rumors of untold riches, just over the horizon, ran swiftly through the Spanish court. Footloose nobles and penniless adventurers eagerly took ship to seek their fortunes. The queen continued to make grants of lands yet to be discovered, usually to captains who undertook to organize an expedition at their own expense.

ESTABLISHMENT OF DIRECT ROYAL RULE   The result in the Americas was wild disorder and bitter quarrels. Columbus soon proved unable to deal with the situation. A royal judge, dispatched from Castile to look into the situation, sent Columbus back to Spain as a prisoner in 1499. The grant of governmental powers to Columbus was canceled; and in principle, though not yet in fact, direct royal administration was extended to the newfound lands on the far side of the Atlantic.

The decision was simply an extension across the ocean of a struggle going on in Castile itself between the royal government and the great feudal nobles, who resisted any increase of royal authority over their lands. The royal government in Castile was making rapid advances, particularly since Ferdinand of Aragon—a much more commanding personality than his wife, Isabella—could give advice and direct policy from behind the scenes. As soon as troubles broke out in Columbus' possessions, therefore, officials took the opportunity to establish direct royal administration over the newly discovered lands.

Such a policy was all very well on paper. But at first the government lacked sufficient income from the New World to pay for the fleets, soldiers, judges, governors, and other officials needed to make royal administration a reality. Hence, the policy of making generous land grants to anyone who would equip an expedition continued to be followed. Such grants sometimes overlapped, since no one knew exactly what was being granted in the first place. Small-scale civil wars and threats of violence therefore continued to break out among the Spaniards in the New World. Royal court decisions and the law applied only spottily, if at all, since there was no way to enforce theoretical rights except with arms in hand.

In other words, the turbulent struggle between king and nobles, which had been decisively won by the agents of the king in Castile just before Columbus sailed, shifted overseas.

ADJUSTMENT OF CLAIMS BETWEEN SPAIN AND PORTUGAL   For a while, news of Columbus' discovery aroused great excitement all over Europe. In 1493 the pope divided the world equally between Spain and Portugal, along arbitrarily chosen meridians of longitude. During the following year, the two governments agreed to modify the pope's line of demarcation by moving it a hundred leagues to the west. The new line brought Brazil within the Portuguese half of the world, but because of the difficulties of measuring longitude, no one was really sure where the line fell in the Far East.

Other European kings did not like to admit the rights of Spain and Portugal, but only the English tried to do anything about it. Henry VII sent John Cabot across the Atlantic to explore more to the north (1497). Cabot discovered no passage to China or the Indies. On the contrary, he found only empty and forbidding forests that offered no obvious attraction to Europeans. After this single venture, therefore, for more than a century the English gave up western exploration as a bad business. No other country even tried.

Discoveries of Vespucci, Balboa, and Magellan

As for the Spaniards, it looked for a while as though the whole venture would soon fall through. Expedition after expedition went out to look for the fabled wealth of the Indies, and each discovered new stretches of the American coast. By 1507 most experts were ready to agree that what had been discovered was not Asia but a new continent. In that year a German scholar, Martin Waldseemüller, published a map on which he entered everything he could find out from the reports of the explorers. For his information about the more southerly parts of the coast of South America, he relied on the report of an Italian captain, Amerigo Vespucci, who had sailed almost as far south as the estuary of La Plata in 1502. In recognition of Amerigo Vespucci's discoveries, Waldseemüller proposed to call the new land America. The name stuck, although at first it applied only to South America, and it was not until after 1600 that Europeans agreed that the term should apply to both North and South America.

Any remaining doubt as to what Columbus had discovered was removed when Vasco Nuñez de Balboa, a Spaniard, crossed the Isthmus of Panama in 1513 and sighted the ocean we call the Pacific. Soon thereafter Ferdinand Magellan, a Portuguese sea captain sailing for Spain, discovered the straits that bear his name, at the tip of South America. He then sailed up the western coast of what is now Chile until he reached the trade-wind zone. With the southeast trade winds at his back, Magellan boldly set out across the vast Pacific. The voyage was long and perilous, for Magellan was heading for the Spice Islands, which he knew to be north of the equator. This required him to steer in a northerly direction, so that somewhere in the mid-Pacific he left the trade-wind zone behind and entered the region of tropic calms, where his ships made slow and halting headway. But Magellan was a skilled navigator and eventually made his way to the Philippine Islands, where he was killed in a skirmish with the natives. His companions continued on their way around the world; and one of the five ships with which he had started finally made it back to Spain, arriving in 1522 after three years at sea.

Such feats of seamanship were exciting and impressive, but left unanswered the question of how Spain's overseas ventures were ever going to pay for themselves. The gold Columbus gathered from the natives of Santo Domingo did not amount to much. Other American products, however interesting, did not command an immediate market in Europe. The Amerindians whom the Spaniards first met were poor and did not even make good slaves, because they died so rapidly from European diseases.

The Conquests of Mexico, Peru, and Chile

Castile's overseas enterprise was saved by the reckless venture of Hernando Cortes against the Aztec Empire of Mexico. Cortes started off from Cuba in 1518 with 600 men and seventeen horses under his command. After sailing for a while along the Mexican coast, he put ashore at Veracruz and set out to march inland toward the Aztec capital, Tenochtitlán. The Spaniards were helped by Indian tribes who resented the Aztec lordship. Montezuma, the Aztec ruler, was nonplused, believing the Spaniards to be supernatural beings. He allowed himself to be taken prisoner and was killed when the Aztecs revolted against the Spaniards in 1520. Cortes was forced to retreat from Tenochtitlán, but the next year, with help from Indian allies, he once more besieged and captured the city. This

MONTEZUMA

In the year 1502 a handsome young Aztec chieftain succeeded his uncle as ruler of Mexico. The Aztecs were a warrior people, chosen, they believed, by the Sun God to feed him human hearts every day so that he would be strong enough to rise again each morning and dispel the darkness. In the year 1325 the Aztecs took possession of a swampy island in Lake Texcoco and made it their stronghold. By Montezuma's time, the island had become the site of a great city, Tenochtitlán. It was connected with the mainland by narrow causeways. Drawbridges allowed the Aztecs to halt an approaching enemy with ease. Even if a foe should camp where the causeways reached the mainland, boats could bring in supplies from distant shores of the lake. The city of Tenochtitlán was therefore a secure base. From it the Aztec warriors raided far and wide, seeking always to take prisoners alive so as to be able to sacrifice them to the Sun god. Peoples and tribes round about soon agreed to pay tribute to keep the great city supplied with food and all its other needs, rather than run the risk of being captured and sacrificed. So Aztec raiding parties traveled farther and farther to find captives for their god and, doing so, rapidly created a large empire.

This was what Montezuma inherited. He was a capable and pious ruler. Each day priests sacrificed human beings to the Sun god by cutting their still beating hearts from their bodies; each day the Sun rose victoriously in the east, refreshed by human sacrifice. But the Aztecs knew of another god, Quetzalcoatl, who had disappeared long ago after promising

time he destroyed it and founded Mexico City nearby, as the capital of the new Spanish domain.

What made Cortes' feat so important to the authorities back home was that he discovered enormous quantities of gold and silver in the Aztec capital. Here at last was something really valuable that could pay the costs of exploration and development. The news made credit easy to find and recruits eager to go on overseas adventures.

Cortes' brilliant and brutal success was quickly followed by Francisco Pizarro's conquest of Peru (1531–1536). Only 180 men and twenty-seven horses started out with Pizarro in 1531. Yet the Inca Empire he conquered was larger and much better organized than the Aztec Empire had been. Gold and silver were even more abundant than in Tenochitlán.

to return. Quetzalcoatl was white and bearded, a rival to the Aztec Sun god. What he would do when he returned, no one knew.

When Montezuma had ruled for fifteen years, disturbing news came from the eastern coast. Ships as big as houses had been seen; they carried white strangers, wearing beards. Was this a sign that Quetzalcoatl was coming back? Did this foretell the overthrow of the Sun god and of his blood-stained servants, the Aztecs?

Many inhabitants of Mexico thought so. Then, in 1519, a few hundred men and some horses actually came ashore and started to march inland. Hernando Cortes was on his way!

What should Montezuma do? Ought he to welcome Cortes as a god? Should he fight him? No one in Tenochtitlán knew. Montezuma tried at first to persuade the strangers to go back where they had come from. When they refused, he tried to cut off their food supply. But that failed, too, because peoples along the way decided that the Spaniards were gods—or at least so powerful that it was best to treat them as gods.

In the end Montezuma did the same. When Cortes came close to his capital, he went out to welcome him, escorted him into the center of his city, and gave the Spaniards everything they asked for. Montezuma soon found out that Cortes was not Quetzalcoatl; but that did not make him harmless. Quarrels began, and Cortes took Montezuma prisoner. When a riot broke out against the Spaniards, Montezuma tried to tell his people to stop. Instead, they stoned him; soon after he died, a helpless prisoner. Within a year the empire he ruled and the Sun god he served vanished utterly, because the Aztecs' former subjects all rebelled, led and organized by Cortes and his men.

Such amazing adventures led other Spaniards to start off in every direction, looking for still more cities of gold. A grant from the Spanish government and a few promises to eager followers were enough to get the necessary credit for equipping an expedition. In such a fashion, Hernando de Soto explored what is now the southern United States and discovered the Mississippi River (1539–1542). Francisco Vásquez de Coronado explored what is now New Mexico, Texas, Oklahoma, and part of Kansas in 1540–1543. Yucatan, the home of the Mayas, was explored a little earlier (1527–1535) without yielding returns comparable to the wealth of Mexico and Peru. Similar energies were spent in conquering Chile (complete by 1561), Columbia (1536–1538), sailing down the Amazon from Peru (1541), and exploring Lower California and other nearby regions.

The Spanish Mission of the Alamo, ca. 18th century. (The Bettmann Archive)

THE ORGANIZATION OF MINING   By 1545 it had become clear that no more great empires remained to be conquered and no more Indian hoards of gold and silver awaited Spanish discovery. The great days of the conquistadors had lasted no more than twenty-five years. It was time for officials and administrators, missionaries and bureaucrats, to take over and make Spain's vast overseas empire of the Americas into a more orderly affair.

The first step was to organize mining to keep a flow of precious metals moving toward Spain. Precious metals would pay for everything and keep the authorities at home happy. Gold was found in small quantities at widely scattered locations, mostly as nuggets in stream beds. But the really important new mines produced silver in quantities that Europeans had not seen before. The richest mine was located at Potosi, in the high Andes. The mine was put into regular operation in 1545. Similar mines in central Mexico came into production soon afterward, but Peru remained the largest single source of precious metal. The Spaniards brought the best European techniques to the mines of the New World. The returns were spectacular. Vast quantities of precious metal kept coming year after year after year.

Safe delivery of the silver was a problem, since pirates from other European nations had no scruples about attacking a treasure-laden Spanish ship on its way home. A convoy system was therefore set up. Silver from Peru was brought by ship to Panama, carried across the isthmus on muleback, shipped again in armed convoy through the Caribbean islands, and then headed for home through the Straits of Florida following the path that Columbus had first sailed in 1492.

Administration according to standard bureaucratic methods became possible as soon as the flow of precious metals had been organized, since the mines paid, and more than paid, for all official salaries. The grants made to the conquistadors in the first days of exploration were canceled. Instead, the Spanish lands of the New World were divided between a viceroyalty of Peru, with its capital at Lima, and a viceroyalty of New Spain, with its capital at Mexico City. The viceroy (that is, substitute king) was appointed from Spain and represented the royal authority in the New World. He was assisted by a council of high officials, but all important business had to be approved by a special Council for the Indies that sat in Spain. Various provinces were carved out of each viceroyalty. In these a subordinate council, like that which advised the viceroys, exercised official authority. Each town had a council too, presided over by an appointed officer of the crown.

The wild excesses of the conquistadors' generation were thus effectively tamed. Lawsuits replaced naked force as the way to get and hold property. What had been the wildest and most unruly part of the Castilian kingdom became the most carefully and exactly governed portion. This surprising transformation was not only the work of mining engineers and lawyers; it was also the work of the Catholic Church.

The Missionary Thrust

The Spanish kings were accustomed to working closely with the Church. At each stage of the long reconquest of Spain from the Moslems, newly won territory had been made part of the kingdom of Castile through the efforts of royal and Church officials. Indeed, royal officials and Church officials were nearly the same thing. In 1478 Ferdinand and Isabella organized a special Church court system known as the Spanish Inquisition. Its purpose was to search out heretics, particularly former Jews and Moslems who pretended to be Christians but secretly remained loyal to their old faiths. Four years later, in 1482, the pope agreed to give the monarchs of Castile and Aragon almost complete control over appointments to all high Church offices in their respective kingdoms.

These new powers became of the utmost importance to the royal administration. In particular, the Inquisition was almost the only institution that functioned freely and uniformly in both Castile and Aragon. Inquisitors had the power to arrest anyone on suspicion and could hold

The Spanish Armada formation as it approached the coast of England. The defeat of the Armada in 1588 by a combination of factors, including inclement weather, was taken by the English as a sign of divine favor and provided considerable impetus to English overseas expansion. (New York Public Library Picture Collection)

a prisoner secretly for months, or even for years, while they inquired into the "correctness" of his religious views. Such methods did indeed reveal a good many Jews and Moslems who pretended to be Catholic. But the same methods could be and were used against any opponent of the royal administration. Even if no heresy could be found, the king's critics might simply disappear for an indefinite period. Efforts to inquire what had happened were likely to lead to the disappearance of the person who did the asking. Such arrests, therefore, quickly broke the back of opposition to Ferdinand and Isabella and prepared the way for greater and greater coordination between the two kingdoms.

THE CHURCH IN THE NEW WORLD   One of the first things the Spanish monarchs did after the news of Columbus' discoveries reached them was to make sure that the Church in the Indies would be under their full control. The pope agreed to this in 1493 and gave the Spanish royal authorities the right to appoint bishops and other Church officials in all their overseas possessions. The Inquisition was not established in the New World until 1569, however, perhaps because it was not needed.

Individual priests and friars accompanied nearly every exploration undertaken by the conquistadors. Believing that millions of souls awaited salvation, the Spanish Church undertook an enormous effort, sending missionaries to every part of the territory that came under Spanish rule. Because the missionaries were interested in the religious welfare of the Indians, they became the special spokespeople for the interests of the Indians. The most famous defender of Indian rights was Bartolemé de Las Casas (1474–1566), a priest, later bishop, who went to Santo Domingo in 1502 and spent the rest of his life trying to plead and argue against enslavement of the Indians. He was successful. When law codes for the Americas were published (1542), Indians were classified as legal dependents, or wards, of the Spanish crown. Their enslavement and mistreatment were prohibited, although Spanish landholders were able to find other ways of controlling Indian labor when it suited them.

Las Casas also made one of the earliest experiments in trying to convert the Indians by setting up a mission. He wished to convert them by persuasion, without use of force. But the Indians usually preferred their own ways, and if left really free would disappear into the forests. Later missions, therefore, combined an element of force with the element of persuasion. Friars and soldiers together rounded up groups of Indians and invited them to accept Christianity. The Indians seldom refused.

Sometimes a group of Indians tried to sneak away from the mission. Then the soldiers went after them and brought them back. But in general the Indians readily submitted to the friars and priests. The priests and medicine men of their old religions had demanded obedience. So did the Christian priests. It was not hard for simple farmers to transfer loyalty and obedience from one to the other, particularly when the native religion and political leadership could offer no effective resistance to the Spaniards.

When the great conquistador expeditions ceased about 1540, missions became the means by which the Spaniards continued to extend their hold over the native peoples. The lack of hoarded gold was no obstacle to the expansion of missions. Each mission was expected to pay for itself. This meant putting the Indians to work. Accordingly the Spanish missionaries set out not only to convert the Indians to Catholic Christianity, but also to teach them new skills.

Farming methods changed little, since the Indians knew a great deal already about how to raise American food crops. But new metal tools— hoes, axes, spades—often made an enormous difference in cultivation. Cattle, sheep, and horses also changed the pattern of land use in some parts of Mexico and South America. The missionaries built great churches with Indian labor and taught the Indians how to make all the things needed for church services and for the daily life of the whole community.

In this way, missions could become self-sufficient very quickly. Indeed, missionaries in Paraguay and in some other parts of the New World were later to make missions financially profitable. Indian labor could, after all, be used to produce goods for export. Such commodities when sold in Europe brought in funds that could then be used anywhere in the world; but this was a later development. Most missions were merely self-supporting. This was enough to permit rapid and continuous expansion of their scope, within limits set by the number of available Spanish missionaries and companies of soldiers needed to back them.

The mission system was important all along the fringes of the Spanish domains in the New World. In the central areas, however, and wherever there were silver mines of any importance, the mission pattern broke down. Indian labor was needed for the mines. It was also needed by the ordinary Spanish immigrant who had come to make his fortune and was not ready to work with his own hands. A common pattern was to lend goods or money to the Indians, who had no idea of what a loan meant and normally could not repay it. Then, as defaulting debtors, they could legally be required to work for their creditors. Low wages and easy credit at the store could then keep the Indians forever in debt and forever bound to work for their creditor. This relationship was called *peonage* and it differed only in legal form from slavery.

In this way, Spaniards were able to compel Indians to work for them as servants, household artisans, and miners, and in other ways. Where this occurred, Indians and Spaniards both came under the spiritual control of parish priests and bishops, as was customary in Europe. In theory, the Church continued to make efforts to protect the Indians, and government officials backed the priests. But in practice, loopholes in the law allowed the immigrant Spaniards to get what they wanted: Indian labor to do the menial and necessary tasks of the new colonial society in which the Spaniards constituted the upper class. Since the Indians ranked at the bottom, half-breeds—with a Spanish father and an Indian mother—came in between. In the regions where Negro slavery became important, other in-between groups arose from intermarriages between Negroes and Indians, and Negroes and Spaniards.

In time these in-between groups became more numerous. This meant that the original simplicity of the Spanish-Indian relationship blurred. But the Church retained its importance always and so did the official bureaucracy. The two supported each other and together kept the society of the New World in order. Every effort was made to be sure that only Catholics in good standing came from Spain to the New World—and religious doubt or opposition to the Church was energetically suppressed in the Americas. The result was an ordered, stately society sustained by both the silver from the mines and the splendor of church services—and carefully controlled by officials appointed from Spain by the royal council.

Portuguese Missions

Portuguese missionary enterprise had a different history. To outflank Islam had been Prince Henry the Navigator's great goal; and when at last Vasco da Gama rounded Africa, the missionary idea was not forgotten. Friars and priests accompanied the Portuguese explorers; and when regular shore stations were set up, missionary churches were established also. The trouble was that the local inhabitants were not willing to accept the teaching of the missionaries. In India and China, Christianity was not entirely unheard of, and Hindus and Confucians had no use for it. They regarded Christianity as the faith of an unimportant group of outsiders, who might indeed have good ships and guns but who certainly did not know the truth about the nature of the universe.

Wherever the Portuguese met Islam—and that was almost everywhere on the shores of the Indian Ocean—the followers of Mohammed were in direct competition with Christian missions. The Moslems usually proved more persuasive, perhaps because they asked local peoples to give up less of their customs and habits than the Christians did. Sufi Islam, after all, had become a very elastic doctrine. Preachers of Islam recognized different ways to God. Christians required observance of all the sacraments. In particular, Christianity prohibited a man from marrying more than one wife, whereas in Africa and in parts of southeast Asia, rich and important men took several wives and indeed measured their importance, in part, by the number of wives they had. This situation made the Christian gospel unwelcome.

Even when Portuguese missionaries won initial success, long-term results were slight. In the kingdom of Kongo, for example, a usurping ruler became Christian in 1506 and took the name Afonso. King Afonso tried hard to spread Christianity throughout his kingdom, but he also wanted to increase his power by monopolizing the export of slaves. This alienated his subjects; and in fact his kingdom soon broke up, leaving little trace of King Afonso's conversion behind.

Africans mostly preferred to keep their old ways and religion. Nothing had happened to African society to discredit traditional rites and beliefs. The additional fact that Portuguese and other Europeans soon became deeply engaged in the slave trade with the Americas may also have helped to discredit Christianity.

In one land, however, Christian missions had a different reception. The land was Japan. St. Francis Xavier reached Japan in 1549 and met with considerable success. The Japanese took a remarkable liking to European novelties and, for a while, even imitated European clothing and other outward aspects of their life. Christianity benefited from this interest in foreign things. A community of Japanese Christians soon came into existence and flourished for about a century.

Nowhere else did Portuguese efforts to spread Christianity meet with much success. The Portuguese Empire remained, therefore, a naval and trading empire almost entirely limited to the ports and the high seas. Nothing remotely resembling the vast inland empire that the Spaniards created in the New World resulted from Portuguese exploration. The mark they made on the world was correspondingly temporary, whereas the Spanish conquest of the Indians of the New World gave shape and definition to the society of most of South and Central America.

Brazil was an exception, for here the Portuguese met with Indians similar to those the Spaniards confronted elsewhere. The Portuguese government did not set up a centralized official control like that which made the Spanish Empire so orderly. Instead, Brazil was divided into a large number of separate local governments. Without silver to pay for everything, officialdom could not keep local energies under control. Efforts to use Indian labor on plantations (especially sugar plantations) proved disastrous, since the Indians died from the unfamiliar diseases brought in by the Portuguese and by Negro slaves from Africa. Soon the Negroes began to bear the main burden of producing sugar.

Missionary enterprise in the backwoods never really got started. Portuguese settlers in Brazil wanted laborers, and they raided inland, far and wide, in search of manpower for their sugar fields. The Spanish pattern of protected missions could not arise under such circumstances. On the other hand, plantation owners usually recognized it as part of their duty to provide Christian services for their slaves. By enslavement, therefore, Brazilian Indians and Negroes from Africa were at least superficially Christianized.

INDIRECT CONSEQUENCES OF EUROPEAN EXPLORATIONS

The great European discoveries changed everyone's outlook on the world, and altered prevailing concepts of the relationships among the major branches of humankind in far-reaching ways. But in addition to conscious changes, there were three worldwide and fundamentally important consequences that resulted from the new patterns of communication, of which contemporaries were largely or completely unaware. These were the so-called price revolution, the spread of diseases to new regions and among new populations, and the spread of American food crops to Europe, Africa, and Asia. Each of these deserves brief explanation.

The Price Revolution

The supply of American silver was so large that the supply of goods that might be bought with coins of silver could not keep up. The result was a rapid rise in prices. More and more silver was needed to buy the same amount of useful goods. Naturally enough, the price revolution was felt first and most strongly in Spain. These prices rose by about 400 percent in a century. In other parts of Europe increases may have been a little less, and they came more slowly. But no part of the European world escaped the effect, since a sharp rise in prices in one market attracted goods from other markets, where prices promptly rose, until some sort of rough balance could be established once more. The effect was not limited to Europe, but spread to the Ottoman Empire and to both India and China.

But as the price revolution spread through the civilized world, it became less important. In Europe more of the people engaged in the purchase and sale of goods than was the case in Asia where the peasant majority bought and sold very little, because they supplied their social superiors with food in the form of rents and taxes in kind. Changes in the price system in China, therefore, did not do much to change relations between peasants and landlords. The same was true in India and in most parts of the Moslem world. In Europe, however, the price revolution disrupted traditional relationships between buyers and sellers, landlords and tenants, government and taxpayers, borrowers and lenders. Some classes benefited, others suffered. Everyone felt uncertain. Nearly everyone believed that greedy, wicked individuals must somehow be responsible for the rise of prices. But in an age when no one understood the relationship between silver supply and price levels measured in silver, it was hard to find out who was responsible or to pin the blame on anyone in particular.

This did not make the general disturbance of traditional day-by-day relationships any less important or easier to accept. When many suffered and everyone faced new uncertainties in economic matters, the European public was eager to find a scapegoat. The fierce religious quarreling that broke out with the Lutheran movement in Germany owes much to the economic dislocation caused by price revolution. It ran through Europe's history for the next hundred years and changed men's lives in detail in innumerable ways. Nothing could be quite the same when prices changed so sharply and, of course, unevenly.

The Spread of Disease

A second, no less important, change was the result of the circulation of disease by ship. Where populations had previously had little contact with the outside world, new diseases brought by sailors from Europe had truly devastating consequences. In particular, the Indians of the Americas suffered enormous loss of life. They lacked any sort of established immunity to the standard childhood diseases of Europe; and thousands died in epidemics of chicken pox and whooping cough as well as from the disease more serious to Europeans, smallpox. On top of this exposure, the Amerindians soon had to face diseases brought from west Africa in slave ships— yellow fever, malaria, and the like.

Exposed to such a series of killing diseases, many Indian tribes died out completely. In Mexico and Peru, where millions of farming peasants lived when Cortes and Pizarro first appeared on the scene, the loss of life was even greater. It has been estimated, for example, that in the central part of Mexico the population was between 11 and 20 million when Cortes arrived. By 1650, when smallpox, measles, chicken pox, and other diseases had done their work, only about 1.5 million people remained, including half-breeds and, of course, all the immigrants from Spain. In other words, more than 85 percent of the population had been wiped out in 130 years. Similar sharp decreases took place in Peru and other parts of South America. The same thing happened wherever a dense population that had not had earlier exposure to civilized diseases came into contact with European sailors.

Civilized populations reacted differently. New plagues and epidemics reached European and Asian port cities by ships. But soon the number of ships and the frequency with which they came and went meant that every active port was infected with a more or less standard assortment of germs, varying only with the climate and living habits of the people.

When diseases became endemic in this manner, heavy loss of life from disease ceased to be an important control on population. Children either died in infancy or early childhood, or else survived with a fair level of immunity to all the standard local diseases. It was not possible any longer for a new disease, or a disease that had not been around for fifty years or more, to arrive in a town and kill half of the inhabitants because the townspeople either never had the infection or had lost their biological immunity to it.

In Europe during the later Middle Ages, after the opening of overland trade routes with China under the Mongols, this sort of occasional pestilence had been very common. The Black Death was among the earliest and most severe, but by no means the only example of sudden outbreaks of plague that might kill off a large proportion of a town's population in a single summer. But after about 1750 communication had become so much more regular, and levels of infection had become so uniform throughout the civilized world, that plagues almost ceased to afflict Europe; and they became much less important in India, China, and the Middle East as well.

The result was a remarkable increase in population. From about 1750 civilized populations seem everywhere to have started to grow at a rate unknown before. The new immunity to epidemic diseases was one of the main reasons.

The Spread of New Crops and Livestock

A third result of opening the world's oceans to shipping was the rapid spread of some important food plants and animals into new regions. The Americas gave tobacco, maize, potatoes, and sweet potatoes to the rest of the world. In return came the domesticated animals of Europe: horses, cattle, sheep, and goats. The horse revolutionized Indian life on the Great Plains of North America, for mounted on horseback the Indians were able to hunt buffalo with much greater success than before. They developed a warlike hunting way of life, similar in some interesting ways to the life of the nomads of the Eurasion steppelands. (This, incidentally, is the kind of Indian who entered modern legends of the wild West. But their way of life was still very new when the cowboys from the east arrived to dispute possession of the plains with them.)

Maize and potatoes came to have great importance in Europe and Africa. Sweet potatoes became a major food crop in southern China as well as in west Africa. Tobacco changed European and Turkish habits and made the fortune of the first English colony in North America.

Taken together, the spread of the food plants from the Americas to the rest of the world greatly increased human food supplies. For example, until maize came from America, Africa had never before had a really high-yielding cereal plant that would do well in the climate of that continent. As maize spread, the food supply expanded and African populations started to grow. This, in turn, allowed Black Africa to withstand the losses due to the slave trade. In southern China, likewise, peasants could plant sweet potatoes on land unsuited for rice paddies and thereby add considerably to the local food resources. Potatoes and maize had similar importance for Europe, although not until after 1650.

The increase in the food supply and the decrease in epidemic diseases, therefore, worked together to allow Old World populations to grow. The depopulation that new diseases brought to other parts of the world made the expansion of civilized settlement easier than it might otherwise have been, since local populations often withered away when put into contact with settlers who brought dangerous new diseases with them. Taking the whole globe into account, the European discoveries therefore tipped the balance between civilization and simpler, more isolated communities by favoring the more complex, more varied, more diseased but also more resistant, populations we call civilized.

CONCLUSION

After about 1550 the first drive and energy of the Portuguese and Spanish expansion slackened. The Portuguese came to depend on tolls and trade profits to support their string of coastal stations in Africa and Asia. The Spaniards had put their new empire on a self-sustaining basis, thanks to the new silver mines. But the period of great, sudden windfalls, of surprising new discoveries, and of derring-do and adventure faded rapidly into the past.

Yet, in the short period of not more than two generations after Columbus returned with the news of his voyage, European discoveries had changed the relationships among the civilizations of the world in a fundamental fashion. The seacoasts of the world had become the most important places where different civilizations met.

To be sure, the frontier between the steppe nomads and civilized peoples, which had played such a large role in history since the time of the Scythians and Assyrians, did not disappear. As a matter of fact India and China were conquered from the north by peoples coming directly or indirectly from the steppe in the centuries after the European discoveries had opened up the world's oceans to shipping.

But coastal ports where European ships put in began to rival the old steppe frontier as a zone of critical importance. Here Europeans had a chance to learn about the strange ways of other peoples, and other peoples had a chance to study European skills and ideas, if they cared to do so. Goods and ideas, settlers, diseases, and art styles could move more speedily by sea than overland, and did so.

At first the new pattern of movement by sea did not seem to make a great deal of difference in the Far East and India. Merchant ships had traversed the calm waters of the Indian Ocean and the South China Sea for many centuries before Portuguese ships rounded the Cape of Good Hope. The newcomers took over part of the trade and seized some strategic ports, but the goods they had to offer were of little interest, and their ideas were quite unconvincing to most of the people who bothered to listen to them at all.

Even their techniques of seamanship and naval artillery, which were clearly superior to what had been known before in these southern seas, did not make the local peoples change their ways. The costs were too high, and too many changes in old skills would have been required. For ordinary trading, the traditional kind of ship construction, already familiar in those waters, was superior because it was so much cheaper. The Portuguese with their floating castles found it easier to settle back and collect tolls from native ships.

In the Americas, by contrast, the arrival of Europeans changed everything. The Amerindian civilizations were ruthlessly decapitated by the conquistadors. Old priests and chiefs were utterly discredited. The Indian rank and file transferred obedience to the Spaniards. Native traditions sank to the village level and most of the lore of Aztec and Inca priests disappeared forever, since the Spaniards paid little attention to pagan superstition, and Indian priests had not committed their doctrines to writing.

Africa found itself more closely tied in with the rest of the world than before. Sea trade opened new possibilities, particularly in west Africa and in the whole southern half of the continent. Previously, connections with the civilized world had run northward across the Sahara or by caravan eastward along the open savanna country. In both cases, the civilization with which African communities came in touch was Islam. With the Portuguese explorations, however, Christian contacts opened up, and Africans often found themselves in a position to choose between Moslem and Christian styles of civilization. Usually they preferred Islam, even though the Moslems were just as eager slave traders as were the Christians.

Islam continued to expand, not only in Africa but in southeast Asia and in southeastern Europe. European discoveries did upset the Moslems' spice trade for a while, but even the trade recovered after a few years. Trade overland between China and the Moslem lands was also affected somewhat by the opening of sea contact between Europe and China. But as long as the Ottoman Turks continued to win victories in the field against Christian armies, it certainly did not seem as though the great explorations had made any vital difference for Islam either.

Yet Islam had been outflanked, just as Prince Henry the Navigator had hoped. The whole of the Americas had been brought, at least potentially, within the circle of European civilization. The southern seas had been taken over by European shipping, and Moslem merchants faced new and dangerous rivals—even if the Portuguese failed to drive them from the seas.

With the benefit of hindsight, we can now see the long-range effects of the great European discoveries had yet to show themselves in 1550, or even a century later than that. It was, in fact, the uses to which Europeans put their discovery of the New World that eventually allowed the far western style of civilization to outstrip its rivals in Asia.

The stimulus to Europe's own development was therefore the most important single consequence of opening the world's oceans to European shipping. New wealth, new ideas, new perspectives, new adventures all poured in upon Europe. The various internal deadlocks that had seemed about to freeze European civilization into a "medieval" mold were soon left behind. Europe plunged recklessly and relentlessly into a self-transformation that made the era 1500–1650 the dividing line between what historians have traditionally called medieval and modern times. We shall examine some of the aspects of that transformation in the next chapter.

CHAPTER 2

Europe's Self-Transformation

Between 1500 and 1650 Europeans began a new age. The Church and religion were transformed by the Reformation, beginning in 1517, and by the Catholic reform that gathered headway a generation afterward. Politics altered almost as drastically as peoples fought and struggled over religious doctrines, dynastic interests, and economic resources. Economic relations were transformed by the price revolution resulting from the influx of American silver, and by new forms of business organization that dominated large-scale enterprises and long-distance trade. Finally, European intellectual horizons of learning enlarged dramatically as voyages of exploration and missionary reports brought in a flood of information about the vast and varied world that lay beyond the seas.

The shock of so many innovations coming so fast was severe. Many people were dismayed and alarmed, and popular movements of the age were all aimed at getting back to a purer, simpler past. But a handful of venturesome persons reacted differently, and found new ways to act and think that took advantage of fresh possibilities that opened before them year after year. Grumbling and protesting, the mass of the European population was dragged along, and had to accept more and more novelties because specialists and experts organized, directed, and controlled human and material resources in such ways as to make new techniques and ideas work better than older, customary methods.

Asians did not respond to novelties nearly so actively between 1500 and 1650. This was, therefore, the time when western Europeans began to pull ahead of other civilizations in several important respects, preparing the way for the dominance western civilization was later to acquire over the rest of the globe.

POLITICS AND RELIGION

Ever since the Roman emperor Constantine had allied himself with the Christian Church in A.D. 312, politics and religion had been closely intertwined in Europe's history. The medieval Church had been in the thick of politics. The popes headed an international government that shared authority with secular rulers differently in different places and at different times. Until about 1300 the power of the papacy tended to increase. Thereafter, royal governments in France, Spain, and England took a larger share in church affairs and left less and less real power to the popes. In Germany, however, no strong national government existed. The Holy Roman Empire of the German nation had been wrecked by the quarrel with the popes. When the empire was restored in 1273, the first man elected to the imperial dignity was Rudolph of Hapsburg, a relatively obscure, petty noble who could not possibly challenge the power of the great dukes and princes who ruled the larger states into which the empire had divided. Rudolph did have the rights of his office, however, including the right to reassign any fiefs that happened to fall vacant due to a lack of heirs. During his lifetime a large fief in Austria fell vacant. Rudolph took it for himself, thus planting the Hapsburg family on lands it continued to rule until 1918.

The emperor's powers were limited. In 1356 a constitutional document called the Golden Bull defined how the emperor should be chosen. Seven great princes were named electors, with the right to choose the emperor. In addition, there was a Diet (general assembly or council like the English Parliament) to which all the princes and free cities sent representatives. Both the electors and the Diet were interested in keeping the imperial government weak, so as to leave as many rights to themselves as they could. Hence the empire remained a confusing collection of states, almost but not quite independent of one another, presided over by an emperor who, most of the time, could not get his subjects to obey him, pay him taxes, or cooperate in common policies.

The Hapsburg Empire
of Charles V

This situation was changed when the house of Hapsburg acquired new and important territories through a series of fortunate marriages. First, Emperor Maximilian (reigned 1493–1519) married the heiress to the Burgundian lands. This marriage brought the Low Countries (present-day Belgium, Netherlands, and Luxembourg) and nearby territories under Hapsburg rule. He then married his son Philip to the heiress of Spain. Their son, Charles V, therefore, succeeded to the crown of Spain in 1516 when Ferdinand died. Charles succeeded, also, in securing election as Holy Roman Emperor when his grandfather Maximilian I died in 1519.

As emperor, Charles V used his authority to bring together a tremendous though scattered territory. Spain was the greatest power in Europe. Beginning in 1502, Spanish soldiers had conquered part of Italy, and the empire overseas began to pay off after Cortes (1521) and Pizarro (1535) started the flow of precious metals from the Americas to the Spanish royal treasury. In addition, the Low Countries were one of the richest parts of the continent. Austria and nearby lands constituted still a third power cluster, plus whatever Charles V could make out of his imperial title to German lands. No European ruler since Charlemagne had presided over such an empire. If the German princes could be brought to heel, as Ferdinand and Isabella had brought the Spanish nobles to heel, Emperor Charles V could hope to become supreme, or very nearly supreme, in all western Europe.

However, Charles V's enemies were as numerous as his subjects and his lands lacked any real cohesion. Spaniards, Dutch, Austrians, and Germans had little in common except the same ruler; and Charles was never able to govern them all from a single center or by the same set of laws. From 1522 he gave his brother, Ferdinand I, responsibility for German and Austrian affairs, taking Spain and the Low Countries as his own personal responsibility.

The big issue in Charles's eyes was who was going to control Italy. The French had invaded that country in 1494, upsetting the balance of power between the dozen or so little states into which Italy was divided. Spaniards came in by sea from the south and captured the kingdom of Naples by 1504. The pope and other Italian rulers twisted and turned, caught between the French in the north and Spanish in the south, but were quite unable to escape foreign control. Time and again, Francis I of France (reigned 1515–1547) marched his armies into Italy. Each time he did so, Charles V went out to meet him, and both sides gathered whatever allies could be found in Italy and elsewhere. Each time Charles

Martin Luther, 1483–1546. (*National Museum, Stockholm*)

won. Bit by bit, Spanish influence seeped northward through the peninsula, snuffing out Italian political independence (except in Venice) and choking off the more pagan aspects of Italian Renaissance culture with the fierce crusading spirit of Spanish Catholicism.

A second problem was almost as critical as the fate of Italy in Charles V's eyes: defense against the Turks. With Constantinople as its capital (since 1453), the Ottoman Empire continued to be a formidable and aggressive military state. After 1499, however, wars waged against the shah of Iran turned Ottoman attention eastward. That did not stop expansion of Turkish power, however, for Sultan Selim the Grim was able to conquer Syria, Palestine and Egypt between 1512 and 1520. In the next generation, Sultan Suleiman the Lawgiver (ruled 1520–1566), brought the Ottoman Empire to its peak. In 1526 he invaded Hungary, killed the king, and took control of most of that land. The Hungarian crown, however, passed to Ferdinand of Hapsburg, who had married the sister of the Hungarian king. The Hapsburgs therefore took over the part of Hungary that escaped Turkish control. This meant that later Turkish campaigns against Christendom pitted the sultan's forces against Hapsburg imperial armies. In 1529, for example, Suleiman besieged Vienna but failed to capture it. Border warfare became normal, and every once in a while the sultan set forth with his field army to settle accounts with the Christians. Suleiman died on such an expediton in 1566.

Defense against the Turks by land was the special concern of Ferdinand rather than of Charles V. This was also the case with the third of

Charles's great problems: how to cope with the disturbance in Germany created by Lutheranism and the religious excitement stirred up by Luther's quarrel with the papacy. From Charles's point of view his wars with the Turks and against the French in Italy were defensive. They were necessary to prevent his enemies from driving his friends and supporters from their rightful positions. However, any systematic effort to suppress heresy in Germany required Charles to take into his hands powers that had not been in the German emperor's hands for centuries. Moreover, his Spanish and Netherlandish subjects were not eager to see their money or soldiers used to strengthen the emperor's position in Germany. It is therefore not really surprising that Charles could spend only a small part of his time and energy in trying to do something about the Lutheran movement. He had too many other matters to attend to.

Yet in European history, the Protestant Reformation that Luther started in 1517 turned out to be far more significant than the long wars over Italy, for the Reformation divided Europe into opposing religious camps and changed the lives of nearly everyone to some degree. To understand what the great dispute was about, we must know something of Luther's life and personal pursuit of salvation; for it was these experiences that made him so certain and so persuasive, and gave him courage to defy the highest authorities of Church and state when they commanded him to change his views.

Luther's Reformation

Martin Luther was born in 1483, a miner's son. He started to study law, but gave it up to become first a monk, then a priest, and in 1508 a professor of theology at the University of Wittenberg in Saxony. Such a career was unusual only because the young Luther advanced so rapidly. But he took religion far more seriously than most people did. He became a monk because he felt the need of assuring his soul's salvation. In the following years he worked hard to win that salvation. But his best efforts seemed fruitless. He remained—in his own judgment—a sinful man who deserved damnation. How could he, or anyone else, escape the just punishment for sin? How indeed?

The question was an agonizing one for Luther, until one day in 1515 he was reading St. Paul's Epistle to the Romans and came upon the verse that says: "The just shall live by faith." This simple phrase struck Luther with the force of revelation. Here was his answer: God asked only faith in Him—total, unquestioning faith. God did the rest. Faith freed men and women of sin. All efforts to wipe out the penalties of sin by penance and good works were futile, and indeed misleading, since sinners might

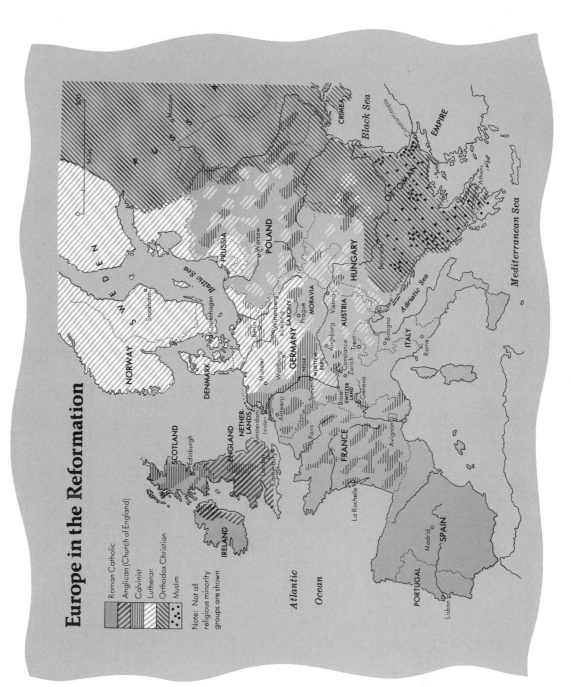

Europe in the Reformation

Roman Catholic
Anglican (Church of England)
Calvinist
Lutheran
Orthodox Christian
Muslim

Note: Not all
religious minority
groups are shown

think that their accounts with God were square when in fact they had failed in the great essential: to have faith and commit all else to God.

The radical consequences of his position became clear to Luther only by degrees. He did not set out to split the Christian Church in two. On the contrary, he always clung to the idea that somehow God would again unite all Christians. When he found his quarrel with the papacy could not be compromised, he appealed to a council of all the bishops, with the idea that this body might reform the Church—always, of course, according to the truth as Luther understood it.

LUTHER'S ATTACK ON INDULGENCES   What triggered the Lutheran Reformation was a campaign to raise money in Germany for the building of St. Peter's cathedral in Rome. One of the ways the popes collected money was by selling indulgences. These were pieces of paper that canceled the penalties of sin. The idea was that the pope could arrange the transfer of merits, accumulated by Christ and the saints, to a soul in need of help. By buying such indulgences, pious persons believed they could relieve themselves or others from having to suffer for their sins in purgatory. The sale of such indulgences had become an important source of income for the popes.

Luther was appalled by such an approach to sin, salvation, and finance. In 1517, therefore, when a seller of indulgences came to a nearby town, Luther pubicly challenged the usefulness of indulgences. He did this in the customary way, by posting a series of theses on the church door in Wittenberg. These theses were short statements about controversial questions that Luther was prepared to defend in public debate with anyone who chose to argue against him.

Learned theologians were soon able to prove that Luther's views led to heresy. If Christians needed only faith for salvation, what happened to the power of priests to channel God's saving grace to sinners through the rites of the Church? Luther eventually admitted in public that on this and other points he agreed with John Huss, the Czech heretic, who had been burned at the stake for his opinions in 1415.

But even when he had been forced to recognize the radical implications of his position, Luther did not change his convictions. He felt, instead, that the pope must be wrong, because he knew that he was right, about faith and salvation—the important thing—and had the words of the Bible to prove it. He put the whole issue before the German public in 1520 by writing three pamphlets in rapid succession: *Address to the Christian Nobility of the German Nation; The Babylonian Captivity of the Church;* and *The Liberty of a Christian Man.*

In emphatic language Luther argued his cause, accused the popes of having twisted true doctrine, and invited the German nobility to reform the Church along the lines laid down in the Bible. Appeal to the Bible

LUTHER'S KIDNAPPING

When Martin Luther accepted the emperor's summons to the Imperial Diet at Worms in April, 1521, he and his friends recalled how John Huss had gone to the Council of Constance a little more than a century before and, in spite of the emperor's pledge for safe conduct, had been condemned as a heretic and then burned at the stake. Parallels with Christ's visit to Jerusalem and the arrest, trial, and crucifixion that followed also flickered in the minds of Luther's followers. But the young emperor Charles V allowed the troublesome professor to leave Worms unhindered, even though he was about to declare Luther an outlaw.

When Luther was nearing his home in Wittenberg, armed horsemen suddenly appeared along a lonely stretch of road, seized the famous reformer, and with oaths and threats carried him off before the eyes of his horrified companions, who thought he was about to be murdered. Indeed, shortly thereafter a body was discovered and identified as the mortal remains of Dr. Martin Luther. His followers were dismayed but not surprised. Such an event fulfilled the parallels they already had in mind.

Yet his close friends soon began to receive letters from the "dead" Luther; and in December he even visited Wittenberg secretly, disguised as a knight. But it was not until March, 1522, eleven months after he had disappeared so dramatically, that Luther returned openly to Witten-

as the only reliable source of religious truth was, in fact, Luther's strongest and most convincing argument. It soon became obvious that many of the practices of the Church did not have any definite biblical basis. For example, confession, which had been defined as a sacrament only in 1215, in the time of Pope Innocent III, was not clearly authorized by any scriptural passage.

The public response in Germany to Luther's words was tremendous. His arguments seemed convincing to most Germans. Nearly everyone agreed that the Church needed reform—and furthermore, no one in Germany really liked to see good German money being shipped off to Rome to build the new cathedral of St. Peter's. Many Germans were eager to agree with Luther when he accused priests of having taken to themselves rights that were in fact enjoyed by every faithful Christian. The salvation of souls was, after all, a matter of highest importance; and if, in fact, berg and publicly took charge of the tumultuous reform movement he had so suddenly called forth.

The inside story then came out. Frederick the Wise, Elector of Saxony, was Luther's immediate sovereign. He did not want to see Luther killed as an outlaw. Yet he also felt that the famous Wittenberg professor of theology was a hothead and troublemaker. While still at Worms, the Elector decided to take Luther into custody secretly, thus making sure that no harm could come to him and that he could do no further harm himself. So that he might be able truthfully to deny that he knew where Luther was, the Elector ordered his servants to capture the reformer without letting the Elector himself know anything about the details.

When one of the Elector's officers explained the plan to him, Luther agreed, for he was in fear of his life and could not afford to defy the pope, the emperor, and his own prince all at once. The kidnapping was therefore arranged as a device for throwing Luther's enemies off the track. Accordingly, as soon as Luther's abductors were safely hidden in the woods, they paused to allow their "captive" to cast off his monk's cowl and put on a knight's clothing. Then the little party rode, by a roundabout way, to one of Frederick the Wise's more remote castles, the Wartburg. There Luther went into strict selcusion until his hair and beard had grown, disguising the monkish tonsure he had worn up to that time.

Luther used his spare time at the Wartburg to translate the Bible into German. He also carried on a busy correspondence with his friends and never lost touch with the Lutheran movement that continued to convulse Germany. As may be imagined, Luther's reported death and subsequent resurrection did nothing to weaken his hold on the popular imagination of Germany.

Luther was right, and the popes had been misleading the Christian community for centuries, something had to be done about it, right away.

The newly elected emperor Charles V therefore made the Lutheran question one of the important items of business to be taken up at his first Imperial Diet, which met at the city of Worms in 1521. Luther came in person, on the strength of the emperor's promise that he would not be harmed. Luther reaffirmed his views, despite their condemnation by expert theologians. This was enough to satisfy the emperor, who persuaded the Diet to put Luther under the imperial ban. This meant that anyone who killed Luther would not be tried in an imperial court. Such an act, in effect, invited his assassination.

But the Elector of Saxony, Luther's immediate sovereign, continued to protect his controversial subject. For safety he sent Luther to the Wartburg castle, where he lived incognito for nearly a year. Luther used this time to translate the New Testament into German. A little later, with help from others who knew Hebrew, he also translated the Old Testament.

Luther's Bible was widely read. Now ordinary laypersons could read the Bible. Many of them tried to puzzle out religious truth from its pages for themselves. The result was sharp disagreement, since different parts of the Bible lend themselves to very different interpretations.

Some Anabaptists decided that infant baptism was an error, because the baptisms recorded in the Bible involved only adults. Other doctrines often combined with this idea. Poor and unhappy people pored over the biblical passages announcing the end of the world, and began to expect the opening of the skies at any minute. If the end of the world was really near, people ought to give up most ordinary pursuits, cease from sinning, and prayerfully await the end.

LUTHER DENOUNCES THE PEASANT REVOLT   Religous views of this kind easily spilled over into social and economic protest. In 1524–1525, peasants in southwestern Germany tried to throw off their obligation to pay customary rents and services to their lords. Radical religious views were part of the movement too. This frightened and angered Luther. He felt that the peasants were distorting the meaning of Christian liberty as he had explained it in his famous pamphlet. Faithful Christians, according to Luther, were free because they served their neighbors spontaneously, not because they had no duties or obligations to others. Luther also feared that the peasants and other radicals might discredit his reform in the eyes of the German nobles and princes, who could not welcome revolution. The result was another pamphlet in which Luther denounced the peasant rebels in extremely harsh language and exhorted their lords to kill them mercilessly.

The peasant revolt was indeed suppressed in blood. Thereafter, the Lutheran movement lost much of the white-hot enthusiasm that Luther's words had stimulated during the first eight years of the Reformation. Instead, Luther and his followers set out to order the Church as it should be ordered—that is, according to the Bible—wherever the secular ruler would agree to undertake the task of reform. Many, but not all, German princes went along with Luther in this task. They had much to gain, for the Lutherans decided that Church property was unnecessary, that monasteries should be suppressed, and that Church appointments should be treated as another (though supremely important) branch of the governmental bureaucracy.

When Luther died in 1546, reform along these lines had been firmly established in most of northern Germany and in Scandinavia. Emperor Charles V had been far too busy in Italy and elsewhere to check Lutheranism effectively. When he did find time to turn to internal German affairs, it was too late. Confiscated lands and abandoned monasteries could not be restored; in such matters the German princes would not submit to the emperor's will without a fight. Charles V tried to use force, but that failed. In 1555 he therefore reluctantly agreed to the Peace of Augsburg, which gave every German ruler the right to impose either Lutheranism or Roman Catholicism upon his subjects.

John Calvin and the Reformed Churches

Luther's challenge to the papacy did not pass unnoticed outside of Germany. Especially among townspeople in France, Switzerland, England, and the Low Countries, long-standing discontents with the papacy and with the Church burst into flame as news of what had happened in Germany spread through Europe. In many places the reform party was unable to gain control of the government.

Without such power they could only form a church, according to their taste, by withdrawing into some sort of separate body of their own. But in Switzerland, where local cantons (or districts) and cities ruled

Jean Calvin, 1509–1564. (New York Public Library Picture Collection)

themselves, religious reformers had only to convince a majority of the city council in order to begin reform.

In this fashion, a fiery preacher, Huldreich Zwingli (1484–1531) started reformation in Zurich in 1518. His ideas paralleled those of Luther on many points, although the two reformers differed on the meaning of the sacrament of the Eucharist. Church reform spread to other Swiss towns, but high in the mountains more conservative communities clung to the old faith. Civil war broke out, and Zwingli was killed in battle. Soon afterward a peace was concluded that left each canton free to choose its own form of religion.

Zwingli's death, however, left the Swiss reformers without a leader. This gap was filled by John Calvin (1509–1564), a Frenchman, who first came to Geneva in 1536 but took up permanent residence there in 1541. Calvin was a far more cool-headed man than Luther. He thought out his opinions carefully and stuck to them with a will of iron. Through his learning and conviction he impressed his views upon all around him.

Like Luther, Calvin took the Bible as the only reliable source of religious truth. In the main, he drew the same lessons from the Bible that Luther had drawn. In his famous book, *Institutes of the Christian Religion,* Calvin gathered together the biblical passages that supported his views on all issues under debate. Calvin arranged his discussion of doctrine systematically so that anyone eager to find out what the Bible had to say about salvation, predestination, faith, and innumerable other questions could discover answers in his book. The *Institutes,* therefore, became a standard reference work for all of the reformed churches.

CALVIN'S DIVERGENCE FROM LUTHER   In some matters, however, Calvin disagreed with Luther. Like Zwingli, Calvin interpreted the Eucharist as merely commemorative of the last supper that Jesus Christ had taken with the Apostles. Calvin also emphasized predestination in a way that Luther did not. Luther accepted the idea of predestination, but never felt it to be particularly important. What mattered was faith in God. Calvin, on the other hand, drew the logical conclusion: some persons have faith and are saved, but some lack that faith and are therefore damned to all eternity. God makes the choice, not the individuals concerned. God does so for reasons that mere human beings cannot understand.

Such a doctrine emphasized the role of God as judge and ruler. It did not, however, persuade Calvin and his followers to sit back and wait for God to do whatever He had decided to do. Instead, Calvinists developed a tremendous moral drive. No one could ever be absolutely sure that God had chosen him or her to be saved. But a person could try to live as though he or she were among the elect, destined for Heaven. Under Calvin's leadership, Geneva became a school of righteousness. Dissent was suppressed. Morality was enforced by preaching and instruction, and when that failed, by the force at the disposal of the city government.

Calvin's ideas about the proper relation between Church and state were quite different from Luther's. After 1525 Luther had fallen back upon the support of the German princes and had given them all but complete control over church administration. Calvin combed the Bible for evidence of how the early Church was managed, and came to the conclusion that ministers and elders ought to be in charge of each separate congregation. General questions should be decided by representative assemblies in which both ministers and laymen took part.

Calvin attracted many earnest young men to Geneva to see and study the godly community he had helped to construct there. Such men spread Calvin's ideas far and wide through Europe. In Scotland, John Knox (1505–1572) was able to convert a whole kingdom by fiery preaching and a skillful appeal to nobles who were restless under royal authority. Elsewhere, however, Calvinism spread by attracting the assent of individuals most of whom lived in towns. Calvinists, therefore, remained a minority in France and the Rhinelands. In the Dutch provinces, Calvinists became the majority during a long war against Spain (1568–1648). In both Poland and Hungary, also, Calvinism had a considerable success, mainly among the nobility. Catholic missionaries later reconverted nearly all Polish Calvinists to Roman Catholicism; and in Hungary the majority also returned to Catholicism, although in the eastern parts of Hungary important Calvinist communities still survive.

England's Reformation

The Reformation in England began when Henry VIII (ruled 1509–1547) came to the conclusion that the reason he did not have a male heir was that he had married his dead brother's widow, Catherine of Aragon (the aunt of Charles V and mother of Henry's sickly daughter Mary). King Henry wanted a male heir to assure the continuance of the Tudor family on the English throne. Also, his eye had caught the pretty face of a young lady of the court named Anne Boleyn, whom he wished to marry.

The difficulty was that the pope refused to annul Henry's marriage to Catherine of Aragon. The Spanish influence in Rome opposed any such act. Moreover, Henry had married his brother's widow in the first place only on the strength of a special dispensation from the pope; it was awkward for the pope to contradict what before had been officially approved. After waiting in vain for a favorable decision, King Henry asked Parliament in 1534 to declare him to be head of the Church of England. This done, the archbishop of Canterbury declared the king's marriage annulled, freeing him to marry Anne Boleyn. But the king was again denied a male heir, for Anne gave birth to a girl, Elizabeth. King Henry soon tired of Anne and had her head cut off on the charge of unfaithfulness. He later married four other wives, one of whom gave birth to a son, Edward VI (reigned 1547–1553).

Although he quarreled with the pope, Henry VIII had no intention of tampering with doctrine or even with rituals. But Lutheran and, presently, Calvinist ideas could not be prevented from seeping into England. Henry opened one important breach in the old order by seizing lands belonging to monasteries, as a way of increasing his income. Under his son, distinctly Protestant phrases were introduced into the officially approved church rituals. Queen Mary (reigned 1553–1558), daughter of Catherine of Aragon and wife of Philip II of Spain, tried to bring England back into the Roman Catholic fold. Her successor, Elizabeth I (reigned 1558–1603), returned to Protestantism, and in 1563 Parliament approved Thirty-nine Articles summing up Christian doctrine. These articles became by act of Parliament the official theological position of the Church of England.

These articles had been drawn up with care so as to allow anti-papal Christians of many different shades of opinion to accept them. They have remained in force ever since. Because Protestantism and English patriotism came to be firmly identified with each other under Queen Elizabeth, most Englishmen and women were well satisfied with the theological compromises of the Thirty-nine Articles. But some enthusiasts felt that the English church needed still further reformation. These "Puritans," as they came to be called, were under strong Calvinist influence. Some felt it possible to work within the established church. Others withdrew to form their own congregations, to preach and practice true and purified Christianity as they understood it.

Roman Catholic Reform

For nearly twenty years the popes in Rome paid little attention to the Protestant movement. They were caught, like all the other rulers of Italy, in the complicated struggle between France and Spain for control of the Italian peninsula. When Charles V's soldiers took and sacked Rome in 1527, how could the pope cooperate effectively with that same emperor to put down the Lutherans in Germany? Moreover, the Renaissance popes were rulers, diplomats, and art patrons—far too much concerned with these affairs to take Luther seriously.

For a long time, too, there was a real ambiguity about the cry for reform. Luther and Calvin never intended to set up separate churches,

St. Ignatius Loyola, 1491–1556.
(*New York Public Library Picture Collection*)

and they always remained true to the ideal of one universal Church to which all Christians ought to belong. When asked what to do about the corruptions of the papacy, their answer was to appeal to a general council. This sounded like a return to medieval ideas for reforming the Church by means of a council, and the popes could not be expected to welcome revival of this issue. They tended to suspect anyone who urged the need for reform of trying to undermine the authority of the papal office.

POPE PAUL III AND THE COUNCIL OF TRENT   Nevertheless, Protestant arguments and the advance of Protestant opinions in so much of Europe could not be overlooked forever. Pope Paul III (reigned 1534–1549) began major reform by appointing scholars and pious individuals to positions of power within the Church. He also approved the establishment of the Society of Jesus (1549), revived the Inquisition (1542), and eventually yielded to widespread demands for a council by calling the Council of Trent (1545–1563, with many recesses).

The Council of Trent took care of the main Protestant challenge by declaring that the Bible was not the only source of religious truth. The tradition of the Church, descending without a break from the Apostles, was of equal validity. In other matters of detail, the Council also explained doctrine in an anti-Protestant sense. The gap between the two camps was thus defined clearly, as had not at first been the case. The Council of Trent also reaffirmed the sovereign power of the papacy over the Church, and entrusted to the pope the task of carrying out practical reform.

THE JESUIT ORDER   The Society of Jesus played an active part in the deliberations of the Council of Trent. This was a new religious order, founded by St. Ignatius of Loyola (1491–1556). Loyola was a Spanish nobleman, who started out to be a soldier. While recovering from a battle wound, he decided to become a soldier for Christ. His first idea was to concentrate on converting the heathen, and for this he needed theological training. Loyola, therefore, took up study at the University of Paris, where he soon formed a small circle of similarly minded young men. They organized themselves into a religious order in Rome and, in 1540, were given papal blessing as the Society of Jesus.

The Society of Jesus differed from other religious orders in several respects. Its members offered themselves for any sort of service and, like soldiers, swore absolute obedience to their superiors. At the head of the order was a general—to begin with, Loyola himself—and the general took orders only from the pope. The Society of Jesus was thus like the royal standing armies that were coming into existence all over Europe: a body of trained and disciplined men at the disposal of the papacy. They quickly distinguished themselves as teachers, missionaries, and diplomats, and became a power in Europe and the world comparable to that of an established state.

To train his shock troops, Loyola developed what he called Spiritual Exercises. Every member of the Jesuit order—as the Society of Jesus is often called—had to undergo special Spiritual Exercises once a year, and in case of need, more frequently. They lasted about a month, during which time the candidate was kept apart from others and commanded to reflect upon his sins, pray for forgiveness, and concentrate his entire attention upon key doctrines of the Church. The Exercises were so emotionally intense as to alter the personalities of those who experienced them. The aim was to strengthen individual character, producing men who would be fully conscious of their religious duty—resolute, self-disciplined, obedient, at all times. St. Ignatius of Loyola was remarkably successful. Thanks largely to the Spiritual Exercises, thousands upon thousands of men who entered the Society of Jesus, from Loyola's day to the present, became new men to a degree seldom equaled by other religious orders or communities.

The Jesuits soon succeeded in checking the advance of the Protestant movement in Germany; and in eastern Europe they were the main agents in reconverting Poland and most of Hungary to Catholicism. Long efforts to bring England back to papal obedience eventually failed. Overseas, however, Jesuits were among the most active and successful Catholic missionaries, both in the Americas and in Asia.

Other important steps were taken to strengthen the Roman Catholic church. Simple catechisms were introduced to teach the doctrines of the Church to everyone. The papal Inquisition sought out heretics in Italy and punished with death those who refused to recant. The Council of Trent created an Index of prohibited books. The popes kept the Index current by adding titles of new books that were judged damaging to the faith. In countries where the rulers cooperated, such books could not be printed or sold legally. School systems were much enlarged. The Jesuits distinguished themselves by making their schools the best in Europe, combining a thorough training in Latin and mathematics with religious instruction.

The upshot of the Protestant Reformation and the Roman Catholic response was to make Europeans far more conscious of religious doctrine than before. Both the new Protestant churches of Germany and England and the revived Catholic churches in France, Italy, and Germany were more devout, learned, and serious organizations than had been true before Luther disturbed the religious balance of his time.

Yet religious division was the exact opposite of what everyone sought. There could be only one true Church and only one correct doctrine. All agreed on that. And the salvation of souls depended, everyone believed, on the correctness of beliefs and action in accordance with those beliefs. With these assumptions, no one could rest quietly when confronted by religious error. Their own immortal souls, and those of all persons around them, depended on suppressing mistaken and misguided opinions. It is not strange, therefore, that wars became religious, as Catholics and Protestants tried to impose their different versions of religious truth on each other.

RELIGIOUS
AND DYNASTIC WARS

Charles V abdicated in 1556 (effective 1558). He retired to a monastery and died soon after. The bulk of his possessions he left to his son Philip II of Spain. His brother Ferdinand I, however, inherited the Austrian lands and the title of Holy Roman Emperor. The two branches of the Hapsburg family continued to cooperate with each other in most matters, just as had been the case in Charles V's lifetime. Between them, Philip and Ferdinand inherited all the concerns that had distracted Charles V: the Turkish danger from the east, the rivalry with France, the Protestant movement in Germany and elsewhere. But Philip II tended to put a different priority upon the problems he faced. The suppression of Protestantism ranked higher for him than it had for Charles V, and the rivalry with France ranked correpondingly lower.

There was good reason for this, since France passed through a period of internal weakness from 1559 to 1598. In the first of these years, the French signed the Treaty of Cateau-Cambrésis with Philip II, giving up the long struggle over Italy and also surrendering French claims to the Low Countries. For the next few years, weak French kings succeeded one another on the throne, and it became more and more obvious that the Valois royal family was about to die out. This raised the question of succession to the throne.

During the same years, Calvinist preaching was particularly active in France, and a party of Huguenots, as the French Calvinists were called, came into existence. They fought a series of low-grade civil wars against a rival Catholic faction, headed by the family of Guise. After the death of the last of the Valois kings in 1589, Henry of Navarre, a Protestant and first of the Bourbon line, laid claim to the throne. In 1594 he gave up his Protestantism for the Catholic faith, saying, "Paris is worth a Mass," and was crowned king. But Henry IV did not become really secure on the throne until he had come to terms with his former Huguenot allies. This he did through the Edict of Nantes (1598), which allowed great nobles and some towns to maintain Calvinist forms of worship and guaranteed them the same political rights as Catholics. Philip II of Spain died in the same year so that he never had to face the strength of a reunited France.

As for the Turks, Philip II continued to wage war against them in the Mediterranean on and off until 1580, when he made a peace that recognized Turkish rights over the north coast of Africa as far as Algiers. This agreement represented a considerable gain for the Turks, though in fact they were never able to control north Africa from Constantinople. Algerian pirates preyed upon any and all ships that came their way, with scant regard for their supposed obedience to the Ottoman sultan.

Philip's struggle against heresy met with much success. As we have seen, the energy and religious conviction of the Roman Catholic church increased greatly, beginning with the pontificate of Pope Paul III (1534–1549). Spanish piety and Spanish ideals played a large part in this revival. Cooperation between the reformed papacy and the two branches of the Hapsburg house remained very close. All of central and eastern Europe felt the impact. Hapsburg officials, Jesuit confessors, and Catholic schools worked together to overwhelm Protestant heresy throughout a broad band of territory that reached from Italy northward across the Alps into Austrian, south German, Hungarian, and Polish lands. Only northern Germany and Scandanavia, together with the parts of Hungary under Turkish rule and areas of the Rhineland under Protestant German princes, escaped the force of this Catholic counteroffensive.

The Limits
of Hapsburg Power

In the western parts of Europe, however, Philip II of Spain met with serious setbacks. His wife, the English queen Mary, failed to bring her country back permanently into the Catholic fold. Worse still, the Netherlands revolted in 1567. Seasoned Spanish troops reconquered the southern part of the Netherlands (roughly, modern Belgium); but in the north the Dutch provinces could not be subdued, because the Dutch held command of the sea and were able to move supplies and troops to any threatened place more easily than the Spaniards could move overland against them.

The rebels received some help from Queen Elizabeth of England. English pirates, such as John Hawkins and Francis Drake, had also begun to prey upon Spanish ships on the high seas and to plunder Spanish towns in the New World. This eventually persuaded King Philip to try to settle accounts with the English, instead of concentrating everything against the Dutch. He therefore sent a great fleet northward in 1588, intending that it should pick up Spanish troops from the southern Netherlands and then attack England.

But Philip's plan failed. When his fleet, the Spanish Armada, sailed through the English channel, it suffered repeated attacks from Queen Elizabeth's ships, whose cannon fire damaged the Spanish galleons so badly that the plan of invading England had to be given up. Instead of trying to fight his way back through the Channel, the Armada's commander decided to return to Spain by sailing north around Scotland and Ireland. But his ships were caught in violent storms. Almost none of them ever returned to Spain.

King Philip's death in 1598 marked a turning point in Spanish fortunes. For nearly a century, Spain had been the greatest power in Europe, as well as mistress of the New World. After Philip's death, a reunited France, led by the new Bourbon dynasty, challenged Spain's political dominance in western Europe. Fifty years later, by 1650, the French monarchy had clearly become more powerful than the Hapsburgs of Spain. During the same years, the naval strength of England and of the Dutch Republic increased on all the oceans of the world at the expense of Spain and Portugal. Within Spain itself, it became more and more difficult for the government to keep up the armies required to defend the imperial position that the country had won between 1492 and 1598.

THE THIRTY YEARS' WAR   On the other hand, between 1618 and 1635, the Austrian branch of the Hapsburg house came close to winning control over all Germany. The progress of the Catholic Reformation in German lands strengthened the position of the Hapsburgs. In 1618, Protestant Bohemian nobles, fearing the consolidation of Catholic power, attempted to throw off Hapsburg control. This action started thirty years of bitter war that soon spread through most of Germany. On the one side stood Ferdinand II, Holy Roman Emperor and champion of Catholicism (reigned 1619–1637). On the other side gathered an unstable collection of Protestant princes. Early in the Thirty Years' War, Ferdinand overcame the Bohemian rebels (1620) and made that extensive kingdom thoroughly subject to his government for the first time. This resulted in a great expansion of his effective power, for Bohemia was richer as well as bigger than the Austrian lands.

Ferdinand also discovered that he could create a vast army by allowing the soldiers to live off the land. Albert of Wallenstein was the imperial general who first showed how effective a force maintained in such a way could be. Each time Wallenstein's army entered a new district, his soldiers plundered it thoroughly. The destruction to Germany was severe. On the other hand, the imperial armies occupied more and more territory.

The intervention of Denmark on the Protestant side (1625) did not check the progress of the emperor's armies; but when Gustavus Adolphus, king of Sweden, entered the field against them (1630), the balance was temporarily reversed. The Swedes won several famous victories, but could not destroy their opponents. In 1632 Gustavus Adolphus died in battle. Two years later Wallenstein, Emperor Ferdinand's most successful general, was assassinated. He had quarreled with his imperial master and may have planned to make himself and his army supreme in Germany.

By now almost everybody was sick and tired of the war, which had become more destructive than any in memory. The aging Emperor Ferdinand died in 1637. He was succeeded by Ferdinand III (reigned 1637–1657), who wanted to make peace. The hope of uniting all Germany again no longer seemed worth the cost. The danger to the Hapsburgs of an over-mighty general, such as Wallenstein, and of an army of plunderers had become quite obvious. Nevertheless, the war went on until 1648. The main reason was that the French intervened in 1635, hoping to keep the Austrian Hapsburgs busy in Germany so that they could not come to the aid of their Spanish relatives, who began a war with France in 1622. The war between France and Spain lasted until 1659, when the reluctant Spaniards were compelled to cede some small territories along the Pyrenees frontier to France, as well as a few towns in the Netherlands.

The Treaty of Westphalia finally ended the Thirty Years' War in 1648, leaving Germany devastated and divided into literally hundreds of separate little states. The Dutch Republic and Switzerland were both formally recognized as separate and independent countries, no longer part of the Holy Roman Empire. France and Sweden emerged as great powers, the one in western Europe, the other in the northeast. The weakened Hapsburgs were no longer a match for the combination of their French, Swedish, and Protestant German enemies. A new era of French predominance in European politics began.

Internal Political Development

In 1500 nearly every ruler in Europe had to persuade his subjects to pay taxes. Usually a meeting of "estates" (Diet or Parliament) authorized the ruling king or prince to collect certain taxes for particular purposes and for a limited period of time. The estates represented the different classes in society that paid taxes or helped to collect them from the peasants: nobles, clergy, and townspeople. Only in Italy did governments have standing professional armies and a large enough income to pay salaries to civilian officials.

By 1650 in Spain, France, Italy, and the Germanies, rulers generally had become absolute monarchs. This did not mean that they could do anything they wanted to do. It did mean that they did not have to consult representative bodies before collecting taxes or before spending tax income for whatever purposes the ruler and his personal advisers thought good. The religious wars in France, the Thirty Years' War in Germany, the Counter-Reformation in Italy, and the suppression of internal revolts in Spain had led to this result.

In fact, European rulers kept the interests of their subjects constantly in mind. They knew very well that their power depended on being able to supply their armies with guns and ammunition, food, clothes, and all the other things soldiers need. Equipping an army depended on industry and on trade. It meant trying to collect as much ready money inside the kingdom as possible, so as to be able to buy whatever might be needed. It meant, in short, close cooperation with capitalists and businessmen.

One important European government did not follow this policy. The Spanish rulers actually persecuted townsfolk who were not good Catholics, and they banished Jews and Moriscos (converted Moslems) from the country. These latter two groups had been among the most active businessmen of Spain, and their departure helped to bring on the economic decay from which Spain began to suffer after 1600. In general, the Spanish

Europe in 1648

Brandenburg-Prussia
Austrian Hapsburg lands
Spanish Hapsburg lands
Swedish possessions
Venetian possessions
Ottoman Empire

Boundary of the Holy
Roman Empire

Battle sites

Approximate division line
between Puritans
and Cavaliers in England,
May 1643

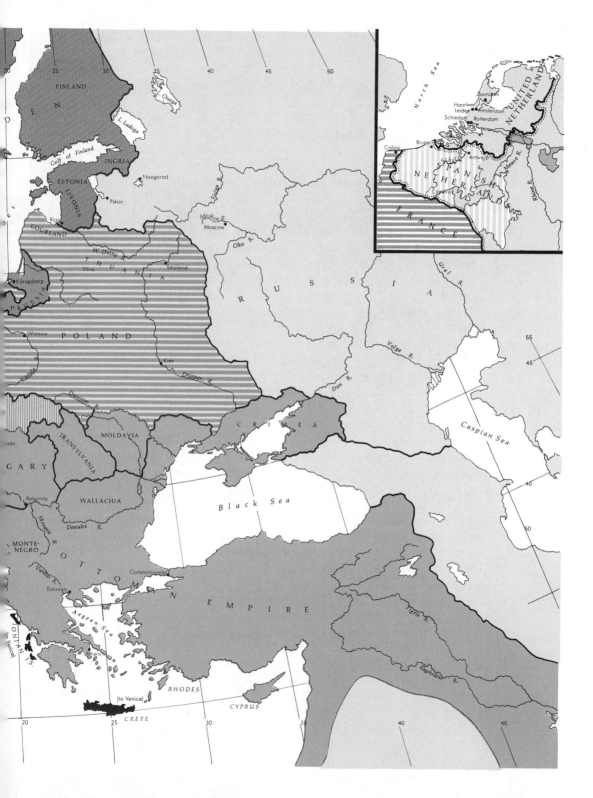

government fostered the interests of the Church and of the clergy more than of any other group in the population. The policy was successful in uniting Spain under the king and gave the Spaniards a cause for which to fight. But it weakened Spain economically, and other kings were not eager to follow such a policy.

The countries that lay around the edges of Europe's center did not become absolute monarchies before 1650. England came close to it under the Tudors (1485–1603). Parliament became almost a rubber stamp for Henry VIII and Elizabeth I. Under the Stuart kings, who succeeded Elizabeth, however, Parliament reasserted its claim to a controlling voice in royal policies and, as we shall see in Chapter 18, civil war led to the establishment of full-blown parliamentary government after 1688. The nobility of Portugal, Ireland, Scotland, and Sweden continued to be able to defy the king and his central government with armed force when it suited them. In Poland and Hungary the nobles kept sovereign political and military power in their own hands, for elected kings of these two countries had no administrative machinery to make their will effective.

Scattered through the heartland of Europe were the remnants of medieval city-states. In the Dutch Republic and in Switzerland, cities managed to create powerful and important new confederations. The Dutch, in fact, became the leading sea power of the world and handled the big business interests of all of Europe. The Swiss were famous soldiers and mercenaries. The Swiss Confederation was dominated by self-governing cities, such as Geneva, Zurich, and Berne, just as the Dutch Republic was dominated by Amsterdam and lesser cities. Venice, in Italy, and a score or so of imperial free cites in Germany carried on medieval traditions of republican self-government; but in these old-fashioned city-states, political power nearly always lodged in the hands of a privileged and wealthy few.

Only a few religious radicals supposed that the people had the right to govern themselves. It seemed self-evident that God had created separate social classes, or, as they were usually called, estates. Some were peasants, some were artisans; other were kings or nobles. Society was like a body: it needed a head, but it also needed feet and hands. Each class, or estate, had its appropriate part to play. If any class refused to fulfill its proper function, then the body politic was diseased. Nothing would go right until the disorder ended. The gap between rich and poor, educated and uneducated, peasant and master, was very great. Differences in clothing showed at a glance who was who. Manners and the way a person walked and talked showed his or her class as well as where he or she had come from. Each rank had its duties as well as its rights, and there was always the possibility of rising through government service, since the king or prince could issue patents of nobility to anyone he chose. A rich businessman could buy such titles or a civilian official might be rewarded for faithful service with a title to nobility.

On top of the whole system stood kings and princes, who recognized no superior but God. They held their positions by God's choice. Hence they ruled by divine right, just as their subjects served and obeyed by doing whatever they were born to do, according to God's will. Revolution, by such standards, was always wrong. Any injustices of this world would be corrected in the next. Only false religion, which might keep souls from Heaven, could justify rebellion. Hence, it is not really surprising that the wars and revolts, of which the century and a half between 1500 and 1650 was unusually full, were justified in religious terms.

A glaring gap in this social theory was that no rules or limits applied to the relations of one ruler with another. Each ruler claimed absolute sovereignty within his own territory. Each claimed the right to make war or peace with any or all neighbors. Scholars tried to find a natural law that would instruct and guide rulers in their dealings with one another. A Dutchman, Hugo Grotius (1583–1645), wrote a famous book entitled *On the Law of War and Peace* with this purpose in mind. But kings and princes followed Grotius' rules only when it pleased them.

In effect, the problem that had troubled Europe since feudal times— how to maintain public peace—was simply shifted to a different level. Rulers who succeeded in suppressing the war making power of the nobility brought a higher level of peace and order to their kingdoms than Europe had known since the days of the Roman Empire. But they used the same military force that kept peace at home to attack one another—with results that could be disastrous, as the Thirty Years' War showed.

THE REALM OF THOUGHT

The basic fact in Europe's intellectual history in these years was the breadth and depth of uncertainty that became apparent everywhere. The Reformation made the question of authority in matters of religion acute for everyone. Discoveries made by European explorers proved that the classical authors of antiquity had often been wrong about geography and knew nothing about the plants and animals of the New World. A series of important inventions, starting just before 1600, also allowed experts to see and measure things far more accurately than ever before. The microscope (invented *c.* 1590), the pendulum clock (invented *c.* 1656), the thermometer (invented *c.* 1607), the telescope (invented *c.* 1608), and the barometer (invented *c.* 1643)—all sharpened human senses and extended the range of observation as dramatically as the explorations a century earlier had done. Discovery of microorganisms in drops of water was no less surprising than the moons of Jupiter: things of which the ancients had never dreamed.

The Search for Certainty

Europeans responded to the tremendous uncertainty of the years 1500–1650 in two contradictory ways. Some, probably the majority, tried desperately to mend the chinks in their world view by finding a total and complete answer to all important questions through an act of faith. Calvin and his fellow Protestants, for example, made one basic assumption: God had told human beings all they needed to know in the Bible. Careful study of the Scriptures would, therefore, answer all important questions. Anything omitted from the Scriptures was by definition unimportant, and the only things that really mattered were the issues of salvation and righteousness with which the Scriptures dealt. The appeal of Calvinism rested largely on the logical simplicity of this assumption and on the skill with which Calvin was able to find answers from Scripture for the burning issues of the day. Roman Catholics, when stirred again to action by the Protestant challenge, also offered a complete system of belief. The more complicated origins of canon law and Catholic theology (based upon the Church Fathers, upon natural reason, upon Roman law, and upon decrees of the popes and councils, as well as upon the Holy Scriptures) were made up for by the greater completeness of the intellectual system and the detailed rules for conduct that Catholic priests could offer the faithful in nearly every circumstance.

The effort to find an authoritative answer for every important question was shared also by the great philosopher of the age, René Descartes (1596–1650). Descartes was a Frenchman, Jesuit-trained. He had a powerful bent for mathematics, and invented analytic geometry by combining the ideas and techniques of algebra and geometry. Descartes believed that mathematical reasoning could arrive at truths that everyone who understood the argument would have to accept. Each step followed logically and necessarily from the one before. A handful of simple self-evident assumptions were all that mathematicians needed to arrive at surprising and useful results. Why not, therefore, try the same thing with the age-old questions of theology and philosophy, about which everyone was quarreling so bitterly?

Descartes eagerly set out and found that he could logically doubt everything except the fact of his own existence. "I think, therefore I am," was his famous phrase. From this slender assumption he then set out to construct a complete philosophy by logical deduction. The existence of God; the nature of the soul; how the world machine, sun, moon, and stars worked; and how animal bodies functioned could all be demonstrated, according to Descartes, by careful reasoning.

The trouble, of course, was that the biblical, the Catholic, and the mathematical answers to important questions did not agree with each other. No one of them, even if complete and persuasive by itself, could command the acceptance of all Europeans. This indeed was what all the argument was about and what gave rise to so much persecution and bloodshed.

A few thinkers responded to this distressing situation by concentrating attention on whatever happened to interest them, leaving to one side the ultimate and important questions. In this way separate sciences and branches of a study made great progress. Sometimes, indeed, scientific progress upset some old idea that had been made part of official Church doctrine. In such cases the difference in outlook came clear between specialists who cared for detail and accuracy and others who felt that overall certainty was the only thing that really mattered. Calvin, no less than the papal Inquisition that condemned Galileo's astronomical discoveries, could not let scientific specialists pull down the sacred doctrine he believed in. But the specialists had a way of winning in the end, because they based their work on more and more exact observation, measurement, and experiment.

The Development of Science

The scientists who took such pains to observe and measure and calculate had special reasons for doing so. Two great theories about the world were in conflict: one was based on Aristotle's logic and other writings while the other, mystical and mathematical, looked back to Plato. Aristotle's way of thinking had been skillfully worked into a Christian mold by the great medieval scholastics, chief of whom was St. Thomas Aquinas. Aristotle's physics snd astonomy, revised in the light of more recent information, had also been well worked out before 1500. There was nothing important left to discover along these lines, a fact that made it all the easier for the Roman Catholic church to accept Aristotelian science as part of official doctrine.

During the Renaissance, however, men had rediscovered Plato and ancient "Pythagorean" writers. During his student days at the University of Padua in Italy, for example, Nicoláus Copernicus (1473–1543) accepted

Pythagorean ideas about the mystical power and special qualities of numbers. He later argued that the earth revolved around the sun because a circular path for the planets was more "perfect" than the complicated movements required by the Ptolemaic-Aristotelian theory that made sun, moon, and planets revolve around the earth. Johannes Kepler (1571–1630) corrected Copernicus' theory by discovering that the path of the planets around the sun was not circular but elliptical. This required exact observation and measurement of the positions of the planets. It also required, or at least was inspired by Kepler's conviction, that mathematical ratios between the orbits of the different planets created the "music of the spheres" of which Plato and Pythagoras had written.

In medicine, too, an extraordinary character, who called himself Paracelsus (1493–1541), challenged the authority of Galen on mystical

Galileo performing his famous experiment dealing with the movement of physical bodies. By dropping two objects of unequal size and weight from the leaning tower of Pisa, he allegedly disproved Aristotle's theory that objects fall at speeds proportional to their weights. (The Bettmann Archive)

grounds. Only then did careful surgeons, such as Andreas Vesalius (1514–1564), discover errors that resulted from the fact that Galen had used pigs instead of human corpses for dissection. Once Galen's authority had been shaken by such discoveries, doctors began to experiment with new drugs and treatments for disease—often, perhaps, more to the injury than to the benefit of their patients. All the same, knowledge increased. William Harvey (1575–1657), for example, laid the foundation for modern physiology by figuring out that the heart was a pump and that it circulated blood throughout the body by means of the arteries and veins. He was led to this theory, however, by the same complex of Platonic-Pythagorean lore that treated the human body as a microcosm of the universe, and the heart as equivalent to the sun around which, by the new Copernican theory, everything else revolved.

The thought of Francis Bacon (1561–1626) and of Galileo Galilei (1564–1642), like that of their contemporary René Descartes, marked the coming of age of a new era in European science. Francis Bacon was a

By the study of the swings of a chandelier in the Cathedral of Pisa, Galileo determined that the period of the swings was regular and predictable. He was one of the first to suggest the use of the pendulum in clocks. (New York Public Library Picture Collection)

successful English lawyer, but in his spare time he set out to invent a new sort of logic that would improve on Aristotle's. He believed that if people would only stop arguing about abstract matters and instead use their senses to observe nature and keep careful count of what they saw, all sorts of new and useful information could be discovered. Bacon was no scientist himself, nor was he, like Descartes, a great mathematician. His ideas remained apart from the mainstream of scientific development; and, in fact, no one ever really followed his inductive method of scientific discovery in arriving at important new ideas and theories. Yet Bacon put a new challenge to old Aristotelian ideas in the field and helped to give English thought its own distinct character, more concrete and down to earth than the theories that had greater appeal on the continent of Europe.

Galileo, on the contrary, was a great practical inventor and discoverer, as well as a theorist. Unlike Descartes, he did not try to use mathematical reasoning to construct a complete system of knowledge. Galileo merely found ways to measure exactly how physical bodies moved, and put his results into mathematical form. He never tried to answer every question the way Descartes did. Instead he stuck to a limited range—to what we call physics and astronomy today. He was an ingenious experimenter and pioneered the use of the telescope, discovering not only Jupiter's moons and Saturn's rings, but sunspots as well—thus, incidentally, disproving one of Aristotle's principles about the perfection of heavenly bodies.

More than any other single person, Galileo can be considered the founder of modern science. He emphasized testing theories by observation and experiment, and argued for his own discoveries and theories with unusual literary skill. Near the end of Galileo's life, the papal Inquisition compelled him to state publicly that some of his astronomical theories were wrong. Galileo submitted in order to keep out of trouble, but in private he made it quite clear that his opinions had not changed just because some officials of the Church made him say he had been in error.

Overall, the tensions and points of friction between those who tried to find complete answers to all questions in a total system of belief and those who kept searching for new information and knowledge in detail proved extraordinarily fruitful. Neither the one nor the other could long relax and assume that there was nothing more to find out, or no new point to defend.

Europeans pursued truth along many different lines. Sometimes, perhaps, the yawning uncertainties seemed dreadfully frightening. But the effort to do something about uncertainties meant rapid increases in knowledge and a restless testing of every idea and belief. The birth of modern science, with all the consequences that it had in later times, was the unexpected result. Human minds had never engaged in more fruitful or more fateful endeavor. The society and technology, the ideas and beliefs, the power and the risks of our own age arise largely from the continued development and practical applications of science as pioneered in the age of Galileo, Bacon, and Descartes.

THE PURSUIT OF BEAUTY

The efforts Europeans made to discover truth were matched by almost equally fruitful efforts to give expression to their sense of beauty. In literature, the century and a half from 1500 to 1650 was the time when most of the existing literary languages of western Europe achieved their definition. Miguel de Cervantes (1547–1616) in *Don Quixote* mocked medieval romances and created modern Spanish. French owed its literary definition largely to John Calvin, who wrote a version of his *Institutes of the Christian Religion* in that language. Luther's Bible defined modern German. The King James Bible (1611), together with William Shakespeare (1564–1616) and other Elizabethan poets, established modern English.

Westminster Abbey. (British Tourist Authority)

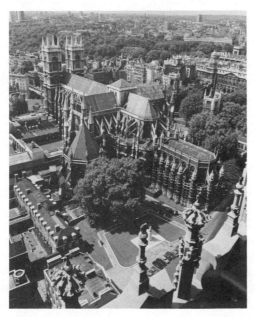

Latin remained the usual language for scholarship and science. It was also used for literary expression by men of letters such as Desiderius Erasmus (1466–1536) and Thomas More (1478–1535). In *Utopia,* More indirectly criticized injustices of the England of his day by describing a never-never land where people behaved rationally.

In the field of art, the force of Italian example was very strong. Especially in Catholic Europe, a more elaborate art style, called *baroque,* spread from Italy over southern Germany and eastward into the Austrian lands and Poland. The same style took root in the New World where great baroque churches attested to the power of the clergy to organize the labor and loyalty of the Amerindians.

Distinct national schools of painting arose in Germany, Spain, and the Low Countries. Painters such as the German Albrecht Durer (1471–1528), the Spaniard Diego Velásquez (1599–1660), the Fleming Pieter Brueghel (1525–1569), the Dutchman Rembrandt van Rijn (1606–1669) were each able to express something of the distinct national character of their homelands.

In Italy, the great days of Renaissance art ended with the disastrous wars that began with the French invasion of 1494. Particularly after the sack of Rome by Charles V's soldiers in 1527, one of the main centers of patronage for art was gone. The Catholic Reformation was less friendly than before to artists and to secular pursuits in general. Nevertheless, in Venice a school of painters carried on, including many well-known artists among its followers—Tintoretto (1512–1594) and Paolo Veronese (1528–1588) being the most famous.

Differing local traditions of art were sometimes mingled in the work of a single artist. The career of Domenico Theotocópuli (1541–1614)—born in Crete, trained in Italy, and active during his mature years in Spain, where he was commonly called El Greco (the Greek)—clearly showed the influence of all three of the environments he inhabited, allowing him to create a style which was distinctly his own.

In northern Europe (particularly in the Dutch provinces), artists took on new roles in society. Paintings intended for private display in homes could be bought and sold like other luxuries. This contrasted with older ideas about art, displayed in churches and other public places and intended to edify and instruct as well as to please the viewers.

In accordance with their new social role, a distinct Dutch school of artists came into existence which, along with Venetian, Spanish, and German schools, added greatly to the variety of European painting. But all these separate schools belonged together in some fundamental ways. They all accepted the techniques of perspective that had first been worked out in Italy about 1440, and all agreed that a good painting should create an illusion of three dimensional reality. These areas of agreement corresponded to the larger fact that Europe continued to have a loose but very real cultural unity throughout this age of sharp transition, despite all the fighting and quarreling in which Europeans continued to indulge.

Music, also, began to broaden. Systematic notation made possible more formal compositions. Court rituals and military parades gave new occasions for musical performances. Improved instruments opened new possibilities for harmony and rhythm. Singing and accompaniments became more closely linked to each other. In Italy the beginnings of opera date from before 1650. Congregational singing was a prominent part of Protestant services. Musical culture spread with Luther's hymns and Calvinist singing of psalms, as well as with the more stately and elaborate organ music that the Roman Catholic church permitted after the composer Giovanni Palestrina (1525–1594) showed what could be done by combining choral voices with organ music.

Europe's artistic life was thus vigorous and varied, open to new ways of doing things. Patterns of thought and patterns of art and literature that had been created in the Middle Ages were not treated reverently, as though they were models that could not be tampered with. Even the ancients, who had been held up as models by the humanists of the Italian Renaissance, were found to be in error on important points. People were thrown back on their own resources—to pick and choose from the past and from what they could find in the world around them.

Such an open situation positively invited experiment and a more or less free personal invention in the fields of art, as well as in thought. In both these fields, Europeans responded to their opportunity much as they were doing in practical lines of activity; that is, with extraordinary energy, imagination, and creativity.

CONCLUSION

The common denominator of all the confusing changes that came to Europe between 1500 and 1650 was this: western Europeans learned how to expand and intensify the energies they could bring to bear in almost every sphere of human activity. Overall, this meant a great increase in the power of the civilization both at home and abroad in contacts with other cultural traditions.

New kinds of organization allowed larger numbers to cooperate in peaceable and in warlike undertakings. The joint stock company, for example, was perfected just after 1600. Under a legal charter, it allowed the shared ownership of a company through the purchase of stock. The joint owners were liable in case of bankruptcy for only the amount of money each of them had invested. And, of course, as long as the company prospered, a joint owner could sell his share, sometimes at a price higher than he paid for it. Modern corporations are built on the same principles. What this kind of business organization did was allow thousands of persons to work together over long periods of time for goals defined by a small group of managers. Savings could be pooled, risks spread out, special skills put to fuller use by this kind of organization than was possible with family businesses or partnerships.

In politics, nothing quite so dramatic as the joint stock company was invented. Bureaucracy and standing armies were not new. But they became much more efficient and took charge of more and more activities. Local self-help and the authority of separate town governments suffered; so did the rights of noble lords over their peasants. On the other hand, it became easier for merchants to buy or sell anywhere within the kingdom without having to submit to local guild rules. Royal and princely governments also learned how to mobilize a larger proportion of the resources of their subjects for public purposes. Everything became more complicated as it assumed a larger scale. A handful of knights, supported by local peasants, no longer had any value on the battlefield. Instead, by the end of the period, dozens of cannon and thousands of muskets were what mattered, along with men carefully trained to use these weapons effectively. Skilled artisans, financiers, miners, smelters, wagon train drivers, riverboat captains and crews of seagoing vessels, tax collectors, army officers, drillmasters, and literally thousands of other specialists were needed to create and maintain such armies. But the cooperation of so many specialists produced more effective armies. Every new invention or improvement that worked spread rapidly, for no government could long afford to be without an armed force that could hold its own against neighboring states.

In thought and in culture, too, Europeans were able to find many new ways to mobilize greater energies. Sale of printed books, for example, allowed a man such as Erasmus to make a living as an author and scholar without having to take a post in a university or with the Church. The theater, too, by charging admission, created a livelihood for actors and playwrights such as William Shakespeare. Together, these changes gave secular literature a wider scope than before. The printing press also had great importance in spreading new ideas more rapidly and more accurately than previously. Luther's pamphlets, for example, made it practicable for anyone in Germany to learn the full details of his challenge to the papacy from Luther's own words—and to hear the arguments of his opponents, also. In less controversial fields, too, the printing press made exchange of information far more efficient. Travelers' reports of new lands, woodcuts portraying newly discovered objects, maps drawn according to the latest news, anatomical and botanical drawings, mathematical proofs, philosophical or theological arguments—any sort of information, in fact—could be made public through printing. This meant that those who cared about any particular line of inquiry could secure the latest and best data or theory much more easily than before, even when they happened to live far away from the place where a new invention or where new information had first been discovered. Once again, human energies over wider areas could be mobilized more efficiently: each new idea or new bit of knowledge that entered European learning gave people more things to think about. And just as the best-supplied and best-organized armies usually won battles, so also the best-informed and most experienced minds usually won arguments—and in doing so, enriched, enlarged, and expanded the intellectual inheritance of Europe as a whole.

Nowhere else in the world were these centuries nearly so full of fundamental novelties and departures from old ways. The appearance of well-armed European vessels along the shores of Asia did not make much difference to the old civilizations of that part of the world. Moslems, Hindus, Chinese, and Japanese were interested in keeping what they had and in keeping any necessary changes to a minimum. Only Europeans found it possible and necessary to question the assumptions of their ancestors so drastically—and so fruitfully.

CHAPTER 3

The World Beyond Europe

1500 to 1700

The pattern of communication created by the conquest of the world's oceans by European seafarers just before and just after 1500 did not upset the age-old balance among the major civilizations of Eurasia all at once. Both the Moslem and Chinese worlds continued to expand their territory very successfully until after 1700. Even the Hindus, although subjected to Moslem rule, gained new self-consciousness and energy through religious revival.

Outside of western Europe itself, the really radical changes during the centuries 1500–1700 were limited to the Americas, where the arrival of Europeans had immediate and disastrous impact on Amerindian peoples. Africa remained apart, although the slave trade brought throngs of Africans to the New World. On the other hand, Australia and Oceania were scarcely affected by European seafaring before 1700.

The new age that began about 1500 favored civilized peoples. This was dramatically evident in Asia and in eastern Europe where the development of guns gave civilized infantry a growing military superiority over nomad steppe cavalry. As a result, by 1700 Chinese and Russian armies had divided almost the entire Eurasian steppe between them. The eclipse of the nomads as a serious element in the military balance of Eurasia made land frontiers upon the steppe less and less critical, while the importance of seaboard regions, where European ships arrived and departed with growing frequency, became correspondingly greater for all the world's peoples.

Yet the challenges that European ideas and techniques offered to other civilized communities were not so pressing that they could not be disregarded, when it seemed easier to do so. Between 1500 and 1700, each of the Asian civilizations chose to take this path. It was especially tempting because the spread of heavy artillery to all parts of the civilized world allowed great imperial states to consolidate their hold over wide territories. Vast and mighty empires seemed in no danger from the occasional visits of European (or any other kind of) ships to their port cities.

Continuities are therefore more evident than revolutionary change in the history of the Asian civilizations during the first 200 years of European overseas expansion. Only in Japan, where an independent style of civilization was still comparatively new, and in Russia, where western Europe's pressure was felt more sharply because the distances were less, did far-reaching and drastic internal changes come to older patterns of life between 1500 and 1700.

THE WORLD OF ISLAM

In 1500 Moslems had no reason to doubt that the tide of world history was running with them, as it had done ever since the prophet Mohammed first proclaimed his revelation of God's truth in Mecca, centuries before. To be sure, the political unity of Islam lay in ruins, and civil war was constant. But this was nothing new. However reluctantly, Moslem thinkers had already come to terms with these political failures.

Moslem Territorial Advances

They could find reason to console themselves by considering the frontier successes that continued to come to Moslem warriors and to Moslem missionaries. In Africa and southeast Asia, Islam continued to expand throughout the two centuries that we are here concerned with. No single great event led to this result. Rather, Islam spread through a series of local conversions—sometimes of a city, of a tribal leader, or just of individuals—until they constituted a majority of the politically powerful persons in the region. Moreover, conversion to Islam was a gradual matter. Reverence for Sufi mystics led to acquaintance with the Koran and the Sacred Law. This in turn was prologue to familiarity with the entire cultural

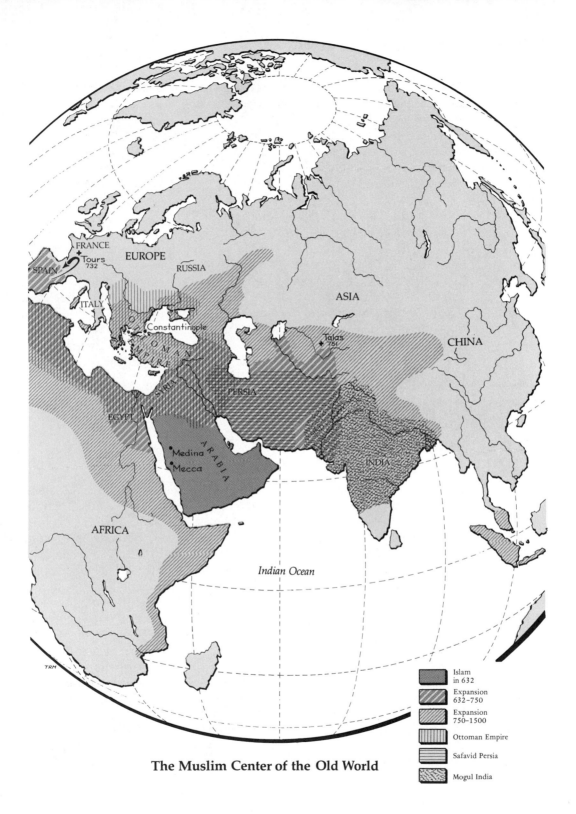

FRANCE
+ Tours
732
SPAIN
EUROPE
ITALY
RUSSIA
Constantinople
ASIA
Talas
751
CHINA
SYRIA
PERSIA
EGYPT
ARABIA
• Medina
• Mecca
INDIA
AFRICA
Indian Ocean

TRM

The Muslim Center of the Old World

▓	Islam in 632
▨	Expansion 632–750
▨	Expansion 750–1500
▥	Ottoman Empire
▤	Safavid Persia
▨	Mogul India

inheritance of Islam. Mastery of the Koran required a knowledge of Arabic, and knowledge of that language opened wide the door to the treasures of Moslem learning.

On the battlefield, Moslem arms also did well. All of India came under Moslem domination after 1565, when the Hindu Empire of Vijayana- gar fell to a coalition of local Moslem rulers. Java became Moslem by 1526 in the same way. Against Christian Europe, Ottoman arms reached their highwater mark in 1683. The long naval duel in the Mediterranean between the Turks and the Spaniards ended with Turkish success. They kept control of the eastern Mediterranean Sea and excluded the Spaniards from north Africa, except for a small foothold at Ceuta, just opposite Gibraltar. By land, Ottoman armies extended their power all around the Black Sea and, year after year, kept up a generally successful local frontier war with the Hapsburgs. In 1683 the Turkish imperial army again besieged Vienna, as in the days of Suleiman the Lawgiver, and again failed to take the city. The long war that followed ended in 1699 with the first really serious defeat the Turks had ever suffered in Europe. By the Treaty of Karlowitz, which ended the war, the Turks had to yield most of Hungary to the Hapsburgs.

Moslem Setbacks on the Steppe

This was not the first really serious territorial loss that the Moslems had suffered at Christian hands. In 1552 the Russian czar Ivan the Terrible, (reigned 1533–1584), conquered the khanate of Kazan. Four years later he also took Astrakhan at the mouth of the Volga River, thus opening the whole of that river to Russian settlement and trade. These victories added tremendous new territories to the Russian state; and the old masters of Russia, the Golden Horde, passed permanently from political existence. Not long afterward, Russian pioneers crossed the Ural Mountains. By 1588 they destroyed the khanate of Sibir and took control of the headwa- ters of the Ob River. Here, in the central regions of the steppe, Moslem states and peoples began to topple like ninepins in the face of Russian guns, backed up by Russian settlers. The reversal of relations between steppe cavalry and civilized infantry was nowhere demonstrated more emphatically, or earlier, than along Russia's eastern and southern fron- tiers. (See map, p. 77.)

Farther east, also, the Moslems suffered a serious setback. By 1515 a new tribal confederation, the Uzbeks, conquered the Amu Darya and Syr Darya valleys. In doing so, they dislodged bands of Persianized Turks who ruled the region. The Turks fled southward into India, and there in time erected the Mogul Empire.

This sort of domino action was age-old and completely traditional. What was different this time, however, was that the region, which the Uzbeks vacated when they moved southward, was taken over by a pagan tribe known as Kalmucks. Instead of becoming Moslem, as the Uzbeks and their predecessors in that part of the steppe had done, the Kalmucks preferred Lamaistic Buddhism. The same faith spread also among the Mongols and held its own among the Tibetans, who had created it in the first place.

Thus a distinct nomad religious community came into existence in eastern and central Asia, holding itself consciously apart from Islam as well as from China. In the end it was the Chinese, not the Moslems, who conquered these communities, although China's victory was not complete until 1757 when the Kalmuck confederacy, ravaged by smallpox as well as by Chinese guns and cavalry, finally broke up. With this defeat, the last significant steppe cavalry force dissolved. The history of east Europe and Asia had definitively entered a new phase.

These setbacks on the steppe did not provoke any sustained countermove on the part of the civilized states of the Moslem world. The steppe was in itself poor and unpromising ground. With the opening of the ocean route between Europe and the Far East, trade caravans, which had formerly crossed the steppe between China and the west, lost much of their importance. Animal packtrains could not compete with the cheapness of ship transport.

Moreover, the steppe route was soon outflanked on the north also. Russian pioneers quickly mastered the art of traveling through the northern forests. They traveled in summer by boat and in winter by sleigh along the rivers that made a series of natural highways. Relatively short and easy portages connected one river system with the next and the native inhabitants—simple hunters and fishers for the most part—offered no resistance to Russian backwoodsmen who carried guns as part of their normal equipment. Hence, by 1638 Russian explorers reached the Pacific Ocean at present-day Okhotsk. They were attracted by furs, which they forced the local peoples to collect for them as a form of tribute. These furs were exported both to China and to Europe, where they were in great demand. Tea and other Chinese goods were then carried back to Russia along the same river route.

Thus the loss of the central portions of the steppe seemed no great matter to the men who controlled the great Moslem empires.

The Rise
of the Safavid State

Far more significant from the Moslem point of view was the great religious and political upheaval that came into the open in 1501 when Ismail Safavi openly proclaimed himself the descendant of the seventh Imam and therefore the true and only legitimate leader of the Moslem community. Ismail was a Shia. That is to say, he belonged to one of the sects of Islam that refused to recognize the legitimacy of the Omayyad caliphs and claimed instead that only descendants of Ali, Mohammed's son-in-law, could legitimately lead the community of the Faithful. The Safavid sect had been in existence for many years and a secret propaganda had spread its ideas far and wide over Iran and eastern Anatolia. Ismail's Turkish soldiers were organized tribally, just as Mohammed's soldiers had been in the first days of Islam. The fanatical spirit of the Shia movement was also similar to the spirit that had kept the original Moslem community together.

As a result, Ismail won a series of rapid victories. In 1502 he took Tabriz in Iran and crowned himself shah. He captured Baghdad and Mesopotamia in 1508, and defeated the Uzbeks in 1510. In 1514 a widespread rising of Ismail's sympathizers took place in Anatolia against the Ottoman sultan. Selim the Grim had to mobilize the whole strength of his imperial army to suppress the Shia rebels. When he had drowned the uprising in blood, Selim drove ahead toward Tabriz to try to stamp out the source of the infection. He was able to defeat Ismail's troops in battle, thanks largely to the Ottoman artillery; but he could not capture Tabriz or destroy his rival.

Instead, Selim decided to eliminate any possible allies Shah Ismail might be able to find within the heartlands of Islam by conquering Syria, Palestine, Egypt, and the part of Arabia where the holy cities of Mecca and Medina were located. This he did in two years' campaigning, 1515–1517. But Iran was just too far away from Constantinople to allow the Ottoman armies to conquer it. The Turkish cavalry had to return to their estates after each campaigning season, and the sultan had to get back to his capital to assert his personal control over the central government. Hence the Ottoman armies operated within definite limits. Vienna lay at one extreme of the Turks' effective campaigning range, Tabriz at the other. Neither city could be captured, given the methods of transport and military organization available to the Ottoman Empire.

THE RELIGIOUS ISSUE: SHIA *VS.* SUNNI   Shah Ismail's claim to be the only legitimate political and religious leader of Islam was profoundly troublesome to all other Moslem rulers. It opened up again all the difficult

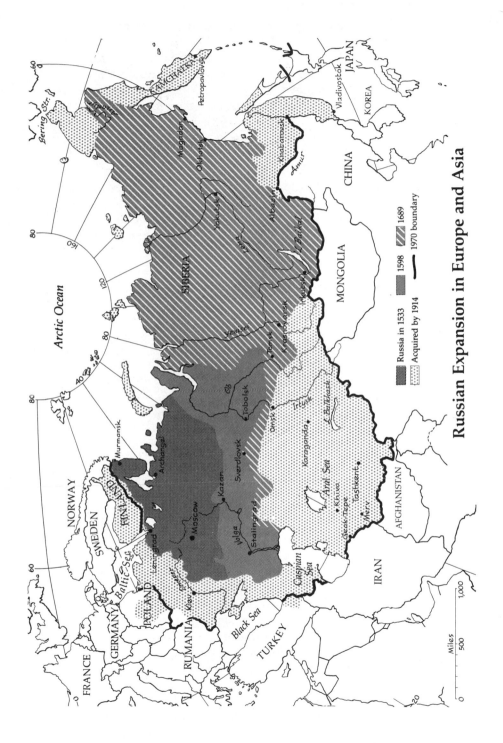

Russian Expansion in Europe and Asia

Russia in 1533
Acquired by 1914

1598
1689
1970 boundary

problems of righteousness in social and political matters. What claim, indeed, did Turkish upstarts like the Ottoman sultans have to rule Moslems? Who was the rightful successor to the Prophet? What was the true and proper basis of religious and political authority?

These questions were strikingly similar to the issue of authority in matters of religion that was raised by the Protestant Reformation in Europe at almost exactly the same time. In Europe, Luther's challenge to papal authority provoked centuries of argument and a strenuous reexamination of biblical and early Christian texts. No universally accepted conclusion was reached, of course; but in the struggle for an answer, the depth and breadth of European knowledge and scholarship were greatly increased.

The Sunni Moslems of the Ottoman Empire responded to the Shia challenge differently. The pattern was defined under Sultan Suleiman (ruled 1520–1566), whom Europeans called "the Magnificent" but who was called "the Lawgiver" by his own people. Suleiman put the full weight of his government behind Sunni orthodoxy. Schools for training experts in Sunni law were set up; and a carefully controlled hierarchy of religious officials, much resembling the hierarchy of the Orthodox church, was established in every Ottoman town. Unorthodox dervish communities were not usually persecuted. Rather, the Ottoman government allowed them to set up special *tekkes* (that is, monasteries of a sort). These were often out in the country, where the dervishes could pursue the mystic vision of God in their own way without dangerously exciting the religious sentiments of the people as a whole.

Suleiman's efforts to reorganize and reinvigorate Sunni Islam worked. Revolt did not break out afresh. Shia believers went underground, pretended to accept the official form of Islam, and passed on their doctrine only to small, secret, initiated groups. This was as before. What was new was the official organization and control of the teachers and lawgivers of Sunni Islam—an intervention on the part of the state in the affairs of religion of which earlier Moslem empires never dreamed.

Ottoman success in controlling Shia heresy was made easier by the fact that the raw religious excitement of Shah Ismail's time faded rapidly. Ismail's heirs soon quarrelled with Shia experts in the Sacred Law who were called ayatollahs. The shahs claimed God-given, absolute power; the ayatollahs wanted to subordinate the shah's government to their own interpretation of God's will. Both did agree, however, that all traces of other forms of Islam should be destroyed.

Accordingly, the Safavid government launched a great effort to make all the shah's subjects into true believers according to the doctrines of the so-called "Twelver"* sect of Shia Islam. Special catechisms and

* "Twelvers" were those who recognized twelve legitimate successors to Mohammed before the line of Ali's descendants came to an end. Other Shia sects recognized different lines of descent from Ali and fewer legitimate successors to the Prophet.

schools taught the people what to believe. The former tolerance of religious variety and even of skepticism—a spirit very much in evidence in some late Persian poetry—abruptly disappeared. Persian culture took on a new, intolerant Shia coloring. The change that came to Iran under the Safavids was therefore similar to the change that came to Italy under the influence of the Counter-Reformation. In both countries, religious uniformity was achieved at the cost of cultural creativity.

The Moslem rulers of India also had to come to terms with the Safavid claim to universal authority over all true believers. Both Baber (ruled 1526–1530), the founder of the Mogul Empire, and his successor, Humayun (ruled 1530–1556), publicly accepted the Shia faith at times when they badly needed help from the Safavids; but both renounced their Shiism when they were not in need of help. Akbar (ruled 1556–1605), who first put the Mogul Empire on a stable basis, tantalized everyone by experimenting with all sorts of religious views. Christian missionaries who came to his court were sure that he was about to become Christian; but in fact he probably thought of himself as the head of his own religious community, experimenting with truth, seeking answers to all sorts of ultimate questions with a more or less open mind.

Akbar's successors adopted orthodox Sunni Islam, and the emperor Aurangzeb (ruled 1658–1707) tried to suppress both Hindu idolatry and Shia error. In doing so, he conquered previously independent Shia states in southern India and expanded the Mogul Empire to its greatest extent. But he also aroused Hindu hostility. Guerrilla actions against the Moguls, which started in Aurangzeb's lifetime, quickly undermined the power of the central government in the years that followed his death.

The Splendor of Moslem Art

Moslem art entered upon a particularly splended period with the development of the Ottoman, Safavid, and Mogul empires. The Safavid shah, Abbas I the Great (reigned 1587–1629), for example, created a new capital for himself at Isfahan and made it one of the architectural wonders of the world. The Taj Mahal in India, built for the Mogul emperor Shah Jahan (reigned 1628–1657), was erected only a little later. Persian miniature painting also attained its highest point in these centuries, when expert craftsmen were gathered together at court and given every facility for their work. Traces of Chinese and European techniques are easy to find, but the gemlike coloring and minute detail of the Persian miniatures make them one of the world's great art traditions.

In India a similar and closely related style of painting developed around the Mogul court. Hindu painters used Persian technique to portray scenes from Hindu mythology, creating what is called the Rajput school of art. Other arts, like carpet weaving, furniture design, and jewelers' work, also attained a very high refinement in the imperial workshops, where only the very best could please.

Moslem Thought and Literature

Intellectually, however, Islam showed far less energy. Formulas inherited from the first centuries of Islam were simply reasserted, memorized, repeated. New thoughts were actively discouraged, perhaps because they threatened always to uncover once again the raw wound created by the Safavid challenge to political and religious legitimacy. Even such subjects as geography, in which Moslems had long taken a special interest, failed to respond to the stimulus of the European discoveries. Pious Moslems refused to read Christian authors, and so the new geographical knowledge that flowed into Europe was disregarded.

Literature escaped stagnation only by calling new literary languages into being at both the Ottoman and the Mogul courts—Turkish at Constantinople and Urdu at Delhi. Turkish and Urdu writers drew heavily upon Persian literary models, for the great Persian poets of the Middle Ages continued to command the admiration of all Sunni Islam. But they were banished from their homeland, for the Shia religious teachers could not abide the delicate ambiguities of religious doubt upon which classical Persian poetry depended for much of its effect.

Weaknesses of Islamic Societies

Despite its brilliant success, Moslem civilization had an important weakness. In almost every part of the Moslem world, just a tiny minority of rulers and landowners really shared in Islamic high culture. Peasants were left out, and of course they were the great majority. Poor townspeople, too, had little in common with the lords and governors who employed some of them to build splendid mosques or tombs or to work in the luxury trades. Western Europe was, by comparison, much more coarse and vulgar. Even peasants entered the market. Refinement in western Europe may have been less; but what there was spread further down the social scale than in the Moslem lands.

In the Ottoman Empire, an important new circumstance arose from the fact that after 1638 the Turks stopped taking children from the Christian villages of the Balkans and training them to become soldiers and administrators of the empire. Instead, new members of the sultan's slave household came to be recruited from among the sons of those who already served the sultan. The result was to cut off what had been an important link between the Ottoman government and the Christian peasantry of the Balkans. As long as the high administrators of the Ottoman Empire had begun life as ordinary villagers, they could never lose a certain underlying sympathy with the communities from which they had come. When, however, officials came to be mainly sons of officials, all sympathy with the peasants disappeared. Discontented peasant boys, who in an earlier time might have become soldiers and administrators of the empire, became brigands instead.

This change weakened Ottoman society. So did the decay of trade and manufactures, which became noticeable about 1650. Perhaps what happened was that the financial and business entrepreneurs of the Ottoman Empire turned away from trade and used their funds instead to buy the right from the government to collect taxes from a district, a town, or even from an entire province. This practice is known as tax-farming. It allowed the tax-farmers to make a handsome profit by collecting more from the public than they had paid for the right to fleece them. On the other hand, funds invested in this way were not economically productive; indeed, it probably became dangerous to invest in trade and manufacturing, for anyone who did make money from such activities was a natural target for the tax collectors. At any rate, the foreign trade of the Ottoman Empire passed almost entirely into the hands of French, Dutch, and English merchants, who took raw materials from Turkey and brought woolen cloth and other manufactured goods into the empire in exchange.

In the Indian Ocean also, the arrival of Dutch and English traders after 1600 began to cut into Moslem sea trade as the Portuguese had never done. The Dutch and English put great effort into developing trade between Asian ports, for their own manufactures were hard to sell in India. The Dutch East India Company (organized 1602) took on the task of managing the agriculture of Java and adjacent islands, forcing local rulers to make their subjects plant whatever crops the Dutch judged would command the best sale in world markets. The English East India Company, organized in 1600, developed a flourishing trade in Indian cotton cloth. English agents made cash advances to Indian weavers and told them what kind of cloth to produce. In this way the English were able to take on the management of cloth production and sale throughout the whole Indian Ocean area.

The increasingly active and dominant role played by European traders in the economic affairs of the Moslem empires was a sign of things to come. But in 1700 no one could have foreseen that the English East India Company would become the successor to the Mogul emperors as rulers of India, or that the might of the Ottoman sultans would crumble before European intervention. Moslem rulers cared next to nothing about who carried the trade from their ports or planned and controlled cotton manufacturing in their dominions. Such activities were the concern of humble folk who, as long as they paid their taxes and kept quiet, did not interest the rulers of the Moslem world in the slightest. The care most European governments (except Spain!) took to foster trade and manufactures differed sharply from the attitudes of Moslem rulers, and reflected the greater sympathy between rulers and townsmen in Europe. Thus, the economic history of Moslem lands also reflects the fundamental weakness of Moslem society: the wide gap between the upper class of rulers and the rest of society.

This gap was nothing new. On the contrary, it was as old as civilization itself in the Middle East. Only the comparison with Europe made the weakness potentially dangerous. Indeed, by every standard except the standard set by Europe's contemporary development, Islam was in a flourishing condition between 1500 and 1700. Moslem dismay, when after 1700 they discovered their weakness, was correspondingly profound.

HINDU REVIVAL

The fact that after 1565 no independent Hindu state survived anywhere except in the remote island of Bali did not paralyze Hindu culture. On the contary, Hinduism entered upon a new stage of development that gave it the ability to withstand Moslem and, later, Christian missionary efforts with ease. What happened was this: two great poets and a famous holy man gave a new focus to Hinduism. The holy man was named Chaitanya (d. 1527). He was born a Brahman but in early manhood began to experience intense mystic experiences, during which his followers believed he actually became the great god Krishna.

A god incarnate was no ordinary thing, even in India. A religious sect soon developed around Chaitanya, important particularly in Bengal, where Chaitanya himself lived. His followers eliminated all caste distinctions. This undercut the main attraction of Islam for Indian minds. Until Chaitanya's time, members of the lower castes, especially in Bengal, had often become Moslem. After the new sect had come into existence, conversion to Islam almost ceased. The emotional conviction felt by Chaitanya's followers found expression in warm manifestations of common feeling in public ceremonies. This proved far more attractive than Islam, even in Sufi form.

The two great Hindu poets, Sur Das (d. 1563) and Tulsi Das (d. 1623), took stories from the two great Hindu epics, the *Mahabharata* and the *Ramayana*, and put them into the common language of northern India. The effect was comparable to what happened when Protestants translated the Bible into the everyday languages of western Europe. Ordinary people memorized long passages from the two poets. Schoolboys studied them. The lessons of piety and good manners their poems emphasized became standard. Hindu self-consciousness and religious uniformity increased.

Of the two, Sur Das was the less influential. He chose to celebrate the deeds of Krishna, and in later life was admitted to Akbar's court. His poems have a Persian touch about them. Tulsi Das, on the other hand, concentrated his religious devotion upon Rama, and escaped all taint of foreignness. Tulsi's poems entered very deeply into all later Hindu religious and cultural life. They emphasized Rama's role as both god and man, and expressed intense personal devotion to him.

This was, indeed, the effect of all three men's work. Worshipers identified themselves with one single figure, who was both god and man at the same time. Other deities and myths in the Hindu tradition were not rejected outright. But in practice each devotee focused his exclusive attention on a single god-man. The result was to create something rather like different sects in Hinduism—some preferring the worship of Krishna, others concentrating upon Rama. But both these deities were held to be incarnations of Vishnu, so there was no ultimate conflict betwen their worshipers.

Devotion to Shiva, the other great god of earlier Hinduism, tended to fade somewhat. So did the crude magic of Tantrism. On the other hand, the most ancient layer of Hinduism—the Sanskrit rituals based on the Vedas and administered by Brahman priests—continued to be necessary for all ordinary crises of human existence. The Brahmans, with their unintelligible Sanskrit chants, had to be called in for birth, coming of age, marriage, and death. Only the followers of Chaitanya refused to honor Brahmans, because they upheld caste and distinctions based upon caste.

In the practical sense, too, Hindus continued to play an important part in the Mogul Empire. Emperor Akbar relied very much upon Hindu administrators and tax collectors, and his successors continued to do the same. Many Hindus continued to possess large estates and served in the Mogul army as warriors alongside the Persian-speaking Turks who constituted the core of Mogul power. The Hindu upper classes tended to take on much of the secular culture of their Moslem rulers. They, for example, were the patrons for whom Rajput painting was produced.

The overwhelming majority of the population of India remained

Hindu. They treated the thin layer of foreign rulers who held the Mogul Empire together as a sort of caste—to be lived with but not to be imitated or listened to, or regarded as anything but what it was: an alien body in the midst of Indian society.

The missionary force of Islam was blunted by such attitudes. Hinduism had found a popular, emotional appeal through Chaitanya and the poets. There was no need to wrestle with Moslem accusations of idolatry any longer. Except in the extreme south, Hindu temples had been destroyed. The new forms of worship took place in public places out of doors, and did not focus on idols but on hymns and prayers and congregational rejoicing. Hindus readily believed that the tremendous antiquity of their sacred texts made them superior to the Koran, or, for that matter, to the Christian Bible. Hinduism, in other words, had nothing to fear from outside, being rooted securely in the feelings of the Indian people as a whole.

In Java, however, Hinduism crumbled before Islam, as we have already seen. On the mainland of southeast Asia and in Ceylon, Buddhism remained vigorous, partly, at least, because it allowed the Burmese, Siamese, Vietnamese, and Singhalese peoples to preserve their national identities in the face of Islamic and other foreign pressures.

THE CELESTIAL
EMPIRE OF CHINA

When the first Portuguese reached the coast of southern China in 1513, the Ming Dynasty was already beginning to suffer from the signs of decay that had often before afflicted Chinese dynasties. Heavily taxed peasants were ready for revolt. Unruly generals intrigued for power. Tax income ceased to flow smoothly to the imperial court, and the nomads along the northern and western frontiers were restless.

In addition, the Ming government had to cope with piratical attacks from the sea that soon assumed a serious scale. The majority of the pirates were Japanese. By 1555 they were strong and numerous enough to sail up the Yangtze River as far as Nanking to besiege that great city. Nothing in Chinese experience had prepared the Ming rulers for this kind of attack. Efforts to organize a Chinese navy that could police the seas and suppress piracy were sometimes successful, but the emperors always decided to economize and disband the naval force when it had done its work. The result was that discharged sailors often joined up with pirate crews—confirming the court's worst suspicions about sailors, and

An example of Manchu art, a landscape by Wang Hui (1632–1717).
(Smithsonian Institution, Freer Gallery of Art)

at the same time making it necessary to organize a fresh campaign to clear the seas of pirates once again.

The Portuguese fitted into this disorderly picture with no difficulty at all. The Chinese soon recognized the fighting qualities of Portuguese ships and made a sort of informal alliance with them. In return for allowing the Portuguese to trade from Macao, near Canton, the Chinese got a promise of Portuguese help against the Japanese (1557). On the other hand, when it suited them, the Portuguese turned to piracy themselves.

In 1592, the Japanese warlord, Hideyoshi, attempted to cap his victorious career by attacking and conquering China. He sent a large Japanese army to Korea, where the Ming armies fought a long, hard campaign against the invaders. The struggle was undecided when Hideyoshi died in 1598. His successors simply withdrew. In an effort to stabilize political conditions at home, the new rulers of Japan, the Tokugawa shoguns, first restricted and then completely closed Japan to contact with foreigners. Strict laws prohibited Japanese ships from sailing to other countries from Japanese ports. Foreigners were also, of course, refused the right to sail into a Japanese harbor. The result was to remove the main pirate threat. The Chinese were therefore spared having to do anything about improving sea defenses—a success which cost them dearly two centuries later when European gunboats began to demand access to Chinese ports.

The Manchu Conquest

Neglect of the sea frontier was inescapable, since the Ming were under increasingly dangerous attack from the north and could not stop rebellion from within. In 1615, Manchurian tribes formed a powerful confederation and began nibbling away at Chinese territories. Then, in 1644 the commander of the Manchu confederation entered Peking, supposedly as a supporter of a Ming general who was trying to put down rebellion. Once inside Peking, however, the Manchus ceased pretending to serve the Ming emperor and instead proclaimed a new dynasty. Manchu forces soon overran the rest of China; but the island of Formosa held out until 1683, when it, too, submitted to the new rulers of China.

Like many steppe conquerors before them, the Manchus tried to keep their own people separate from the Chinese. Special garrisons of Manchu soldiers were set up at strategic places, mostly outside big cities, and high military command was rigorously reserved for Manchus. The civil administration, nevertheless, remained entirely Chinese. Indeed, the Manchus were already half won over to Chinese culture before they invaded the country and had none of the Lamaist foreign taint that made the Mongols so unpopular among the Chinese. However, many Mongols were fitted into the ranks of the Manchu army, for there were not enough Manchus to control all of China. Some Chinese also served as soldiers, but they always remained in subordinate posts.

The new emperors busily set out to improve defenses against the steppe peoples to the west and met with such solid success that by 1755 the danger from the steppe was forever destroyed. Incidentally, the Chinese Empire as we know it today was created by the Manchu annexation of Tibet, Sinkiang, Mongolia, and, of course, Manchuria too. The territory administered by the Chinese emperor almost doubled as a result. Traditional China acquired a fringe of half-empty borderlands in which to expand. The process is still under way today.

The Manchus also cultivated Neo-Confucian learning and conformed gladly to Chinese imperial precedents in all matters affecting the internal administration of the country. Population grew rapidly, both because of an improved level of internal peace and because introduction of the sweet potato and other American food crops allowed the Chinese to cultivate hilly lands, especially in the south where rice paddies could not be created.

Christian Missions to China

All foreigners were barbarians in Chinese eyes. They became worthy of courteous attention only when they had taken the pains to learn Chinese and become gentlemen. The first European to accomplish this feat was Matteo Ricci, a Jesuit missionary, who hoped to convert China to Christianity by winning over the emperor and his court. In 1601 Ricci gained permission to travel to Peking, where his mastery of Chinese learning made him acceptable to the officials and scholars who governed China.

Other Jesuits followed Ricci and soon proved that they had more accurate knowledge of astronomy and calendar making than the official court astronomer did. A Jesuit accordingly was appointed to this office, giving the mission an official status from which it could not easily be removed. Correct calculation of the calendar was thought to be of great importance, since lucky and unlucky days for undertaking new enterprises depended on having a calendar that accorded correctly with the motions of the heavenly bodies.

The Chinese also found European geographical knowledge interesting and delighted in mechanical toys and pendulum clocks that the Jesuits imported from Europe. But these were trifles. Educated Chinese felt sure that everything important was already well taken care of by traditional Confucian wisdom. Jesuit efforts to convince the Chinese of the truth of Christianity therefore fell on deaf ears, though poor children and others who were helped by the missionaries with food or medical service did sometimes become Christian.

The missionaries themselves faced an interesting dilemma. How could the technical terms of Christian theology be translated into Chinese? Or, put in another way, how did Chinese religious ideas and terminology fit into a Christian framework? Was ancestor worship idolatrous? Or was this only a family ceremony, honoring but not worshiping the dead? The Jesuits, after some hesitation, decided that ancestor worship was not worship at all, but a simple civil ceremony. They also decided that the Chinese word "Tien," usually translated "Heaven," was a suitable equivalent for the Christian word "God." These decisions meant that the Jesuits could point out to a Confucian scholar that he was already half-Christian and did not need to change family custom to become fully Christian by admitting the truth of divine revelation as recorded in the Bible and interpreted by Catholic tradition.

Such arguments did not convince many Chinese, and they profoundly shocked other Christians who had come to the Far East to convert the heathen and wished to have no truck with pagan ways. Serious controversy began in 1628 and dragged on until 1742. The Jesuits, of course, tried to defend their policies, and in doing so wrote extensive accounts of Chinese society and civilization. Learned Europeans in this way acquired a remarkably full, often idealized stock of information about China.

As a result, appreciation for Chinese art and admiration for Chinese principles of government found a considerable lodgment in Europe. Even more important, quite a few Europeans tried to understand Chinese civilization as a whole and in itself, apart from their own inherited prejudices and opinions. This marked a new kind of relationship between different civilizations. Nothing could stand in sharper contrast to the sublime self-satisfaction of the Chinese educated class, who continued to believe that nothing of value could come from mere "south sea barbarians."

China's Cultural Conservatism

Given such attitudes, little really new could arise in Chinese culture. Scholars became more and more rigorous, and set out to scrape away Buddhist and Taoist ideas in order to get back to the authentic Confucian point of view. Paintings and poetry continued to be produced in quantity, for every cultivated man had to be able to paint and write good verse. But all this fell into well-worn, thoroughly traditional patterns. Experts agree that the works of the writers and artists of the Ming and Manchu periods were inferior to earlier paintings and poems. Prose tales, smelling of the street, did get printed for the first time, and a new dimension to

The arrival of the ambassadors of the Dutch East India Company in Japan, from a 17th century engraving. (The Bettmann Archive)

Chinese culture thus entered the literary record. But that is about all that changed.

Chinese social structure remained what it had been ever since Sung times. Growth of manufacturing and trade was matched by the increase in agriculture that resulted from the use of American food plants. Merchants and businessmen accepted the low social station to which Confucian doctrine assigned them. As soon as they could, they escaped by buying land and sending their sons to school to become gentlemen. Upward social mobility fed energetic and capable men into government and strengthened the existing social order at the same time.

Thus the Manchus brought stability within a busy, prosperous, and extremely successful traditional order. Confucian ideals asked for nothing else. In 1700, reality came closer to matching the universally accepted principles of Chinese society than at most times before or any time since.

JAPAN'S SHARP SHIFTS OF POLICY

The Japanese welcomed the first Europeans to visit their shores more warmly and with a livelier interest in what the strangers had to offer than any other Asian people. St. Francis Xavier arrived in Japan in 1549, only six or seven years after the first Portuguese adventurers had come. His proud and imperious bearing impressed the Japanese. The Jesuit mission he inaugurated soon met solid success. Japan lacked any national religion of its own. Its religious loyalty was divided among Buddhist sects, Neo-Confucianism, and the still undeveloped imperial cult of Shinto. This undoubtedly helped the progress of Christianity.

Another contributing factor was the political division of the country. Local lords found it very much to their advantage to welcome missionaries. Missionaries could attract European ships to the ports where they were well treated and could warn them away from places where Christian preaching was not permitted.

European ships were important in two ways. They had guns for sale, and a European cannon or two could knock down castle walls with ease. This often made all the difference in the local wars that had long been chronic in Japan. In addition, the Chinese government officially prohibited trade with Japan, because Japanese pirates were raiding the Chinese coast all the time. But a Japanese gentleman needed silks and other elegancies from China. The Portuguese were able to import such commodities and carried Japanese silver to China in exchange. Portuguese merchants profited handsomely from this trade and cooperated closely with Christian missionaries to make sure that both silk and guns were channeled exclusively into friendly Japanese hands.

Unification of Japan

Nevertheless, only a minority of the Japanese nation accepted Christianity, and the missionaries suffered, as well as profited, from their involvement in politics. This became obvious when, after a series of more and more violent wars, the whole of Japan came under the control of a successful warlord, Toyotomi Hideyoshi (1537–1598). Hideyoshi started out as a stableboy, but his ruthlessness and ability carried him to supreme power by 1590. He viewed foreign missionaries as political rivals and in 1587 issued a decree banishing them from the country. Yet, strangely enough, he did not enforce his own decree. Perhaps he was afraid that if he acted too harshly against the missionaries, the Portuguese would break off trade relations just when he was eager to build up his armaments for the invasion of China.

In 1592 Hideyoshi launched his great adventure on the Asian mainland by invading Korea. Early victories were followed by a long and difficult stalemate, and when Hideyoshi died in 1598 the Japanese forces were quickly withdrawn. The reason was that his followers soon quarreled. Each lord wanted all of his troops on hand at home. In a great battle fought in 1600, one of Hideyoshi's lieutenants, Iyeyasu Tokugawa, came out on top.

Iyeyasu Tokugawa was a much more cautious man than Hideyoshi. After his victory, he sought only to keep what he had won by making his new position as secure as possible. He made Tokyo his capital and planted reliable family retainers as fief holders in most of Japan. In outlying regions, however, he permitted independent "outside lords" to retain their possessions. Iyeyasu kept careful watch on all fief holders and required each ruling family to leave hostages in Tokyo to guarantee good behavior. The imperial family and court continued to exist at Kyoto, but the Tokugawa family made sure that the emperors had as little to do with the realities of power as possible.

The new system of government is referred to as the Tokugawa shogunate, because the head of the ruling Tokugawa family took the title *shogun* (commander of the imperial army). The regime lasted until 1867. Succession rested within the Tokugawa family, regulated by family rules. But the family possessions were so extensive that what amounted to a bureaucracy of officials had to be invented to administer the lands held by members of the Tokugawa family. Hence, while old feudal forms survived, something quite different grew up underneath.

The Closing of Japan by the Tokugawa Shoguns

During the first decades of Tokugawa rule, the family was deathly afraid of renewed struggles for power among the warrior class. Hideyoshi's son, for example, was killed in 1615 to eliminate a possible rival. A code of conduct for warriors, emphasizing loyalty to the feudal superior, was formally published in 1615. Active persecution of Christians began in

1617. When a body of Japanese Christians revolted in 1637, the shogun reacted by stamping out every trace of the foreign religion he could discover. Since the Japanese Christian community had reached a quarter of a million or more, this involved large-scale violence and much bloodshed. All foreign missionaries were killed. Japanese Christians who refused to renounce their religion were also executed, with great cruelty.

At the same time, the shoguns established a new policy of total isolation from the rest of the world. In 1636 Japanese were forbidden to leave the home islands. Anyone who did so was refused the right to return. In 1638 Portuguese traders were driven from Japan. Three years later arrangements were made with the Dutch whereby a single ship was allowed to come to Nagasaki once a year. Even then, it could only dock at an island in the middle of the harbor. In this way the shogun felt that foreign intrigues could be prevented, and supplies needed from abroad could be carefully controlled.

Intervention in Japanese political-military affairs, which had allowed the first Christian missionaries to attain such important successes, thus backfired after less than a century, to the bitter cost of their converts. At the same time, Japan lost an opportunity to create a sea empire in the Far East similar to the Japanese Empire created during World War II; for the shogun's policy of isolation compelled Japanese mariners to stay home and stop raiding and trading across the seas surrounding Japan which they had begun to dominate.

Divergent Forms of Japanese Culture

A time of such profound political shifts might be expected to create important new forms of cultural expression. That was, in fact, the case. Hideyoshi's age was a time for bigness and brashness. Hideyoshi himself was a great egoist, a religious skeptic, and flamboyant in everything he did. He built a bigger palace than had ever been seen before in Japan; and when he invaded Korea, he announced that his aim was the conquest of the whole world, beginning with China.

Japanese artisan skills developed rapidly in Hideyoshi's time. Chinese and Korean captives established or expanded new industries in Japan, such as fine pottery manufacture and silk weaving. Eager efforts to imitate European gunsmiths were also successful, though shortages of iron always hampered Japan's armament. City life developed with the new wealth that came from overseas ventures, as well as from trading within Japan.

The Tokugawa regime was tamer and much more conservative. In

1608 Iyeyasu made Neo-Confucianism official. His successors continued to patronize this Chinese school of learning. Its emphasis upon deference toward superiors seemed to justify the Tokugawa system of government. Yet the active, unruly life of the cities, which had taken such a spurt of growth in the age of the civil wars, did not disappear with the end of political disorder. On the contrary, peace provided still greater opportunities for trade within the Japanese islands.

The merchant class and other city dwellers, therefore, continued to support the popular, vigorous, and, at least occasionally, crude and sensuous culture that had come to the fore in Hideyoshi's time. In strong

TALE OF THE FORTY-SEVEN RONIN

Kira, the shogun's secretary, was a proud and haughty man. He mocked the clumsiness of Asano, a country noble who did not know the proper rituals for court behavior. One day, when Kira commanded Asano to fasten his shoe and then criticized the way the bow had been tied, Asano grew angry, drew his sword, and slashed the secretary's arm.

Great was the dismay at court. Not only had Asano wounded the shogun's secretary, he had also defied court ritual—for no one was allowed to draw his sword in anger at court. Asano's only honorable course was suicide, which he performed in the traditional manner (hara-kiri) by cutting his abdomen open with the same sharp sword.

But this was not the end. Asano had forty-seven faithful followers, his *ronin*. They were fighting men with no fiefs of their own, who depended on the gifts of their lord for a livelihood. Now, thanks to Kira, Asano was dead. The ronin's duty was plain: revenge! But Kira was crafty and strong. He had his own ronin to protect him; and after Asano's death they were all especially alert, expecting some effort at revenge.

Asano's forty-seven ronin therefore decided to wait. They pretended to forget their lord and went in for drunken brawling. Then, when two years had passed and Kira's men were lulled into carelessness, the forty-seven ronin assembled one night and attacked the secretary's palace, killed his bodyguard, and cut off Kira's head. The revenge was sure; but, as before, court ritual had been broken. What to do?

To escape being treated like criminals, the forty-seven ronin followed their master's example and each committed hara-kiri. Thus they lived up to the Japanese warriors' code, faithful even unto death.

contrast to this tradition, the samurai class cultivated a heroic ideal, from which all forms of self-indulgence were banished. Loyalty and courage, even to the sacrifice of personal life and fortune, were the supreme virtues. Suicide by harakiri was an accepted and admired solution for any personal failure to live up to the warrior ideal. In the realm of art, this ideal found its own appropriate expression in the manufacture of magnificent swords and in such spare entertainments as the "tea ceremony" or the art of flower arrangement.

Japan therefore developed a curiously double face under the Tokugawa regime. Officially all was controlled, traditional, and strongly colored by Chinese models. But underneath, in the cities particularly, a sharply different cultural tone prevailed. Friction between these two worlds could not be avoided. Constant tension mirrored political strains, never entirely suppressed, between the Tokugawa family and the outside lords, and between the shogun and the emperor.

This situation kept Japanese minds open to new thoughts in a way that was not true to China. In China practice and theory matched one another so closely, after the Manchu conquest had again established a strong imperial authority, that no one could doubt the essential rightness of China's inherited wisdom and skills. The Japanese, on the contrary, had plenty of reason to wonder about a system that valued warrior skills above all others, yet gave the samurai no chance to use their skills— and which officially put merchants at the bottom of the social scale, but in practice allowed them to grow richer than any warrior. Such disproportions between theory and practice meant that the Tokugawa government was like a corset for Japanese society, enclosing something quite at odds with, and very difficult to fit inside of, the official framework.

RISE OF THE
RUSSIAN AUTOCRACY

The effectiveness of firearms, together with the furious energy of war captains such as Hideyoshi, united Japan. Russia's dramatic expansion over all of northern Asia was likewise the direct result of the revolution in warfare that came with the spread of gunpowder weapons.

For more than 200 years, Moscow and other Russian towns, except only for Novgorod far in the north, paid tribute to the heirs of Genghis Khan, rulers of the Golden Horde, who made Kazan their capital. When Ivan III, the grand duke of Moscow, repudiated his subjection to Kazan in 1480, he continued to collect tributes that had once been forwarded to the Golden Horde. Ivan simply used them to support his own army and his own set of officials. This made Moscow by far the most powerful of Russian cities. But the Muscovites found themselves militarily inferior to their western neighbors, the Swedes and Poles, whose wealth and armament, commercial development, and level of culture were all superior to those existing in the Russian lands.

This presented Ivan IV and his successors with a difficult problem. Constant effort was needed to keep their western neighbors from taking over Russian lands. Russia required large and well-equipped armies, but the government could not afford to pay for everything that was needed. The solution that Ivan IV adopted was a violent revolution from the top. He seized the lands of most of the old, noble families of Russia and assigned them to his own personal followers. These men were required to serve the czar (literally Caesar or emperor), as Ivan started to call himself, as soldiers and officials without salary. To make their lands worthwhile, peasants had to cultivate them and pay rents. To assure the necessary labor power, the Russian government passed laws that made it more and more difficult for peasants to run off into the woods or southward to the open steppe. In this way a burdensome form of serfdom, approaching slavery, was fastened upon the Russian peasantry.

In theory there was a rough sort of justice in the system. The peasants served their lords, who in turn served the czar; and the czar served God by protecting the Russian lands and the Orthodox faith from foreign encroachment. Moreover, the system worked, though not without difficulty. As long as Ivan IV lived, he kept his western enemies more or less in check, losing only minor border territories to them. Meanwhile, as we have seen, Russia profited enormously by expansion south and east at the expense of the steppe nomads. But Ivan left an incapable son to succeed him, and the son died without a direct heir. A confused period, known as the "Time of Troubles," followed. Poles invaded and occupied Moscow for a couple of years, and claimed the crown for the king of Poland. The Swedes also overran important new territories inland from the Baltic coast.

The Time of Troubles

Inside Russia, the greatest confusion reigned. Old noble families were interested in getting power back into their own hands. Far to the south, a rude, democratic Cossack community of warriors had arisen in the steppe. The Cossacks joined the fray, opposing the nobles and sympathizing with the peasants, but also robbing them as they marched to and fro across the countryside. The new "service nobility" that Ivan the Terrible had created lacked cohesion and leadership, once the legitimate line of czars died out. Several pretenders, each claiming to be the son of Ivan the Terrible, only added to the confusion.

In this situation, merchants and townspeople, together with the leaders of the Orthodox church, played a critical role. The Poles were Catholic, and their invasion of Russia was partly a crusade to bring that land under the pope. In 1595 the pope agreed to permit the eastern churches to continue to conduct services in Church Slavonic, and to keep some other peculiarities of ritual—making the sign of the cross with three fingers instead of two, for example. These concessions persuaded the high clergy of the Ukraine to accept the papal claim to headship of the entire Christian Church. Those who followed them were known as Uniates, and the branch of the Roman Catholic church that thus came into existence was commonly referred to as the Uniate Church.

Russian national feeling, however, was deeply committed to the idea that the one true Orthodox Christian faith had found refuge in Russia after the fall of Constantinople. To admit that the pope's claims to rule the church were right seemed a dreadful heresy to most Russians. Hence it was not difficult for the head of the Russian church, the patriarch of Moscow, to rally widespread popular feeling against the invaders. He was aided by the merchants and townspeople, who in turn rallied the service nobility and peasant sentiment behind a movement to throw the Poles out of Russia and to reestablish a czar to defend the true Orthodox faith.

In 1613 a national assembly representing different classes of the Russian state chose a new czar, Michael Romanov, the son of the patriarch of Moscow. Reorganized Russian forces soon drove back the Polish invaders and reestablished the autocracy. The Romanovs, like the Tokugawas, were cautious rulers and adopted a policy of keeping strangers at a distance, as far as possible. Japan could close its doors completely, being an island. Russia had more difficulty in isolating itself because of its long, open land frontiers. All the same, the first Romanovs reduced communication with the outside world. Foreign traders were required to live in special ghetto quarters in the towns, for example, and contact with them was reduced to a minimum.

Church Reform

But the pressure from the west was unrelenting. In particular, Jesuit missionaries, who had been extremely successful in eliminating Protestantism from Poland, kept up an assault upon Orthodox "errors" that could not be neglected. The trouble was that the Russian church books were full of mistakes that had crept in through errors of translation or of copying.

Jesuit scholars delighted to point these out, and some of them were so obvious that they could scarcely be denied. Yet Russian clerics could not admit that the Jesuits were right without seeming to endanger their whole claim to Orthodoxy.

In 1667 a new and masterful patriarch, Nikon, decided to "take the bull by the horns." He set out to revise the Russian prayer books and service manuals by going back to the Greek originals and correcting whatever errors had accumulated over the centuries. Since the Greek church was undeniably older than the Roman church, the appeal to Greek church books seemed like an effective reply to Catholic propaganda.

On the other hand, any change in the familiar phrases of the church services shocked many Russians. An important party, known as "Old Believers," refused to accept Nikon's reforms and, indeed, accused him of being Antichrist. The czar soon quarreled with Nikon, but even after deposing him, maintained the policy of church reform. What to do with those persons who refused to accept the revised forms of church ritual then became a serious problem. The czar resorted to persecution, but this simply drove religious dissent underground.

Communities of Old Believers spread over Russia and became particularly numerous in the fringe areas, where the power of the state was weak. Some groups developed extreme doctrines, expecting the end of the world at any minute and seeing in the acts of the czar fulfillment of the prophecies in the book of Revelation.

Costs and Gains of Russia's First Encounter with the West

Russian society thus came to be sharply divided. The upper class accepted the restored czardom and the revised forms of church worship. But they ruled over a "dark and deaf" peasantry who felt that their masters had betrayed true religion as well as elementary social justice. Peasant revolts expressed the anger of the lower class, but the uprisings always failed. Such experiences merely confirmed the Old Believers in thinking that Antichrist was on the march and that the end of the world was truly at hand. Expecting God to set right the injustice from which they suffered, they remained, for the most part, sullen but passive when a new czar, Peter the Great (ruled 1689–1725), undertook still another revolution from the top to bring Russia more fully into touch with the western European world. But since Peter did not begin his reform until 1698, we shall wait until a later chapter to consider his career and its importance for Russia and the world.

One point, however, deserves emphasis here. The very real and profound troubles that Russia had in coping with the west and in keeping the Poles and Swedes in check had the effect of making the Russians extremely successful in their dealings with the peoples to the south and east. Thus the time when Russia's problems with the west were especially acute was also the time when the vast Russian Empire took shape. Siberia and the Russian Far East in the Amur Valley were occupied under the first Romanovs. Even more important, the Ukraine was annexed to Russia in 1667.

Russia in fact became, with China, the principal gainer from the gunpowder revolution that undermined the battle effectiveness of steppe cavalry. In 1689, after minor collisions in the Amur Valley, the two powers signed the Treaty of Nerchinsk, defining boundaries and regulating trade between them. By this treaty a buffer zone, including Mongolia and the lands around the Ili river, was declared off limits for both the signatories. But by thus delimiting the zone of nomad life, the two great agricultural empires of Russia and China were also signing the death warrant of independent nomad power.

However costly in themselves, Russia's troubles in adjusting inherited ways so as to repel western attacks therefore paid off handsomely across Russia's other frontiers.

THE NEW WORLD

The Amerindians, like the Russians, had to change their ways drastically between 1500 and 1700 to adjust to the presence and activity of western Europeans. Moreover, the gap between Amerindian and European society was too great to allow the inhabitants of the New World to gather the same kind of compensation that came to the Russians. Instead, wherever they came into close contact with Europeans, Amerindian communities suffered cruel disruption and soon lost all effective independence.

Spanish Empire in the Americas

In the most highly developed regions of the New World—Mexico and Peru—Spanish policy was to convert the Indians to Christianity but otherwise to leave their village communities alone. Nevertheless, as disease cut into the native population, the Spaniards and their descendants needed to use a large proportion of the remaining Indian manpower to keep their mines and other economic enterprises going. Ways were found of breaking into the Indian villages despite the legal protections that Spanish law gave the natives.

In particular, Indians might become debtors and then could legally be required to work off the debt. So, in practice, it was easy for Spanish ranchers to keep their Indians constantly in debt and thus assure themselves of a steady supply of labor. The mine owners had more difficulty, for their labor needs were much greater. Labor shortage, however, promoted laborsaving improvements. As a result, the Mexican mines became among the most technically advanced in the world. After about 1650 the tremendous destruction of population by disease came to a halt. But by then the population of central Mexico had been reduced from between 11 and 20 million persons to a mere 1.5 million. Recovery was slow at first, for death rates remained high.

Despite the drastic depletion of the Indian population, Spanish America, before 1700, became the seat of a flourishing provincial version of Spanish Catholic civilization. Mexico City and Lima were great cities by European standards—far larger and more impressive than anything yet established by English or French colonists. Universities were founded to train priests and lawyers needed by the Spanish regime. The universities kept up close connections with the European world of learning and imported such novelties as the philosophical speculations of Descartes soon after they burst upon the European intellectual scene.

The Indians were excluded from such activity; but their own cultural traditions were shattered beyond repair. Only simple village crafts—basketmaking, weaving, or the like—survived. Everything else disappeared with the overthrow of the priests and rulers who had governed the Amerindian civilizations. Thus Spanish power and Spanish culture were secure and unchallenged in the New World, even though only a few persons of Spanish birth or descent shared in them fully.

Portuguese Brazil

In Brazil, the Portuguese settlers created a much more complicated and disorderly society by importing large numbers of slaves from Africa to work the sugar plantations, upon which the prosperity of the colony soon came to depend. Since few Portuguese women left home, Portuguese men married African or Indian wives and recognized their children as legitimate. A gradation of racial mixtures therefore emerged in Brazil that was more complex than the Spanish-Indian blend. Moreover, since the African slaves brought their own cultural traditions with them to the New World, African elements enriched the Indian and Portuguese cultural traditions to make the Brazilian heritage unique.

Brazil's political history was also more complex than the bureaucratic regularity that prevailed in the Spanish Empire. First the French and then the Dutch tried to take over Brazil and were driven out by the colonists themselves. A bold buccaneering spirit led the Brazilians to penetrate deep into the Amazon forests, looking for slaves for the sugar mills and, later, also for gold and diamonds, which were discovered in the interior of the continent. Recurrent friction with Jesuit missionaries who controlled the Guarani Indians of Paraguay and with Spaniards who settled along the Rio de la Plata gave local bands of Brazilians an excuse to raid and plunder far and wide. By doing so they extended the boundaries of their colony at a rapid rate.

French and British Colonies in North America

By comparison with the Spanish Empire and even with Brazil, the British and French colonies in North America were still poor and undeveloped in 1700. Nowhere had settlement penetrated far from the coast. Colonial society was, for the most part, a crude, simplified version of the English and French model. Permanent settlement began at Jamestown in 1607 and at Quebec in the following year. But the infant colonies grew slowly at first. The easy wealth the first settlers expected was not to be found. Conditions were hard, food short, the climate unfamiliar. The arrival of religious dissenters (Puritans) in Massachusetts, beginning in 1620, added a new strain to the English settlement of the New World. The Puritans became a body of hard-working, disciplined people, ready to undertake the heavy labor of cultivating even the stony soils of New England.

Like the Spaniards, the French put great emphasis upon converting the Indians to Christianity and tried to protect them from unscrupulous traders. But European diseases proved fatal, even when communicated by well-meaning priests. As a result, the Indians of Canada and the northeastern United States did not long survive close contact with the strangers.

The French in Canada soon found a profitable trade in furs. Explorers learned how to travel by canoe along the waterways of the continental interior. By going up the St. Lawrence River to the Great Lakes and then portaging from Lake Michigan to the Mississippi River, the French outflanked the English colonists, who were blocked from the deeper interior by the Appalachian Mountains. The government of New France (the possessions of France in North America) was closely controlled from Paris. Governors, appointed by the king, managed all important affairs.

The English colonies were much more varied. Virginia and Massachusetts had both been founded by companies chartered by the king of England. New York was acquired from the Dutch in 1664 by conquest, having, however, already been granted to the king's brother, the duke of York. Pennsylvania was founded on the strength of a royal grant to William Penn; and many of the other colonies started through grants to other proprietors.

Between 1640 and 1660, England was troubled by civil wars. In 1688 the mother country suffered another revolution and plunged into European wars. During most of this time the colonies were allowed to go their own way with only occasional efforts at supervision from England. Moreover, efforts to centralize control in London met with strong local resistance. When the royal charters for Virginia and Massachusetts were canceled, for example, and governors were sent out from England to conduct the public affairs of the colonies, they found themselevs face to face with representative assemblies whose members were used to running their own affairs. Hence nothing like the orderly dignity and systematic thoroughness of Spanish or even of French administration ever prevailed in the English colonies. Instead, they became a refuge for religious dissenters (Catholic, Quaker, and Puritan) as well as for other misfits of English society.

Relations with the Indians were left largely to local decision. The settlers early found that they could not make the Indians work for them. They sometimes tried to treat the Indians fairly. William Penn was the chief exemplar of this policy. But in general, the settlers trampled on Indian rights and took what they wanted or could use without troubling themselves about what their actions might do to the Indians.

The fact was that the Indians could not defend themselves or make their wishes effective politically except by trying to play off the French against the English. But even with French guns and diplomatic encouragement, desperate acts of violence against the encroaching English could not restore Indian lands. Such attacks, however, convinced almost all the colonists that the Indians were cruel and dangerous enemies who could not be trusted.

Everywhere along the frontier where Indian communities were confronted by the newcomers, the Indians withered and drew back, unable to offer much resistance. Disease was always a factor. In addition, the Europeans had vastly superior knowledge and skills that put the Indians at a disadvantage they could never overcome.

AFRICA AND OCEANIA

The improvement of transportation, which resulted from the opening of the world's oceans by European explorers just before and immediately after 1500, meant that all the simple societies of the earth that lay within easy reach of a coastline were in the same sort of danger as the Indians of North America. There were obstacles of distance which it took time to overcome, especially in the Pacific, where the smaller islands were, in general, not explored or disturbed by European sailors until after 1700. Australia, too, remained effectively isolated behind the Great Barrier Reef that made approach from the north difficult for sailing ships. The coastlands of the Arctic were but slightly disturbed by the activities of English traders in Hudson Bay (from 1670) or in the White Sea (from 1553). In these parts of the world, age-old hunting and collecting societies continued to live in their accustomed ways, without noticeable disturbance from outside.

Africa and the Slave Trade

The African continent was much more complicated. Ships could not penetrate far into Africa, except along the Nile, because rapids near the mouths of all the African rivers interrupted navigation. Diseases dangerous to Europeans made the interior distinctly unattractive for white people. Moreover, there was little occasion for them to think of traveling inland because slaves, Africa's main export, were delivered to the ports by Africans themselves.

Effects of the slave trade on African life in the interior are scarcely known. Many villages must have been destroyed and many thousands of people must have died either on the way to the ports or on shipboard while crossing the ocean. Yet nothing suggests widespread depopulation. Perhaps the spread of American food plants, particularly maize, more than made up for the loss of life caused by slave raids. Furthermore, slave raiding and trading broke down local isolation. Relatively large military-political units took shape in most parts of Africa, and the migration of Bantu-speaking tribes southward brought large new territories into the circle of "Black Africa," at the expense of Bushmen and Hottentots.

Portuguese efforts to convert Africans to Christianity met with little success, though slaves were nearly always introduced to Christianity by their masters in the New World. This was, indeed, one of the principal

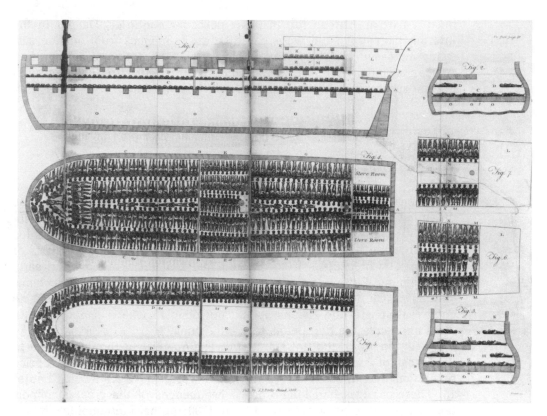

The horrors of the African slave trade are well illustrated in this 1808 engraving of a slave ship. (*Library of Congress*)

grounds upon which Europeans justified the slave trade, for souls saved from eternal damnation seemed (to some people) a fitting return for a lifetime of bodily servitude. Islam, on the other hand, continued to win fresh converts in both east and west Africa, though many tribes remained pagan by choice and rejected Islamism as well as Christianity.

African society and native culture, therefore, did not crumple up and decay at the touch of either Moslem or European strangers in the way that Amerindian society did. One reason was, again, disease. In Africa it was the strangers who died of unfamiliar infections, not the Africans who had accustomed themselves to survival in spite of malaria, yellow fever, and other tropical diseases that killed off Europeans regularly. In addition, the level of African civilizations in west Africa and along the coast of east Africa was such that the arrival of new sorts of strangers, even when they had better ships and guns than had ever been seen before, did not make very much difference. Long-distance trade had been a part of African life in these parts for centuries. Deeper in the interior, the simpler old ways could go on. Influences from outside certainly increased, but there was nothing utterly disruptive or new in that. African societies therefore were able to survive their first collision with Europe successfully, as Amerindian societies were not.

CONCLUSION

The appearance of European sailors, soldiers, and settlers in the Americas disrupted and, in time, destroyed the earlier Amerindian societies. Nowhere else, however, did the opening of the oceans to European ships have anything like such drastic consequences. In the civilized ports of Asia, mixing of peoples from different parts of the world was already quite familiar. European skills and knowledge did not persuade Moslems, Hindus, or Chinese to abandon familiar ways. There seemed to be no good reason why the Asians should not cling to what seemed good to them and leave the Europeans to do the same.

Yet the world did not stand still. The opening of the oceans led to the spread of American food crops, to population increase, and to a price revolution that affected all the civilized world, as we saw in Chapter 15. These changes had long-range consequences of the greatest importance. Within the 200 years from 1500 to 1700 another fundamental change took place within the Eurasian continent: the age-old superiority of cavalry to infantry came to an end. This was the result of the development of guns and muskets, which allowed foot soldiers to fire volleys that could break up an ordinary cavalry charge.

In Eurasia, consequently, the advantages that steppe nomads had enjoyed ever since 700 B.C., when attacking farming peoples, ceased to exist. Rapid expansion of civilized control over the steppe regions resulted. Nevertheless, before that happened both India and China underwent one final conquest from the steppes. In India the conquest led to the establishment of the Mogul Empire, beginning in 1526, and in China to the establishment of the Manchu Dynasty that ruled from 1644 to 1912.

The development of guns and muskets also meant, in all civilized countries, that central governments had growing advantages over more local authorities. Cannon could knock holes even in well-defended castles and city walls. But siege guns were expensive and conspicuous, which made it easy for a central authority to monopolize them. Local leaders, accordingly, had to submit far more completely than had been customary.

Everywhere in the civilized world, therefore, the size of political units and the effectiveness with which a single ruler could impose his will on distant parts increased sharply between 1500 and 1700. Almost all the buffer zones between the separate civilized communities of Eurasia were rapidly gobbled up by one or another civilized government. Russia and China were the two powers that gained most from this situation; their territorial expansion in fact paralleled Spain's empire-building in the Americas both in time and geographic scale.

Improved communication among all the coastlines of the world increased the pace of social change everywhere. Many small and weak communities disappeared completely. In fact, only in Africa (and perhaps in New Zealand) were local peoples able to withstand and, in time, react successfully to the challenges that sudden exposure to civilization presented to previously isolated peoples.

These changes in world relationships were fundamental and vastly important for human history. Yet it would be wrong to emphasize the novelties too much. Each of the major civilized traditions of the Old World continued along familiar and well-worn paths. Moslems continued to win converts along almost every frontier. Hindus underwent a religious revival that assured the continued vitality of that cultural tradition despite political subjection to Moslem rulers. The Chinese underwent the crisis of going from the rule of one dynasty to another in a completely traditional fashion. They did so rather more quickly and painlessly than had often been the case in earlier centuries, and emerged so strong and prosperous as to arouse the admiration of many Europeans when they learned how the Chinese governed their "Celestial Empire."

The western European world, to be sure, showed signs of a growing expansive power. European settlement of the Americas began to make inroads upon the continental vastnesses of North and South America. Until long after 1700, most of the New World was not occupied by settlers of European origin; but it was clear enough, all the same, that Amerindian populations could not stop westward expansion across North America, nor prevent occupation of the temperate parts of South America.

On Europe's eastern flank, Russia became more and more closely tied to the west. The relationship irritated the Russians, for they wished to keep their Orthodox faith and defend their cultural independence from western Europe. But they had to do so by borrowing western skills, importing western workers, and becoming more like the western nations of Europe. Russia's experience between 1500 and 1700 was thus a foretaste of the dilemmas other civilized peoples confronted later on when Europe's power compelled Moslems, Indians, Chinese, and Japanese to pay attention to what had happened in that remote peninsula of Asia called Europe.

Dispersal of Agriculture

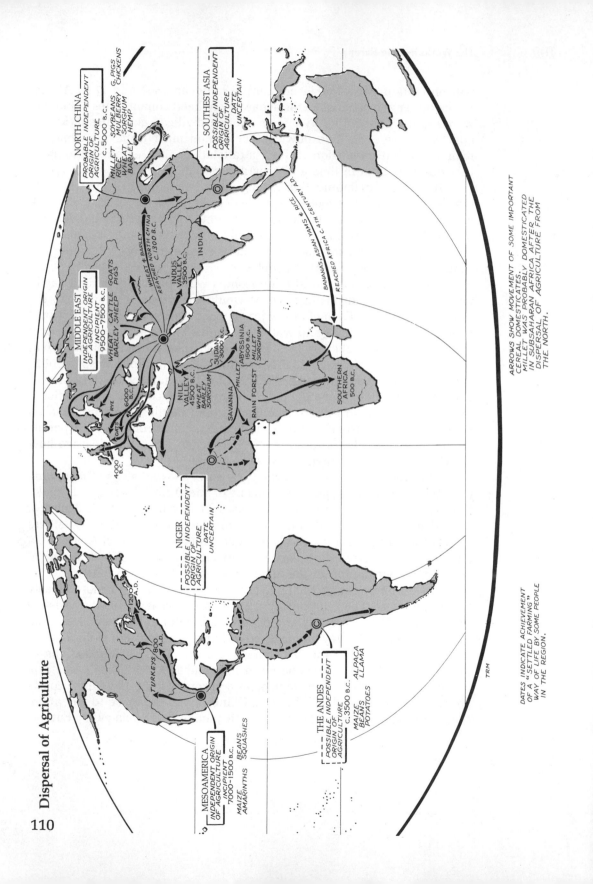

ARROWS SHOW MOVEMENT OF SOME IMPORTANT
CEREAL DOMESTICATES.
MILLET WAS PROBABLY DOMESTICATED
IN SUB-SAHARAN AFRICA AFTER THE
DISPERSAL OF AGRICULTURE FROM
THE NORTH.

DATES INDICATE ACHIEVEMENT
OF A "SETTLED FARMING"
WAY OF LIFE BY SOME PEOPLE
IN THE REGION.

TRM

NORTH CHINA
PROBABLE INDEPENDENT ORIGIN OF AGRICULTURE
c. 5000 B.C.

MILLET
RICE
WHEAT
BARLEY
SOYBEANS
MULBERRY
SORGHUM
HEMP
G. PIGS
CHICKENS

SOUTHEST ASIA
POSSIBLE INDEPENDENT ORIGIN OF AGRICULTURE
DATE UNCERTAIN

BANANAS, ASIAN YAMS & RICE
REACHED AFRICA C. 4TH CENTURY A.D.

INDIA

WHEAT & BARLEY
REACHED NORTH CHINA
c. 1300 B.C.

INDUS
VALLEY
3500 B.C.

MIDDLE EAST
INDEPENDENT ORIGIN OF AGRICULTURE
INCIPIENT
9500–7500 B.C.

WHEAT
BARLEY
GOATS
SHEEP
CATTLE
PIGS

6000
B.C.
RYE
OATS

4000
B.C.

NILE
VALLEY
4500 B.C.
WHEAT
BARLEY
SORGHUM

SUDAN
3000 B.C.

ABYSSINIA
1500 B.C.
MILLET
SORGHUM

SAVANNA
MILLET

RAIN FOREST

SOUTHERN
AFRICA
500 B.C.

NIGER
POSSIBLE INDEPENDENT ORIGIN OF AGRICULTURE
DATE UNCERTAIN

MESOAMERICA
INDEPENDENT ORIGIN OF AGRICULTURE
INCIPIENT
7000–1500 B.C.

MAIZE
AMARINTHS
BEANS
SQUASHES

TURKEYS
900
A.D.

1200
A.D.

THE ANDES
POSSIBLE INDEPENDENT ORIGIN OF AGRICULTURE
c. 3500 B.C.

MAIZE
BEANS
POTATOES
ALPACA
LLAMA

THE USE OF PLANTS AND ANIMALS IN AGRICULTURE

Slash-and-Burn

For slash-and-burn farmers, leafy forests are the only kind of terrain suitable for farming. They slash the bark to kill the trees; a few years later they burn the dead tree trunks and branches and use the ashes as fertilizer. Slash-and-burn methods were first used in the Middle East before 7000 B.C.

1. For this kind of agriculture, farmers used land with thick and leafy forest growing on it. Such land produced a good grain crop.
2. To kill the trees, farmers slashed the bark all around the tree trunk. Sunlight reached the ground, filtering through the dead trunks.
3. Farmers raked away dried leaves to expose soft loam underneath. They scattered seeds on the loam and covered these with loose soil.
4. At first no competing plants existed in newly cleared forest patches, so only desired food-producing grasses could grow.
5. When the grain ripened, farmers harvested it with sickles and stored seeds in jars or baskets.
6. After a few years of cultivation in this way, farmers burned the dead tree trunks and scattered the ashes as fertilizer.
7. Each year more airborne seeds came onto the cleared land. These grew into plants that competed with planted seeds, so a satisfactory crop could no longer be raised.
8. Slash-and-burn farmers then moved on and found a new patch of forest land where they could repeat the whole cycle.

CROPS   Wild grain reseeds itself by allowing the ripe kernels to break off from the spike and fall to the ground. When people began to harvest grain, only kernels with tougher spikes could reach the storage area without being shaken to the ground and lost. And only kernels that reached the storage area were available for seed next season. This meant a very rapid seed selection for kernels that had tough spikes. New types of grain arose with spikes so tough that they could not seed themselves without human help. People, too, soon came to depend on these kinds of grains for food.

HIGHLIGHTS   The significance of slash-and-burn agriculture is that:

Human beings brought seed-bearing grasses into regions in which they did not naturally grow and eliminated the mixture of grasses and other plants found in nature.

Slash-and-burn farmers created food for themselves instead of finding or killing what grew naturally, as hunters did.

A new interdependence arose as human communities came to depend on plants, while the plants in question came to depend on human action for their biological existence.

Irrigation

Irrigation is the process of channeling water onto dry land to make arid soil fertile. This was the basis for Middle Eastern river valley civilizations along the Tigris-Euphrates, Nile, and Indus rivers, beginning 3500–2500 B.C.

1. Rivers, like the Tigris and Euphrates, that start in high mountains and flow through plains cut into the land in their upper reaches, but drop gravel, sand, and silt

as they flow more slowly across the plains.

2. In spring the river floods; and as it rises above its normal banks, it widens out, flows more slowly, and leaves large deposits at the edges of its usual bed. This creates natural levees.

3. When the flood subsides, the river returns to its bed, trapped between the levees. It continues to deposit gravel and sand. In time therefore it flows above the level of the surrounding plain.

4. When the flood subsides, stagnant water lies in shallow pools and swamps outside the levee on both sides of the river. As the year passes, these swampy pools evaporate until the annual flood comes to fill them again.

5. When the swamp water gets low, a channel cut through the natural levee can allow river water to reach the lower land lying on each side of the stream.

6. With construction of bigger channels, diked on each side to direct the flow of water, wide regions can be irrigated by following the contour of the land downstream. This is known as arterial irrigation.

7. Irrigation along the Nile differs. The lower Nile carries only fine silt which sinks too slowly to form natural levees.

8. The Nile flood comes slowly and gently, so that dikes can channel the flow of water onto the land and from field to field. This is called basin irrigation.

HIGHLIGHTS   The use of irrigation is important because:

As long as floods occurred, the same fields could be cultivated year after year. Comparatively large populations could then live in a relatively small space.

The operation of an arterial irrigation system required much human labor for construction and maintenance. Centralized control and planning were needed as canals became longer and deeper and irrigated more land.

Massed human labor, responding to centralized organization, created the material basis for the first civilizations.

Field and Fallow

Field and fallow is a method of farming in which a piece of land is plowed and sown with seed during one growing season, then plowed and allowed to remain idle during the next. It was probably first developed in Middle Eastern river valleys a little before 3000 B.C.

1. Field and fallow farmers used animals to pull a simple plow through the soil. This allowed them to cultivate more ground than when human muscles alone supplied digging power.

2. This method effectively kept down weeds by plowing the fallow field in summer time, killing competing plants before they formed seeds.

3. As a result, the fallow field had few weeds the next year to spoil the grain. The former grain field, left fallow, was cleared of weeds in turn by being plowed.

4. By plowing and planting the grain field at the start of the growing season, then plowing the fallow field, then harvesting

Slash and burn agriculture, Venezuela. (Tim Asch/ Anthro-Photo)

the ripened grain, labor was spread more evenly through the year.

CROPS AND DRAFT ANIMALS
The main crops of early field and fallow farming were the same as for slash-and-burn: wheat and barley. The big change was the use of animal power. Castrated bulls, called oxen, were used for plowing because of their strength and tameness, acquired at the expense of their normal biological power of reproduction. (Compare this to changes in domesticated grain crops.) Oxen also had horns to which it was easy to attach a simple plow.

The scratch plow had three essential parts: a beam or rope which attached the plow to the oxen, a share that dragged through the soil, and a handle which plowmen used to "steer" the share through the soil. The scratch plow had to be light enough for a man to steer, so it did not work well in heavy clay soil.

HIGHLIGHTS Field and fallow farming meant that:

Effective weed control and cultivation of more land allowed an ordinary farmer to harvest more grain than his family could eat.

This surplus grain could support a class which did not produce its own food but worked at other things. Such specialists created the earliest civilizations.

Farming had been women's work until the invention of the plow brought men into the fields with their animals. This made men, as in the hunting days, the main providers of food within families and assured male dominance in society at large.

Vegetative Root

In vegetative root farming, roots were cultivated for food, sometimes on flooded areas of land. Vegetative root agriculture probably began somewhere in southeast Asia. The date of origin is quite uncertain. It may have begun as early as 13,000–9000 B.C., before slash-and-burn agriculture got started.

1. Vegetative root farming probably started near the edge of rivers or lakes where fishermen had settled in permanent villages.
2. A live shoot from the parent plant was partly buried in the moist or flooded ground so that it would take root.
3. In tropical climates all stages of growth may be found on a single patch of land at any given time.

CROPS Many different kinds of crops were grown in vegetative root agriculture. Taros, yams, and manioc have large tuberous roots that store large amounts of starch. They were cultivated by primitive man because they were easy to use: a single root makes a meal for two or three people. Such roots can be fried, boiled, or baked. They can also be made into a soup, a paste, or a cake; and manioc is processed to produce tapioca.

HIGHLIGHTS Vegetative root farming is significant because:

Vegetative root agriculture solved the weed problem by raising a few individually large plants. Weeds could simply be pulled out by hand.

Since staple root crops provide mostly starch, fish or some other food source was necessary for the human diet.

This type of cultivation flourished mainly in tropical climates where plants can ripen at all times of the year, since the roots are not easily stored.

Rice Paddy

Rice paddy cultivation requires the land to be under water while the rice plants grow, but at harvest time fields are drained dry. This procedure causes competing plants to be either drowned or baked out, thus keeping weeds down. Rice paddy cultivation began somewhere in China or southeast Asia, perhaps about 3000–2500 B.C.

1. Since rice paddy land must be perfectly level, farmers have to cut down the higher portion and fill in lower parts of a field until water will stand at a uniform depth.

2. Only regulated amounts of water are wanted on the field. A rice paddy must therefore be surrounded by waterproof dikes with sluices and channels to control water flow.

3. After this preparation, fields are plowed and planted with seedlings sprouted in a special nursery. The water which flows gently into the fields prevents the growth of weeds that live on land, carries dissolved minerals, and supports a complex interaction of organisms that keep the soil fertile.

4. When the rice is ready to ripen, the farmer stops the water from flowing into the paddy, and it dries out. This kills weeds that flourish in water.

5. The rice is harvested with sickles; and if water remains available, a second crop of rice can be planted in the same growing season.

CROPS Rice has the enormous advantage of producing more food per acre than any other crop, particularly when double-cropping is possible. This allows a very dense population to come into existence. The high food yield from rice paddies, in turn, supports the abundant labor force needed to construct and maintain paddy fields with the elaborate conduit system that brings water into fields and keeps it there as long as it is needed. The rice plant requires a mean temperature of 70° F., a good deal warmer than wheat.

HIGHLIGHTS The importance of the rice paddy is that:

The alternation between flooding and draining achieves both weed control and fertilization of the soil.

The labor required to build rice paddies ties the farmers to the land permanently. Nowhere else can they hope to secure as much food for their labor.

Dense population depending on rice paddy cultivation can be compelled to support distant governments, since farmers cannot leave the land nor hide harvest from tax collectors. This makes state-building easy.

Moldboard Plow

The moldboard plow turns the soil over in furrows instead of merely breaking it up into loose bits as the scratch plow does. The moldboard plow came into existence in the moist climate of northwestern Eu-

An Egyptian shadoof for irrigation. (*New York Public Library*)

Harvesting flax. (*Ronald Sheridan's Photo-Library*)

On a field plowed year after year in the same way, this builds up ridges in the centers and makes shallow ditches called balks on each side. The plow thus creates a drainage system on flat, water-logged fields.

HIGHLIGHTS   The moldboard plow changed farming methods because:

Moldboard plow agriculture opened the flat, abundantly watered plains of northwestern Europe to cultivation on a large scale for the first time.

With the moldboard plow, a rotating three-field system with winter crop, spring crop, and fallow could be used.

In northwestern Europe, the soil could be plowed with the moldboard plow at any time of the year. A single farmer could therefore cultivate more land and raise more food than in lands where plowing was seasonal. This helps to account for the rapid rise of Latin Christendom after A.D. 1000.

Elimination of Fallow

Between 1600 and 1750, Dutch and English farmers discovered that they could plant certain valuable new crops on land previously left fallow, and still keep down weeds or even increase and improve the soil's fertility. These new crops were used mainly for animal feed.

rope about A.D. 100; but it came into general use slowly, between A.D. 500 and 1000.

1. **Construction of the Moldboard Plow.** The moldboard plow has a share and a beam essentially the same as the scratch plow. (See Field and Fallow.)
   Two new parts were added to this. A colter that slices vertically through the earth from above runs just ahead of the tip of the share.
   A moldboard, lying behind the share, turns the furrow, cut from the earth by the combined action of the colter and plowshare. This exposes earth three to ten inches below the surface.

2. **Use of the Moldboard Plow.** Four to six oxen were needed to pull the moldboard plow, and such a team cannot turn quickly or easily. Long, narrow fields were, therefore, the only efficient shape for cultivation.
   The moldboard turns the furrow to one side only. As the plow comes and goes the length of the field, it turns the slices toward a center furrow, or ridge.

1. One way to use the fallow productively was to plant a fast-sprouting cover crop, like clover, alfalfa, or vetch, that can get started early in the growing season and smother competing plants.

2. A second way of using fallow was to plant crops in rows, and then cultivate between the rows often enough to destroy weeds.

3. Agricultural "improvers" used manure and other materials to fertilize their fields: chalk, lime, seaweed, ashes, even soot and sometimes sand were tried with good results.

Harvesting rice. (United Nations)

CROPS New crops came into use with the elimination of fallow. Nitrogen-fixing bacteria flourish in the roots of clover, alfalfa, and vetch. When the top part of these plants had been used for cattle food, the roots remained with extra nitrogen that the bacterial action had taken from the air and made into plant protein. This assured a noticeable improvement in the field's fertility. Turnips were the most important row crop; cabbages, beets, and later potatoes were also raised in this way.

HIGHLIGHTS The elimination of fallow meant that:

The new crops, suitable for fields formerly left fallow, were mainly used for animal feed. This allowed a vast increase in animal products with an improvement of the human diet.

The nitrogen-fixing crops incidentally improved fertility for grain raising, thus increasing cereal yields also.

With more and better fodder, farmers could develop specialized breeds of dairy, meat, and draft animals.

Scientific Agriculture

During the nineteenth century, the application of science and technology to agriculture became conscious and widespread. From western Europe and North America, scientific efforts to improve agriculture spread throughout the world.

CROPS AND FARMING METHODS Fertilizers and food additives supply chemicals needed for plant and animal growth. A German professor, Justus von Liebig (1803–1873) was the first to analyze plants chemically and experiment with artificial fertilizers. Scientific study of animal nutrition began only in the twentieth century with the discovery of vitamins.

Geneticists can alter plants and animals to suit human uses. Mendelian theories of inheritance (named after Gregor Mendel, whose ideas were published in 1866 but forgotten until 1900) enabled experimenters to create strains of hybrid corn in the 1920s that greatly increased U.S. farm yields. In the 1960s other experimenters invented new kinds of rice, giving Asians a chance to increase their food production very greatly.

Machinery allows farmers to plow, plant, and harvest large areas quickly. Farmers had always used simple machines, from the digging stick on up. But only with the industrial revolution could big, complicated, factory-made machinery come to the fields. The first practically successful farm machine was the McCormick reaper, patented in 1834.

Food storage and distribution were also altered by the application of science. Canning depends on heat to sterilize food and prevent decay. It was discovered in France in 1809, but came into common use in the United States only with the Civil

The moldboard plow at work. An illumination from the Duc de Berry's Book of Hours. *(Musee Conde Chantilly/Photographic Giraudan)*

War, 1861–1865. Freezing, another important method of preserving food, came in after World War I.

HIGHLIGHTS The significance of scientific agriculture is that:

Fewer hands produce more food in less time. As a result, in the parts of the world where scientific agriculture has spread, most people eat food produced by others.

Until about 100 years ago, most human beings worked as farmers. Now most live in cities and work at other tasks.

American Crop Migration

With the opening of the world's oceans to shipping (1500–1600), the Old World received several important new food crops from recently discovered lands.

MAIZE The center for early domestication was probably in Mexico and Central America. Corn was taken to Europe by Spanish explorers in the sixteenth century, and from there it reached the Middle East. The Portuguese are credited with introducing corn into Africa and India. Magellan is supposed to have brought it to the East Indies via the Pacific Ocean.

POTATOES Potatoes were native to the Andes in South America and were first domesticated by the ancient Peruvians. They were introduced into Europe twice: first by Spanish sailors and a second time by Sir Francis Drake after his circumnavigation of the globe in 1580. From western Europe, potatoes were introduced to the North American colonies, central and eastern Europe, and the Middle East. As was the case with corn, the potato came to Africa with the Portuguese and to southeast Asia and China by way of the Pacific.

SWEET POTATOES Sweet potatoes probably originated as a cultivated crop in the Caribbean region. Spanish explorers brought them back to Europe before white potatoes arrived from the more distant coasts of Peru. Sweet potatoes never became very important in Europe. But in southern China, the sweet potato, introduced across the Pacific in the six-

The Harvesters, *by Pieter Brueghel.* (*Metropolitan Museum of Art, Rogers Fund, 1919*)

Modern harvesting done by machine. (*USDA photo by John Shite*)

teenth century, became a crop of basic importance. In parts of Africa, too, sweet potatoes rivaled corn in importance.

Eurasian Crop Migration

As food crops were introduced into Europe, Asia, and Africa from the New World, the crops and agricultural methods of the Old World also spread to the newly explored areas.

In many parts of the world, European settlers brought with them the equipment of agriculture that was familiar to them in their homelands. They simply displaced the peoples they found living there, as in most of North America and in Australia.

In some parts of the world, however, older forms of agriculture were little affected by the skills and knowledge that opening the oceans diffused around the world. This was the case with rice paddy cultivation, which continued unchanged and spread slowly in southeast Asia and to some Pacific islands.

In between were regions where new crops or domesticated animals radically altered older life-styles. An example was the rise of Plains Indian cultures in North America after they learned to use the horse, introduced by Spaniards.

The American and Eurasian crop migration had several effects:

Efficient crops and techniques of cultivation spread all around the globe into vast new regions climatically suited to them.

Human food supplies increased in amount; and in many places there was an improvement in quality as well.

The diffusion of agricultural techniques caused by regular oceanic movements of people, plants, and ideas tended to equalize the level of development within each climate zone all around the globe.

CHAPTER 4

Europe's Old Regime

1650 to 1789

Between 1648, when the Peace of Westphalia ended the Thirty Years' War, and 1789, when the French Revolution began, Europe passed through a period of calm. But it was a calm and quiet time only by comparison with the storms that had gone before and those that came after. Wars did not cease, but they were conducted by professional armies with a decent respect for the fact that an enemy province might change hands at the peace table—and who wanted to acquire a smoking ruin? Challenging new ideas did not cease to arise in Europe; but they were advanced by professional writers and scientists who did not feel they had to go out and make their ideas come true, without delay, in the way the religious reformers of an earlier age and the political reformers of the age that was to come tried to do.

It was an age of moderation and compromise. People agreed to disagree on many matters and found, somewhat to their surprise, that they could do so and still get along with one another. An elaborate code of manners made this possible by cushioning collisions among individuals and between classes. Good manners often required men and women to disguise their feelings and betray their private characters by acting out a role. But individuals did in some degree become what they pretended to be—noble king or humble servant as the case might be; and the web of pretenses imposed by good manners did smooth over difficulties and helped to keep violence in check.

The restless energies that had helped to tear Europe apart in the age of religious wars was turned outward. The result was an enormous expansion of European empires in the Americas, in India, and throughout the forest and steppe zones of Eurasia. What had been a strictly west-European civilization ceased to be so, when both Russian nobles and American settlers in the foothills of the Appalachians came to share the culture and tradition that continued to have its center and main focus in northwestern Europe. European civilization, in short, became Western civilization, no longer tied to its original geographical cradleland.

Calm did not involve inactivity or the end of rapid change. It meant, instead, that innumerable small groups of professionals were able to go ahead and work along their own lines without bothering too much about how their ideas or actions would fit into the overall picture of European or Western civilization. Intellectual pace-setters gave up the effort to find an absolute, universal truth and to fit the whole of society into its mold. This had been the great ambition of the Reformation age; but after about 1650 people more and more gave up the attempt, having seen too much violence and cruelty mobilized in the name of too many kinds of religious doctrines, each claiming to be the one and only truth.

Kings and princes organized violence more effectively than ever before by maintaining professional standing armies. Most rulers claimed absolute power within their frontiers. But, so-called absolute monarchs faced all sorts of practical limits to their power. Many local groups possessed traditional rights and privileges that had come down from medieval times. In addition, the soldiers and officials, who made royal absolutism effective, acquired a vested interest in maintaining their own special rights and roles. As such they resisted unwanted changes, even when those changes were decreed by a ruler who in theory held absolute power.

Absolutism was also counterbalaned by the development of communication networks that ran across political boundaries among people with similar interests or pursuits. Clerics, bankers, and merchants had maintained such networks for centuries. What happened during the Old Regime was that scientists, writers, musicians, agriculturists, and others developed regular means of exchanging professional information about new discoveries and achievements. Thus, by one of the contradictory compromises characteristic of the Old Regime, Europe was divided into hundreds of separate states, each in theory completely independent of all the others. Yet it was also more united in matters of culture than before (when religious barriers had divided Europe into hostile parts) or after (when national differences did the same).

SOCIAL AND ECONOMIC CHANGES

Europe met with extraordinary success under the Old Regime. This showed up most dramatically in the way European settlers, merchants, and monarchs extended their reach into new regions of the earth. Expansion abroad was matched at home by stepping up the pace and intensity of economic activity so that larger populations lived better at the end of the Old Regime than at its beginning and had some important new commodities at their disposal.

Population Growth

Population growth was fundamental. In the eighteenth century every part of Europe began to undergo such growth. Epidemic diseases became less common and less severe. The last important plague in Europe raged sporadically between 1663 and 1684. Thereafter, one of the factors that in earlier times had kept down population almost ceased to function, and the modern population explosion started, averaging a growth rate of about one percent per year.

Medical science had little to do with the first stages of this change, for doctors knew too little about the causes of disease to be very effective in stopping it. Quarantine of ships and of travelers from foreign parts may have been helpful sometimes (although often the fleas or rats or other carriers of disease were left alone because no one knew they were dangerous). Not until 1796 was the first successful inoculation against smallpox discovered by an English doctor, Edward Jenner (1749–1823); and several decades passed before his idea of deliberately infecting people with a weak form of the disease became an accepted practice.

The Agricultural Revolution

Improved methods of agriculture were more important than medical science in forwarding population growth. Two valuable American food crops, potatoes and maize, slowly but surely came into their own in Europe during the Old Regime. Maize became important in southeastern Europe; potatoes in the north and west, where cooler climate and sandy soils were particularly favorable to them. In such regions, potatoes could produce nearly four times as many calories per acre as oats or rye, the only cereals that would ripen in Europe's less favored regions. Nearly four times as many people could therefore find nourishment by eating potatoes instead of oatmeal or rye bread. Only in Ireland did an almost total shift occur. Elsewhere, potatoes and maize supplemented bread in a significant way, but never entirely drove the older staples from the diet of even the poorest classes.

In addition to new crops for human nourishment, European farmers learned how to farm much more efficiently. By planting clover, alfalfa, or hay on grainfields, it became possible to do without fallowing. In medieval times, about a third of the arable land had to be left fallow each year to allow the extermination of weeds and recovery of fertility after two successive crops of grain. But by planting such fields with clover or alfalfa, the soil was restored, thanks to the activity of nitrogen-fixing bacteria that infest the roots of these plants; and at the same time, good winter fodder for horses and cows could be produced.

Better winter food meant larger and stronger animals. Improved plows, carefully designed to do the work with the least effort, could be pulled by a single team of horses, where four to six oxen had been needed in medieval times. Another crop, turnips, when planted in rows, allowed a careful farmer to cultivate his land repeatedly during the growing season and thus cut down on weeds, while still getting a valuable fodder crop from the land. Drainage and flood control works, systematic experiment with a wide variety of fertilizers, and improved designs for such things as farm wagons, scythes, spades, and plows all increased yields or reduced the cost of production. In either case, the effect was to create a larger food supply with which the growing city populations could be fed.

SIGNIFICANCE OF AGRICULTURAL ADVANCES   Holland and England were in the forefront of agricultural improvement. Other parts of Europe lagged behind, and in some regions there was almost no change at all. Nevertheless, the agricultural improvers of the seventeenth and eighteenth centuries showed that great increases in yields and profits could be secured by using new methods, new crops, and new implements of cultivation. Improving farmers pioneered the idea of systematic experimentation. They tested results by keeping accurate records of how much seed, how much labor, and how much yield per acre were involved in using a new technique. And they communicated their results to other interested landowners through agricultural journals and newsletters, so that any really valuable discovery could spread rapidly and widely.

Always before, agriculture had been in the hands of persons who assumed that what their predecessors had done was the only way things could be done. Disproving this notion was one of the most fundamental breakthroughs of modern times. Simple as it may seem today, the idea that farming methods could be improved directly challenged age-old ways of life that tied the overwhelming majority of mankind to a fixed routine. And when a majority of the members of any society begin to alter their ways in important respects, then the scope and pace of historical change may enormously increase. This, of course, is exactly what has happened in modern times.

Looking backward, it is clear that an agricultural revolution had to come ahead of the better-known industrial revolution, which has been reshaping European and world society during the past 200 years. Without far-reaching changes on the land, Europe's industrial development could not have advanced as it did; for the industrial revolution required both food and labor to come from the countryside—and in ever-growing quantities. What permitted this to happen was the systematic application of the experimental method to techniques of farming, pioneered by a few hundred improving farmers, landlords, and scientists in England and Holland, beginning soon after 1650.

Trade and Finance

Growing populations and improved agriculture sustained and were in turn, sustained by a rising curve of commerce. Important improvements in transportation made it easier to carry goods to market. Canals, for example, linked the major rivers of France. All-weather roads, smooth enough to allow wheeled vehicles to pass at any time of year, came slowly into existence as road builders learned how to drain the roadbed, cover the surface with gravel, and fill in holes before they got too big. Regular stagecoach connections between major cities were established so that anyone able to pay the price could travel scores or hundreds of miles at will and be more or less sure of arriving on schedule at their destination. The net importance of these improvements is hard for us to imagine. But if you try to think of what life would be like without wintertime roads and without public transportation, the significance of these improvements for everyday life will become apparent.

Trade and commerce and all other economic enterprise were also stimulated by improvements in banking methods. Devices were found for assembling larger and larger quantities of capital. This capital was used to organize larger and more expensive undertakings. The effect was to allow Europeans to mobilize goods and manpower for common enterprises on an ever-larger scale. War was always their biggest undertaking; and Europeans learned how to fight wars on credit, thereby mobilizing more and more of their resources in the pursuit of victory and empire.

NORTH AMERICA AND THE CARIBBEAN, 1763

THE IDEA OF A "NATIONAL DEBT"   The decisive invention here was the concept of a "national debt." Until about 1700, bankers and rulers tended to treat government borrowing as the personal debt of the reigning monarch. The new king or prince did not always feel obliged to pay off his predecessor's obligations. High interest rates were one consequence; and lending money to rulers remained a highly speculative business. In England, however, as we shall soon see, the king's powers over government were sharply reduced after 1689; and succession to the throne passed from one relatively distant heir to another until it lodged in the House of Hanover in 1714. The result was that bankers began to make a clear distinction between the king's personal debts and the public debt.

The Bank of England was organized in 1694, in large part, to manage the public debt. Its "bank notes," (that is, promises to pay a given sum in metallic currency on demand) soon became standard currency for large transactions. And, most important of all, anyone could buy a government bond and collect interest on it, secure in the knowledge that the Bank of England and the whole financial community of London would see to it that the interest would be paid on schedule. In this way, the spare cash of a large proportion of the English public (and foreigners too) could be used in time of emergency to help finance unusual public expenditures. Interest rates for government borrowing became much lower. In other words, national resources could be mobilized more efficiently than ever before.

Other governments lagged behind England in developing an efficient central bank and establishing public debts—but not by much, for the advantages of such a system for waging war were enormous.

Techniques of Manufacture

Expenditures for war went, very largely, into the hands of merchants and manufacturers who supplied Europe's armed forces with hundreds of items they required. New and expanded industries and transport systems resulted, some of which could be put to ordinary peacetime uses with little or no adjustment.

Between about 1650 and 1750, western Europeans faced a growing crisis as a result of the rapid disappearance of forests. Timber, fuel, and rough pasturage traditionally had come from Europe's forests. But as more and more people put greater demands upon the forests, big trees became scarce. The consequences of this scarcity for shipbuilding and metallurgy—both industries requiring large quantities of wood—were particularly important. The only solution for shipbuilding was to import timber, either from northern Europe—Sweden or Russia—or from the Americas. But English ironmasters discovered a far more effective way to solve their difficulty in getting enough fuel for their smelters by inventing a new form of fuel—coke.

Ordinary coal, which existed abundantly in parts of western Europe, was useless for smelting iron ore. It had too many chemical impurities to be capable of producing a usable steel. Even a trace of phosphorous, for example, if allowed to penetrate the molten iron, would make a brittle and generally useless product. As a result, iron ore had always been smelted with charcoal; and to produce enough charcoal for Europe's iron smelters required enormous amounts of wood. For several decades in the early eighteenth century, therefore, Sweden and Russia had a special advantage in the iron and steel industries, since they still had enough forests to fuel the forges.

As early as 1709, an English ironmaster, Abraham Darby, discovered that he could purify coal of the objectional chemicals by burning it part way, just as wood had long been partly burnt to make charcoal. The coke that resulted from this could then smelt iron ore just as charcoal could. But for a long time, the Darby ironworks kept the method for making coke secret, and consequently the new technique did not come into general use until after 1750. When it did, coal, which was already an important fuel in western Europe for heating houses and for various industrial processes, acquired a much greater significance than before.

NEW SOURCES OF POWER   Steam engines, which converted the energy of coal into mechanical motion, were invented as early as 1710 to drive pumps needed to lift water from coal mines. But the first such engines were extremely inefficient. Only when James Watt (1736–1819) invented an engine that did not have to be cooled to make the steam condense (1769) did steam power become really significant. Even then, the problem of making pistons and cylinders fit closely was very hard to overcome, so that the age of steam and power-driven machinery scarcely got started before 1789. (see Chapter 6.)

Watermills, windmills, and larger and better-designed ships were far more important sources of power than steam in the days of the Old Regime. But because horse power remained the fundamental source of power for agriculture and land transportation, the most weighty improvement of all was the increased size and strength of horses; and horse power multiplied as improved agricultural methods provided more and better fodder for their nourishment.

Overall, new techniques increased the amount of power—both muscular and mechanical—at the disposal of Europeans several times over, between 1650 and 1789. This progress was fundamental. It opened all sorts of new possibilities for everyday activity.

PRECISION TOOLS AND LUXURY CRAFTS   In other directions, too, European skills reached new levels during the Old Regime. Clockmakers, gunsmiths, lens grinders, glass blowers, jewel cutters, diemarkers learned how to shape metal and other hard materials very precisely. One of the great triumphs of Europe's technology was the invention of a clock so accurate and so insensitive to the pitching motion of a ship at sea that it could keep time within a few seconds for months on end. This invention, in turn, allowed ships' captains to calculate longitude. The first chronometer (as such clocks were called) accurate enough to measure longitude was invented in 1761 by an Englishman named John Harrison (1693–1776). He built upon a long tradition of mechanical ingenuity going back to the Middle Ages when the first mechanical clocks were built in church steeples to keep time for the whole town.

European artisans and inventors were also eager to borrow, and even improve upon, foreign skills when they found them useful. Two noteworthy examples are the discovery of how to make porcelain in imitation of the Chinese who long kept the process secret; and the establishment of cotton manufacture in Europe in competition with Indian artisans. Since Indian weavers lived more cheaply than European workers could afford to live in the harsher climate of the north, it was only by inventing labor-saving devices that European manufacturers could come close to rivaling Indian production costs. They began to do so, with startling success, from about 1770; but, as in the case of the steam engine, the main impact of the new technology in textiles came later.

Luxury trades in the age of the Old Regime actually introduced much of the everyday equipment of an ordinary American household of the twentieth century. Light, strong, and handsome furniture, "china" dishes, big windows filled with transparent glass, and printed wallpaper were among the new household items introduced between 1648 and 1789. Taken together, they made a more comfortable, cleaner, and attractive life possible—at first only for the upper classes and then, with mass production, for larger and larger numbers of people.

Territorial Expansion

The advance of European settlement in North America is familiar. By the time the English colonies won their independence, they numbered about 4 million inhabitants—nearly half the population of England at the time. The frontier of settlement reached and, in places, had even crossed the Appalachian Mountain barrier. Far in advance of settlement, fur traders had explored the American west as far as the Rocky Mountains and the Mackenzie River, while Russians and Spaniards competed along the Pacific coast of North America. Claims overlapped, but in practice a gap remained between Russian and Spanish spheres of influence, for Russian fur traders never did much south of Vancouver island, while San Francisco remained the northernmost regular Spanish settlement.

In Latin America, the decline of the Amerindian population reached its low point about 1650, after which a slow and then more and more rapid growth of population set in. Settlement in the Rio de la Plata region and in the interior of Brazil resembled what was happening at the same time in North America. In the la Plata region, ranching was more important than farming; in Brazil the discovery of gold and diamonds (*c*. 1695) far in the interior sparked the exploration and partial settlement of the vast Amazon Basin. The Brazilian coast and the islands of the Caribbean supported profitable sugar plantations, worked by slaves brought across the Atlantic Ocean from Africa. The importance of the sugar islands in international trade was extraordinary. Indeed, in 1763 the French preferred to give up all of Canada in order to keep the island of Martinique; and as late as 1773, British records show that trade with the Caribbean Islands was more valuable than trade with the mainland North American colonies.

THE EASTWARD MOVEMENT IN EURASIA   Overseas expansion in the Americas was matched by eastward expansion in Eurasia. The Austrians and Hungarians, for example, conquered a thinly settled land from the Turks in 1699; and for seventy-five years thereafter, the Austrian government and Hungarian nobles shared the task of planting settlers on the grasslands of central Hungary. Farther east it was principally the Russians who took over the task of occupying the steppelands north of the Black Sea and bringing them into cultivation. Other settlers crossed the Ural Mountains into Siberia or traveled down the Volga River toward the Caspian Sea. It is impossible to know how many pioneers took part in this eastward movement, but the number was probably as great as or greater than the number of settlers and slaves who crossed the Atlantic.

CHARACTERISTICS OF FRONTIER SOCIETY   On the frontier, whether in the New World or in eastern Europe, society was simpler than near the centers of European civilization: population was scant in proportion to land and other resources, and all the different levels and ranks, into which European nations divided, tended to break down. Two alternatives presented themselves. The first was for individuals and families to go off, more or less on their own, even though this meant giving up many of the advantages of civilized life—since schoolteachers, professionals, and other specialists could not support themselves in such a poor, crude, free-and-equal environment. The American frontier and parts of Siberia were, in fact, populated in this way. This produced a lawless, rough, half-barbarous frontier population, with a great ability to help itself and a fierce unwillingness to submit to anyone who was, or seemed to think he was, in any way superior.

The other alternative was to maintain some sort of social subordination by using force. In Europe, the poor had to work for the rich to be able to eat. On the frontier, the only way to make some people work for others was to enslave them. Slavery and other forms of forced labor, such as peonage and bonded servitude, played a big role in the New World. Such legal devices permitted a few plantation owners to remain far more cultured than was possible where rude equality prevailed. The same pattern dominated the eastward movement, where the legal powers of landowners over their serfs expanded throughout the period when settlement on new ground was most rapid and labor shortages were most critical. From the point of view of the Russian government, no other policy was possible. Landlords were needed to staff the government and to fill up the officer ranks in the army. A strong and efficient army was needed to fend off attackers from the west and to overpower rivals in the south and east. The looser, freer, and more individualistic type of society that flourished in the English colonies of North America could and did arise only because the colonists never had to support a trained and well-equipped army in order to defeat the Indians. Serious quarrels among the European states over possession of lands in the New World did of course arise; but they were fought out between England, France, and Spain mainly with soldiers trained, equipped, and paid for by the home governments.

POLITICS AND WAR

Intensification and expansion also dominated the politics of Europe. Until 1715 France held the center of the stage and led all other European states in developing an efficient army and bureaucracy. Between them, French soldiers and French officials were able to call on far greater resources—whether to fight a war or to build a palace at Versailles worthy of Louis XIV, the Sun King (reigned 1643–1715)—than any other state in Europe could do.

French Territorial Expansion

Early in Louis' long reign an armed uprising nicknamed the *Fronde* (French for "sling") broke out (1648–1653). Louis was thoroughly frightened when armed men struggled in his bedroom for control of the boy king, and when he grew up and took power into his own hands, he decided to permit absolutely no rivals within France. This required him to maintain an armed force, year in and year out, far superior to anything his own

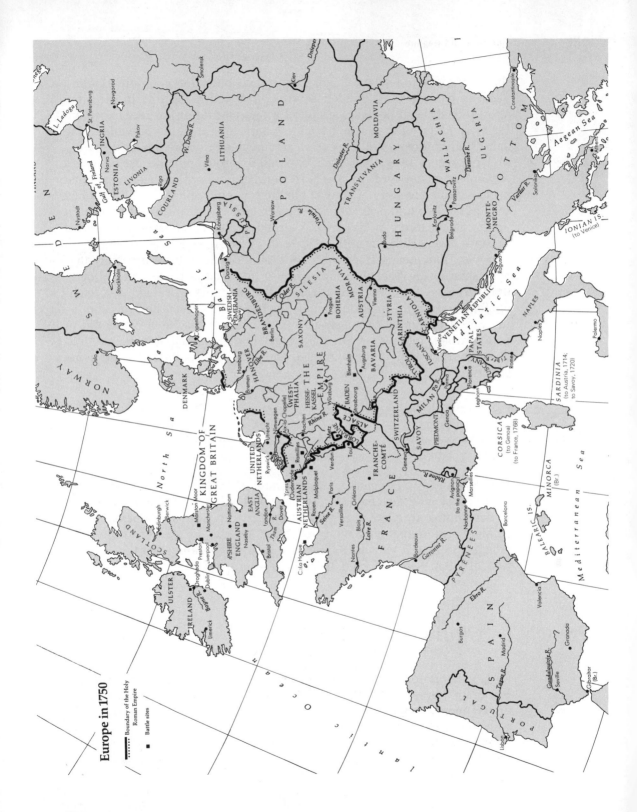

Europe in 1750

Boundary of the Holy
Roman Empire
Battle sites

130

nobles or any foreign ruler could bring against him. Louis was able to keep such a standing army because France was a rich land, and ever since the Hundred Years' War, the king had been legally entitled to collect taxes as he saw fit.

Louis XIV was a serious and hard-working monarch. He chose ministers who tried to develop French resources in every way possible. In particular, the controller general of finance, Jean Baptiste Colbert (in office 1662–1683), encouraged new industries, regulated old ones, adjusted taxes to make them more uniform and easier to collect, and always tried to make the king of France as rich and powerful as possible. The royal government and administration thus took over many functions that in earlier times had rested with guilds in separate towns or with other local authorities. The result, with Colbert's careful management of finances, was spectacular, for Louis XIV became able to maintain the greatest army and the most splendid court Europe had yet seen.

The king set himself the task of extending his kingdom to its natural frontiers, that is, to the Pyrenees, the Alps, and the Rhine. In 1659 he signed a treaty with Spain that drew the frontier line along the watershed of the Pyrenees. During the rest of his reign Louis tried to reach the Rhine; but his efforts were checked by the Dutch and after 1689 by the English and Dutch together. In 1700 Louis undertook the last great venture of his reign, for in that year the king of Spain died without direct heirs and left a will assigning his kingdom to one of Louis XIV's grandsons, Philip of Anjou. When the French tried to make good the claim to the Spanish throne, a general war broke out. England, Holland, the Austrian Hapsburgs, and many other rulers of Europe joined in a Grand Alliance to stop the French. The war was hard fought and strained French resources to the limit. In the end a compromise was agreed to by the Treaties of Utrecht and Rastatt (1713, 1714). Philip's claim to the Spanish throne was recognized by all concerned, but Spanish possessions in Italy and the Low Countries (present-day Belgium) were transferred to Austria; while the British, as their part of the bargain, acquired Gibraltar from Spain and Nova Scotia and Newfoundland from the French.

The result of the War of the Spanish Succession showed that the Austrian Hapsburgs and the British government had both caught up with the French when it came to waging war and managing the state. The power of the Dutch, by comparison, faded; so did the power of France's traditional allies—the Swedes, the Poles, and the Turks. From 1715 onward, the French advantage over neighboring states was gone. Instead, governments closer to the expanding edge of European civilization gained the advantage. By bringing new territory under their control, they could add to their resources, while the French were stopped by one or another coalition of enemies from doing anything similar themselves.

British Territorial Expansion

In the west, the country that benefited from these new possibilities was Great Britain. Great Britain was itself a new creation resulting from the union of England, Scotland, and Ireland in 1707. Britain's main expansion took place overseas in the Americas and in India. Each time the English fought the French in Europe, the struggle extended across the oceans of the earth and into the colonies. Sometimes fighting in the colonies began before war started in Europe. The most important instance of this came in 1754, when the French and Indian War began in North America two years before a full-scale war was joined in Europe between France and Great Britain. The upshot of this so-called Seven Years' War (1756–1763) was British victory in both America and India. By the Peace of Paris (1763), the French surrendered Canada and India to the British.

To be sure, the Spanish, Portuguese, and Dutch empires still existed. But the British had secured the right to trade with the Spanish colonies as part of the Peace of Utrecht in 1713, and they actually controlled much of the trade with South and Central America. Ever since 1689 when William of Orange, a Dutchman, became king of England, cooperation between the Dutch and British had become close and habitual. The same was true of British relations with Portugal. Hence British trade and British naval supremacy seemed unchallenged overseas after 1763.

Yet when quarrels between the government of George III (1760–1820) and thirteen of the British colonies of North America led to open warfare in 1776, not only the French, but also the Spanish and even the Russian governments, challenged Britain's predominance at sea, either by engaging in outright war or by an "armed neutrality" aimed against British naval power. Eventually the British had to yield. Through a second Peace of Paris in 1783, they agreed to the independence of their former American colonies and saw French power reestablished in North America in the Louisiana territory—a land that seemed much more promising than the snowy wastes of Canada to statesmen interested in sugar and other tropical products.

Despite this setback, British overseas trade and the empire built around that trade continued to be the largest in the world. British power and wealth increased with great rapidity. British business methods and parliamentary government, which had taken fresh hold on England after the "Glorious Revolution" of 1688, also began to arouse admiration among some Frenchmen who came to think that the successes of the British government—and the failures of their own after 1715—resulted from the superiority of the British constitution.

Eastern European Expansion

In eastern Europe, expansion overland matched western expansion overseas. Not one but three new empires rose to greatness at the expense of older and less well-organized states. The rising powers were the Austrian Hapsburgs, based in the Danube Valley; the kingdom of Prussia, based in the eastern reaches of the north German plain; and the Russian Empire, based far to the north and east.

RUSSIAN AGRICULTURAL EXPANSION   Of the three, Russia had the most favorable position, being situated like Britain at the outermost edge of the European world where expansion into new and vast territories was quite easy. Yet Russia had special problems too. Agriculture was inefficient. Peasants who worked as serfs for masters they disliked could not be made to work carefully so as to make the most of what they did have. In addition, Russia had inherited a civilization and style of life from medieval times that derived in part from Byzantium and remained always a little different from the life of western Europe. After the Time of Troubles (1610–1613) when Polish armies seized Moscow for a short time, the Russian government tried to safeguard the national tradition by holding westerners at arm's length.

The policy worked pretty well. In particular, after a long competition with the Poles, the czars of Moscow took over the Ukraine (1667) and thereby added a broad and fertile agricultural land to their dominions. The problem, however, was to find settlers to cultivate its empty expanses, and then to find markets for the grain it could produce. Not until 1774 were these two problems really solved; for in that year, after a successful war against the Turks, the Russians made a treaty that gave them the right to send ships through the straits at the mouth of the Black Sea. Thereafter, a great boom came to the Ukraine; the Russian government began to profit from its rich new agricultural base.

THE WESTERN WAYS OF PETER THE GREAT   Long before then, Russia's upper classes had accepted many west-European ways. This was the result of deliberate policy on the part of Czar Peter I, the Great (reigned 1682–1725). Not until 1698, when he returned from a visit to western Europe, did Peter try to revolutionize his country. But once started, he never rested. He forced every courtier to cut off his beard and put on Western clothes. He tried to teach the Russian court ladies to behave like French court ladies. He also required every man of noble rank to serve the state in one capacity or another. Some acted as civil administrators, but most served in the army or navy. To equip his armed forces, Peter built factories to make all the things soldiers and sailors required, from cannon to uniform cloth and gaiter buttons.

The overriding goal Peter sought was military strength. He achieved it. After a long and difficult war, he compelled the Swedes to give up important territories along the Baltic Sea (1721). Without waiting for the peace, Peter built a new capital city on the newly acquired coast, and

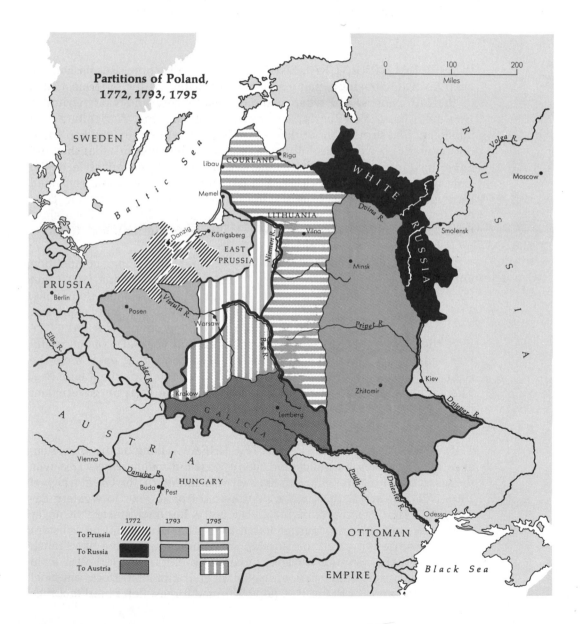

named it St. Petersburg. Here he had a "window on the west" through which French governesses and German tutors soon swarmed to educate the children of the nobility in European manners and ideas.

One of the reasons that Peter could achieve such a sharp break from the Russian past was that many, perhaps most, peasants regarded him as Antichrist. In their eyes, therefore, it did not matter how wicked his actions might be. Each new shock simply seemed another sign that the end of the world was at hand, when God could be counted on to right all wrongs. The great conservative mass of the Russian people therefore remained remarkably passive while their ruler ordered them and their noble masters about. Even when Peter laid hands on the Holy Orthodox church itself, deposed the patriarch of Moscow, and put the church under the administration of ordinary state officials, there was no outcry. The Russian church had already lost its hold on popular religious feeling due to Nikon's reforms of the preceding generation.

The other secret of Peter's success lay in the way he trained the nobles to serve him. He required noblemen's sons to serve as privates in special "Guards" regiments. There they learned all the newfangled ways of court. Those who caught the ruler's eye or had any unusual qualities were sent off to perform any of hundreds of special jobs for the impatient czar. Diplomats, factory managers, governors of a province, commanders of a fleet—any or every job might open; and for those who did well, wealth and power came with the job. Nor was noble birth the only path to advancement. Peter was always short of skilled subordinates. He welcomed foreigners, roughnecks, adventurers of any background into his service. They could go as far as luck and their own abilities would carry them. This policy created a nobility almost completely alienated from the rest of Russian society and correspondingly dependent on the czar.

THE GREATNESS OF RUSSIA UNDER CATHERINE   Peter's successors, mostly women, had to rule over the Russian lands by keeping on good terms with the nobility. Catherine the Great (reigned 1762–1796) had the least claim to the throne, yet was by far the most successful. A German princess by birth, Catherine came to power when a clique of courtiers murdered her husband, Czar Peter III. She lived to see Russia become a European power of the first rank. By intervening in Swedish politics, she made Sweden a dependency and nearly conquered Turkey. She destroyed Poland by arranging three successive partitions of that country among its neighbors—Russia, Austria, and Prussia.

Nearly all of the nobles and officials, army officers and tax collectors, who served the Russian state in Catherine's time, believed that what they did was worthwhile. They opened up new land to agriculture, built new towns, and in general made Russia more powerful, modern, up-to-date. As for the common folk, they had to work for the future and for the benefit of the state—if need be, against their will. The gain seemed worth the cost to nearly all the nobles. Russia's future greatness and its superiority to the pygmy states of western Europe seemed assured.

Austrian Expansion

The other growing states of eastern Europe were Austria and Prussia. Austria was ruled by the Hapsburg family, whose claim to the title of Holy Roman Emperor had become traditional. But the real strength of their state rested on the Hapsburg hereditary lands of Austria and Bohemia. From this core, Austrian power expanded eastward and southward by driving back the Turks, beginning with victory in a long war (1683–1699). After 1714, when the Hapsburg rulers added the former Spanish possessions in Italy and the Low Countries to their other territories, the great power status of the Hapsburg Empire was assured. But it never achieved administrative unification. Each separate duchy, principality, or kingdom kept its own forms of government and administration. To be sure, the empress Maria Theresa (ruled 1740–1780) and her son Joseph II (ruled 1780–1790) tried hard to make the same laws and rules apply everywhere in their dominions. Yet they fell far short of success. The Austrian lands, like Germany and Italy generally, remained divided by all sorts of local differences. This weakened the empire and made it impossible to bring anything like the full resources of the various Hapsburg lands to bear on any common enterprise as the French, British, and Russians were increasingly able to do.

Prussian Expansion

Prussia, on the other hand, was the most strictly centralized and carefully administered state in Europe. From the time of Frederick William, the Great Elector (ruled 1640–1688), everything was subordinated to making the army as strong as possible. The result was to make Prussia a far more powerful state than its sandy soil and scant population could otherwise have supported. A symbol of Prussia's rising importance came in 1701 when Frederick, whose highest title had been Elector of Brandenburg, became king in Prussia.

In the War of the Austrian Succession (1740–1748) and again during the Seven Years' War (1756–1763), Prussian soldiers proved their mettle to all Europe. In the first of these wars, Frederick II the Great, king of

Prussia (ruled 1740–1786), seized the province of Silesia from Austria and made his conquest stick. In the Seven Years' War he faced a far more dangerous coalition, for the French and Austrians, rivals for centuries, combined forces against the Prussians, and the Russians also joined them. Nevertheless, with help from Great Britain in the form of money and supplies, the Prussian army staved off defeat until Russia changed sides (1762), and the French and Austrians at length gave up the struggle and made peace. Prussia thus escaped from what had seemed overwhelming odds, and—as we have seen—Frederick II lived to divide Poland with his former enemies, Austria and Russia, making his state greater still.

NEW CHALLENGES TO ROYAL ABSOLUTISM

Prussia under Frederick the Great, Austria under Joseph II, and Russia under Catherine the Great all were ruled by monarchs who claimed to be absolute and also "enlightened." This meant, first of all, that they were not believers in traditional Christianity. It also meant that they tried, or talked about trying, to use the state to promote wealth and well-being among the people as a whole. It meant, too, administrative centralization and concentration of authority in the hands of officials who were themselves told what to do by the ruler or by his ministers. These political principles worked rather well in eastern Europe in the eighteenth century. But in western Europe, royal absolutism failed to cope successfully with the more complex societies that prevailed in France, England, and Holland.

France

In France, which had once been the model of efficient government for the rest of Europe, all sorts of vested interests prevented the king and his ministers from changing established ways of doing things. Many key government officials bought their offices. As a result, they could not be shifted around by the king. Under these conditions the administration lost its flexibility. French taxes ceased to produce enough money to keep the French government in funds. The army and navy suffered, and the French had to endure humiliating defeats at the hands of the British and Prussians. A growing number of writers were openly critical of the way things were run. In particular, professionals and business leaders were

Versailles, The Hall of Mirrors. (French Government Tourist Office)

inclined to feel that they had too little voice in making governmental decisions. They began to look across the channel toward Great Britain, where people like themselves played important roles in Parliament and helped run the government.

England

Britain's internal political development was almost exactly opposite to the French experience. When the Stuart kings first came to the throne in 1603, they tried to build an efficient royal government like the French. This soon got them into trouble with Parliament, a medieval institution that got in the way of efficient administration by refusing to grant needed taxes and by defending unruly groups that refused to obey the king in matters of religion and taxation. Indeed in 1642, relations between Charles I and Parliament got so bad that civil war broke out. Parliament won, and in 1649 a special commission decided that King Charles should be executed for failing to keep his promises to Parliament. But cutting off Charles's head solved nothing and, in fact, shocked many Englishmen.

Legal quarrels over the rights of the king as against those of Parliament were only part of the dispute. Many Englishmen believed that the church needed to be reformed and purified along Calvinist, biblical lines.

MARIA THERESA AND
THE HUNGARIAN DIET

In 1740 a young queen, Maria Theresa, succeeded to the throne of the Hapsburgs. Her father had spent years trying to get his various subjects to promise to obey his daughter; but the Hungarians were stubborn. According to their ancient constitution, the Diet had to approve a new king; how could they accept a woman as their ruler? A king was supposed to command in battle; no woman could do that. Nevertheless in 1723, seventeen years before she actually came to the throne, the Diet had reluctantly voted to accept Maria Theresa as heir.

The question of what the Hungarians would do became acute soon after Maria Theresa became queen. Prussia attacked the Hapsburg lands, backed by France and Bavaria. An army had to be raised and Hungarian help was required. Maria Theresa journeyed to Pressburg (called Bratislava today) where the Hungarian Diet was meeting. She appeared before the assembled nobles, carrying her infant son in her arms, and appealed for help.

In a sudden burst of enthusiasm, the Hungarians promised to fight for her cause, and did in fact take the field against the invaders with considerable success. The Hapsburg power was saved, although Maria Theresa did lose the valuable province of Silesia to the Prussians. For the rest of her long reign, Maria Theresa remained grateful to the Hungarians for coming to her help in time of need. She therefore did nothing to hurt the interests of the nobles or to alter the ancient Hungarian constitution that protected the nobles' privileges.

Called Puritans by their opponents, they dominated both Parliament and the army that Parliament raised with which to fight the king. But victory in the field presented Parliament with the difficult task of deciding how church and state should be reorganized. The members of Parliament could not agree. When the army made Oliver Cromwell—Parliament's greatest general—Lord Protector, a military dictatorship was fastened on England. But this soon became unpopular and indeed violated Cromwell's own convictions.

When Cromwell died (1658), the regime fell apart. Almost in desperation, a group of generals and other political figures called the Stuart heir to the throne. Charles II (reigned 1660–1685) had grown up in France and had no wish to be exiled again. In general, he kept on reasonably good terms with Parliament. Nevertheless, King Charles tried to escape

Parliament's financial control by making a secret arrangement with Louis XIV, whereby the French paid a considerable sum of money to Charles in return for keeping England quiet while Louis attacked his neighbors in order to make the Rhine his frontier.

When James II came to the English throne in 1685, suspicion between king and Parliament caused a crisis once more. James was a Roman Catholic, and Parliament suspected that he wanted to make England Catholic again. They also suspected treasonable relations with France. In 1688, therefore, a coup d'état was organized. William of Orange came from Holland and claimed the throne jointly with his wife, Mary, who was the daughter of James II. The coup was successful, but Parliament made the new monarchs agree to a Declaration of Rights that defined the limits of royal power in a sense favorable to Parliament. Thereafter, the kings of England reigned but did not really rule. Taxes had to be authorized by Parliament before they could be collected legally. No royal standing army could be maintained in England; the army's allegiance was to Parliament.

William was a vigorous king, but he was mainly interested in wars against Louis XIV on the continent. As long as his new kingdom supported such wars, he was well content to leave the government in the hands of ministers agreeable to Parliament. Queen Anne (reigned 1702–1714), George I of Hanover (reigned 1714–1727), and George II (reigned 1727–1760) followed the same policy. They found it simpler to govern when their ministers could get support for their acts in Parliament. Indeed, both the kings, George I and II, did not speak English easily and stayed away from most of the meetings of the ministers at which government policy was discussed. They were satisfied to give the responsibility for choosing ministers to Robert Walpole, an ordinary member of Parliament who was able to win the confidence of both the monarch and of a majority in Parliament. In common speech he came to be called prime minister; and the group of ministers he selected were referred to as the cabinet.

Rules and traditions of parliamentary and cabinet government were not perfectly defined until after George III (reigned 1760–1820) tried to take a personal hand in governing his kingdom. The king was able to get personal supporters elected to Parliament and to choose his own ministers. But he roused opposition when his plan to bring the American colonies under tighter control led only to rebellion and a disastrous war with France. The fact that George III soon afterward became intermittently insane hurt the king's cause even more and gave control of the British government back to Parliament and parliamentary leaders.

The advantages of the British system of government as it developed under the Old Regime were real. Members of Parliament represented the major propertied interests of the country. The election process allowed rising new interests to make themselves heard in Parliament at the expense of other groups whose importance was declining. In this way a rough match between political decision-making and the balance of British society as a whole could maintain itself, as it were, automatically. Moreover, closer partnership between government and the upper classes made popular support for government policies more reliable than was the case in a country like France.

The result was that an awkward representative assembly that in 1600 had looked like an outmoded survival from medieval times became, by 1700, the sovereign body controlling one of Europe's greatest and most rapidly growing states. The brilliant successes that came to the British government and nation in the decades that followed made parliamentary and cabinet government a model for all those on the European continent who disliked their own royal, absolute governments.

Autocratic Russia, where society was divided between nobles and serfs and where the military model dominated all administration, stood on one flank of Europe and, with Prussia, represented one extreme of social and political organization. Great Britain, where the middle classes were more powerful than in any other great state and where religious and other kinds of pluralism were more widespread than in most other parts of Europe, stood at the other extreme. The rest of Europe fell somewhere between.

Thus we see how Europe's enormous success under the Old Regime—and the territorial expansion that registered that success—meant the inclusion, within the circle of Western civilization, of greater variation, socially and economically as well as politically, than in earlier ages.

EUROPEAN CULTURE

Pluralism and internal variety were also characteristic of Europe's culture under the Old Regime. Different social classes and different nations, not to mention different professions and different cliques and parties, tended to develop their own distinct styles of thought and behavior. General patterns existed, but only vaguely and never in a way that prevented individuals and small groups from following their own particular bent.

French art and literature won a leading place in all Europe, particularly after the Polish and Russian upper classes in Catherine's time came under the influence of French culture. But there was also a Spanish-Italian-Austrian sphere of influence, built around the Hapsburg dynasty and carrying on the traditions of the Catholic Counter-Reformation into the eighteenth century. Finally, the English and Dutch made up a circle of their own, and by 1770 romantic poets had declared Germany's cultural independence of France as energetically as they knew how.

Science remained much more international, though French followers of Descartes clashed with English Newtonians; and the German Leibniz also quarreled with Newton on grounds that were at least partly nationalistic. However, in scientific matters, observation and measurement offered a means for settling most disputes quite quickly; whereas in fields where taste was the only thing to go by, preferences based on language, religion, personal whim, or local connections tended to create and support a number of separate cultural circles.

The leading characteristic of the culture of the Old Regime was growing professionalism. Writers became able to live from the sale of their work, creating a new, independent profession apart from both church and government. Painters and musicians still depended, usually, on noble patronage or on a church appointment. Scientists sometimes held university posts, and sometimes governments competed for their services. The Swiss mathematician Leonhard Euler (1707–1783), for example, took a job as professor at the University of St. Petersburg when only twenty-three years of age; then, at Frederick the Great's call, he moved to Berlin in 1741, but returned to St. Petersburg in 1766. The prestige of scientists rose very high. Isaac Newton (1642–1727), the great English mathematician and physicist, was treated as a public monument during his own lifetime and, when he died, was buried in Westminster Abbey with England's kings and queens.

Natural Science

Modern science got an enormous new energy after 1650. The task of observing, recording, and classifying all the plants and animals of the world was immense. In addition, with new instruments like the microscope and telescope, thermometer, barometer, sextant, marine chronometer, and others, Europeans had the tools to observe and record facts far more exactly than ever before. This great task of assembling information and arranging it in some sort of order was what kept most scientists busy and gave the whole enterprise of science such excitement. Everybody could understand what was being done; and no one could doubt any longer that Europe's knowledge far outstripped other peoples' knowledge, or even what the ancients had known. Making useful, workable classifications was, of course, the big problem. The two most successful classifiers were the Swede Linnaeus (1707–1778), who invented the system for classifying plants by genus and species that is still used today; and the French naturalist, Georges Louis Leclerc de Buffon (1707–1788), who wrote a forty-four–volume *Natural History* in which he dealt with both animals and plants.

The Newtonian Era

But the aspect of scientific discovery that mattered most for later ages was more mathematical and abstract. The key figure was Isaac Newton, born in the year that Galileo died and, in a real sense, Galileo's intellectual successor. Newton was a great mathematician and, among other things, developed calculus. A German, Gottfried Wilhelm Leibniz (1646–1716), also invented calculus and developed the kind of notation used today. Later, a nasty quarrel broke out between followers of the two great men over the question whether Leibniz had gotten his original idea from Newton or not.

Newton's greatest work was, however, in physics and astronomy. He experimented with sunlight and discovered that he could split it up into the colors of the rainbow and then recombine it into white light by use of prisms. He invented a reflecting telescope that was superior in some ways to those using transparent lenses. But Newton's fame rests mainly on the theory of gravitation, as developed in his *Principia* (full title, *Philosophiae Naturalis Principia Mathematica*), first published in 1687. By assuming that all bodies attract one another with a force that varies inversely with the square of the distance between them, Newton was able to show that the motions of the moon and of the planets, as well as the motion of falling objects near the surface of the earth, obeyed exactly the same laws. He put these laws in mathematical form, so that when appropriate data as to mass, distance, and velocity could be supplied, motions became predictable into the future and could also be projected back into the past.

The marvelously simple world machine that Newton's theory revealed struck contemporaries with the force of a new revelation. The motions of the heavenly bodies suddenly fitted in with everyday things like the curving path of a thrown ball, or the arc of a falling apple. Everything could be explained with a few simple mathematical formulas. Some wondered about the mysterious nature of "gravitational force" that could work invisibly at a distance; others feared the mechanical, impersonal nature of Newton's vision of the universe. But when innumerable observations backed up his theories, and when planets and cannonballs kept on behaving as Newton's formulas predicted, who could doubt the essential accuracy of the new theory? Many felt, in the words of the poet, Alexander Pope: "God said, 'Let Newton be,' and all was light!"

Scores of other ingenious experimenters and mathematical minds of the first rank surrounded Newton, in England and also on the continent. The scientific community founded special societies, the most famous of which was the Royal Society of London, where gentlemen interested in natural science could meet and exchange ideas. These societies corresponded with one another and published records of their meetings and of papers submitted to them from a distance. As a result, a lively network of communication among scientists and scholars came into existence, running from London to St. Petersburg, and from Florence and Rome to Stockholm. A distant outsider like Benjamin Franklin (1706–1790) could communicate the results of his experiments with lightning and win recognition throughout the European world for proving lightning to be a form of electricity. The existence of such a network for communicating scientific results guaranteed the continued flow of data and ideas and made science a truly international enterprise.

No theoretical breakthroughs comparable to the importance of Newton's work came until after 1789. Chemistry, however, achieved a new precision with the work of Antoine Lavoisier (1743–1794). He measured the weight of matter entering into and coming out of chemical reactions with greater accuracy than ever before. On the basis of such measurements he was able to explain what happened in an ordinary fire, for he detected and measured the consumption of oxygen from the air and the discharge of carbon dioxide and other gases into the air. Lavoisier also kept clear the distinction between an element and a chemical compound and introduced many of the names used still by chemists (for example, oxygen). As a result of such work, chemistry was poised, by the close of the Old Regime, for all the technical and practical triumphs that came in the nineteenth century.

Social Theory

Newtonianism changed Europeans' view of the world in fundamental ways. It was hard to believe that God stood ready to intervene at a moment's notice in human affairs when the vast spaces of the universe all obeyed the same laws of motion. God seemed to be a master mathematician and craftsman who created the world in accordance with natural laws. He could not be expected to spoil his own handiwork, or admit its imperfection by intervening to work a miracle. Thus, the whole world view of the Reformation era was called into question.

As prevailing views of God and his way of controlling the universe, changed, political theory had to be readjusted. The idea that God personally chose kings to rule and intervened in everyday affairs to reward and punish his people by sending them good and bad rulers seemed less and less convincing. But if God did not choose kings, what right had they to rule? The best answer theorists could find was to suppose that a contract, implied rather than real, between ruler and ruled gave kings their right to govern. But the practical force of any such theory depended entirely on the terms of the contract. Thomas Hobbes (1588–1678), for example, argued that individuals, fearing one another, made a contract that transferred absolute power to their rulers; John Locke (1632–1704), on the contrary, asserted that subjects had the right to overthrow a ruler who broke the terms of the contract by endangering their lives, liberty, or property, since the only purpose for submitting to a ruler's authority in the first place was to assure the protection of these natural rights. Jean-Jacques Rousseau (1712–1778) carried the argument to its democratic extreme by arguing that the social contract requires kings or other rulers to obey the "general will" of the people. If rulers failed to do so, it was a duty as well as a right to overthrow them.

Others concentrated their attention on economics and tried to find natural laws that governed human behavior in the marketplace. Two Scots, John Law (1671–1729) and Adam Smith (1723–1790), were particularly bold in their speculations. Law had a chance to put his theory of bank credit and currency management into practice in France, where his policies provoked a speculative boom and bust that discredited his ideas—perhaps unjustly—as well as his practice. Adam Smith was content to be a professor at Glasgow; but his treatise entitled *The Wealth of Nations*, published in 1776, became fundamental to all later economic theory. Smith's view was like Newton's in an important sense. He believed that if individuals were left alone to follow their private preferences in economic matters, enlightened self-interest would, in fact, create the best possible pattern of production and exchange. Just as gravitation kept the planets in their orbits, so Adam Smith believed private calculation of personal advantage was a universal force that operated behind all particular phenomena and made the economic machine work as it did.

Philosophy and Literature

Formal philosophy underwent a remarkable deflation during the Old Regime. At its beginning, René Descartes (1596–1650), Baruch Spinoza (1632–1677), and Gottfried Leibniz (1646–1716) still hoped to use mathematical rigor to reason out a complete system of truth that would explain everything in the whole world. Their disagreements focused attention on the question of how anyone can know anything at all. The more carefully critics considered this matter, the more uncertain knowledge of any kind seemed. John Locke (1632–1704), George Berkeley (1685–1753), and David

Hume (1711–1776) made it increasingly difficult to believe that human minds could ever really know anything about the nature of things. Immanuel Kant (1724–1804) rescued philosophy from this dead end by pointing out that, even if the nature of things was forever unknowable, still the nature of the knowing mind could be explored. And since nothing that did not fit in with the capacities of the mind could ever be known, to understand the qualities and capacities of the mind, in fact, allowed a philosopher to know the character and limits of all that could be known.

Such abstract ideas interested only a few; but there were others who called themselves "philosophers" and who wrote about social and political problems and often sought to reform the world around them. These philosophers were closely connected with the world of literature. They used novels, plays, or poems to convey their ideas more effectively to the audience they wanted to interest. The main center for this kind of "philosopher" was in France where, especially after 1715, there seemed much to criticize in government and society.

Charles-Louis de Secondat, Baron de Montesquieu (1689–1755) was among the first to voice dissatisfaction with the French government. He wanted the nobles to play a larger part, and argued that good government required the separation of legislative, executive, and judicial functions. His ideas, together with those of John Locke, were particularly influential among the men who wrote the Constitution of the United States.

The most famous of the French "philosophers," however, was Voltaire (real name, François-Marie Arouet, 1694–1778). Voltaire wrote plays, poems, histories, as well as pamphlets and books. His central idea was that reason and good sense would show people how to behave—if only priests and others who had a vested interest in appealing to human fears and superstitions would let the light of reason shine forth freely. He set himself, therefore, to attack religious superstition and to spread the light of reason. Everything he wrote contributed in one way or another to this general aim.

Voltaire and others like him believed they were helping humanity by spreading science and truth. The task of enlightening others, although immense, seemed very much worthwhile. Progress and social improvement could only come through the spread of reason and knowledge. One of the most powerful ways to spread knowledge was the preparation of a great encyclopedia. The articles, arranged alphabetically, dealt with almost everything under the sun. The main figure responsible for producing the French encyclopedia, published between 1751 and 1772, was Denis Diderot (1713–1784). Similar works were soon produced also in English and German. Like ordinary dictionaries, which also were first compiled in the Old Regime, this sort of reference work allowed anyone to look things up accurately and rapidly as never before.

This is not the place to try to describe the literary work of Europe's major writers in any detail. Poetry and drama—both tragedy and comedy—remained vigorous in France and in England too. The three great "classical" dramatists of France flourished under Louis XIV: Pierre Corneille (1606–1684), Molière, whose real name was Jean Baptiste Poquelin (1622–1673), and Jean Racine (1639–1699). John Milton (1608–1674) and Alexander Pope (1688–1744) were perhaps the two most important English poets of their age. England also saw the birth of the modern novel with the works of Samuel Richardson (1689–1761) and Henry Fielding (1707–1754). Other countries of Europe failed to produce writers of Europe-wide reputation, until a brilliant group of Germans emerged toward the end of this period. Chief among them were Gotthold Ephraim Lessing (1729–1781), Johann Christoph Friedrich von Schiller (1759–1805), and Johann Wolfgang von Goethe (1749–1832).

These German writers and important English literary figures like Robert Burns (1759–1796) and William Wordsworth (1770–1850) tended to seek inspiration from everyday language of the people. They declared that personal emotion and self-expression were the key to great art. Such "romantic" ideas stood in self-conscious opposition to the "classical" rules of correctness which had been fashionable in earlier times. Like the criticism of the "philosophers" and the smoke of the new steam factories, the "romantic" movement pointed ahead toward the age which was to follow the overthrow of the Old Regime.

Art and Music

The Old Regime was not an age of major innovation in art, but during that time European music did evolve rapidly toward a "classical" form.

Palaces, like that built for Louis XIV at Versailles, were designed for grandeur and perfection. Size and formal balance of doors, windows, and decorative elements were the ways which architects chose to achieve these goals. Soon after 1700 a lighter, more graceful style called rococo came in, and exact balance of each part was deliberately abandoned. Then, toward the close of the eighteenth century, a reaction toward more "classical" simplicity and geometric regularity took place.

These shifts of style spread over most of Europe from France, where taste was, for the most part defined. In painting there was somewhat greater variety. Antoine Watteau (1684–1721) in France, Thomas Gainsborough (1727–1788) in England, Francisco Goya (1746–1828) in Spain, and Meindert Hobbema (1638–1709) in Holland—each embodied different national traditions. Yet differences, though real, were slight. The ideal of painting that had been defined so brilliantly in Italy, during the Renaissance, continued to be the norm for all of Europe.

What happened to European music between 1648 and 1789 was rather like what had happened to painting about two and a half centuries before. European musicians, first of all, had new or newly perfected instruments at their disposal. The violin and harpsichord were the most important. The scientific study of sound opened a better theoretical understanding of musical pitch, scales, and timbre. All this gave musicians the tools of their trade, just as Italian painters in Renaissance times had developed oil paints and canvas easels as the basic tools of theirs.

Using the new tools, a series of great composers created musical forms and works that still are performed regularly. Johann Sebastian Bach (1685–1750), George Frederick Handel (1685–1759), Wolfgang Amadeus Mozart (1756–1791), and Franz Joseph Haydn (1732–1809) are the most famous and familiar. Two general remarks about their achievement must suffice here. First, instrumental music became central and singing secondary, although, of course, all sorts of combinations of instruments and voices were experimented with. Few other musical traditions have given such prominence to instrumental music; but then, few other musical styles have had instruments so flexible and various to put through their paces.

Second, secular music—opera, symphonies, etc.—became as elaborate as and perhaps even more important than church music. This reflected musicians' roles as entertainers at royal courts and great noble houses. The fact that they were classed just above the rank of servants explains the relatively low social status held by Mozart and Haydn. Fuller recognition of music among the arts had to wait for the development of concert halls open to the public and supported by the purchase of tickets. This did not become usual until after 1789. Until musicians had a way of making a living by public performance, they had to exist either on the patronage of the rich or by holding church positions (as Bach, for example, did).

Religion and the Churches

Any brief survey of the cultural life of an age is likely to stress what was new and different and leave out the things that remained more or less the same. This is misleading for most people are more influenced by the stable, old, and familiar ideas and styles of thought than they are by anything new, however attractive it may seem. This is particularly true in the period we have been considering, when so many radical new ideas were put before the European public, yet affected only small minorities in most cases.

We may be sure that nearly all Europeans remained Christian in some sense or other. The official churches, supported by the different governments of Europe, all continued to claim that their own version of Christian doctrine offered the one and only true path to salvation. Children were taught the catechism in school or at their mother's knee; and even those who in later life rejected some or all of what they had been taught in childhood remained deeply influenced by their religious training. Most people never really made up their minds between the traditional doctrines of Christianity and the impersonal "deist" view that portrayed God as the creator of the universe, who then abandoned His handiwork to let it run itself like a great machine. Many, particularly in the lower classes, never heard deist views expressed and thus remained loyal to traditional Christian ways of understanding the world. Still others reacted strongly against the new scientific vision of reality and consciously reaffirmed their faith in a personal and immediate relationship between God and individual human beings.

The powerful new religious movements of the age were all of this sort. In England, George Fox (1624–1691) founded the Society of Friends (or Quakers) on the strength of his own personal experience of God and of commanding visions that ordered him to preach to the public. The sect he founded had no clergy at all and put great emphasis upon following one's own "inner light." Occasional persecution only hardened Quaker convictions. In the following century, John Wesley (1703–1791) took up a career as traveling evangelist after he, too, experienced a conversion and felt his "heart strangely warmed within him." His followers were known as Methodists. Both Quakers and Methodists became important in the English colonies of North America, where established churches were weaker than in England itself.

On the continent, Philipp Spener (1635–1705) founded Pietism. This was a religious movement that flourished within the Lutheran and Calvinist churches of Germany. Details of doctrine seemed unimportant to Spener and his followers. What mattered was direct personal experience of God, to be had through meditation and prayer and Bible study, conducted privately or within the family, as well as in public. German Pietism influenced Wesley and nearly all of Protestant Germany.

The Roman Catholic church was disturbed by Quietism and Jansenism, both of which were eventually judged to be heretical and were therefore suppressed. Quietism was founded by a Spanish priest, Miguel de Molinos (1640–1697). He was a mystic and taught that the soul should wait quietly for God to come. Jansenism was named for a Dutch priest, Cornelis Jansen (1585–1638), but the main leader of the movement was a Frenchman, Antoine Arnauld (1612–1694). The Jansenists wanted to go back to St. Augustine's teachings, putting much stress on predestination and personal piety. They came into sharp controversy with the Jesuits; and for some years France was divided between those who sympathized with the Jansenists and others who went along with the Jesuits. The pope ruled against the Jansenists in 1713, and their center, Port Royal, just outside Paris, was closed down. But the Jesuits' victory left them many enemies in France. They also fell into disfavor with the rulers of Spain and Portugal for refusing to submit to royal decrees; and the combined pressure of the governments of Spain, Portugal, and France persuaded the pope to suppress the order in 1773. The Jesuits survived, however, by taking refuge in Russia and Prussia, until in 1814 the papacy recognized their order once again.

Movements like these and the reaction all over Europe to Louis XIV's suppression of Huguenots in France (1685) showed the continuing hold Christianity had on men's minds. Europe's other religion, Judaism, began to undergo a fundamental transformation toward the end of the Old Regime, when the longstanding isolation of Jews from gentiles in German towns began to break down a bit, and individual Jews ventured out into the wider worlds of business, literature, and the arts. Moses Mendelssohn (1729–1786) was the main pioneer in opening intellectual communication between Jews and other Germans.

CONCLUSION

Even from this brief survey, it should be clear that Europe acquired knowledge and power at a faster rate than ever before during the Old Regime. Expansion on all fronts continued without halt; and with expansion went intensification, increasing variety, complexity, and an ever faster rate of change. The political and social balance that had been struck after the religious wars was never rigid and unchallenged. But by 1789 industrialism, arising primarily in England, and democratic political ideas, at home mainly in France and in America, had both begun to challenge the old order. Breakdown came with the French Revolution and the quarter century of war that the Revolution provoked.

Yet the eagerness with which later generations attacked the remnants of the Old Regime that survived the revolutionary struggles should not blind us—their descendants—to the positive achievements which that phase of Europe's long history had to its credit. No earlier age had been more brilliant or successful; the painful break with Europe's medieval frame, which had been the business of the Renaissance and Reformation, really paid off during the Old Regime when relative calm at home allowed Europe to take on the world—and to try to understand and appreciate, as well as trade and fight with, peoples of every kind. The impact Europeans had on the rest of the world will be the theme of the next chapter.

CHAPTER 5

World Reactions to Europe's Expansion

1700 to 1850

Between 1500 and 1700, European merchants, explorers, soldiers, missionaries, and other adventurers had made their presence felt along almost every habitable coast. When first the newcomers appeared, local peoples often greeted them with curiosity and sometimes with hospitality, although both Moslems and Chinese were suspicious and aloof from the start. As soon as Europeans in any way threatened, or seemed to threaten, things that local peoples held dear, rulers reacted by trying to break off relations and withdraw from what had become a disturbing contact. The increasing power that Europeans acquired during the Old Regime meant that they threatened more and more to upset other people's ways. Almost everywhere, except in Russia, the response was to cut off or to cut down on contact with the source of the trouble. This was the policy of Asian and African peoples and states from 1700 to 1850.

WITHDRAWAL FROM CONTACT WITH EUROPEANS

Stronger and more remote peoples could insulate themselves from Europe's influence successfully; but weaker or less favorably situated peoples could not. Thus, each of the great Asian civilized societies was able to cut off effective communication with Europeans, even when—as in the case of Moslems of India and of the Ottoman Empire—they had to endure the physical presence of foreigners in their midst. Their policy was to pay no attention to anything the Europeans had to say and to adhere to old tradition and patterns of behavior, in the hope of seeing the intruders go away after a while. The Japanese and Siamese carried this policy to its logical extreme by completely prohibiting contacts with Europeans. The Chinese confined trade to a single port, Canton, and entrusted the task of dealing with foreigners to a special group of merchants, the Co-hong.

In other parts of the world, however, weaker and simpler societies were not always able to withdraw. This was the fate of the Amerindians, for example, and of peoples of the Pacific Islands, of Australia, and of South Africa. In all of these regions, Europeans or people of European descent and culture kept pursuing the retreating natives, taking their land for farms or ranches, spreading diseases, and destroying traditional social discipline by defying it without punishment.

In the African interior, tropical diseases and comparatively well-organized kingdoms blocked European penetration. The simple geographical fact that sub-Saharan Africa's rivers have falls near their mouths created a barrier to inland travel. By requiring any traveler to come ashore and walk, the river falls exposed strangers to local human hostility and to mosquito-borne infections. As a result, the interior of Africa remained proof against European penetration until after 1850, although the slave trade left almost no part of the continent unaffected.

Taking the world as a whole, the cost of withdrawal from disturbing contacts with Europeans was heavy. Closed minds, fearful of having to face awkward facts, could only repeat what had been thought and done in earlier ages. That was no way to cope with Europe's eager acquisition of new skills and knowledge. As a result, the gap between European accomplishments and the achievements of the rest of the world widened rapidly.

By the years 1850–1860, the great civilizations of Asia found themselves helpless in face of Western superiority, which by then had become literally overwhelming. Hence, the effort to hold fast to old tradition and familiar ways of doing things backfired in the long run by requiring the non-Western peoples of the world to suffer an extremely painful and prolonged breakdown of their various styles of life after 1850. But between 1700 and 1850, no one could foresee what was coming; and in the Far East particularly, the policy of withdrawal and insulation seemed to work fairly well.

Population Growth

Another dimension of the worldwide scene between 1700 and 1850 made the "stand pat" policy easier in the short run and more dangerous in the long run that would otherwise have been the case. This was the upsurge of population that set in among civilized peoples at a rate seldom equaled before. Japan was an exception, for the custom of allowing unwanted newborn children to die from exposure—usually in some remote and unfrequented spot—kept Japan's population constant. But in China, in India, and in at least parts of the Moslem world, population spurted upward.

Three worldwide factors contributed to the remarkable growth of population. One factor was the fading away of epidemic diseases. A second factor was that American food crops enhanced the food producing capacity of heavily populated parts of the world. Sweet potatoes in south China, maize in Africa and southeastern Europe, the potato in northern Europe and Russia came into their own between 1700 and 1850. Many millions of people came to depend on these crops.

A third factor was that the development of artillery allowed a few centers of political authority to control larger empires more effectively than in earlier ages. Thus, the Manchus in China established a higher level of peace and order over a larger territory and for a longer time than the world had ever seen before. In other parts of the world, kingdoms and empires were less majestic in scale. Nevertheless, rulers in Europe and Asia were in a better position than ever before to suppress banditry and small scale raiding. In all probability, therefore, loss of life through local violence lessened at a time when deaths from disease were decreasing and new food crops were spreading.

In the short run, as long as fresh land lay uncultivated or more intensive tillage allowed food production to keep pace with growth of population, things went along smoothly, and traditional ways of life were strengthened rather than weakened by growth in numbers. But when limits to traditional methods were reached, population did not stop growing. Mass desperation on the part of the peasantry, on a scale that traditional political methods could not cope with, was an inevitable result.

The world still finds itself affected by this crisis. It set in at different times in different parts of the earth, beginning, for example, about 1775 in China and about the same time in some of the European provinces of the Ottoman Empire. From the point of view of the great civilizations of Asia, therefore, this development meant that European pressures from outside became irresistible after 1850, at a time when fundamental internal problems were building up toward massive peasant revolt. Only Japan, where population was harshly and deliberately kept in check, escaped this difficulty.

With the benefit of hindsight we can see clearly how non-Western peoples eventually paid a heavy price for putting off fundamental transformation at home to take account of new things the restless Europeans kept on discovering. But at the time, when Europe was not yet equipped with the additional force that developed with the Industrial Revolution, the policy of withdrawal and conservative loyalty to traditional ways seemed adequate for coping with the problems that faced Moslem, Chinese, and Hindu peoples. A policy that was able to keep expectation and reality more or less in touch with each other during a century and a half should not be hastily condemned.

THE WORLD OF ISLAM

From the time of the prophet Mohammed until about 1700, the general course of history conformed to Moslem expectations. In spite of some serious defeats and disasters—such as the breakdown of political unity among Moslems, dating from A.D. 750, or the Mongol sack of Baghdad in A.D. 1258, Moslem missionaries and conquerors kept on adding new lands to the realm of Islam. No large or important territories had been lost by Mohammed's followers. Border wars with the Christians in Europe and against Hindus and other unbelievers in Asia and Africa tended for more than a thousand years to favor the Moslem cause. Who, then, could seriously doubt that Allah continued to favor his people as he had in the days of the Prophet and the first caliphs?

Moslem Military Power Fades

It was, therefore, a tremendous blow to Moslems when the political and military balance rather suddenly reversed itself after 1700. In 1699 the Ottoman Empire was forced to make a humiliating peace with the Austrian Hapsburgs and surrendered most of Hungary. This was the first time the Ottoman Turks had been compelled to retreat before Christian arms.

Immediately thereafter, the Mogul Empire in India began to founder. Aurangzeb died in 1707, leaving his empire distracted by revolt. Mogul power never recovered. Exactly half a century later, British traders emerged as the strongest military power in all of India. The East India

Company made the Mogul Emperor its puppet, but everyone knew that Moslems no longer really ruled India.

The third great Islamic empire was the Safavid, based in Iran and Azerbaijan. It, too, suffered a breakdown, beginning in 1709 with an Afghan revolt. Drastic political disorder invited the intervention of Russian, Chinese, and even British agents. Old-fashioned Moslem cavalry continued to charge across the landscape, brave and bold as ever; but their defeats and victories more and more depended on supplies of powder and shot that came from foreign, usually Christian, sources. The old independence and power were irremediably gone.

The overthrow of steppe warriors as a major force in the Eurasian balance of power lay behind these dramatic military-political setbacks. More than any other civilization, the Moslems had opened themselves up to the steppe. Their victories in India and in Europe had depended in large part on migration of steppe warriors from central Asia to the frontiers, where holy war against infidels promised booty. But when cavalry ceased to be decisive on the battlefield, the whole military-political tradition of the great Moslem empires became outmoded.

THE JANISSARY CORPS   Only the Ottoman Empire made a serious effort to develop an efficient infantry equipped with guns. But the Janissary corps, which won many famous victories by its discipline and firepower in the age of Suleiman the Lawgiver, fell behind European troops from the time when its members ceased to be recruited from the Christian villages of the Balkans. Village boys, pulled up by the roots from their places of origin, could be kept under a severe discipline and, as slaves of the sultan, were trained to serve him well. But after 1634, the corps came to be recruited instead from sons of Janissaries, and the character of the troops changed quickly. Because the sultan found it difficult to pay his soldiers a living wage, the Janissaries worked at various artisan trades during the winter when they were not in the field.

This soon resulted in merging the Janissaries with the Moslem artisans of the towns. By 1700 or 1750 most Moslem artisans in the European provinces of the empire held appointments in the corps. Positions were bought and sold freely, and little check was kept on whether or not the purchasers had military training or would submit to discipline. The efficiency of the corps could not survive such practices; but the Janissaries nevertheless had the sultan and his ministers at their mercy. To protect their own privileges and traditions, they were ready to riot and revolt. They absolutely refused to allow any new body of troops to come into existence that might challenge their power at home.

THE INDIAN ARMIES   Such experiences did not encourage other Moslem rulers to try to build up infantry forces that could make firepower really effective in battle. Neither the Mogul nor the Safavid rulers actually tried. The Mogul armies were poorly equipped, poorly trained, and poorly led by comparison with European armies of the Old Regime. But with European guns, uniforms, and drillmasters, Indian soldiers proved quite effective. Ironically, it was this that made it possible for the English East India Company to dominate India so easily. A mere handful of Company employees from the British Isles were able to train *sepoy* (that is, native Indian) troops in the European manner—and thus by 1763 created what was by far the most efficient army in India.

Hindu rebels in central India, called Marathas, also weakened the Mogul power. Sikhs, too, made good their independence in the northwest. Local governors, who in theory owed their position to the emperor's appointment, became independent in all but name. Invaders from the north, first Nadir Shah from Iran and then Afghan raiders, crossed the mountains and plundered northern India.

Many Moslem princes, faced with Hindu unrest at home and the danger of Afghan raids from the north, fell back on British protection. The East India Company adopted the policy of "indirect rule." Existing states and tax systems were allowed to stand as long as a British resident at court was kept informed and allowed to give advice, which, in most cases, had to be followed. This cost the Company less, opened the doors to trade, kept the peace, and aroused a minimum of local hostility.

However, the iron hand within the velvet glove appeared from time to time. In 1818, for example, British troops put down the last Maratha bid for genuine independence. And in the years 1839–1842, a British army invaded Afghanistan, across India's northwest frontier, to enforce the Company's will. By that time the mighty Mogul Empire had become a shadow, and Moslem rule over India had become a hollow pretence. Moslem princes and their hangers-on had to submit. The Hindu majority was indifferent and politically inert, seeing little difference between one kind of foreign master and another. As long as the discipline of their Indian troops held, the British position in India was unshakable.

The Growth of Russian Power

In central Asia and the former Safavid lands, Afghans, Uzbeks, Persians, Kazaks, Kalmucks, and Azerbaijani Turks engaged in a general melee. Successful captains like Nadir Shah (ruler of Persia 1736–1747) built vast empires that crumbled as fast as they had been constructed. Until after 1750, the power that made the greatest gains in this confused situation was China. A series of successful military campaigns extended China's northern and western borders to their present limits.

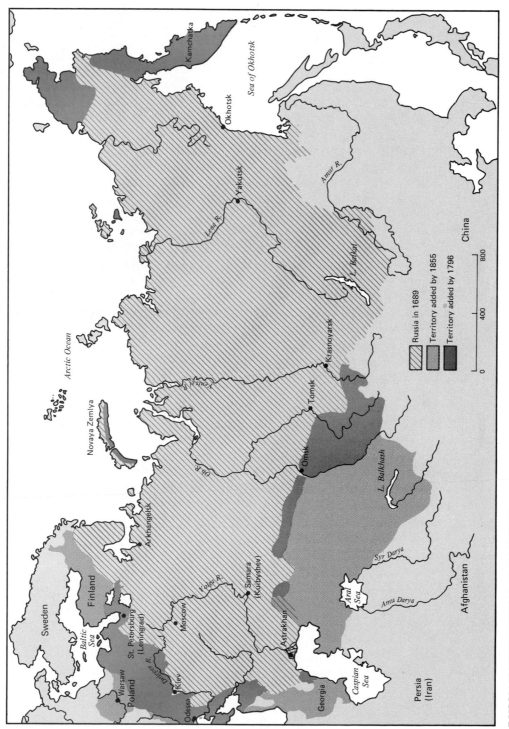

Russia in 1689

Territory added by 1855

Territory added by 1796

0   400   800

Arctic Ocean

Novaya Zemlya

Kamchatka

Sea of Okhotsk

Okhotsk

Yakutsk

Lena R.

Amur R.

L. Baikal

Krasnoyarsk

Yenisei R.

Tomsk

Ob R.

Omsk

L. Balkhash

China

Syr Darya

Aral Sea

Amu Darya

Afghanistan

Sweden

Finland

Baltic Sea

St. Petersburg (Leningrad)

Warsaw

Poland

Kiev

Dnieper R.

Odessa

Moscow

Arkhangelsk

Volga R.

Samara (Kuibyshev)

Astrakhan

Georgia

Caspian Sea

Persia (Iran)

RUSSIAN TERRITORIAL EXPANSION 1689–1855

ALI PASHA OF JANINA

Ali Pasha of Janina (1740–1822) was one of several upstarts who took control of outlying regions of the Ottoman Empire just before and after 1800. Ali's power centered in the wild mountains of the western Balkans, where Greece and Albania meet.

In some ways Ali was thoroughly old-fashioned. He was an Albanian chieftain's son; but when he was about fourteen years old, his father was killed by a neighboring tribe. Ali and his mother had to flee for their lives into the barren mountains of southern Albania. Soon a group of outlaws gathered around them, and Ali's mother led the band until her son became old enough to take command himself.

As soon as he could, Ali set out to revenge himself. Eventually he succeeded in destroying all those who had taken part in killing his father. But this was only a start. By hook and by crook—and by applying a good deal of simple violence—Ali extended his domain over most of what is today Albania and much of western and northern Greece. He built up a private army and ruled as a complete despot. As he rode through the streets of his capital, Janina, or traveled in the country round about, he often would order his bodyguard to kill on the spot a man whom he accused, rightly or wrongly, of misdoing. Ali never learned to read. He also never learned to trust anyone. He administered his government entirely on the basis of his memory of faces, names, and places.

All of this was quite traditional. But there was another side to Ali's career that made him very different from any earlier Albanian or Moslem despot. His power reached its peak during the disturbed era of the French Revolution, when French, Austrian, English, and Russian diplomats and secret agents were unusually active in the Ottoman Empire, as well as elsewhere. Therefore Ali frequently played host to rival representatives

After that date the southward advance of Russian power became the most significant result of the continuing upheaval. Long leaps forward, such as that which brought Peter the Great's authority to the southern shore of the Caspian in 1723, were sometimes followed by withdrawal. But shifts back and forth usually tended to favor Russia, because Russian armies and administration, tempered by participation in Europe's rivalries, were generally superior to anything the Moslems of central Asia could create.

Major landmarks of Russia's advance were the annexation of Georgia in 1800 and occupation of the Amu Darya Valley, south of the Aral of the European great powers, trying always to get promises of support and supplies of arms from them.

Ali also was interested in ideas, and he could not help wondering what it was that allowed revolutionary France to defeat its enemies so often. It was hard for French agents to explain the power of the slogan "Liberty, Equality, Fraternity" to a man like Ali, who assumed that French successes in battle must be due to supernatural help. When he discovered that some of the revolutionaries were deists and did not accept Christianity, he was delighted. Ali's own relgious background was a heretical form of Islam, which taught that traditional Islam and Christianity were both in error. Consequently, Ali felt that his religious opinions and those of the latest thinkers of Paris were really in agreement. If only he could find out the rituals through which the French got in touch with their God, then his armies, too, might be as successful as Napoleon's!

Ali never gave up this hope. Near the end of his life he entered into negotiations with a secret revolutionary society that helped to start the Greek War of Independence in 1821. To be sure, he was looking for help against the sultan in Constantinople, who had resolved to destroy Ali's power. The Greek revolt did not save Ali. Instead, he helped the Greeks because the Turks decided to concentrate on overthrowing him first. This allowed the Greeks to set themselves up solidly in the south. The eventual success of their revolution was made possible by the long siege of Janina that was required before Ali's power collapsed in 1822, after which he was killed.

Clearly, the effort to build a bridge between the world of an Albanian tribal chieftain and that of democratic French revolutionary thinkers was not a success. Yet, since Ali's time, many others have made a similar attempt to bridge the gap between their own traditional ideas and those of the Western world. In this sense, the despotic, old-fashioned, religious heretic of Janina was a forerunner of our own age.

Sea, in 1849. The net result, shortly after 1850, was to bring the Russians against the Chinese frontiers in central Asia, while Afghanistan and Persia (Iran) constituted a buffer zone, separating the Russian frontiers from the outposts of British power in India's northwest provinces. These two countries suffered from continual intrigues and violence as local chieftains tried to play off Russian against British agents. The old tribal life survived, but what had once been the crossroads of the world had by 1850 become a backwater, bypassed by everything that really mattered.

OTTOMAN RETREAT   The case of the Ottoman Empire was more complex. It, too, had to keep on retreating. Loss of Hungary in 1699 was followed by further losses to Austria in the Balkans in 1718; but the military tide was temporarily reversed in 1739–1740 when the Turks won several battles against Austrian commanders who had acted rashly. This victory came at an unfortunate time for the Turks, because it convinced them that with only minor adjustments their old military establishment could cope with European arms. Hence, for the following quarter century, the Turks dropped efforts at the military reform. Therefore, when the Russian armies, rested from their campaigns of the Seven Years' War, invaded the Ottoman Empire in 1768, the Turks found themselves woefully unprepared. Russian soldiers were completely successful and dictated a peace, at Kuchuk Kainarji in 1774, that gave them control of the Black Sea and the right to pass freely through the straits.

Turkish response to this blow was ineffective. Some thought the situation called for military reform along European lines, but preliminary efforts in that direction were stopped in their tracks by Janissary revolts. Local governors became independent in all but name. Serbs, Greeks, and Arabs rose in revolt. It looked as though the last days of the Ottoman Empire were at hand.

What saved Ottoman power until 1918 was the diplomatic intervention by the great powers of Europe. First the French and then the British came to Turkey's aid—sometimes with diplomatic notes, sometimes with a fleet, and sometimes with military instructors and advisers who tried to make the Turkish armies able once again to cope with the empire's defense. Success was only partial. Outlying parts of the empire became independent (Egypt from 1809, Greece in 1830) or autonomous (Serbia from 1815, Romania from 1828). Algeria, which had never been administered regularly from Constantinople, was annexed by the French in 1830. On the other hand, the sultan's administration became stronger in the parts of the empire left to him. The unruly Janissary corps was destroyed in 1826 and a new Turkish army took shape. Efforts to reform the law and administration in accordance with European ideas never achieved success, although sweeping proclamations to that effect were issued in 1839.

The Moslem Reform Movement

Most Moslems felt deep doubts about trying to imitate the West. To do so ran against their deepest prejudices. It meant admitting, in effect, that Islam was not the true faith, for Islam was embodied in the Sacred Law; and the Sacred Law did not allow good Moslems to imitate European laws and customs. If Allah ruled the world and if he had revealed his will to Mohammed, as every Moslem believed, then it was folly to abandon the ancient ways. No doubt, shortcomings on the part of the faithful had angered Allah and persuaded him to withdraw his favor from the Moslem community. The answer, clearly, was to go back to the rigor of the Prophet's day, to follow every jot and tittle of the Sacred Law and wait patiently until Allah's favor was restored.

WAHHABI REFORM   In different parts of the Islamic world many Moslems drew this conclusion. Efforts to get back to the purity of the original Islam created disturbances in China, in Java, and in parts of Africa; but the most successful and influential reform movement, appropriately enough, started in Arabia itself. The spokesman of reform was Mohammed ibn-Abdul-Wahhab (1703–1792), whose followers are often referred to as Wahhabis. A local chieftain of the Saud family became the military leader of the movement and spread its power through most of Arabia. This brought on a collision with the Ottoman sultan, who claimed possession of the two sacred cities, Mecca and Medina. In 1818 Mohammed Ali, pasha of Egypt and only nominally subordinate to the sultan, sent troops, trained in European style, against the Wahhabis and defeated them with ease.

Yet this setback did not destroy the reform movement. On the contrary, Moslems in India and other parts of the Islamic world became interested in the Wahhabi reform only after it ceased to be identified with a strictly Arab military cause. The essence of Abdul-Wahhab's message was simple. He wanted an exact and faithful obedience to the Koran and the Sacred Law—and the ruthless discard of all the Sufi incrustation that had grown up in Moslem practice since the prophet Mohammed's day. The movement had a strong puritanical element in it. In particular, the prohibition of wine was taken in the strictest sense, as were all the other injunctions of the Koran. The Wahhabi reform remains to the present day a great force within Islam and affects the conduct of millions of Moslems. This is true even in parts of the world where observance of Wahhabi principles has never become official, such as is the case in modern Saudi Arabia.

Moslems unaffected by the Wahhabi movement remained passive for the most part. After all, other disasters had come and gone. This one, too, would finally pass. Allah would show his power only when it pleased him to do so. The wise do not demand reasons for God's acts. Such arguments pressed to their logical extreme seemed to prove that efforts at reform were futile and meaningless, since everything had to wait for Allah to show his hand.

Only a tiny minority took seriously the idea of borrowing Western skills. Even when such individuals held high positions in government, they could not make their will effective. Until the twentieth century, no Moslem ruler was able to create a clique of administrators whose careers depended on continuance of radical reform, as Peter the Great had done in Russia. Hence, efforts to borrow Western ways always flagged. Too few believed in such a program to make it work.

Art and Literature

Under the circumstances no one would expect to find important new art or literature arising within the Islamic world. Even the effort to stay safely within old forms fell short, for political upheaval meant that steady royal patronage for artists, architects, and poets could not be depended on. Yet the breakdown of these traditional patterns had a negative virtue, since it opened the way for new beginnings. Ottoman Turkish, for example, was cast into new and simpler literary molds, far closer to everyday speech, by Akif Pasha (1787–1845). His literary efforts did not win much

Christian missionaries in India. Gordon Hall, an American missionary, dies of cholera in a remote Indian village, 1826. (New York Public Library Picture Collection)

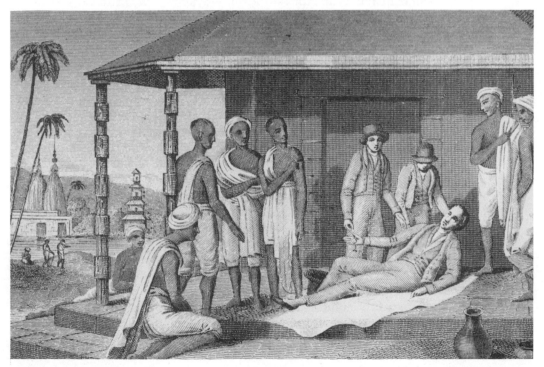

admiration, but his deliberate act of cutting Persian and Arabic words out of written Turkish created the literary language used in Turkey today.

Moslem Missionary Work

The bad fortune that came to the Moslem heartlands between 1700 and 1850 was scarcely compensated for by the fact that in Africa and southeast Asia, conversion to Islam continued to advance as it had for centuries. Individuals and small groups, especially those who began to take part in trade, found Islamic law useful. Acceptance of Islam offered a convenient way of entering into the great world at large. Arabs from Oman, in southern Arabia, became active in the slave trade of east Africa, operating mainly from the island base of Zanzibar. European commercial activity in that part of the world was unimportant. On the other side of the Indian Ocean, Malay pirates and traders sailed the South China Sea and traded with the islands nearby—Mindanao, Borneo, and points between. These traders acted as missionaries of Islam, as their predecessors had done for centuries. But conversion of these regions was a poor substitute for the dominion over the entire Indian Ocean, which had once rested in Moslem hands. On the sea, as on the land, Moslem fortunes were at a low ebb indeed.

HINDU AND BUDDHIST ASIA

Hindus and Buddhists of southeast Asia found the presence of Europeans far less hard to take than the Moslems did. Both Hindus and Buddhists had already been forced to subordinate themselves to Moslem strangers, who expected to rule and to trade and who were ready to use force, when needed, to get their way. The European trading companies behaved in the same way.

From the Hindu point of view, habits that had been developed to deal with the Moslems worked perfectly well when applied to Europeans. The intruders were treated as another caste; and appropriate rituals were at hand to remove any defilement that might come to a pious Hindu from having to deal with them. Hindu religion was strong and vibrant, and therefore could easily resist Christian missionary efforts. Since religion and the entire way of life were intimately bound together, this meant, in effect, that Hindus were not inclined to inquire into European ideas or, indeed, into any other aspect of their civilization.

Hindu-European
Cultural Interaction

The British, however, were curious. Until 1837 the language of administration in India remained Urdu, the mixed Persian-Turkish speech used by the Moguls. This meant that British officials and the Hindu clerks who worked for them both had to learn Urdu. As a result, the British tended to view India through a more or less Moslem pair of spectacles. But a few individuals became interested in the other languages of India. The greatest pioneer was Sir William Jones (1746–1794), who translated works from Persian, Arabic, and Sanskrit and founded the Asiatic Society of Bengal. He noticed the relationship between Sanskrit and European languages, a discovery that excited much attention in European learned circles and started quite a vogue for the study of Sanskrit. Enthusiastic scholars assumed that, as the oldest recorded form of Indo-European speech, Sanskrit must be closer to the original thought and language of their own ancestors.

European scholarly interest in Sanskrit studies was also fanned by the attraction many Europeans felt for Hindu philosophy and mystical doctrines. Filled with doubts about the truth of Christian dogma, yet repelled by the mechanical emptiness of a Newtonian universe, many sensitive Europeans became interested in Hindu doctrines emphasizing the illusory nature of the world of sense. Interest in India became, in fact, a trait of the romantic movement, especially in Germany.

CHRISTIAN MISSIONS   Christian missionaries provided a second and quite different channel for interaction between Hindu and European worlds. To be sure, until 1813 the East India Company carefully excluded Christian missionaries from its trading posts. The theory was that any attack upon local religious customs would damage trade and endanger the Company's position. In 1813, however, Parliament required the Company to admit missionaries freely. Once on the spot, the missionaries decided to put their message in the local vernacular language and, for the purpose, had to develop printing presses and standards of literary usage. The modern written Bengali language got its start in this fashion, though it was soon taken over by Hindu writers for their own purposes. Mission schools were also set up, in which secular subjects were taught as well as Christian doctrine, thus bringing Indian minds into contact with the European intellectual world.

RAMMOHUN ROY   Neither Hindus nor Moslems were much attracted to the doctrines of Christianity. Indeed, in one famous case, a Christian missionary lost his own faith after arguing with learned Hindus and emerged a Unitarian, convinced that all the great religions of the world conveyed essentially the same message. This was also the conclusion arrived at by the first Indian who studied and tried to understand the cultural world of Europe. His name was Rammohun Roy. Born a Brahman, he first learned Urdu in order to qualify for a government job. He then learned English. This led to Greek and Latin, and soon his Bible studies required him to acquire a smattering of Hebrew also. As soon as he could afford to do so, Rammohun Roy resigned from his government job to devote himself more fully to religious studies. From Christianity he turned to the study of Islam, and the comparison of both with his inherited Hindu faith convinced him that all three religions needed to be revised in the light of modern knowledge. The truth conveyed by each of the world's great religions boiled down, he thought, to a simple belief in one God. Unitarians in England and America were much impressed by Rammohun Roy's message, which he brought to England just before his death in 1833. His efforts to reform Hinduism were not very successful. Yet he did persuade the British authorities to prohibit the custom of *suttee*, according to which a widow had been required to sacrifice herself on her husband's funeral pyre.

Rammohun Roy was the first of a long line of prominent Indians who learned English, and through English became acquainted with European civilization. In 1835 the East India Company set up schools to teach English and other European subjects. This opened the door wide for later generations of Indians to straddle two cultural worlds—one English and official, the other Hindu and private.

By and large, Indian Moslems stayed away from the new schools, leaving the pursuit of government clerkships to Hindus. Schooling in India was often defective, and graduates were usually more interested in getting a job in a government office than in interpreting Western civilization to their own people or in reforming Hindu customs in the light of European ideas or examples. Yet, for all its defects, the schools and administration of India began a process of interaction between Hindu and European civilizations on a scale and with an intimacy that was not achieved elsewhere until much later.

Buddhist Retreat and Isolationism

Nothing of this sort bridged the gap between the Buddhist peoples of southeast Asia and the outside world before 1850. These people lived in Ceylon, Burma, Thailand, Laos, Cambodia, and Vietnam. All of these kingdoms found themselves squeezed between the vigorous and expand-

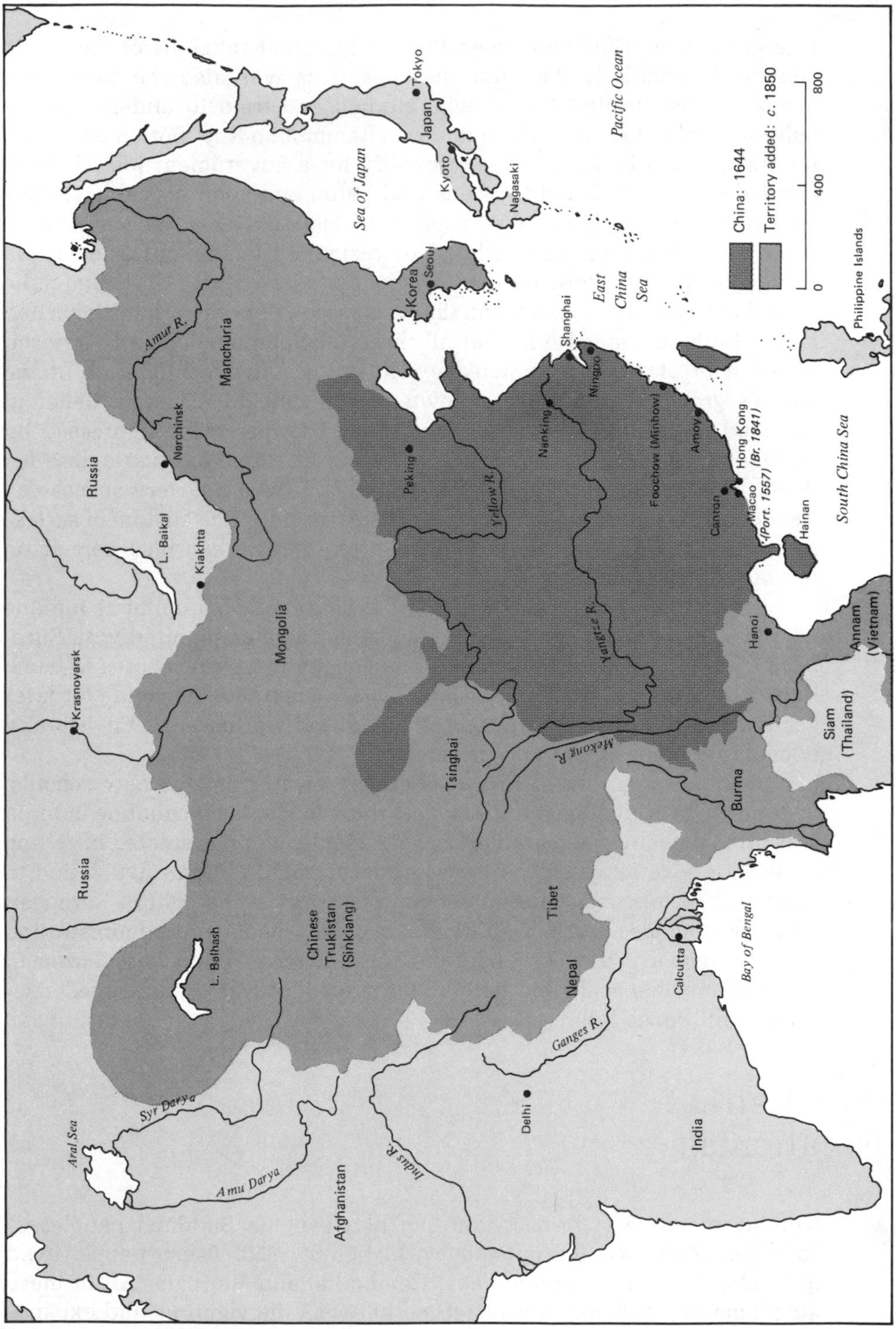

Tokyo
Japan
Kyoto
Nagasaki
Sea of Japan
Pacific Ocean
East China Sea
China: 1644
Territory added: c. 1850
0
400
800
Philippine Islands
Korea
Seoul
Manchuria
Amur R.
Russia
Nerchinsk
L. Baikal
Kiakhta
Krasnoyarsk
Mongolia
Peking
Yellow R.
Shanghai
Ningpo
Nanking
Foochow (Minhow)
Amoy
Hong Kong
(Br. 1841)
Macao
(Port. 1557)
Canton
Hainan
South China Sea
Yangtze R.
Hanoi
Annam
(Vietnam)
Siam
(Thailand)
Mekong R.
Tsinghai
Burma
Tibet
Chinese
Trukistan
(Sinkiang)
L. Balhash
Nepal
Calcutta
Bay of Bengal
Ganges R.
Delhi
India
Aral Sea
Syr Darya
Amu Darya
Afghanistan
Indus R.

CHINA, MANCHU DYNASTY

ing land power of China on the north and an aggressive European, primarily British, seapower. The Chinese emperor claimed a vague traditional lordship over all of the southeast Asia, as well as over the British and other European traders who visited Chinese ports. In the years 1766–1769 the Chinese sent an army into Burma to try to enforce Peking's authority, but without lasting success.

British seapower was more difficult for these states to deal with. In 1802, for example, the kingdom of Kandy in Ceylon submitted to British guns. The Burmese had to give up part of their coast lands after a short war (1824–1826), and Thailand lost control of Malaya when local Moslem rulers shifted allegiance from the king of Siam to the East India Company's agents at various times between 1768 and 1824.

However disagreeable, neither Chinese nor British pressure persuaded the Buddhists of southeast Asia to do anything drastic to change their traditional ways. Like the Moslems of Afghanistan and Iran, these peoples and kingdoms were far enough off the beaten track so they could afford to hold fast to old-fashioned ways, although their power of self-defense was clearly inadequate to keep European intruders away.

CHINA'S REVERSAL OF ROLES

China prospered under two exceptionally long reigns. The K'ang-hsi emperor occupied the imperial throne from 1662–1722 and made the Manchu dynasty secure for the first time. The Ch'ien Lung emperor ascended the throne in 1736 and abdicated in 1795 so as not to reign longer than his famous predecessor; but in fact, he continued to fulfill the emperor's role until his death in 1798. The Chinese ideal of stability and decorum was almost perfectly summed up in these two reigns. Virtue as defined by Confucius flourished. Scholarship was vigorous. Imperial patronage of pottery works produced the finest porcelains ever manufactured in China. Painting and poetry flowed from thousands upon thousands of brushes.

Peace prevailed at home; and along the distant frontiers of central Asia, Chinese armies overthrew the last nomad power that dared to defy the celestial emperor's will. Russia, by the Treaty of Kiakhta (1727), recognized the forward movement of Chinese frontiers to include Mongolia and Chinese Turkistan. Having made the northern border secure, the Chinese turned attention to the south and invaded, with varying success, Tibet (1751), Burma (1766), and Nepal (1792).

Population grew rapidly from about 150 million in 1700 to about

430 million in 1850. An increase in artisan manufactures and exports no doubt provided employment for a small part of the new population of China; but the great majority lived in the villages where rice lands were close at hand.

China's Confucian Mold

Until about 1775 all seemed well. More people simply increased China's vast bulk. New land could be found for cultivation by moving higher up the hill slopes or deeper into swamps and other marginal lands. Everyone who worked hard enough could eat, and the peasants asked for nothing more than that. Their increasing numbers supported many landlords, whose sons studied the Confucian classics, sat for the imperial examinations, and, if they worked hard enough, could hope to pass the necessary tests and get jobs in the government. Since government jobs meant a chance to accumulate wealth, as well as the enjoyment of power and prestige, competition for appointments was intense.

The investment of time and energy in study was correspondingly immense. Study of the classics began in earliest youth and was often pursued day in and day out until middle age, since failure the first time did not mean that a student could not try the examinations again. The extraordinary effort required to pass the tests molded the rulers and leaders of Chinese society to the Confucian ideal and completely closed their minds to anything not tested in the examinations.

The government also patronized scholars directly. Men, famous for their learning, were assigned the task of editing ancient texts and compiling reference works of the most diverse sorts, such as bibliographies, familiar quotations, dictionaries, encyclopedias, lists of "best books," and the like. The grandiose scale of these labors is hard for us to believe. In 1726, for example, a famous encyclopedia of 5020 volumes was completed (although it should be pointed out that a Chinese volume was smaller than those European printers usually produced). By comparison with the bulk of such labors, however, really new work was hard to find. The attention of China's rulers was firmly fixed upon the past. It seemed self evident that the more ancient anything was, the more valuable it must be.

Of course, not everyone passed the examinations, and among those who did not make it a more self-indulgent cultural underworld came into existence. Novels or romances, the most famous of which is *The Dream of the Red Chamber* by Ts'ao Hsueh-Chan (d. 1764) reflected the life of such leisured but ineffective individuals. But since this sort of writing was regarded as unworthy of a scholar, the book was never published in the author's lifetime. It portrays the inner life of a large Chinese family, with an intimacy modern readers find delightful but which seemed like undressing in public to Ts'ao Hsueh-Chan's contemporaries.

CHRISTIANITY DISCREDITED   As for European ideas and skills, Chinese scholars and officials had no time for such trifles. Until 1715, to be sure, the emperor often found it useful to employ Jesuit missionaries on various technical tasks at which they excelled, such as casting cannon and making a map of China with reference points established by astronomic observations. But in 1715, after years of bitter quarreling, the pope decided that the Jesuit view of Confucian rites was in error. This was a deep insult to the emperor, who only a few years before had come to the exactly opposite conclusion. Since a key point at issue was how the word "God" should be translated into Chinese, it seemed, to indignant Chinese, that the pope was trying to tell them how to use their own language. No greater insult could have been offered to an emperor who prided himself on his scholarship.

Thereafter, the Christian mission was completely discredited at court. The Jesuits were allowed to stay because they knew how to keep the calendar correctly; but they were forbidden to make converts. Christian missions, as far as they continued to operate at all, had to do so in defiance of the law. Limited underground preaching appealed mainly to poor and discontented groups in the cities. But in the eyes of the scholar class, this only discredited European ideas that much more.

The Peasant Revolt

In 1774 a peasant revolt disturbed the peace of China. It was put down, but secret societies, such as the White Lotus, which was associated with this revolt, kept on multiplying. The reason was that poor peasants no longer could live in traditional ways in those parts of the country where the growing population had begun to press on the supply of cultivable land. If loans to peasants to tide them over a bad season could not be repaid, creditors could acquire whatever land the debtors had once possessed. This soon created an angry, landless class ready for revolt. The result, therefore, was a series of disturbances—some small, others more serious—that kept the imperial authority on the defensive. The government's long success in maintaining peace and prosperity thus began to backfire after 1775 in a most distressing way.

Trade Problems Lead to War

At almost the same time, China's foreign trade began to present a serious problem too. In 1757 the emperor had decreed that Canton should be the only port at which foreign ships might put in. China's main European trading partner was the East India Company, which enjoyed a legal monopoly of Britain's trade with China. Dutch, French, and, after 1784, United States ships also put in at Canton occasionally; but the Chinese were able to keep them all under control by giving an association of merchants, the Co-hong, a monopoly of all dealings with strangers.

From the European point of view, the great problem was to find something the Chinese wanted to import. Chinese-made goods commanded a lively market in Europe and elsewhere, but about the only thing the Chinese wanted in exchange was silver. Europeans were reluctant to see their good silver disappear into China; and it was not until a brisk market for opium developed in China that the Europeans discovered a commodity they could offer instead. Opium was produced cheaply in India, and it gave the English just what they needed to make the China trade really profitable for the first time.

In 1834 the British government canceled the legal monopoly the East India Company had long enjoyed and tried to put trade with China on the same basis as trade with any other part of the world. A swarm of private traders therefore descended on Canton, eager to get in on the profits to be made from the opium trade.

The Chinese imperial authorities soon took alarm at the spread of the opium habit. They forbade the production or sale of the drug, but this simply drove the trade underground. European merchants began dealing with all sorts of shady characters and smuggling became a large-scale, organized gangster affair. In 1839 the Chinese decided to crack down. A special commissioner came from Peking with instructions to break up the illegal trade. He seized 30,000 chests of opium within a few months and seemed on the point of cleaning up the whole mess when he collided with British authority.

THE OPIUM WAR   The point at issue was trifling. Some English sailors had engaged in a brawl at Canton and killed a Chinese. The Chinese demanded that one of the sailors be handed over to them to be executed. From a Chinese point of view this was only common justice and an ordinary assertion of sovereignty. From the British point of view, however, handing over a man to be executed without trial and without any proof of his guilt was an appalling miscarriage of justice. The British ship's captain therefore refused. He was backed up by a commissioner of trade, appointed by the British crown. When the Chinese then tried to use force,

The Opium War. A 19th century Chinese illustration of the Imperial Chinese Commissioner Lin Tse-hsu supervising the destruction of ca. six million dollars worth of opium seized from the British in June 1839.

the British government decided to send a detachment of the royal navy to the scene.

British naval vessels and marine landing parties found the Chinese coast almost completely at their mercy. Chinese ports lacked harbor defenses, and Chinese troops could not move rapidly enough from one threatened place to another. When clashes did take place, the Chinese soldiers proved far inferior to the British detachments. In 1842 the bewildered and indignant Chinese had to make peace. By the Treaty of Nanking they opened four additional ports to British trade, agreed to levy a uniform 5 percent tariff on imports, ceded Hong Kong to the British, and officially recognized that Queen Victoria was not—as the Chinese had always before pretended—paying tribute to the emperor when British ships put in at Chinese ports.

UNEQUAL TREATIES   The French and American governments soon made similar and even more advantageous treaties with China. In 1844, the Americans secured the right of extraterritoriality. This meant that American citizens would be tried by American law, even on Chinese soil, and before American consuls. In the same year, the French secured official toleration of Christianity and of missionary activity in the port cities. By the principle of the "most favored nation clause," which was inserted into each of these treaties, any concession to one foreign power became a concession to all. Thus a mere five years from the time when the clash had begun, China found itself the victim of unequal treaties and unable to stave off the intruding foreigners.

The shock to Chinese feelings was immense. The Celestial Kingdom, to which all barbarians ought to pay tribute, had suddenly ceased to occupy the center of the world. New and strange powers, unknown to Confucius, had burst upon the scene. The ancients offered no rules for how to cope with such a situation. Stunned surprise and utter dismay were all that Chinese scholars and officials could feel at first; and in their state of shock they had no time to turn toward more constructive action before a new and violent civil war flamed up, the Taiping Rebellion which, for fifteen years (1850–1864) tore at the vitals of the empire.

The suddenness of China's fall needs to be emphasized. Until 1839 the internal troubles of the country remained marginal. Tried and true Confucian patterns of conduct seemed to be working well; and China's superiority over the barbarian world was completely taken for granted by every educated Chinese. The intellectual class, in other words, had been so homogenized that no one had any idea of how to deal with the crisis that burst so suddenly. The great bulk of China sprawled helpless, blind, angry—completely unprepared for the reversal of roles that events had thrust upon the nation.

THE LAND
OF THE RISING SUN

Japan's history from 1700 to 1850 was in almost every respect the exact opposite of China's. While China fought a series of victorious frontier wars, Japan remained at peace. While China's population nearly tripled, Japan's population remained almost constant and may even have decreased slightly. While Chinese scholars fixed their gaze upon their own past to the exclusion of everything else in the world, Japanese intellectuals explored several different kinds of learning and paid considerable attention to what was going on in Europe, even though the official policy of isolation remained rigidly in force.

Political Insecurity
of the Shogun's Power

From the beginning, the Tokugawa shoguns had to face some awkward problems that refused to go away. Nothing like China's smug self-satisfaction could, therefore, arise in Japan, since both the ruling clique of the Tokugawa family and the "outside lords," who had been excluded from any part in the central government realized that the whole system might fall apart again. Only the bitter memory of Japan's long civil wars and the political watchfulness of the shoguns kept the peace. But memories of a time when the Tokugawa family was just the equal, not the superior, of other noble families never died; nor could the Japanese forget that the emperor, kept in seclusion by the shoguns, was in theory supreme. No doctoring of the historical record could hide the fact that the shoguns' power was a usurpation.

Economic Disbalance
between Warriors
and Merchants

Another difficult problem arose from the success with which the shoguns kept the peace. The warrior class had no occupation when there was no war. It was a matter of policy (as established by Iyeyasu Tokugawa in 1603) to require all important lords to spend part of the year in the capital, Tokyo, where they would be directly under the eye of the shogun; and when they were not in residence they were required to leave hostages behind in the form of sons and other close relatives. Hence, all of the fief holders had to keep houses in the capital, where they had nothing much to do.

Two consequences followed. First, fief holders had to convert at least a part of their income, which was in rice, into money that could be used in the capital to keep up the family establishment. This required merchants to buy surplus rice in the countryside and sell it in the cities, above all in Tokyo, the new magnet to which population and other resources flowed. Second, the merchants who organized the distribution of rice and other necessary commodities grew rich; but the fief holders had to sell at the merchants' price and buy at the merchants' price—and therefore grew poor. At least they found themselves too poor to live up to the standard of luxury that rapidly developed in Tokyo and other cities. Special amusement quarters catered to the taste of rich merchants for song and dance, good food and company. Warriors, whiling away their time idly in town, could not resist such attractions; and when they could not afford them, they ran recklessly into debt.

The result was a sharp discrepancy between what was and what most Japanese felt ought to be. The warriors and rulers were poorer than the merchants who, according to Confucian ideas, were social parasites and pests, ranking, by rights, below the least worthy peasant. The fief holders and the peasants agreed in deploring what had happened and tried all sorts of ways to remedy the injustice. Sometimes the government resorted to outright confiscation of merchant fortunes. More often a repudiation of debts was decreed, in whole or in part; or the currency was debased to make repayment of debts easier. All such measures failed. The merchants quickly made good their losses by charging more for services rendered. As long as the fief holders were not allowed to remain all year round on their lands, the merchants' services were literally indispensable, and they were, therefore, always able to regain the upper hand economically.

Toward the end of the period, some of the fief holders tried to solve their economic problem by developing mining and other enterprises on their holdings. New crops and skills spread—particularly the cultivation of silk worms. Japan, for the first time, became self-sufficient in silk. Another practice was to marry into a merchant family, thus refreshing the depleted fortunes of the noble warrior stock and endowing the merchant with a new respectability. Blurring of class lines in this fashion was forbidden by the warrior code of behavior, but the temptation was great on both sides and instances multiplied.

Official Ideology

The shogun's policy in face of these difficulties was to sit tight and hope for the best. Neo-Confucianism was official. Study of other schools of thought was formally prohibited. Great emphasis was put upon loyalty; and the code of approved conduct for the warrior class was spelled out exactly, both in formal decree and in literature and drama. The famous story entitled "Tale of the Forty-seven Ronin," for example, kept alive memory of an incident that took place in 1703.

But the moral of the "Tale of the Forty-seven Ronin" was, to say the least, double-edged, for Asano's followers were admired for faithfulness to their lord even when it caused them to act against the policy of the central government. Such loyalty could, obviously, justify rebellion. Moreover, the more the official line stressed loyalty to superiors, the more awkward it became to justify the shogun's own disloyalty to the emperor. Public demonstrations of loyalty to the emperor thus became a way of expressing dissatisfaction with the shogun. But the government found it impossible to suppress sentiments that were outwardly so correct and proper.

THE DEVELOPMENT OF SHINTO   Accordingly, a school of thought arose that stressed the divine origin and descent of the imperial house. By degrees experts elaborated rites and ceremonies to celebrate the great events recounted in Japanese legend. These practices are referred to as *Shinto*, and evolved rapidly to the level of an organized religion—complete with priests, different sects, and rituals for everyday human emergencies of birth, marriage, and death. Borrowing from Christian and Buddhist rituals seems to have gone into the development of Shinto. An even stronger element was preference for an authentic Japanese instead of a borrowed Chinese doctrine.

The development of Shinto cults among the Japanese public at large was matched by the labors of a handful of scholars who set out to learn about Western thought. The medium was Dutch, for—as we saw in Chapter 3—a single Dutch ship was permitted to put into Nagasaki harbor each year and to carry on a carefully supervised trade. Foreign books were smuggled into Japan by this route, and a few persons learned how to read them and even made Japanese translations or adaptations of some medical and mathematical texts.

Admirers of Dutch learning and those who cultivated Japanese tradition got along with one another quite well. Both opposed the official Neo-Confucian orthodoxy of the shogun's government; both were supported more or less secretly by the "outside lords," who never quite gave up their jealousy of the Tokugawa family; and both were looking for alternative lines of action for their country. Hence, when foreign pressures did persuade the shogun to open Japan again to foreign trade (1854), a few individuals in Japan were already familiar with some of the basic characteristics of Western civilization.

The Life of the Arts

Japan's remarkable social structure was reflected in the arts. On the one hand, official culture conformed closely to Chinese models. Japanese painters, whose work can scarcely be distinguished from the work of Chinese masters, flourished at court. Literary scholarship along Chinese lines was brought to bear on the Japanese past. Chinese characters were used to write Japanese, and Chinese words were imported wholesale into the Japanese language to carry the proper Confucian distinctions. All this Chinese influence made Japan seem little more than a provincial variant of Chinese civilization.

On the other hand, there was a vigorously vulgar artistic life in the amusement sections of Tokyo and other cities, designed to appeal to the taste of merchants and other uneducated, wholly Japanese persons. Kabuki plays and the arts of geisha girls were examples of this sort of cultural tradition. In addition, artists produced cheap, multicolored prints that have since won the admiration of art critics and historians. They allow lively glimpses of the delights of city life as known in old Japan. In addition, novels and tales of adventure which were produced at this time gave literary expression to the same life-style.

Toward the end of the Tokugawa period, blurring of the distinctions between paintings done in the Chinese manner and the more popular styles faithfully mirrors the breaking down of the distinctions between merchant and warrior classes. Japan, therefore, saw the emergence of a more varied, complex, and pluralist society and culture—in a small way similar to the expanding pluralism of Western civilization—immediately before the nation plunged into new complexities by opening itself wide to imitation of and borrowings from the West in 1854.

THE WORLD'S LESS-DEVELOPED REGIONS

The largest human population that remained on the fringes of civilized life lived in sub-Saharan Africa. Actually, the peoples of that continent were much involved with the larger world, but only indirectly and without knowing much about the outside world, or themselves being known by it.

Effects of the Trade in African Slaves

Moslems from the north and east, European slave traders along the western coasts, and Dutch settlers in the region of the Cape of Good Hope, far to the south, ringed Africa completely. The effects of the slave trade were felt almost everywhere. Small communities were broken up; larger kingdoms expanded. Some African states specialized in the slave trade, raiding their neighbors to capture victims, who were then sent down to the coasts. Other kingdoms arose mainly to defend an area from such raiding. But everywhere the effect was to push African tribes and peoples toward more complicated, larger-scale political organization. Trade and state building required specialization; and specialization, as always, enhanced wealth and skills and foreshadowed the spread of civilized social complexity into even the remotest parts of Africa.

Bantu-speaking tribes continued to move southward along the grasslands of eastern Africa. Powerful new tribal federations were formed along the advancing Bantu frontier. The Zulu from 1818 and the Matabele from 1835 were the two most famous such federations. They relied mainly on their cattle for livelihood, although they raised some maize as well.

Dutch settlers (known as Boers) established a ship's victualing station at the Cape of Good Hope in 1657. The colony grew slowly and was transferred to British control in 1814. In 1835 the Boers of the Cape region began a great trek northward into the interior of South Africa, in large part to escape British control. The advancing Boers met the advancing Bantus at about the line of the Orange River, but the superior weapons that the Boers possessed gave them a clear advantage when it came to open clashes. The effect of Dutch and Bantu expansion on the Hottentots, who had previously lived in this part of Africa, was disastrous. They survived mainly as half-breeds, contributing to a population later known as "Cape Colored."

The spread of American food crops was the other great change that transformed the African scene in these centuries. Maize and sweet potatoes became the staples of west African agriculture, and maize spread throughout the continent. An expanding food supply may even have stimulated enough population growth to make up for the losses of the slave trade. Although millions were sent to the New World to labor in the plantations of Brazil, the Caribbean, and the southern colonies on the

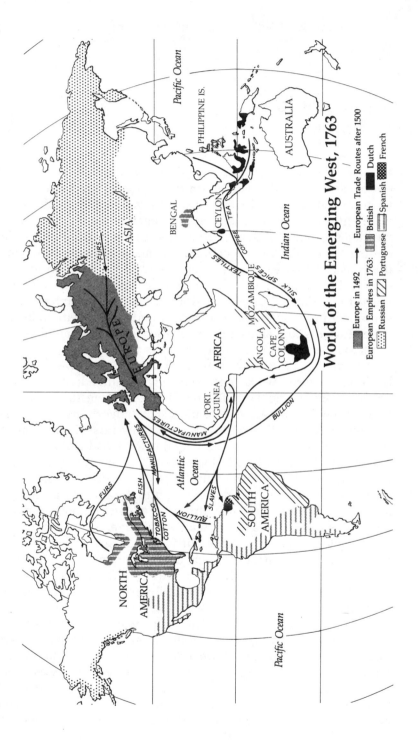

World of the Emerging West, 1763

Europe in 1492 → European Trade Routes after 1500

European Empires in 1763: British · Dutch
Russian · Portuguese · Spanish · French

North American mainland, there is no sign of general depopulation of African territories.

Growing antislavery sentiment began to check the trade soon after 1800. In 1807 the British government forbade the importation of slaves into any British possession, and the United States followed suit by prohibiting the slave trade in 1808. The British even used their navy to try to suppress the remnants of the trade that continued after this date, intercepting ships bound for Brazil, for example, and after 1822 interfering also with the Arab trade in slaves that centered in Zanzibar. The result for the Africans was, presumably, less fear in the night. But local violence and disorder of the sort that had been fostered by slave raiding continued to make life difficult in the interior of Africa.

Explorations of the Pacific

The lands of the Pacific were thinly occupied by comparison with Africa. After the first few years of oceanic discovery, European ships stopped exploring for a long time. The reason was that nothing worthwhile attracted ships to the barren coasts of such lands as Australia, where the native inhabitants were hunters and gatherers and had nothing to offer Europeans in trade. In addition, there were serious problems for European vessels that wished to sail for long distances across an ocean so vast as the Pacific. Until an accurate marine chronometer had been invented (1761), the longitude of a small island could not be measured. Hence, the chance of returning to the same speck of land in the vastnesses of the open Pacific was slight. Moreover, on long voyages the crew suffered from scurvy—a serious disease brought on by lack of vitamins. No ship's captain could therefore afford to cruise around looking for an island that ought to be somewhere in the general area where the ship was, but whose exact location no one could tell for sure.

In the eighteenth century, organized European navies took over the work of exploration, and within a short time had charted the coastlines of nearly the whole Pacific area. The first official explorer was Captain Vitus Bering of the Russian navy. He made two voyages, in 1728 and 1741, and discovered the straits that bear his name, the Aleutians, and the Alaskan mainland. Russian fur traders soon followed in Bering's wake and set up trading posts on the American side of the straits. The French sent Captain Louis Antoine de Bougainville to cruise in the Pacific, 1767–1769; the British countered with Captain James Cook, who made three voyages to the same regions between 1768 and 1779. Captain Cook carried with him the first really successful marine chronometer and was able, therefore, to plot the longitude as well as the latitude of the coasts and islands he explored. The first usefully accurate maps of the Pacific region resulted from his careful labors. He also required his sailors to eat sauerkraut in order to protect them from scurvy by providing a supply of vitamin C in their diet. Later the British navy discovered that lime juice was even more effective as a protection against scurvy, whence the nickname "Limey" for British sailors.

SETTLEMENT PATTERNS IN THE PACIFIC AREA   Whalers soon followed the explorers, with the result that Tahiti and Hawaii and other less famous islands of the Pacific had to put up with the boisterous manners of whalers and other sailors who put ashore for a bit of relief from the cramped quarters of their ships and from the smell of whale oil. Diseases brought to the Polynesians by the mariners had the usual effect of spreading devastating epidemics, from which the old island life never recovered.

Around the shores of the Pacific, too, European settlers and traders began to leave their mark before 1850. Spanish missions moved north to Nootka to counter the Russian advance into Alaska. But the imposing Spanish Empire in the Americas began to break up after 1808 as local revolts gained headway. Not long after Mexico became independent of Spain (1821), the United States attacked (1846) and took over California. Almost immediately, the discovery of gold (1848) started a rush into that remote land.

Across the Pacific, in Australia, European settlement dated from 1788, when the British government sent the first shiploads of convicts there to make a new life for themselves on the other side of the world. Beginning in 1793, free settlers began to arrive. The effects of the arrival of the newcomers upon the Australian aborigines were drastic. They were driven toward the northern parts of the continent, where deserts and heat made the land unattractive to the English. New plants and animals introduced by the Europeans upset the existing balance of nature in dramatic ways, so that, for instance, a plague of rabbits resulted from the absence of the natural predators which in other parts of the world keep the rabbit population in check.

The last important area of European settlement was New Zealand, where British colonists arrived for the first time in 1840. The Maori tribes, who lived in New Zealand, were more able to cope with the shock of contact with Western civilization than were the native Australians. As a result, after the usual losses from disease and social disorganization, the Maoris, with the help of the new food resource supplied by the potato, made an astonishing recovery. In recent years Maoris have entered freely into the public life of New Zealand and now enjoy ordinary citizen rights.

Amerindian Retreat

The fate of the Amerindians was generally similar to that of the Maoris. Some tribes were utterly destroyed, but most survived as a shattered remnant. As late as 1890, some of the Plains Indians in North America attempted armed resistance to the white settlers, but this was the last flicker of a century or more of hopelessly one-sided struggles. Repeatedly, Indians were assigned lands by treaty arrangements, only to see white settlers press into the areas supposedly reserved for the Indians. Only poor and unpromising land, which the white settlers did not want, was allowed to remain in Indian possession. In South America, too, the last flicker of warlike resistance to advancing settlement came between 1841 and 1871, when the Araucanian Indians met defeat at the hands of Chileans who proceeded to extend their frontiers to the southernmost tip of South America.

By far the largest number of Amerindians, of course, served the Spanish society of Peru, Mexico, and adjacent regions in various humble capacities. When revolution broke out among the whites of Spanish America (after 1808), it did not much affect the Indians. Indeed, until after 1850, the Indian element among the peoples in Spanish America remained passive politically. They continued to submit quietly to the demands imposed upon them by persons of Spanish descent.

Only in the remoter recesses of the Amazon jungles and in parts of the frozen Arctic did primitive life continue unaffected, or almost unaffected, by the presence in the New World of persons who shared the skills and ideas of Western civilization. Civilized ways had a remarkable reach: for example, metal hatchets, traded from hand to hand, often penetrated far beyond any face-to-face encounter between European traders and the people who ultimately put the hatchet to use. Moreover, even simple tools sometimes transformed life patterns in surprising ways. In this sense, we can be sure that by 1850 no part of the inhabited globe was immune to the impact of civilization; and the regions where isolated, simple societies still survived were shrinking faster than ever before.

CONCLUSION

By comparison to the state of the world in our own time, the globe remained a relatively spacious place in 1850. It took months for persons, goods, or news to move from one side of the earth to the other. What occurred in China had no immediate impact upon what happened in Europe, Africa, or America. A lag in reaction time and defects in communication gave local peoples room to maneuver without immediately attracting the attention and intervention of world powers. The Industrial Revolution, upon which Europe had already begun to launch itself by 1850, soon took care of this lag in communication, inaugurating a new age which we will consider in the last part of this book.

Before we do so, however, we must return to Europe and the West for a closer look at the two great movements that were to transform the world in the period after 1850: the Democratic and the Industrial revolutions.

CHAPTER 6

The Democratic and Industrial Revolutions

1776 to 1850

In 1776 the states of western Europe were threatened by the giant power of Russia. Vast resources and an enormous population had been organized by the despotic government of Catherine the Great to support an immense army, which was as well trained and equipped as any in Europe. Moreover, Russian power was on the move. Poland lost its eastern provinces to Russia in 1772; Turkey had been humbled in 1774; Catherine was laying plans to create a new, dependent Greek empire on the ruins of the Ottoman state; and only a royal coup d'état in Sweden in 1772 prevented that country from becoming a province or protectorate of the Russian Empire. Joseph II of Austria judged it better to cooperate with the Russians against the Turks than try to oppose them. The Prussians, unable to find any allies to help them stop the Russian advance, came to the same conclusion and joined with Russia and Austria three separate times—in 1772, in 1793, and in 1795—in successive partitions of Poland. When an independent Poland had thus been completely erased, the Russian frontier and the eastern boundaries of Prussia and Austria coincided, leaving no buffer zone between.

Three-quarters of a century had shown how rapidly the Russians could learn all they needed to know about Western military skills and organization. By 1775 they had come abreast of western European states in these respects, with the result that Russia's size was no longer a handicap but an immense advantage. The Germanies, divided among more

183

than 300 sovereign states under the shadowy leadership of the Holy Roman Emperor, were clearly in no position to check Russian power. Even a onetime giant such as France seemed dwarfed by Russia's size and resources—quite apart from the fact that rivalry with England and frictions among the different classes at home made it impossible for the French government to devote more than passing attention to the rise of Russia.

EMERGENCE OF EUROPE'S NEW REGIME

Three-quarters of a century later, the aspect of Europe was strikingly different. By 1850, Russia was definitely old-fashioned. The czar's empire had fallen behind western Europe once again, in military matters as well as in industrial and political organization. The restless drive to expand Russian power in every direction, which had been so much in evidence in Catherine's reign, had given way to a conservative policy aimed at keeping things as they were. Internal difficulties were beginning to trouble the Russian state, which was still built upon serfdom for the majority and privilege for the few.

The fundamental difference between the situation in 1775 and the situation in 1850 was that the peoples of western Europe had been able to raise themselves again to a new and higher level of wealth and power, and in doing so outstripped Russia and the rest of the world. Thus western Europeans postponed by a century having to face up to states as large as Russia and as well organized as they were themselves.

This remarkable reassertion of the primacy of western Europe was carried through on two fronts. No one planned it; no one foresaw the result. France took the lead in politics; Britain took the lead in economics. Between them, they revolutionized the life of Europe and moved that continent from the Old to the New Regime. The change in politics was simple in principle. Government and people came into closer partnership than before. As a result, the energies of a larger proportion of the total population could be brought to bear upon common, deliberately chosen goals. Routines of local life, particularly of village life, were broken in upon; service to the nation in war and, less spectacularly, in peace became the duty of every citizen simply because the government was now "his" government and not the king's. Where the Old Regime had settled for political passivity on the part of the lower classes, the New Regime allowed and expected activity. The power, wealth, and energy at the disposal of governments that succeeded in taking their peoples into this kind of active partnership increased far beyond the limits imaginable to Louis XIV or Catherine the Great.

This "Democratic Revolution" gained much of its success from the fact that it got under way at the same time as an Industrial Revolution. The essence of the Industrial Revolution was the discovery of new ways to use mechanical power for producing useful goods. In particular, steam engines were used to drive textile and other kinds of machinery. Increased supply of power permitted the design of larger machines and new processes. As more and cheaper goods were produced, consumption increased. Then transportation and communication were revolutionized by the use of steam and electricity. As a result industrialized nations became able to draw food and raw materials from all over the world to feed themselves and their factories. The pioneers of industrialization reaped enormous wealth. Some of the new wealth became available for state purposes, with the result that western Europeans could be both strong and rich at the same time. When total production leaped upward every decade, harsh and difficult choices between private and public, civilian and military, use of resources did not have to be made.

Europe's power and wealth under the Old Regime had also expanded rapidly. What happened from the 1770s on, therefore, was nothing new, although the pace of economic and technical change increased decade by decade. Internal balances between industry and agriculture and between the middle class and the aristocracy shifted sharply in favor of the former. This led to political transformations which gave the middle classes the leading role in public life because they, more than any other segment of society, were able to voice the public opinion to which the new governments of Europe paid attention.

Thus the New Regime that emerged by 1815 from the upheavals and wars of the French Revolution was, in a sense, a middle-class regime. Business people and professionals took over roles formerly reserved for nobles. High social status, wealth, and office were often earned by individual skill, luck, education, or personal characteristics. Such flexibility, in turn, allowed abrupt shifts of social energies into new activities—whenever they became profitable or seemed important for some other reason.

All the characteristics of the Old Regime that had distinguished Europe from other civilizations thus emerged from the crucible of the Democratic and Industrial revolutions in exaggerated form. In changing itself once again, western Europe remained true to its changeable past and became more emphatically than before the center of the entire world.

THE AMERICAN REVOLUTION

As long as the English colonies in North America had to contend with unfriendly Indians and with French rivals in Canada and Louisiana, differences of opinion with the British government—intense enough at times— were always settled short of an open break. The British navy and, in time of war, British soldiers were too necessary for the colonists' protection to make it safe to quarrel with the mother country. After 1763, however, French power no longer existed in North America. This meant that the colonists no longer had anything to fear from their neighbors. The Spaniards were weak and distant; and without the French to arm them, the Indians could not hope to put up much resistance either.

The government of George III felt that the colonists had become too independent. In particular, British ministers in London thought the colonies should help to pay for the war that had just been won by submitting to taxes imposed by Parliament. The colonists objected. They had not been consulted and were not represented in the English Parliament. As the colonists saw matters, Englishmen had fought the Civil War of 1642–1649 to win the right of paying only those taxes agreed to by their elected representatives. They concluded that the sacred rights of English-

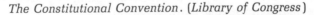

The Constitutional Convention. (*Library of Congress*)

men were endangered by the tyranny of King George, who was, in any case, trying to manipulate elections to Parliament in order to make it a rubber stamp for his own royal will.

Many people in England agreed with the colonists' arguments. Even when the dispute led to public violence and then to war, a party in Parliament criticized the king and sympathized openly with the rebellious colonists' cause. On the other hand, some people in the colonies believed that nothing justified open resistance to the king. Argument was fierce; and when fighting broke out, the patriot cause tended to become more radical. Not merely the "rights of Englishmen" but the "Rights of Man" were called upon to justify resistance to the British government. The theory that government derived its just powers only from the consent of the governed was formally proclaimed by the colonists in the Declaration of Independence (1776). Liberty and equality became the watchwords of the patriot group, although few of them took liberty and equality to mean the abolition of slavery or equalization of property. The words had, instead, a limited political meaning: the right of ordinary men of sound mind and modest wealth to take part in choosing representatives to shape governmental policy.

France Supports the Revolution

The French were fascinated by the American uprising. The theoretical debate about political rights thrilled the ears of some, for their own position as subjects of an absolute monarch displeased many Frenchmen. In addition, by helping the colonists the French government could hope to undo the disasters of the Seven Years' War. Even if their own colonial possessions could not be recovered, at least the British position overseas would be weakened if the rebels could win their independence.

After helping the rebels in unofficial ways, the French finally went to war in 1778. French soldiers joined the ragged forces under General George Washington's command with such effect that, when the British surrendered at Yorktown (1781), more French than Americans were on hand to witness the victory. Moreover, the French fleet made things extremely uncomfortable for the British at sea, and French diplomacy also brought the Spaniards and the Dutch into the war against King George. When the Russians, too, began to organize a diplomatic offensive against the British among all the Baltic powers, Great Britain was almost completely isolated. In 1783, therefore, King George made peace, recognizing the independence of the rebellious colonies and ceding Florida to Spain.

American Constitutional Government

Victory in war presented the colonists with the problem of governing themselves effectively. During the war, the Articles of Confederation (1777) had been agreed to by each of the colonies. This document committed them to a permanent union to be called The United States of America. But the separate colonies or states kept control of taxation with the result that the central authorities suffered from a crippling lack of income. The experience of the immediate postwar years did not solve the problem, although the decision made in 1785 to transfer control over the western lands to the federal government meant an important increase in its powers. In 1787, on the initiative of the state of Virginia and with the endorsement of the Congress of the United States, a new constitutional convention assembled. After four months of discussion, the delegates agreed upon a constitution that gave greater powers to the federal government. Having been ratified by two-thirds of the separate states, the new system of government began operation in May, 1789.

Such a rational way of setting up a new government, after discussion and deliberation on the part of representatives of the people at large, seemed an extraordinary demonstration of political wisdom to many Europeans of the day. The rude and simple Americans had proved able to make a government according to reasonable principles and along lines to suit themselves. To be sure, there were skeptics who waited confidently for the arrangements embodied in the Constitution to fall apart. Aristocrats found it hard to believe that the passions of common people would not upset orderly government. After all, the political experience of centuries seemed to show that republican government could only succeed in small city-states, and that monarchy was required to keep a large, sprawling country together.

THE IMPACT OF THE AMERICAN REVOLUTION   But whether they looked hopefully and with sympathy upon the American experiment in rational self-government or waited, instead, for its failure to prove the folly of trying to subordinate the operation of government to popular approval, no European interested in political questions could remain indifferent. Theories of the rights of man and of the citizen had been talked about for decades in French drawing rooms and all over Europe. Now the Americans had been bold enough to act on them. The more successful the Americans seemed, the more restless Europeans felt in finding themselves subject to the authority of rulers they had no part in choosing, and over whose actions they had no legal control. The United States of

America, in other words, became a shining beacon, proving to those who wished to believe it that reasonable citizens could govern themselves without any need for kings, nobles, or priests.

The idea that government is, in fact, a human creation and can be changed by human wills is accepted everywhere today. It is therefore hard for us to realize how exciting such an idea seemed in 1789. Nearly all of Europe was then ruled by kings and emperors who claimed to have been entrusted with their power by God. They ruled with the help of nobles and officials. These were privileged classes in the sense that many laws applied differently to them than they did to commoners. Differences of clothes and of manners also distinguished the privileged classes from the rest of society. They expected to be treated as superior beings by the common people.

The old idea that society was a great organism, requiring some at the head, to do the thinking, while others were the hands and had to do the work, no longer convinced people of the middle class that they should remain in the walk of life to which they had been born. Too many of their superiors were clearly incompetent. Too many individuals had, in fact, changed status. Legal theory and practical fact were too far apart. To such persons the simple truths, acted on by the Americans, alone seemed worthy of free and rational minds. Government that failed to win the consent of the governed had no rightful claim to exist and should be changed. Or so it seemed to a vocal and energetic minority, especially in France, where the failures and rigidities of the government by no means ended with victory against the British in 1783.

THE FRENCH REVOLUTION

The widespread dissatisfaction with the way France was run became critical when Louis XVI (reigned 1774–1792) found himself in serious financial difficulties. The war with Britain (1778–1783) had cost a lot of money; and the French tax system could not produce the extra amounts needed to keep the government from bankruptcy. In theory, of course, Louis XVI was an absolute monarch and needed only to decree a new tax to make it legal. In practice, however, the bureaucracy that was supposed to serve the king had developed a will of its own. Many official posts were sold at auction. Those who purchased an office naturally felt that they owned what they had paid for and refused to change the way things were done unless the change was somehow clearly to their own advantage. In particular, high courts had the right to "register" the king's decrees. Originally, these courts were merely supposed to make sure that if any new decree

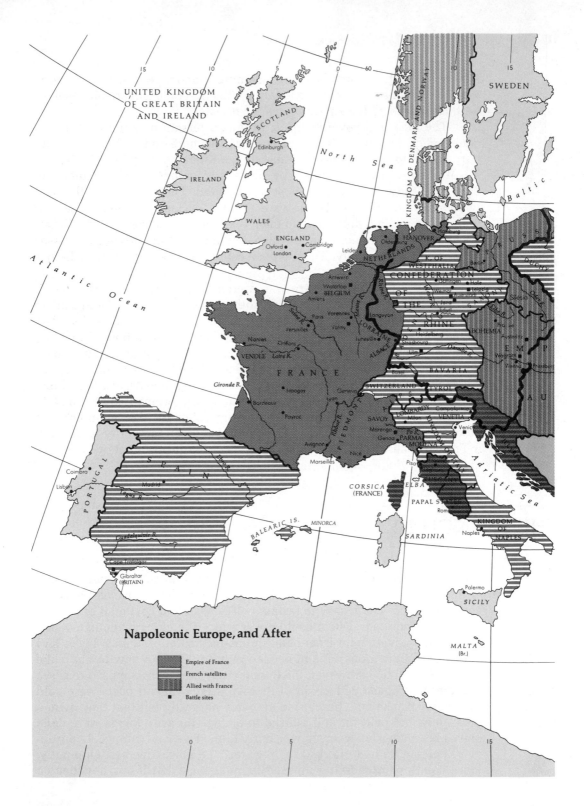

Napoleonic Europe, and After

Empire of France
French satellites
Allied with France
■ Battle sites

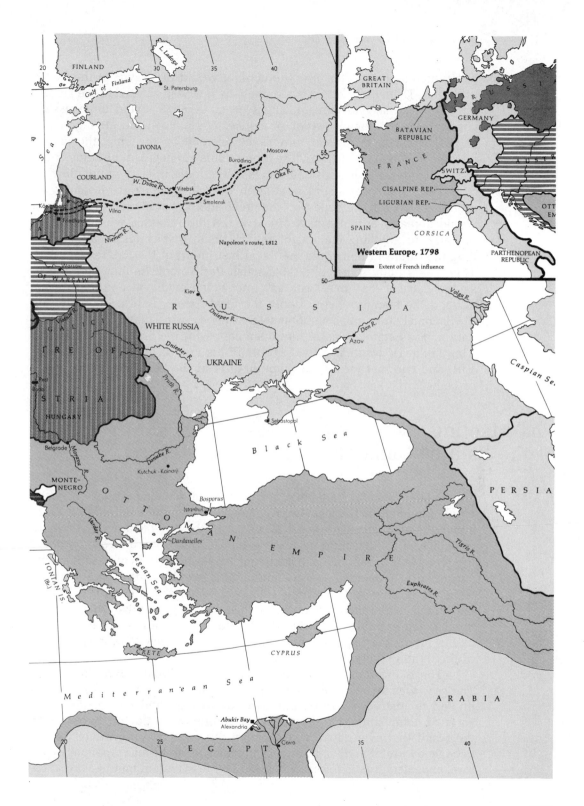

FINLAND

L. Ladoga

Gulf of Finland

St. Petersburg

LIVONIA

Moscow

Burodino

Vitebsk

Smolensk

W. Dvina R.

Oka R.

COURLAND

Köningsberg

Friedland

Vilna

Niemen R.

Napoleon's route, 1812

OF WARSAW

Warsaw

GALICIA

RE OF

STRIA

HUNGARY

WHITE RUSSIA

R U S S I A

Dnieper R.

UKRAINE

Dniester R.

Pruth R.

Kiev

Don R.

Azov

Volga R.

Caspian Se

Belgrade

Morava R.

MONTE-NEGRO

Danube R.

Kutchuk - Kainarji

Sebastopol

B l a c k   S e a

P E R S I A

O T T O M A N   E M P I R E

Vardar R.

Bosporus

Istanbul

Dardanelles

Tigris R.

Euphrates R.

IONIAN IS. (Br.)

A e g e a n   S e a

CRETE

CYPRUS

M e d i t e r r a n e a n   S e a

A R A B I A

Abukir Bay

Alexandria

E G Y P T

Cairo

Western Europe, 1798

GREAT BRITAIN

RUSSIA

GERMANY

BATAVIAN REPUBLIC

F R A N C E

SWITZ.

CISALPINE REP.

LIGURIAN REP.

AUSTRIA

SPAIN

CORSICA

OTT. EM

PARTHENOPEAN REPUBLIC

▬▬▬ Extent of French influence

contradicted some other law, the conflict would be drawn to the king's attention. Then, if the king wished, the new law was entered in the statute books, or, on second thought, might be modified to avoid unnecessary confusion in the administration of justice. When, however, the high court of Paris refused to register new taxes decreed by the king, the judges became great popular heroes. The king's ministers decided that they could not afford to push through new taxes in the teeth of such opposition.

The royal government next tried calling together an assembly of notables (1787) in the hope that the great and powerful men of the realm would agree to accept a new tax law. But the notables were unwilling to agree to anything that might require them to pay larger taxes. The king next tried to revive the medieval institution of the Estates-General. This was a body rather like the English Parliament. Its members represented each of the three "estates" into which medieval political theory divided the country: clergy being the First Estate, nobility constituting the Second Estate, and commoners—everybody else—making up the Third Estate. The Estates-General had been called for the first time 1302 when King Philip IV wanted to get support in his quarrel with Pope Boniface VIII, and had met for the last time in 1614 at the beginning of the reign of Louis XIII.

The Meeting of the Estates-General

The Estates-General had been a gathering of representatives from the whole kingdom of France. But in 1789 great uncertainties existed as to how to choose representatives from each of the three estates. Even more critical was the question as to how the Estates-General would vote. If the representatives from each estate met separately and voted separately, conservatively minded clergy and nobles would control the Estates-General. If, however, all three estates met together, individual nobles and many of the clergy could be expected to sympathize with reform-minded representatives of the Third Estate who wanted to assure that in the future the king and his ministers would consult representatives of the nation regularly.

These uncertainties provoked a burst of political debate in France. The case was argued in numerous pamphlets. Each electoral district was invited to instruct its representatives in writing, and consequently all sorts of complaints and programs for reform were put on paper, with the result that even those who had not felt especially aggrieved before became aware of serious political injustices. A great many people therefore, expected drastic reform when the Estates-General met in May, 1789.

REVOLT OF THE THIRD ESTATE   King Louis and his ministers agreed that, up to a point, reform was needed. New taxes certainly were necessary; but Louis XVI never decided what else ought to be done. The king was a good mechanic, who liked to tinker in his workshop. He was a well-meaning man, but weak-willed. In the spring of 1789, he failed to decide how the Estates-General should sit and vote; and even after the first ceremonial meetings had taken place, he hesitated. Then, in June, he decided to order each estate to meet and vote separately; but before he got round to announcing his decision, someone locked the doors of the room where the Third Estate had been accustomed to assemble. The representatives reacted by jumping to the conclusion that a plot was afoot to dismiss them entirely. On June 20, 1789, they moved to a tennis court nearby and amid great excitement solemnly swore an oath that they would never disband until they had made a constitution for France.

Such an act was revolutionary. The representatives of the Third Estate, in effect, had announced their intention of curbing royal absolutism. Yet King Louis reacted mildly. He first went ahead and announced his decision that the representatives should sit and vote separately by estates. The Third Estate refused to accept his ruling. In the next few days, a growing number of clergy and nobles began to attend the meetings of the Third Estate. A week later the king yielded and ordered the representatives of all three estates to meet together and to vote individually. The Estates-General thus became the National Assembly, committed to making a written constitution for France just as the Americans had recently done for the United States.

The National Assembly

Excitement ran high all over France. Louis XVI was by no means sure that the National Assembly could be trusted, and some of his advisers wanted him to call up soldiers and dismiss the troublesome representatives by a show of force. Troop movements stirred the people of Paris to action. They set up their own revolutionary authority, the Commune, to control the city; and on July 14, 1789, a great crowd attacked the Bastille—a royal fortress in the heart of Paris—and captured it. In later times this event was celebrated as the birthday of the Revolution. It brought a new element into action—the people of Paris, who in the years that followed often demonstrated in favor of radical measures and on several critical occasions were able to silence the opposition.

The example of Paris proved infectious. Radical-minded reformers took control of other cities. Peasants, too, took the law into their own hands and began to attack their lords' houses. Often they set out to burn the charters that listed the obligations they owed their lords, in the belief that if the documents were destroyed the lords would never again be able to collect the rents and services listed in them.

The National Assembly responded by "abolishing feudalism" in the course of a hectic night, August 4–5, 1789, when, one after another, excited representatives renounced special rights and privileges. From that time onward, all Frenchmen were, at least in theory, equal before the law. All were citizens, owing the same duties and obligations to the state and enjoying the same rights and protection from it. Legally separate classes or estates and privileged corporations had been abolished. Liberty and equality had dawned. Before long, a third slogan was added to the revolutionary program: fraternity, meaning the brotherhood that ought to exist among free and equal citizens. These three ideals stirred enthusiasm not only in France but in other parts of Europe. The English poet, William Wordsworth wrote:

"Bliss was it in that dawn to be alive"

—and many young men in Germany and Italy, as well as in England, felt the same.

FINANCIAL PROBLEMS   Events, however, refused to stand still in order to allow the National Assembly to draw up a constitution for France. In particular, the government's financial problem would not wait. As a stopgap, the Assembly decided to issue paper currency that would be redeemed by the sale of church lands. But issuing paper currency proved such an attractive solution to the financial problem that more and more "assignats," as the bills were called, were printed to meet pressing government obligations. Even when in addition to the church lands, the property of runaway nobles and the royal domains were put up for sale, the face value of assignats far exceeded the value of the lands that were sold. As a result, the paper currency could not be retired as intended. Inflation and rapid rise in prices resulted; wage earners suffered, but some businessmen and borrowers benefited.

The National Assembly's decision to sell church lands and reorganize the church as a branch of the state, by paying salaries to priests and bishops, was flatly condemned by the pope. This made the first great split in the revolutionary ranks: for the many Frenchmen and women who remained good Catholics could not support the Assembly in opposition to the pope. Louis XVI was among those who refused to accept the drastic reorganization of the church. But for the time being, he was helpless. His secret appeals for assistance sent to the other monarchs of Europe produced no result, although when discovered later, they proved that the king had become a traitor to the Revolution.

The Constitution of 1791

By the summer of 1791 the new constitution was finally ready. It made France a limited monarchy. Supreme authority was conferred upon an elected legislative assembly. It controlled taxation, exercised supreme judicial authority, and had the power to call royal ministers to account. Essential sovereign rights, in other words, were transferred from the king to the elected representatives of the French people. The king, nevertheless, kept important powers, such as the right to choose his ministers and to appoint army officers and diplomats, as well as a veto on legislation, which could, however, be overridden by the Legislative Assembly.

These provisions did not last, but the reorganization of local government written into the Constitution of 1791 proved durable. All France was divided into departments of about the same size. Church dioceses, judicial districts, and department boundaries were all made to coincide. All sorts of monopolies and special privileges were swept away. Simple, uniform administration, linking the individual private citizen with the government directly, was made to prevail all over France.

The effect of these changes was that in time of crisis the central government could demand more from each citizen than the government of the Old Regime had ever dreamed of doing. The thick tissue of privileged bodies that had grown up during the Old Regime meant that the king's ministers had seldom been able to touch citizens individually, but had always to deal with guilds, town governments, high courts, provincial assemblies, and the like. Thus, the overthrow of privilege and the dawn of liberty, of which the revolutionaries were so proud, turned out to have a meaning they did not expect. Liberty, equality, and fraternity could mean intense, equal, and unlimited service to the state—whether as a conscripted soldier or as a taxpayer.

The fatal flaw in the Constitution of 1791 was that Louis XVI, who no longer had the slightest sympathy for the Revolution, could not be trusted with the powers assigned to him. In June, 1791, the king tried to flee abroad in disguise. But the royal party was recognized and compelled to return. The National Assembly was not prepared to do without a king. Outright republicanism was almost unthinkable still. All the same, when the new Legislative Assembly met in October, 1791, suspicion of the king's good faith in accepting the Constitution ran deep.

Matters came to a crisis as a result of the outbreak of war against Prussia and Austria. King Louis and a circle of conservative "aristocrats" had tried to get these rulers to intervene against the Revolution for months, and so welcomed war when it came in April, 1792. Oddly enough, the most extreme radical faction represented in the Legislative Assembly also welcomed the war. An organized party of enthusiasts for the Revolution—called Girondins because some of their most conspicuous spokesmen came from one of the new departments in southern France, known as Gironde—were eager to bring liberty, equality, and fraternity to the other peoples of Europe. They also believed that foreign war would compel French citizens to rally to the cause of the Revolution, and would help to silence internal frictions that were threatening civil war.

The expectations of the Girondins turned out to be as false as those of the king. Revolutionary enthusiasm was not enough to win battles, and when the Austrians and Prussians began to advance into France, rumors that King Louis was in treasonable correspondence with the enemy roused the Paris crowds to fresh action. Under the leadership of Georges Jacques Danton, they surrounded the legislators and demanded that they suspend the king. Reluctantly the Legislative Assembly obeyed and organized new elections for a convention to revise the Constitution once again.

The Radical Phase:
The Convention

Opinion shifted rapidly in the days of crisis that followed. To be sure, in September, 1792, French armies turned the tide, and a few weeks later started to march into the Austrian Netherlands (Belgium), where they were received as liberators. The Prussians also retreated, so that soon after the National Convention met in September, 1792, French armies stood victoriously on the banks of the Rhine. But Louis' treasonable correspondence with the Austrians and the Prussians had been discovered. Accordingly, when the National Convention met, its first act was to abolish royalty and declare France a republic. In the following months, "Citizen Louis Capet" (Louis XVI) was brought to trial before the Convention, condemned for treason, and beheaded (January, 1793).

This event shocked all of Europe. Kings and nobles everywhere felt threatened, and even those who had sympathized with the first stages of the French Revolution found it hard to justify the acts of the Convention. Britain, Holland, Sardinia, and Spain promptly joined Austria and Prussia in war against France. Discontent inside France became widespread, and the threat of revolt and civil war hung over the deliberations of the Convention.

The Convention was also hampered by bitter factional fights within its own ranks. The Girondins, who had been the radicals of the year before, were challenged by a new faction, known as Jacobins, whose principal spokesman was Maximilien Robespierre. The Jacobins were or became leaders for the Paris crowds, and part of their power depended on being able to summon a mass demonstration from Paris to back up their policies. The Girondins, in reaction, tended to become identified with the provinces, where, on the whole, less radical views prevailed. Danton tried to stand above party and, as a result, alienated both sides. Many delegates to the Convention belonged to neither faction, but swung back and forth as the emergency of the moment seemed to require.

In the summer of 1793 it looked as though the Revolution would go down in defeat. The most successful French general, Charles François Dumouriez, with part of his army, went over to the enemy. In the south the British besieged Toulon, and the Prussians advanced across the Rhine toward French soil. A rash of revolts spread through France, particularly after the Girondins had been excluded from the Convention in June, leaving the Jacobin party in full control.

The Reign of Terror

The crisis roused the Jacobins, supported by the people of Paris, to heroic effort. Executive power was concentrated in the hands of a Committee of Public Safety, of which Maximilien Robespierre became the leading spirit. A Reign of Terror began. Hasty trials of anyone suspected of disloyalty to the Revolution led to mass executions. Universal military service for all male citizens was decreed. Frantic efforts to assemble and equip vast new armies quickly bore fruit. By the fall of 1793 the revolutionary forces were once more on the offensive, and the most dangerous internal uprisings had been suppressed.

The effort to turn back the danger required strong, centralized control. Special "representatives on mission" carried the authority of the Convention to the provinces. Local dignitaries and officials were summarily executed if they seemed disloyal or merely inefficient. Jacobin societies sprang up in all important towns. These societies carried on a vigorous correspondence with the Jacobin club in Paris and, in effect, served as local propaganda agencies to spread enthusiasm for the latest policy decreed from Paris. The Jacobin societies also made it their business to oversee the activities of local officials. If they detected any lack of zeal, a letter to the Jacobin club in Paris would lead to prompt dismissal or even to the execution of the accused. The same system worked inside the army to keep check on the officers.

In this fashion, something close to total mobilization of the French nation was achieved. Close mutual support between "the people," organized into the Jacobin societies, and their government achieved amazing results. The massed forces of the European Old Regime could not stand against the revolutionary armies. Everywhere the French took the offensive. The Revolution was once more secure.

Success in battle did not, however, solve the question of how France should be governed. Robespierre talked of a "Republic of Virtue." This frightened many delegates to the Convention, who were not sure they were virtuous enough to satisfy Robespierre. The Paris populace, on the other hand, wanted to extend equality to economics. In particular, the Parisians were angry at the rise of food prices, believing that greedy bakers, or grain dealers perhaps, were responsible. Robespierre hesitated, and eventually refused to go along with the Paris crowd. He tried to eliminate awkward criticism by executing the leaders of the Paris Commune in March, 1794, and Danton in April, 1794. His own turn was not long delayed. In July of the same year, some of his colleagues on the Committee of Public Safety arrested him. When news spread through Paris, a group of Robespierre's admirers tried to free him, but Paris, as a whole, did not rise. In the confusion which his supporters created, the man who had become identified with revolutionary extremism was shot, dying a few hours later (1794).

Reaction and Consolidation

The politicians who conspired against Robespierre did not intend to end the Reign of Terror or to change policy in any important way. But Robespierre's overthrow sparked a sharp reaction all over France. Summary revolutionary justice was halted. Soon the Jacobin hold on the Convention was broken; their meeting place was closed in November and the surviving Girondin deputies were recalled. When a new constitution was drafted and approved in October, 1795, the Convention ended its sessions.

GOVERNMENT BY THE DIRECTORY   The new government, the Directory, was headed by five directors whose authority was checked by two representative bodies, the Assembly of Elders and the Council of Five Hundred. Stability at home and energetic pursuit of victory abroad was the policy the Directors followed. With the help of brilliant young generals such as Napoleon Bonaparte, who led a ragged army into Italy and utterly defeated the Austrian forces there (1796–1797), the Directory at first met with general success. Prussia and then Austria made peace. According to the resulting treaties, revolutionary France, in a few short years, had achieved Louis XIV's ambition of extending French territory to the Rhine. Moreover, a client state in Holland, the Batavian Republic, and another in northern Italy, the Cisalpine Republic, extended French influence and revolutionary principles even further into Europe. Plans for fundamental

NAPOLEON'S CORONATION

Napoleon Bonaparte was born in Corsica. As a boy he was both very poor and very proud, for his family claimed noble rank but had little money. When he went to France he felt like an outsider, for the Corsicans spoke a language more like Italian than French. Napoleon never lost the feeling of being an outsider, even when he rose to undisputed power over all of France and a large part of Europe.

In 1804 Napoleon was approaching the peak of his career. Only Britain opposed him in war. At home, most Frenchmen admired his victories. Napoleon decided that he should make his power hereditary. But Napoleon was also a son of the French Revolution, and the French revolutionaries had set out to overthrow the hereditary privileges of kings and nobles. How could the Corsican upstart become a monarch without betraying his principles—and those of his most devoted followers?

Napoleon's answer was to put the question to a vote. If the people of France wanted him to hold hereditary power, then his rule would be based not on empty tradition or ancient privilege but on the will of the people. The vote was taken, and the people overwhelmingly approved the proposal that Napoleon should become emperor of the French.

From the time of Charlemagne, emperors had been crowned by the pope. Napoleon decided that his new title required a coronation, and he demanded that the pope come to Paris for the ceremony. After some hesitation, the pope agreed; and on December 2, 1804, the solemn ceremony took place in Notre Dame Cathedral at Paris.

But there was another difficulty for Napoleon. In the traditional ceremony, the pope put the imperial crown on the emperor's head. This seemed to say that the imperial crown was the pope's gift; and, again, Napoleon's revolutionary principles made any such idea unacceptable. For the French revolutionaries had also attacked the Church and denied that political rule came from the hand of God, or from any bishop, priest, or pope.

Napoleon solved this problem, too. As the ceremony of the coronation approached its climax, the imperial crown was carried forward. Just as the pope was about to pick it up and place it on Napoleon's head, the emperor himself leaned forward, seized the crown, and placed it on his own head. No one but Napoleon himself was going to crown the new emperor of the French!

reorganization of the Germanies were left undefined; but France, Prussia, and Austria all were eager to get rid of the hundreds of separate sovereign states into which that land had been divided ever since 1648.

Great Britain remained a problem. The British navy guarded England's shores, and no French superiority on land could force the British government to make peace or recognize the territorial gains won by revolutionary arms. In 1798 Napoleon proposed to invade Egypt, as a way of threatening India and bringing pressure on the English to make peace. The Directors feared Napoleon's popularity and were glad to see him leave the country. They therefore promptly agreed with Napoleon's plan.

Soon afterward British diplomacy and subsidies raised a new coalition against the French. The Russians joined in, for the first time, with the Austrians and Prussians, and sent armies to fight in Italy and Holland. The French were driven out of Italy, and Russian armies even crossed the Alps but failed to invade France when supplies gave out. Napoleon's first victories in Egypt had been well publicized at home; later failures were overshadowed by the news of French defeats in Italy. Accordingly, when Napoleon suddenly appeared in France in November, 1799, he seemed to be a savior and had little trouble arranging a coup d'état that made him First Consul and the effective ruler of France.

NAPOLEONIC RULE   Napoleon soon restored French power in Italy. The Russians had already gone home, due to quarrels with the Austrians. After defeating the Austrians, consequently, Napoleon found himself in a position to make peace with all the enemies of France. He even negotiated an agreement with the papacy in 1801, by which the pope recognized the loss of the church lands in France and made it possible for a Catholic once more to support the French government in good conscience. This was followed in 1802 by the Peace of Amiens whereby the British government gave up the struggle to undo the achievements of the French Revolution in Europe. Napoleon was universally acclaimed at home, became consul for life in 1802 and, two years later assumed the title "Emperor of the French."

Thus monarchy had been restored to France; but Napoleon was at pains to refer every change in his regime to the vote of the people, and always claimed to rule only by virtue of the popular will. In large degree, the claim was justified. The French were proud of the greatness Napoleon thrust upon them, and appreciated the peace and order he maintained at home.

The fundamental changes the Revolution had made were consolidated and written into law—the famous *Code Napoléon*—that gave exact definition to property and personal rights as they emerged from the revolutionary upheaval. Napoleon maintained a strictly centralized administration, appointing prefects over each department and mayors over all important towns. A special police kept track of suspects by means of a vast card file. Public opinion was managed by carefully controlled news releases. Discontent could not find open expression and, in fact, few French citizens felt anything but pride in what their nation, under Napoleon's leadership, was able to do.

Abroad, matters were different. The Peace of Amiens soon broke down, and Napoleon started a new war against Great Britain in 1803. Austria, Russia, and Sweden joined Britain against Napoleon in 1805; but the Austrians met crushing defeat at the Battle of Austerlitz. The next year Napoleon defeated the Prussians and, in 1807, arranged a peace at Tilsit with the young czar of Russia, Alexander I. When Austria resorted to arms again in 1809, Napoleon was once more victorious. By marrying the Austrian emperor's daughter, Marie Louise, in 1810, he entered the most select and exclusive ranks of European royalty.

In 1810 Napoleon's power reached its peak. He controlled Italy and Germany, having made both Austria and Prussia into second-rate powers and his allies. He had created the Grand Duchy of Warsaw on the ruins of the former Polish kingdom. His relatives were established on thrones in Spain, Italy, and Holland; and the Russian czar agreed to cut his country off from British trade as part of Napoleon's grand plan for bringing Great Britain, the "nation of shopkeepers," to its knees by economic boycott.

NATIONALIST RESISTANCE TO FRENCH RULE   Nevertheless, there were serious weaknesses in Napoleon's position. The British navy was undefeated, and British subsidies were always available to foment any resistance against the French anywhere on the continent. Overseas ambitions that Napoleon had briefly nourished after the Peace of Amiens had to be abandoned. Accordingly, he gladly sold Louisiana, recently acquired from Spain, to the United States in 1803. In Europe itself, the French provoked popular resistance in Spain. Soon a British expeditionary force added weight to the guerrilla warfare waged by the Spaniards. In Germany and Italy, many people asked themselves why France should be so powerful and their own nations so weak. National feeling, in other words, began to turn against the French and made the rising against Napoleon, when it came, strong and irreversible.

The breaking point occurred in 1812 when Czar Alexander quarreled with Napoleon and went over to the British side. Napoleon organized a great army to invade Russia and marched to Moscow. But winter closed in and Russian resistance did not end. The proud French army had to withdraw, suffering enormous losses from cold and hunger en route. News of this defeat set all Germany ablaze. The Prussians entered the war against Napoleon; soon the Austrians did the same. A great battle at Leipzig, in 1813, ended in allied victory. Napoleon faced defeat.

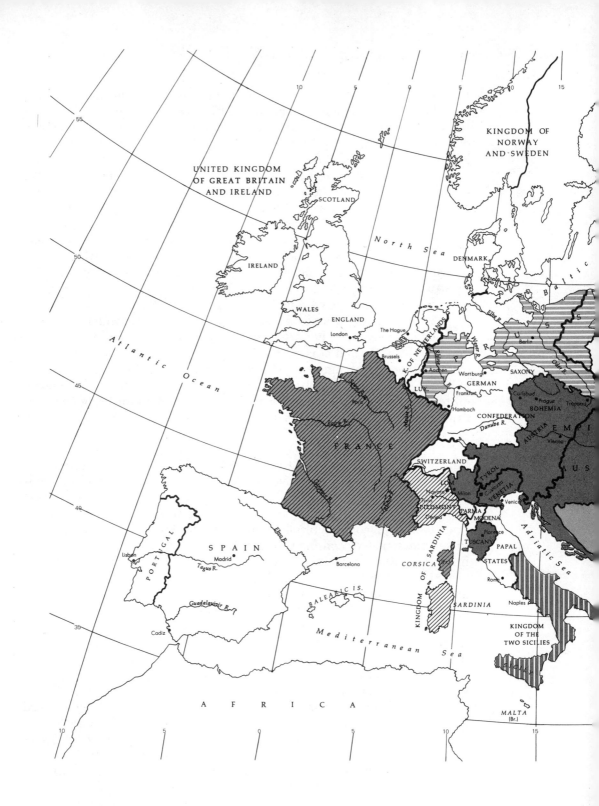

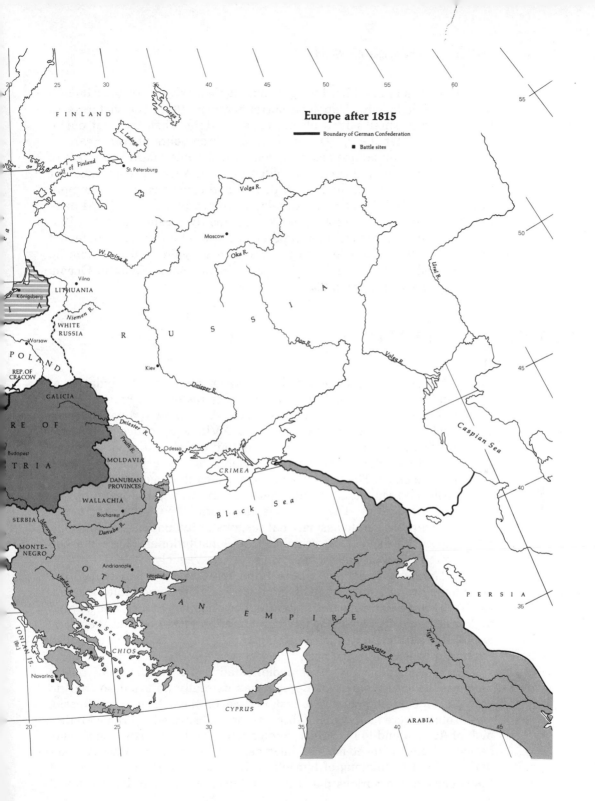

Europe after 1815

■■■■■ Boundary of German Confederation
■ Battle sites

FINLAND

L. Ladoga

L. Onega

Gulf of Finland

St. Petersburg

Volga R.

Moscow

Oka R.

Ural R.

W. Dvina R.

Vilna

LITHUANIA

Königsberg

Niemen R.

WHITE RUSSIA

R U S S I A

Warsaw

P O L A N D

REP. OF CRACOW

GALICIA

Don R.

Volga R.

Kiev

Dnieper R.

Dniester R.

Prut R.

Odessa

Caspian Sea

RE OF TRIA

Budapest

MOLDAVIA

DANUBIAN PROVINCES

CRIMEA

WALLACHIA

Bucharest

SERBIA

Danube R.

Morava R.

Black Sea

MONTE-NEGRO

O T T O M A N

Vardar R.

Andrianople

Istanbul

E M P I R E

P E R S I A

Aegean Sea

IONIAN IS. (Br.)

CHIOS

Euphrates R.

Tigris R.

Navarino

CRETE

CYPRUS

ARABIA

The allies found it hard to agree among themselves, but nevertheless the alliance held until Napoleon surrendered in 1814. The victors sent him to Elba, a small island off the coast of Italy. Then they set out to make peace, after the upheavals of twenty-three years of war. Scarcely had the peace conference met at Vienna when fierce quarrels broke out. Napoleon took advantage of the situation and secretly embarked for France. On his arrival, the French people and armies rallied once more to his banner, but the news of Napoleon's return brought the allies back together again. British and Prussian troops swiftly organized; and at Waterloo, in Belgium, not far from the French border, they met and defeated the French (1815). Napoleon surrendered once again, and this time he was shipped off to St. Helena, far away in the South Atlantic Ocean. He died there of cancer in 1821.

The Congress of Vienna

The Congress of Vienna resumed its task of restoring the balance of power in Europe. The Bourbon monarchy was restored in France, in the person of Louis XVIII, brother to Louis XVI. (According to royalist principles, Louis XVI's son counted as Louis XVII, even though he never reigned.) The restored king issued a constitutional decree, giving legislative power to elected assemblies. In general, he made little attempt to turn back the clock. The basic revolutionary idea that people and government could and should cooperate remained in force. To be sure, not all the people were allowed to vote in elections; only the wealthy and better educated were invited to assume that responsibility. But despite this limitation upon the democratic principle, the constitutional decree marked the restored Bourbon government of France as vaguely "liberal."

In Germany and Italy, where Napoleonic reforms had erased old boundaries, return to the Old Regime was equally impossible. Instead, Austria took over the task of guarding Italy against France and passed to Prussia the task of watching the Rhine frontier. The Prussians, therefore, annexed broad territories in the Rhineland in return for giving up Polish territories to Russia in the east.

By these and many other complicated deals a balance of power between the major states of Europe was carefully adjusted so that no one of them could dominate the rest. France, on the one side, and Russia, on the other, were the two chief threats—or so it seemed to Prince Metternich of Austria and to the British foreign minister, Lord Castlereagh, who, between them, arranged most of the important compromises. Czar Alexander was fond of thinking of himself as Europe's savior, and at different times entertained various plans for establishing a new order. He toyed with the idea of uniting Germany and Italy in accordance with the will of their people. With himself as king, he restored Poland. A great crusade against the Turks attracted him, too. But most of all, he pinned his hopes on a Holy Alliance of Christian monarchs who would work in harmony and consult with each other regularly in order to end the warfare that for too long had brought such havoc to Europe. (See map, p. 202–203.)

Revolution *versus* Reaction in Europe

Alexander's vision boiled down to no more than an agreement among the powers to meet at intervals in the future in order to agree upon joint action when any crisis required it. Congresses did meet until 1822, but after that date Great Britain withdrew and the system fell to the ground. In the meanwhile, Metternich had been able to persuade Alexander that a wicked conspiracy to spread "the revolution" existed in Europe. Instead of toying with liberal ideas, therefore, the czar became wholeheartedly reactionary. As a result, the three eastern monarchies of Austria, Prussia, and Russia became stalwart defenders of the status quo. France and Britain, on the contrary, were more sympathetic with revolutionary outbreaks, and refused to agree to international intervention aimed at suppressing liberal revolutionary movements. This lineup became clear when Britain refused to go along with proposals to put down the Latin American revolutions that had broken out in the Spanish empire of the New World. Britain, indeed, looked kindly upon President James Monroe's declaration (1823) that European intervention in the New World would be considered an unfriendly act by the United States. The Greek revolt against the Turks, which broke out in 1821, also commanded widespread sympathy in France and England. Russia, too, after Alexander's death (1825) could not refrain from supporting the rebels. The result in 1830 was an international guarantee of Greek independence.

In July of the same year, an almost bloodless revolution in France brought a new "citizen king," Louis Philippe, to the throne. Two years later, the Reform Bill of 1832 passed the British Parliament.

This bill reapportioned representation in Parliament so that it more nearly corresponded to the distribution of population and gave the vote to middle-class taxpayers. The result was to confirm the liberal character of these two states and make middle-class political leadership secure. Germany and Italy remained a dubious battleground where liberal and conservative principles clashed. Farther east, Austria and Russia alone remained opposed to the liberal idea that government should be responsible to the people.

In 1848, a fresh round of revolution, beginning in France, spread over most of Germany and Italy and into Austria as well. Metternich was overthrown, but the revolution failed to establish representative government in Germany or Italy because agreement on national unification could not be reached. By about 1850 among Germans and Italians most of the aspirations inherited from the great days of the French Revolution itself had been exhausted through repeated failures. Revolutionary enthusiasm was soon to find a new socialist form. As far as Europe was concerned, the era of the French Revolution had come to an end.

The change from 1789, however, was great. In all the western parts of Europe, a closer partnership between government and people had brought the urban middle classes actively into politics. Public opinion mattered as never before. Governments rose and fell on the strength of it; and when supported by the enthusiasm of their people, governments had proved able to reach deeper into society and bring greater energies to bear, both in war and in peace, than any governments of the Old Regime had been able to do. Problems were identified, discussed, and then acted upon in the light of public opinion that found its voice mainly through newspapers. This procedure allowed an extraordinary outpouring of energy. Cityfolk, instead of being merely subjects, had become citizens, responsible for the conduct of public affairs in their own right and through their representatives. The farmers and peasants of the countryside remained quiet, generally, and did not take much part in political and public affairs. But then, the problems of the day, aside from war and diplomacy, all centered around the transformation of urban life that came with the Industrial Revolution.

THE INDUSTRIAL REVOLUTION

The term "Industrial Revolution" was popularized about 1880 by an English historian, Arnold Toynbee, and he applied it to the reign of George III (1760–1820). At the time, however, what contemporaries noticed were the wars and political upheavals of the age. The fact that cotton manufacturers in Manchester were making money by building new machines in dark and unpleasant factories hardly attracted the attention of anyone who was not in the cotton business.

Yet from the vantage point of our own age, it seems clear that the changes in the ways factories made things in Manchester and other cities had great importance for the world's history. By harnessing inanimate forms of energy, ingenious inventors and manufacturers added a new dimension to human power over nature. The use of coal and steam, later of electricity, was like the discovery of agriculture in Neolithic times; and a whole range of new possibilities opened up in both cases. Agriculture led to settled villages and then to cities and civilization. What power-driven machinery may lead to, we have still to find out. But it is already clear that where development of the new techniques has advanced most rapidly, human beings have been freed from the age-old round of the farmer's year. Instead of regulating our lives according to the simple necessities of planting and harvesting, industrialized societies have cut most of the population loose from the soil and have enabled them to live in cities under conditions very different from those their ancestors knew. The immensity of the change in the everyday experience of ordinary people has not been fully explored even now, some 200 years after the critical breakthrough occurred.

Invention of Steam Engines

Improvements in spinning and weaving machinery had been made throughout the eighteenth century. But the fact that wool and linen production was firmly established as a cottage industry carried on in the homes of innumerable artisans—some of them part time—set limits upon the size such machines could attain. The first steam engine started operation in 1712. It was invented by Thomas Newcomen to pump water from a coal mine. Other engines were built for the same purpose in following years without making much difference to anyone.

But when James Watt improved Newcomen's engine by making it unnecessary to cool the cylinder to make the steam condense, the consumption of coal became much less extravagant. When he further designed simple ways to convert the back-and-forth motion of the piston in its cylinder into rotary motion that could be transmitted by gears or drive belts to other kinds of machines, the critical point in the Industrial Revolution had been achieved. Watt took out his first patents in 1769, but fully satisfactory performance of his engines came more slowly.

As soon as Watt tried to make large numbers of engines, he encountered new difficulties. The piston had to fit snugly into its cylinder or else the steam escaped around the edges wasting energy. Filing down a piston by hand to make it fit a cylinder exactly required skill and patience in extraordinary degree. No two cylinders were ever alike; each fit had to be separately achieved. A few clumsy strokes of the file could spoil a piston entirely. This made large-scale production of steam engines impossible until a skilled mechanic, Henry Maudslay, in 1797 invented a lathe that could cut metal accurately within a thousandth of an inch.

The importance of this first "machine tool" can scarcely be exaggerated. It and others designed later for special purposes allowed skilled artisans to make parts for steam engines and other machines accurately. Instead of having to make each separate machine fit together by trial and error, standard parts could be assembled to make a standard machine that really worked. And even after temporary breakdown, standardized spare parts could be supplied, so that with relatively simple adjustments the whole machine would work again.

These things seem elementary to us, but it took time and skill to make such methods routine. For a long time, small adjustments with file and chisel had to be made by the skilled "engineer" who put the machine together or repaired it after breakdown. The first manufacturer who clearly worked out the theory of replaceable parts was Eli Whitney (1765–1825), an American; he was the inventor of the cotton gin and a manufacturer of muskets.

Labor in the Machine Age

A second problem raised by the new machines was human rather than mechanical. When steam power was turned on in a new factory, all the machines leaped to life; but if their attendants were not on hand, something could go wrong and serious damage might occur. This called for mass punctuality. But weavers and spinners, accustomed to working in their own cottages on their own time and when they felt like it, could not easily get used to living by a clock. As a result, owners and managers used very high-handed methods to force their workers to submit to the routine requirements of the new machines. Women and children were easier to control, and were often strong enough to tend the new machines; but the conditions under which they lived and worked, the brutality of the methods by which overseers forced them to be punctual and careful, and the long hours they were required to stay at their machines seem shocking today. Wages were low, barely above starvation levels. Workers' unions were illegal in Great Britain after 1799. In France the National Assembly had prohibited them, too, along with guilds and other combinations in restraint of trade.

The problems of factory life were multiplied by the rapid growth of industrial towns on or near coal fields. Housing was miserable and high-priced. Family life often broke up. Especially when the factory work force was wholly or mainly female, as was the case in many textile plants,

*The pit head of a British coal mine in the early 19th century, painted
ca. 1820. (The Bettmann Archive)*

men had no satisfying role to play in the family. They could not live on
their wives' earnings and keep their self-respect. In addition, elementary
city services—water supply, garbage removal, and schools—did not exist,
and at first no one thought it necessary to provide them.

EARLY ADJUSTMENTS TO INDUSTRIAL LIFE   But human inventiveness, so active in creating new machines, was not absent in the social
field either. Reformers began to demand legislation to protect the working
people from oppressive hours and dangerous conditions in the factories.
In Great Britain the first such laws did not get through Parliament until
1833, and effective inspection and enforcement came even later. Organization of city services and local governments in the new industrial towns
became systematic only after 1832. British workers could hardly afford
to wait that long, since the great boom in textiles and coal, in ironworks
and related industries, started with the wars of the French Revolution
(1792–1815). In Great Britain, therefore, two generations of industrialism
passed before anything in the way of legislative regulation helped to
improve human living conditions.

In the new factory and mining towns that began to spot the English
countryside so hideously, the dreariness of working-class life was relieved
in two meeting places: the church and the pub. Methodist chapels offered
evangelical religion and elementary experience in self-government. A surprising number of later labor union leaders and labor politicians of Great
Britain got their start as lay preachers in Methodist chapels, or were

the sons of Methodist lay preachers. Pubs offered a different kind of assembly place, where alcohol helped to reconcile the laboring poor to their lot in life. In a later generation, labor unions and self-help societies such as the Rochdale Pioneers, from which the modern retail cooperative movement descends, also came into existence.

In Britain, therefore, the harshest impact of the new industrialism had become a thing of the past by 1850, through a combination of working-class self-help and regulation from Parliament. In other countries, adjustment was delayed. Without fail, the first stages of industrial development saw a widespread breakdown of older social patterns, with corresponding human distress. But as industrialism spread from Great Britain to the European continent, governmental and official regulation came faster and more sweepingly, leaving less to local makeshift and private initiative.

The Napoleonic Wars and the British Economy

Britain prospered enormously during the French wars (1792–1815). Government need for uniforms put special demands upon the textile trades. As a result, mechanization spread from cotton mills, where it had started, to woolen mills. In the 1780s cotton mills—because they engaged in a new manufacture in England—did not displace artisans, but opened new jobs for unskilled women and children. However, as soon as the extraordinary war demand ended, use of power machinery in woolen manufacture brought about the destruction of a great cottage industry in England. This involved much suffering on the part of poor weavers who could not compete with the price of mill-made cloth, but could not afford to pull up roots and leave their patch of land and little cottage either.

Military demand for guns and ships and all the equipment needed for land and naval forces had parallel consequences for the metal trades. New methods and larger-scale operations opened new uses for power-driven machinery. Mines went deeper, and more engines were needed for pumping. On every hand, fresh uses for steam power were found. The result was greater production and lower costs.

Sharp alternation between boom and bust hastened the transformation of the British economy. What made these alternations was the letting of massive government contracts for war supplies whenever the British government took on a new campaign or signed a treaty promising to supply the forces of one of their continental allies for war against the French. But whenever a campaign ended or an ally made peace with the ever-victorious French, such programs were canceled. Boom conditions then suddenly gave way to equally dramatic periods of depression. The effect of such conditions was to push and pull labor and resources into new industries and open the way for radically new techniques in periods of boom. Then in periods of depression, all the less efficient firms and old-fashioned methods had to be given up, since they could not compete with newer and more productive methods that had been pioneered in the boom times. The long-drawn-out Napoleonic wars therefore acted as both a whip and a carrot to reshape the British economy. It emerged in 1815 far more developed than any other in the world.

THE WARS AND THE FRENCH ECONOMY   Until about 1780, France kept pace with Great Britain in the development of new industrial methods. War stimulated some branches of the French economy, too; but France lacked extensive coal fields and was not in a good position to take advantage of the new steam power. Early steam engines were extremely wasteful of coal by comparison with those designed later. It was therefore much cheaper to bring labor and raw materials to the coal than to try to ship vast amounts of coal any distance from the place where it was mined. This handicapped the development of French industry during and after the war years of 1792–1815.

In addition, the vast conscription of manpower into the army and into government service drew human energy and inventiveness away from the grubby industrial process and into war and administration. Hundreds of thousands of Frenchmen spent the best years of their lives stationed in distant parts of Europe, either as garrison forces or simply marching to and fro. Many died, and those who lived did not learn the habits of the new industrialism or become interested in its skills and opportunities. In 1815, therefore, the demobilized French soldiers went back home to small farms, small towns, and an economy not nearly as much transformed by the war as Britain's.

OTHER PARTS OF EUROPE   Much the same was true of other parts of the European continent. The coal fields that run in a belt across Belgium, the Ruhr region of Germany, Saxony, and into Silesia, the Ukraine, and central Asia were a great treasure for the future; but until railroads opened up the continental interior, the cost of transporting bulky goods for more than a few miles overland made the industrial value of these coal fields almost nil. Coal fields and iron deposits, located on or near navigable water, were England's good fortune at a time when sea transport was inexpensive and easy and transport overland was still prohibitively expensive. In Belgium, however, where many of Napoleon's cannon had been forged, coal beds close to navigable rivers provided the basis for rapid development of industry on the British model after 1830.

Postwar Industrial Progress

In the postwar period, to 1850, Britain kept the lead in industrial growth. The years 1815–1818 were difficult, for government spending decreased sharply and new markets were not immediately at hand to take up the slack. Overseas sales helped, for machine-made British goods were definitely less expensive and often better than handmade products. As a result, the Indian cotton industry was almost wiped out by the competition of British-made cloth, carried halfway round the world. The trade of Latin America also fell largely into British hands. British arms and diplomacy sometimes helped trade too, as we have seen in the case of China. After prolonged diplomatic conversations, the Ottoman Empire, too, was opened freely to British goods in 1839, with the result that Ottoman artisans, for the first time, found themselves exposed to competition they could not meet.

The development of speedy, cheap mechanical transportation, in which the British pioneered, laid the groundwork for the later rise of Germany and the United States, not to mention Russia and other continental nations, to the first rank industrially. The key invention was the steam railroad. The first successful steam locomotive was built in 1804, but the first railroad was not built until 1825. Development was rapid thereafter, and by the 1840s railroad building spread to the continent of Europe.

Railroads speeded overland transportation and lessened costs enormously. People and goods could move scores or hundreds of miles in a few hours. Iron ore and coal, even when separated by long distances, could be brought together to provide the basis for iron and steel production; and they, in turn, provided the fundamental material from which a larger and larger number of new machines were made. Railroads themselves became consumers of vast amounts of iron and steel. Bridges and steamships, storage tanks for the coal gas with which the cities were lighted, and literally thousands of other new uses for iron and steel developed, one after the other, between 1815 and 1850.

Some Key Inventions and Breakthroughs

The extraordinary development of the iron industry that dominated the European industrial scene between the 1780s and 1850 required the use of the new fuel—coke—for smelting ore. Throughout the eighteenth century, Europe's iron and steel production had been limited by the scarcity of charcoal, which was the traditional fuel used for smelting iron. Darby's coking method for iron smelting was kept secret for a long time (see Chapter 4), but from about 1750 it became generally known in England. The necessary fuel for the vast development of the iron industry thus became available.

As so often is the case with discoveries, the invention of coking involved useful by-products that changed European life in quite unforeseen ways. "Coal tars" left behind by the coking process provided important chemical raw materials for dyes, aspirin, and dozens of other products manufactured in the second half of the nineteenth century. Even before 1850, "coal gas"—produced by turning coal into coke—provided a cheap source of illumination for houses, streets, and public places of assembly. Inexpensive artificial light, in turn, opened all sorts of possibilties. Nineteenth-century theater and concert life, for example, would have been inconceivable without the utilization of artificial lighting for stage and concert hall.

Two other key inventions are worth mentioning here. In 1814 the first cylinder press was installed in the printing office of the *London Times*. This made high-speed printing possible. Newspapers, in turn, created a link between government officials and other social leaders on the one hand and the public on the other. The flexibility and energy of nineteenth-century European society could not have been achieved without this sort of close linkage between the top and middle ranges of society.

A second key invention was the development in 1836 of a breech-loading handgun. The Prussian army was the first to adopt the new style of weapon. Superiority of the "needle gun," as it was called, was proven in 1866 when Prussian soldiers lay down on their bellies to fire at their Austrian foes, who had to stay on their feet to reload their muskets in the old fashion.

With this invention, therefore, the training of European armies had to be altered. Instead of standing close-massed in ranks, loading and firing on command, as had been necessary with muzzle-loading weapons, a far looser, open order became the key to success on the battlefield. New forms of discipline for the effective control of skirmish lines were called for; but it took European military experts a long time to adjust tactics to the requirements of breech-loading weapons.

Innumerable other inventions changed the character of human activity in less dramatic ways. The camera (1839), electric telegraph (1844), horse-drawn reaper (1834), screw propeller for ships (1836), revolver (1835/1836), bicycle (1839), sewing machine (1846) are only a few of the new devices that were introduced or improved during these years. Invention became deliberate and expected. Ingenious inventors tinkered in their backyards or basements, hoping to make a fortune by some lucky patent. Few of them had much acquaintance with science or theory. Invention was still the province of the commonsense mechanic with a deft hand and three-dimensional imagination. Complicated mathematical calculations as well as academic physics and chemistry were largely irrelevant to the sorts of inventions that changed the texture of life in European cities between 1789 and 1850.

Rural Conservatism

In the countryside the impact of the new inventions was delayed. Even after Cyrus McCormick invented the horse-drawn reaper in 1834, farming went on much as before. In Europe, particularly, farms were often too small and peasants too ignorant to take advantage of the reaper. Better transportation made it easier to get their produce to market; and growing city populations with ready money tended to push up farm prices in the more densely populated parts of Europe. More intensive cultivation, better seed, better tillage, and better rotations of crops all combined to increase Europe's food production sufficiently to keep pace with the rapid growth of its cities and population. Simplifying rights to particular parcels of land had been part of the legal reforms of the French Revolution, and this made agricultural progress much easier. Wherever the *Code Napoléon* applied, every particular piece of land was assigned to a single owner, and all overlapping and competing rights were abolished. In other words, the last remnant of manorial agriculture disappeared from western Europe; only in the Austrian and Russian empires did the older collective types of tillage survive until 1848 or even later.

Most Europeans remained on the land. Even in Britain, farming and occupations directly related to agriculture continued to engage a majority of the population until after 1850. This meant that European society as a whole was supported and stabilized by a generally stable and increasingly prosperous rural population. Farmers and peasants were, in general, willing to let city dwellers and their traditional superiors, the nobility or gentry, run political affairs, as long as the work on the farm went well and prices were not too bad.

Such basic stability, in turn, gave scope for city dwellers to push and pull against the conservative spirit of the landed element—lords and gentlemen, receivers of rents, the traditional rulers of European society. In France, home of the Revolution, landed classes never recovered real strength. Elsewhere in Europe, the balance varied with time and place; but in general it was the city people—rooted in industry and commerce, rising to new wealth and self-confidence with every successful new venture—that advanced, and the landed conservative classes that retreated.

CONCLUSION

Between 1775 and 1850, western Europe developed two new and strikingly successful sources of power. One was political: the closer alliance between government and people (at least, the upper and middle classes), pioneered in the United States (1776–1789) and carried triumphantly forward by the French (1789–1815). Even the defeat of Napoleon in 1815 did not reverse this Democratic Revolution–for Napoleon's enemies were able to defeat him only by taking their own public into partnership in some degree or other; and the restored French monarchy continued to try to find public support among the same groups that had been most important in supporting the revolutionary regime.

Western Europe's second major innovation was technical: the Industrial Revolution, pioneered mainly in Great Britain. Here the central fact was that inventors found ways to use inanimate sources of power—coal and steam primarily—to drive all sorts of new machines and perform other services for mankind's convenience. Cheaper, sometimes better, and far more abundant goods were the first result; radically changed living conditions for urban dwellers were a second, sometimes less pleasant, by-product of the new forms of industry.

Thus, the manufacture of more and cheaper goods plus a closer cooperation between political leaders and the public at large combined to produce far greater disposable power for those countries and peoples who were successful in making these twin transformations take root in their midst. Great Britain led the way; but Belgium and, after a few years, Germany and the United States followed close behind. France lagged industrially, and so did all of Mediterranean and eastern Europe. Other civilizations fell even further behind and, by 1850, found themselves entirely incapable of resisting the new kinds of power that western Europeans were able to bring to bear against them—commercially, diplomatically, and militarily.

Such an upsurge in Europe's power set the stage for the collapse of other civilizations' effective independence. Improved communication and transport laid the technical basis for closer and closer interaction of all parts of the world. After about 1850, the separateness that allowed Chinese, Japanese, Indian, and Moslem peoples—not to mention the inhabitants of Africa, Australia, and the Americas—to maintain their own distinct ways of life no longer existed. Such a change in human relationships marks the end of one historic era and the beginning of a new, globally cosmopolitan age, in which we ourselves are living. The inauguration of this new age was the real significance of Europe's Democratic and Industrial revolutions.

DISEASES AND THEIR EFFECTS ON HUMAN SOCIETIES

Disease has played a very big part in human history. In all modern wars, more soldiers died of disease than from enemy action until World War II. Whole societies have sometimes been destroyed by epidemics. Unfamiliar diseases prevented successful European settlement in many tropical lands. Elsewhere European diseases, spreading like wildfire among local peoples, often cleared the way for settlers.

This essay explores the way people and diseases have altered their relationships across the ages. Lack of exact information means that we have to guess details; but there are some general principles—for example, the difference between endemic and epidemic disease—that go far to explain what happened.

The Case of the Vanishing American: 1519–1650

When Cortes invaded Mexico, the inhabitants of Montezuma's empire numbered more than 11 million persons. They lived close together in villages wherever good land for cornfields existed. They had never been exposed to Europe's "childhood" diseases: smallpox, chicken pox, measles, mumps, and whooping cough. One after another, these diseases spread among the Indians, killing adults as well as children. But the Spaniards, having almost always had such diseases in childhood, did not suffer. By 1650 the population of central Mexico, where Montezuma had once ruled, was about 1.5 million; at least 10 million persons had disappeared.

Why did so many Indians die of diseases the Spaniards and other Europeans did not find so very serious? The answer lies in the different disease history of the two populations. In Europe, smallpox, measles, and the rest had become *endemic*. This means that the disease was always around so that in the first years of life nearly everyone caught it. Natural immunities inherited from the parents made recovery more likely. Many children died all the same, but they were quickly replaced by new births. In Mexico and the rest of the Americas, the new diseases became *epidemic*. This means that old and young alike fell ill. Because they lacked any sort of inherited immunities, many died. When a large proportion of adults died, all activity began to fail.

HIGHLIGHTS The consequences of this disease pattern in the Americas were vast.

A handful of Spanish conquistadors and missionaries easily controlled large populations. Their resistance to diseases killing so many Indians seemed to prove that God was with them.

In Massachusetts and Virginia, weaker Indian communities simply disappeared, leaving empty land for English settlers.

Similar disease patterns often arose elsewhere. A population among whom a particular disease was endemic always had an advantage in any new encounter with another population among whom the disease was unknown.

How Europeans Acquired Their Childhood Diseases

Medical records are too vague to allow us to know exactly what disease hit when. But general considerations tell us a good deal. We assume that different diseases first broke out in different parts of the earth and among separate human communities. In any one area, a new disease begins as an *epidemic*. Either it kills everybody, and the disease germ itself disappears, or enough people survive the first epidemic to raise children who inherit some immunity to the disease. If enough of them survive childhood exposure to be able to reproduce themselves, after four or five generations the new disease will become *endemic*.

The spread of disease endemic in one human community to another where it is not endemic depends on how far and how often people travel between the two communities. Most major changes in disease distribution ought, therefore, to take place when people change the pattern of their travel and communication in some important way. (The arrival of the Spaniards in Mexico is such a case.)

Our question then becomes: When did people *first* venture upon important new kinds of travel and communication? About 100 B.C. to A.D. 200, caravans regularly traveled across Asia along what Eu-

The Bubonic plague in Europe, ca. 14th century.
(*Bettmann Archive*)

ropeans called the Silk Road. During this period ships also sailed the southern seas, connecting the east Mediterranean lands with south China via India and Malaya.

The disease consequences are clear. Severe epidemics hit both the Han Empire of China and the Roman Empire of Europe in the first Christian centuries. Serious depopulation resulted. Depopulation eventually made trade unprofitable, until regular movement along the caravan routes almost petered out. This was probably the time when most of our familiar childhood diseases became endemic among all the civilized populations of Eurasia.

HIGHLIGHTS

The distribution of infectious diseases depends on the patterns of movement and contact among human populations.

Important changes in human travel are likely to trigger new patterns of disease distribution.

The epidemic impact of new diseases upon a dense population without immunities may destroy the conditions needed to sustain the trade and travel that triggered the epidemic in the first place.

This natural cycle had much to do with the decline and fall of classical civilization of the Han and Roman empires, though military and other factors also played a part in the collapse.

The Black Death: A Different Disease Pattern

When infection passes direct from person to person, the transition from epidemic to endemic requires from four to five human generations. The pattern differs when there is another carrier for the disease. For example, the infectious organism for bubonic plague is carried by rats and is spread further by fleas. It is endemic among wild rats in parts of India and

China. From time to time, the disease takes hold as an epidemic among the dense rat populations of cities. When enough rats die off, their fleas may try to live on humans, thus spreading the epidemic to humankind, too. Immunities do not build up, for the disease disappears among humans when an epidemic is over, only to emerge again from the regions where it is endemic among wild rats.

Why then did bubonic plague cease in western Europe after 1718? Probably because changes in the ways Europeans got along with rats and fleas checked the spread of the disease. First, public quarantine of ships, houses, or whole cities where plague broke out made it illegal for anyone to leave the quarantined area until after a fixed time—usually forty days—had elapsed without fresh outbreaks of the disease. Second, improved cleanliness made

it harder for fleas to take up residence on human bodies. Third, with better housing people encountered rats less often. What really stopped bubonic plague were the changes in European habits that made contacts between human beings on the one hand and rats and fleas on the other less common than before. In Asia and other parts of the world where no such changes took place, bubonic plague continues to threaten fresh epidemics.

HIGHLIGHTS

Some epidemic human diseases are endemic among animal population.

In such cases, the natural shift from epidemic to endemic forms of disease does not occur as far as humans are concerned.

One method of protecting ourselves from the diseases carried by animals is to reduce human contacts with the animal carrier.

The Impact of Scientific Medicine

During the past 150 years, scientists discovered how infectious diseases spread. With the identification of disease-causing bacteria and viruses, new methods of preventing disease became possible. Chief among them is inoculation with a weakened form of the disease-causing organism. This induces the human body to build up antibodies in the blood that make infection unlikely. In this way a long list of former killers, like yellow fever, smallpox, and infantile paralysis, have become unimportant.

In other cases, chemicals have been discovered that check the disease within the human body. In this way malaria, pneumonia, syphilis, and other diseases have been brought under control. These artificial immunities have extended hu-

An Aztec warrior striken with smallpox. (American Museum of Natural History)

287.

mankind's freedom from infectious disease enormously, increasing the average length of life by many years.

Today scientific medicine allows control of most infectious diseases. This means that on top of the disappearance of epidemic disease as a major killer of humankind, many endemic diseases also have been (or are being) eliminated. An enormous improvement in the quality and dependability of human life results. Yet there is another side. Less infectious disease means longer life. Babies that would have died in infancy grow up to have children of their own; and their children do the same. Very rapid growth of population results. One of the most distinctive characteristics of modern times is the runaway population explosion.

Because the causes of the bubonic plague were not fully understood, a variety of folk remedies were developed in an attempt to prevent infection. (Bettman Archive)

Smallpox vaccination in 1870. (Library of Congress)

Growth of dense human populations created a fertile field for new infections, and several examples of recent disease transfers from animal populations to humans are known. Most of these were quickly eliminated by simple medical counter measures. But one new virus, which interferes with the immune reaction of human bodies, has not been brought under control. The Acquired Immune Deficiency Syndrome (AIDS) epidemic results. Increasing numbers of people began to die of AIDS in the 1980s, despite efforts by medical scientists to find a cure.

HIGHLIGHTS

Between about 1650 and 1850, epidemic diseases ceased to be important killers. Modern communications spread diseases around the world, and the epidemic-to-endemic shift occurred almost everywhere.

Since 1850 scientific medicine also brought the main endemic diseases under control.

Sustained population growth (about .1% per year) began about 1750 when epidemic diseases had been largely checked. Galloping population growth (up to 1.5% per year) took over as many of the important endemic diseases were also brought under control.

Disease and disease-control did not act alone. Increased quantity and quality of food supplies also contributed to modern population growth, and so did other changes in the condition of human life.

The State
of the World,
1850

From the time when civilizations first began until 1850, the world had been big enough to find room for a dozen or more different civilizations, as well as for literally thousands of other societies. Patterns of communication and transportation set definite limits to the size of states. The Ottoman Empire, for example, could not grow beyond the radius of a three months' march from Constantinople for the simple reason that, if he had to march more than three months to reach the scene of combat, the sultan could not bring his armies into the field for long enough to win a decisive victory. Comparable limits existed for other empires in other parts of the world. The limits of political dominion were only outward signs of the limits to other forms of communication. Such limitations defined the circles within which people could interact continuously with one another and thus create and maintain a single civilization.

EUROPE'S
IRRESISTIBLE INVENTIONS

By 1850, however, these old limits upon human interaction had been broken through. European inventions made worldwide interaction possible. Railroads opened up the possibility of penetrating the continental interiors of all the world, making the most remote village no farther removed from the outside world than the nearest railroad station. The electric telegraph opened still more amazing horizons, for all that was needed was to string wires across the lands and oceans of the world to create instantaneous communication around the entire globe. Steamships had a less revolutionary impact, for the oceans had already become highways for contact between the world's habitable coasts. Still, cheaper and faster ocean transport did make the worldwide net of communications and contacts so much the tighter.

In 1850 these new means of communication had been invented but had not yet been used outside of Europe and North America. Their global effect, therefore, lay still in the future. But the Europeans clearly had both the will and the means to catch all the world in this new net of their devising. The Industrial Revolution had affected weapons, as well as transport and communications. The result was that European governments controlled ships, guns, and soldiers—all of which were so much superior to the forces any other people in the world could put into the field that armed resistance to Europeans had become all but impossible. The Chinese, to their surprise and dismay, discovered this fact in the Opium War of 1839–1842. The Turks learned that same lesson during the Napoleonic Wars, when French, British, and Russian forces took turns at being enemy or friend to the sultan, but always enjoyed a clear upper hand when it came to military action. In India, British power was supreme by 1818. In central Asia, Russian advance was checked only by distances and the limited interest that the Russian czar felt in adding new deserts and barren steppelands to his domain. In the Americas there had been no contest from the time that the conquistadors first set foot in the New World. And the same was true in Australia. Of the inhabited continents, sub-Saharan Africa alone remained unexplored by Europeans in 1850, but this was because of geographical obstacles, not because local peoples were able to oppose European penetration by force.

LEADING ROLE OF EUROPE

Hence, by 1850 no part of the world could prevent Europeans from moving in if they wished to do so. Moreover, there was a second and no less powerful weapon in the European armory: cheap goods. With the help of machine production, it was possible for European factories to turn out a host of consumer goods—saws, hatchets, scythes, pocketknives, sewing machines, cooking pots, textiles, and hundreds of other items that were cheaper and better than anything which local artisans could produce

A later 19th century steam locomotive. (Santa Fe Railway photo)

by hand. European traders wished to sell such goods freely in order to get raw materials and other supplies they needed in return. Local peoples often welcomed the new goods. Local governments had little choice but to admit the Europeans. The futility of trying to prevent trade was sharply demonstrated by the Chinese defeat in the Opium War, and no other major civilized government ever again made the attempt.

But the availability of cheap machine-made goods, which could be supplied in almost any quantity if the demand was brisk enough, brought about a fundamental disruption of traditional society in all those parts of the world where artisan handicrafts had become important. Every civilized society, in other words, stood at Europe's mercy, for the disruption of handicrafts meant the breakdown of traditional city life; and cities were always and necessarily the centers of civilization.

The world had become one, in a way never known before. What happened in Peking, Delhi, Accra, or Constantinople depended on what was thought and done in London, Paris, New York, and Hamburg. The possibility of isolating one civilization from another had disappeared. All humankind had become part of a single worldwide interacting whole. Europeans played the lead role and, to begin with, enjoyed most of the advantages of this new world balance. The three major Asian civilizations suffered catastrophic breakdown, all at the same time and within a mere fifteen years, 1850–1865. During the same period, the less highly developed parts of the world felt the impact of European enterprise more forcibly than ever before; and disruption of tribal and other forms of local society was widespread, though not quite universal.

WORLD COSMOPOLITANISM

Europe and the Western world beyond Europe remained for a long time almost unaware of what was happening to the rest of humanity. From a Western point of view, it all looked like progress and the spread of Christian civilization, or the advance of science and technology. Inherited ways of thinking and doing, modified though they were by the Democratic and Industrial revolutions, provided a general framework for European life and thought that did not seem to need fundamental revision. How could it be otherwise when the world lay open to European curiosity and enterprise as never before; when everything seemed to work in Europe's favor; and when people of European culture could find nothing in the world that seemed equal, or nearly equal, to their own achievements?

Yet enough time has now passed since the end of the separateness of world civilizations and cultures to make it plain that the worldwide interactions that started to take on such intimacy after 1850 were not entirely one-sided. World cosmopolitanism required Westerners to get used to living with people of backgrounds different from their own, just as much as it required the rest of humankind to get used to the Westerners. The last part of this book will, therefore, explore this interaction, insofar as our present place in time and space allows us to understand what happened.

CHAPTER 7

The Decisive Years

1850 to 1865

Interaction among the world's civilizations attained a new level of intensity between 1850 and 1865. During that short period of time, the impact of Europe's Industrial Revolution began to hit home in all parts of the globe. In particular, the great Asian civilizations found themselves unable to keep intrusive Europeans and/or Americans from doing more or less whatever they wanted to do, even on Chinese, Indian, Moslem, and (in much lesser degree) Japanese soil. This discredited old institutions, habits, and customs among more and more of the leaders of Asian opinion; but what to put in place of ancestral practices was hard to agree upon. A time of troubles thus began, when almost everywhere outside the Western world people found themselves forced to experiment with new and unfamiliar ways of coping with daily emergencies. As a matter of fact, the world has not yet emerged from this time of troubles. We ought, therefore, to study the years 1850 to 1865 with particular attention, if we want to understand how the world arrived at its present condition.

THE BREAKDOWN
OF TRADITIONAL
SOCIAL ORDER

The opening up of the world's oceans by European seafarers marked the start of modern times, not only for Europe but for all the world. The oceans ceased to be barriers to movement and became, instead, connecting links bringing individuals of diverse and different backgrounds into contact with one another, on a scale and with a regularity that had never been possible before. Within thirty years after Columbus' first voyage in 1492, the main breakthroughs took place: Vasco da Gama's voyage round Africa in 1497 and Magellan's circumnavigation of the globe, 1519–1522.

Just as sharp a break came when new techniques of transportation and communication allowed Europeans to penetrate the continental interiors of the earth more or less at will, beginning about 1850. In the next fifteen years the traditional civilizations of Asia collapsed, in the sense that their leaders no longer could follow customary patterns, but more and more had to react to European initiatives.

To be sure, western Europe was not particularly affected, at least to begin with. Europeans were mightily reassured by the fact that their diplomats, armies, navies, missionaries, merchants, explorers, technicians, scientists, and settlers were able to break in upon almost every other human society on the face of the earth, without bothering about how their behavior might interfere with local customs or interests. This seemed to prove Europe's superiority beyond all doubt.

Indeed, by 1850 they were so sure of themselves that few Europeans really tried to understand the foreign peoples and different civilizations they met. In the 1700s, many Europeans were ready to admire the wisdom of Confucian sages, but the ways of the "heathen Chinee" struck their descendants of the 1800s as merely peculiar. Armed with such smugness, Europeans were not, therefore, particularly affected by the opening up of the continental interiors of the world, which took place during the fifteen years between 1850 and 1865.

But the rest of the world's peoples were deeply affected, for they found themselves plunged into a buzzing, blooming confusion where their forefathers' tried and true rules of conduct no longer worked. As a result, in the 1850s traditional political, social, and economic patterns of life broke down in China, Japan, India, and the Ottoman Empire. These breakdowns were by-products of the Opium War of 1839–1842, and of two other wars: the Crimean War of 1853–1856 and the Indian Mutiny of 1857–1858.

In the next decade both Russia and the United States entered upon a particularly painful transformation. In Russia the abolition of serfdom in 1861 gave legal expression to changes that ran from top to bottom of Russian society—changes that were triggered by the fact that Russia's Old Regime had failed in the Crimean War. In the United States the Civil War of 1861–1865 and the emancipation of the slaves in 1863 gave far more violent expression to the growing pains through which the American nation passed in these same years.

EUROPE'S IRRESISTIBLE IMPACT

This widespread and sudden breakup of traditional social orders had worldwide as well as local causes. For one thing, the impact of the Industrial Revolution (which had gotten under way one-half to three-quarters of a century earlier in Great Britain) began to be felt in the far parts of the world only after 1850. Being delayed, the impact, when it came, took a double form: one military, one economic. First of all, by 1850 European weapons and military organization had become overwhelmingly superior. Mobility and firepower came easily to armies and navies equipped from Europe's new industrial workshops.

Secondly, after gunboats and marine landing parties had battered down political barriers, European merchants found themselves, all of a sudden, in a position to supply goods at lower prices, and often of better quality, than could be produced locally. A flow of such goods quickly changed consumers' tastes and ruined local artisans. With their ruin, the traditional social structure of towns and cities was damaged beyond repair. This presented most of the world's peoples with a painful crisis. Societies and governments that lacked power machinery and factories had to find ways of creating them, or else submit to foreign economic domination. The old routine of doing nothing in particular, and of paying no attention to what Europeans were up to, became quite impossible to follow when Europe's guns, and the will to use them, opened the way for Europe's cheaply manufactured goods.

Industrialism was not the only factor causing change, of course. Europeans were far better organized than were the other peoples of the world. Standing armies and navies, well-equipped and carefully trained, could operate thousands of miles from home and still get reinforcements, supplies, and strategic directives—if not always when most needed, at least eventually. As for trade, corporations and other kinds of companies coordinated the efforts of scores or of hundreds (and sometimes of thousands) of individuals across as well as within national boundaries. As a result, common purposes could be carried out anywhere in the world and across decades or even longer periods of time. No other civilization could operate nearly so well at a distance.

In addition, Europeans were sure they were right: Adam Smith and others had proved that free trade was a good thing. If trade benefited Europeans more than others in the 1850s and 1860s, it merely proved how well thrift and a shrewd eye for business paid off. Moreover, the precious blessings of exposure to Christian civilization justified, in European eyes, the political subordination of native peoples whose own past had kept them in heathen darkness.

A third piece of Europe's moral armament for its great venture of smashing the idols long held dear by other peoples of the earth was the value Europeans placed upon heroic achievement. Both as individuals and as citizens or subjects representative of the nation back home, Europeans valued deeds of daring and took risks most of us would shrink from. As in the days of the conquistadors, incredible expeditions carried tiny companies of adventurers into strange and hostile parts of the globe, blazing trails for the administrators who followed afterward. Nineteenth-century Europeans took their vision of heroism mainly from the Greek and Roman classics. Schoolboys read Plutarch, Livy, and Caesar, and then tried to act on the model the ancient heroes offered them; and this was so whether the schoolboys pursued their activities in darkest Africa, in heathen Asia, or in desolate Australia—or whether, indeed, they were merely chasing a fox across the hedgerows of England.

The combination of such traits made the mid-nineteenth-century Europeans literally irresistible. As Thucydides said of the ancient Athenians: "They were born into the world to take no rest themselves and to give none to others."

Europe's Civilized Rivals

At the same time, we can point to special areas of weakness that afflicted Europe's civilized rivals, China and Islam in particular. Both these great civilizations had been psychologically on the defensive for centuries.

CHINA   Ever since the Chinese had driven the Mongols out of their country (1368), the overriding aim of Chinese rulers and thinkers had been to keep themselves pure by preventing foreigners from again bringing in new and uncivilized habits. To be sure, the Manchu rulers were foreigners and the Chinese never quite forgave them for that. But at least the Manchus had the grace to accept Chinese civilization and tradition as fully and completely as any foreigners could. Foreigners who did not take the pains to meet the Chinese on their own terms by mastering the Confucian classics and the Chinese language were of no interest or concern to China's upper classes, except when they became unruly and had to be punished.

Such a policy worked very well indeed until about 1775, as we saw; it made China great and prosperous. But it had also allowed China to fall behind the European world in innumerable ways. Therefore, when military collision came, in the 1840s, Chinese minds and traditions were completely unprepared to face the crisis. Sticking to successful past methods seemed the only thing to do. It hurt dreadfully to acknowledge that foreigners had knowledge and skills that were actually superior to Chinese knowledge and skills. To admit such a thing was to admit that the whole policy of Confucian China had been a mistake. Indeed, the more obvious it became that something vital was lacking in traditional Chinese civilization, the more traitorous it became to say so in public—up to the time when it was too late to avoid being trodden upon by European intruders.

ISLAM   Islam had a similar though different history. The great divide, as far as Moslem skills and knowledge went, came about 1500. In 1499 the Safavid Shah Ismail challenged the prevailing compromises of Islamic society. But in the Ottoman Empire, where Islam's main contact points with Europe lay, this revolutionary religious movement was kept under control by administrative devices and military force. Debate was hushed up. Official Sunni Islam became dependent on the administrative structure of the Ottoman Empire. As a result, the official guardians of truth and knowledge could no longer afford to think freely and seriously for themselves. Heresy was too easy to fall into. It seemed safer and better to memorize the Koran and ancient commentaries upon it.

But this intellectual attitude also required Moslems to turn their attention away from the new thoughts evident all over Christian Europe in the age of the Renaissance and the Reformation, and to pay no attention to anything outside the official canon of Sunni Islam. Consequently, all the dazzling new ideas and techniques that grew up right next door to the Ottoman Empire made no difference to Ottoman and Islamic society until, once again, it was too late to catch up and keep pace with the restless Europeans. Territorial retreat became necessary instead. Only complicated diplomacy prevented complete collapse. Time, the will, and the means to catch up with Europe were as utterly lacking in Islamic lands as in China.

JAPAN AND INDIA   Japan and the Hindu communities of India were in a less awkward position. The Hindus already had been overrun by Moslems. The religious ideas and caste organization of Hindu society made it easier for them to get used to having Europeans—in this case the British—ruling them and interfering in their economic and political affairs. One foreign master was much like another, after all; and if Europeans offered jobs in the government to clerks who could learn how to get along in an English-speaking world, there were plenty of bright and ambitious young men who were eager to qualify themselves, as soon as suitable schools had been set up.

Japan's case was almost the opposite. The Japanese had never been conquered. Japan's rulers deliberately opened the country to contact with Europeans and Americans, because they knew that traditional defenses against foreign attack were no longer effective in keeping the foreigners out. It seemed better, therefore, to learn the Westerners' secrets as quickly as possible. Only so could Japan be safe again from the danger of foreign conquest. After a shaky start, Japan's efforts along these lines proved remarkably successful. The nation was thus able to keep its traditional social structure and safeguard old values while working hard to modernize technology and government along Western lines.

Everywhere else in the non-Western world, among civilized and uncivilized peoples alike, the collision between Western ways and local traditions led to the disruption of old patterns of leadership. This was painful and confusing enough, but the difficulty grew greater as new ideas, new ideals, and new leaders struggled to cope with the ever-present white foreigners, who were always wanting something and would never take No for an answer. A century of paralysis, or near-paralysis, resulted. Moslems, Indians, and Chinese, not to mention the other less numerous and less mighty peoples of the earth, all found themselves helpless, unable to act together effectively for any clear and attainable goal. Anger and frustration were inevitable. Dismay, despair, and passive retreat while waiting out the storm were no less inevitable. Few individuals were able to act constructively amid the chaos surrounding them as a result of the sudden collapse of traditional guidelines and landmarks in every walk of life.

Westerners, by contrast, had few or no hesitations before 1914. Some thinkers and artists did, indeed, foreshadow the collapse of Europe's New Regime—bourgeois, capitalist, parliamentary, reformist, progressive, and smug. But the great majority paid no attention. Westerners kept any doubts they may have had strictly to themselves when dealing with people who were less powerful than they were.

This extraordinary contrast dominated the history of the world from 1850 to about 1950. Then a new era set in. Western empires in Asia and Africa collapsed as local peoples reclaimed their independence; and

Westerners' self-confidence suffered serious shock from the disasters of two world wars.

But for a century before 1950 our contemporary doubts about the uniqueness and superiority of Western civilization did not enter into the picture. Instead, triumphant Europeans asserted their power everywhere; and in a short fifteen years, between 1850 and 1865, old barriers to their supremacy everywhere crumbled.

THE CRIMEAN WAR
AND ITS CONSEQUENCES

The Crimean War, 1853–1856, was one of the silliest wars ever fought; yet its consequences were extraordinarily important for Russia and for Europe as a whole, for the Ottoman Empire, and even for India. The struggle began with a quarrel between Roman Catholic and Orthodox Christian churchmen over control of the holy places in Palestine. The Ottoman Turks were nominally in charge; but when the French backed the Roman Catholics and the Russians backed Orthodox claims, the sultan found himself in a delicate position. Turkish fear of the Russians was deep-seated. If the czar made good his claim to protect Orthodox interests in Palestine, the next step would be interference between the sultan and his Orthodox subjects in the Balkan Peninsula, where Serbs, Bulgars, and Greeks all belonged to the Orthodox Christian faith. English diplomats feared the same thing; and English journalists stirred up popular excitement in Great Britain by pointing with alarm to the consequences for the balance of power in Europe if the Russians should advance into the Balkans or, worse still, seize Constantinople and the Straits between the Black Sea and the Aegean Sea.

Hence, when Russian demands provoked the Turks to declare war on Russia, France and Britain came to the sultan's aid. Austria intervened by sending the Russians an ultimatum, requiring them to withdraw from the provinces which later made up Romania or face the threat of Austrian attack. When the Russians did withdraw their troops from this territory, Austrian forces marched in. As a result, the Turks and Russians had no place to fight; and if British and French journalists had not been so bloodthirsty, the war might have ended before the French and British land forces even entered into action.

Instead, the French and British mounted an amphibious attack on the Crimea, hoping to eliminate the main Russian naval base at Sevastopol. A difficult campaign ensued, for both the Russian and the Allied forces had to operate at the end of very long supply lines. Supply and

THE LADY WITH THE LAMP

When Florence Nightingale was seventeen years old, she heard a voice calling to her and believed that God had spoken. But for seven years she could not discover what she was called upon to do. Gradually, she decided that her mission in life was to nurse the sick; but her parents refused to permit her to do such a thing, because at that time nursing was a very lowly occupation, and Florence Nightingale came from a wealthy English family.

But Miss Nightingale was nothing if not determined. She refused to marry and secretly read all she could about nursing and hospital administration. The more she read the more she was sure that hospitals needed to be reformed, and that God had chosen her to accomplish the task. Eventually her parents gave way, and in 1851—when she was thirty-one years old—Florence Nightingale left home and went to Germany to get her first practical experience of nursing. The German hospital in which she worked was run by Protestant deaconesses, and it came nearer to her standards than any English hospital of the time.

On returning to England she began to set up a hospital, but she had scarcely started when the British government blundered into war against Russia, in the Crimea. Soon newspaper reports describing dreadful conditions in British military hospitals flooded into London. Officials of the government turned to Miss Nightingale and asked her to help. With

medical services were not set up to take full advantage of the new resources of science and industrial mass production; but the telegraph made it possible for journalists to send back daily news reports of everything that went wrong. Shortcomings revealed during the Crimean War made the British—and to a lesser degree the French also—realize the need for fundamental reorganization of their army supply systems and of their promotion policy for officers. Modern nursing started at this time, when Florence Nightingale organized emergency measures to help the British wounded: The French and British, who had been rivals ever since 1688, even became accustomed to cooperating with each other; they soon extended the practice to China, as we shall see. After a winter's siege, Sevastopol surrendered and peace followed. The Russians were humiliated, but made peace anyway because, after Czar Nicholas died in 1855 his successor, Alexander II, felt that far-reaching internal reforms had to come first, before revenge would be practicable.

As far as Europe was concerned, the most important consequence thirty-eight nurses to assist her, in 1854 she sailed for the battle zone, and within a month had 5000 wounded and sick soldiers to look after.

To begin with, there were almost no medical supplies or facilities. But Florence Nightingale and her nurses set to work, cleaned things up, and did the best they could with what they had. They all put in long, hard hours; and Florence Nightingale worked harder than anyone else. Late at night, when her tasks for the day were done, she inspected each ward, carrying an oil lamp so as to be able to see. The sick and wounded soldiers soon nicknamed her "The Lady with the Lamp." She became a national heroine, universally admired and everywhere acclaimed.

Florence Nightingale used her position to demand, plead, and argue for a more adequate medical setup for the British army. Even after the close of the Crimean War, when she returned home and hid from her public admirers, Florence Nightingale continued to work from behind the scenes for much needed reforms and improvements. Modern ideas about military hospitals and medical administration, as well as the modern profession of nursing, were created very largely through her work.

But after her hectic days in the Crimean War hospitals, she always remained out of the public eye—and most people assumed she had died. Actually, she worked at home with high officials of the British government until the 1870s. Thereafter she "retired" and spent much time in religious exercises. She lived until 1910, dying at the age of ninety. Having been idolized for two short years, during the Crimean War, Florence Nightingale remained mysterious, strong-willed, and independent all her life.

of the Crimean War was the bitter feeling that arose between Austria and Russia. The conservative alliance that had kept Russia, Austria, and Prussia together since 1815 broke up completely. The Russians felt that their help in 1849, when a Russian army had invaded Hungary to put down rebels against the Hapsburg authority, had been repaid with the basest ingratitude. Instead of backing the status quo against any efforts toward change, as the Russians had done for forty years, the new czar was unwilling to raise a finger in their support when Prussia challenged the traditional Hapsburg leadership of central Europe. The result was the unification of Germany under Prussia between 1866 and 1871. Much of the world's history since then hinges upon German efforts to make up for the lateness of their arrival upon the European scene as a united nation; but it seems best to postpone exploration of this by-product of the Crimean War until the next chapter.

Here we are concerned with the consequences of the Crimean War for Russia and the Ottoman Empire and with the echo that the Turks' victory over Russia had in India.

Russian Reaction
to Defeat

Russia's reaction to the defeats that the czar's armies suffered in the Crimea was confused and not very successful. The whole system of government had been built around the army, which had shown itself unable to defend Russian soil. Something was obviously wrong. Russia had again fallen behind the Western powers, and heroic efforts to catch up, as in the days of Peter the Great, seemed called for. But agreement on what had to be done and how to do it was never reached.

At first, "liberals" had the upper hand in trying to meet the difficulty. The great problem, as they saw matters, was the absence of real freedom in Russia. What was needed was to unleash individual initiative by changing laws that made most Russians serfs. Accordingly, in 1861, the government abolished serfdom and divided legal ownership of the land between landlords and their former serfs. Yet before the emancipation laws were put through, an opposite "Slavophile" point of view made itself heard at court. As a result, instead of assigning the land to individual ownership, as liberals would have done, the law assigned ownership of the serfs' fields to the village community as a whole. Provisions were made for periodic reassignment of fields among the villagers. This arrangement was customary in most of central Russia. The reform of 1861 gave it full legal force and thus set off Russian ways more sharply than ever from the patterns of land ownership current at that time in western Europe.

ATTEMPTS AT SOCIAL REFORM   This result was what Slavophiles wanted. Their idea was to treasure everything distinctively Russian. Some believed that in this way Russia could bypass the capitalist, individualist stage of society characteristic of nineteenth-century western Europe and move directly into socialism—the social order of the future, according to their way of thinking. They argued that Russia might thus be able to leap ahead and, instead of being backward and despised, would find itself in the forefront of European social and historical development. Other Slavophiles feared and detested socialism and revolution; they believed in the past for its own sake and resisted every change, including the abolition of serfdom.

Both liberals and Slavophiles tended to extremes. They agreed that something fundamental was wrong with Russia, but disagreed on practically everything else. In between was a body of officials and piecemeal reformers—practical administrators who worked within the limits of the possible. Their trouble was that the limits of the possible seemed uncomfortably narrow. Russia's poverty made any large-scale program for industrial development, or even for constructing an adequate railway network, prohibitively expensive. Tax income was not large enough to finance the necessary undertakings, and private enterprise and capital were not available. Moreover, fear that reform, if pressed too vigorously, might awaken the sleeping giant of the Russian peasantry and provoke some vast outburst of peasant discontent soon hampered reform, even when changes did not cost much money.

Half measures and the endless delays of bureaucratic decision-making won no friends for the moderate middle road of gradual reform. Impatient young men, often priests' sons and students, began to gather in secret groups to talk of how Russia should be reborn. The spirit of revolution was fed by the fact that reform soon petered out. In 1864 the czar proclaimed a law setting up limited local self-government. Thereafter, the steam went out of the reform effort.

The basic fact was that the peasants were not satisfied with emancipation as handed down in 1861. They believed that the land was theirs by right. Some convinced themselves that wicked landlords had twisted the czar's intentions by keeping back part of the land. And while the peasant majority nursed its grievance, half in secret, the rest of the Russian society fell into hopeless disagreement. Fierce debate over whether Russia should imitate the Western nations or not, and how imitation should be carried through if it should be tried at all, continued to distract Russian public policy until 1917.

In central Asia and the Far East, Russian armies were still able to advance and, in fact, annexed important new territories in the years 1850–1865. But at home everything was in confusion. Straightforward programs of economic development, aimed at catching up with the West, seemed impossible. Where would the money come from that was needed to build railroads, factories, mines, and steel mills on the scale that would be required to come abreast of Great Britain or France? But without such a program, really adequate defense against the Western powers was impossible, as had been shown in the Crimean War. On the other hand, the only justification for the czar's autocratic government was that compulsion and authority were needed to protect Russia from her enemies. If the czar's government could no longer perform that function, what claim had it to the obedience and service of the Russian people? After the scoffing irreligion of Peter the Great and Catherine II, it was hard to fall back on the theory of divine right; but the only alternative theory was popular sovereignty, which was too risky. The people, if consulted, would want to overthrow the landlords; the czar's government was not ready, as it had been in the days of Ivan the Terrible and Peter the Great, to lead a revolution of that kind, with or without the support of the people.

The effect of the Crimean War on Russia, therefore, was to open up a series of painful riddles. Cooperation between monarch and nobles, operating mainly by means of the military-civil bureaucracy, in which nobles occupied all important posts, had made Russia great in the eighteenth century. After the death of Catherine the Great (1796), however, this cooperation slowly wore itself out. For a while, the conservative policy of Alexander I (reigned 1801–1825) and Nicholas I (reigned 1825–1855) hid Russia's inner strains. But the failure of Russian arms in 1853–1856 discredited the czarist regime at home as well as abroad—without, however, provoking thoroughgoing breakdown, thoroughgoing reform, or thoroughgoing reaction. Instead a patchwork of half measures disfigured the Russian ship of state. Meanwhile, the western nations of Europe built up their power through the Industrial and Democratic revolutions, leaving Russia to flounder, falling further and further behind.

The Consequences of Ottoman Victory

The Ottoman sultan, though among the victors of the Crimean War, was no better off. The war left a Turkish debt, owed mostly to French and British bondholders. For a few years, the sultan's government met interest payments on the bonds by floating new ones; but when investors became more cautious, the cycle broke—and indignant creditors, with the help of their home governments, fastened a foreign-managed "Ottoman Public Debt Administration" upon the helpless Turks (1881). This administrative corporation had the right to collect specified taxes, mainly customs dues, to pay off the bondholders. It operated on Turkish soil without being subject to Turkish control. The victor of 1856, in other words, emerged from the war with a "ball and chain" of debt, from which the Ottoman government was never afterward able to escape.

Special privileges for foreigners were nothing new in Turkey. Europeans resident in Turkey had enjoyed the right to be judged by their own law from the time the Ottoman sultan first concluded treaties with Christian nations. The Turks took it for granted that foreigners, not being Moslems, could not be tried by Moslem courts. When the sultan was mighty and Christian traders existed on sufferance, the system worked well enough, from a Turkish point of view. When power relations were reversed, however, European consuls often gave protection to persons whose claim to be British or French subjects was very dubious. Shady characters sometimes escaped Turkish justice in this way. On the other hand, the unfairness of Turkish judges, especially when called upon to

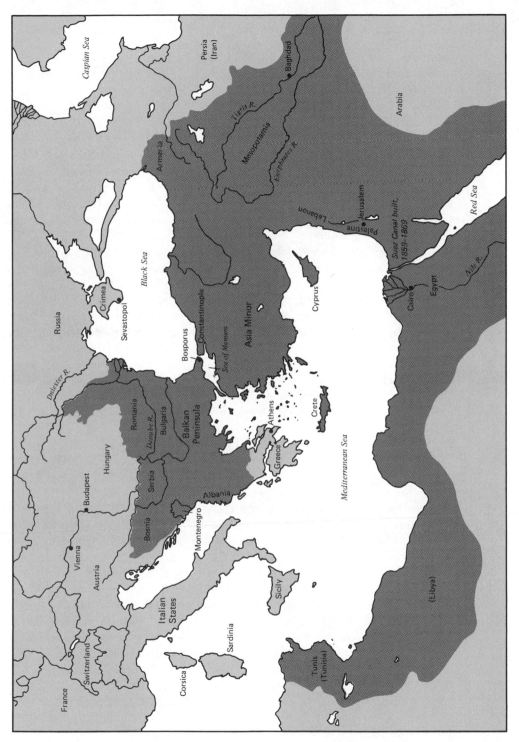

Caspian Sea

Persia
(Iran)

Baghdad

Tigris R.

Armenia

Mesopotamia

Arabia

Euphrates R.

Red Sea

Lebanon

Jerusalem

Palestine

Suez Canal built,
1859-1869

Nile R.

Black Sea

Cyprus

Egypt

Cairo

Crimea

Sevastopol

Bosporus

Constantinople

Asia Minor

Russia

Sea of Marmara

Dniester R.

Romania

Bulgaria

Balkan
Peninsula

Athens

Crete

Danube R.

Serbia

Greece

Hungary

Mediterranean Sea

Budapest

Albania

Vienna

Bosnia

Montenegro

Austria

Italian
States

Sicily

(Libya)

Switzerland

Sardinia

Tunis
(Tunisia)

France

Corsica

OTTOMAN EMPIRE 1865

237

decide a quarrel between a Christian and a Moslem, gave European consuls grounds for extending their protection to persons who could not hope for a fair trial before a Turkish court.

MOSLEM REFORM   The basic trouble with the Ottoman Empire was the lack of sympathy between Moslem rulers and Christian subjects. This, indeed, had been the real cause for the outbreak of the Crimean War. The Turks and their allies feared that if Russia were allowed to "protect" the interests of Orthodox Christians in the Ottoman Empire, before long the Russians would win over the loyalty of the Christians and be in a position to snuff out Turkish power in the Balkan Peninsula whenever the czar wanted to do so.

The British ambassador to Turkey, Lord Stratford de Redcliffe, felt sure that energetic reform could cure this situation. If new laws were applied fairly to all the sultan's subjects—Moslem, Christian, or Jew— then the possibility of creating a stable, strong state would arise. Without reform, Lord Stratford felt, even the best efforts of the British government to prop up Turkish power would be in vain. The French and Austrian ambassadors agreed. Accordingly, just as the war was ending in 1856, the sultan proclaimed the equality of all his subjects before the law. Efforts to spell out this principle in detail continued for the next ten years. The European ambassadors and advisers wanted systematic codes of law. One by one, such codes were drawn up, usually modeled on the French *Code Napoléon*.

But the reform program did not work. The sultan's Christian subjects did not trust their Turkish masters. Secret revolutionary movements soon sprang up, or took on new life. Prince Michael of Serbia (reigned 1860–1868), for example, plotted a general rising of all the Christian peoples against the Turks. The Turks, for their part, felt that the only people who benefited from the reform were Christians and Jews. They found it hard to give up the Sacred Law. After all, if Islam were the true religion— and who could doubt that and remain a Turk?—then the Sacred Law was in fact sacred, and no one had any right to annul its provisions. How then could the sultan take it upon himself to proclaim some newfangled nonsense about the equality of Jews and Christians? How indeed?

Nearly all Turks and other Moslems in the Ottoman Empire, therefore, tended to feel that the reform laws were meant for window dressing only. If the foreign ambassadors demanded such things, let them have them; but when it came to real, day-to-day personal relations, especially in the provinces, old habits persisted and the provisions of the law codes were simply disregarded. This, of course, justified revolutionary conspiracy on the part of Christians; and the existence of such conspiracies, in turn, justified the Turks in disregarding the law.

OTTOMAN SOVEREIGNTY   Turkish efforts at reform were damaged, also, by the fact that the European powers continued to chip away at Ottoman frontiers. Romania became independent as a result of the diplomatic settlement of 1856. This was no great loss, since the provinces had been effectively freed from Turkish rule since 1828; but the Turks did not like giving up their claim to these rich territories. Turkish troops were pulled back from Serbia in 1867, after troubles between the garrison of Belgrade and the Serbian populace provoked diplomatic intervention by the European powers. Turkish power over Lebanon was similarly hedged in with irritating restrictions after 1861.

On the other hand, the telegraph and, eventually, the railroad made it possible for the sultan to control what went on in remote provinces of his empire far more closely in the second half of the nineteenth century than had been possible before 1850. Hazy areas still existed in Albania, Armenia, Iraq, and Arabia, where tribal or other forms of traditional local government competed with the authority of the sultan's governors. But even in the eastern portions of the empire—where tribalism was strongest—the authority of local chiefs tended to retreat into the desert regions, where nomadic life made any other kind of government impractical. This constituted a solid gain for the central government of the empire.

Some progress also was made toward modernization of the Ottoman army. Turkish troops, trained and equipped in the European fashion, had done well against the Russians in the Crimean War, and Turkish tradition made soldiering come easy. But the Ottoman government never even tried to build the industrial base needed to equip Turkish troops from home production. Instead, they relied on foreign-made equipment.

From 1839 on, the Ottoman government officially accepted the principles of free trade. This meant giving up any attempt to protect local artisans from the competition of European machine-made goods. As railroads were built inland, the disruption of artisan life, which resulted from this policy, moved inland too. But no one in authority cared very much, or even understood what was going on. Local resentments were fierce enough, but usually found expression in rival nationalisms. Christian artisans, after all, suffered as well as Moslems. Each group blamed the other— and let it go at that.

In the aftermath of the Crimean War, therefore, the Ottoman Empire formally and publicly cut loose from the traditional Islamic ordering of society. Legal reform, along European lines, officially left the Sacred Law behind; but distrust among the different religious and national groups within the empire made the new laws unenforceable. The trouble was that laws imported wholesale from the West did not fit Ottoman society. Few Turks believed in the reform program; and Balkan Christians soon pinned their hopes on national independence.

The spread of nationalism was, of course, profoundly subversive of the Ottoman state, for the various nationalities that lived together under the sultan could not separate into independent nation-states without first destroying the empire. Yet this was what reform led to. How, then, could Turks and other Moslems support a program that asked them first to give up their religion and cultural identity, and then to watch their Christian subjects throw off Turkish control? But there seemed no alternative. The old traditions of Ottoman government were dead and gone; and the heirs of that tradition could not come up with any practical line of action.

Reforms in India

India, also, suffered drastic change between 1850 and 1865. The central event was what the British called the Sepoy Mutiny of 1857–1858. This was a rebellion of Indian soldiers, called sepoys, and it led to the suppression both of the Mogul Empire of Delhi and of the East India Company. The revolt, in turn, was touched off partly by news of Turkish (that is, Moslem) victories against Christians; but this was not the main cause.

The Indian soldiers, whom the East India Company hired to sustain its power in India, had many grievances. What started the mutiny was a rumor to the effect that a new drill routine would require the soldiers to violate religious taboos. To be exact, the British planned to pack powder charges for new muzzle-loading army muskets in little paper packets. In this way, an even amount of powder could be put in with each shot. To protect the powder from moisture, the paper was soaked with grease; and the Indian sepoys discovered—or assumed—that this was pig's fat, which was prohibited for Moslems, or else beef fat, which was prohibited for Hindus. The only way to open the packages was to bite off a corner, which, of course, meant ritual defilement.

This particular collision between new techniques and religious taboos was only one of many. British policy in India had changed. Before 1800 the East India Company went to great lengths to avoid offending local customs and respected all religious traditions. Christian missions, for example, had been forbidden, and the Mogul administrative language, Urdu, had been maintained even in provinces ruled directly by the company. Once British power in India became clearly superior to any rival (1818), the original grounds for this policy disappeared. Moreover, the Company came under attack at home for not admitting missionaries and for allowing various "wicked customs and heathen habits" to go on unchecked.

In 1837 it was decided to shift the language of administration from

Urdu to English; but the change came slowly, since it required the establishment of schools to teach English to clerks and other subordinate officials of the government. But by the late 1840s, British power really began to bite into traditional Indian life. James Andrew Ramsay, Lord Dalhousie, governor general of India from 1848–1856, put the whole force of the East India Company's administration behind such improvements as building a rail and postal system uniting all India, as well as the construction of telegraphic and road communications, irrigation projects, and similar public works. He also annexed important new territories, acting on the principle that when a ruling prince died without a direct heir, his territory ought to come under direct Company administration.

The Sepoy Mutiny of 1857 interrupted these enterprises, but only briefly. The soldiers acted in fear and anger. They knew vaguely what they were against: all the newfangled nonsense their British masters were bringing in so energetically. But they had no positive program, and the sharp differences between Moslems and Hindus failed to come into the open only because of their common enmity to the British.

For a few weeks the whole British position in India seemed threatened, for the Company kept very few white troops in India. Reinforcements soon arrived, however, and one by one the centers of resistance were reduced. Within two years, British power was fully restored. The British Parliament took the occasion to reorganize the government of India, bringing it under a cabinet minister in London.

The new regime plunged ahead with remodeling Indian government and law. The overriding idea was to unite the country by a system of communications and administration and to station enough English troops in the land to make sure that any local disturbances—such as those that started the mutiny—could be snuffed out before the flame of rebellion spread. In addition, the British hoped and believed that a just and fair administration, acting in accordance with published laws, would remove grievances and make the Indian people loyal and obedient subjects. In 1853, recruitment into the Indian Civil Service was put on the basis of competitive examination, with the result that intellectually inclined graduates of Oxford and Cambridge, trained in the traditions of the English upper classes, began to govern India. Legal reforms, separating administrative from judicial functions, followed. In 1861 legislative and executive councils were established, in which British administrators and Indian subjects sat together to decide local problems of government.

In this way India came under the rule of a benevolent despotism, inspired by liberal principles. Those things that British custom assigned to the sphere of government were usually carried through with thoroughness, impartiality, and efficiency. But whatever belonged, by British practice, to the private sector was left strictly alone. The results were oddly lopsided. Efficient, limited government was superimposed upon age-old custom. Custom gave way where it had to, but elsewhere remained little changed, since whatever was "private" in British eyes lay beyond the self-imposed limits of their jurisdiction. Private custom stood in the way of modern industrial development, for example. But because the government took British ideas of free trade and private business initiative for granted, public authorities did nothing to develop that sort of modernity.

Military security, however, was very much a part of the government's concern. In addition to making it routine to station significant numbers of British troops in the country, the government of India set out to erect a protective sphere of influence on every side of the subcontinent. The British occupied Aden, at the mouth of the Red Sea, in 1839; they intervened in Persia and Afghanistan to make sure that only rulers friendly to them should hold power there; they made similar arrangements in Zanzibar and Oman (1862). The situation in Egypt was more complicated, for there French influence competed, and sometimes cooperated, with the British. The great struggle was over whether or not to cut a canal through the Isthmus of Suez. In 1854 the ruler of Egypt agreed to let a French company build a canal; but the British opposed the scheme and managed to delay matters for several years. As a result, the Suez Canal was not opened for traffic until 1869. When the canal was completed, the British government bought the shares that had been assigned to the Egyptian government and thus secured an effective voice in the management of the canal company. With the opening of the Suez Canal the "life line of empire," connecting Great Britain with India, ran through the Mediterranean. In that sea, British naval power had to compete with French, Italian, and other navies; but further south, beyond Suez, the shores of the Arabian Sea and of the Persian Gulf were firmly under British influence by 1865.

The new regime in India, together with British diplomatic activity in Arabia, Persia, and Afghanistan, reduced the eastern heartland of the Moslem world to nearly the same state of helpless dependency that afflicted the Ottoman Empire. By supplying a few guns, or refusing powder and shot to a stubborn sheik, the British could make and break dynasties and kingdoms along the shores of Arabia and the Persian Gulf. To the north lay Russia, whose appetite for Moslem territory was never in doubt. In 1849–1854, the czar's troops pushed back Persian frontiers, occupying the Syr Darya valley. Then the outbreak of the Crimean War interrupted their advance. After the war, the Russians resumed expansion at the expense of the Kirghiz people, who lived as nomads on part of the central Asian steppe.

In such a situation, most Moslems despaired of public life and military-political action. They concentrated instead on a more rigorous and exact performance of private religious observances. The central inspiration for this movement came from Arabia, where Abdul-Wahhab had founded a rigorist movement in the eighteenth century. At first, the Wahhabi reform was closely tied up with the military career of the Saud family; but when Egyptian armies defeated the Saudis in 1818, Wahhabism began to spread more widely among Arabs and Indian Moslems. Turks and Persians, on the other hand, were not interested. The narrow emphasis upon Koranic lore could not appeal easily to these two peoples, whose native speech was not Arabic, and whose ancestors had brought the changes to Islam that the Wahhabi reformers set out to undo.

COLLAPSE OF THE FAR EASTERN CITADELS

Both the Manchu emperors of China and the Tokugawa shoguns of Japan found themselves in deep trouble in 1850. The key problems were internal. In China, the great mass of the peasantry had begun to stir. In Japan, it was the "outside lords" who were becoming restless. But in both cases, traditional methods of government seemed ineffective in meeting the new challenges. Dismay and uncertainty grew among the inner circle at court. No one knew what to do or how to do it.

China

China's case was by far the most critical. In 1842 the emperor had been forced to make terms with the British and to open key Chinese ports to European trade. Eight years later an obscure prophet, Hung Hsiu-ch'üan, announced the establishment of the "Heavenly Kingdom of Great Peace" in Taiping. Hung Hsiu-ch'üan had spent a short time in a Protestant missionary school; later he began to see visions, mixing old Chinese ideas with Christian teachings about the end of the world and the Second Coming of Christ.

In ordinary times the words of such a man as Hung Hsiu-ch'üan would not have attracted much attention, but in 1850 he was able to arouse smoldering discontents that had been accumulating for years. The Taiping movement was mainly a peasant revolt. Millions upon millions of poverty-stricken Chinese peasants responded to the promise of a heavenly kingdom, interpreting it to mean the end of rents and taxes. But, of course, it was impossible to create or maintain an army without some kind of income. Hence, when an army became necessary to hold off and then drive back Manchu forces, the Taiping movement came face to face

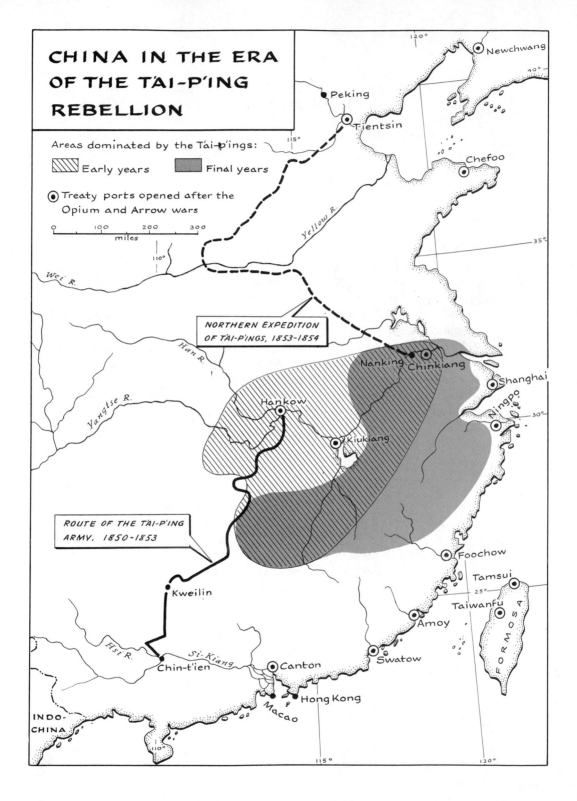

CHINA IN THE ERA OF THE TAI-P'ING REBELLION

Areas dominated by the Tai-p'ings:

Early years   Final years

⊙ Treaty ports opened after the Opium and Arrow wars

0   100   200   300
miles

NORTHERN EXPEDITION OF TAI-P'INGS, 1853-1854

ROUTE OF THE TAI-P'ING ARMY, 1850-1853

Newchwang

Peking

Tientsin

Chefoo

Wei R.

Yellow R.

Han R.

Yangtse R.

Nanking   Chinkiang

Shanghai

Hankow

Ningpo

Kiukiang

Foochow

Tamsui

Kweilin

Taiwanfu

Amoy

FORMOSA

Hsi R.

Si-Kiang

Chin-t'ien

Canton

Swatow

Macao   Hong Kong

INDO-CHINA

with the crisis that always besets a successful peasant rebellion: how to organize a new government that can be strong enough to survive when the rebelling peasants want only to be left alone and not have to pay anybody anything.

The Taiping leaders never solved this problem. Hung Hsiu-ch'üan himself was a seer of visions, not an administrator. Some of his followers proved to be good generals, but they never had help from a regularly organized government supporting them in the rear. Consequently, the Taiping armies had to live by plunder. This hurt their popularity with the peasants and eventually allowed the forces of the imperial court to win. For several years, however, when the vision of the Heavenly Kingdom of Great Peace was still fresh and bright, the weakness at the heart of the Taiping movement was not apparent. From their point of origin in the southern part of China, the Taiping forces moved northward, reached the Yangtze River, and in 1854 captured Shanghai. By then much of south China was in Taiping hands, and the peasants of the north were only waiting for the arrival of their liberators to join in the revolt.

Moslems in the western provinces of China organized a revolt of their own; so did other minority groups. Banditry broke out in other provinces. Then, on top of these disasters, new quarrels with the British and the French led, in 1857, to hostilities and fresh humiliation for the Chinese at European hands. The Treaties of Tientsin (1858) restored peace briefly. But when the Chinese delayed making some of the concessions promised by those treaties, the French and British organized a military raid on Peking, and in 1860 burned down the emperor's summer palace. Such an act confirmed Chinese opinions of the "south sea barbarians," but for the time being the imperial government had to give in on all points of dispute. New treaties admitted British, French, American, and Russian diplomats, missionaries, traders, and adventurers to the capital and to any other part of China they cared to visit.

During these same disastrous years, the Yellow River changed its course. Instead of flowing to the sea south of the Shantung Peninsula, as it had done for centuries, the river broke its banks and found a new course to the sea far to the north of its former channel. But before the river settled into its new banks, vast and destructive floods spread over the lower plain of the Yellow River. Millions of Chinese died as a result. Yet the floods helped to save the Manchu government. When the Taiping soldiers started north for Peking, still in the first flush of their early successes, and when the peasants everywhere were still ready to welcome them as liberators, the floods stopped the advance.

Thereafter, the Taiping cause began to suffer defeats. The framework of Manchu administration had never broken down completely; so the emperor was able to keep soldiers in the field, even if they were dispirited and inefficient fighters. Soon quarrels broke out in the ranks of the Taiping army. Hung Hsiu-ch'üan expected miracles; none came. Instead the imperial forces began to win victories until, by 1864, the Taiping Rebellion was crushed. Hung Hsiu-ch'üan poisoned himself.

Millions upon millions of people died as a result of the disorders and natural disasters that descended upon China in these years. This calamity, by itself, made life a little easier for those who survived. There was more land to go around and innumerable old debts washed away in the confusion. Thus the Chinese had a breathing space after 1865. Nevertheless, the government failed to use it effectively.

It is easy to understand why. The Taiping rebels had been put down by traditional measures. In the next few years, military operations against the Moslems and other unruly groups also proved successful. To be sure, the Westerners remained a thorn in China's side. Yet their impact was blunted by the poverty and disorder of the countryside, which interfered with trade and made missionaries' lives unsafe. Nearly all of China's rulers and learned men heartily disliked and despised the bad manners of the white barbarians from Europe and America. They hoped in time, to be able to drive them away. In the meantime, the best thing to do was to neglect the intruders as much as possible.

This policy was foredoomed to failure, for China's weakness was too great. The traditional order that had achieved such brilliant heights a century before could not survive internal crisis and Western assault.

Commodore Perry meets the Japanese Commissioners in the 1885 illustration. (*New York Public Library Picture Collection*)

And the peasant crisis had not been solved, only postponed; still less had the Western challenge been met. The old order, as in Moslem lands and in India, was in hopeless disrepair. Yet no one knew what to do; agreement on new courses of action could not be achieved; confusion and bafflement reigned, as in the other lands that were feeling the effect of Western superiority.

Japan

Japan followed a very different course. A small, power-seeking clique of reformers set out to make Japan safe by making it strong. This required modern industry to supply an army and navy. But modern industry required new skills and knowledge; and these in turn required a new kind of school system and many other changes in traditional Japanese life. But once launched on the path of radical readjustment, the Japanese leaders never flinched from undertaking the next necessary step.

The first landmark of this extraordinary development came in 1854, when the shogun gave up the policy, in effect since 1638, of shutting Japan off from ordinary contact with the outside world. What triggered this decision was a United States naval mission, sent to Japan under the command of Admiral Matthew C. Perry. When the American warships first appeared in 1853, they were rebuffed; but the next year, when Admiral Perry returned, the Japanese government meekly agreed to open two ports to foreign ships. In 1858 Japan agreed to a detailed commercial treaty with the United States, to which Holland, Russia, Britain, and France later adhered.

The shogun's weakness in knuckling under to the foreigners made a good rallying cry for patriotic warriors and clan leaders who were jealous of the position long held by the Tokugawa family. They focused their loyalty upon the person of the emperor. The ideas of Shinto, which had developed into an increasingly public religion, provided popular justification for the restoration of the emperor's powers. Behind the scenes, however, informal alliances and rivalries among the military clans stood at the center of politics.

The shogun's position was undermined by uncertainties about the right of succession, for direct heirs of the Tokugawa line had died out. The individuals who occupied the shogunate in its last years were weak and ineffective persons. In addition, they were by no means sure that the new policy of opening the country to foreign contacts was wise or safe. Consequently, they were divided and halfhearted; their rivals became more and more united around patriotic slogans—and the hidden figure of the emperor.

The upshot was a coup d'état in 1867. The shogun abdicated, and a new, young emperor officially took command of affairs. Members of what were called the "outside clans" took over all the key positions around the emperor's person. Yet on their way to power, the new rulers of Japan had a sobering experience. In 1864 a combined British, French, Dutch, and American fleet bombarded and destroyed several Japanese coastal forts, as a way of showing the displeasure of the Western powers at widespread antiforeign outbreaks in Japan. This demonstration of Western naval superiority convinced the men who took control in 1867 that anti-Western policies, without the power to defend the country, were not going to work. They therefore gave up their anti-Westernism, at least for the time being, in order to learn how to be strong.

Having once made this decision, there was no turning back and remarkably little hesitation. Whatever was needed for the creation of a strong, modern army and navy, Japan had to have. When it turned out that this meant an entirely new industrial technology with drastic educational, social, and political reforms, the Japanese leaders never faltered. Peasants and commoners obeyed; the leaders commanded; and modern Japan began to emerge with amazing rapidity, within a single generation.

The Japanese were, of course, aware of China's difficulties when they made their fateful decision to open their country to Western contacts. The news spread throughout southeast Asia, where the British pushed into Burma and the French went into Annam, Laos, and Cambodia in the 1860s. When China trembled, these satellite states shook. Their rulers made little effort to resist the force of European arms. Siam remained independent, more as a buffer between French and British imperial spheres than because of any inherent strength that the ruling dynasty commanded. For another decade Korea, alone, remained an independent, hermit kingdom; but in 1876 that last, remote bastion of the Far Eastern circle of civilized communities also opened its ports to Western trade.

CIVIL WAR IN AMERICA

During the short period of time when these far-reaching changes were taking place in Asia, the United States of America came of age as a full-fledged participant in Western civilization. The national borders attained almost their present shape after a war with Mexico (1846) led to the annexation of California and Texas and territories in between. The Gadsden Purchase (1853–1854) added a strip of land in the extreme south of what is now New Mexico and Arizona, to facilitate construction of a

The American Civil War: Confederate dead behind the stone wall of Mayre's Heights at Frederichsburg, Virginia, captured by Union forces on May 3, 1863 during the battle of Chancellorsville. (National Archives)

transcontinental railroad. In 1867 the federal government purchased Alaska from the Russians, thus attaining the country's present continental limits.

For a while it seemed uncertain whether a federal government would prove capable of holding such an enormous territory together. Loyalties to the separate states were strong; in the 1850s sectional loyalties began to create larger and scarcely less powerful political blocs. The issue that crystallized sectional feeling was slavery. In the southern states, preservation of the "peculiar institution" of Negro slavery attracted fanatical support; partly, at least, because the southerners were fearful of what would happen if the slaves were freed. Visions of economic disaster, if not of bloody revolution, haunted their dreams. In the northern states, meanwhile, dislike of slavery increased. It seemed uncivilized, inhumane, and a disgrace to America. Fanatical abolitionists matched southern fanaticism; compromise became more and more difficult.

In 1860 the Union fell apart. Abraham Lincoln was elected President, but without an absolute majority. Moreover, his support was wholly in the North and West; the South feared and distrusted him as spokesman and leader of the new Republican party. Southern states decided to withdraw and form their own confederacy, appealing to the same principles that had been used to justify the American Revolution. But Lincoln and the North refused to admit that withdrawal was permissible. War ensued: long, bloody, and desperate. The war was popular in the sense that both governments commanded strong emotional support from the rear. In the end the North won because of superior numbers and superior industrial output; but until almost the very end, the southern will to resist was never in doubt. Such tenacity raised difficult problems for a national government that professed to derive its just powers from consent of the governed.

At first, slavery was not officially the issue, but in 1863 Lincoln decided to publish an Emancipation Proclamation. Thereafter the advance of Union armies into southern territory meant liberation of the slaves. Full citizen rights were conferred upon the liberated slaves by the Thirteenth, Fourteenth, and Fifteenth Amendments to the United States Constitution. These were adopted between 1865 and 1870; but in practice, systematic discrimination against the new black citizens continued to be a marked feature of American life.

The long years of civil war created a great demand for everything needed to equip huge armies. Rapid expansion of railroads also opened a vast new market for iron and steel mills. The result was a tremendous boom in the North that quickly made the United States an important industrial producer. American factory technology came abreast of the latest English and European practices and in some fields, such as the mechanization of agriculture, the United States took the lead over the rest of the world. As a result, dramatic increases in the export of wheat became possible, even during the war years when large numbers of farm boys fought in the armies and had to be fed, without themselves helping to produce the crop.

Victory for the North, therefore, meant victory also for an expanding industry and for mechanized agriculture. Hoe cultivation and hand-picking lasted in the cotton fields of the defeated South for another eighty years or so; but it was precisely this style of agriculture and the society built around it that had been defeated. America's future was not to rest with a sharply divided society, in which the forced labor of slaves maintained a few plantation owners. A much more varied and complex society prevailed, in which market prices and individual shrewdness—at least in theory—regulated production and consumption.

This new and growing American society differed in some respects from the pattern familiar across the Atlantic in England and western Europe. Aristocratic elements were almost absent from the American scene, and barriers to the rise of individuals from one social class to another were weaker in the United States than in Europe. Despite such differences, Americans shared the skills and ideas of western Europe, and the eastern seaboard of the northern United States had almost caught up with England and France by 1865. Moreover, the United States had begun to expand toward its political frontiers by planting technically skilled communities all across the continent. The energies of the American people were engaged in this task throughout the next generation, when, except in the defeated South, both the work and the means to perform it stood ready at hand; and no really important doubts troubled the public mind.

America's success contrasted sharply with the doubts and difficulties that afflicted Russia, China, India, and the Moslem world. Yet it would be wrong to forget that the nation's success simply side-stepped the problems created by the South's defeat. That part of the United States took little part in the industrial upsurge. The South remained backward, poor, and ignorant—only a marginal sharer in the busy, greedy, restless and increasingly urban world of the North, which had come into its own so suddenly during the Civil War years.

THE REST OF THE WORLD

Improved communication and transportation, which brought Western power to bear upon the Asian civilizations between 1850 and 1865, also had consequences for the rest of the world. In Australia and New Zealand, for example, English settlement advanced inland very rapidly. This was particularly stimulated by the discovery of gold in the interior of Australia in 1851. The news set off a gold rush comparable to the California gold rush of 1849. The surviving British colonies of North America, except for Newfoundland, federated in 1867 to become the Dominion of Canada. The promise of a transcontinental railroad brought British Columbia into the new dominion; but an additional motive was a fear of the United States, where patriotic Irishmen and others wished to even old scores with the British by liberating the rest of North America from Queen Victoria's rule.

Africa

In South Africa the frontier of European settlement also moved inland after the "great trek" (1835–1837), when several thousand Dutch-speaking Boer families moved northward to escape British control. The Boers set up their own republics in the interior of South Africa and used their superior weapons to subdue the Bantu tribes they encountered. The Boers often treated the Africans harshly, though not as harshly as frontier settlers treated the American Indians in the United States. But the Bantu peoples whom the Boers encountered in the interior did not die off and disappear in the way that American Indians did. African spears were no match for European rifles, to be sure; but the Bantu tribal life, based on farming and cattle raising, survived.

Northward, the geography of sub-Saharan Africa became known to Europeans between the 1770s and the 1880s through the work of a heroic company of explorers. David Livingstone, the most famous of them, crossed the continent (1853–1856) and discovered Victoria Falls on the Zambezi River. His later trips made clear the layout of the African great lakes. An American, Henry Morton Stanley, explored the Congo River system (1874–1877). But not until the 1880s were all the main features of the African continent made known to European map makers.

The exploration of Africa was inspired by missionary and humanitarian feeling as well as by national rivalries and scientific curiosity. European political and commercial influence lagged behind exploration. As a result, the scramble to divide Africa among European states did not gain momentum until after the years with which we are here concerned. Except in the south, where the Bantus had to submit either to the Boers or to the British, and in the north, where the Algerians were forced to submit to the French, the various African peoples remained politically independent, and most of them were not yet profoundly affected by the European presence along the coasts.

Latin America

In Latin America, the years 1850–1865 were not of especial significance except in Mexico. In 1861 the Mexican government stopped payment of interest on government bonds. France, Spain, and Great Britain decided to intervene. The French sent enough troops to install a Hapsburg archduke, Maximilian, as emperor of Mexico in 1864. Mexican "liberals" resisted the French. Their main enemy had been the church, whose lands they wished to confiscate. French intervention widened and deepened the conflict. For the first time, peasants of Indian descent began to take part in the resistance to Maximilian.

When the American Civil War ended in 1865, the United States government made clear that it regarded French interference in Mexico (or anywhere else in the New World) as an unfriendly act. Napoleon III soon decided to withdraw his troops from Mexico. As a result, Maximilian was captured and killed (1867); and the liberals, led by Benito Juárez (d. 1872), himself a Zapotec Indian, came to power. The revolution did not go very far; but the Indian and mestizo (part Spanish, part Indian) majority asserted itself politically for the first time by challenging the dominance of a small upper class of purely Spanish descent.

CONCLUSION

Although Latin America was not particularly transformed between 1850 and 1865, and although these years were not particularly critical in western Europe, in most of the rest of the world the period was crucial. The Moslem and Far Eastern worlds were shaken up badly. Russia and the United States reacted to Europe's Industrial and Democratic revolutions in sharply different fashions. Everywhere barriers to the advance of Westerners came tumbling down. As never before, world-girdling communications bound all people together into a single interacting whole. A new age of global cosmopolitanism, centered upon western Europe, leaped into being—full-grown and armored. Humankind could never be the same, nor could Europe. We shall devote the next chapter to a closer look at what was going on in Europe, before turning back to study the world's reactions to European expansion in the period before World War I.

CHAPTER 8

Europe

1850 to 1914

European political, economic, and cultural life in the second half of the nineteenth century and the first few years of the twentieth century was, for the most part, buoyantly self-confident. This was the great age of the European middle classes, who saw themselves and the rest of humankind becoming richer and wiser and, perhaps, even better as time went on. Not everyone believed in progress, but most Europeans who wrote and spoke about such matters took the idea pretty much for granted.

There were solid reasons for such confidence. New machines and new knowledge, especially in the physical sciences, came forward at an accelerating pace; and each new device or idea seemed clearly better than what it supplanted. Human life also became more comfortable, and health improved with the advance of medical skill. In politics, wider and wider circles of the population began to take part in elections and party organization. Education became more nearly universal. Riches increased, and even the poor and unskilled began to experience some benefits from Europe's advancing wealth.

To be sure, there was an underworld to all this progress. Women were legally subordinated to men in such matters as the right to hold property and to vote. Poor people were afraid of unemployment, and they suffered severely in time of illness. Labor in factories and mines was often dangerous and poorly paid. Strikes and the rise of socialist political parties expressed the discontent of industrial workers. Such problems were troublesome indeed for the European middle classes, but what toppled them from their privileged position as leaders of society was international instability. Each of the major European governments engaged in rivalries overseas, trying to build up its political and economic power in Asia, Africa, and other distant regions of the earth. Similar rivalries existed on European soil too, dividing France from Germany, Russia from Austria, and lining up each Balkan nation against others in a tangle that puzzled and dismayed the diplomats of western Europe.

The upshot in 1914 was the sudden outbreak of World War I, and through that war the breakup of much that had been characteristic of nineteenth-century Europe.

POLITICAL CHANGES

In the spring of 1848 a rash of revolutions spread across Europe, starting from Paris and reaching all the way to Berlin and Vienna. Before the end of 1849 the liberal hope of establishing free and constitutional governments in Europe had failed. In France, the Second Republic had come into existence when King Louis Philippe resigned; but in June, 1848, bloody fighting broke out in the streets of Paris between the poor, who wanted improvements in their economic lot, and the regular army. After the "June Days" the French middle classes, as well as the propertied peasants in the countryside, wanted a strong government. They therefore elected Louis Napoleon, the great Napoleon's nephew, first as president of the Republic (1848) and then in 1852 as emperor.

The failure of the 1848–1849 revolutions meant a split in the ranks of those who opposed the system of society and government that had emerged from the Congress of Vienna (1815). All over Europe, middle-class liberals lost confidence. King, officials and landlords continued to run the government without paying much attention to liberal demands for a voice in public affairs. Worse than that, in central Europe elected representatives had been unable to agree among themselves as to where national boundaries ought to run. Nasty quarrels between Germans and Czechs, Germans and Hungarians, Hungarians and Croats—to mention only the most bitter—made it clear that these nationalities would not willingly agree to work together peaceably. What, then, happened to the liberal ideal of popular self-government when representatives of the popular will had failed so miserably?

A second fear eroded the liberal faith. Could the lower classes be trusted? Could workers, whose numbers grew rapidly with the onset of the Industrial Revolution, really take part in self-government? Would they try to seize the property of others and vote for socialist or communist agitators? Many business leaders and professionals concluded that revolution was dangerous and futile. Cooperation with nobles and monarchs and with the army and police seemed necessary to keep the lower classes quiet and in their place.

Some radicals stuck to the older faith in popular self-government, and even welcomed the idea of expanding the ideal of equality to include economic equality. The most important spokesmen for this position were two young writers, Karl Marx (1818–1883) and Friedrich Engels (1820–1895), who published a fiery little pamphlet in 1848—just before the revolutions began—entitled *Communist Manifesto*. It explained how all history had been a class struggle. First slaveholders, then feudal lords, and finally capitalists had dominated society by getting hold of the "means of production" (that is, first land and then, in more recent times, machinery and money). But, Marx declared, the capitalist system would bring its own destruction by concentrating wealth in fewer and fewer hands, while making more and more workers propertyless.

Marx had in mind, in making this prediction, the fact that machine-made goods had been driving small artisans out of business all over Europe and in other parts of the world. Such people often did lose their property, tools, and shops, and had to start working for others for wages. Many artisans resisted the process, hanging on grimly to the bitter end, in hopeless competition with machines. By assuming that the destruction of independent artisans would go on unchecked until a tiny number of great manufacturers controlled the whole industrial process, Marx envisioned a time when the propertyless proletariat, millions strong, would find it easy to seize the means of production from the capitalists. Such a revolutionary act, he thought, would inaugurate the final socialist or communist stage of history, when universal brotherhood, freedom, and equality would prevail.

This vision of the future gave a more radical definition to the French revolutionary ideal of democratic equality. When political parties arose which accepted the Marxian program, they called themselves Social Democrats. Because of Marx and his followers, from 1848 onward the Democratic Revolution had a socialist as well as a liberal wing.

Unification of Germany and Italy

Middle-class liberals who feared socialism found an alternative in nationalism. Socialists emphasized the international brotherhood of the working class. But most persons, including members of the industrial working class, proved more interested in identifying themselves with a great and power-

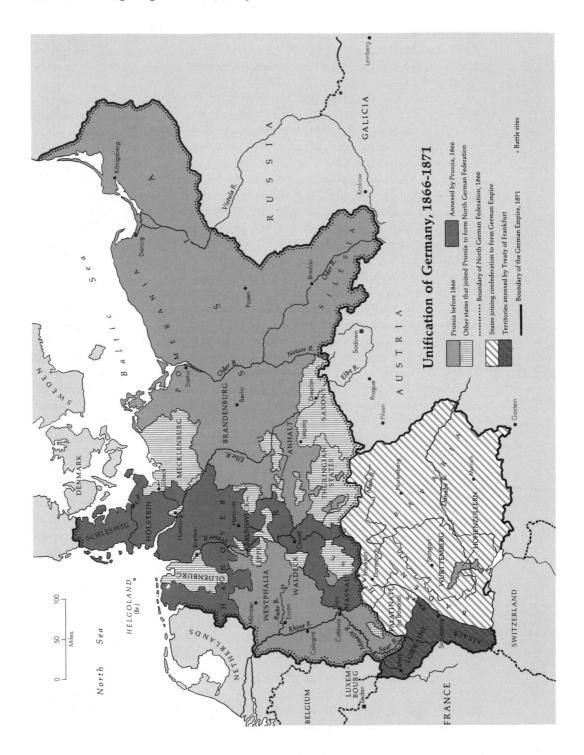

Unification of Germany, 1866-1871

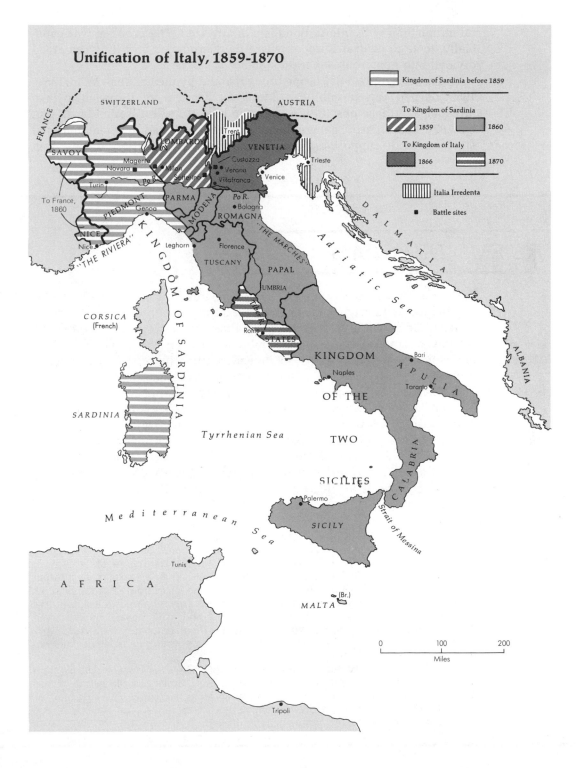

Unification of Italy, 1859-1870

Kingdom of Sardinia before 1859

To Kingdom of Sardinia
1859   1860

To Kingdom of Italy
1866   1870

Italia Irredenta

■ Battle sites

SWITZERLAND

AUSTRIA

FRANCE

SAVOY

LOMBARDY

Trent

VENETIA

Magenta
Novara
Milan
Custozza
Verona
Villafranca

Turin
Po R.
Solferino

Trieste

To France, 1860

Genoa

PARMA

Po R.

Venice

NICE

MODENA

Bologna

ROMAGNA

Nice

"THE RIVIERA"

"THE MARCHES"

D A L M A T I A

Leghorn

Florence

CORSICA
(French)

TUSCANY

PAPAL

UMBRIA

A d r i a t i c   S e a

Rome

KINGDOM

STATES

KINGDOM

Bari

OF

Naples

A P U L I A

SARDINIA

SARDINIA

OF THE

Taranto

ALBANIA

Tyrrhenian Sea

TWO

C A L A B R I A

SICILIES

Palermo

Strait of Messina

M e d i t e r r a n e a n   S e a

SICILY

Tunis

A F R I C A

(Br.)

MALTA

0   100   200
Miles

Tripoli

ful nation than with internationalism of any kind. The problem was especially acute in central Europe, where the Germanies and Italy remained divided into numerous separate states.

The realignment of Europe brought about by the Crimean War (1853–1856) opened new possibilities. Moreover, leaders bold enough to take advantage of these possibilities arose in both Italy and Germany, so that by 1871 both these "geographical expressions" had become national states. Liberals supported the movement for the unification of Italy from

THE EMS TELEGRAM

In the summer of 1870, Count Otto von Bismarck, Prussian prime minister, wanted war with France. He figured that if the independent south German states could be made to fight alongside Prussia and the newly established North German Confederation, patriotic enthusiasm would make the final unification of Germany easy. So, indeed, matters turned out. But starting a war without seeming to be the aggressor took some doing.

Bismarck's chance came when Spaniards offered the vacant throne of their country to a prince of the house of Hohenzollern. The prince was a distant relative of King Wilhelm of Prussia. The French objected, and the prince promptly backed down. Everything seemed over. But the French wanted assurance from the king of Prussia, who was taking his ease at a holiday resort named Ems. What happened next is best told in the language of a telegram sent from Ems to Bismarck in Berlin by the king's aide:

> His Majesty the King [of Prussia] wrote me: "Count Benedetti [the French ambassador] approached me on the promenade and asked me—eventually in a very insistent manner—to authorize him to telegraph immediately saying that I promised for all time to come that I would never again give my consent if the Hohenzollern family should again become a candidate [for the Spanish throne]. I let him know, at the end a bit sternly, that no one could give such an assurance for all time. Naturally I said to him that I had received no new information, and since he was more currently informed from Paris and Madrid than I he very well knew that my government again was out of the running.
>
> His Majesty has, since then, received a message from the prince [that is, from the candidate for the Spanish throne]. Since His Majesty had said to Count Benedetti that he expected news from the prince, the king himself, thinking back to the aforesaid encounter, instructed Count Eulenberg and myself not to receive Count Benedetti again, but to inform him through an

the beginning. In Germany, they first opposed Otto von Bismarck's reliance upon "blood and iron" instead of elections as a way of settling matters. But when Bismarck turned out to be successful in defeating Austria (1866) and uniting north German states under Prussia, most of his liberal critics were silenced. He went on to pick a quarrel with France and defeated Louis Napoleon (1870), and then persuaded the south German states to join in a new German Empire (1871), with Prussia's king as emperor. In face of such a string of successes, liberal opposition to Bismarck's use of trickery and force evaporated. As "national liberals" they proved eager

adjutant that His Majesty had just received from the prince the information that Benedetti had already had from Paris, and that the king had nothing more to say to the [French] ambassador.

His Majesty puts it to your Excellency [Bismarck] whether the new demand of Benedetti and its rejection should not be shared with the press and our ambassadors.*

When he got this telegram, Bismarck saw his chance. He edited the king's message and gave it to the press in the following form:

After the news of the renunciation of the Hohenzollern prince [of his candidacy from the Spanish throne] had been officially communicated to the imperial French government by the royal government of Spain, the French ambassador at Ems demanded additionally of His Majesty the King [of Prussia] that he authorized him [Benedetti] to telegraph Paris that His Majesty promised for all time to come never again to give his consent, if the Hohenzollern family should again return to candidacy.

His Majesty thereupon declined to see the French ambassador again and informed him, through an official adjutant, that His Majesty had nothing more to communicate to the ambassador.*

The result was all that Bismarck wished. Both sides felt insulted. The French rushed to declare war but Prussia and the other German states were far better prepared. Soon the Germans won great victories and started to besiege Paris. In a surge of patriotic feeling, the rulers of the separate German states gathered at Versailles in January, 1871, to proclaim King Wilhelm of Prussia the emperor of Germany.

Thus a powerful, new, united Germany had its birth just outside Paris, in the palace which Louis XIV had built as a sign and symbol of the grandeur of France.

* The bracketed interpolations and translation are from *Bismarck, the Hohenzollern Candidacy and the Origins of the Franco-German War of 1870* by Lawrence D. Steefel, published by Harvard University Press.

to cooperate with conservatives, such as Bismarck, to make a success of the new German Empire.

Count Camillo Cavour (1810–1861) engineered the unification of Italy by using much the same methods Bismarck used in Germany. The difference was that Cavour was a liberal who believed in parliaments and constitutions; and that the kingdom of Sardinia, around which Italy united, was only a second-rate power and could not engage Austria by itself with any hope of success. Cavour, therefore, reached an agreement with Louis Napoleon of France, according to which the French agreed to help the Sardinians in war against Austria. Louis Napoleon wanted glory such as his uncle had won in Italy. He also wanted to upset the Vienna settlement—and believed that it was good politics to be on the side of the people, when possible. He furthermore made Cavour promise to give France two small bits of territory, Nice and Savoy, that would extend the French frontiers to the Alps.

Then Cavour picked a quarrel with Austria in 1859. The French came to his aid and defeated the Austrian armies in northern Italy, but tried to make peace before Italy's unification was complete. That did not satisfy Italian nationalists, who provoked popular uprisings all through central Italy. A dramatic expedition of volunteers known as the "Redshirts," led by Giuseppe Garibaldi against the kingdom of Naples, brought the south into the new kingdom of Italy.

In the northeast, Venetia remained under Austrian control until 1866, and the pope continued to rule Rome until 1870. But the pope's power over Rome depended on the presence of French troops. These were withdrawn when Louis Napoleon blundered into war with Germany. The Italian government then moved in and made Rome the capital of united Italy; but the pope refused to recognize their right to do so. Feuding between the papacy and the government of Italy continued until 1929, when a treaty gave full sovereign powers to the pope within the part of Rome where he lived (that is, the Vatican palace and some nearby areas). In return, the pope surrendered the papacy's historic rights to rule Rome and the papal states of central Italy.

New International Alignments

The loser in Italy and in Germany was Austria. And Austria lost largely because her old allies, Russia and Prussia, refused to continue to support the status quo in central Europe. Yet Bismarck was a thorough conservative in the sense that he believed in strong, authoritarian government, just as the Russian czar and the Hapsburg emperor did. As a result, when he had succeeded in creating the new German Empire around the

Prussian kingdom, Bismarck was eager to restore the conservative alliance with Austria and Russia that had kept Europe's boundaries stable between 1815 and 1859.

For a short period, the Hapsburg emperor, Franz Josef I (reigned 1848–1916), dreamed of revenge; but after the defeat of France in 1870–1871, he gave this up and, in 1879, agreed to an alliance with Germany. The major reason behind this move was that Austria suffered from internal frictions among the many different nationalities that made up the empire. In 1867 a constitutional settlement between the Hungarians and the rest of the empire sharpened the political appetites of Czechs and other Slavs who wanted similar privileges for themselves. With such internal problems, the Hapsburg monarch badly needed all the outside support he could get, and the German alliance of 1879 served this purpose admirably.

In 1882 Bismarck also brought Italy into the alliance, making it a Triple Alliance; and in 1887 he succeeded in making a secret treaty with Russia. Behind all of Bismarck's diplomatic activity after 1871 was his wish to keep France from being able to start a war of revenge with any prospect of success. French pride had been deeply hurt by the German victory in 1870–1871. In addition, the Germans had taken the border provinces of Alsace and Lorraine from France and made them part of the new German Empire; but despite the fact that many inhabitants of these provinces spoke German, the majority considered themselves to be French. French patriots, therefore, refused to forget the lost provinces; but as long as Bismarck was in charge of Germany's foreign policy, the French could find no allies and thus had to swallow their pride. Instead they concentrated on building an empire in Africa and southeast Asia, an enterprise that kept them constantly at odds with British empire-builders, who were trying to do the same thing.

Bismack left office in 1890 after a new emperor, Kaiser Wilhelm II (reigned 1888–1918), came to the German throne. Wilhelm had great ambitions for his country. By 1890 enormous economic success in building the world's most efficient industrial system had created a public that wanted to see Germany, too, start building an empire overseas. Naval officers argued that a powerful fleet was needed to make Germany a really great power. Wilhelm agreed and thought that Germany should cut its ties with Russia and come to an understanding instead with the British. Accordingly, he dismissed Bismarck and set out to make Germany not just a European but a world power.

Wilhelm entirely failed to persuade the British to make a deal that would give Germany world power. Instead, everything that Bismarck had most feared started to happen. First the French and Russians made an alliance (1893); then the French and British settled their colonial disputes (1904); and eventually the British and Russians did the same (1907). The result, therefore, was to align three great powers—France, Britain, and

Russia—in a ring around the Triple Alliance of Germany, Austria, and Italy. Moreover, Italy gave clear signs, even before 1914, of not being reliable from a German point of view. The more Germany built up its navy and claimed the right to an equal voice in European councils about colonial matters, the firmer grew the hostile ring. The result was a series of diplomatic crises beginning in 1905 (first Moroccan crisis) and ending in 1914 with the crisis that triggered World War I. The alliance system worked in such a way that any quarrel anywhere in the world tended to line up the European great powers on opposite sides; and each time one or the other side backed down, it did so with the resolve not to do so next time. In 1914, therefore, the governments of Europe moved toward war as though hypnotized. Doing so, they plunged Europe and the world into a new and violent era, in which many of the familiar landmarks of Europe's past came tumbling down.

ECONOMY AND SOCIETY

The central fact of Europe's history between 1850 and 1914 was the rise and progress of industry. Germany's great industrial boom left all other European nations behind. Russia, too, from about 1890 began to see the rise of large-scale modern industry, with consequences for the internal stability of the czar's government, which we will study in Chapter 10. Everywhere cities grew in size and rural life became less important; yet it is worth remembering that, in 1914, most Europeans were still farmers or gained their living directly from farming. Only Great Britain had become a nation with more than half its population living in towns and cities away from the land.

Conservative Social Forces

The agricultural elements of European society were basically conservative. Patterns of command and deference, as between upper and lower classes in European society, survived as strongly as they did because so many people either still lived in villages or had left them recently. The authority of the father over his children and of men over women was also an inheritance from rural custom, and continued to define the daily conduct of most Europeans, even those who lived in great cities.

Religion was another important conservative force. Early in the nineteenth century, many persons reacted against the religious skepticism that had been so prominent among the leaders of the French Revolution. When liberal and nationalist movements came to the surface again, most churches opposed them. After some hesitation, Pope Pius IX (1846–1878) repudiated all the new movements he saw rising around him in Europe. To get support for his views, he summoned the first Vatican Council (1869–1870). The Council obediently proclaimed the infallibility of the pope, in matters of faith and morals, at the very time that the papal government of Rome was being shattered.

Papal policy presented the governments of western Europe with awkward problems. Bismarck tried to compel German Catholics to obey the laws of the new German Empire instead of obeying the pope; but this merely drove all German Catholics into a single, opposition political party. Eventually Bismarck backed away from the fight because he felt that the socialist threat was even greater. In Britain, the Catholic issue took the form of the Irish question. Ireland was Catholic and oppressed, as well as poor; but Irish members of Parliament frequently held the balance of power between the liberal and conservative parties. In France the great issue was control of schools. This came to a crisis between 1901 and 1905 and ended in the legal separation of church and state and the suppression of most church-run schools.

Another problem that affected all European governments was created by the low cost of American grain. The price of grain became an acute issue after 1870 when railroad construction and the development of steamships made it possible for wheat from the American Middle West, or from the Argentine pampas, to be delivered to European ports at prices below European production costs. The British adhered to a free trade policy and, as a result, nearly ruined British agriculture. Other European governments imposed special tariffs to protect peasants and landowners. This, of course, raised food prices for the cities and hurt the working class in the towns.

New Problems of Industrialism

To be sure, problems of this kind were familiar to European political leaders. Church and state, tariffs and taxes, had been at the heart of European politics for centuries. Problems raised by the galloping growth of industrialism, however, were far more difficult because they were so new. Everywhere, even in Russia, governments tried to win the support of the working class. By 1914 the idea that all adult males ought to have the right to vote in elections for some sort of representative assembly was accepted by all European governments, although in Germany and in Austria, as well as in Russia, such representative assemblies had only

A 302 cm. cannon being test-fired at the Krupp armament works. (*Library of Congress*)

limited powers. In eastern Europe, emperors, their ministers, and other high officials kept ultimate decisions in their own hands, and neither trusted nor were trusted by ordinary workers.

RISE OF SOCIALIST PARTIES   Karl Marx and other revolutionaries advocated one extreme solution to Europe's social problems. In 1864 they organized the International Workingmen's Association, the First International, in order to spread the doctrines of the *Communist Manifesto* and prepare the way for socialist revolution. But before Marx attracted many followers, the revolutionaries quarreled bitterly among themselves.

Moreover, in 1871, the city of Paris went through another crisis. Many Parisians felt that the government, which had made peace with the Germans and given up Alsace and Lorraine, was full of traitors. The city had been besieged for several months and suffered accordingly. A coup d'état, followed by municipal elections, brought a revolutionary Paris Commune to power. Its leaders remembered the heroic days of 1793 when Paris had rallied all of France against foreign tyrants. They were eager to try the same thing again, but never had a chance. Instead, the French government sent in troops and suppressed the Commune, after bloody fighting. The end result was to discredit socialist plans for a popular rising to take power from the capitalists. The models offered by the French Revolution, when Paris crowds had been able to make and break governments, were becoming seriously out of date. As a result, the First International broke up in 1876.

Marx did not despair, however. Separate national parties, strongly under the influence of Marx's ideas, came into existence in most European countries during the 1860s and 1870s. The most important of these was the German Social Democratic party, organized in 1875. Bismarck responded by outlawing socialist agitation, and until 1890 the German party existed outside the law. In 1889 a Second International was founded to unite the socialists; but in spite of much talk about international solidarity, each national party went its own way in all essentials. By 1914, socialist parties had substantial representation in all of Europe's parliamentary assemblies. A French socialist had even cooperated with bourgeois politicians as a member of a short-lived government. A few socialists suggested that violent revolution might not be necessary. Reform might be able to win the rights workers were fighting for and introduce socialism gradually.

NON-SOCIALIST INITIATIVES   From the other side of the political fence, conservatives, such as Bismarck, tried to blunt the effect of socialist propaganda by doing something about the grievances and hardships workers suffered. A series of social insurance laws resulted, whereby the state undertook to make payments to employees who fell ill or suffered disabling accidents. Such policies, combined with improvements in municipal services and the legalization of unions and of socialist parties, had the effect of reconciling many workers to their lot in life.

Great Britain followed a different path. Early experiments with socialist schemes for remaking the whole of society collapsed in the 1830s and left British workers deeply distrustful of what Karl Marx and his fellow revolutionaries were hoping to accomplish. Instead, beginning with the 1850s, labor unions arose, aimed only at improving working conditions through negotiation with employers or, if necessary, through strikes. The leaders of these unions, which to begin with were limited to skilled trades, avoided politics as a matter of principle. When the right to vote was extended to some (1867), and then to all (1884), of the British lower classes, miners and industrial workers supported Liberal party candidates for Parliament, as a rule. Between 1900 and 1906, however, the unions changed policy and began to support a new Labour party; but unlike socialist parties on the continent, the Labour party paid little attention to Marxist ideas and always expected to carry out its program through parliamentary legislation, not through violent revolution.

Tensions between industrial workers and the rest of society were thus eased, though not erased, between the 1870s and 1914. Like the middle class before them, the working class had secured legal ways to make their interests heard, even in the highest quarters of government. During these years, socialism seemed well on its way to making the kind of elaborate compromises with older vested interests that revolutionary liberalism had made in the decades 1850–1870.

New Forms
of Industrial Organization

Adjustment to industrialism was not merely a matter of fitting the new working class into the preexisting structure of European society. New legal forms for business had to be invented. The limited liability company (or, as we call it in the United States, the corporation) met this need. Banking practices and the supply of capital were as critical as the supply of labor or of raw materials. Also, the boundaries separating private enterprise and profit from state operations and taxes had to be defined and constantly readjusted.

BRITISH LAISSEZ FAIRE   In general, British practice stood at one extreme. Until late in the nineteenth century the British government was reluctant to intervene in economic and social questions, and lacked a large, well-trained bureaucracy like that which most continental European governments had inherited from the eighteenth century. Having allowed workers to develop unions, pubs, and chapels and having seen business leaders develop the corporation, free trade, and the gold standard for currency, British politicians felt, for the most part, that the economic machine should be left to run itself with minimal interference or regulation by government. This policy is called "laissez faire"—a term borrowed from French economic theorists of the eighteenth century. The British economy did, indeed, run itself; but British manufacturers tended to fall behind what the Germans were able to do, partly, at least, because the Germans took it for granted that the forms of industrial organization that had worked so well between 1775 and 1850—and had given Britain the lead over all the world—could be improved upon.

GERMAN PLANNING   The Germans came late to the industrial scene, for until railroads made low-cost overland haulage of heavy goods possible, German coal fields were of little value. But from about 1850, German industry grew rapidly, and by 1900 Germany had outstripped Great Britain in almost every branch of production. Three factors help to explain how Germany could be so successful.

First, a few important German industrialists grasped the idea that theoretical science could help them in important ways. Beginning in the 1890s a few German corporations, mainly those working in chemicals and electricity, began to pay salaries to university-trained chemists and physicists whose only task was to discover new ways of doing things, or new products that could be manufactured and sold.

However familiar today, before 1914 this was a radical idea. Why pay good money to someone who, if successful, would outmode the machinery the company depended on for its profits? Why indeed? In earlier times, when an inventor hit upon some new method by tinkering in his attic or backyard, he secured a patent. This meant that no one else could use the invention without paying a fee. Then the inventor either sold the patent to someone else or went into business independently, hoping to make as much money as possible from the invention. A successful effort to find a still better device would simply spoil the patent. From this point of view, it was absurd to hurry on the day when the company's patents might become valueless because of some new invention!

Yet the absurdity was amply justified by results. Just because they made old methods and machinery obsolete faster than anyone else, German electrical and chemical industries outstripped those of other countries before 1914. Their lead over other nations resulted directly from the use which German captains of industry made of the well-trained scientists and engineers who emerged from German schools and universities.

Secondly, German banks and businesses organized cartels on a scale unequaled elsewhere. A cartel is an agreement among producers of given commodities, coal for example, to divide the market among themselves and to sell at fixed prices. Such arrangements often led to increased profits; indeed, that was the aim. They also allowed managers to plan production schedules more exactly, and this sometimes evened out the "boom and bust" pattern that was so wasteful in British and American industry. Credit, also, was more highly centralized in Germany, so that financial as well as production planning operated with larger units and over longer time spans than was common in other countries. A firm could go deeper into debt and wait longer for returns on some new technique or product than was possible with the banking practices that prevailed in England. But, since some new technologies were very expensive and could not be tried except on a large scale, this meant that German financial arrangements and cartel organization could, if the managers so desired, take risks and introduce new things that small-scale businesses could not afford.

In the third place, the German government played a much more active role in economic policy than the British government did. Railroads were owned by the state, and freight rates could be adjusted to encourage or discourage any particular undertaking. The location of steel mills or of other important plants depended not only on geography but also on exactly how much it cost to haul a ton of ore or of coal from its place of origin to the place of manufacture. In setting up freight rates, military considerations were often taken into account. The German general staff cared where its ammunition came from and wanted to see a rail network that would permit troops to reach a threatened frontier faster than the enemy could bring up its forces. Thus the officials who managed the railroads and decided freight rates had a powerful tool at their command to affect the way German industry developed. They used this power to make Germany both prosperous and militarily strong.

INDUSTRIALISM ELSEWHERE   Other European governments fell somewhere between the British and German extremes. No country relied as much on private initiative as did the British; none was nearly as successful as the Germans in manipulating and directing the growth of industry by governmental and semigovernmental (banks and cartels) action. Southern Europe fell behind. Coal fields were lacking there, and until 1914 industry was based overwhelmingly on energy derived from coal. Water power and petroleum were only beginning to offer alternatives, and southern Europe was not particularly well endowed with either oil fields or waterfalls. Eastern Europe, being poorer agriculturally, had always lagged behind the western nations and continued to do so, despite the opening up of a few large mines and factories in Russia.

Underlying everything was a rapid expansion of population. During the nineteenth century, some 60 million people left Europe for America and elsewhere. In spite of this exodus, the population of the continent rose from about 187 million in 1800 to about 401 million in 1900. Factors that affect population are not fully understood, but it seems clear that one important cause for this extraordinary growth in numbers was the progress of medicine, which allowed doctors and public officials to take effective steps against diseases spread by contaminated drinking water. This check on the spread of disease allowed more babies to survive infancy; they grew up to have children of their own, thus setting off a population explosion of the sort that has become familiar, all around the globe, in our own time.

THOUGHT
AND SCIENCE

Europe's continued self-transformation under the twin impulses of the Industrial and Democratic revolutions in the years 1850–1914 must be counted as extraordinary. All the internal strains and struggles, one piled on top of the other, added up to progress in the eyes of nearly everyone who lived at the time. A similar extraordinary achievement transformed science and the arts. There too, vigor and variety, in a reckless effort to expand the limits of the possible, were evident at every turn.

It seems useful in the period 1850–1914 to divide European thought and science into three schools: the "hard," the "soft," and the "crazy," or, in more formal language, the systematic, the evolutionary, and the irrational. The "hard" sciences were mathematics, physics, chemistry, astronomy, and economics. In each of these fields, the goal was to discover laws or patterns of behavior that were true everywhere and at all times. The fundamental point of view behind these efforts had been worked out in the 1600s by the great pioneers of modern science: Galileo, Descartes, Newton. What scientists in the later nineteenth century did was to generalize the scientific laws they had inherited from their predecessors, and find innumerable practical applications in industrial technology.

The Systematic Sciences

On the theoretical side, mathematicians were able to do such surprising things as work out several non-Euclidean geometries and rules for converting one mathematical system into another. Chemists worked with matter and discovered how its building blocks could be combined and recombined according to more or less predictable patterns. Physicists were able to discern how mechanical motion, heat, light, and the entire spectrum of electromagnetic radiation were all forms of energy, and worked out rules for converting one into the other. The key figure in this development was a Scotsman, James Clerk Maxwell (1831–1879), who first realized that light belonged in a much wider spectrum of electromagnetic radiation. No single chemist had quite the status of Maxwell among the physicists; but a Russian, Dmitri Mendeleev (1834–1907), first arranged the elements into a "periodic" table. This table showed gaps where hitherto unknown elements were needed to fill out Mendeleev's overall pattern. Later research discovered all of these missing elements. This confirmed in striking fashion the correctness of the pattern Mendeleev had first perceived.

Toward the end of the nineteenth century, both physicists and chemists had begun to zero in on the electron. At one and the same time, the electron was the smallest building block of matter (in which chemists were interested) and a particle that radiated energy (which physicists found so fascinating). Puzzling problems multiplied. Electrons sometimes seemed to act like waves rather than like tiny billiard balls. Matter sometimes spontaneously sent off radiation. And radiation itself seemed sometimes to come in quanta, or bundles.

THE THEORY OF RELATIVITY   From a quite different angle of approach, astronomers also had turned up unexpected data. The planet

Mercury seemed not to obey Newton's laws of motion perfectly. Most puzzling of all, light sent out from the moving platform of the earth seemed to travel at exactly the same speed, no matter what direction it followed. This contradicted common sense, as well as Newton's laws of motion, since in some directions the earth's motion should have added to the speed of light launched from its surface, and in other directions should have reduced the speed with which the same light traveled through space. Yet nothing of the sort could be detected, even with extremely sensitive instruments.

In 1905 a German Swiss, Albert Einstein, (1879–1955), proposed a special theory of relativity to explain some of these puzzles. Ten years later he followed his first suggestion with a more general theory, and gave the fullest explanation of his ideas in a book published in 1929. Einstein took the four basic terms of Newtonian physics—space, time, matter, and energy—and suggested that they were not fixed, firm, and separate frames within which all natural objects existed, but were, instead, all mixed up with each other. It followed that measurements of space, time, and motion were relative to one another and that matter might be converted into energy, and vice versa, according to a simple mathematical formula, $E=mc^2$; that is, energy equals mass times the speed of light squared. Thus, at the very end of the period with which we are here concerned, Einstein arrived at the greatest generalization of all by giving a new definition to the basic terms of the physical sciences.

ECONOMIC THEORY   Economics rates as a "hard" science, despite having to do with unpredictable human beings, because economists kept on trying to find universal laws that would explain, impersonally, how markets worked. They even hoped to learn how to predict what would happen, in the way that physicists, chemists, and astronomers were able to do. In this they were faithful to Adam Smith's habit of mind. In limited degree, they were successful in much the same way that the other "hard" sciences were successful. This is to say, succeeding theorists were able to bring more and more kinds of data into their system. A grand synthesis was achieved in the 1880s by an Englishman, Alfred Marshall (1842–1924), who introduced the concept of "marginal utility" as a master key to analyze fluctuations in prices, interest rates, wages, and rents. But Marshall's system, impressive and closely reasoned though it was, never explained adequately the boom and bust pattern of the business cycle.

The prestige of the "hard" sciences was reinforced by their practical applications. Chemistry, in particular, allowed the creation of new industries and new products, such as dyes, drugs, electroplated metal, and many more. Incandescent electric lights, invented in 1879 by the American, Thomas A. Edison (1847–1931), began to replace gaslights in homes and offices; other electrical inventions, such as the phonograph and the tele-

Albert Einstein, 1879–1955. (Library of Congress)

phone, followed one after the other. Yet, as we have already seen, it was not until the end of the period, and then only in a limited way—mainly in Germany—that scientific theory and technical processes of manufacturing were systematically brought together. The potentialities of this combination had not really been grasped by anyone before 1914.

The "Soft" Sciences

By comparison, the "soft" sciences seemed impractical, since they had no distinct applications in industry, even though new ideas about the human past, present, and future certainly did change behavior, and in this way altered the conditions of European life almost as much as the technical changes for which the "hard" sciences were responsible.

The basic philosophical approach common to the "soft" sciences was newer than the effort to discover mathematical, timeless, and universal laws that characterized the "hard" sciences. The "soft" sciences all emphasized change through time; but not until after 1800 did anyone try to work out the full implications of a world of ceaseless and universal change. More than any other single man, the German philosopher, Georg Wilhelm Friedrich Hegel (1770–1831), was responsible for developing such a vision of reality. According to Hegel, everything changes always, and does so by a series of reversals or movements from one extreme to another. To use his own terms—a thesis confronts its antithesis and in time both are absorbed into a synthesis, which in turn becomes a thesis for the continuing unfolding of reality.

THE THEORY OF EVOLUTION   The concept of development through time particularly fitted biological and human affairs. Early in the nineteenth century, geologists discovered numerous fossils of plants and animals different from living forms. Studies of the distribution of different species of plants and animals also showed a pattern of resemblances and differences that made traditional ideas of the separate creation of each species hard to believe. Charles Darwin (1809–1882) put these observations together to develop the idea of organic evolution. In his great book *On the Origin of Species* (1859), he argued that since many more living creatures are launched upon life than ever survive to adulthood, there is a struggle for survival that goes on constantly. In such a struggle, some variations help the organism to survive. These survivors tend to spread, because more such individuals grow up to reproduce their kind. In different environments different features help survival, so that in time such differences may become great enough to make what had been a single species separate into two or more different species.

Darwin's theory aroused angry debate because of its implications for religion. Some Protestants argued that belief in the literal truth of the account of creation in the Book of Genesis was fundamental to Christianity, since if the Bible could err in one passage, how could one believe it at all? The debate was complicated by the fact that scholars in Germany had already begun to subject the text of the Bible to critical methods that had been developed, ever since the Renaissance, for the study of ancient manuscripts. By treating the Bible as the work of human beings, such scholars had begun to unravel the various strands from which the biblical text had been put together long ago. But that sort of study, too, seemed to call the truth of Christian doctrine into question.

Some persons responded by arguing that religious truth, like everything else, develops and changes through time. Truths and insights valu-

Charles Darwin, 1809–1882. (*New York Public Library Picture Collection*)

able for one generation might cease to have the same meaning or importance for later generations. God's revelation, according to such ideas, could be a progressive and gradual process, even including the most recent and shocking discoveries of a scientist such as Darwin, or a philosopher such as Hegel. "Modernist" doctrines of this sort were emphatically repudiated by the Roman Catholic church at the first Vatican Council of 1870. Protestant churches divided, some pinning their faith on the literal truth of the Bible, others admitting, in varying measure, the idea that religious truth and knowledge had changed and developed through time.

THE STUDY OF MAN   The social sciences, with the exception of economics, emphasized the idea of development. History achieved a new accuracy in detail as a result of seminar training in German universities, pioneered by Leopold von Ranke (1795–1886). The mass of facts that rapidly accumulated was kept in a sort of loose order by the idea of progress—in particular, the progress of limited constitutional government, of equality before the laws, and of personal, individual freedom. The historian who, more than any other, put this vision of the European past into focus was Lord Acton (1834–1902). Sociology was developed by a Frenchman, Auguste Comte (1798–1857), who also believed in progress. Anthropology, likewise, when it emerged from the study of primitive customs and religions, was organized by such pioneers as Lewis Henry Morgan (1818–

1881) in terms of a supposed development from savagery through barbarism to civilization. Behind and beneath these sciences lay the study of early civilizations, revealed with greater and greater detail by archaeologists. And geologists probed still deeper into time through their study of sedimentary rock layers.

The result of the combined efforts of so many specialists was to create a panoramic vision of the nature of things in which change was universal. The whole human adventure on earth shrank to the proportions of a last-minute flourish, when measured by the geologic time scale or by the scale of organic evolution. But in a world in which everything changed—even the established truths of religion—what was there left to believe in, except the fact of change itself?

Irrationalism

This chilling conclusion troubled many people even before 1914, when the violence and destruction wrought by the First World War shocked millions more. There had been a small number of thinkers throughout the nineteenth century who emphasized the weakness of reason, the emptiness of progress, the folly of the age. Apostles of despair were listened to mainly by literary people and artists, who responded more to their feelings than to abstract thought. But the handful of philosophers who used their power of reasoning to argue how weak or useless reason really was, hardly mattered to scientists and professional specialists.

Yet, in Vienna, shortly before World War I the psychologist, Sigmund Freud (1856–1939), began to explore subconscious levels of the human mind. He found sexual drives and jealousies at the bottom of many kinds of behavior and concluded that human conduct was, for the most part, controlled by dark, elemental impulses over which we have only very limited conscious control. Freud's ideas won little attention before World War I, beyond the circle of a small group of his personal followers. The widespread impact of his ideas came later. Other thinkers, the Italian Vilfredo Pareto (1848–1923), for example, emphasized the irrational aspects of social behavior and argued that myths and exaggerated slogans were the only means political leaders could use to mobilize their followers to action. Another school of thought tried to apply Darwinism to human affairs, and interpreted history as a struggle for survival in which only the fittest could expect to last. Often this theory was thought of in racial terms, with the comforting (for Europeans) conclusion that the white race must be superior because it was at that time able to conquer everybody else. Others applied the idea of struggle for survival to conflicts between rich and poor, and concluded that any sort of political intervention to

The Empire State Building, erected between 1929 and 1931, was the world's tallest building at the time. (N.Y. Convention & Visitors Bureau)

help the poor or weak members of society was dangerous in the long run because it would allow the unfit to survive.

Such ideas, together with those of Freud and others who emphasized the irrational side of human life, directly challenged the theory of democratic government. In the eighteenth century, when democratic political ideals were first clearly set forth, everyone assumed that all persons were fundamentally rational and could judge in a reasonable way the alternatives their political leaders set before them. If this was not, in fact, the case, then the original justification for democratic self-government would have to be abandoned.

Answers to this and other ultimate questions were not found; but European thinkers never drew back from any line of inquiry because it was too dangerous or too shocking to those in authority. A tremendous range of attitudes and ideas churned through questioning minds. New perspectives, new theories, new information competed for attention as never before in human history. In this, as in other respects, the years between 1850 and 1914 were something of a golden age for Europe's prosperous middle class.

ART AND LITERATURE

Artists and writers valued originality above all else in the nineteenth century. Nearly all of them felt that superior craftsmanship within an established style was unworthy of true artistic genius. The result, of course, was that as time passed it became harder and harder to rebel, because there was no established standard of taste against which to measure the personal originality of the artist.

From a historian's point of view, this characteristic of nineteenth-century artistic life makes it particularly hard to say anything that is the least bit meaningful about countries, periods of time, or groups of artists. And outstanding individuals in the arts were so numerous it is hard to know whom to mention. There is some justification for making a distinction between the first half of the nineteenth century, when "romantic" art flourished, and the second half, when "realism" dominated the scene. But romantic attitudes lasted throughout the century, if by "romantic" we mean the effort to express inward personal feelings through art and an urge to explore remote times and places, fantasy, folklore, and things strange, new, and mysterious. Realists may have paid more attention to the lives of poor and humble people and dealt more frankly with ugly and brutal sides of human life than their predecessors usually cared to do. But this was a matter of degree. Moreover, realists who seized upon ugly and disgusting matter for their art were, in their own way, romantics. They too projected inward feelings upon the world. They too sought out strange and mysterious themes by exploring the slums of Europe's new industrial cities.

Impact of New Techniques

One general factor that altered many forms of art during the century was the development of new techniques and materials. In architecture, for example, steel and concrete allowed buildings to rise much higher than before. The Eiffel Tower, 984 feet tall, erected in Paris for a world's fair in 1889, was a particularly dramatic example of what could be done with steel. Skyscrapers, first developed as office buildings in Chicago in

Monet, Women In Garden. (*The Louvre*, *Paris*)

Renoir, By the Seashore. (*Metropolitan Museum of Art*, *The H. O. Havemeyer Collection*.)

Manet, Die Barke.

the 1880s, gave practical use to the new techniques of construction. Musicians exploited a series of new instruments; and painters acquired innumerable new tints as a result of chemical discoveries. Some of them also tried to apply scientific theories of light and vision to their work, by using tiny specks of different colors which, when seen from a distance, blended into a livelier, more interesting surface than could be attained by painting with solid colors. Literature, of course, was limited to words that could be understood, and language changed slowly even in the nineteenth century. In this sense it was the most conservative of the arts.

PAINTING AND MUSIC   Painting, on the contrary, was the most radical. Until about 1875, the basic idea of how to paint a picture, which had been first defined in Italy in the 1400s, continued to be taken for granted. A picture, according to this tradition, ought to look like "real life," and rules for giving an illusion of three dimensions on a flat two-dimensional surface had been carefully worked out. In the latter part of the nineteenth century, however, a cluster of great artists, who worked mostly in France, began to reject this idea. They wished to make their paintings not a "pretend window" to be looked through, but a thing to be looked at for its own sake. Violent colors, quite unlike those of nature, and distorted patterns vaguely resembling familiar objects were perfectly all right when the point of the picture was to be looked at for itself. Accordingly, such painters as Paul Cézanne (1839–1906), Vincent van Gogh (1853–1890), and Paul Gauguin (1848–1903) cut loose from older rules and restrictions and began to explore the possibilities of two-dimensional patternmaking by using paint on canvas.

In the decade immediately before the outbreak of World War I, a new generation of artists began to abandon familiar shapes and to twist fragments of visual experience in playful and novel fashions. Henri Matisse (1869–1954) and Pablo Picasso (1881–1973) were among the most effective of these innovators. Strangely, the way they filled their paintings with twisted bits of familiar shapes and forms, seen from different angles or, as it were, at different times, seemed like a prophecy of the way in which traditional European culture was about to break up under the shock of World Wars I and II. Art often seems to hold a mirror to society. Europe's painters did so in the prewar years with unusual sensitivity and power. In this case, at least, the restless striving for new, original, and personal styles of expression achieved singular success.

Musicians made attempts to experiment with such novelties as the twelve-tone scale, but with small success. The hold of the classics, from Johann Sebastian Bach (1685–1750) to Ludwig van Beethoven (1770–1827), was never shaken. Richard Wagner (1813–1883) tried to create a supreme art that would combine music, poetry, and dramatic spectacle. He found subject matter for his operas in Germanic folklore and pagan myth, believing that here could be glimpsed and expressed the innermost spirit of his own nation. Wagner gathered a circle of admirers around himself, but his notion of the priest-like role his art ought to play offended as many people as it attracted. Older, more classical ideas were upheld by Johannes Brahms (1833–1897) and, in some degree, also by Gustav Mahler (1860–1911).

LITERATURE   Literature was divided into separate compartments by language differences. This makes generalization difficult. No great and commanding figures arose in Germany after the death of Johann Wolfgang von Goethe (1749–1832). His masterpiece, *Faust*, retold the story of how the devil tempted Dr. Faustus with unlimited knowledge and power if he would sell his soul; but in Goethe's version, Faust escaped damnation because of his true love for a simple girl, Marguerite. This long poem, the second part of which was published only after Goethe's death, was soon recognized as a world masterpiece.

In English, the novels of Charles Dickens (1812–1870) were immensely popular in his own time but may seem long-winded today. A cluster of great "romantic" poets flourished in the first half of the century: William Wordsworth (1770–1850), Samuel Taylor Coleridge (1772–1834), George Gordon, Lord Byron (1788–1824), John Keats (1795–1821), and Percy Bysshe Shelley (1792–1822). Robert Browning (1812–1889) and Alfred, Lord Tennyson (1809–1892) scarcely achieved the same heights in the latter part of the century.

French literature was abundant as always. Major novelists included Victor Hugo (1802–1885), Stendhal, pen name for Marie Henri Beyle (1783–1842), and Honoré de Balzac (1799–1850) in the first part of the century; and Gustave Flaubert (1821–1880), Emile Zola (1840–1902), and Anatole France (1844–1924) in the second half. French poetry took a new turn with the work of Charles Baudelaire (1821–1867), who was an admirer of the American, Edgar Allan Poe. Both men were misfits who tried to find escape in the beauty of words and the images they could arouse in imagination. The next generation of French poets are commonly called "symbolists," because their poems conveyed meaning indirectly and by symbolic suggestion—if, indeed, they conveyed any distinct meaning at all. The famous symbolists are Stéphane Mallarmé (1842–1898), Paul Verlaine (1844–1896), and Arthur Rimbaud (1854–1891). French experimentation with sentences that were not quite sentences and with words whose meaning rested on the associations the reader brought to them was influential upon English and American writers after World War I. In this sense, as in art, France led the way and the rest of Europe followed.

In the nineteenth century, literary figures of world reputation are hard to find in Italy or Spain; but in Norway, Henrik Ibsen (1828–1906) shocked and fascinated European audiences with plays that were written in prose and dealt in a realistic manner with such topics as woman's rights. European drama from Renaissance times had been poetic, full of high-flown language and heroic posturing. Ibsen's effort to capture ordinary, everyday speech and to deal with everyday situations thus represented a rather sharp break with tradition—in its way, almost as great a break as the changes painters were making in art.

In Russia, a cluster of famous novelists burst upon the scene in the mid-nineteenth century. Ivan Turgenev (1818–1883), Fëdor Dostoevski (1821–1881), and Count Leo Tolstoi (1828–1910) were the greatest. Turgenev's realistic sketches of Russian country life brought that strange, rude society alive for a Western reader as nothing else did. Dostoevski explored the feelings of his characters in extraordinary detail. He illuminated Russian society from within, as Turgenev did from without. Tolstoi, in later life, founded a cult around himself that glorified the simple life. His greatest work, *War and Peace*, dealt with Russia's struggle against Napoleon in the "Fatherland War" of 1812.

The United States also entered the international "republic of letters" in the nineteenth century. Among the more distinctive American voices, those of Ralph Waldo Emerson (1803–1882), Henry David Thoreau (1817–1862), Walt Whitman (1819–1892), and Mark Twain, pen name for Samuel Langhorne Clemens (1835–1910), deserve mention along with Edgar Allan Poe (1809–1849).

CONCLUSION

The overwhelming impression that this hasty survey should leave is one of richness, variety, and confusion. European artists and thinkers reached for the sky. They did not quite make it; but, in failing, they expanded enormously the range of human achievement and knowledge. Their successes, however, created the problem with which we still struggle, for the great ideals of truth, beauty, and goodness tend to get lost amid so many truths, so many beauties, and so many private, personal, or partial kinds of good and evil. The historian's problem of what to choose for attention becomes everyone's problem. Amid so many competing voices and ideals, where should one turn? How does it all fit together? Does anything make sense? Answers were not forthcoming before 1914—and what has happened since that date has only added to the confusion in which Westerners, and humankind, find themselves.

Yet, for most of those who lived at the time and for us looking back the gains in knowledge, power, and sensitivity were probably worth the cost. The nineteenth century, of all centuries, was an age of progress.

Where it will lead remains to be seen; but, in and of itself, European civilization attained a final flowering between 1850 and 1914, before submerging itself, like the other civilizations of the world, into the still emerging cosmopolitanism of the twentieth century.

Europe kept its traditions and its sublime self-confidence longer than other civilizations were able to do. In a paradoxical way, Europe was, therefore, both ahead and behind the rest of the world. Ahead, because what the rest of the world had to become accustomed to and adjust to was what the Europeans were doing and thinking. Behind, because until after 1914 Europeans remained smug and self-contained within the broad limits of their inherited tradition of civilization and had not yet come to realize, as other peoples had been compelled to do, that their way of doing things was only one of many ways and not always or necessarily the best.

CHAPTER 9

World Reactions to Europe's Achievements

1850 to 1914

Three developments changed the lives of nearly all humanity between 1850 and 1914. These were, first, the very much improved forms of transportation and communication; second, rapid population growth; and third, the imbalance arising from Europe's superiority to the rest of the world in a wide range of critical skills.

TRANSPORTATION AND COMMUNICATION

Before 1850, in nearly all parts of the world, human beings lived in local communities. News from outside a radius of twenty to fifty miles arrived only occasionally. Since it was difficult to carry goods for long distances, nearly all the basic requirements of life had to be found approximately within the same radius. Most people were farmers and raised nearly everything they consumed in their own fields. Usually the surplus produce which they sold did not travel far, but was used in local towns. Because transportation was slow and expensive, people lived where there was food, rather than trying to bring food to where they lived.

Rural localism was modified by the fact that water transportation was comparatively cheap. This allowed the maintenance of large imperial states, such as China, Russia, and the Ottoman Empire. Canals, rivers, and seas made it possible to feed large populations in the Chinese capital at Peking, Russia's capital at Moscow (later at St. Petersburg), and the Ottoman capital at Constantinople by transporting food and other supplies by water across hundreds of miles. A state that depended largely on land transportation, such as the Mogul Empire of India, had to be weak, since wagons and animal packtrains simply could not bring enough supplies to a central point to make the emperor definitely stronger than local governors.

When railroads began to spread from Britain (1840s) to the European and North American continent (1850–1870) and then to other continents (1870–1910), the age-old limits upon the movement of goods and people disappeared. Cities, hundreds of miles away, became easy to get to. And when the growing railroad systems were connected with oceangoing steamships, the lands and seas of all the world were caught up, by degrees, in a single transportation network.

The effect upon human society was similar to the evolutionary emergence of animals with a central nervous system. Human communities had sprawled over the earth's surface throughout historic time, like a Portuguese man-of-war or some other loosely coordinated assemblage of cells and organs. Stimuli passed from one segment to another, but in a slow, haphazard fashion; and because conductivity was low, many stimuli failed to pass from one part of the world to another for long periods of time. The advent of railroads, steamships, and telegraph wires, and the appearance of newspapers with a mass circulation and of telephones meant that stimuli began to travel enormously faster and more purposefully.

Experts could communicate with experts all around the globe. The price of wheat in Chicago, of jute in Calcutta, of coffee in São Paulo, and of money in London governed decisions made halfway across the world. Technical skills, political ideas, and artistic styles moved at lightning speed by attracting the experts' attention. Sudden change could reach out to extremely remote regions of the earth. In the 1880s, for example, Japanese experts deliberately went shopping for a constitution and, after careful study of European and American models, decided that the constitutional arrangements of Bismarck's Germany were best for them. Sometimes stimuli went the other way. Thus, Parisian artists in the 1890s borrowed motifs from African ceremonial masks, plundered from west Africa by French soldiers and sold in the Paris "flea market" at prices that even a poor artist could afford.

When it began, the new communications and transportation network was mostly controlled by Europeans. And as railroads were built inland, the effect was to extend the reach of European goods and of Europeans' political, military, and financial advantages. Nevertheless, the opening of the Suez Canal in 1869 and of the Panama Canal in 1914 changed the world's strategic patterns in a way that foreshadowed the weakening of Europe's dominance. The Suez Canal put the Middle East back into the center of Old World communications, where it had been before Europe's sailors had opened up the oceans; and the Panama Canal strengthened America's position in the world by improving the flexibility of the naval and military power of the United States. But neither of these changes did much to undermine the reality of Europe's dominant position before 1914.

POPULATION GROWTH

Population growth acted in most parts of the world to check and limit the impact of the new communications and transportation. Poor peasants, on the edge of starvation, took little advantage of the possibilities opened to them by railroads and telegraphs. They continued to live much as their ancestors had done. This constituted a massive conservative force in world society. Yet the peasantries of the earth also nursed a potential for revolt. Inert and helpless they were, but hungry and resentful, too; and as their numbers increased, the old ways of life became more and more impossible to maintain, since tiny holdings had to be divided and divided again among the members of each new generation.

Why world population spurted upward so dramatically is not clear. Medical measures to check disease were important in some parts of the world; but they scarcely affected the immense numbers of rural Chinese and Indians before 1914. Increased food supplies due to better seeds, better methods of cultivation, or, in some parts, better fertilizers, irrigation, new crops, and pest control had some bearing on population growth. The pacification of great regions of the earth, brought about by improved communications, also allowed many persons to survive who in an earlier age would have perished through local violence. Famine relief was also important, especially in India where railroads made it possible to transport large amounts of food to regions where crops had failed. Lessening of epidemic diseases, through a more or less continual exposure to small doses of all sorts of infections, was another factor behind the world's population explosion. This resulted from improved transport, which circulated disease germs as well as goods and ideas throughout the world.

Traditional authorities could not cope with rising population pressures in Asia, but neither could European administrators in India or missionaries in China. Only Japan was able to absorb its rapidly rising population into new industrial occupations. But in the Americas, Africa, and parts of southeast Asia, there was still room for expansion. Between 1850 and 1914, in all of these regions, uncultivated land could be brought under cultivation without much trouble and without any basic change in familiar farming methods.

For this reason, African and American societies did not undergo any very acute upheaval before World War I. The establishment of European political administration in Africa made only minor differences to most Africans. Old ways, minus the slave trade, local wars, and some customs of which Europeans disapproved, went on much as before. The same was true in the New World, both for newcomers of European or African descent and for the Amerindian peasantry of central America and northern South America.

IMPACT OF EUROPEAN SKILLS

The impact of improved communications and of population growth was largely unconscious, in the sense that no one decided in advance what to do about them. The third worldwide phenomenon, the impact of superior European skills upon other peoples, was very much a matter of conscious decision-making. People living outside of western Europe had to come to terms, in some fashion or other, with the facts of European superiority over local society and civilization. Although peasants could and did neglect the question, their cultural and political leaders could not afford to do so.

It is useful, perhaps, to distinguish between the attitudes of an "inner ring" of peoples who shared the European inheritance in greater or less degree, and an "outer ring" of peoples who did not. Russians and Balkan Christians to the east were partially in and partially out of the circle of European civilization, and felt both ashamed and proud of this fact. Overseas, the United States and the British Commonwealth countries, together with those parts of Latin America where Spanish and Portuguese settlers did not depend on Amerindians and Negroes to do the manual labor, also belonged to the "inner ring." Their problem was to catch up with Europe by settling the empty lands around them, after which the refinements of civilized life—which were still only poorly developed in these regions—could (they hoped) be expected to grow automatically.

The "outer ring" faced a much more difficult decision. Chinese, Hindus, and Moslems had to weigh the costs of giving up essential parts of their own treasured past in order to try to catch up with Europe's power.

Japan chose to borrow from the west, and soon forged ahead. No other proud and old civilized people was able or willing to make the hard decisions such a policy required: instead, these communities hesitated, worried, floundered, and endured.

Africans south of the Sahara, and Amerindians in the middle regions of the New World, were subjected to European rule during the period with which we are now concerned. This was nothing new for the Amerindians. In their most developed centers, Amerindians had seen the Spaniards destroy their political leadership and higher culture before 1600. African kingdoms and tribes, however, were only brought under the control of European administrators during the later years of the nineteenth century. The degree to which African cultures and political organizations were altered by the arrival of Europeans differed a good deal from case to case. In general, the British tried to keep as much of the preexisting political and social system as possible; whereas the French, like the Spaniards in the days of the conquistadors, were more inclined to impose their own patterns of government and education upon their African subjects.

Weaker peoples found the conditions created by improved world communications all but impossible to survive. In Australia, for example, the aborigines, who had inhabited that continent for many thousands of years, could not adjust their ways to those of the intrusive whites. The same was true of Tasmanians and of some of the Pacific islanders; of Eskimos; and of Amerindian tribes who inhabited most of North America and the more southerly parts of South America. In these regions, contact with the outside world resulted in destructive epidemics of disease and paralyzing breakdowns of custom. In most cases these populations did not die out utterly, but their customary framework of life fell apart drastically and dreadfully.

HOW THE "INNER RING" GOT ALONG

The United States of America was by far the most important overseas member of the "inner ring," corresponding, in many ways, with the vast overland semi-European power, Russia. Russia's relations with the Balkan Christians and with the western Slavs (Poles, Czechs, Slovaks) were similar to the relations of the United States with Canada and Latin America; and interesting parallels as well as important differences may be detected in the internal development of the two societies.

U.S. Domestic
and Imperial Growth

Both the Democratic and Industrial revolutions had already gone a long way in the United States by 1850. Americans could proudly claim to be the earliest pioneers of rational self-government, and "Yankee ingenuity" in matters industrial was as great as any in the world. What was lacking in the United States was capital, population, and cultural refinement. With the end of the Civil War (1865), Americans set out to remedy all three deficiencies as fast as they could.

Capital came from Europe, especially England, in the form of short- and long-term credit. In addition, shrewd industrialists like Cornelius Vanderbilt (1794–1877), Andrew Carnegie (1835–1919), John D. Rockefeller (1839–1937), and Henry Ford (1863–1947) quickly learned how to accumulate capital by plowing profits back into their businesses. They were free to set prices at what the market would bear. When very expensive plants became necessary to produce steel or oil or motor cars, competition among firms (which in theory was supposed to keep prices close to the cost of production) worked imperfectly. Large profits reinvested in new enterprises thus created vast fortunes very rapidly. By 1914 the United States, although still a "debtor nation" in international money markets, had already begun to export large amounts of capital to the Caribbean, Mexico, Hawaii, and other foreign parts.

Population growth came from European immigration, as well as from the natural increase of people already living in the United States. As the decades passed, the flow of immigrants to North America from the British Isles and from Germany and Scandinavia slackened. Other nationalities from southern and eastern Europe became more numerous. Italians, Poles, Czechs, Croats, Jews, Greeks, Ukrainians, the many other ethnic groups swarmed across the ocean into the growing cities of the United States. There they provided labor for new factories, construction work, and the more menial services which city life required.

POLITICAL PROBLEMS AT HOME   Both the growth of capital and the flood of immigration created problems for a democratic political system. Farmers and small businesses often felt that the railroads and other big moneyed interests were squeezing them unfairly. Public regulation of railroad rates (1887) did something to remove the grievance; but a long agitation for cheaper money and credit failed to take the United States dollar off the gold standard. Similarly, popular movements aimed against immigrants succeeded only in closing the doors against Chinese and Japanese "cheap labor." Labor unions achieved a stable national existence after

1886, when the American Federation of Labor was founded. At first only a few skilled trades were organized. In these occupations immigrant labor, lacking the necessary skills, was not much of a factor.

Political collisions between old and new immigrants and between workers and capitalists were cushioned by the fact that, until 1890 or so, the United States still had an agricultural frontier where public land could be acquired easily and quite cheaply by anyone willing to cultivate it. Hardships and grievances could never be very bitter when such a

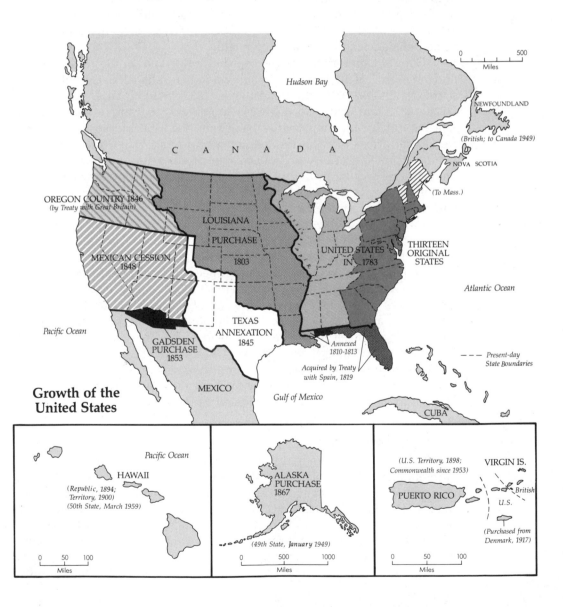

Growth of the United States

resource permitted the discontented to start afresh. Settlement of the western parts of the country tended to bypass the arid regions of the southwest, at first. As a result, Arizona and New Mexico were not organized as states until 1912, at a time when American expansion had already been carried overseas to the Philippine Islands and Puerto Rico, which were acquired from Spain after a brief and victorious war (1898) against that decaying empire.

U.S. EXPANSION ABROAD   With the Spanish-American war and with American diplomatic and military interventions in Panama, Nicaragua, Haiti, Mexico, and other Latin American states that swiftly followed, the United States joined the circle of imperialist powers. Germany, too, entered the field at about the same time, demanding its "place in the

Latin America, 1828
After the Wars
for Independence

sun." Great Britain, in effect, made room for the Americans and for the Japanese as well, who also built up a navy and began to create an empire for themselves in the Far East after a victorious war against China (1894–1895). The British simply gave up any pretense of controlling the seas in the Japanese and American parts of the globe. German rivalry close at home was too dangerous for any other policy to seem practical. The result was to keep British and American policies harmonious, even in the absence of any formal treaty of alliance. This was a fact of the greatest importance for the lineup of powers in World War I.

CULTURE AND SOCIETY IN THE UNITED STATES   On all these fronts, the United States met with success. In the material sense, there was no doubt that the nation was catching up fast with the most advanced European countries. But cultural equality was harder to attain. Captains of industry, such as Vanderbilt, Carnegie, Rockefeller, and Ford, all arranged that a large part of their personal fortunes should be used to support institutions intended to improve the quality of American cultural life. As a result, universities, libraries, symphony orchestras, opera companies, and similar organizations sprang up like mushrooms in every large American city after about 1890. But real cultural creativity lagged behind the physical and financial support Americans provided so eagerly.

Before 1914, few artists or thinkers of the first rank lived in the United States. As a matter of fact, quite a few highly cultivated Americans, such as the novelist Henry James (1843–1916), preferred to live in Europe because they found their compatriots crude and unsympathetic. American culture had not really escaped from provincialism in 1914, in spite of all the money and conscious effort devoted to its cultivation.

One of the backward aspects of American life was concentrated in the Old South. After the Civil War, halfhearted efforts to bring blacks into full participation in public life failed. By the late 1870s, relations between whites and blacks settled down to patterns not so very different from those that had prevailed in the days of slavery—patterns which enjoyed the legal sanction of so-called "Jim Crow" laws. Black sharecroppers, therefore, hoed cotton and tobacco in nearly the same way that slaves had done before 1863; and their education, skill, voting rights, and familiarity with newer aspects of modern life were not much greater than what had existed under slavery. In search of greater opportunities, some blacks did move into cities, mainly in the South. In fact, it was black musicians in New Orleans who invented jazz, the first truly original and compelling cultural innovation that bears the stamp *Made in America*. But in 1914 jazz remained hidden in the back streets of New Orleans, Memphis, and Chicago; the majority of people in the United States, along with the rest of the world, discovered it only after World War I.

Canada and Australia

In almost all respects, Canada lagged behind the United States by a generation or so, but followed much the same curve of development. Australia and New Zealand differed in one important respect: from the 1880s both countries passed laws that made it difficult for anyone not of British origin to immigrate. This slowed population growth. In addition, elaborate laws for the protection of workers slowed down the development of industry in comparison to what was happening in the United States in the same period. When the separate Australian colonies united to form the Commonwealth of Australia (1901) and New Zealand also became a fully self-governing dominion (1907), both countries were almost entirely agricultural. They were divided between vast stretches of nearly empty sheep pasture and an extraordinary concentration of population at two or three port cities, where import-export businesses and the processing of raw materials for export were concentrated.

Clearly, such societies had a long way to go before they could hope to equal European complexity and sophistication. But, as in the case of the United States and Canada, the people from "down under" often asserted the superiority of their way of life to that of the Old World, where—they quite correctly pointed out—high civilization had been built partly upon the exploitation of the poor by the rich.

South Africa

A different situation prevailed in South Africa. The Boer descendants of Dutch settlers kept their own language and, until 1901, defended their rural way of life, with guns in hand, against British intrusion. First the Boers withdrew inland; then when diamonds (1867) and gold (1886) were discovered on Boer soil, they tried to disfranchise the English-speaking miners who swarmed to the scene. Meanwhile, British empire-builders decided that all of eastern Africa, from Capetown to Cairo in Egypt, ought to come into British possession. The most active advocate of such an expansion was Cecil Rhodes (1853–1902). After making a fortune in gold mining, Rhodes turned to politics. His schemes led to a hard-fought war between Boers and British (1899–1902). In the end, the British won, but only after cutting off supplies for the Boer fighters by putting their women and children into specially guarded "concentration camps," and by burning the farmhouses and buildings.

Another feature of South African life was the presence of large numbers of Bantu-speaking Africans, as well as the people known as "Cape

Coloreds" whose ancestry mingled European, Indonesian, and Hottentot strains. When the Union of South Africa was established (1910), Boers, British, and "Cape Colored" populations all secured voting rights; but the Bantus were excluded. Boers regarded the Bantu as servants and inferiors; the British, when they did not share Boer attitudes, thought that tribal government should be maintained to make the transition into modern life easier and smoother.

South America

The situation in South America was again different. Argentina, southern Brazil, and Chile all remained hospitable to immigrants from Europe. But the distances involved made passage more expensive than to the United States, so fewer people made the attempt to immigrate to those countries. Agricultural expansion inland, largely dependent on railroad construction, was rapid; and foreign capital, much of it British, was important. But the absence of coal fields severely handicapped the development of industry.

The miners, coffee growers, and entrepreneurs of the southernmost provinces of Brazil treated the rest of that enormous country, where black and Indian populations were numerous, as a sort of colonial domain. In addition, Brazilians, in alliance with Argentina, overthrew a remarkable regime in Paraguay, where, after the destruction of the Jesuit missions, three military dictators in succession organized the Guarani Indians into a tightly disciplined army. The war was bitterly fought (1865–1870) and ended only when the Paraguayans had suffered enormous loss of life.

Somewhat later Chileans again proved that a population of European descent, and therefore possessing European skills, could exert superior military power. For Chile defeated Bolivia and Peru (where most of the population was Indian) in a war (1879–1884) aimed at seizing undisputed control of the valuable guano deposits of the coastal desert. These deposits, made from bird droppings, were rich in nitrogen, and before 1914 constituted the cheapest and best source of artificial fertilizers.

Russia

Overseas countries inhabited mainly by people of European descent enjoyed the advantage of having weak neighbors. In trying to catch up with Europe, they could, therefore, afford to pay little attention to building up military power. This was not true of Russia, whose landward frontier

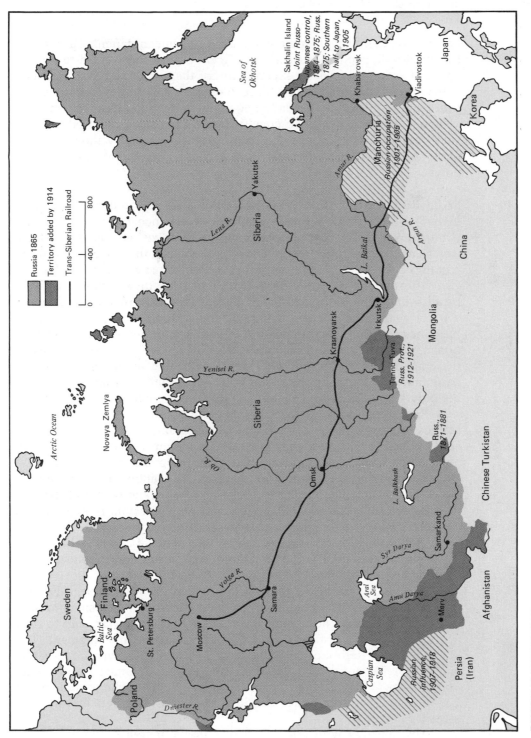

RUSSIAN TERRITORIAL EXPANSION 1865–1914

against western Europe had always been difficult to defend. Throughout the nineteenth century, Russia was a great power and wished to remain so. But this required heavy expenditure for the army and navy; and such expenditures left little to spare for building up industry. Yet modern industrial plants were vitally needed to equip the army and navy with efficient weapons. Financing railroad construction on the scale required by Russia's vastness also strained the resources of the country though it was obvious that without railroads Russia could not remain a truly great power.

FAILURE OF AUTOCRATIC GOVERNMENT   This difficulty was tied in with more strictly political problems. Ever since their defeat in the Crimean war (1856), many Russians had wanted to see changes in their government. But a Polish revolt (1863–1864) stopped the movement toward creating some sort of representative system of government in Russia. Czar Alexander II (reigned 1855–1881) had tried to win the Poles over by allowing partial self-government. Instead, the Poles revolted and fought a bitter guerilla war before being put down. The rulers of Russia drew the conclusion that it was dangerous to dabble with representative institutions. Absolute Russian dominance over all the subject nationalities of the empire seemed the only way of strengthening the state. Unbending autocracy, supported by the secret police and a strong army, looked like the only kind of government that could prevent open revolt.

Reaction fed revolution. Students plotted to overthrow the czar and his government. Efforts to rouse the peasants failed; so in 1879 a small circle turned to terrorism and embarked on a plan to assassinate leading officials. In 1881 the czar himself was killed by one such terrorist.

This confirmed the worst fears of Russian reactionaries. In the next years, energetic police measures broke up most of the revolutionary circles. But the government could not rely only on repression. To keep strong, an active policy of building railroads and industry seemed absolutely vital. But Russia, like the United States, was short of capital. The people were already severely taxed to maintain the army and bureaucracy at existing levels.

A solution was found through the diplomatic alliance with France, concluded in 1891. The French government allowed the Russians to float large loans in Paris. These loans enabled the Russian government to start a crash program of railroad building and industrial development. The Trans-Siberian Railroad, built between 1891 and 1903, was the greatest single achievement; but, in addition, many new armaments and textile plants came into existence in Moscow and St. Petersburg; and in the Ukraine, coal and iron mines provided the basis for a new and modern steel industry.

The difficulty with this policy was that it increased the danger of revolution. Factory workers, often miserably treated and badly housed, responded readily to preachers of revolution. A Marxist party, the Social Democrats, founded in 1898, vigorously exploited this fact. Soon after, in 1901, a new terrorist group, the Socialist Revolutionaries, organized themselves, intending to appeal primarily to the peasants by advocating abolition of landlord rights.

As long as the Russian government remained successful abroad and the czarist police and army functioned with reasonable efficiency at home, the plans and hopes of Marxists and other revolutionaries were not important. And Russia was, on the whole, successful abroad. Stretches of central Asia were annexed to the czar's empire between 1865 and 1876. A victorious war against the Turks in 1876–1877 had a less satisfactory outcome because the European powers whittled away the "Big Bulgaria" the Russians had created in the Balkans. But even so, the czar annexed Bessarabia (1878). In the following years he added Merv (1884) in central Asia, and acquired extensive rights in Manchuria and Outer Mongolia, in the Far East.

In 1903 the Marxists quarreled among themselves. A fiery and stubborn young leader, Vladimir Ilich Ulyanov (1870–1924), who went by the revolutionary alias, Lenin, insisted that the party must become a secret group of professional revolutionaries who would obey without question whatever instructions the elected leaders of the party judged to be advantageous at the moment. Some of the delegates at the Party Congress refused to agree; but a majority, the Bolsheviks, accepted Lenin's doctrine. Most of the rank and file of the party, however, followed the anti-Leninist, or Menshevik, group.

Russia's internal situation changed suddenly in 1904–1905, when the czar's armies and navy met crushing defeat at the hands of the Japanese in the Far East. Failure in war provoked revolution at home. The Czar soon yielded, and declared that he would govern henceforth with the advice and consent of an elected duma (parliament). However, when the crisis had passed and the army came back to European Russia, reaction set in. The powers of the duma were reduced, and the government set out to improve the equipment of the Russian armies by getting armaments from France and retooling factories at home. The Russian rulers badly wanted a breathing space, such as that which had followed the Crimean War. Instead, a series of crises in the Balkans (1908, 1912–1913) led the Russian and Austrian governments to such a pitch of rivalry that when still another crisis arose in the summer of 1914, neither one nor the other would yield. The result was World War I and the downfall of both empires.

ART AND INTELLECTUAL LIFE   Yet, while Russia's public life was thus heading toward a fateful explosion, Russian writers, musicians, and scientists moved as equals in the world of Paris or Berlin. Their numbers were fewer, perhaps, than those of the West, but the genius of the novelist Fëdor Dostoevski (1821–1881), of the musician Pëtr Ilich Tchaikovsky (1840–1893), and of the chemist Dmitri Mendeleev (1834–1907) equaled anything their Western contemporaries achieved. This did not erase Russia's deep-seated love-hate feeling toward Germany, France, and England. Inner uncertainties expressed themselves either in extravagant praise for Russia's own peculiar past or in equally sharp rejection of that past in order to erase the remaining differences that separated Russia from the West.

Many Russian writers had a guilty feeling about the peasantry, whose harsh, poverty-stricken lives cut them off from sharing in the polite culture, as well as in the political life of the country. Yet efforts to reach the peasants merely roused their suspicion. The famous novelist, Count Leo Tolstoi (1828–1910), in his old age pretended to live like a peasant; but Tolstoi's playacting was no more effective in communicating with the mass of Russian society than earlier revolutionary preaching had been.

THE ASIAN "OUTSIDE RING"

The gap between the Russian upper classes and the Russian peasantry was like the gap that opened between those Chinese, Japanese, Hindus, and Moslems who mastered aspects of European civilization and the majority of their compatriots. In this, as in many other respects, Russia stood halfway between Europe and the societies of Asia.

China

In China old ways of thought survived almost unshaken among the ruling class until 1895. After the severe crisis of the Taiping Rebellion (1850–1864), China enjoyed a kind of respite. But the respite was not well used.

The trouble was that no educated Chinese who had spent his formative years studying the Confucian classics really could believe that fundamental changes should be made in the way China was governed. Some reforms were made and often entrusted to foreigners. Thus, for example, a customs service was organized in 1863 by an Englishman, Robert Hart, who made it the most efficient branch of Chinese government. Other new enterprises, such as a nationwide postal system (introduced 1896), began as branches within the customs service, which, in fact, served as a training school in the methods of a modern bureaucracy.

Gestures were made toward creating a modern army and navy, but they remained halfhearted. Between 1875 and 1878, Chinese armies were able to reconquer Moslem and Turkish areas of central Asia, thus restoring China's boundaries to their former limits. Chinese control over Tibet and Mongolia was infirm, but never formally surrendered. On the other hand, the Russians advanced into Manchuria, the French took over Annam (1883), and the British conquered Burma (1886), thus shearing off outlying territories which had previously recognized Chinese suzerainty.

Missionaries from Europe and the United States penetrated considerable distances into inland China, and in the 1880s railroads began to open up the Chinese interior to Western goods. In the north, some coal and iron mines, equipped along Western lines, also started operation. But none of these things altered the fundamental Chinese conviction that their own ways were superior.

Then Japan and China quarreled over Korea. War broke out in 1894, and the Japanese won a series of rapid victories. This was a crushing blow to Chinese pride. For half a century, the Chinese had been forced to live with the fact that Western barbarians possessed the secret of winning wars. The Chinese had not really tried very hard to find out what that secret was. But now it was all too evident that the Japanese, who had started at no better technological level than the Chinese, had somehow learned that secret. Inaction could no longer be justified; something drastic had to be done.

REACTION TO FOREIGN POWERS   The urgency of action was all the greater because Europeans began to make plans for dividing China into spheres of influence. Germany appeared on the scene and in 1897–1898 secured concessions from the Chinese government in the Shantung Peninsula. This set off a frantic scramble on the part of other imperial powers, each eager to pin down its rights to local concessions. Control of railroad rights-of-way into the interior was the prize immediately at stake. Russia gained control of the railroads in Manchuria; Britain planned to open up the Yangtze with riverboats and railroads; the French concentrated in the south, driving a railroad northward from Hanoi to Yünnan. The Germans, as latecomers, concentrated in the region nearest Peking, where foreigners had hitherto been kept at bay. As for the United States, it advocated an "Open Door," meaning the right of every foreign power to enjoy equal access to all parts of China.

China's first reaction was a last, desperate effort to throw out the foreigners. A secret society, the so-called "Boxers," preached hatred of all outsiders, but made the mistake of relying on magical protection against European bullets. When the Boxers attacked the European legations in

Peking, tiny staffs fought them off until a relief expedition could be sent in from the coast. The Boxers were then shot down ruthlessly. The Chinese government was required to pay an indemnity for the losses suffered by the Westerners.

Failure of the Boxer Rebellion forced the reluctant Chinese to face the necessity of change. In 1905, accordingly, the imperial government abolished the ancient system of recruitment to the ranks of officialdom. Examinations testing mastery of the Confucian classics were abandoned. The effect upon Chinese life was profound. Young men who formerly had pored over the pages of the ancient sages now swarmed into missionary schools and colleges, hoping to prepare themselves for government jobs by finding the secret of Western greatness. Many young Chinese went to Japan, and the United States decided to use its share of the Boxer indemnity payments to bring Chinese students to study at American universities.

Obviously, it took time for Western-style education to take effect, since the language barriers to be crossed were unusually difficult. But the impatient Chinese could not wait for a new generation to arise, trained in Western-type schools. Revolutionary secret societies had long been a feature of Chinese life; and after the war with Japan (1894–1895), they took on new life. Sun Yat-sen (1866–1925) was the leader of one such group. He searched the political writings of Western and Japanese authors—hunting for ideas that might work in China—and came up with a hodgepodge of nationalist and socialist ideas.

In 1911 revolution broke out in China. The next year the emperor (a six-year-old boy) abdicated, and the Manchu Dynasty came to an end. Confusion only increased. Sun Yat-sen, now leader of the Kuomintang party, challenged more old-fashioned war lords who, for their part, probably dreamed of establishing a new imperial dynasty rather than carrying through a thoroughgoing revolution. Foreign diplomats and business interests added to China's troubled times; and the Japanese, who had meanwhile taken over Korea, showed signs of wishing to put a puppet of their choosing on the Chinese throne. The outbreak of World War I, in 1914, freed the Japanese from having to take European diplomatic objections to their further advance too seriously. The war did not simplify the complex China situation in any other way.

Japan

Japan's history contrasted in every respect with China's unhappy experience. In 1867 the die had been cast for radical reform with the "restoration" of the emperor. By good luck, the young man who took the title *Meiji* for his reign (1867–1912) proved to be unusually wise, judicious, and strong-willed. Over and over again, in time of crisis, his decisions as to which advisers to appoint to office were of critical importance. Under the Meiji emperor, Japan was therefore able to pursue a consistent policy. It did so with a truly amazing success.

REFORMS IN GOVERNMENT   The first and central aim of the whole undertaking was to make Japan strong, so that the nation would no longer have to fear foreign gunboats. Very quickly the clique of warriors who engineered the overthrow of the shogun recognized that this required far-reaching changes in the Japanese social scene. Thus they "abolished feudalism" between 1869 and 1871. This meant destroying the rights of the warrior class to collect rice rents from the peasants. The dispossessed warriors received handsomely engraved government bonds instead.

A postal service, a daily newspaper, and a ministry of education, whose job it was to set up schools that could train the Japanese in what they needed to know about the West, quickly followed. In 1872, universal military service was decreed. It takes a moment to realize how radical this was in Japanese society, where the right to bear arms had always been a jealously guarded privilege of the warrior class. Now peasants and merchants, even the despised outcasts who had traditionally been charged with menial tasks, were admitted to the ranks of the army. Appointment and promotion within the officer ranks were made to depend not on birth or traditional status but on competence and seniority. This established a career open to talent, appealing especially to poor peasant sons. It also provoked an armed rebellion on the part of disgruntled warriors of the old school (1877); but the new army stood the test by defeating the rebels. After the victory, the old order of things disappeared beyond all hope of recall.

The Japanese never looked back. In 1889, the emperor proclaimed a new constitution designed to resemble Bismarck's imperial system in Germany. Voting rights were limited to the richer classes. The elected diet (parliament) had only modest powers. The diet did, however, give the Japanese who mattered politically a way of making their will known to the highest circles of government. This was exactly what it was intended to do. Next came revision of the laws according to European patterns of justice. And in 1897, Japan attained respectability by putting its currency on the gold standard.

All the while, energetic efforts to introduce modern industry continued, so as to be able to supply and maintain a modern army and navy. Usually the government tried new things first. Then, when a factory had begun to turn out the desired product, the government sold it, sometimes at very low prices, to private capitalists. This meant, in effect, that the costs of starting up enterprises were carried by the government, which,

芝浦製作所
第二工場
發電機
製作場

A silk reeling factory in Japan is an example of early Japanese industrialization during the Mejii Restoration. (Courtesy of Toshiba Corporation, Tokyo, Japan)

with its tax income, was able to bear initial losses. But once private owners took over, more or less free market prices came into play. This required considerable efficiency on the part of the Japanese firms, for European and American factory-made goods were only lightly taxed on entry into the country. As a result, by 1914 some Japanese products, particularly textiles, were beginning to compete quite successfully with European and American products in the export markets of the Far East.

The Western powers recognized Japan's success by giving up extraterritorial rights (1899) which had been secured by the first treaties after the opening of Japan. Two years later, Great Britain concluded a military alliance with Japan; and in 1904–1905, the Japanese amazed all Asia and most of Europe by defeating the Russians. They annexed Formosa in 1895 after defeating the Chinese and took over control of Korea in 1910 by suppressing a Korean revolt aimed at driving them out of the country.

Throughout, the Japanese peasantry remained obedient, hard-working, poor to the edge of hunger, but energetic and ambitious all the same. At first, capital for industrial development came mainly from the peasants in the form of heavy taxes. Later, industry financed itself from profits, which came from the Japanese consumers. later still, when Japan was able to build up a substantial export trade, the burden shifted, in part, to Koreans, Chinese, and others.

This success story was made possible by the unwavering social discipline of the Japanese. The imperial authority, exercised by a changing circle of ministers and informal advisers, operated upon a society in which the habit of command and obedience had been cultivated for centuries. Military clans had formerly been in control; now it was shifting cliques of upstarts, eventually diluted by a sprinkling of ordinary commoners, who gave commands. The aim was much the same; that is, military strength and greatness, not any longer for a single clan, but rather for Japan as a whole.

Universal elementary education opened Japanese minds to many aspects of Western civilization beyond the merely technical. But the idea of equality or of liberty, as developed in the West in the nineteenth century, made little impression. The Democratic Revolution, in other words, did not come to Japan with the Industrial Revolution. Instead, the speed and smoothness with which the Japanese adopted Western industrial and military technology depended on the survival of old-fashioned inequality.

India

Hindu India was like Japan in one respect. A considerable number of Indians went to European-type schools and acquired some familiarity with European civilization. Yet the differences between Japan and Hindu India were far greater than the likenesses. The liberal principles of British administration in India required the government to keep its hands off most economic matters. These were thought to belong, as in England, to the sphere of private enterprise. But, except for a small number of Parsis (believers in Zoroastrianism) and other foreigners, no one in India was ready or able to start up modern industry or bring in new techniques, as the Japanese government did so successfully.

Consequently, despite a fine railroad network, a remarkably honest government, and legal freedom to act, industrial development came very slowly to India. The government's policy of allowing free trade meant that Indian manufacturers were exposed to competition from British factories. The Japanese labored under the same handicap at the beginning, when their tariffs were fixed at a very low rate by treaty agreement

A workshop in an Indian diamond field. (*Bettmann Archive*)

with the Western powers. Free trade alone was not to blame, as Indian nationalists have often claimed. It was, basically, the lack of any will on the part of any significant group of people to do anything about the down-to-earth business of factory production. To British-educated Indians, the prestige of work in a government office was so great that any other career seemed unattractive.

Population growth made famines serious. Systematic countermeasures, begun in 1883, had the effect of keeping more people alive in time of crop failure. But this failed to solve the problem, and indeed only made it worse. Too many persons remained alive to be fed properly from the available land, given the existing level of agricultural skills.

In the sphere of politics, Hindu India was more active. In 1885, the Indian National Congress met for the first time. Delegates discussed political questions and petitioned for a larger share in government policy-making. The Congress leaders took the ideals of the British liberal parliamentary tradition seriously. And although they did not get all they asked for, little by little the British did bring Indian representatives into the higher councils of government.

In 1905, political agitation showed a different face. The British decided to divide the large and wealthy province of Bengal into two. This roused suspicion that the British were really trying to create a predominantly Moslem state in one half of Bengal (what is now East Pakistan) and a Hindu state in the other half, in accordance with the ancient precept of "divide and rule." Protests were organized, not only among the educated upper class but also among the rank and file of Calcutta and other cities. A handful of terrorists tried to use assassination as a way to register their feelings. The British responded with repression but, in 1911, decided that the wiser course was to unite the two halves of Bengal once more.

Except for this flare-up of popular agitation in Bengal, most Indians remained untouched by political debates. When the capital was moved to Delhi in 1911, the new king of England, George V, came to India to be crowned Emperor of India. A splendid gathering of Indian princes seemed to prove the loyalty and contentment of the Indian peoples under British rule.

Islam

Indian Moslems seldom attended British schools, and few of them entered the Indian administration. They played larger roles in the army but, by and large, the Moslems of India found it hard to accustom themselves to Christian rule. This was also true of other Moslems, even though by 1914 a very large part of the Islamic world was under the political control of Europeans. The French began to move into north Africa in 1830, capturing Algiers in that year. In 1881 they took over Tunis to the east. In 1912 the French protectorate over Morocco, to the west, received international recognition, although only after German opposition had twice triggered international crises. French power also reached southward across the Sahara and overran most of the Moslem kingdoms of west Africa; and Moslem areas of Africa which escaped the French were conquered by the British.

Italy took Tripoli in 1911 after a war with the Turks; and Egypt fell under British control in 1882. When a sectarian leader proclaimed himself the Mahdi (that is, divinely appointed leader of all true Moslems) and drove Egyptian administrators out of the Sudan, British arms were summoned to impose Anglo-Egyptian control throughout the region. The Red Sea and Persian Gulf shorelines were also under British influence; so was the southern portion of Persia and Afghanistan. Most of these lands retained nominal independence, but by giving and withholding subsidies and supplies, the British were able to put their friends in power and keep their enemies harmless.

From the landward side, Moslem states fared no better. The Russians and Chinese, between them, squeezed out the last independent khanates of central Asia by 1884. Russia controlled the northern third of Persia as a result of a general agreement reached with Britain in 1907. In the

Balkans, the Ottoman Turks lost ground to Bulgars and Albanians, as well as to the Serbs and Greeks who had won their indepedence in the first half of the century. No ray of hope relieved this dismal record of defeat and retreat. Everywhere Moslems continued to suffer defeat in war. Military failure was all the harder to endure because from the days of the Prophet Mohammed, success on the battlefield and the blessing of Allah had been closely linked in Moslem minds.

INTERNAL PROBLEMS   Turks, Persians, and Afghans still ruled nominally independent states. Each had all the makings of a nation, with a history, language, and military tradition of its own. But the two strongest of these nations, the Turks and the Persians, faced a dilemma; for if they became out-and-out nationalists, they stood to lose an empire over other peoples.

In 1908, for example, a secret society of army officers and reformers, who went by the name "Young Turks," started a revolution in the Ottoman Empire. They wished to make the empire over into a secular state. In this fashion they hoped that the age-old conflict between Moslems and Christians would disappear. Everyone, it was hoped, could learn to be a good "Ottoman," whatever his religion might be. The Young Turks took it for granted that Turks would continue to rule the state. When elections resulted in a parliament in which Bulgars, Greeks, Armenians, Albanians, and other nationalities all stubbornly defended their own self-interests, the Young Turks resorted in disgust to a coup d' état. They then established an authoritarian regime whose leading figures turned more and more to Pan-Turkism as a substitute for Ottomanism. The idea was to arouse the Turkish-speaking subjects of the Russian and Chinese empires to a sense of their common destiny with the Ottoman Turks. The leaders of the Young Turks began to dream of a vast Asian empire, in which Turks would be a majority of the population and rule the state. This brought the Turkish government into World War I on the German side, since Pan-Turkism could only become a political fact after the dismemberment of the Russian Empire.

As for the Persians, their subject nationalities were mostly of Turkish speech. What made such Turks "Persian" was the Shia form of Islam they had inherited from the Safavid period. Any shift from the traditional religious basis of the Persian state therefore threatened an immediate breakup, which no Persian welcomed.

The Arabs and the Indian Moslems were, of all Moslems, the most confused. They found it hard to choose between the ideal of a local nation-state—Egypt, Syria, etc.—and the ideal of a Pan-Arab empire. More important, they could not decide between trying to build a strong secular state and remaining faithful to the Sacred Law of Islam. Yet the fact remained that one interfered with the other; and, wanting both, the Arabs got neither.

Up to 1914, they remained sullen and angry, almost untouched by either the Industrial or the Democratic revolutions. As for the Moslems of India, they had only a choice of evils. Having no country of their own, they feared the Hindu majority around them as much as, or more than, they disliked being subjected to British rule.

There were parts of the world where Islam continued to prosper. In much of Africa and in southeast Asia, the faith of Mohammed continued to make converts, despite the competiton of Christian missionaries. Islam offered peoples emerging from isolation all the benefits of a civilized faith: literacy, a world view that answered all fundamental questions, and a code of conduct that could be used to guide everyday behavior. It had the further advantages of allowing a man to marry more than one wife (an important consideration among polygamous peoples) and of not being associated with the politically dominant whites from Europe. But continued Moslem missionary success in these regions of the world offered small comfort to the Moslems of the heartlands. They scarcely knew what was happening in such distant parts, and the knowledge would have been of no benefit in solving their own pressing problems.

AFRICANS
AND AMERINDIANS

The European explorers who crisscrossed the interior of sub-Saharan Africa between 1850 and 1880 were only the advance guard for other Europeans who followed hard on their heels, eager to bring the blessings of Christian civilization to the heart of the "Dark Continent." These blessings took different forms. Mission schools and hospitals relieved ignorance and pain. Traders supplied cheap cotton cloth, tin cans, and other useful commodities. Officials and soldiers repressed the slave trade and overthrew native rulers, or reduced their powers by giving advice that could not be disregarded without risking punishment.

In some parts of Africa, minerals were discovered and African labor was put to work in the mines or in performing other tasks for European capitalists. However, wages often failed to provide an inducement to make Africans work, since they had little use for the things money could buy. Consequently, in places like the Congo, Europeans resorted to forced labor, which was not very different from the slavery which had just been abolished. Nevertheless, when news leaked out about the way King Leopold of Belgium was treating the Congolese, widespread protests in Europe persuaded the Belgian government to abandon the system of compulsory labor.

European Destruction
of African Kingdoms

The French and British were the most active imperial powers in Africa, as elsewhere in the world. The French expanded southward from north Africa, and by the 1890s had brought most of western Africa under their rule. French ambitions extended eastward, toward the Nile, with the idea of linking up eventually with a toehold on the Red Sea at Djibouti, which was already in French possession. This, of course, collided head on with the Cape-to-Cairo ambitions that Cecil Rhodes and other British imperialists had conceived. The critical confrontation came in 1898 at Fashoda (present-day Kodok) on the Upper Nile. A French party reached this town early in the year, just before the British—having defeated the Mahdi and his fanatical Moslem followers—proceeded south up the river to make sure of control of the Nile sources. After a few tense weeks, the French government yielded. Anglo-Egyptian control of the entire length of the White Nile, all the way to Lake Victoria, was assured.

A major reason for the French backdown in 1898 was the agreement, already in the making, which brought the British into friendly understand-

An artist's impression of Stanley's famous meeting with Livingstone.
(*New York Public Library Picture Collection*)

"DR. LIVINGSTONE, I PRESUME?"

David Livingstone prepared himself to become a Christian missionary by earning a medical degree so that he might minister to men's bodies as well as to their souls. He wanted to go to China, but the London Missionary Society sent him to Africa instead. There he became a pioneer and explorer, pushing into new territories where white men had seldom or never been before. His published journals made him famous, for they described the new lands he visited with charming simplicity and scientific precision.

In 1866 he started from Zanzibar on what turned out to be his last adventure. He wanted to solve the ancient puzzle: where did the Nile start? Illness delayed him; his servants ran away; and he had trouble finding a boat with which to cross Lake Tanganyika. Years went by with no news of Livingstone's whereabouts. Everyone in the outside world assumed that he had died somewhere in the interior of Africa.

Henry Morton Stanley was another adventurer. Born in Wales, he ran away to sea and jumped ship in New Orleans in time to enlist in the Confederate army in 1861. Captured in 1862, he changed sides and enlisted in the Union army instead. Later he became a famous journalist, traveling to trouble spots all round the world. In 1871, the *New York Herald* commissioned him to find Livingstone, dead or alive. Stanley organized an expedition at Zanzibar and plunged into the interior of Africa as Livingstone had done more than four years before.

After months of difficult travel, Stanley found him, living quietly by the shores of Lake Tanganyika. But the two men, both British born, had never met. And there was nobody to introduce them. So Stanley, according to his own report, broke the ice by saying: "Dr. Livingstone, I presume?"

The two men did some exploring together and discovered that Lake Tanganyika drains westward into the Congo River, not northward into the Nile. Then Stanley returned to Zanzibar with the news of Livingstone's survival and with fresh installments of his journals to prove it. But Livingstone stayed behind, determined to continue his search for the sources of the Nile. He died on the quest two years later (1873), after months of fever.

ing with the French in order to oppose German power. German ambition
was asserted in Africa as well as in China, with the result that part of
Togoland and Tanganyika became German; and German control of Tanganyika interrupted the Cape-to-Cairo route of which Rhodes had
dreamed. In 1908, Belgium acquired the Congo from King Leopold, who
had organized a private company to develop the Congo region. Portugal
and Spain also possessed African colonies. The Italians tried to build
an empire in the northeast corner of the continent by conquering Ethiopia.
However, an invasion attempt failed in 1896 when Ethiopian warriors
rallied under King Menelik and defeated the Italians, who then had to

content themselves with two patches of desert near the mouth of the Red Sea, supplemented (1911) by Tripoli in the north.

Ethiopia, in the east, and Liberia, a state founded in 1822 by slaves sent back to Africa from the United States, were the only African states— other than the white-ruled South Africa—to remain independent in fact as well as in law. Egypt retained a theoretical sovereignty, but British control made this a hollow pretense. It would be misleading to suggest that the boundaries drawn by European diplomats corresponded very closely to human reality on the ground. Sometimes the new administrative frontiers divided peoples with a common language and traditions. Often they grouped very different peoples under a single administration. But European officials could not change customs all at once, even when they wished to do so.

THE "NEW" AFRICA   Perhaps the most striking thing about the Africa that was subjected to Europeans between 1850 and 1914, was its great variety. Wide racial differences existed, especially in eastern Africa. Literally hundreds of languages were spoken. Most were local, used only by a single people; but Arabic and Swahili were spoken up and down the east coast; while in the interior of Africa, the Bantu family of languages extended over much of western and southern Africa. There were tribes, and powerful war confederacies, as well as villages in which no political authority existed. A few well-organized bureaucratic kingdoms, like that of Buganda, also awaited European explorers; but most of the better-organized states were soon attacked and destroyed by the European empire-builders.

By 1914, Africa's variety was half hidden by a veneer of European administration. But even after 1900, when the struggle among the great powers for control over Africa came to a stop because practically the whole continent had been apportioned, isolated rebellions and desperate wars, sometimes fought to the bitter end, continued to trouble the European administrators. The British, for example, fought no fewer than five wars against the Ashanti before they annexed their land and made it into the northern part of what they called the Gold Coast and what is called Ghana today. The Germans crushed a revolt in Tanganyika in 1905 by destroying the tribe that had challenged their authority. But such events were unusual. Most of the African continent submitted peaceably enough to European control.

Amerindian Peoples

The other large human population existing on the fringes of civilization between 1850 and 1914 lived in the central portion of the Americas, between Peru and Bolivia on the south and Mexico on the north. They

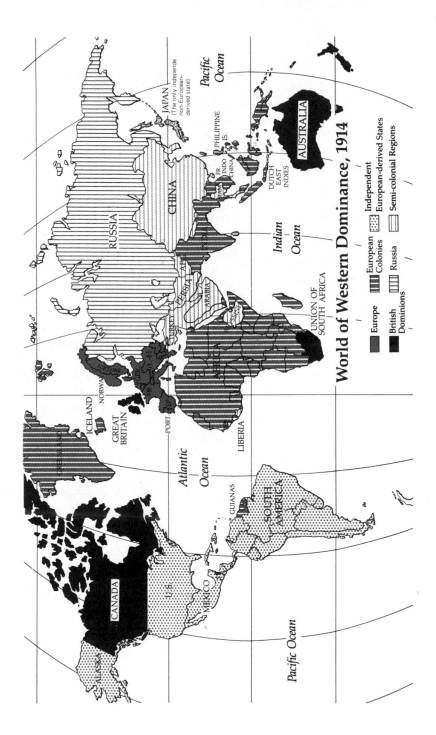

World of Western Dominance, 1914

Europe | British Dominions | European Colonies | Independent European-derived States | Russia | Semi-colonial Regions

JAPAN (The only independent non-European-derived state)

Pacific Ocean

RUSSIA

CHINA

PHILIPPINE

FR. INDO CHINA

DUTCH EAST INDIES

AUSTRALIA

Indian Ocean

PERSIA

ARABIA

UNION OF SOUTH AFRICA

AFRICA

ICELAND

GREAT BRITAIN

NORWAY

SWEDEN

PORT.

LIBERIA

Atlantic Ocean

GREENLAND

BR. GUIANAS

SOUTH AMERICA

CANADA

US

MEXICO

ALASKA

Pacific Ocean

were the descendants of Amerindians, who had inhabited these regions before the Spaniards came, with some admixture of Spanish blood. When Spain fell under French control in 1808 as an incident in the Napoleonic wars, "loyal" Spaniards in the Americas refused to recognize the authority of Napoleon's puppet government in Madrid. Even when the French were driven out of Spain (1814), the Spanish colonies in America remained in turmoil. Fighting between liberals and conservatives led to a liberal victory and the establishment of republican governments. By 1824, the success of the Latin American revolutions was established. More stable governments gradually emerged.

In the parts of the Spanish empire inhabited chiefly by people of European descent, the liberal ideals that had come to the front during the revolutionary years offered no special difficulties. The church was the main target of the liberals; control over church lands was a principal bone of contention among military and party leaders. In the regions where Amerindian populations were a majority, however, the liberals faced a special problem. Should the ideals of self-government extend also to the Amerindians? In South America, the white ruling classes answered this question in the negative. In Mexico, on the contrary, the answer was in the affirmative. Benito Juárez—the liberal champion against Emperor Maximilian and the French from 1860 to 1872—was of Indian parentage and got much of his support from the Indians and men of mixed blood. Later, to be sure, Mexico came under the control of Porfirio Díaz (1876–1911), who favored foreign investment and the landowning class more than the poor. In 1911 he was overthrown by a revolutionary movement, aimed against United States capital as well as against the rich at home. Resulting diplomatic disputes between the United States and Mexico led in 1916 to minor military skirmishes along the border between the two countries.

Meanwhile, the ruling cliques of Peru, Ecuador, Bolivia, Colombia, and Venezuela quarreled vigorously among themselves for control of the government. But they always stopped short of appealing to the Amerindian villagers—partly, perhaps, because the peasants would not listen and partly because the whites feared for their position in society if ever the Amerindian majority should enter actively into politics. Therefore, being unable to mobilize wide support in their countries, all such regimes remained comparatively weak and were often unstable, as was shown by the victories won by Chile whose population was predominantly white against Peru and Bolivia whose populations were predominantly Amerindian (1879–1884).

CONCLUSION

In spite of the survival of remote Andean villages almost untouched by world events and the existence of similar village communities in some other parts of the globe, it still remained true that the world had become united as never before. Between 1850 and 1914, Europe, like a great spider, had spun a web of rails and telegraph lines around the globe. All humankind was caught in it. Struggles to escape, to withdraw, to get back to the good old times when strangers and outsiders didn't matter, were in vain. In the next chapters we will survey the whole globe, decade by decade, to see what people have, to date, done with the unparalleled opportunities and difficulties this new state of the world created for humanity and for each segment, class, group, and individual that, taken together, make up humankind.

TRANSPORTATION AND COMMUNICATION

To those who lack long-range means of travel and communication, walking is the only way to go and talking face to face the only way to communicate. The people to get along with, guard against, trade with, and pay attention to are those living nearby; and such people are referred to as neighbors.

Through most of history this was the case, although from the beginning of civilization, ships and pack animals gave some people a longer reach. Writing, wagons, and mounted messengers came later; but by 500 B.C. transportation and communication reached a limit that lasted for about 2000 years. Using relays of horses or simple sailing vessels, a person could travel about 100 miles a day, whether by land or by sea.

Then, beginning about 500 years ago, a series of new inventions transformed transportation and communication. Greater speed changed the definition of "neighbor," until today all of us have become neighbors throughout the habitable globe.

Breaking the Ocean Barriers

Between 1400 and 1500, Europeans learned how to make ships that could travel safely across stormy seas and in waters where tides ran swift and high. Strongly built hulls, a big rudder, and multiple masts with sails that could be put up or down, according to the strength of the wind, all played their part in making ships safer and more maneuverable.

With such vessels, long voyages across the oceans became easy. But how to get back? This required new methods of navigation, which would allow a ship to find its position by observing the sun or the stars. European sailors—especially the Portuguese—worked out this problem, too, by 1500.

Finally, how to protect oneself against strangers, whether on sea or land? The answer was to put cannon on board ship. Strong hulls, built to hold up against heavy waves, could also withstand the recoil of heavy guns.

HIGHLIGHTS

When all these things came together, travel across the oceans lost most of its terror.

Within less than thirty years (1492–1521), European seafarers broke through the vast ocean barriers that had previously divided humanity into separate continental blocks.

The North Atlantic is a stormy ocean. When European sailors learned to master its waves and currents, no sea was difficult for them.

The opening of the oceans by European ships started new kinds of interaction among the peoples of the world. Trade, migration, and exchange both of diseases and of new food crops all took new paths.

Printing

Printing from wooden blocks was invented by the Chinese before A.D. 800. Since Chinese writing uses thousands of different signs or characters, it was easier to carve a whole page at a time than to assemble separate bits of type made in advance.

In Korea and in Europe, however, alphabetic writing required only a small number of different signs. Therefore it made sense to cast type for each letter in multiple copies ahead of time, and then to assemble the movable type into words.

In Europe the first book printed in this manner was made in Germany by Johann Gutenberg in 1454.

HIGHLIGHTS

Printing made it possible to produce large numbers of copies of a text cheaply and accurately. This had revolutionary effects in Europe but a conservative effect in China.

In China, printing was used to reproduce the Confucian classics and commentaries upon them. Wider familiarity with these texts simply strengthened Confucian ideas and attitudes.

Among Europeans, an intensified interaction of old and new ideas and information shook established beliefs. Printing spread the Protestant Reformation. It also spread information that came pouring in after the opening of the oceans. Europeans also used printing to reproduce Christian and pagan classics, making them more easily available.

Inland Transport

Since the invention of ships, water transportation had always been much cheaper than land transport, and often faster as well. Canals could extend the advantages of water transportation inland, even where natural riverways were absent. Locks allowed barges to travel up over a watershed, crossing from one river basin to another. In northwestern Europe, canal-building became important for inland transportation between 1750 and 1850. Canals could carry heavy loads cheaply once they were built; but in many cases construction and maintenance were costly.

Roads used by wheeled vehicles must have some kind of drainage; otherwise the rain softens the surface, mudholes develop, and the road soon turns into a quagmire. The Romans built narrow roads of paving stones. After 1700, Europe-

An illustration of a Viking ship. (*Library of Congress*)

ans discovered a much cheaper way of making durable roads by scattering gravel on the roadbed so that rain could drain away without leaving mudholes behind. Smooth roads allowed higher speed, so stagecoaches carried goods and passengers as much as 100 miles a day, reaching the old limit civilized peoples had known ever since they tamed the horse.

HIGHLIGHTS

Cheaper movement of heavy goods by water and faster movement of goods and passengers by land intensified interaction across longer distances.

Rapid economic development resulted, with remarkable growth of both industry and agriculture.

Nationwide solidarity and cooperation set in more intensively than before.

As a result, national wealth and power increased, especially in the states of northwestern Europe, England, France, and the Netherlands.

Popular Press

Early presses were worked by men using their own muscles to press a sheet of paper against a bed of ink-covered type. Even with the help of carefully designed levers this went rather slowly. A few hundred printed sheets per hour was all that could be printed, as long as the press worked by moving back and forth, toward and away from the typeface.

Faster printing came by making the type fit onto a curved, cylindrical surface. Such a cylinder could print by spinning around while a long sheet of paper rolled past. Cylinder presses made on this principle could print many thousands of sheets in an hour.

HIGHLIGHTS

High-speed printing gave birth to mass circulation newspapers and magazines. Newspapers and magazines read by millions created a new kind of interaction between the government and the public. Mass circulation newspapers often appealed to crude and ill-educated readers by simplifying problems, distorting facts, rousing emotions.

But government action supported by the aroused will of a whole people attained much greater force than had been possible before and used greater resources, both human and material, to carry through common purposes.

Steam Railroad

Railroads reduce friction between wheels and the ground by concentrating comparatively large weights on very narrow, hard rails. This principle was first used mainly in hauling coal, both inside the mines and on the surface. Men or children and animals could drag heavy coal wagons along wooden or metal rails.

The railroad came into its own when steam power was set to work moving whole trains of cars along metal rails. More powerful locomotives and carefully prepared roadbeds allowed the trains to reach speeds up to 100 miles per hour.

HIGHLIGHTS

Railroads could carry people and goods overland faster than ever before and often more cheaply than by other methods of overland transport.

Railroads linked up with ocean-going steamships to deliver cheap grain to European ports from America and Australia. This damaged European agriculture and forced millions of European peasant farmers to emigrate to America.

The rise of Germany and of the United States as great powers depended on the development of the continental interiors of Europe and North America. Railroads opened up these interiors between 1850 and 1914.

Global Communication

Smoke signals and fire beacons spread alarms in very ancient times. Semaphore

A Chinese war junk, ca. 19th century. (Illustrated London News, *March 21, 1857*)

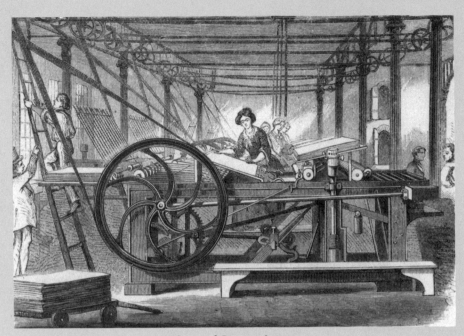

A 19th century printing press. (Library of Congress)

flag stations carried more complicated messages during the Napoleonic wars. But from the 1830s the electric telegraph offered a far superior way of sending messages over long distances.

By interrupting an electric current according to a prearranged code, messages could be transmitted instantly wherever a copper wire could reach. Waterproof cables, laid across the ocean beds, soon linked continent with continent. Key points in the world came into instantaneous contact with one another.

After 1876, telephone communication speeded up the process, since words can be spoken faster than a telegraph operator can send letters by code. Over long distances, however, background noise often made spoken words unclear when telegraph signals could get through.

A modern high-speed printing press. (Laimute Druskis)

Telegraph and telephone extended the range of human communication enormously, by linking up the globe into a single communications network.

Person-to-person interaction became possible anywhere on the earth where telegraph wires reached.

Orders for purchase and sale could reach around the world. This created a world market for standard bulk commodities like wheat.

Central command and precise control, both in peacetime diplomacy and in war, became possible for the first time.

Mass Communication

Wireless communication uses electromagnetic waves to transmit messages at the speed of light. Complicated transmitters and simpler radio and television receivers allow massive communication at low cost. The only important limitation is that electromagnetic waves travel in straight lines and, unless bounced off reflecting layers of the atmosphere, soon leave the earth. Sending stations can be connected by wires, however, to relay a given signal.

Radio and television stations create a new form of mass communication, since the same messages can be sent into millions of homes at small cost to the sender.

Political propaganda by radio and television exercise a strong influence, especially in countries where the government maintains control of sending stations.

Radio and television tend to reduce class and regional differences within the radius of the broadcast.

Air and Space Travel

Flying changed patterns of long-distance travel fundamentally. Old barriers fell. Mountains, deserts, and valleys ceased to

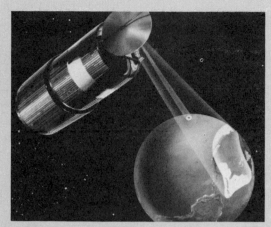

An illustration of the Westar IV communication satellite. (Western Union Corporation)

matter much for overland travel; harbors, tides, and shoals ceased to affect travel overseas. For long flights earth became a sphere, making the Arctic a particularly strategic region. This is because major population concentrations are in the northern hemisphere; and the shortest air routes between distant population centers always follow the bulge of the earth northward toward the Arctic. The earth became still smaller when rocket propulsion opened the possibility of escape from earth's gravity and exploration of the solar system.

Air and space travel changed transport routes and shortened time of travel between distant portions of the globe.

In case of a war, air and space travel mean that every state's borders are in danger.

Humanity's exploration of the earth and space beyond the earth continues with consequences—psychological, political, economic, and ecological—still unknown and unknowable.

CHAPTER 10

World Wars of the Twentieth Century

1914 to 1945

The two world wars of the twentieth century, World War I, 1914–1918, and World War II, 1939–1945, were similar in many ways and should be discussed together. Both began in Europe and pitted Germany against a coalition of allies; and in both wars Germany was eventually defeated. But Germany's defeat came only after American resources and manpower were brought into action on European soil; and by 1945 the national power of the United States had clearly outstripped all other nations, not just in Europe but all round the globe. American predominance was temporary, to be sure. But the rise of the United States, together with that of the Union of Soviet Socialist Republics (USSR) and of Japan, marked the end of the era of world leadership by nations of western Europe—an era that dated back to the sixteenth century.

The wars marked the end of an era in another sense as well. Before 1914, democratic and parliamentary government, together with the private pursuit of profit in the marketplace, seemed the wave of the future—the path of progress along which all peoples might be expected eventually to travel on the way to a peaceful and prosperous future. However, the wars showed that things were not that simple. The brutality and bloodshed of warfare itself—an experience more shocking in 1914 than in 1939— was obviously incompatible with the old confidence in civilized progress. In addition, it became clear that politically organized effort, overriding the rules of private profit, could increase production and magnify national

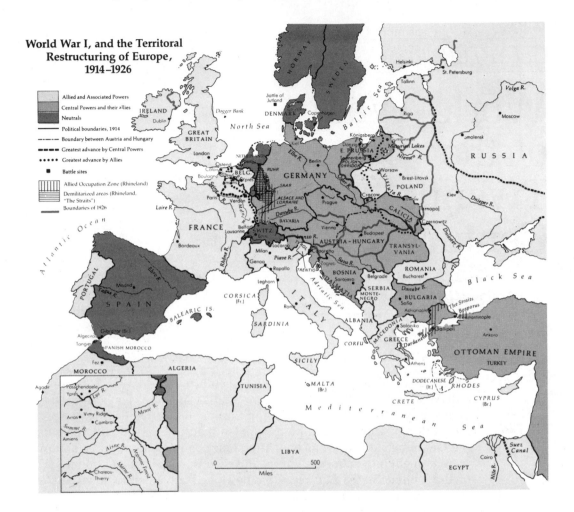

World War I, and the Territoral
Restructuring of Europe,
1914–1926

power far more efficiently than anyone had previously imagined. Managed economies worked wonders, more spectacularly in World War II than in World War I, making a return to unregulated private pursuit of profit impossible.

Democratic and parliamentary government also met with new challenges. The communist regime of Russia after 1917 and the Fascist regime of Italy after 1922 both emphasized an ideal of *solidarity*—class solidarity for Lenin and his followers in Russia, and national solidarity for Mussolini and his followers in Italy. Communists and Fascists agreed that democratic parties and elections simply allowed selfish pursuit of private interests. This, they claimed, was both wicked and inefficient. Instead, some sort of socialist management or corporate organization of human effort would get more done and leave the old liberal, bourgeois selfishness of pre-war society behind. Fascism was discredited by the defeat of Germany and Italy in World War II; and during and after World War II, Russian communism began to look more and more inefficient. But the pre-1914 assurance that the democratic, liberal, and parliamentary recipe for good government was universally applicable and adequate for all situations could never be recovered.

Finally, the experience of World Wars I and II altered popular attitudes toward war. In 1914, the prospect of a short, victorious campaign was welcomed by millions of civilians who were called up to serve in the national army in accordance with mobilization plans laid down long in advance. War seemed a test of fitness, a way of asserting and preserving national greatness, and a useful instrument of statecraft. Years later, after two global wars, and after millions of people had been slaughtered, the glory and heroism of war diminished almost to the vanishing point. Yet fear of war did not prevent continued preparation for war. Instead, an ever more costly arms race broke out after 1945 even more vigorously than before 1914. And today, though nuclear weapons have made World War III suicidal, that arms race continues.

In all these respects, the two great wars of the twentieth century constitute a turning point in world affairs, whose full implications and long-range consequences we do not yet know. But it looks as though they will mark the end of what used to be called the modern era of world history—an era that began about 1450 and ended, perhaps, in 1945. We have no name for the new era, if indeed the course of future events will make it seem proper to call the period since 1945 a new era. We who live through it can only wonder and wait to see how things turn out.

OUTBREAK OF WORLD WAR I

In Sarajevo, the capital of Bosnia, on June 28, 1914 an angry young man named Gavrilo Princip shot and killed Archduke Francis Ferdinand, heir to the throne of Austria-Hungary. Princip was a Serb, and the Austrians held the Serbian government responsible for the assassination. Friction between Serbia and the Austro-Hungarian monarchy was already acute. Serbs lived on both sides of the border between the two countries, and Serbian nationalists wanted to unite their people into a single sovereign state. But when Princip resorted to murder, the Austrian government decided to teach the Serbs a lesson. They believed, mistakenly, that other

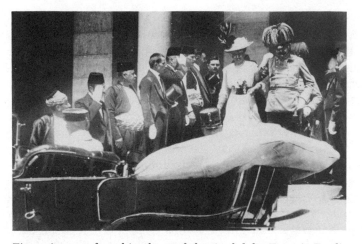

Five minutes after this photo of the Archduke Francis Ferdinand and his wife Sophie was taken, both were assassinated by Gavrilo Princip. The death of the Archduke proved to be the one crisis which the major European powers were unable to resolve without war. (UPI/Bettmann Newsphotos)

European governments would not support assassins; and, indeed, if Austrian demands on the Serbian government had been more moderate, or if the Serbian government had not gone very far towards meeting Austrian demands, it is likely that the crisis would have remained limited to the Balkan cockpit where it started.

But the rival alliances into which the European great powers had divided since 1907 came immediately into play, making a diplomatic crisis into a catastrophe. Russia backed the Serbs; Germany backed the Austrians; France rallied to the Russian side against Germany; and Great Britain, after hesitating and trying to find a peaceful solution through negotiation, finally came in on the side of France and Russia. Only Italy, which had been formally allied with Germany and Austria, held back. Thus the crisis escalated into full-scale war, breaking out between July 28, when Austria declared war on Serbia, and August 3, 1914, when Great Britain declared war against Germany and Austria.

One reason for the way things turned out was that the great powers of the European continent all had carefully worked out mobilization plans. These could be put into effect by a simple order, but once started, could not be altered without risking paralyzing confusion. Each plan was designed to bring a maximal number of soldiers into action in the shortest possible time, using railroads to deliver soldiers and supplies to strategic locations in accordance with very precisely calculated timetables. Whichever army got going soonest with the largest forces would be able to impose its strategic plan on the enemy, and, according to plan, could then expect to win a decisive victory in a matter of a few weeks. Everything depended on speed, numbers, and the quality of troops and materiel brought to the field of battle. Delay or hesitation, once the first mobilization order had been given, was too risky to contemplate. As a result, the Austrian decision to attack the Serbs provoked Russian mobilization, quickly followed by German and French mobilization; and once rival mobilization plans went into action, there was no turning back.

As events showed, the German war plan was the most effective. A vast German army began to march across Belgium, intending to cross into northern France, surround Paris, and then take the French army, deployed along the German frontier, in the rear. The plan worked for the first few weeks, but as the Germans approached Paris, early in September, a gap opened between two of the advancing columns, and the French were able to attack through the hole that had opened up in the German front. Fearing that their vanguard might be cut off, the Germans decided to withdraw behind the Marne River on September 9.

Stalemate
and Intensified War Effort

This meant that the German plan had failed, but the French plan for attacking Germany directly across the frontier had also failed disastrously, and Russian armies, advancing into East Prussia, were turned back by September 15 as well. Even the Austrian forces assigned to conquer the little state of Serbia were unsuccessful. Machine guns and rifle fire proved far more lethal against attacking infantry than anyone had expected. The only thing to do was to dig in furiously, for even hastily built trenches could protect soldiers from rifle and machine gun bullets.

In France, accordingly, a system of trenches came into existence by the end of 1914 that ran unbrokenly from the Swiss frontier in the south to the shores of the English channel in the north. Efforts to break through proved futile throughout the ensuing four years, though both sides tried, over and over again, to win decisive victory on this, the Western, front. In the East, geographic distances were such that trench systems never ran continuously along the entire front. Armies were therefore able to take the offensive and move scores or even hundreds of miles at a time, forward and back. But until 1917 stalemate also prevailed on the Eastern front. Even the most smashing victory soon petered out because an advancing army inevitably ran out of supplies, while the defeated forces recovered their fighting capacity by getting closer to their own sources of food and ammunition.

In this unexpected situation, European governments saw two ways of winning. One was to find new allies, thus extending the front, and

Trench warfare on the Western front: A wounded British soldier is prepared for evacuation. (National Archives)

strengthening one side at the expense of the other. By 1916, diplomatic pressure, promises of territorial gains, and *coup d'état* in Greece divided most of Europe between the two sides. Italy, Romania, and Greece joined the Allies; Bulgaria and Turkey joined the Central Powers. Even after Serbia was overrun by a combined German, Austrian, and Bulgarian offensive in 1915, the Serbian army fought on, based on Greek soil; and the Central Powers, despite their initial victories in Belgium and northern France, and subsequent advances into Polish territory in the east, remained almost completely surrounded by hostile forces. Until 1917, when the United States entered the war, the policy of finding new allies therefore proved ineffective in tipping the balance one way or the other in any decisive fashion. It simply engaged more countries and peoples in the struggle and made the eventual peace settlement more complicated.

The second way to win the war was to intensify mobilization, bringing more men into combat and equipping them with more and more artillery and other heavy weapons. Military experts agreed that a really massive preliminary bombardment by thousands of guns could smash the enemy's trenches and permit a decisive breakthrough. The flaw in this plan was that surprise became impossible as the open trenches of 1914 were turned into ever more elaborate underground fortifications, and became able to withstand even a prolonged bombardment.

Consequently, an energetic British effort to win the war by building a new mass army equipped with hitherto unheard of quantities of artillery turned out to be in vain. A long and bloody Battle of the Somme in 1916 only sufficed to relieve pressure on the French, who were barely able to withstand an intense German assault aimed at the fortress of Verdun. But as before, the end result was stalemate.

Despite these failures, mobilization of the rear to provide more and more shells and other supplies for the front had important consequences for European countries. In effect, the principal combatant governments learned to make their nations over into a single war-making firm, maximizing output of goods and soldiers needed for the war effort by subordinating everything else to a national plan. Rationing of scarce goods, allocating critical materials, and keying industrial production to the needs of the armed forces all came into being. The effect was to raise war-making capacity to unimagined heights: but all for naught, as one attack after another failed to achieve expected results.

Nicolai Lenin [Vladimir Ilich Ulyanov], 1870–1924. (Bettmann Archive)

THE SEALED TRAIN

Vladimir Ilich Ulyanov took the name "Lenin" when he became a revolutionary. The czarist government arrested him; later he fled from Russia and lived in Switzerland. He was there when World War I broke out. Switzerland remained neutral, completely surrounded by warring nations.

News of the March 1917 uprisings in Petrograd, the Russian capital, made Lenin desperate to get back. He wanted to take command of the Bolshevik party he had founded and carry the revolution onward to more and more radical stages. He wanted to end the war by overthrowing the landlords and capitalists, first in Russia and then in all the world. But how could he hope to escape from his Swiss refuge?

German agents in Switzerland knew a lot about Lenin and his plan for "turning imperialist war into class war." They thought, "Why not help Lenin to get back home and let him stir up the Russians to fight one another instead of fighting us?" The German Supreme Command had no objection. When the kaiser heard of the plan, he suggested that Lenin should be sent copies of all his latest speeches!

But Lenin was afraid. Perhaps the Germans only wanted to capture him by offering to let him ride a train through Germany to neutral Sweden. And his enemies might discredit him as a German agent if he took advantage of such an offer. All the same, he simply had to get back if all his dreams and life's work were not to fail.

1917–1918:
The Years of Decision

Some governments were, nonetheless, better equipped than others to manage the mobilization of resources that had become necessary. The Austro-Hungarian monarchy, for example, had to depend on help from Germany to make up for gaps in home production of artillery and other war goods. Internal frictions among the different nationalities of the empire became more intense as the war went on and paralyzed the state by 1918. Turkey, too, depended on Germany for war supplies; and frictions between the Turkish government and some of its Arab subjects turned into a critical weakness by the last months of the war.

But the most important country that got into serious trouble on the home front was Russia. The czarist government achieved remarkable results in increasing its armament production; but by 1917 food and other

On April 9, 1917, Lenin settled the issue. He would accept the German offer, provided the Germans would seal off the train so that no one could get on or off while passing through German territory. In this way, Lenin hoped that he could escape the charge of cooperating with the Germans. A train was made ready at once, and about twenty Russian revolutionaries, chosen by Lenin, got on board.

The trip lasted several days, with long delays in various switching yards. Each time the train stopped, the little group of Russians wondered whether they would all be arrested or perhaps killed. But the delays were caused by the fact that the German authorities had to clear the plan for sending Lenin and his friends to Russia through Sweden with officials of the Swedish government. By April 13, all was ready. Lenin crossed the Baltic to Sweden by ferryboat. The travelers continued by rail to Stockholm and then to Finland and so at last to Petrograd, Russia's capital. They arrived there on April 16, exactly a week after leaving Switzerland.

Both Lenin and the Germans got what they wanted from this deal. Lenin not only got back to Russia; within seven months he won supreme power and a chance to put his ideas into practice. From the start, his propaganda against the war proved very effective. Many Russian soldiers listened to Lenin and stopped fighting the Germans. As a result, the Russian army melted away and Germany was able to concentrate its remaining strength on the western front.

essential civilian commodities began to disappear from the cities where all the guns and ammunition were manufactured. Total food production declined because so many men were taken from their villages to serve in the army. Those who remained on the land began to consume more of what they raised, because there was nothing for them to buy in town.

Economic hardship fostered political discontent. Revolutionary parties had long existed in Russia; and the handful of Marxists who followed Lenin (original name, Vladimir Ilich Ulyanov, 1870–1924), soon began to win mass support in the hungry cities. Distrust and demoralization weakened the czar's government, and in March 1917 strikes by armament and other industrial workers in the capital, together with mounting criticism from the upper classes, persuaded the czar to abdicate. A provisional government then proposed to hold elections for a Constituent Assembly that would draft a new constitution for Russia; but in the meanwhile the war had to go on.

Shortages simply got worse; and when Lenin proclaimed the slogan "Peace, Land, Bread" more and more Russians responded. "Peace" was obviously needed to set things right. "Land" invited peasants on landlords' estates to seize control of the fields they cultivated. "Bread" meant life itself to hungry city dwellers, though how anyone would be able to deliver it to them was never made clear. But given the situation in Russia, Lenin's slogans were irresistible. In particular, peasants drafted into the army decided that they had to get back to their villages in a hurry so as to be sure of getting their share of the land. Desertions therefore multiplied, and the discipline of the army wavered. Continuation of the war became impossible.

On the night of November 6–7, 1917 Lenin seized power in the capital city of Petrograd (formerly St. Petersburg, later renamed Leningrad). Red Guards, organized by workers in the factories of the city, were the instrument he used; but the real basis of Lenin's power was the appeal of his propaganda, and the small corps of dedicated revolutionaries he had shaped into the Bolshevik faction of the Russian Social Democratic (that is, Marxist) party before the war. But Marxist doctrine held that proletarian, socialist revolution was destined to occur first in the most industrialized countries, not in a predominantly peasant land like Russia. And when Lenin took power, he confidently expected revolution to break out at any moment in Germany, France, and England. To hurry socialist revolution along, he declared peace unilaterally, denounced capitalist governments for continuing the war, and made public secret treaties according to which the czar's government had agreed to share the spoils from the Austrian and Ottoman empires with France, Britain, and Italy.

Disintegration of the Russian army became almost complete after Lenin took power, and the Germans were therefore able to advance eastward more or less at will. But they did not want to go too far; instead they wished to profit from Russia's collapse by concentrating their forces on the Western front, where decisive victory remained to be won. Small bodies of German troops remained in the east, and in 1918 the Germans signed a peace treaty with the Bolsheviks at Brest Litovsk that separated Poland, the Ukraine, Transcaucasia, and the Baltic provinces from Russia.

Success in the east was meaningless, however, unless the Germans could also defeat the French and British in the west. That became far more difficult after April 6, 1917 when the United States became a belligerent. Throughout the war, Americans had prospered by supplying food and munitions to the allies; and when the Germans responded by declaring unrestricted submarine warfare in the Atlantic, and began to sink American ships, President Woodrow Wilson asked Congress to declare war. It took time to train American soldiers and send them to France, but as the Russian army disintegrated, a new American army was coming into being, thus counterbalancing Russia's collapse.

Moreover, American military power was matched by a powerful propaganda, designed in part to counteract Lenin's appeals for socialist

World War I American soldiers march in London. (National Archives)

revolution. In January 1918, President Wilson summed up American war aims in fourteen points, including the "right of national self-determination" and the establishment of a League of Nations that would settle future international quarrels peaceably. America, Wilson declared, was fighting a war to end war and make the world safe for democracy. It was a program quite as revolutionary in central and eastern Europe as Lenin's Marxism, and it appealed powerfully to war-weary people everywhere.

Early in 1918, German troops began their final offensive on the Western front. For a while it looked as though a decisive breakthrough might be possible, but the weary French and British held, and fresh American units hurried into battle. Soon the balance tipped in the Allies' favor, and the Germans started retreating. Before the battle line reached the German border, however, revolution broke out in the rear of the German army, and a new, socialist German government signed an armistice on November 11, 1918. The war was over at last, for Turkey, Bulgaria, and Austria had also admitted defeat in the preceding weeks.

THE PEACE SETTLEMENT: 1918–1923

The armistice ended the fighting, but said nothing about the terms of peace. Peacemaking was complicated by the fact that both Russia and the United States rejected treaties defining postwar territorial arrangements the Allies had made during the war. President Wilson advocated "open covenants, openly arrived at," and wanted to draw national boundaries anew on the basis of majority preferences among the local populations. Lenin continued to denounce the whole capitalist system and expected further revolutions to bring fellow Marxists to power in other European countries. The communist government of Russia simply refused to have any dealings with the Allied and Associated Powers, to give the victors the name they officially assumed at the peace conference. This meant that peace could not come to eastern Europe until 1921, when civil wars in the Ukraine and elsewhere had been fought to a finish. It took even longer for peace to come to the Near East, where a Greek-Turkish war lasted until 1923.

In the Far East, upheaval continued in China throughout the interwar period, though Japanese expansion was temporarily checked in 1922. During the war, Japan had conquered German colonial holdings in the Far East, then demanded special privileges in China, and when the Russian empire seemed about to break up also sent an army into Russia's Far Eastern provinces.

Moreover, the victorious allies entered the peace-making process with differing aims. The United States wished to check the Japanese and establish democratic governments in Europe so as to be able to get back to what soon came to be called "normalcy." The British government had similar goals and also wished to get control of Palestine and Iraq so as to safeguard the route to India. The French wanted the return of Alsace and Lorraine, provinces taken from them in 1871; but more important, they wished to make sure that Germany could never again become so powerful as to threaten French security. The Italians wanted territories along the Adriatic and in the eastern Mediterranean that they had been promised in 1916 in return for their entry into the war.

But the victors were only partly in control of the situation. Throughout eastern Europe, where the Austrian, Ottoman, and Russian governments had ruled before the war, confusion reigned. Socialists and national-

EUROPE AFTER WORLD WAR I

ists collided; and rival nationalities disputed rights to nearly every territory and province. Germany, too, was in turmoil. Everywhere socialists split between those who supported Lenin's recipe for the future and moderates who preferred to cooperate with the western powers. The choice for central and eastern Europe rested, in a sense, between Wilson's ideal of democratic, national self-determination and Lenin's ideal of proletarian revolution. But French and British wishes also mattered; and they, burdened with war debts owed to the United States, hoped to punish the Germans and make them pay for the costs of the war by imposing heavy reparations payments.

When the Peace Conference met at Paris in 1919, therefore, the problem was how to combine Wilson's principles of democratic self-determination with punishment for Germany, while hoping that Lenin's challenge to the existing social order would soon disappear. It made for an unsatisfactory peace. The Treaty of Versailles, presented to the Germans for their signature in 1919, imposed unilateral disarmament and sliced off bits of German territory to allow Poland access to the sea, while prohibiting German Austria from ever uniting with Germany. Nearly all Germans felt that such provisions violated Wilson's promises. Even more deeply resented was the "war guilt clause" which declared that Germany had been responsible for starting the war and therefore had to pay reparations for all the war's costs. This provision was unenforceable in practice and threw a monkey wrench into the new League of Nations, upon which President Wilson pinned his hopes for future peace.

Further east in Europe, events on the ground mattered more than decisions at Paris. The collapse of German power in 1918 provoked complicated civil wars in ex-czarist lands among communists, "White" Russians, and various kinds of nationalists. France and Britain sent expeditionary forces to Russian ports and gave some help to the "Whites." The United States likewise sent a few soldiers into the Far Eastern provinces, as much to watch the Japanese as to oppose the communists. But war weariness was almost as intense in the west as in eastern Europe itself, and by 1920 the contestants were ready to make peace. Resulting treaties set up independent states throughout the western borderlands of the old Russian empire. Russia's frontiers with the newly independent states of Finland, Estonia, Latvia, Lithuania, and Poland conformed pretty closely to the existing military lines of demarcation. But the Ukraine, Transcaucasia, and the Far Eastern provinces all returned to Russia, not at once, but within a very few years.

Hunger and disease were rampant, and in 1921 Lenin announced a "New Economic Policy" whereby private trading was allowed. It looked as though the communist principle of public ownership of the means of production had proved unworkable, just as critics in the west had always said. Lenin's ideals, as much as Wilson's, had indeed been compromised.

Europe seemed about to settle into a new mold, giving France primacy on the continent, thanks to German disarmament and to alliances the French concluded with most of the new states of eastern Europe.

To the south, the treaty prepared at Paris for the Ottoman empire proved unenforceable. Turkish national feeling rebelled against the provisions of the treaty that assigned territory on the eastern shore of the Aegean to Greece, and when the Greeks tried to enforce the treaty, Kemal Mustapha organized a makeshift Turkish army, which defeated them and proceeded to drive all Christians from the Asian side of the Aegean. A million and a half refugees fled to Greece. In return, Turks and Bulgarians were expelled from Greek soil to make room for the newcomers. The Treaty of Lausanne ratified and regulated the mass exchange of populations in 1923.

The Arab lands of the Ottoman empire were assigned as mandates to France (Syria and Lebanon) and Britain (Palestine and Iraq). A mandate was a new legal invention, requiring the administering power to treat the territory in question as a temporary trust under the supervision of the League of Nations. Eventually, it was assumed, mandated lands would become capable of democratic self-government. Former German colonies in Africa and the Far East were also made into mandates and assigned to one or another of the victors, including Japan. Local populations sometimes resisted, as happened in Syria, but not for long.

Palestine presented a more complicated problem. During the war, the British government had endorsed the idea of establishing a national home for Jews in Palestine. This Zionist ideal had begun to gain momentum among European Jews from the 1890s; but Arabs in Palestine opposed the idea vigorously. The new British administrators antagonized both parties by vainly trying to find a compromise.

In the Far East, Japan's wartime activities in China and the Russian Far Eastern provinces had aroused American opposition. Britain, allied with Japan since 1903, felt compelled to cooperate with the United States. When the Japanese faced up to this fact, they decided to draw back. The decisive negotiations took place in Washington in 1922 where a naval limitations treaty defined the number of warships the principal naval powers of the world could have. A 5:5:3 ratio for capital ships was agreed upon between Britain, the United States, and Japan. Japan's overall inferiority nevertheless assured the Japanese navy of the preponderance in Far Eastern waters it already enjoyed, since neither the British nor the Americans could ever expect to concentrate their whole fleet so far away from home bases. But the Washington treaties of 1922 did nothing to stabilize conditions in China, where local disorders dating back to the overthrow of the Manchu dynasty in 1911 continued to distract the country.

The peace settlements, 1918–1923, were therefore imperfect and partial. Seeds of future troubles were all too apparent, especially in Europe,

THE LONE EAGLE

Charles Augustus Lindbergh, born in Detroit (1902) and raised in Minnesota, was too young to take part in World War I, but learned to admire the aviators who dueled in flimsy airplanes high above the trenches in France. As soon as he could, he enlisted as a flying cadet in the United States Army Air Corps. When he graduated, the Air Corps put him on reserve status, and he got a job flying the mail between St. Louis and Chicago.

After doing this for two years, learning a lot about wind and weather and the ways of airplanes, he decided to compete for a prize offered for the first nonstop flight between New York and Paris. Backers in St. Louis paid for a plane built to his specifications. They named it *Spirit of St. Louis*.

On May 20, 1927, all was ready. A few minutes before 8:00 A.M., Lindbergh lifted the overloaded plane off the grass of the Roosevelt airfield at Garden City, Long Island, New York, and headed for Paris. Flying in those days was rather hit-or-miss. For long hours Lindbergh could not be sure where he was, for everywhere the ocean looked the same. He could figure out how far he had gone through the air, but had to guess how much the winds were blowing his plane from its compass course.

A second problem was sleepiness. He took off early in the morning and landed in Paris late in the evening of the following day, after more than thirty-three hours in the air. The noise of the engine and the whistle of the wind sounded monotonously; yet Lindbergh had to stay awake and keep the plane headed on a steady course. Otherwise he might waste

where a disappointed Italy became the seat of a Fascist government in 1922, and where German resentment against the treaty of Versailles was deep and abiding.

STABILIZATION AND RENEWED CRISIS: 1923–1933

Russian economic recovery came slowly under the New Economic Policy. The communist regime was weakened first by Lenin's incapacity (an assassin's bullet followed by a stroke) and then by his death in 1924. The precious gas by swerving to and fro across the ocean, or might even plummet into the sea and drown.

The struggle to stay awake was his most difficult task, for the plane functioned perfectly and his guesswork about the winds turned out to be very nearly right. He sighted Ireland on the second day, and could then fly on to Paris by following the map from point to point across southern England and northern France.

As he approached Paris a new problem arose. A vast crowd streamed out to greet him as news of his approach spread through the city. (His plane had been recognized over Ireland, and newspapers had followed its progress hour by hour thereafter.) And it was getting dark. How could the weary aviator see the landing place? Cars with their headlights gleaming were hastily arranged to show Lindbergh where to land; and the police kept the runway clear until the plane touched down safely.

Then the crowd broke through police lines. Excited people even started to tear the canvas skin off the *Spirit of St. Louis* for souvenirs. Lindbergh was completely taken aback. He struggled to get his plane safely locked in a hangar. Then he collapsed from fatigue. He awoke to worldwide renown.

Lindbergh's later life was anticlimactic. He soon came to hate the publicity and hero worship that surrounded him. In 1932 his eldest son was kidnaped. This caused a second wave of intense public excitement and ended in tragedy, for the kidnaper killed the child. Lindbergh was later accused of being too much impressed by Hitler's achievements, and President Roosevelt refused to allow him to fight in World War II. Thus politics clipped the "Lone Eagle's" wings; Lindbergh became an inconspicuous civilian consultant to airplane manufacturers.

United States, too, withdrew from European affairs in 1920 when the Senate refused to ratify the Versailles treaty. Relations between the two remaining victors, France and Britain, also unraveled, when the French attempted to enforce their rights under the Versailles treaty by occupying part of Germany in 1923 in order to compel the delivery of reparations. Economic collapse then threatened to provoke either a communist or a fascist revolution in Germany, and this prospect brought the United States back into action. An economic settlement of sorts was agreed upon, (the Dawes Plan) whereby American bankers lent money to Germany, thus allowing the Germans to pay reparations to France and Britain, who, in turn, paid installments on their war debts to the United States. This arrangement worked for a while, and even provoked a burst of industrial prosperity in Germany. The United States, too, enjoyed a tremendous postwar boom as new mass-produced consumer goods—automobiles, radios, and washing machines, and so forth—came into more and more American homes and changed old patterns of living profoundly.

In 1929 boom turned into bust, following a rhythm that had existed for centuries, but which no one really understood. Bank failures in Austria triggered panic in the United States. Suddenly the loans that had sustained the German recovery were no longer available. The same financial panic closed off credit for factories in the United States, so manufacturers had to shut down or cut back production drastically. In earlier times, crises of this kind had been endurable, because most economic activity was agricultural, and many of the people thrown out of work when factories shut down could go back to relatives on the farm and wait until new jobs opened up again. In the 1930s this was no longer possible in countries like Germany and the United States. Too many people lived in cities, without relatives in the country they could turn to.

Private charity and public relief were the alternatives if unemployed workers were not to starve. Idle factories unable to produce goods, and idle workers unable to buy what they needed to live, were hard to explain or endure. Marxist prophecies about the crisis of capitalism seemed to

A Nazi party rally. Adolf Hitler stands in the center flanked by Hermann Goering on his right. In the foreground is Julius Streicher, editor of the virulently anti-Semitic newspaper Der Stuermer. (*Library of Congress*)

be coming true. The situation was made more acute by the fact that beginning in 1928 the Russian government, now controlled by Josef Stalin (1879–1953), had launched a vast Five Year Plan of industrial development and continued to announce new victories in the struggle to build modern power plants and factories at a time when economic depression made life miserable for millions in the west. Russian peasants paid the cost of Stalin's forced pace of industrialization by providing both labor and food for the industrial effort without getting anything back in return; but this was not clear at the time.

DRIFT TOWARD WAR: 1933–1939

Economic suffering and discontent in Germany and the United States triggered drastic political departures. In Germany, Adolf Hitler (1889–1945) and the National Socialist German Workers' Party (Nazis, for short) came to power in January 1933. In March of the same year, Franklin D. Roosevelt (1882–1945) became president and launched what he called the New Deal to cope with the depression. Hitler and Roosevelt, despite the many contradictory currents that flowed among their supporters, had this in common: they both fell back on World War I methods of national mobilization to meet the crisis of the depression and were fairly successful in doing so. On other matters, the two regimes differed profoundly, for Hitler was a fanatic nationalist, intent on undoing the Versailles settlement, while Roosevelt was a democrat and an optimist, with no very deep convictions about international affairs.

Hitler set out to establish a fascist dictatorship, far more efficient and powerful than the original fascist regime in Italy. Between 1922 and 1927, Benito Mussolini (1883–1945) had fastened the dictatorship of his Fascist party on Italy; but Mussolini's praise of national solidarity at home and imperial expansion abroad met with a mixed reception among Italians. Old patterns of peasant life still prevailed in the south, and the Roman Catholic church together with other conservatives acted as a second restraining force. Mussolini's efforts to build a Mediterranean empire at the expense of Yugoslavia and Greece were successfully checked by France and Britain, acting through the League of Nations. But in 1933, when Mussolini attacked Ethiopia, to revenge the defeat Italian soldiers had suffered in 1896, the League huffed and puffed but failed to prevent the Italians from conquering the whole of Ethiopia by 1936.

Before coming to power, Hitler partly modeled his Nazi party on Mussolini's Fascists; but national socialism, as defined by Hitler, differed from Italian Fascism in being racist. Hitler proclaimed the superiority of the so-called Aryan race and asserted that German Aryans had been corrupted by Jews and other inferior races. One of his goals on coming to power in 1933 was to drive Jews from all walks of German life. He also wanted to restore German military power and had to cope with all the millions of unemployed whose votes had helped him come to power. Vast public works, especially road building, reduced unemployment; and after 1935, when Hitler felt it safe to denounce the Versailles treaty and begin rearmament openly, the unemployment problem disappeared.

By 1936, French and British protests against Italy's invasion of Ethiopia made Mussolini into Hitler's ally; and between 1936 and 1939 Italy and Germany helped a fascist government, headed by Francisco Franco (1892–1975), come to power in Spain after a bitter civil war. The demoralization of the French, torn by domestic strife and unwilling to accept a wartime style of national mobilization, had become plain. Hitler therefore turned attention to building up the German armed forces so as to be able to undo the territorial settlement of 1919 on Germany's eastern border. Appealing to the right of national self-determination, Hitler annexed Austria and then dismembered Czechoslovakia in 1938; in 1939, he turned on Poland. But this time resistance was better organized, and when Hitler persisted, World War II broke out.

In the United States recovery from the depression remained precarious until late in the 1930s, when armament programs designed to face up to German and Japanese threats had the effect of mopping up remaining pockets of unemployment. The Americans began rearmament reluctantly, but events in Europe together with a resumption of Japanese expansion on the mainland of Asia tipped the balance of opinion within the United States.

Japan's aggression against China began in 1931. It was triggered, at least in part, by the fact that after years of disorder and sharp division among local war lords, China seemed about to unite under the leadership of Chiang Kai-shek (1887–1975). Chiang came to power first by cooperating with, and then expelling communists from, the Kuomintang party in 1927, killing a good many of them. Survivors found refuge in the countryside. Under the leadership of Mao Tse-tung (1893–1976), they eventually made their way to the province of Yenan, on the Russian border, where a trickle of supplies from the Soviet Union helped them keep Chiang Kai-shek's troops at bay. In the rest of China, however, old war lords were compelled, one by one, to come to terms with Chiang's forces or face defeat.

Before China's unification could be completed, however, the Japanese intervened in Manchuria. Swiftly they occupied the entire province and proclaimed a descendant of the Manchu dynasty as Emperor of Manchukuo. The League of Nations denounced but failed to check Japan's aggression, and neither the Chinese nor the Americans were willing to

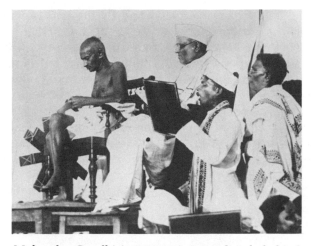

Mohandas Gandhi (1869–1948). Immediately behind him is Jawaharlal Nehru (1889–1964), prime minister of India between 1947 and 1964. (Library of Congress)

recognize the new state of affairs in the Far East. Instead, animosity increased and in 1936 the Japanese invaded north China, pushing southward along the coast and trying vainly to subdue the vast bulk of China completely. Rapid build up of heavy industry in Manchuria helped to support the Japanese armed forces, which began to play a more and more independent role, not only on the mainland of Asia but within Japan itself. The so-called "China incident," committing the Japanese army to operations on the mainland, merged into World War II after 1941. Indeed the conventional date for the beginning of the war, September 1, 1939, is arbitrary. Active operations in Asia dated back to 1932, when, from a Far Eastern point of view, the war really started.

Before describing World War II, a few words should be said about other parts of the world and how they fared during the interwar years. Africa remained quiet under colonial rulers. Even Italy's conquest of Ethiopia had little obvious effect on the rest of the continent. India, on the other hand, became the scene of a struggle between British imperial rulers and the Congress Party, whose leader, Mohandas Gandhi (1869–1948), demanded independence and national self-determination. He preached passive resistance, relying on "soul force" to overcome opposition. The British found Gandhi's campaigns very embarrassing, for how could they support democracy and self-determination in Europe and deny it in India? Several times Gandhi went to jail after defying British regulations; but this only increased his following in India. On the other hand, Indian Moslems were uncomfortable with Gandhi's movement, fearing that an independent India would become a Hindu India in which their religious identity and social status might be penalized. By the late 1930s some Indian Moslems had begun to demand an independent state of their own, separate from India. This may have strengthened the British position in India in the short run; but in another sense it simply consolidated opposition among another segment of the Indian population against continuation of British imperial rule.

In Latin America, the interwar years brought no very conspicuous changes. A bitter war between Paraguay and Bolivia ended in 1935 when mediators arranged a new boundary between the two nations. Further north, relations between Mexico and the United States entered upon a comparatively friendly era after 1933, when President Roosevelt proclaimed a Good Neighbor policy, which meant, in effect, that old United States claims to compensation for properties confiscated by the Mexican government during and after the revolution of 1911 would not be pursued any further.

Elsewhere, in the islands of the Pacific and in the British Dominions of Canada, Australia, and New Zealand, for example, life went on quietly for the most part. World affairs were dominated by the drama of European politics where Hitler's challenge to existing international relationships had become obvious and urgent by the mid-1930s. When war began in Europe in September 1939, the struggle soon spread round the globe, making it a world war, more truly than in 1914–1918.

WORLD WAR II: HITLER'S INITIAL VICTORIES, 1939–1941

France and Britain reluctantly came to Poland's aid in September 1939 when the German army launched its attack. Memories of World War I weighed on everyone's mind, in Germany as well as elsewhere. No rejoicings like those of 1914 took place. But Hitler had prepared the ground for victory this time rather more skillfully than the German government of 1914 had done. First of all, he signed a nonaggression treaty with Russia on August 23, 1939, just a week before the war began. Secret clauses partitioned Poland between the two powers and provided that Russia would supply Germany with food and other raw materials needed for the war effort. Stalin, who had previously been among the most vehement of Hitler's enemies, had changed sides and by doing so prevented a repetition of the World War I blockade, which had done a good deal to weaken the German war economy.

Blitzkrieg

Hitler had also prepared his armies for what the Germans called "Blitzkrieg"—lightning war. This referred to the use of tanks, trucks, and airplanes to speed up the pace of military action. Columns of tanks, supported by motorized infantry and low-flying airplanes, could break through on a narrow front, penetrate many miles into the rear, and, by attacking headquarters, disrupt the enemy command and control system. In such a situation, it was always unclear just who had surrounded whom, for tanks needed fuel and ammunition in enormous quantity and without it were helpless. But troops cut off from headquarters, with an enemy in the rear, and with hostile airplanes overhead, were likely to panic; and an armored column, probing the enemy rear, could often capture the gasoline it needed to keep on advancing. Blitzkrieg tactics had been dreamed up by British officers at the very end of World War I, but it was the Germans who developed the idea and the machinery needed to restore mobility to warfare and overcome the long standstill in the trenches that had prevailed during World War I.

Hitler hoped and believed that blitzkrieg would bring quick victory and make war profitable once again. His long-range goal was to seize territory in eastern Europe to assure the German "race" of a sufficiently large geographic space to become a world power. This meant displacing Slavs of course; but in 1939 he also had to cope with the French and British, who, to his surprise, had not backed away from war when news of the nonaggression pact with Russia reached them. Nevertheless, the allies were unready to attack; instead they manned prepared fortifications along the French border and waited for something to happen.

Happen it did. First of all, the Russians set out to improve their position by recovering control of lands lost after World War I. Stalin sent soldiers into Estonia, Latvia, and Lithuania, and tried to do the same to the Finns, but they resisted, and even drove back an invading Russian army in the winter of 1939–1940. The French and British saw an opportunity in this situation to end the cooperation between Russia and Germany by sending an expeditionary force across Norway into Finland while simultaneously attacking oil fields in the Transcaucasus, thus cutting off oil supplies for both Russia and Germany.

But before the allies were ready to act, Hitler seized the initiative by first sending troops into Norway and Denmark, and then, in May, attacking France, Belgium, and Holland. It was 1914 all over again with the difference that tanks and airplanes moved much faster than men and horses, and this time there was no eastern front for the Germans to worry about. French morale soon cracked, and in a mere six weeks the campaign was over. Most of the British expeditionary force escaped from the

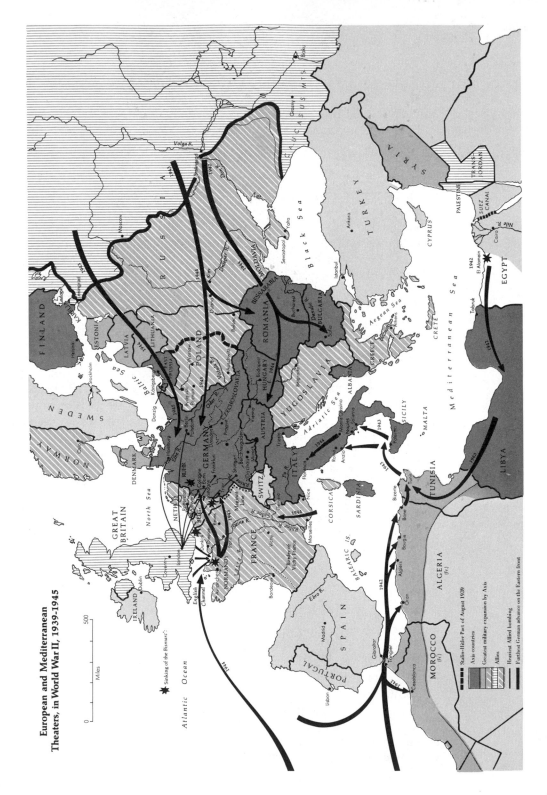

European and Mediterranean
Theaters, in World War II, 1939-1945

★ Sinking of the Bismarck

★ Heaviest Allied bombing

Stalin-Hitler Pact of August 1939

Axis countries

Greatest military expansion by Axis

Allies

Farthest German advance on the Eastern front

beaches of Dunkirk in small boats. After this surprising turn of events, the British public reacted to the disaster as though it had been a victory. But for the French there was no escape. Instead they concluded an armistice on June 22, 1940 in the same railway car in which the armistice of 1918 had been signed. To all appearance, Hitler had won.

But Britain refused to admit defeat. The Norwegian campaign, and British failures to stop the Germans from seizing control of that country, had provoked a change of government. Winston Churchill (1874–1965) became Prime Minister and brought a new resolution and recklessness to the British war effort. He embarked on all-out mobilization and mortgaged the future by buying what Britain could not produce for itself in the United States and elsewhere. Most of all, his speeches rallied the British people against the Nazis, even when German success seemed assured by the fact that the resources of most of the European continent lay at Hitler's beck and call.

Hitler was not prepared to mount an invasion of Great Britain. The German navy could not control the English Channel, and that meant that landing barges were vulnerable to naval attack. Hitler, nevertheless, ordered preparations for an invasion and launched heavy air attacks on British airfields. When that failed to drive British planes from the skies, the Germans attacked London and other cities, without changing the strategic situation. In September 1940, Hitler's invasion plan had to be postponed—as it proved, forever.

Invasion of Russia

Prolonging the struggle with Great Britain threatened to distract Hitler from his main goal—seizure of territory in the east on which to build a great Germany. He therefore decided in November 1940 to attack Russia, thinking that when the communist power had been destroyed, Britain would have lost another potential ally and have to make peace. This decision proved fatal to the Nazis, and in retrospect seems amazingly reckless. Why invite a war on two fronts when Stalin was doing everything he could to cooperate? But at the time, almost every military expert believed that the Russian army was poorly led and lacked the will to fight. The Red army's poor performance against the Finns seemed to prove what pre-war treason trials, followed by massive purges of disloyal officers in the late 1930s, had led outsiders to suspect. Hitler therefore counted on a swift and easy victory against Russia, like the easy victories he had already won against Poland and France. And by attacking communist

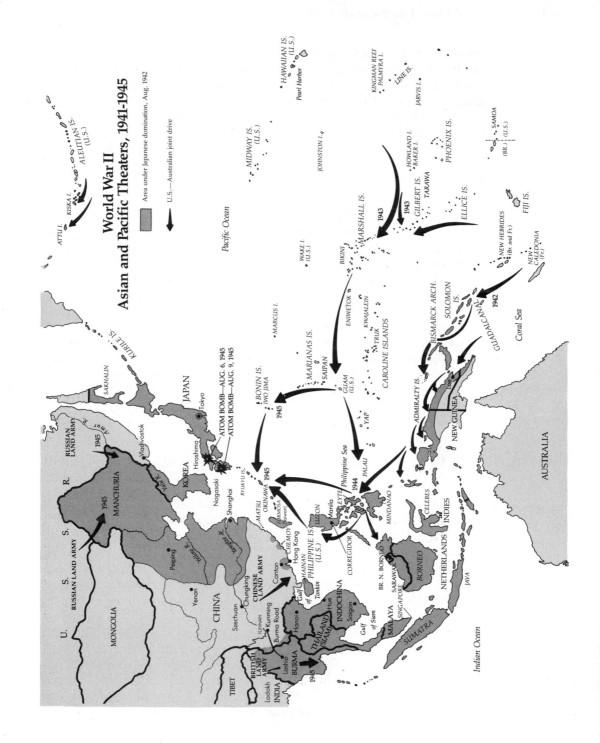

World War II
Asian and Pacific Theaters, 1941-1945

Area under Japanese domination, Aug. 1942

U.S.—Australian joint drive

Pacific Ocean

ALEUTIAN IS. (U.S.)
KISKA I.
ATTU I.

HAWAIIAN IS. (U.S.)
Pearl Harbor

KINGMAN REEF
PALMYRA I.
LINE IS.
JARVIS I.

MIDWAY IS. (U.S.)

JOHNSTON I.

PHOENIX IS.

SAMOA (U.S.)
(BR.)

HOWLAND I.
BAKER I.
GILBERT IS.
TARAWA
1943
1943

ELLICE IS.

MARSHALL IS.

NEW HEBRIDES (Br. and Fr.)
FIJI IS.

NEW CALEDONIA (Fr.)

WAKE I. (U.S.)

BIKINI

MARCUS I.

ENIWETOK
KWAJALEIN
TRUK
CAROLINE ISLANDS

1942

Coral Sea

KURILE IS.

SAKHALIN

Amur R.

JAPAN
Tokyo

RUSSIAN LAND ARMY
1945
Vladivostok

1945

U. S. S. R.

MANCHURIA

1945

MONGOLIA

Amur R.

Yalu R.

KOREA
Hiroshima
Nagasaki
Shanghai

ATOM BOMB—AUG. 6, 1945
ATOM BOMB—AUG. 9, 1945

BONIN IS.
IWO JIMA
1945

MARIANAS IS.
SAIPAN
GUAM (U.S.)

OKINAWA 1945
RYUKYU IS.
MATSU
FORMOSA (Taiwan)

PALAU
YAP

Philippine Sea
1944

ADMIRALTY IS.
BISMARCK ARCH.
SOLOMON IS.
GUADALCANAL

NEW GUINEA

AUSTRALIA

Peiping
Yenan
CHINA
Chungking
Szechuan
Kunming
YUNNAN
Burma Road

Yangtze R.
Hwang R.

CHINESE LAND ARMY

CHEMOY
Hong Kong
Canton
HAINAN
Gulf of Tonkin

LUZON
Manila
CORREGIDOR
PHILIPPINE IS. (U.S.)
LEYTE
MINDANAO

CELEBES

BR. N. BORNEO
SARAWAK
BORNEO

NETHERLANDS INDIES

JAVA

TIBET
Ladakh
INDIA

BRITISH LAND ARMY

BURMA
Lashio
1945

Loimi

INDOCHINA
Hanoi
THAILAND (SIAM)
Hue
Saigon
Gulf of Siam

MALAYA
SINGAPORE

SUMATRA

Indian Ocean

346

Russia, he could again live up to his principles, for one of the main themes of Nazi propaganda had been denunciation of communism.

Before beginning the invasion of Russia, however, Hitler was distracted by a brief Balkan campaign. What happened was this: shortly before the end of the campaign in France, Mussolini declared war against France and Britain. Fighting in north Africa between British forces stationed in Egypt and Italian troops in adjacent Cyrenaica (Libya) followed; and the Italians suffered some embarrassing defeats. Then in October 1940 Mussolini attacked Greece, hoping to restore his damaged prestige. Once more the Italians were defeated; and in the spring of 1941 British troops arrived from Egypt to help the Greeks. This threatened the German flank, so Hitler ordered an attack on Yugoslavia and Greece in April 1941. As before, victory came quickly and the British were driven back to Egypt.

On June 22, 1941, a few weeks later than first planned, the German war machine was finally ready for the assault on Russia. As before, blitzkrieg tactics worked wonders at first. Vast Russian armies surrendered without much of a fight. But the Russian spaces were immense, and German columns could not advance more than about 100 miles at a time without pausing to bring up supplies. Roads were miserable, and the deeper the Germans got into Russia, the more difficult it became to deliver everything needed to renew the offensive. Russian morale wavered but did not crack, and eventually the onset of cold weather began to hamper German mobility, for the Nazi army was not equipped for winter operations, lacking even the proper clothing for subzero temperatures. By December 6, 1941, although the Nazis were within a few miles of Moscow and had almost surrounded Leningrad, Hitler had to call off the offensive, ordering the German armies to hold fast everything they had conquered.

Easy victories had stopped. Instead the Germans faced a two-front war once again, and their situation was worsened by the actions of the United States, where sympathy for Britain and hostility to the Nazis led President Roosevelt to offer Hitler's enemies all help short of war. Americans started by selling armaments and other strategic goods to France and Britain. Then, when the British began to run out of funds, Congress passed the Lend Lease Act (March 1941), whereby the United States offered to supply what Britain and Hitler's other enemies needed without charge, on the theory that they were contributing to the security of the United States by opposing Hitler and should not be required to pay back the costs of things actually used up in the course of the struggle. Then, when the war ended, whatever was left over could be returned or paid for at some agreed price. In this way, war debts, like those that had plagued international relations between the wars, would not accumulate, and by becoming "the arsenal of democracy" the United States might not have to send its own soldiers into battle.

Pearl Harbor and Initial
Japanese Victories, 1941–1942

Affairs took a new turn on December 7, 1941, just the day after the German offensive in Russia halted, when the Japanese attacked the American naval base at Pearl Harbor. All the anchored U.S. battleships were sunk; but U.S. aircraft carriers were at sea and remained unscathed. The attack was a profound surprise. It had been decided upon as a sort of desperation measure, in response to the United States' decision to embargo the export of oil and scrap iron to Japan. The Japanese armed services then foresaw a time when shortages of oil would prevent them from continuing their operations in China and Vietnam. The American embargo had, indeed, been designed to compel the Japanese to draw back from China; instead it caused them to risk everything on the Pearl Harbor attack.

Japanese strategists thought that if they could paralyze the U.S. Pacific fleet, then it would become possible for them to capture oil fields in the Dutch East Indies (Indonesia) and thus assure themselves of sufficient oil to maintain the army and navy indefinitely. By creating a vast "Co-Prosperity sphere" throughout southeast Asia, China, and islands

The battleship U.S.S. Nevada in Pearl Harbor under attack by Japanese aircraft. (Official U.S. Navy Photograph)

of the Pacific, the Japanese hoped that they would be able to hold off counter attack indefinitely. Given existing methods of warfare, and the difficulties of landing on a defended beach, this was not an unreasonable thing to believe.

For six months after Pearl Harbor, everything the Japanese military had counted on seemed to be coming true. A series of brilliantly successful campaigns brought the Philippines, Malaya, Burma, and the Dutch East Indies under Japanese control, and the Japanese also garrisoned a number of smaller islands of the southwest Pacific. "Asia for the Asians" was a slogan that appealed to the inhabitants of former British, French, and Dutch colonies; but the Japanese had difficulty in converting hostility to European colonialism into active support for what amounted to an empire of their own. Moreover, Chinese resistance continued, and the population of India, after hesitating, settled down under British management to create a vast new army needed to protect its exposed frontier in Burma from any further Japanese advance.

TURNING THE TIDE: AMERICAN MOBILIZATION AND ALLIED OFFENSIVES 1942–1945

Despite these initial successes, the Japanese were no match for American power, once the resources of the United States were fully geared for war. And the American response to Pearl Harbor was all-out mobilization, harnessing all available manpower and know-how to the task of creating a truly formidable army and navy as quickly as possible. How to manage an all-out war effort had already been worked out by the British, building on World War I precedents. By borrowing, and improvising for itself, the American government was therefore able to achieve a remarkably efficient system for channeling resources into the war effort, all in conformity with strategic plans devised by the Chiefs of Staff. Production goals, once seemingly impossible, were soon achieved and surpassed. American industrial and agricultural productivity was so great that the flow of Lend Lease goods to Britain, Russia, and other allied powers actually increased while the American armed forces were being built up and then sent into action overseas.

Hitler declared war on the United States just after the Pearl Harbor attack, even though the Japanese had not informed him of their plans and refused to attack the Soviet Union in the Far East, despite German requests that they do so. Hitler's declaration of war made it easy for the United States to confirm and strengthen cooperation with Britain and

THE SECOND BEST IS NOT THE PACIFIC

In July 1942, the war was going badly for the Allies. Japan controlled a vast region of the Pacific. The Germans' second summer offensive in Russia was thrusting toward the Volga. In the north African desert, other German soldiers were at Egypt's doorstep.

Earlier in the year, America, Britain, and Russia had agreed upon their strategy for 1942. Anglo-American forces were to land in northern France and open a second front to relieve the Russians. Everything else was to be subordinated to that effort. But by July, the British decided that the plan would not work. Landing craft and other supplies were lacking. Reinforcing the defenses of Egypt and of India seemed even more important than landing in France, for it took only a little imagination to believe that the Axis' next move would be for Japanese forces to move into India while the Germans drove past Egypt to meet them somewhere in the Indian Ocean.

The Americans were very reluctant to change the agreed-on plan. What if Russia should collapse or make a separate peace? But without the British, a landing in France was clearly impossible. What to do? On July 10, the chiefs of staff recommended that in such a case major effort should be shifted to the Pacific against the Japanese.

This brought President Franklin D. Roosevelt up against the most important strategic decision of the war. If he accepted the advice of his with the Soviet Union by deciding, in spite of the Japanese attack at Pearl Harbor, to concentrate first against Germany, on the ground that if Hitler were left alone to defeat Russia in a second campaign, he would become difficult or impossible to overthrow. As a result, Allied military campaigns were far better coordinated than anything the Germans, Italians, and Japanese were able to achieve.

Results of American mobilization and allied planning began to show towards the end of 1942. By far the biggest action came in Russia, where a second German advance was turned back at Stalingrad on the Volga, beginning in late August. The Russians had to rely almost entirely on their own resources, for Lend Lease shipments were still small, owing to shortages of shipping. But they were able to produce tanks and guns, thanks to factories in the Urals and still further east that had been built just before the war; and once the harshness of Nazi rule became clear, the Russian population rallied behind the communist regime.

chiefs of staff, the British and Russians would be left to fight the war against Germany on their own. Each of the great Allied nations would in effect be conducting its own war, with little real cooperation. This seemed unwise. It seemed even more unwise to concentrate on Japan when everyone agreed that the Germans were a more serious threat to the long-range security of the United States.

On July 15, 1942, President Roosevelt talked the problem over with his friend, Harry Hopkins. The two men sat in the White House on a summer's evening, wondering what to do. In the end, Roosevelt decided to try once again to work out a plan for joint action with the British. He sent Harry Hopkins and General George C. Marshall to London to make the attempt. Ten days later, they agreed on a landing in north Africa. In greatest haste, a vast expedition was made ready under the supreme command of a young American general, Dwight D. Eisenhower. As a result, on November 8, 1942, less than four months after the decision had been made, American and British troops went ashore in French north Africa.

The Russians were not fully satisfied with this second front. But British and American cooperation became closer and more intimate than ever before. Soon afterward, the turning point of the war came: at Stalingrad in Russia; at Guadalcanal in the Pacific; and in north Africa. And as the Allies took the strategic initiative, they made it a genuinely cooperative effort—all because President Roosevelt had decided on July 15, 1942, that even if a landing in France was not possible in 1942, "the second best is not the Pacific."

On other fronts, too, the balance began to favor the allies in the second half of 1942. Japan's victories ended in June, when the Americans won a sea battle off Midway island, and later in the year, hard fighting on Guadalcanal, in the southwest Pacific, led to a second American victory, this time on land. Against Germany, the first important Anglo-American success came in the Atlantic, where German submarines threatened for a while to sink so many ships as to prevent the successful deployment of American forces overseas. By midsummer 1942, that danger had been largely overcome; and in November the Americans and British were able to combine forces for a large-scale landing in north Africa. A few weeks earlier, British troops had won a decisive victory in Egypt over a combined German and Italian army; and by May 1943 the whole southern shore of the Mediterranean was in Allied hands. From there, the Anglo-American forces invaded first Sicily (August) and then the Italian mainland (September). By this time, most Italians were anxious to make peace, and a *coup d'état* in Rome overthrew Mussolini. Prompt German reaction,

Churchill, Roosevelt, and Stalin at Yalta. (*Library of Congress*)

however, meant that northern Italy remained under their control. A German taskforce even freed Mussolini from prison, but he was no more than a hollow puppet from then on.

On the Russian front, a third German offensive, launched in July 1943, was quickly turned back, and from that time onward, it was the Russian army that advanced, while the Germans fought desperately to hold them back. Lend Lease deliveries began to supplement Russian home production significantly by 1943; in particular, American trucks, shoes, and food kept the Red Army mobile.

Problems of the Peace

Russia's growing military success meant that concerting plans with American and British leaders became necessary. A conference at Tehran (November 1943) brought Stalin, Roosevelt, and Churchill together for the first time, and they were able to agree on future strategy. In particular, the United States and Britain promised to attack across the Channel in 1944, in spite of the very great technical difficulties of landing on the French coast. Everyone expected that a successful landing would lead to Germany's defeat, since the Russians promised a massive offensive in the east to coincide with the landings in France.

On June 6, 1944 Allied landings on the Normandy beaches proved successful, and within a few weeks German armies were driven from France. But the allies barely got across the German border before bad weather set in, and in December Hitler was even able to launch a counter-offensive. Russian armies in the east got into Poland, but had to stop short of Berlin, the German capital. Victory in Europe was thus delayed until May 1945 when Russian and American forces finally met at the Elbe river. Hitler had killed himself a few days previously. With his death, the Nazi movement collapsed utterly, though only after murdering millions of Jews and others in special extermination camps, and bringing massive destruction on most of Europe.

How to arrange the postwar map of Europe was hard for the allies to agree on. Until Hitler had been destroyed, differences could always be papered over, as happened at Yalta in February 1945, when Roosevelt, Churchill, and Stalin met for a second time; but when German resistance finally collapsed, hard decisions had to be made, and it soon became obvious that the sort of "friendly" governments the Russians wanted in

An atomic bomb explodes over Nagasaki, August 9, 1945. (U.S. Department of Defense)

eastern Europe were undemocratic by British and American standards. For a while, the United States continued to hope that such differences could be amicably settled, especially since they wanted Russian help against Japan.

Towards the end of 1944, however, the limitations of Japanese war-making ability became clearer and the American wish for Russian help in the Far East diminished accordingly. United States submarines succeeded in sinking so many ships that the Japanese became unable to tap the resources of their "Co-Prosperity sphere." Moreover, beginning in November 1943, the Americans learned how to send taskforces thousands of miles from base with everything needed for a successful assault on a defended beach. This meant that the Japanese defense perimeter in the Pacific became vulnerable, since even the bravest garrisons, cut off from home, could not survive very long without food and ammunition. With giant steps the Americans were therefore able to advance first towards the Philippines, then towards the Japanese home islands.

The final blows came swiftly. On August 6 and 9, 1945 American airplanes dropped newly invented nuclear bombs on Hiroshima and Nagasaki. Then, on August 9, the Russians began marching into Manchuria. These disasters persuaded the Japanese government to sue for peace on August 15. Formal surrender was arranged on September 2, 1945, just five years and a day after the war in Europe had begun.

CONCLUSION

World War II was over, at least officially. Urgent unsolved questions remained; and in the hurly-burly of everyday decision making, no one really took time to wonder whether the two world wars of the twentieth century, and the changes they had brought about, marked the end of an era. But with nearly half a century's perspective, it seems probable that historians will need a new label for the period since World War II.

The modern era that began with the great European voyages of discovery in the latter part of the fifteenth century was marked by the rise of western Europe to world predominance. But European world power came to an end with the breakup of colonial empires in the aftermath of the war, and with the rise of new superpowers, east and west of the old center of world leadership. To be sure, both the USSR and the USA inherited or borrowed a great deal of their culture and skills from western Europe; but neither Americans nor Russians were quite the same as the peoples of the west European nations who had lorded it over the rest of the earth before the wars.

The era of the two world wars also marked an end to the delicate balance between public and private enterprise that had characterized bourgeois Europe. That balance had initially been struck in a few city states of Italy and the Rhinelands in the fourteenth century; it had spread to the Netherlands, England and France during the sixteenth and seventeenth centuries; and had then been imperfectly imitated in central and eastern Europe. It gave wide scope to private accumulation of capital and pursuit of gain by buying and selling at prices negotiated anew for each deal in accordance with the best estimate of personal advantage each party could make at the time. Intervention in the market by political and military authorities was always important. Taxes and tariffs affected market prices, often in very important respects; and fixed "fair" prices for food and other necessities were often enforced as well, especially in times of crisis. But as compared to other times and places, bourgeois Europe gave the market far freer scope than usual.

The two world wars reversed this trend, sharply. Rationing, price control, direction of labor, compulsory military service, planned industrial production all took over. In each of the principal belligerent countries, military and civilian planners set out to make economic production fit strategic war plans. Careful calculation and management proved able to achieve wonders. Goals that seemed impossible were in fact achieved, over and over. As long as everyone agreed that the effort was worth while, and millions of common folk willingly put up with all the discomfort and deprivation that wartime conditions involved, the efficiency of what we may call "command" economy as against the traditional "market" economy was undeniable.

Bourgeois society could never be the same after such a demonstration of what state intervention in the market was able to achieve; although the problem of maintaining general agreement on the political goals to be pursued turned out to be far more difficult than it was to agree that wartime enemies must be defeated. After 1917, the Soviet Union defiantly rejected bourgeois free-market rules and set out to build a new socialist society. The nations that remained "capitalist" and democratic compromised between free-market and command principles for the management of their economies. But everywhere the role of the state and of deliberate public planning was much increased as compared to conditions before 1914, while the scope for strictly private pursuit of profit was correspondingly reduced by all sorts of new regulations and controls aimed at narrowing gaps between rich and poor, or in other ways advancing political goals. In this respect, as much as in the displacement of world leadership from western Europe to the United States and the Union of Soviet Socialist Republics, the world wars of the twentieth century seem likely to mark a new era in world history.

We will discuss some of its characteristics in the remaining chapters of this book.

CHAPTER 11

The World Since 1945

In coming close to our own time, problems of historical perspective become acute. We are creatures of place and time, inevitably, and can only look about us and try to pick out what matters most, or seems likely to matter most, in the rush of recent events.

Overall, rivalry between the United States and the Soviet Union seems one obvious, dominating feature of the post-World War II world. Diplomatic rivalry has spilled over into an arms race of enormous technical complexity—a race that threatens the very survival of humanity, if nuclear warheads should ever be used on anything like the scale that is now possible. World politics and international relations have been fundamentally altered by this new reality and by the fear it creates.

Another obvious feature of the post-World War II world is massive population growth, more rapid in poor and predominantly agricultural lands than in the industrially developed, richer countries. This was accompanied, at least until the 1970s, by sustained economic expansion that brought rising standards of living to many millions of persons, so that, even in the poorest countries, growing numbers of human beings were at least able to find enough food to remain alive. Economic growth rested partly on the diffusion of new skills, especially agricultural skills, and partly on the diffusion of improved forms of economic management, both national and transnational in scale.

A third obvious feature of our time is the growth of cities with all the changes in daily experience that city living brings. It is worth reminding ourselves that until about 1950 most human beings still inhabited villages and worked in the fields. After that date, city dwellers, depending on food raised by others, became more numerous than rural folk; though in some poor countries city living still remains a minority way of life. Many changes go along with this shift from rural to urban existence. Weakening of family ties is perhaps the most important. New, individual life-styles, much influenced by TV and movies, also find greater scope in cities than in villages. Sports, sex, and crime achieve new visibility and, perhaps, new importance. But contrary currents also arise: religious revivalism, seeking to get back to a true, pure way of life is one expression of the revulsion against the urban breakdown of traditional values. Efforts to maintain and strengthen ethnic and other local identities run in a parallel direction. Which current predominates varies from time to time and from one part of the world to another.

Finally, it is worth reminding ourselves that any effort to understand what goes on around us is likely to overlook something that will seem critically important in time to come when its consequences and implications become apparent, while some of the things that seem most important to us may shrink to triviality in the light of subsequent events. The rivalry between Americans and Russians, for example, may prove to be less important for the history of the world than something happening in Africa or China—or in space. Everything depends on how things turn out: and this we cannot know. We need to realize, always, how surprising human affairs are likely to be, as much in the future as in the past. Who, for example, could have anticipated the consequences of Columbus' voyages? Or of Christ's teaching? Who could imagine the role of gunpowder when it was new? Or of agriculture when it began? Discoveries, inventions, and the teaching of new doctrines continue among us and are likely to transform human life in the future at least as surprisingly as ever happened in the past. Consequently, modest, tentative judgments about what really matters is all we can hope for.

WORLD POLITICS SINCE 1945

Even before hostilities ceased in World War II, quarrels among the victors had broken out. The Conference at Yalta (February 1945) where Roosevelt, Churchill, and Stalin met for a second time, made vague promises on paper without solving the differences between Russia and the Anglo-American powers over the postwar settlement in Europe. By July 1945,

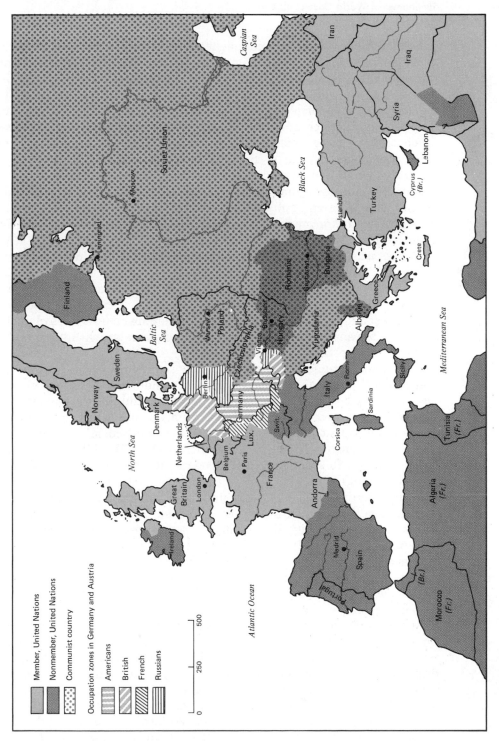

POST-WAR EUROPE 1949

when the Allied heads of government met at Potsdam, just outside Berlin, frictions were sharper, but the need to end the war with Japan, arrange for peace treaties, and settle the military administration of defeated Germany kept the alliance from breaking apart. But in the course of the next year, open quarrels, openly arrived at, prevailed. Stalin carved out a sphere of influence in eastern Europe wherever the Russian army was in possession of the ground. A matching Anglo-American sphere of influence formed in the rest of Europe, though by the end of 1946 it was clear that Great Britain could no longer afford to play the role of a great power. The result was that by 1947 the Americans confronted the Russians across what Churchill aptly termed an Iron Curtain, splitting Europe into communist and noncommunist parts. Europe's most powerful nation, Germany, was divided between the two blocs.

In Asia a similar division took place. Japan fell within the American sphere of influence, whereas China, thanks to the victory of Mao Tsetung's Red Army over Chiang Kai-shek's forces, became communist in 1949. Korea and South East Asia, like Germany, were divided between communist and noncommunist regimes, depending on how lines of demarcation between rival occupying forces had been drawn at the end of the war.

In China and adjacent lands the new communist rulers were fervent nationalists, although that fact was partly hidden at the time by their use of Marxist revolutionary phrases. In India and Africa, however, nationalism remained separate from communism, so when these lands became independent after World War II, they and some other poor and ambitious countries began to constitute a "Third World" that belonged neither to the Russian nor to the American side in what came to be called the Cold War.

But Third World peoples remained poor and weak compared to Japan and Europe. In the rich countries, where administrative and industrial skills had attained high development, the ravages of war were swiftly repaired by applying to the tasks of reconstruction the same sorts of management that had worked so well in war. In western Europe, reconstruction was facilitated by generous grants from the United States—the so-called Marshall Plan, 1948–1952. American officials required Europeans to plan recovery from war damages on a continent-wide basis; and enough Europeans were ready to think beyond national boundaries to sustain forms of international cooperation that evolved into the European Economic Community by 1957. This rather clumsy association, uniting France, West Germany, Italy, Belgium, Holland, and Luxemburg, nevertheless managed to agree on important economic policies that sustained a prolonged surge of prosperity in western Europe, and even accepted Great Britain, Ireland, Denmark, Greece, Portugal, and Spain as members when those countries applied for admission between 1973 and 1984.

Recovery in eastern Europe involved greater hardships, since outside assistance was not forthcoming. Nevertheless, the planned economies of the Soviet Union and of its new satellite countries, Poland, Romania, Hungary, Czechoslovakia, and East Germany, made a remarkably rapid recovery too, even though living standards remained far lower than in western Europe.

Japan's Economic Boom

Japan's economic revival began as a by-product of a war in Korea, 1950–1953. The communist rulers of North Korea invaded the southern part of that country in 1950, apparently under the impression that no one would really try to oppose this expansion of their power. But American commitment to legal settlement of international issues through the United Nations was still a lively hope; and American distaste for any further spread of communism, after Mao Tse-tung's success in China, was intense. As it happened, the Russians had walked out of the United Nations in protest over another issue and so were unable to veto the decision to oppose North Korea's attack on the south. The United States then took the lead in organizing a United Nations army to defeat the communists. When victory seemed almost complete, the Chinese Red Army intervened and drove the U.N. forces back to something close to the original dividing line between North and South Korea. Then, after lengthy negotiations, a truce was agreed upon in 1953, perpetuating Korea's division into two rival halves.

A plant worker at Nissan, September, 1982. The construction and export of small, relatively inexpensive automobiles by the Japanese is one of the most prominent features of Japan's post-war industrial recovery. (Michal Heron)

During this war, U.N. forces found it convenient to order all sorts of supplies from Japan. The resulting demand for goods set Japan's economy off on a postwar boom that eventually left all the rest of the world behind. The secret of Japan's phenomenal success in building ships, cars, electronic devices, and other high-tech goods remains unclear. Somehow, old patterns of life and work, dating back to the feudal past, came together with a modern educational system and national management of key aspects of the economy so as to allow the Japanese to excel everyone else. In many branches of light industry, their principal rivals, in fact, were other Far Eastern lands—South Korea, Taiwan (where Chiang Kai-shek's Chinese nationalists found refuge after 1949), Hong Kong, and Singapore. Beginning in the late 1950s, European and American factories proved unable to match the quality and price of many different kinds of goods produced by these new Far Eastern competitors. If this situation persists, it will mark a fundamental change in world balances, ending an era, at least 200 years old, in which European and then American factories drove artisans of other lands out of the market by offering cheaper and sometimes better goods for sale than could be produced locally even by the most highly skilled workers.

A factor in Japan's extraordinary economic success in the postwar period was that the peace treaty concluded in 1947 prohibited armaments. Japan, like western Europe, found shelter under the umbrella of American armed forces, and became free to concentrate on producing civilian rather than military goods. This may be an advantage. On the other hand, recent military research and development has led to important new industrial products and processes in such fields as communications, computers, airplane manufacturing, and atomic reactors. But most of the new weapons have no civilian use, and resources devoted to their production in the Soviet Union and in the United States have therefore been subtracted from the civilian economy. Yet in a world where overproduction can become a problem in periods of depression, even that may not be a disadvantage.

The real issue, probably, is organizational: how efficiently different firms and nations are able to combine the efforts of large numbers of persons to get things done cheaply and well. By that measure, Americans and Europeans are not far behind the Japanese; and all of them are far ahead of Third World peoples. Wealth and power therefore have remained concentrated in American, European, and Japanese hands; and world politics has turned largely on their decisions, and especially on the decisions of the American and Soviet governments, whose armed forces, population, and organizational skills left everyone else behind.

News reporting focuses on quarrels and confrontation: the more violent the more interesting. This is liable to distort our judgment. The fact is that since 1945 the world has not suffered any really major war, and most of the wars that have been fought have not lasted long nor killed very many people. Compared with past human behavior, this is unusual. Twenty-one years separated World War I from World War II; the post-World War II period of approximate peace has already lasted twice that long.

The Arms Race

One reason for this record is that all concerned are profoundly afraid of all-out war. The atomic bombs dropped on Hiroshima and Nagasaki in the last days of World War II announced a new level of destructive power; and those formidable weapons were far surpassed when the Americans and Russians both discovered how to build vastly more powerful H-bombs after 1950. War took on a completely new guise when, after 1957, the great powers also acquired rockets, capable of carrying city-destroying nuclear missiles to any part of the earth's surface. No effective means to intercept intercontinental rockets existed; hence outbreak of war between the two great powers threatened the sudden destruction of most of the population of the two combatants, all within a few minutes of the start of hostilities. Recent calculations even suggest that a few hundred nuclear explosions might alter the atmosphere and disturb the conditions for life on earth so radically that human and all other higher forms of life would perish utterly. No one wants that sort of disaster; and so far the two governments have managed to back away from situations in which resort to ultimate force seemed likely, such as the confrontations over Berlin (1948–1949) and Cuba (1962).

Efforts to control the arms race have not been very successful. In 1972 the two great powers signed a Strategic Arms Limitation Treaty (SALT) that prohibited research and development of some new forms of weaponry; but negotiations to reduce or to limit the total number of nuclear weapons failed when the United States refused to ratify a second treaty in 1980. Efforts to prevent the spread of nuclear weapons to other countries have not prevented Britain, France, China, and probably Israel and India from developing nuclear arsenals of their own; and several other countries—Pakistan, Libya, Iraq, Argentina, and Brazil for example—may have secret nuclear arms programs as well. How the balance of war and peace will tilt if these and perhaps still other countries acquire nuclear weapons is hard to forsee: But no one doubts that world politics will be altered, perhaps disastrously, if almost unimaginably powerful means of destruction come within the control of fanatical and insecure governments.

One of the ironies of the situation is that the overwhelming destructive power of existing nuclear weapons does not give Russians and Americans the ability to control other governments, even those close by and partly dependent on aid or trade with them. Yugoslavia actually succeeded in breaking away from the Russian orbit after 1946, before the nuclear stalemate had set in. When the stalemate became clear to all concerned, China broke openly with the Russians in 1960, while Poland and Romania exhibited various degrees of independence without directly defying the Russians or overthrowing their local Communist party dictatorships. The American alliance system, NATO (North Atlantic Treaty Organization), also showed signs of weakening, and France withdrew from full membership in 1966.

Nevertheless, NATO and the Russians' military alliance system, the Warsaw Pact, maintained a balance of armed forces in Europe that neither side was eager to test. On both sides of the Iron Curtain, combined, multinational military commands, modeled on those that had proved so effective in World War II, remained in place, prepared to spring into action if war should break out on European soil.

Within Europe national sovereignty was seriously compromised by these new forms of military organization, as well as by the European Economic Community that regulated the internal economic policies of west European nations. Clearly, Europe's rival nationalisms, that had been so prominent during the nineteenth century and sustained World Wars I and II in the twentieth, were weakening. But in other parts of the world, nationalism boiled to the surface, sometimes assuming religious, or quasi-religious forms, and sometimes hiding behind Marxist revolutionary phrases.

Independence in the Third World

Asian and African nationalisms were directed, initially, against European colonial government. In some parts of Asia and Africa, agitation for political independence had developed before World War II. This was particularly true of India, where Mohandas Gandhi had mobilized millions in his campaigns of nonviolent resistance to British rule. A fundamental turning point came in 1946, when a newly elected Labour government in Great Britain decided to give up empire and encourage local peoples to set up governments of their own. In India, political parties and leaders already existed who were ready to take on the tasks of government. Independence therefore came quickly (1947), although not without provoking mass riots between Hindus and Moslems. A new state, Pakistan, was carved out of British India to accommodate the millions of Moslems

CONQUEST OF MOUNT EVEREST

Mount Everest rises 29,028 feet above sea level, higher than any other mountain on earth. Icy winds blow fiercely around the high slopes of the mountain; temperatures of 30 or 40 degrees below zero are common near the top. Not only that, the air gets thinner with every increase in altitude. Men whose bodies are built to breathe at or near sea level cannot get enough oxygen into their bloodstream to keep their muscles strong at altitudes as high as Everest's peak. For many years, this seemed to make it impossible to climb to the earth's highest point.

But the word *impossible* was a challenge. Improved equipment for dealing with rock, ice, and snow at high altitudes allowed skilled mountain climbers to get higher and higher. In 1921 the first effort was made to use these skills on Everest. The expedition did not get anywhere near the top, but proved one very important thing: tanks of oxygen, strapped to a climber's back, allowed oxygen-starved muscles to revive their strength in spite of the thin air. So the extra weight was worthwhile; and with this discovery, the conquest of Mount Everest became a real possibility.

But difficulties were immense. Between World Wars I and II, five Everest expeditions set out, each better equipped than the previous one had been; and five times they failed. Then World War II interrupted mountaineering in the Himalayas until the 1950s. All the early expeditions had approached Mount Everest from the north, only to reach an impassable face near the very top. In 1951 a new route, approaching from the south, was reconnoitered. A Swiss expedition tried this approach in 1952 and almost reached the top before bad weather interfered. The next spring a British party, helped by Sherpa tribesmen who were accustomed to living at very high altitudes, renewed the assault.

Day after day the climbers leapfrogged higher. Toward the top, the party divided up into small groups of two or three men. One such group went on ahead to explore the best line of ascent and set up a camp, from which the next group could take off and do the same thing over again. On May 28, a camp only 1,100 feet below Mount Everest's crest was set up. The honor of making the final climb fell upon two men: Edmund Hillary, an Englishman, and Tenzing Norgay, a Sherpa. Starting from the advance camp in the early morning, the two men reached the highest point on the surface of the earth before noon, May 29, 1953. Unlike many of those who had tried before, they got back down safely.

Thus another landmark in the restless effort to test strength and skill by doing what has never been done before entered the record of human achievement.

who preferred a state of their own to citizenship in a predominantly Hindu India.

Elsewhere it took longer to find parties and persons who could govern. The first black African state to become independent was Ghana (1957), and in the course of the next decade all the other British and French colonies of Africa also became independent sovereign states. For a while the French resisted granting independence to their African colonies; but a long and nasty uprising in Algeria (1954–1962) at length persuaded them to imitate the British policy of transferring power to local leaders as soon as they showed signs of being able to govern.

In southeast Asia, events followed a similar course. The French, Dutch, and British at first sought to maintain their empires; but when armed resistance developed, the Europeans decided that restoring their rule was not worth the cost. Consequently, Burma, Indonesia, Malaya, and Vietnam, along with several smaller countries, all became independent soon after the end of World War II, although Vietnam was divided between a communist north and a noncommunist south. When guerrillas from the north threatened to overthrow the government in the south, the United States decided on armed intervention to stop this new advance of communism. The result was a long and desultory war, 1964–1973, in which the Americans were never successful in winning heartfelt support from the Vietnamese people—or even from all Americans at home. The North Vietnamese, in contrast, appealed to deepseated national and revolutionary feelings, and in the end compelled the Americans to withdraw, despite the enormous technological superiority that American troops enjoyed over their guerrilla enemy.

Complexities in the Middle East

By far the most complicated political situation, however, developed in the Middle East. European imperial control of Arab lands, extended after World War I by the system of mandates, had already worn thin before World War II broke out; and countries like Iraq and Egypt won at least formal independence in the late 1930s. During the war, Palestine and Syria remained under British and French administration respectively, at least in theory. But Jewish settlers in Palestine wanted full sovereignty for themselves, particularly after news of the wholesale destruction of Jews in the Nazi death camps reached them. A national homeland, where Jews could enjoy the protection of an armed state of their own, had always been part of the Zionist ideal. Now it seemed urgent to achieve that goal, since the wartime fate of Jewish minorities in Europe showed how vulnerable they were, not just to discrimination, but to genocide as well.

The Jews therefore organized for seizure of power, by force if necessary; while the Palestinian Arabs tried to oppose them with an armed force of their own.

The British could not control the situation and decided to withdraw, calling on the new United Nations to decide what should happen in Palestine. In fact, action on the ground proved decisive. Jewish armed groups seized control of part of the country; other parts remained in Arab hands; and in 1948 the United Nations ratified what had happened by recognizing the territory the Jews controlled as a new sovereign state of Israel. Arabs in Egypt, Syria, and other neighboring lands had tried, vainly, to prevent the Jews from achieving independence. They all refused to recognize the new state of Israel until 1979, when Egypt did so. The issue was further embittered by Arab refugees from the part of Palestine the Jews had conquered who organized the Palestine Liberation Organization (PLO) to fan Arab resentment and seek revenge. Israelis, for their part, wanted to expand the territory under their control so as to secure more nearly defensible frontiers and come nearer to reconstituting the biblical Kingdom of David.

Arabs were far more numerous, but the Israelis, reinforced by Jews

Crowds at the Wailing Wall in Jerusalem, traditionally the place for Jews to mourn the Roman destruction of the Temple in A.D. 70. The Wailing Wall is all that remains of the foundation of the Temple Mount begun by Solomon and continued by Herod. That portion of Jerusalem containing this wall was taken by Israeli troops during the 1967 war. (Martin E. Fischer)

who streamed into the country from all parts of the Moslem world and from much of Europe, were better organized and had the advantage of financial support and a supply of arms from the United States and elsewhere. As a result, renewed warfare in 1956, 1967, and 1973 led to further Israeli victories. The Israelis took possession of Jerusalem and all the territory west of the Jordan river, though other governments, even those most sympathetic to Israel, did not recognize the annexation of this additional territory. In 1982 the Israeli army invaded Lebanon to disperse PLO encampments near the border and strengthen the political position of the Christian minority in that country. This time, however, success eluded them. The PLO was badly damaged, but radical Moslem groups among Lebanon's population gained new scope and power in an on-going civil war by opposing the Israelis. American efforts to mediate failed; and in 1985 the Israelis withdrew.

Moslem anger at what happened in Palestine after World War II was only part of the dismay that pious followers of Mohammed felt at the course of public events. Ever since the 1920s, the governments of Iran and of Turkey had tried to modernize by abandoning the traditions of Islam in order to import skills and ideas from the European world. Ironically, success—even partial success—in modernizing provoked a powerful popular reaction against godlessness and the repudiation of Islam. Preachers of traditional religion easily convinced ex-peasants, concentrated in vast city slums, that return to Islam was the only way to salvation. In Iran, where oil wealth allowed the government to modernize very rapidly, popular revolution broke out in 1979. A new pious regime came to power, inspired by the teaching and preaching of Ayatollah Khomeini, who sought to impose the Sacred Law of the Shia version of Islam in every detail. In Turkey, however, modernization had started sooner and came more slowly, so the shock was smaller. Moreover, Turkish Moslems were divided among many different sects. Disagreeing one with another, they could not carry through a popular revolution as the Iranians, who were almost all Shiites, had done.

Nevertheless, the Iranian revolution sent a quiver of excitement throughout the Moslem world. For the first time in two centuries, Moslems could argue convincingly that the wave of the future did not require abandonment of the faith and customs of their forefathers after all! Khomeini's example showed how to act on the belief that Allah still ruled the world and would reward his faithful servants as in former ages! Buoyed by such hope, Shiite Moslems in Syria and Lebanon became more assertive. Similar responses occurred in Afghanistan and throughout the Arab lands. The failure of Israel and the United States in Lebanon in the 1980s was connected with this resurgence of Moslem and specifically of Shiite piety. The Soviet Union, for its part, invaded Afghanistan in 1979 to prevent Moslem revolutionaries from overthrowing a puppet communist government there. Guerrilla resistance to the Russian invaders proved as stubborn as anything the Vietnamese had offered to Americans in the decade before.

But, to cap the complexity of Middle Eastern affairs, the revolutionary Iranian government set out to liberate fellow Shia believers from the secularizing rule of the government of Iraq. War broke out in 1980, fueled by oil revenues available to both sides. Other quarrels, based partly on

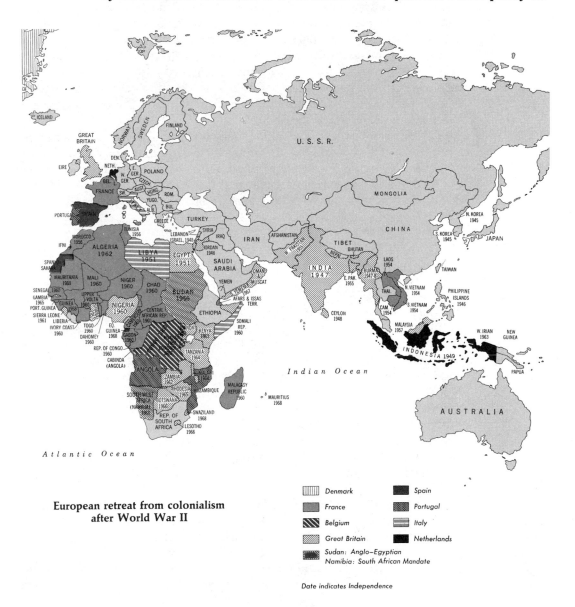

**European retreat from colonialism
after World War II**

Denmark

France

Belgium

Great Britain

Sudan: Anglo–Egyptian
Namibia: South African Mandate

Spain

Portugal

Italy

Netherlands

Date indicates Independence

ancient religious differences, divided Libya from Egypt almost as bitterly as Iran opposed Iraq. Unity was a distant hope within the Moslem world. Ironically, the more Islamic nations and governments tried to make political action conform to their faith, the bitterer their divisions became.

Other parts of the world lagged behind the Middle East in mingling religion with politics. Nonetheless, renewed commitments to traditional religious identities made themselves felt elsewhere. The clash between India and Pakistan was heavily colored by religious differences, for example; and some guerrilla movements in Africa and Latin America assumed a religious or at least partly religious overtone—sometimes Christian, sometimes Moslem, and sometimes mixing in Marxist ideas as well. In other places, more traditional, secular forms of Marxism roused warmer response; but in spite of their theoretical internationalism, Marxists, too, quarrelled, as short-lived wars between Vietnam and China and between Vietnam and Cambodia showed.

Still, despite these and other local wars and guerrilla actions, the overall pattern of world politics since 1945 was more peaceful than in most past ages. Fear of atomic annihilation was a powerful restraint; but the remarkable economic expansion that took place after World War II also had much to do with the general climate of politics.

POPULATION GROWTH AND ECONOMIC EXPANSION

The modern worldwide population expansion dates back to about 1750, but after World War II its pace accelerated so much that experts began to speak of a population explosion. The main reason for the sudden surge in human numbers was that death rates in poor countries dropped very suddenly when the World Health Organization (WHO), set up in 1948, helped local governments to apply scientific public health measures on a worldwide scale. Diseases like malaria, cholera, tuberculosis, and many others, that had traditionally snuffed out a great many lives, were sharply reduced, thanks to new antibiotic drugs and other treatments. The greatest triumph came in 1980, when the World Health Organization was able to proclaim that smallpox, one of the most lethal of all human diseases, had been entirely eliminated.

Worldwide application of scientific medicine to human health problems, beginning in the late 1940s and 1950s, allowed far more infants to survive than before; and they, in turn, began to have children by the 1970s and 1980s. The result was indeed extraordinary. World population had reached about 2.5 billion in 1950; by 1985 the total had almost doubled to just under 5 billion. Such figures stagger the imagination and make the decades after World War II unique in world history. By the mid-1980s statistics seemed to show that dropping birth rates had begun to reduce the global pace of population growth; and if that trend continues, the population history of the three postwar decades will stand out as unprecedented and unparalleled. But, short of war or some other global catastrophe, even if future birth rates continue to decline, population will increase for a long time to come, simply because so many millions of children are still coming of age in the poor countries of the earth and will themselves begin to have children in the years ahead.

The rapidity with which human numbers increased, especially in the poorer, mainly agricultural countries of the world, created difficult problems. Whenever increasing numbers of young villagers could not find enough land to cultivate in the way their parents had done, they faced awkward choices. Some remained at home, cultivating smaller plots of land more intensively than before. Other millions sought escape from creeping impoverishment by migrating to towns and cities. But with so many rural youths coming in from the countryside, jobs became hard to find. Nearly always, conditions of life for newcomers to the cities were bleak and unsatisfactory. Inevitably, millions of such people felt that something was fundamentally wrong with the world, and competing remedies—religious, revolutionary, or a combination of the two—found ready response. Political upheavals and guerrilla movements of the most diverse kind fed on such discontents; and, of course, wherever prolonged violence broke out—in Vietnam, Ethiopia, El Salvador, Afghanistan, and Lebanon, for example—economic disruption intensified the crisis and hardened opposition among rival groups.

The surprising thing, really, is that nearly doubling the world's population since 1950 provoked so little violence. One reason was that the improvements in public health, which allowed more people to survive, were matched by improvements in agricultural methods, which expanded the total food supply and thus allowed more people to get enough to eat—somehow. In effect, scientific agriculture ran a race with scientific medicine, allowing increasing food production to keep up with increased human numbers on the global scale, even though local supplies did not always match local needs. Agricultural scientists developed genetically redesigned seeds that gave larger yields, especially when used with chemical fertilizers. Sometimes irrigation was possible, or improved implements gave better results. The spread of more efficient agriculture to much of Asia and through parts of Latin America and Africa constituted what has been called "the Green revolution." It allowed growing populations to survive, however precariously. Nevertheless, vulnerability to drought, flood and other natural stresses increased as agricultural production intensified. The race between population growth and increased food production continued to skirt disaster.

Migration of Populations

A second aspect of postwar population history introduced another kind of strain on world relationships. After a decade-long "baby boom" in the late 1940s and early 1950s, birth control checked population growth in all the developed countries of the earth. As a result, the demographic gap between poor and rich tended to increase. In some places, Hungary for example, replacement of existing population became problematic; in all the rich countries—European, American, Japanese alike—as children became fewer, the elderly became more numerous, making relations among age groups different from before. In addition, fewer young people seeking work meant that the nasty jobs were hard to fill, and this opened an opportunity for migrants from the populous poor countries, especially those located nearby. In Europe, such immigrants were often Moslem: Turks in Germany, Algerians in France, Pakistanis in Britain. In the Soviet Union, too, Moslems from central Asia grew in numbers while Russians and other peoples of European origin saw birth rates plummet. The United States, for its part, attracted growing numbers of immigrants from Latin America and the Caribbean islands, who played a parallel role in American society.

Assimilation of these immigrants was unlikely, at least in the short run; and just how relations between old inhabitants and newcomers will work out in future is an unsolved question for everyone concerned. The fate of immigrant communities in rich countries affects the countries of emigration too, sometimes emptying out poor villages and destroying traditional ways of life, sometimes allowing old ways to continue in seriously overcrowded circumstances, thanks to money sent back home by the emigrants. Improved transport and communication means that migrants do not need to break off contact with their places of origin. Instead, they can return frequently, thus creating a new sort of link between rich and poor lands. Intensified frictions compete with better understanding across ethnic and cultural barriers in these circumstances. As usual in human affairs, the upshot remains problematical.

Changes in Subsistence Agriculture

Another postwar change of far-reaching importance was the awakening of the peasant mass of humanity to new possibilities of political and economic action. As population grew and as new methods of cultivation spread, traditional patterns of subsistence agriculture retreated. Even poor peasants had to try to find something to sell so as to be able to buy what they needed for the new kinds of farming. For the first time in history, agriculture was fully, or almost fully, incorporated into the exchange economy that dominated the globe. This was true in communist as much as in noncommunist lands. Instead of depending mainly or entirely on what each family could produce for itself, as most peasants had always done before, rural as well as urban dwellers began to produce goods or supply services for others, getting what was needed for his or her own life in exchange.

From the very beginning, the power and wealth of civilized society had depended on occupational specialization; but for thousands of years, specialization affected only a few. A minority of rulers, priests, artisans, soldiers, and other city folk consumed food that others had raised, while the rural majority supplied that food by paying rents and taxes in kind. They seldom had much left over after attending to their family's needs. Thus, until the last few centuries, most human beings worked in the fields and consumed only a part of what they produced, while supporting the few who engaged in other occupations. They did so without getting much of anything in return except the (often undependable) benefits of peace and order.

Nevertheless, as discussed in earlier chapters, slowly and gradually improved transportation allowed human beings to exchange goods over longer distances. As a result, market relations gradually began to affect the lives of more and more persons. The process accelerated after A.D. 1000 with improvements in shipping, and got into high gear in the eighteenth century, with the Industrial Revolution. But even after the Industrial Revolution it took a long time for the vast rural mass of humanity to enter actively into the network of economic exchange. The process is not complete even today; but the tiny communities of hunters and gatherers who still survive in the Amazon basin, the Kalahari desert, or on the Arctic sea ice, and the larger numbers of herders and subsistence cultivators who continue to exist in remote regions have become a small minority in the world as a whole. The vast majority of human beings, urban and rural alike, depended instead on a flow-through economy, exchanging goods and services with strangers, sometimes across thousands of miles and despite political boundaries.

Advantages were real but risks were great. In particular, any interruption in the smooth exchange of goods and services became potentially devastating to hundreds of millions of persons. The depression of the 1930s showed how paralyzing bad times could be in countries where subsistence agriculture had almost disappeared. In the postwar decades, this kind of vulnerability spread from the highly industrialized countries to all the world.

New Techniques
of Economic Management

In partial compensation, techniques of economic management improved so that the old pattern of alternating boom and bust was damped back to minor proportions throughout the first thirty years of the postwar era. This was achieved, in large part, by using in peacetime methods of management and control that had been developed to fight the two world wars of the twentieth century. New kinds of statistics and new modes of data processing, made easy by computers, allowed managers to adjust the flow of goods and services, both on the level of great private corporations—sometimes operating across national boundaries—and on the national, governmental level as well. Goals varied: but whether it was full employment, maximal profit, or fulfillment of production quotas assigned by a Five Year Plan, managers could come considerably closer to achieving their purposes than before. In the rich and powerful noncommunist countries, official manipulation of indirect economic regulators, like interest and tax rates, sustained a boom from the mid-1950s to the mid-1970s. In Communist countries, official plans for economic development achieved parallel results by assigning resources to particular projects in accord with a system of priorities.

Communist
and Capitalist Patterns

The communist pattern of economic change got results by relying mainly on official rules and commands; the capitalist pattern mixed governmental commands and rules with private pursuit of gain as affected by changing market prices. Communist command economy worked best when an underemployed rural population could be set to work in mines and factories to exploit new resources. But when careful rationing of labor, raw materials, and machinery became critical, as happened in the Soviet Union from about the 1970s onward, the system of command began to look clumsy, since there was no measure of efficiency that could be easily brought to bear as long as prices were set at arbitrary and often unrealistic levels.

The managed economies of the capitalist nations had their own weaknesses. In particular, unequal rewards among individuals and firms—and among different nations and regions of the globe—put great strain on the system. Even when economic expansion made most people at least a little better off, those who found themselves at the bottom of the income scale were liable to feel jealous of the rich. Poor countries were especially sensitive to the difference between their own level of life and that of richer lands. Theories of underdevelopment that blamed the gap on continuing capitalist exploitation or on past political colonialism were attractive to peoples and governments that could not manage their economies very well at home. Their difficulties were only partly due to low levels of skill, or to local social traditions that ran against the grain of market behavior. Crushing disadvantages handicapped small and weak countries because changing prices for their exports could reward or hurt them in ways completely beyond local control. Efforts to escape dependence on the export of a few commodities by developing industries and other new forms of economic activity required the borrowing of large sums of money. Such loans were difficult to repay, even when the borrowed money was profitably spent; and when, as often happened, it was ill spent, repayment became all but impossible.

Problems of a Global Economy

A second difficulty in the economic system that arose after World War II affected communist and capitalist methods of management alike. On both sides of the Iron Curtain, national governments were the main units of economic management. But economic relationships were worldwide, and insofar as what happened depended on international exchanges, no one government—not even the government of the Soviet Union or of the United States—was able to manage affairs at home very effectively.

This became evident in the 1970s when both the superpowers discovered that they needed to import critically important goods at prices they could not control. As old oil fields at home ran dry, the United States, along with most other countries of the noncommunist world, began to import more and more oil from abroad. Then, in 1974, a new association of oil producing countries (OPEC) suddenly raised the price of oil by about four times. The resulting shock to the world economic system was considerable. Poor countries had difficulty paying for more expensive oil and had to cut back on activities that used the precious fuel. A few oil-rich governments, located mainly in the Middle East, found themselves with more money than they could use at home. And the industrially developed countries of western Europe, Japan, and the United States had to adjust to the new level of fuel prices by changing the way they used oil and other resources.

The long postwar boom faltered under the strain. All the governments concerned preferred inflation to taxation, with the result that rising prices changed the rules of economic behavior in ways many people found confusing and unjust. Even when OPEC nations ceased to cooperate with each other, and the price of oil dropped, the international economic system did not recover its former expansiveness. Inflation continued, rapidly in some countries, more slowly in others, while a heavy debt burden weighed down the poorer countries of the world. The discrepancy between national economic management and a growing dependency on goods and services coming from outside national boundaries was not overcome. In effect, the rich and powerful countries of the world were given a small taste of the weakness and dependency that poorer countries had always known. International agencies, like the World Bank, and regional international unions, like the European Economic Community, were too weak and too local to manage the world economy effectively. No one was in charge; no single policy could prevail. Thus the limitations of economic management on the national scale, as developed during and after World War II, became increasingly apparent; but no one knew what to do about it.

LIMITATIONS OF THE SOVIET SYSTEM   The Russians, too, ran into increasing difficulty in the 1960s and 1970s. Their dependency on foreign supplies was even more vital than that of the United States, for the collective farms of the Soviet Union failed to produce enough grain to feed their people comfortably. In 1963, after a bad harvest, the USSR had to buy millions of tons of grain from the United States; and grain shortages at home had to be made good by massive foreign purchases in other years as well, whenever bad weather hurt the crops. The weakness of Soviet agriculture was due less to geography than to their policy-makers' long-standing preference for industry, especially heavy industry and arms production. Indeed the strength and weakness of the Soviet system rested on the fact that communist managers could and regularly did disregard market prices and real costs of production by giving special importance to a particular goal, and by then assigning to it all the labor and resources needed for its accomplishment—regardless of what happened to other, competing activities and needs.

Yet the necessity to import food was even more embarrassing than the Americans' need to import oil. It advertised shortages and put Russian economic planning at the mercy of the weather and fluctuating grain prices that were set partly by other governments and partly by supply and demand on the world market. The limitations of communist-style economic management, even on the territorially vast scale of the Soviet Union, thus became glaringly apparent shortly before the American-style of nationally managed capitalist economy began to show its no less real limitations in the 1970s.

The Russians also found it difficult to cooperate smoothly with their neighbors, despite the fact that Communist parties, all theoretically committed to the international solidarity of the working class, came to power in eastern Europe and China after the end of World War II. But in practice each new Communist government wished to develop its own national economic system, minimizing dependency on outsiders, including the Soviet Union. Advantages of specialization were thereby reduced, and since prices were arbitrary in each communist country, trade agreements became occasions for political negotiation. Sometimes the Soviet Union drove a hard bargain, offending neighbors who felt exploited. Sometimes advantages ran the other way, when the USSR granted generous terms to a communist regime facing discontent at home and in need of aid. Poland benefited in this way in the 1980s; Cuba did the same, more because of its geographical location at America's doorstep, than because of internal unpopularity of the communist government that came to power there after 1958. But economic subsidies, however helpful to unpopular governments, could not buy loyalty to the Soviet Union, as the Poles' simmering discontent showed.

PROBLEMS IN THE CHINESE ECONOMY   The most important neighboring country with which the Soviet Union had to deal was China. Until about 1960, efforts at cooperation continued, but the Chinese communists wanted aid for economic and military purposes which the Russians were

Mao Tse-Tung (1893–1976), Chairman of the Chinese Communist Party and de facto *ruler of China between 1949 and 1976. Mao's influence upon China has been compared in scope to that of Confucius. (Bettmann Archive)*

unwilling or unable to give. Friction between the two governments became open in the 1960s, when Mao Tse-tung accused the Russians of not being true Marxist revolutionaries any longer. Russian aid was withdrawn, and border quarrels actually led to a brief armed encounter in 1969. Meanwhile China attempted to exemplify Mao's revolutionary ideals by making a "Great Leap Forward" on the strength of its own resources. Backyard furnaces to smelt iron and organized assault on class enemies disturbed Chinese society without achieving economic advance. After Mao Tse-tung died (1976), a reaction brought new men to power who sought support from the United States to counterbalance the threat they felt from the Soviet Union. Greater reliance on market prices at home provoked a rapid increase in China's agricultural production, but efforts to check population growth by imposing penalties on those with too many children showed that the government was by no means liberal or prepared to rely on the market to adjust population to available resources.

THE THIRD WORLD   China's enormous population—a quarter of the human race—makes its future important to every other nation. India, Africa, and Latin America are the other poor and populous lands where more than half the world's population struggles to survive. Here, as much as in the rich and powerful countries of Europe and America, the future of humanity will be decided in time to come. Increased production, intensified exchanges, more skillful management may suffice to accommodate the increasing population of these lands, or even raise local living standards slightly, as has been the case since World War II. On the other hand, vulnerability to major disaster increases with economic development that depends on continuous circulation of goods and services among millions of persons and across long distances. If major disaster does strike, in time to come the economic expansion of the decades since 1950 will seem as exceptional as the population history of those same decades. So far at least, and compared to any earlier age, the economic history of the post-World War II world looks like a triumph of management and luck in the face of rapid technological change and the enormous pressure of a doubling of the world's population.

THE IMPACT
OF COMMUNICATIONS

Despite the importance of economics, human lives depend only partly on material goods. Wealth and poverty, contentment and distress arise from what people expect for themselves and others; and that, in turn, depends on communications. In villages where traditional subsistence agriculture prevailed, food might become scarce each year in the weeks before the harvest, while in bad years everyone starved. But as long as economic differences between families remained slight and reflected how hard each family worked, no one was likely to feel poor. Hardships were part of life: normal, natural, and expected. Custom and habit sustained individual lives and defined what to expect, individually and collectively.

Buying and selling introduced new complications and new possibilities of economic differentiation. Contact with townspeople who never worked in the fields and yet often lived far more comfortably than villagers often made rural life seem harsh and unattractive. Landlords and money lenders, where they existed, led an even easier life without working at all. Civilized societies lived with these contrasts for many centuries, and village custom somehow accommodated the inequity, usually by treating urban folk and landlords as a different, alien sort of being. By refusing to compare themselves with such outsiders, villagers could retain their own community values and way of life, regardless, or almost regardless, of what happened outside the village itself.

This sort of psychological insulation of rural from urban standards of living arose and flourished when communications were slender, so that the great majority of individuals lived out their lives in a village context and encountered outsiders only a few times a year and in more or less standard ways—raiding, paying rents and taxes, or buying and selling as the case might be. Until quite recently, therefore, expansion of market relations among villagers did not necessarily disrupt local patterns of life, even if more buying and selling did introduce new material goods and technical possibilities into rural society.

As long as villagers' communication with outsiders continued to be mainly oral and face to face, this ancient accommodation between the rural majority of humankind and the urban minority survived. Printing, although extremely important for urban specialists, was slow to affect rural communities. After all, peasants could not read until someone decided that schooling was useful, even for poor and humble countryfolk. In European lands, rural schooling was seldom available before 1850, and in other parts of the world, school systems that reached into the villages came a good deal later, and, indeed, have not become universal yet.

In the twentieth century, however, new and powerful communications shortcuts arose in the form of movies, radio, and TV. Movies existed before World War I but came into their own during the 1920s as a new form of popular entertainment. Radio networks began to attract large audiences during the 1930s in Europe and America and became important in poor countries after World War II. TV broadcasting started in the 1940s, but soon caught up with radio in the sense that broadcast stations became nearly universal, even though receiving sets, since they cost more, remained far fewer. But display in public places made TV broadcasts available to hundreds of millions, both in city streets and buildings and in innumerable village squares. The same was also true for movies and for radio broadcasts, although cheap receiving sets made it far easier to own a radio privately and use it in the home. From the 1970s, recorded tapes added still another dimension to the new forms of communication and made smuggling prohibited messages across political frontiers comparatively easy.

An important feature of all these means of communication was that they did not depend on literacy and schooling. As long as the movie or broadcaster used a language familiar to listeners, messages came across very much in the way face-to-face encounters had always brought messages to the attention of ordinary people in everyday life. TV's visual images reinforced spoken words with a different sort of communication, comparable to the effect that travel to new lands and experience of strange societies might otherwise have on those watching the screen.

The full force of these new modes of mass communication has yet to be felt. Their political impact was sufficiently obvious that nearly all governments monopolized the control of broadcasting within national boundaries and sometimes used jamming stations to interfere with messages coming from abroad. In west European and some other democratic lands, laws prescribed more or less equal access to radio and TV for rival parties during election campaigns. But decisions about how to present the news, made on a daily basis by some sort of official or quasi-official authority, had enormous power over public opinion, and gave those in control of the media a systematic advantage against all rivals.

In Communist countries and in other lands where a single party or military faction ran the government, access to radio and TV was tightly controlled to prevent dissenters from broadcasting criticism of official policies and points of view. In such circumstances, tapes sometimes played an important role in spreading a rival version of the truth. Ayatollah Khomeini's leadership of the Moslem revolution in Iran, for example, rested very largely on taped sermons in which he denounced the shah's godlessness from the security of a French villa. These were then smuggled into the country and played on tape recorders to secret gatherings and in private homes, convincing most Iranians of the righteousness of the revolutionary cause.

The United States was unusual in consigning control of radio and TV to private companies whose main concern was making money from paid advertising. The political or social impact of their programming took second place to the aim of appealing to the largest possible audience, so as to increase advertising income. Even political campaigns began to be conducted with the powerful aid of paid advertisements. Equal

LET'S NOT GET TOO CASUAL ABOUT THIS THING.

A television set with a telecaption attachment for those with impaired hearing. Devices such as this have made it possible for television to become available even to those with aural handicaps. (Courtesy of the Closed Caption Institute)

access rules for formal political speechmaking by the major candidates and parties modified without cancelling the commercialization of American elections imposed by the way the country's radio and TV networks were managed.

Sports, criminal violence, and sex proved powerfully attractive in the competition for mass attention that American broadcasting companies engaged in. Programs often set out to shock viewers by pressing against the conventional and legal limits on what could be broadcast. Movies went even further, and a new market for pornographic films arose when legal rules against them were voided by American courts.

What the effect of such programming may be on actual conduct and attitudes is a matter of considerable debate in the United States and elsewhere. No one knows for sure, but it is hard to doubt that family relations and religious attitudes have been changed by movies, radio, and TV, working alongside other aspects of contemporary life. The cult of physical fitness as much as the prevalence of crime in the streets of American cities probably reflects the power of the media to affect popular patterns of behavior.

In the world's rich countries, modern communications fostered the emergence of a distinct youth culture, expressed and propagated primarily by musical recordings and performances celebrating sexual and other forms of sensory indulgence. In the 1960s, when those born during the postwar baby boom came of age, the gap between youths and older age groups widened. This was especially true in the United States, where the Vietnam war heightened the collision between the ideal of sensual self-expression, on the one hand, and the values of military discipline and self-sacrifice on the other.

Poor countries, in general, could not even afford blue jeans—the uniform of America's youth culture; and in communist countries, official censorship screened out most of the message, though official exhortations to work hard so as to achieve the goals of the current economic plan did not find ready acceptance among young people either. But dissent, where it existed, found almost no public expression, so differences among age groups, that figured so prominently in Japan, western Europe, and the United States, were pretty well hidden from view.

Another important feature of modern communications is that they readily cross political boundaries, whether or not governments approve. Agitation via the media which led to the Iranian revolution of 1979 offered by far the most spectacular example of successful defiance of a government. News and information services directed to foreign listeners are broadcast by the world's leading governments with the aim of affecting public opinion in foreign countries in ways favorable to the sending nation. What effect such broadcasts have is hard to measure; but it means that no government, not even the most tyrannical, can be completely sure of controlling public opinion among its own people by censoring the news disseminated through its own broadcasts and newspapers since messages from other sources can be received via the airwaves.

Propaganda from governmental sources soon breeds skepticism among a population subjected to it. This blunts the effect of official efforts to control public opinion without making such efforts entirely futile.

Effects of American Media

A more subtle yet perhaps more powerful effect on human consciousness arises unintentionally from entertainment programs whose messages, political or otherwise, are only implied. This side effect makes the widespread showing of American movies and TV programs in foreign lands one of the most significant cultural phenomena of our time. Mass media exports are not an American monopoly: other countries have some success in exporting entertainment as well. Great Britain produces several programs shown in the United States, for example; and there are some other established exchanges, for example, the circulation of Egyptian films to other Arab lands, and of Russian films within the communist bloc. But these are all dwarfed by the sale of suitably dubbed American films and tapes to the TV stations and movie houses of other countries. Since costs had been met already by their showing within the United States, the producers of these programs can afford to offer them abroad at comparatively cheap prices. American films and tapes have held popular attention by appealing to elemental human emotions, by having no overt political message and, above all, by being available in abundance, whereas in smaller countries locally produced programs simply cannot fill all the broadcast time.

The effect of such broadcasting in poor and backward countries is even more uncertain than the effects within the United States itself. Many foreign viewers perhaps react to screen portraits of the streets of Los Angeles and other American cities as a sort of never-never-land and treat the whole thing as a fairy story. But patterns of personal behavior, exemplified in westerns, soap operas, and other staples of the American entertainment business, are likely to suggest new possibilities to viewers in distant lands where family traditions and expectations are profoundly different from those prevailing in the United States. How the old and new will combine remains to be seen. Change in patterns of personal behavior, rapid and unpredictable in its results, seems sure to follow from the mingling of such discrepant elements. It is still too soon to tell.

Countercurrents to the mass culture of the broadcast media as commercialized in the United States are powerful and obvious. Most of the world's governments produce at least a few radio and TV programs of their own, intended to assert and maintain local traditions and values. Some countries prohibit American entertainment entirely, so its circulation becomes clandestine. This is true of the Soviet Union and of most other communist countries for example. Many Moslem lands also prohibit or censor American programs.

Even within American society itself, and in other countries where the mass media are not strictly controlled by official authority, private persons and organizations deliberately reject some or all of the values implied by commercialized mass entertainment. Religious groups, seeking to uphold old certainties, are by far the most important of these counterweights in American society. Some of them use radio and TV to propagate their teachings in direct competition with secular entertainment. Ethnic groups also sometimes seek to maintain their unique heritage despite the attractions of the American melting pot and rely on radio as well as ethnic newspapers to do so.

All this is a counterpart, within American society, of similar movements in the world at large among peoples who wish to be modern, rich, and powerful all right, but wish also to maintain their customs, their language, their religion, and their uniqueness against all the temptations and corruptions of the outside world. Since nearly everyone feels pulled in both directions—towards the new and towards the old—how any particular group or country will choose between alternatives in time to come remains very uncertain. It is silly to suppose that American mass culture will prevail everywhere; it is equally foolish to deny that those who reject it most strenuously, like the Iranian revolutionaries, will nevertheless be influenced in reaffirming their own tradition by what they oppose.

CONCLUSION

Thus we end where we began: unsure of where the world is going. Rapid change is sure to continue, at least for a while. Human consciousness is in flux as never before, thanks to new patterns of communication that have arisen within the past generation. Human numbers increase and press on the means of subsistence more acutely than in any former age. Ecological disaster on the one hand and atomic annihilation on the other may upset or destroy the world as we know it. But human intelligence and adaptability allowed our forerunners to muddle through somehow. Future generations are likely to do the same. Time alone will tell.

CHAPTER 12

Thought and Culture Since 1914

Since 1914 deep and far-reaching changes have come very quickly in the way people think and act. From country to country, great differences appear; and even within a single country, different age groups and different economic classes, different races and different religious bodies sometimes disagree with one another about nearly everything. Or so it seems to anyone who reads the newspaper headlines and listens to all the quarreling voices that compete for public attention all round the world.

General trends are hard to detect. Certainly, communication has increased. We know far more about events in distant parts of the earth than our grandparents or great-grandparents did; and far more people travel than ever before. This may tend to even out differences—but only in the long run. In the short run, as people become more aware of their many differences, more frequent contacts often merely underline the things that split humankind into so many quarrelsome parts.

Since World War I, scientists have mastered new secrets at a great rate; atomic physics, genetic codes, psychological motivation, humanity's evolutionary past—these and many other fields have opened important new vistas since 1914. Yet we have also learned how much human action depends on irrational and unconscious impulses. Artists have tried to express and explore the subconscious levels of life, both in words and through the visual arts.

Some people feel that the result of so much change amounts to a breakdown of all civilized traditions. Others argue that the Western world is undergoing one more internal transformation, like the shift from medieval to early modern or from the Old Regime to nineteenth-century industrial and liberal society. At the moment, no one knows which of these judgments will stand up in time to come. Caught as we are in the midst of it all, no one is wise enough to foresee the outcome or understand everything that is happening. In this chapter, therefore, we can only make an attempt to point out some things that seem important, and may turn out to be so—or may not.

THOUGHT AND CULTURE

From close up, at any rate, it looks as though specialization and professionalization of art and thought had run riot since 1914. Artists who are so original that no one understands them are easy to discover in any art colony. Scholars whose interests are so specialized that only a few others in the entire world can understand what the argument is about also exist on many university campuses. On the other hand, the gap that used to exist between local folk cultures and the concerns of the upper classes was probably no greater than the gap between experts and the masses in our own day. What has happened is that the popular level of culture has achieved visibility through the mass media of communication, whereas before, popular culture passed from generation to generation invisibly, by word of mouth and by example.

Taking the world as a whole, the dominating fact about popular culture is the break it represents with folk traditions of every kind. Wherever economic conditions allowed, peasants and ex-peasants left traditional local styles of living behind them as fast as they could. New city-made clothes and gadgets of all kinds tend to be the first things that matter. People emerging from traditional peasant ways of life may find their most fascinating introduction to civilization in studying an illustrated mail order catalogue or the advertisements in a glossy magazine. This allows them to learn about what can be wished for. The next thing is actually to possess a bicycle, then household appliances; and the climax is a car. But to have a car in such societies is still reserved for a tiny few who have made it all the way to the top.

Mass Media
and Popular Culture

Somewhere about midway in this curve of rising expectations, people start to pay serious attention to the mass media. To begin with, it was nearly always government initiative that brought the radio and roads to the countryside and to urban slums. During World War II, for example, the United States Information Service distributed thousands upon thousands of cheap radio speakers to villages in many different parts of the world. These radios were hooked up to a central radio station and were usually planted in a public place near the center of the community. In many regions of the world where official propaganda and news had never penetrated on a regular basis, it now became possible to speak daily to the villagers. An entirely new kind of political life thus became possible.

Even the busiest politicians have to stop talking sometimes. This means that national radio and television hookups must fill the time with other sorts of material. This opened the way for exposing hundreds of millions of human beings to new forms of cultural expression. Popular music, and popular TV programs, differing from country to country, did something to close the gap between city and village populations. Performers attracted a following among the vast numbers of persons who became able to listen to them or see them on the screen. And new art forms arose as well: westerns, crime shows, soap operas, quiz shows, jazz, rock music, and the like.

The most original creation of American popular culture was jazz. This originated in the black ghettos of New Orleans, Memphis, and Chicago. It came to the attention of whites in the 1920s, and spread widely through Europe and round the world. After years of resistance, even the Russians have begun to let jazz be heard in public. Popular music in the jazz tradition soon cut loose from its folk roots and became big business. One style succeeded another as popular performers vied for attention by more and more extravagant forms of expression.

In the 1950s a counter-current manifested itself. Students and other Americans became interested in folk music found mainly in the South and picked up old songs or invented new ones. Thus, while most of the world was trying to leave oral folk traditions behind, in the United States, at least, an influential group tried to recover something of the old simplicities of folk culture.

STANDARDIZATION OF LANGUAGE   An important by-product of mass media culture is standardization of language.

A few "world languages" attained greater importance with the rise of mass communications. English has profited most, for United States and British radio programs, movies, and phonograph records have spread literally around the world. Russian has met with great success inside the borders of the Soviet Union, where all the other nationalities have learned Russian and use it increasingly in daily encounters. In other parts of the world, the pattern is unclear. In India, for example, government effort to make Hindi a national language has met with organized local resistance, and English still retains some importance for the well-educated. The future of European languages in Africa remains completely uncertain; but in Latin America, Spanish and Portuguese seem to be overwhelming the Indian languages that still survive. In China and Moslem lands, however, the old classical languages, enriched by new coinages to fit new conditions, have had their power reinforced by the advent of mass media. The end result, in all probability, will be to reduce quite sharply the number of living languages. Speech patterns familiar to only a few people will have trouble resisting the new means of communication.

Links between popular mass culture and highbrow thought and art seem unimportant. Artists sometimes have tried to find roots for their work in the folkways of their nation. Thus, for example, a Mexican school of painters, of whom Diego Rivera (1886–1957) was the most famous, sought to arouse popular response by reviving pre-Columbian styles of art. In the 1930s, Parisian artists experimented with creating visual surprises by cutting out parts of magazine advertisements and pasting them together in absurd or shocking patterns. In the 1960s, "pop" art tried similar techniques with paint and canvas, and in a different way, the revival of folk music in the United States tried to accomplish the same thing.

In times past, when schoolteachers were the most important link between popular and highbrow culture, upper-class tastes tended to seep downward with the passage of time. Perhaps a similar process will continue if the persons who manage the mass media, searching for something new to put before the public, find use for what began as inaccessible highbrow stuff. But it is certainly not clear that seepage downward will be the prevailing movement. Popular mass culture may instead crowd out at least some aspects of upper-class culture, or transform it. So far, neither process seems very important. Instead highbrows go one way and the mass media go another. At any given moment in time there seems to be little in common between the two levels of thought and feeling.

THE SCIENCES

Although enormous amounts of new data have been gathered since 1914, the hard sciences that allow prediction have not achieved any radically new breakthrough since Albert Einstein proposed his theories of relativity in 1905 and worked them out in 1915. All the same, it took physicists some time to get used to the sort of universe that Einstein's formulas implied; and ordinary people found it still more puzzling to be told that space and time were not clearly separate, and that waves and particles, as well as matter and energy, were somehow the same thing.

Advances in Physics

In the 1930s, new machines were invented for accelerating electrons and other charged particles to great speeds. With these instruments, exploration of atomic nuclei became possible. High-speed particles could be made to hit an atom nucleus, and special instruments could then record information about the fragments that resulted from the collision. By measuring sizes and speeds, scientists could figure out what had been in the nucleus before the collision took place. As time went on, more and more powerful accelerators were constructed, and the number of particles that could be detected and measured increased.

For a while, it seemed possible to explain all observations by making a geometrical model of atomic structure. A Danish physicist, Niels Bohr (1885–1962), developed the idea that the nucleus was surrounded by revolving electrons, moving in more or less fixed orbits at different distances from the nucleus. Bohr's atom was a little like a miniature solar system, with the nucleus as sun and the electrons as planets. But during the 1930s, various new observations could not be fitted into this geometrical model. Physicists gave up the whole effort, preferring mathematical and statistical expressions to describe subatomic relationships. To ordinary people who habitually think of physical matter in spatial, geometrical terms, this breakdown of visual models was very puzzling. Fanciful names for subatomic particles made advanced physics into a sort of Alice-in-Wonderland world, where quarks come in flavors and leptons spin and collide with dozens of other odd entities.

Even though the language of physics, as it became more mathematical, became more unintelligible to everyone but experts, practical applications did not cease to arise. During World War II, for example, Einstein's formula for the equivalence of matter and energy was translated into the controlled release of nuclear energy. The atom bombs dropped on Japan in 1945 were the first and most dramatic result of this application of theory. Atomic reactors that energize electrical generators and drive submarines are among the more important later applications of the nuclear techniques that physicists and engineers began to explore during World War II.

The potential importance of these inventions staggers the imagination. Total destruction of human life is one possibility. An almost unlimited supply of energy, once the cost of constructing atomic power plants is met, might be another. In either case, old limits on human powers have been broken through; whether for good or ill remains to be seen.

Earth Sciences

A second area in which scientists have been unusually active since 1914 is exploration of the earth and space. New ways to explore the atmosphere and the regions of space close to the earth were introduced, mainly after World War II. As a result, new data have come in much faster than anyone has been able to put them together into a tidy theory.

The first rocket to put an artificial earth satellite into space went up from Russia in 1957. Since then, hundreds of rockets have thrust their payloads into orbit around the earth, where they perform many new tasks: photographing the surface of the earth; relaying radio and TV waves around the earth; measuring gravity, magnetic fields, and other variables with a new precision; and observing the heavens without the fuzziness created by the atmosphere. Other rockets escaped earth's gravity entirely, extending probes toward Venus, Mars, and more distant orbiting bodies. These probes sent back limited information about earth's fellow planets. Far more spectacular, however, was the assault upon earth's nearest neighbor in space, which saw the United States reach the moon with a series of manned flights, beginning in 1969. The Russians, for their part, landed an unmanned vehicle on the moon in 1970, which traveled short distances across the surface and sent back information about what it encountered. American moon flights not only put in position various "sensors" (devices which respond to physical stimuli) to detect moonquakes and other changes on the moon, but were also able to bring back samples from different regions of the moon's surface.

Spectacular photographs and a lot of detailed information about the moon resulted from these efforts. In addition, space explorers wrote a new chapter in the record of human venturesomeness and technical achievement. But so far, theoretical understanding of earth and sky has not been much affected by these first efforts to extend humanity's dominion into the fringes of earth-space. Perhaps there has not yet been enough time for the new data to challenge old theories; but even when existing theory cannot explain observed phenomena—for instance, the discovery that sources of radio waves in stellar space are not the same as sources of visible light—no new general interpretation has yet emerged.

Exploration of the world's oceans also achieved a new thoroughness and scope after World War II. Accurate plotting of ocean bottoms revealed a complicated pattern of ridges and deeps, together with differences in the underlying rocks. These new observations prove that North and South America are slowly drifting away from Europe and Africa, making the Atlantic wider and the Pacific narrower, inch by inch. Earthquakes and mountain-building can be related in important ways to this newly discovered pattern of continental drift; and the possibility of understanding and perhaps some day predicting movements deep within the bowels of the earth now seems open.

But this is still in the future. So far, the principal practical application of the new data which earth scientists have gathered so successfully is better weather prediction. Satellites are capable of photographing wide areas of the earth continuously and can transmit the picture to the ground. This technique allows the paths of storms to be plotted and their course predicted with much greater precision than before. In addition, the military significance of photographic reconnaissance from space is obvious. Orbiting cameras make national secrets much harder to keep than they used to be.

Molecular Biology

In biology, a dramatic new idea was broached in 1953 when Francis H. C. Crick and James D. Watson proposed that biological inheritance was carried from one generation to the next by large molecules that took the form of spiral chains. Even though these chains could be very long, they had a relatively simple repetitive structure. Small changes in the exact order in which sets of atoms appeared in such a molecule made all the difference between the genetic inheritance of one kind of animal and another, or, for that matter, between the simplest of living forms, such as bacteria and algae, and human beings.

Many other, less spectacular discoveries extended detailed understanding of biological processes. More and more of what happened in living tissues could be explained in chemical terms. Numerous applications of this knowledge came in medicine, as doctors invented chemical treatments for conditions that previously had been incurable. Some breakthroughs came by accident. In 1928, for example, Alexander Fleming noticed in some "spoiled" experiments that the growth of certain kinds of mold destroyed germs. This led to the discovery of penicillin (1929), the first of numerous antibiotic drugs that have since saved innumerable lives.

THE DOUBLE HELIX

As a senior in college, James Dewey Watson decided he would try to discover the chemistry of genes. Genes were what carried biological inheritance from one generation to the next; but though biologists had been talking about them for a long time, no one knew exactly what genes were. From the University of Chicago, Watson went to Indiana for a Ph.D. in genetics; then he was awarded a postdoctoral fellowship for study in Europe. He resolved to use it to get started on his dream project: to unravel the chemical structure of genes.

At Cambridge, England, he found a colleague in Francis H. C. Crick. Crick was thirty-five years old, brilliant, and brash. Watson was also brilliant and brash—and eleven years younger. The two men hit it off from the start; and they agreed that to get at the secret chemistry of heredity, the thing to do was to construct a model of a molecule known as *DNA*. DNA is short for deoxyribonucleic acid—a material found in the nucleus of all living cells.

But DNA molecules are among the biggest known to exist. These enormous molecules were made up of hundreds of thousands of atoms, grouped in thousands upon thousands of subassembly blocks. How could anyone hope to discover how such a thing was put together? It was like trying to assemble the millions of parts of a big computer while blindfolded, for even the giant DNA molecules were far too small to be seen. Other research biologists thought that the staggering complexity of DNA would have to wait until the structure of smaller molecules—like the proteins that also exist in all living cells—had been worked out.

But Watson wanted to find out about genes, and he believed that DNA, not proteins, held the secret. So he plunged stubbornly ahead. When Crick and Watson started on the project, they had the advantage of others' work. The separate building blocks out of which DNA was made were already known. The proportions of each kind of material in DNA had

Computers and Their Applications

The development of workable electronic computers was another important breakthrough that came at the close of World War II. Designs for computers were fairly familiar from the work of nineteenth-century mathematicians; and the principle of storage and retrieval of information was been measured quite accurately. Most important of all: a way to fix DNA molecules into crystal form had been invented. This allowed x-ray photographs to be taken of the molecules. The difficulty was that what showed on such photographs was not a shape or even a shadow of the molecule itself, but patterns of x-ray reflections as they bounced off the various atoms that made up a DNA molecule.

Such bits of information added up to a vast puzzle. What could be done with it? What Watson and Crick did was to make guesses, and then try to build a model—out of wire and bits of metal—that would have a place for everything that had to fit into the giant DNA molecule. They made several false starts: leaving not enough space for all the necessary building blocks, or attempting a chemical bond between next-door neighbors that would not work. But in less than two years, they hit upon what turned out to be the right form—a double helix—after seeing some new x-ray photographs of DNA that had been made in London.

By the beginning of April, 1953, the model had withstood all tests. The two young men were ready to announce their discovery. They did so by publishing a short article—only slightly over 900 words long. It began:

> We wish to suggest a structure for the salt of deoxyribose nucleic acid (DNA). This structure has novel features which are of considerable biological interest.[*]

This was grandiose understatement. Biologists everywhere soon realized that the double helix form allowed reproduction of similar molecules. By splitting the two strands of the double helix apart, a new strand could form to fit the old half. Thus the structure of the DNA unraveled part of the mystery James Dewey Watson had set out to solve. He had in truth learned something about the chemistry of genes—the innermost machinery of life itself.

[*] J. D. Watson and F. H. C. Crick, "Molecular Structure of Nucleic Acids," *Nature* 171 (1953): 737.

well understood before transistors made it possible to make a machine that would really work. In the years since 1945, several different generations of computers have come into existence, each more flexible and with greater storage capacity than its predecessors.

The uses of computers are many. Banks, libraries, income tax collectors can use them to keep track of individual accounts. In science, much more complicated uses arise, for computers can make calculations and pick out answers that fit given conditions much faster than human minds, unaided, can. This, in turn, makes various kinds of mathematical information available to scientists and engineers that simply could not be had if they were forced, as before, to sit down and figure out each step with pencil and paper.

Another frontier of inquiry opened by computers is investigation of how the human brain handles its input and output of data. There are some resemblances between the way a computer works and the activity of the brain. As computers become more flexible, they resemble brains more closely, so that theoretical insight into the one seems likely to rub off upon investigation of the other.

Understanding of the structural limits of languages and of logic is also likely to be affected by computers. Sociology and history may be transformed in the future as data describing individual human lives are put on tapes and become available for analysis by computers. At least in principle, this ought to make possible statistically precise generalizations about different aspects of social behavior among a population whose individual life histories have been recorded in detail.

Advances in the Social Sciences

Computers thus span the gap between the hard and soft sciences. They may in the future make some of the soft sciences a good deal less soft,

An office equipped with computer terminals. The impact of the computer upon the creation, processing, and transmission of information might be compared to that of machines upon agriculture and business. (NCR Corporation)

that is, make possible more nearly accurate prediction of human behavior. Predicting election results has already become almost a science, thanks to computers. Other similar changes may follow, particularly in economics, since data on exchanges of money and of materials ought, again in principle, to permit far more accurate forecasting of future economic conditions than has yet been achieved.

MARXIAN STRAITJACKET IN COMMUNIST LANDS   In the hard sciences, little difference exists between the communist and noncommunist worlds. Stalin did, for a while, try to impose Marxian linguistics and Marxian biology upon Russian scientists; but the effort was given up after Stalin's death. Physicists, chemists, mathematicians, and earth scientists have little trouble understanding one another or agreeing upon new discoveries as they are made, no matter on which side of the political fence.

The soft sciences are different, for Marxist doctrine limits and directs communist research. The fact is that many of the predictions Marx and Lenin made have not come true. Workers in capitalist countries have not become poorer and poorer, for example; and communist revolution has come not to the highly industrialized lands but to peasant countries, or countries just beginning to emerge from peasant status. Yet communists treat the writings of Marx and Lenin as though they were sacred scripture. Efforts to apply the doctrine to particular circumstances left plenty of room for invention and differences of opinion. But the basic truths, communists claimed, had been laid down forever and ever, and if the facts failed to conform to the doctrine, it was too bad for the facts. The "real" revolution and the "real" impoverishment of the workers would show up sooner or later.

NEW PERSPECTIVES IN ECONOMICS, HISTORY, AND ANTHROPOLOGY   This attitude made honest thought about society impossible. In the Western world, however, the half century following World War I gave birth to at least three far-reaching new ideas. The first was the "new economics," developed since 1936 by John Maynard Keynes (1883–1946) together with his critics and followers. Keynes set out to explain what went wrong during the great depression of the 1930s, when unemployed workers and unemployed machinery in Britain and elsewhere sat side by side with unsatisfied human wants. Keynes argued that governmental intervention could counteract the boom and bust pattern that had proved so harmful. During World War II his ideas gained new scope and precision in actual practice, when the British and American governments did intervene and directed economic activity into new channels with great success. After the war, economic management by using indirect methods favored by Keynes became normal in the entire noncommunist world, though practice often departed from anything Keynes and his fellow economists ever dreamed of.

A second new concept of general importance was the widened historical vision that archaeology, anthropology, and exploration of the history of the non-Western world made possible. In 1914 most Westerners still knew little and cared less about other civilizations. Indeed, many Europeans and Americans believed that the Asian peoples had no history. They thought that after a first spurt of change, nothing new had happened in Asia. Progress, they believed, was limited to the West. But as changes came to all the world, this naïve misunderstanding of the facts lost any shred of plausibility. Many careful scholars, both Westerners and Asians, set out to discover and write histories of all parts of the non-Western world.

At the same time, archaeologists discovered evidences of the beginnings of civilization in Sumer (1920s), China (1930s), and India (1920s). In 1914 Egypt had seemed the oldest civilization. By the 1940s it was known that this was not true, because the ancient Egyptians had borrowed some important ideas from the Sumerians. In the 1950s archaeological discoveries in Africa began to reveal new details of prehuman and human evolution.

The result of these lines of inquiry was to make it possible to see all the separate histories of nations, civilizations, barbarian peoples, and savages as part of the larger adventure of humanity. Much disagreement over details and even over the pattern as a whole remained. Oswald Spengler (1880–1936) and Arnold J. Toynbee (1889–1975) suggested that civilizations rose and fell according to a standard pattern, each remaining distinct from the others. This book, on the contrary, has tried to portray different civilizations and other less complex societies all at once, in the belief that they acted and reacted upon each other from the beginning. Still other patterns have their supporters: for instance, the Marxian view that all societies pass through slave, serf, and wage stages of development. But whatever room for argument remains—and it is very wide—it still holds true that a far more spacious and inclusive vision of the human past has become available as a result of progress in historical study in the past half century.

FREUDIAN PSYCHOLOGY   A third important change in Western thought about humanity and society is connected with the name of Sigmund Freud (1856–1939). His most important books were written before 1914; but his ideas attained wide circulation only after World War I. The details of Freud's effort to describe the unconscious levels of human minds are not likely to last, because the structure and function of the brain seem not to match the different levels of mental activity that Freud tried to distinguish. But the significant thing was this: Freud showed in thoroughly convincing ways that people often act under impulses that come from below the threshold of consciousness. Language sometimes simply disguises real motives. Freud's second lasting discovery was that one of our deep urges is sexual, and that this drive spills over into many other kinds of behavior and relationships.

In the 1920s, such ideas were new and shocking to many people. The implications of Freud's insights for politics and economics even yet have not been fully taken into account. Democratic theory, after all, assumes voters to be rational and able to choose rationally. Economists expect the same. But if unconscious levels of human motivation are in fact important on a private and personal level, then unconscious drives must also affect public behavior in ways we do not really understand.

ART AND LITERATURE

Although social scientists were, and still are, slow to react to the new ideas that Freud brought before the public, writers and artists in Western lands reacted at once and with considerable enthusiasm.

The communists, once again, stood aside. In Russia and other communist states, art was supposed to serve political purposes by helping to shape the new consciousness that communism required. It was a branch of propaganda, a kind of engineering of the soul. In the first years of the Russian Revolution, wild experimentation had been allowed, even encouraged. But from the 1920s, official directives instructed writers and artists what to do. Uplifting, inspirational subjects were prescribed; what was produced was often dull and trite.

Dullness and triteness were exactly what Western artists and writers were most anxious to avoid. Novelty, experiment, adventure to the limits of intelligibility attracted them. To do what others had done seemed a confession of failure, of lack of genius. Self-expression on the part of the artist and remorseless analysis of his or her subject were characteristic of the most famous writers and artists of the age.

Old Genres in New Forms

In the 1920s both artists and writers experimented with new forms. Painters had only to carry on with the effort begun before World War I. Bits and pieces of ordinary visual experience were jerked out of context or distorted to the point where recognition by the viewer became hit and miss. Symbols aimed at affecting the subconscious mind were deliberately sought after. A desire to surprise and shock was a second goal pursued by many artists. The greatest names had already emerged to fame before World War I: Pablo Picasso (1881–1973), Georges Braque (1882–1963), and Henri Matisse (1869–1954) among them.

Nonobjective paintings that made no effort whatever to look like anything else carried the breakaway from the Renaissance ideal to its logical conclusion. Piet Mondrian (1872–1944) and Vasili Kandinski (1866–1944) were among the pioneers of this kind of painting. The ideal of nonobjective painting was "pure design," mathematical, geometrical, like music in its underlying principles.

In Germany an influential group of architects and industrial designers, the Bauhaus School, arose in the 1920s, inspired by the same ideas. The so-called "international style" of architecture resulted. It was characterized by the free use of new materials such as concrete, steel, and glass for walls, and by spare, rectangular, functional shapes. One great advantage of the new style was the lower costs of construction. Walls of glass were lighter, less expensive, and resulted in bright, open interiors. The Bauhaus style spread round the world within a couple of decades. Nearly all the world's airports, for example, are in this general style, as well as thousands of new buildings in every important city of the world outside of the communist countries, where brick and mortar (more recently, concrete) continued to be preferred to glass.

Writers such as the novelist James Joyce (1882–1941) or the poet Thomas Stearns Eliot (1888–1965) experimented with words. By inventing new words, using fragmentary sentences, and stretching grammar, they and other writers tried to affect subconscious levels of their readers' minds in much the same way that artists were trying to do. But even in the hands of a master, tinkering with language risked unintelligibility; so this was not a very promising field to explore—nothing to compare with what painters were able to do. Accordingly, in the period after World War II, this line of literary development almost stopped. Writers, instead, concentrated on other ways of breaking with the past. One technique was the shock value of exploring previously forbidden themes, such as sex. Another was to celebrate the anti-hero, that is, to create a fictional character who did not impose his will on people and things around him in the way heroes had done since the time of Homer, but became instead the helpless victim of circumstances.

Amidst all this striving for novelty, there were some writers who clung closer to old themes and conventions; among them were the playwright George Bernard Shaw (1856–1950), the poet Dylan Thomas (1914–1953), and the novelists Thomas Mann (1875–1955) and William Faulkner

(1897–1962). It is impossible to predict which of these artists will turn out to be the more important authors of the age.

New Genres in Old Forms

If popularity is any standard to depend upon, the really outstanding authors of the post-World War I period were the writers of murder mysteries. This branch of literature became popular before World War I with the tales by Arthur Conan Doyle (1859–1930), which told how a gentlemanly detective, Sherlock Holmes, used his powers of observation and deduction to solve mysteries. Hundreds of authors followed in Sherlock Holmes's footsteps, and millions of people read their works.

Still another new form of writing that came to the fore after 1914 was children's literature. Better understanding of how children grow from year to year made it possible to write more effectively for different age levels. Some stories became so well known as to populate the English-speaking world with a host of new characters: Pooh, Dr. Doolittle, Charlie Brown, and many more. Talking animals and clever children, generally speaking, took the place of the witches and fairies of older nursery tales.

Comic books, too, first gathered together from already published newspaper strips and then printed as an independent form of literature, also became very popular, appealing mainly to young and not fully literate readers.

Perhaps the most influential form of writing in the last fifty years has been manuals on how to raise infants and small children. Once upon a time, knowledge concerning the care and feeding of infants was handed down from generation to generation without being written down. In the 1920s, however, the movement of people from country to city meant that millions of young women married later in life after forgetting how their own mothers had looked after them as children; and they had no close relative nearby to pass on traditional lore. In addition, new information about vitamins and infant health gave doctors something new to say to mothers. The result was a rash of "How to" books. Millions of middle-class American mothers raised their babies according to instructions laid down in such books. Since then, "How to" books have covered a vast range of other subjects, replacing or supplementing older "hands-on" ways of transmitting practical skills from one generation to the next. The impact upon the national life was tremendous. In other countries, such manuals had less importance, perhaps; but everywhere the breakdown of oral tradition, linking the generations, required books of this kind.

RELIGION AND PHILOSOPHY

Most of the recent developments in science and thought have paid little attention to traditional religion. Yet Christianity, Judaism, Islam, Hinduism, and Buddhism remain. They are massive facts of the human scene. Their power over human minds is probably as great as ever. After all, religious groups also can use the mass media to spread their doctrines.

Among Christians, the most striking development of the years since World War I was the growing willingness of different sects and denominations to seek common ground. For a long time, this ecumenical movement was the work of Protestant groups, especially in the English-speaking world. Pope John XXIII (1958–1963) brought the Roman Catholic church into much more sympathetic relationship with this movement. He summoned the second Vatican Council (1962, 1963), which defined Roman Catholic relationships with Jews and with other Christian sects in a conciliatory way.

While the well-established Christian churches began to emphasize the points that they have in common, new sects—with strong and uncompromising views—continued to arise and flourish, especially among poor and disadvantaged people. Jehovah's Witnesses is an example of one of these sects in the United States. This sect has also won converts in Africa and Latin America among peoples emerging from traditional peasant life, who felt the need of new, clearly defined guidelines for conduct and belief.

Martin Luther King (1929–1968), the most influential spokesman for the non-violent acquisition of American black civil rights until his death by assassination in 1968. (AFL-CIO News)

Perhaps, therefore, the movement toward reconciliation and unity is about evenly balanced by the rise and spread of new uncompromising sects. But even if this is true (and statistics seem unavailable to prove one thing or another), the existence of these two contradictory Christian movements is evidence of the vitality churches continue to enjoy.

Church and Society

A second important, new emphasis within Christianity was the result of efforts to apply Christian principles to changing social, political, and economic conditions. Missionaries in Asia and Africa tended to shift away from emphasis on simple religious conversion, and instead put medical and educational service in the forefront. In the English-speaking world, members of the clergy took leading parts in movements for social reform. The Labour party in England, for instance, was deeply colored by Methodism; and the civil rights movement in the United States, whose most famous leader, Martin Luther King, Jr. (1929–1968), was himself a Baptist minister, attracted much church support.

All round the world, Marxism rivaled Christianity (and other religions) by offering an atheistic explanation of the human condition. Marxist parties were nearly always anticlerical; and where they came to power they tried to undermine Christian faith by propaganda and sometimes by active persecution as well. Nevertheless, in Russia and in other east European lands where communist governments came to power, Christianity retained considerable influence among the people.

The Nazi movement in Germany also challenged Christian principles by glorifying teutonic paganism and rejecting Christian morality. A few Germans, inspired by Christian ideals, plotted actively against Hitler; indeed, Christian faith proved the most effective rallying ground for the German opposition to nazism. In other European countries, too, Christian belief played an important role in inspiring resistance movements against the Nazis during World War II. As a result, after the war, powerful new Christian-Democratic parties emerged in all the important countries of western Europe. These parties have, in fact, dominated the post-World War II governments of Italy and West Germany.

On the other hand, in Spain and some of the Spanish-speaking countries of South America, the church pursued a conservative if not downright reactionary policy. In these lands the church remained a target for liberal and anti-clerical reformers.

A third issue for Christians was how to react to secular thought and science. Many Protestants rejected Darwinian evolution and put their faith in the literal accuracy of the Bible. This was challenged by "Modernists" who believed that religious truth (like other kinds of truth) evolved over time, so that Bible writers were mistaken on some points and headed in the right direction on others.

Among Roman Catholics, modernism had been prohibited by the Vatican Council of 1869–1870. Yet a Jesuit philosopher and archaeologist, Teilhard de Chardin (1881–1955), developed an evolutionary philosophy which included religion. In this, as in other ways, the gap between Protestant and Roman Catholic thought seemed to be narrowing, as both found it possible to adjust to the progress of science without giving up continuity with older tradition and doctrine.

Judaism

Among Jews, the Nazi persecution in Germany, climaxing in the death camps of World War II, had tremendous impact. Nearly all European Jews were uprooted. Of those who survived, many went to Israel after the war or followed earlier emigrants to the United States, South Africa, Argentina, and elsewhere. The Israeli war of independence in 1947 provoked another wave of persecution that ran through the entire Moslem world. As a result, nearly all "oriental" Jews were forced to flee to Israel.

Within Israel, opinions differed widely as to how a Jewish state ought to handle religion. Secular-minded Jews, who want a modern, industrial, and socialist society, predominated; but there were also Orthodox Jews who regarded any departure from rabbinical rules as religious heresy.

The outbreak of vicious anti-Semitism in Nazi Germany and the rise of Israel as a Jewish state persuaded many Jews in other lands that it was neither possible nor desirable to try to merge into the general population by giving up all ties with traditional Judaism. This "assimilationist" idea had flourished in Germany ever since the later 1700s, when special laws against Jews began to be repealed. Intermarriages between Christians and Jews had become quite common, and differences between Jews and other Germans were less than in almost any other land. If Hitlerism could break out in Germany, therefore, the whole ideal of assimilation into secular society and of ceasing to be a separate social group seemed to be proved dangerous and false.

At the same time, in the United States and England, widespread reaction against the Nazi barbarism discouraged open expression of anti-Semitic feelings; and various social barriers against Jews tended to fall, one by one, without the public outcry and legislation that was needed to batter down discrimination against American blacks. In Russia, however, traces of old anti-Semitic feelings, which had been strong before World War I, survived in spite of official communist disapproval.

Islam

The ecumenical movement among Christians tried also to reach out toward Jews in order to soften the historic clash between the two faiths. This was not true of Islam. Few Christians knew much about the faith of Mohammed, and the Moslems had no interest whatever in associating with Christian clerics whom they regarded, as they did the Jews, as hereditary enemies and preachers of false doctrine.

Yet Islam found itself in an embarrassing position. The Moslem Sacred Law, like the Jewish law, was at the heart of traditional religion. Its rules were plainly incompatible with Western thought and made it next to impossible to build up a strong Moslem state. Still, to reject the Sacred Law meant losing the past. The Turks tried to do so in the 1920s. But in the 1950s Islam began to come back and even won official recognition in Turkey, because voters remained Moslem despite the efforts of the revolutionary government to discredit the faith. On the other hand, in Arabia where red-hot Wahhabi reformers had come to power in the 1920s, the discovery of vast oil reserves brought huge sums of money into the country. With this new wealth some of the warmth of the Wahhabi faith vanished, at least in court circles. Pakistan was a religious state, carved out of British India in 1947, because its citizens were Moslems. But when it came to deciding what a Moslem state ought to be like, the old dilemma of how to treat the Sacred Law proved insoluble. A military coup d'état brought Westernized army officers to power who systematically sidestepped the issue by concentrating on inherited quarrels with Hindu India.

Throughout the Moslem world, communist doctrine collided with traditional religion. Marxist atheism and materialism contradicted Mohammed's revelation, and neither side tried to disguise the fact. As a result, there were few communists in Moslem lands. Only people who were willing to throw away their cultural heritage could become communists, and this was always a small minority. The mass slaughter of the Indonesian communist party in 1966 was a bloodthirsty demonstration of how Moslems feel about Marxists.

The collision between Islam and the modern secular outlook achieved new intensity in Iran in 1979 with the victory of Shia fundamentalists over the shah's government. But how to apply the Sacred Law under contemporary conditions remains problematic, and how to combine the pursuit of holiness with other goals has not been resolved. For the Iranian revolutionaries, like other people, want wealth and power as well as wishing to obey Allah; and the two are difficult to combine.

This is the crucial dilemma of the world of Islam. No resolution of the problem seems in sight.

Hinduism, Buddhism, Confucianism, and Shinto

Hindus and Buddhists, on the contrary, saw no vital contradiction between Western, secular ideas and their traditional religions. Long ago, both these faiths made room for an infinite variety of doctrines. Atheism was nothing new or shocking to Hindus and Buddhists. Buddha was an atheist, and many Hindu philosophers were, too. Marxism thus was able to fit in as another partial truth—mistaken, of course, inasmuch as Marxism taught that the material world was real—yet, perhaps, useful in its own limited way if it helped social reform or forwarded national independence.

As a result, Indians living in the southern part of India, where various local languages survived, often became Marxists as a way of protesting against domination from the north, where Hindi was the common speech. Similarly, in Vietnam and other parts of southeast Asia, all kinds of half-way-houses between Buddhism and communism existed, without any particular sense of strain being felt on either side.

Confucianism in China and Shinto in Japan, however, appear to be dying faiths. The schools that once trained generations of Chinese in the Confucian Classics were abandoned after 1905, and a new generation grew up with little acquaintance with that past. Since 1949 the communists have done all they could to discredit old ways of thought. Maoism was deliberately invented to replace Confucianism, but in many ways it resembled what it displaced. Anything else would be strange, for Mao was educated in a traditional way until his twenties, when, as a young college student, he first met Lenin's ideas and began his career as a Marxist. Other Chinese communist leaders, as well as many in the rank and file, have a similar personal history. Massive carryover from the Confucian past is, therefore, inescapable, even if doctrines have been officially and fundamentally changed.

As for the worship of the sun goddess and of her divine descendant, the emperor of Japan, the events of World War II thoroughly discredited that form of Shinto. After the war, the emperor publicly denied his divinity, and the crown prince of Japan married a commoner. Nothing much remained of the old Shinto beliefs. Traditional religion was represented in Japan mainly by remodeled forms of Buddhism. Buddhism's main rival was Marxism; but Japanese Marxists do not yet seem to have invented their own national brand of the faith, as have the Russians and Chinese, not to mention the Yugoslavs and other east Europeans.

CONCLUSION

Human societies, thought, and culture have changed very fast and fundamentally since 1914. No end is in sight, although past ages of really rapid and far-reaching change have all been relatively brief—a matter of two or three generations, usually. But this time, older limits have been left behind. The majority of human beings no longer must work in the fields to feed a privileged few who are doing other things. For the first time in history, modern machines and methods allow a few to feed everyone else. Cultural consequences of this fundamental change remain unclear. All we think and do reflects and contributes to this basic departure from life patterns that prevailed throughout previous civilized history. It makes our age a time of adventure into the unknown on a greater scale than before—perhaps more than ever before.

How future generations will evaluate the time in which we live is impossible to know, but interesting to wonder about. If the pace of change levels off eventually, as seems inevitable in the long run, it is possible that our remote descendants will regard this as a great, heroic time in which the ground rules of their own societies were laid down by us—stumbling, uncertain, and anxious though we be. Confusion, which seems to dominate every aspect of our age, even its science, can be immensely fertile. It offers future generations a multitude of models from which to pick and choose. Such, perhaps, may be the long-range historical importance of the twentieth century.

BREAKTHROUGHS IN THE USE OF ENERGY AND FUEL

Muscles came first: arm, leg, and tongue. Then were tamed a few big animals strong enough to carry heavy loads or pull great weights. The horse, ox, camel, and water buffalo were the most important of these sources of power; and until two hundred years ago they remained, with human muscles, the most important sources of power humans knew.

Yet from very early times people also tapped inanimate forms of power. Fire, for example, unlocked chemical energy—and from Paleolithic times, hunters used fire to warm themselves and to cook. Later civilized peoples made fire to bake pottery and smelt metals as well.

This was only the beginning. Wind, water, coal, electricity, and most recently nuclear energy have all been put to work for men's purposes with consequences— good and bad, foreseen and unforeseen— that have entirely transformed our natural environment.

Natural Power of Water and Wind

The Romans made the swift-flowing river Tiber grind grain into flour to feed the swollen populace of their city in the first century B.C. The principle was simple: a paddle wheel half in and half out of the river revolved as the flowing water pressed against each paddle.

Windmills worked on a similar principle but were invented later. The earliest known came from central Asia, where Buddhists used them to launch prayers to heaven. Later, windmills were put to more material uses—for grinding grain, pumping water, and driving other machines.

HIGHLIGHTS

Wind and watermills provided a new source of mechanical power that could be put to many uses.

The great advantage was that, once a mill had been built, the power cost nothing and it could be put to work whenever the water flowed or the wind blew.

The main disadvantage was that, for many centuries, no one had a steady flow of grain to be ground or wood to be sawed. The superior work capacity of water and wind was wasted.

Since it was expensive to build mills initially, they were not much used until the sixteenth and seventeenth centuries in Europe, when improvements in transportation did make it possible to keep water and windmills steadily at work.

Explosive Power of Gunpowder

Gunpowder is a chemical mixture that does not need to take oxygen from the air in order to "burn." When ignited almost all of it turns into gas. The effect, in an enclosed chamber, is explosive.

The Chinese discovered gunpowder about A.D. 1000. They used it first to blow up fortified gates by filling hollow chambers of bamboo with the explosive mixture and pushing them under the closed gates. Soon afterward the Chinese began experimenting with hollow metal pots, filled with gunpowder and open at one end, which they used as primitive guns.

Europeans started similar experiments in the thirteenth century, having learned about gunpowder probably from China via the Mongol Empire. By 1500, Europeans excelled in the manufacture of big guns, perhaps because they already had a highly developed metallurgy. Peaceful

A water mill constructed in the 19th century.
(Virginia State Travel Service)

pushed the piston back. James Watt in 1776 improved upon this method by using valves to let the steam both into and out of the cylinder. A heavy balance wheel carried the piston back, expelling the old steam and readying the cylinder for the next rush of high-pressure steam.

The steam engine was soon put to work at many different tasks, like pumping, driving trains, and activating machinery in factories.

uses for explosives, as in mining for instance, came later, mainly in the nineteenth and twentieth centuries.

HIGHLIGHTS   Gunpowder altered warfare and government in far-reaching ways all over the world.

> Big guns were expensive, and only a few rulers could pay for them. Those who did could knock down their rivals' castle walls. Large terrritorial states could be built with the help of big guns.
> Handguns became important in warfare only in the seventeenth century. Infantry armed with guns overcame the age-old superiority of steppe cavalry. This allowed the Russian and Chinese empires, in the eighteenth century, to divide the steppelands of Eurasia between them.

Expansive Power of Steam

Modern steam engines let steam under pressure flow into a cylinder, closed at one end by a close-fitting piston. Steam pressure then makes the piston move. There were different ways of bringing the piston back again. The earliest type of engine in common use allowed the steam to condense, so that atmospheric pressure

HIGHLIGHTS   Steam engines could be set up where fuel was easily found.

> Since coal fires were the easiest way to produce steam, available coal beds became the prime factor controlling the location of heavy industry after 1850, when the steam engine came into its own.
> Because the steam engine was invented in Great Britain, the British achieved a head start over all other peoples in exploiting the potential of the new, cheap, and flexible source of power.
> The many possibilities opened by the use of steam power between 1776 and 1850 made this the era of the Industrial Revolution in Britain and western Europe.

Gunpowder was invented by the Chinese, who used it in the manufacture of fireworks and weapons.
(Library of Congress)

A French musketeer. (Library of Congress)

Electricity as a source of power is clean, and it can be precisely controlled.

In time, electricity opens the possibility of modulating power at short intervals. This allows refinements in manufacture otherwise unattainable.

In space, electrical power can reach down to the level of individual molecules and atoms by ionizing them. This opens the possibility for new kinds of processes, like silver-plating.

Electrical power also allows worldwide instantaneous communication, making precise information readily available to government, business, and other decision-makers.

Enormous Power of the Atom

All humanity's earlier adventures in harnessing diverse forms of energy have been

Instantaneous Power of Electricity

Lightning and static electricity awed and puzzled humankind from earliest times, but not until the nineteenth century did anyone begin to learn how to control the power of electrical currents. Electric motors on a toy scale were known as early as 1831, but it was the 1880s when engineers began to conceive of building large-scale dynamos to supply electric current to large numbers of customers.

Electric power was first used for interior lighting. But in the twentieth century more uses for electricity in industry have been found, with the result that heavy cables have largely replaced steam engines as energy sources in modern factories.

An electrical storm. (NOAA, National Oceanic and Atmospheric Administration)

dwarfed by the most recent breakthrough: the controlled release of nuclear energy. The first successful experiment took place in Chicago in 1942, and atomic energy was initially used for making the bombs dropped on Nagasaki and Hiroshima at the close of World War II. Peaceful uses of atomic energy include the generation of electricity and underground blasting.

Atomic energy was developed by highly-trained scientists acting on extremely abstract mathematical theory. Theory and practice had been closely linked in the development of electrical power too, but not as deliberately and consciously or on such a scale as in this case.

HIGHLIGHTS

By converting matter itself into energy, atomic power offers an almost limitless supply of energy.

Such a storehouse of potential energy can be used for any and all of the peaceful purposes to which electrical and other forms of power have been put.

At the same time, atomic energy has the potential for destroying all higher forms of life.

Systematic application of scientific theory to the improvement of techniques was carried through successfully in unlocking atomic energy. The development of new products and manufacturing processes is faster than ever.

Costs of Power Over Nature

Humanity's enormous triumphs in using power for its own purposes involve unexpected and unwished-for costs. Too rapid changes in machinery strained modern society by asking people to alter their habits too fast; too reckless a use of power in manufacturing products has upset the natural environment in ways we do not fully understand.

The use of nuclear reactors to produce electricity, while not without risks, has facilitated the production of generally low-cost energy. (American Electric Power Service Corporation)

Still, some of the risks are clear. Carbon dioxide added to the atmosphere by burning coal and other fuels alters the way sunlight reaches the earth. A "greenhouse effect" may melt glaciers, raise sea levels, and alter climates.

The risks of nuclear radiation are more obvious and sure. Disposal of radioactive wastes from nuclear power plants is difficult, and the risks of accidental disaster are immensely dangerous, as the Russians found out in 1986 at Chernobyl. Nuclear warheads, fired in anger, threaten to destroy all human life by disrupting the balances of nature irremediably.

The State
of the
World Today

At the close of this sort of survey of recent events, it is well to remind ourselves of how blind we are likely to be to new things that will attain great importance in years to come. Perhaps some obscure groups of men hold the future in their hands, as Buddha, Christ, and Mohammed once did. Or some scientific discovery may give people undreamed-of power to influence the way others behave; and by using that power, they may then alter themselves and their fellows in ways we cannot imagine.

No one knows what the future will bring; until it comes, the meaning and shape of the past remain unclear. Each generation must reshape its past to fit its present and assist transition to the future. New nations have to discover, or invent, a history; and in the same way, as humanity changes itself, its past as well as its future alters shape, values, and meaning.

If this book helps its readers to shape their understanding of the past in a way that seems reasonable and convincing, it will have succeeded in its purpose. Other histories have been written and will be written from other points of view. People living today in other parts of the world will not share the ideas that underlie this book. Yet even when one knows this, and knows that future generations will disagree in still other ways, the effort to see the human past whole and complete, as it *really* was and according to the best and fullest evidence we can discover, is not absurd. Accuracy and scope do improve as time passes. Errors and naïve exaggeration can be reduced. And by recognizing how partial and imperfect our own best efforts to understand the past (or the present, for that matter) must be, we can react more intelligently, with less surprise or anger, to other communities from other parts of the world, who think and act differently from ourselves.

Relativity in physics has improved human knowledge and power; relativism in social judgments can paralyze society if everyone simply says, "Everything goes; it makes no difference." A wise and true vision of human affairs will show, however, that it does matter how people behave. People have quarreled endlessly and differed deeply on matters of faith and morals. Nevertheless, across generations and centuries, a rough but effective process of selection has taken place, resulting in better tools, better ideas, and better attitudes. Certainly, unless people are willing and able to work together in groups, they cannot long survive as individuals. Conformity to local habit and custom is, therefore, absolutely necessary. Individuals who refuse to conform become criminals or madmen.

The real pinch comes when conformity to one group creates conflict with another group. Gang fights, race riots, international wars, and all other kinds of organized violence arise from collision between loyalties. Every individual in a modern society belongs to many different classes and groups, each claiming personal loyalty and demanding conformity to its own standards of conduct.

There are no rules as to how to thread one's way among these competing demands—none, at least, that the study of history provides. What that study can make clear is that communities have lived with this dilemma for a very long time, and have tended to build for themselves larger and larger political units within which some sort of peace could be maintained. The process goes on. Your lives will be part of it; so, in all probability, will your children's lives and your children's children's. Unless, of course, the unimaginable devastation of nuclear warheads brings the whole human adventure to a sudden end.

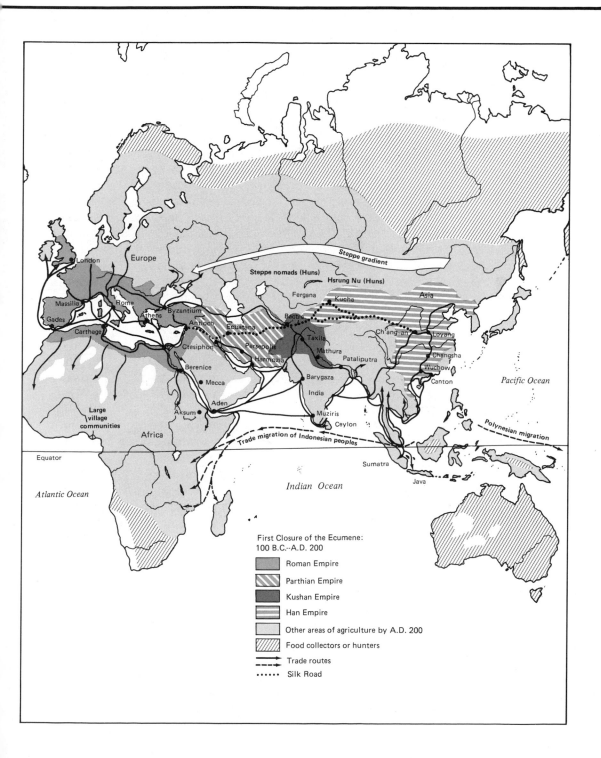

First Closure of the Ecumene:
100 B.C.–A.D. 200

- ▨ Roman Empire
- ▨ Parthian Empire
- ▨ Kushan Empire
- ▨ Han Empire
- ▨ Other areas of agriculture by A.D. 200
- ▨ Food collectors or hunters
- → Trade routes
- ⋯→ Silk Road

Steppe gradient

Steppe nomads (Huns)

Hsrung Nu (Huns)

Europe

Asia

London

Massilia

Rome

Gades

Athens

Byzantium

Carthage

Antioch

Ecbatana

Ctesiphon

Persepolis

Harmozia

Berenice

Mecca

Aden

Aksum

Large village communities

Africa

Fergana

Kucha

Bactra

Taxila

Mathura

Pataliputra

Barygaza

India

Muziris

Ceylon

Ch'ang-an

Loyang

Changsha

Wuchow

Canton

Pacific Ocean

Polynesian migration

Trade migration of Indonesian peoples

Equator

Atlantic Ocean

Indian Ocean

Sumatra

Java

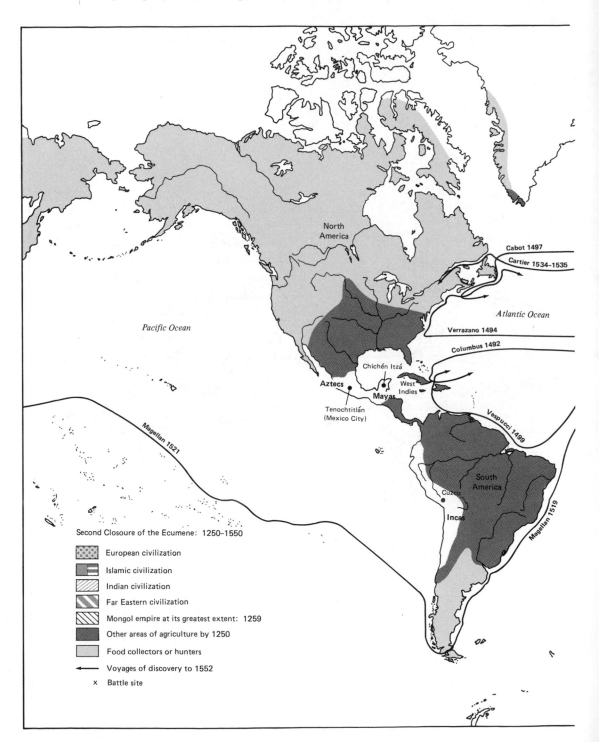

North America

Cabot 1497

Cartier 1534–1535

Atlantic Ocean

Pacific Ocean

Verrazano 1494

Columbus 1492

Chichén Itzá

Aztecs

West Indies

Mayas

Tenochtitlán (Mexico City)

Vespucci 1499

Magellan 1521

South America

Cuzco

Incas

Magellan 1519

Second Closoure of the Ecumene: 1250–1550

European civilization

Islamic civilization

Indian civilization

Far Eastern civilization

Mongol empire at its greatest extent: 1259

Other areas of agriculture by 1250

Food collectors or hunters

Voyages of discovery to 1552

×   Battle site

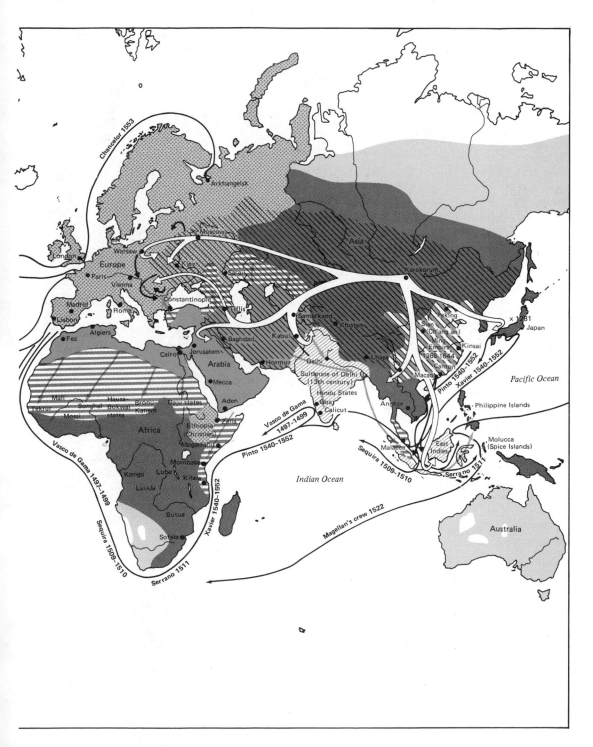

Chancelor 1553

Arkhangelsk

Moscovy

London

Warsaw

Europe

Paris

Kiev

Vienna

Sarai

Constantinople

Madrid

Rome

Tiflis

Lisbon

Algiers

Samarkand

Fez

Baghdad

Kabul

Khotan

Cairo

Jerusalem

Arabia

Hormuz

Delhi

Sultanate of Delhi
(13th century)

Mecca

Hindu States

Mali

Hausa
states

Bornu-
Kanem

Dalu states

Aden

Goa

Calicut

Tekrur

Songhai

Bokwai

Mossi

Zaila

Africa

Ethiopia
(Christian)

Mogadishu

Kongo

Mombasa

Luba

Kilwa

Lunda

Butua

Sofala

Asia

Karakorum

Peking

Sian
(Ch'ang an)

Ming
Empire
1368–1644

Kinsai

Canton

Macao

Lhasa

Angkor

× 1281

Japan

Pacific Ocean

Pinto 1540–1552   Xavier 1540–1552

Philippine Islands

Molucca
(Spice Islands)

East
Indies

Malacca

Serrano 1511

Sequira 1509–1510

Vasco de Gama
1497–1499

Pinto 1540–1552

Indian Ocean

Vasco de Gama 1497–1499

Xavier 1540–1552

Sequira 1509–1510

Serrano 1511

Magellan's crew 1522

Australia

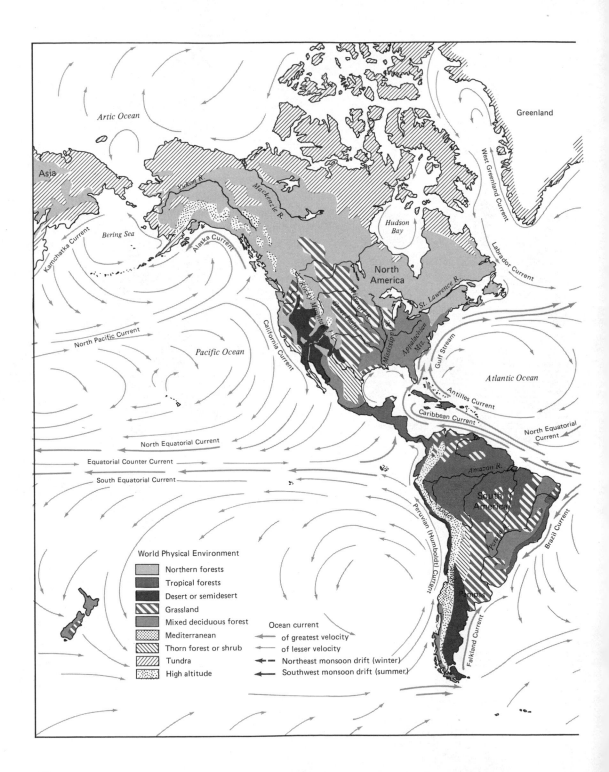

World Physical Environment

- Northern forests
- Tropical forests
- Desert or semidesert
- Grassland
- Mixed deciduous forest
- Mediterranean
- Thorn forest or shrub
- Tundra
- High altitude

Ocean current
- of greatest velocity
- of lesser velocity
- Northeast monsoon drift (winter)
- Southwest monsoon drift (summer)

Artic Ocean

Greenland

Asia

North America

Hudson Bay

Bering Sea

Kamchatka Current

Alaska Current

West Greenland Current

Labrador Current

Yukon R.

Mackenzie R.

North Pacific Current

Pacific Ocean

California Current

Rocky Mountains

Great Plains

Missouri R.

Mississippi R.

St. Lawrence R.

Appalachian Mts.

Gulf Stream

Atlantic Ocean

Antilles Current

Caribbean Current

North Equatorial Current

North Equatorial Current

Equatorial Counter Current

South Equatorial Current

Amazon R.

South America

Peruvian (Humboldt) Current

Paraná R.

Brazil Current

Pampas

Falkland Current

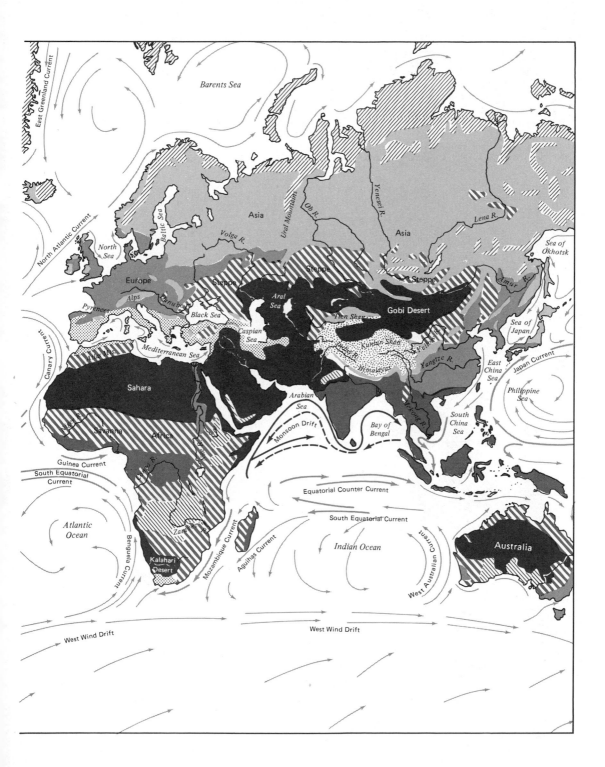

417

Index

1500 to the Present

Index

Prehistory to 1500